Success and Failure in Public Governance

NEW HORIZONS IN PUBLIC POLICY

General Editor: Wayne Parsons
Professor of Public Policy, Queen Mary and Westfield College,
University of London, UK

This series aims to explore the major issues facing academics and practitioners working in the field of public policy at the dawn of a new millennium. It seeks to reflect on where public policy has been, in both theoretical and practical terms, and to prompt debate on where it is going. The series emphasises the need to understand public policy in the context of international developments and global change. New Horizons in Public Policy publishes the latest research on the study of the policymaking process and public management, and presents original and critical thinking on the policy issues and problems facing modern and post-modern societies.

Titles in the series include:

Economic Decentralization and Public Management Reform
Edited by Maureen Mackintosh and Rathin Roy

Public Policy in the New Europe
Eurogovernance in Theory and Practice
Edited by Fergus Carr and Andrew Massey

Politics, Governance and Technology
A Postmodern Narrative on the Virtual State
P.H.A. Frissen

Public Policy and Political Institutions
The Role of Culture in Traffic Policy
Frank Hendriks

Public Policy and Local Governance
Institutions in Postmodern Society
Peter Bogason

Implementing European Union Public Policy
Roger Levy

The Internationalization of Public Management
Reinventing the Third World State
Edited by Willy McCourt and Martin Minogue

Political Leadership
Howard Elcock

Success and Failure in Public Governance
A Comparative Analysis
Edited by Mark Bovens, Paul 't Hart and B. Guy Peters

Success and Failure in Public Governance

A Comparative Analysis

Edited by

Mark Bovens

Utrecht University, The Netherlands

Paul 't Hart

University of Leiden, The Netherlands

B. Guy Peters

University of Pittsburgh, US

Section Editors:

Erik Albæk, Andreas Busch, Geoffrey Dudley, Michael Moran, Jeremy Richardson

NEW HORIZONS IN PUBLIC POLICY

Edward Elgar

Cheltenham, UK • Northampton, MA, USA

Published by
Edward Elgar Publishing Limited
Glensanda House
Montpellier Parade
Cheltenham
Glos GL50 1UA
UK

Edward Elgar Publishing, Inc.
136 West Street
Suite 202
Northampton
Massachusetts 01060
USA

A catalogue record for this book is available from the British Library

Library of Congress Cataloguing in Publication Data
Success and failure in public governance : a comparative analysis / edited by Mark Bovens, Paul 't Hart, B. Guy Peters.
     p. cm.—(New horizons in public policy series)
   Includes bibliographical references and index.
     1. Political planning—Europe, Western—Case studies. 2. Europe, Western—Politics and government—Case studies. 3. Steel industry and trade—Government policy—Europe, Western—Case studies. 4. Medical policy—Europe, Western—Case studies. 5. Financial institutions—Government policy—Europe, Western—Case studies. I. Bovens, M. A. P. II. 't Hart, Paul, 1963– III. Peters, B. Guy. IV. New horizons in public policy

JN94.A792 P53 2001
338.94—dc21

00–065405

ISBN 1 84064 088 X
Printed and bound in Great Britain by MPG Books Ltd, Bodmin, Cornwall

Contents

viii   *Contents*

PART VI   COMPARISONS, CONCLUSIONS, REFLECTIONS

Tables

Figures

Foreword

How well do governments govern? And why do some policy makers appear to be much better at it than others? These simple questions have formed the starting point for this research project. They have captured our attention for years, and the idea for this volume builds upon some of our prior work. In contrast to those earlier efforts, which were focused very much on the darker sides of government and public policy and which were mostly conceptual,[1] the present study adopts an even-handed, empirical, comparative perspective. We have selected four critical challenges to the governance capacities of national governments, and have invited no fewer than 24 experts to evaluate and explain governance performance in six European states. For each sector, a common analytical framework was adopted to facilitate cross-national comparison. In addition, comparisons across the four sectors are made possible by the fact that each of these four analytical frameworks was focused squarely on the same issues of policy evaluation and explanation.

The seeds for this mammoth effort were sown in Luton, England in 1996, when two of the general editors were both invited to a seminar about policy disasters in Britain. An old acquaintance was renewed, and a mutual fascination discovered. This led to a series of brainstorming sessions in Leiden, Utrecht and Oxford, and eventually to the key questions and design of the study. Meanwhile, we managed to recruit four leading experts in the policy sectors we had identified as prototypes of the four critical challenges we wanted to study. They agreed to act as 'sector editors', bearing responsibility for the acquisition of six national case studies each. Case authors were found and the bulk of the now voluminous group of participating researchers met at the March 1999 ECPR workshop sessions in Mannheim to discuss first drafts. Two of the four sectoral groups convened later that year at Nuffield College, Oxford for another session. The final months of the project involved the usual frantic exchanges between general editors, section editors and case authors, negotiating about the format, substance and – most of all – the length of the manuscripts.

In the course of this process we have incurred several debts. First of all, we want to thank our colleagues Erik Albæk, Andreas Busch, Geoffrey Dudley, Michael Moran and Jeremy Richardson for their dedication to this project in their role as 'middle managers'. They have been squeezed at times between the rigid demands of us general editors and the pleas of case authors for maximum flexibility. We have enjoyed this collaboration very much, and the project would not have been where it is now had it not been for their expertise and perseverance. Moreover, Jeremy Richardson's Centre for European Politics, Economics and Society at Nuffield College sponsored a crucial meeting of authors. The support of the Centre is gratefully acknowledged. In addition, financial or administrative support for the project was kindly provided by the Netherlands Science Foundation, the Department of Public Administration at Leiden University, and the Department of Legal Theory at Utrecht University. Our research assistant for this project, Martijn van der Meulen at Leiden University deserves special mention. In the hectic months towards the completion of the manuscript, he was fast, reliable, cheerful and extremely well organized where we at times were none of the above.

The single most important person in this project has been the late Vincent Wright. He has been a source of inspiration and succinct analytical advice during the design stages. Drawing on his seemingly limitless networks of colleagues around Europe he has selflessly helped us find the talented individuals to fill the slots in our 4×6 chapter matrix. On top of that he also provided financial support and hospitality for an early editorial meeting at Nuffield College. He has been 'around' in not just ours but many of our colleagues' professional lives for so many years, and always in such an unfailingly helpful way. For this reason we respectfully dedicate this volume to his memory.

A final work on the annotation and bibliographies. Each section of the book has its own master bibliography at the end of the section. This is done mainly because the references for parts II to V are highly sector-specific. Collapsing these very divergent types of sources in one central bibliography would, we feel, complicate rather than facilitate active use by the readers.

Mark Bovens, Paul 't Hart, B. Guy Peters

NOTE

1. Hogwood, B.D. and G.G. Peters (1985), *The Pathology of Public Policy*, Oxford: Clarendon; Bovens, M. and P. 't Hart (1996), *Understanding Policy Fiascoes*, New Brunswick: Transaction Publishers; Gray, P.D. and P. 't Hart (eds) (1998), *Public Policy Disasters in Europe*, London: Routledge.

Contributors

Erik Albæk is Professor of Public Administration at Aalborg University, Denmark. His research has focused on agenda setting, evaluation, utilization of social science knowledge in public policy making, and the welfare state. His most recent book (with Lawrence Rose, Lars Strömberg and Krister Ståhlberg) is *Nordic Local Government: Developmental Trends and Reform Activities in the Postwar Period* (The Association of Finnish Local Authorities, 1996).

Marc Balaguer is a visiting fellow in the Sociology Department at Harvard University. Before this he worked for several years in the Social Welfare Department of the Catalan government, and in University Pompeu Fabra. He has published on poverty measures and equality and social policy.

Mark Bovens is Professor of Public Administration at the Utrecht School of Governance, Utrecht University of the Netherlands. His present research focuses on accountability and citizenship in the public sector, electronic governance, normative policy analysis and constitutional theory. His most recent book is *The Quest for Responsibility: Accountability and Citizenship in Complex Organisations* (Cambridge, University Press, 1998).

Viola Burau is Lecturer in Comparative Public and Social Policy at Brunel University, UK. Her research interests lie in the comparative study of public policy, health politics in Europe, particularly the relationship between professions and the state, as well as methods of comparison. She has done research on health care reform and doctors, and the governance of nursing.

Andreas Busch is University Lecturer in German Politics at the University of Oxford. At the time of writing he was Assistant Professor in the Department of Political Science of Heidelberg University and John F. Kennedy Memorial Fellow (1997/8) at the Center for European Studies, Harvard University. His research interests are primarily in the fields of comparative politics and political economy. His most recent book (coedited with Dietmar Braun) is *Public Policy and Political Ideas* (Edward Elgar, 1999).

William D. Coleman is Professor of Political Science and Director of the Institute on Globalization and the Human Condition at McMaster University, Hamilton, Canada. Among his recent work is *Regionalism and Global Economic Integration: Europe, Asia and the Americas* (edited with Geoffrey Underhill; Routledge, 1998).

Geoffrey Dudley is a Research Fellow in the Centre for European Politics, Economics and Society at the University of Oxford. He is co-author (with Jeremy Richardson) of *Why Does Policy Change? Lessons from British Transport Policy 1945–1999* (Routledge, 2001).

Leo A. van Eerden is an Assistant Professor in the Department of Finance and Financial Sector Management at Vrije Universiteit Amsterdam. His research focuses on the management of systemic risk and financial regulation.

Richard Freeman is Lecturer in European Policy and Politics at the University of Edinburgh. He has written a number of chapters and articles on the politics of HIV and AIDS and on prevention in health policy, and is the author of *The Politics of Health in Europe* (Manchester University Press, 2000).

Peter Garpenby is Senior Researcher at the Centre for Medical Technology Assessment, Linkoping University, Sweden. His research is on the medical profession in Sweden, implementation of health care reform and the diffusion of medical technology, and has published on these topics in various academic journals.

Pablo González Alvarez is a doctoral student at CEACS/Institute Juan March and Nuffield College, Oxford University. His doctoral thesis focuses on the relations between federalism, the welfare state and inequality. Other research interests are the relations between social capital, political institutions and institutional performance as well as the links between social classes and electoral behaviour.

Mariska de Groot graduated in political science at Leiden University in 1998 and now works with the Dutch association of hospitals, where she is engaged in the development and implementation of a new system for financing hospitals and medical specialists.

Stephen Harrison is Professor of Social Policy at the University of Manchester, UK. He previously taught at the University of Leeds. His research interests encompass the politics of medicine and management, health services policy and organization, and public user involvement. He is the author (with C. Pollitt) of *Controlling Health Professionals: The Future of Work and Organization in the National Health Service* (Open University Press, 1994).

Paul 't Hart is Professor in Public Administration at Leiden University, the Netherlands, Research Director of the Leiden University Crisis Research Center and has published widely on public sector crisis management, policy evaluation and group dynamics in politics. A recent book (coedited with Pat Gray) is *Public Policy Disasters in Europe* (Routledge, 1998).

Jacint Jordana is Associate Professor in the Department of Political and Social Sciences at the University Pompeu Fabra, Barcelona, Spain. Among his research interests are industrial relations, public policy analysis and decentralization politics. Recent publications include 'Industrial Relations in Spain: Does Regional Diversity Awaken Union Tendencies to Divergence?', in J. Wets (ed.), *Cultural Diversity in Trade Unions: A Challenge to Class Identity?* (Ashgate, 2000).

Patrick Kenis is Professor of Organization and Policy Studies in the Faculty of Social and Behavioural Sciences, Tilburg University, the Netherlands. He has published articles on organizations, networks and public policy in different policy areas. He is coeditor (with Bernd Marin) of *Managing AIDS: Organizational Responses in Six European Countries* (Ashgate, 1997).

Michael Moran is Professor of Government at the University of Manchester, United Kingdom. He has published monographs on the regulation of industrial relations, financial markets and the medical profession. His most recent book is *Governing the Health Care State: A Comparative Study of the United States, United Kingdom and Germany* (Manchester University Press, 1999).

Mikel Navarro Arancegui is a Professor of Economics in the ESTE School of Management, University of Deusto (Spain). His research includes studies on industrial competitiveness and policy and the Spanish economy. He has published many books and articles on these subjects.

Sofía A. Pérez is Associate Professor of Political Science at Boston University. Her research interests centre on understanding institutional change in advanced industrialized economies, and her current research project focuses on the effect of financial and monetary integration and labour market institutions in Europe. She is the author of, among other publications, *Banking on Privilege: The Politics of Spanish Financial Reform* (Cornell University Press, 1997).

Luisa Perrotti is Assistant Professor of Political Science at Insead, Fontainebleau, France. Her research interests are in the areas of European integration and comparative politics and public policy. She has coedited (with V. Wright) *Privatization and Public Policy* (Edward Elgar, 2000).

B. Guy Peters is Maurice Falk Professor of Government at the University of Pittsburgh, USA and Senior Fellow of the Canadian Centre for Management Development. Among his recent publications are *Institutional Theory in Political Science* (Pinter, 1999) and *European Policy Coordination: The National Dimension* (Oxford University Press, 2000).

Jon Pierre is Professor of Political Science at the University of Gothenburg, Sweden, and an Adjunct Professor at the University of Pittsburgh, USA. His current research interests include governance, institutional analysis, public policy and public administration. His recent publications include *Debating Governance* (Oxford University Press, 2000) and (with B. Guy Peters) *Governance, Politics and the State* (Macmillan, 2000).

Jeremy Richardson is the Nuffield Professor of Comparative European Politics, Director of the Centre for European Politics, Economics and Society, and a Fellow of Nuffield College, Oxford. He is Editor of the *Journal of European Public Policy* and author of several books and articles on aspects of public policy.

Ana Rico works as a Research Fellow in the European Observatory on Health Care Systems (EOHCS). Prior to joining the Observatory she was Assistant Professor of Public Policy at the Pompeu Fabra in Barcelona. She has published in the field of health economics, health policy and political science.

Gabriel Saro Jauregui is Researcher at the Juan March Institute (Madrid). He specializes in industrial and finance policies and has published various articles and chapters on these topics.

Hans Schenk is Professor of Industrial Policy at Tilburg University and chairman of GRASP Research at Erasmus University Rotterdam, the Netherlands. His research interests include industrial policy, competition and regulation, mergers and acquisitions, behavioural and evolutionary theories of the firm, capital markets and banking. Among his recent publications is 'Industrial Policy Implications of Competition Policy Failure in Mergers', in K. Cowling (ed.), *Industrial Policy in Europe* (Routledge, 1999).

Monika Steffen is a Researcher at the Centre National de la Recherche Scientifique (CNRS) and is affiliated to Institute of Political Studies, University of Grenoble, France. Her work focuses on health policies and international comparisons in Europe, including the conditions in Eastern Europe. She is author of *The Fight against AIDS. A Public Policy Comparison: France, Great Britain, Germany, Italy* (Presses Universitaires de Grenoble, 1996).

Adam Tickell is Professor of Geography at the University of Bristol, and has previously worked at the universities of Leeds, Manchester, and Southampton. He has published widely on finance, governance and economic geography. He is currently completing a major research project on policy transfer in international finance.

Hannah Tooze completed her Ph.D. at the Centre for German Studies, University of Birmingham and now works in the private sector as a consultant to government.

Bent Sofus Tranøy is a doctor in political science at the University of Oslo, where he was a senior researcher at the National Research Project on Power and Democracy when his chapter was written. He has published on economic policy, environmental policy and the comparative method and has recently coedited (with Dag Harald Claes) a book on the Europeanization of Norwegian policy (Fagbokforl, 1999).

Margo Trappenburg is Associate Professor at the Utrecht School of Governance, Utrecht University, the Netherlands. Her recent interests include political philosophy, health care ethics and health care policy. A recent publication is 'Lifestyle Solidarity in the Health Care System', *Health Care Analysis*, 2000, 8 (1), 65–75.

Bert de Vroom is Associate Professor of Sociology of Public Policy, Faculty of Public Administration and Public Policy, University of Twente, the Netherlands. He has published widely on horizontal governance, AIDS policy, labour market and welfare policy. Among his recent publications is 'The Netherlands: The Strong Civil Society Response', (with Ineke Kester and Armand van Wolferen) in P. Kenis and B. Marin (eds), *Managing Aids: Organizational Responses in Six European Countries* (Ashgate, 1997).

David Wilsford is currently President of the Institute for American Universities in Aix-en-Provence, France. His research includes institutional theories of public policy and health policy. Among other works, he is the author of *Doctors and the State: The Politics of Health Care in France and the United States* (Duke University Press, 1991).

PART I

Evaluating and explaining public governance:
general introduction

1. The state of public governance

Mark Bovens, Paul 't Hart and B. Guy Peters

1   A CHANCE MEETING

The White Horse in Broad Street, Oxford, has entertained thousands of visitors to that university city. One chilly, rainy evening in early autumn two such visitors found themselves sitting next to each other in one corner of this pub. Their dark blue plastic bags indicated that both had spent a good part of their afternoon (and their paycheques) in the nearby bookshop. Noticing their common interest, they struck up a conversation and eventually decided to share a meal. When discussing the dinner options, one of them, Cassandra, said that she would eat anything as long as it was not beef. She was still concerned about the 'mad cow disease' that had plagued British cattle some years before, and commented in passing on the failure of the British and some other governments to detect and control the disease in its cattle herds earlier than they did. Her companion, Candide, replied that he would nevertheless be quite happy to order a hamburger for dinner. He felt the British government had not done all that badly in coping with BSE. He argued that, once the dangers of beef had been made clear beyond question, the government did indeed respond quickly and effectively to control the problem. It put a plan in place that removed both the apparent cause of the problem and restored public confidence (at least within Britain) about food safety. The root of the problem was the scientific uncertainty surrounding the disease, and it was made more complex by the anti-British political posturing in Europe, not by government mismanagement.

Their disagreement on the beef issue stimulated a much wider discussion on the successes and failures of public policy making. Candide proved to be fundamentally optimistic about the capacity of governments to design and implement public policies that were effective and just. He believed that there was a corpus of knowledge and experience in the public sector that could produce genuine success and improve the lives of citizens through collective action. He thought that the experience of the past several decades showed a steady, if not uninterrupted, progress. Cassandra disagreed vehemently. Her views about government and its capability to ameliorate the conditions that vex the public were much bleaker. She believed that there were too many unknowns,

3

too much social and political inertia, and too many internal dysfunctions, to expect the public sector to be intelligent, reliable and therefore effective in solving public problems. These different vantage points made it hard for them to agree on almost anything that came up in their little debate. Here is how they went on:

Cassandra
'Well, we may argue over whether or not the Mad Cow problem was a policy failure, but surely you'll agree that there are just too many things that go badly wrong in public policy. Look at all those billions spent in the sixties and beyond on all those so-called strategic industries. Mining, shipbuilding and steelworks: many European governments gave them virtually blank cheques, and still they went under, and thousands of jobs were lost. We should also consider all these white elephants of physical planning and construction projects that nobody wants, that are outrageously expensive, or that simply fail to come about even though there is a great need for them. A guy named Peter Hall wrote an entire book about these in the seventies. Things like the Concorde project, the London airport and ring road stalemates. Later on in Britain there was the Humberside bridge that nobody uses, and the tremendous cost escalation of the Channel tunnel, which is probably why I had to pay more than three times what it costs to fly to get my car over here. Or look at financial policy here in Britain, whether it is the Poll Tax fiasco, the Barings bank collapse, Black Wednesday or the failure of the Major government to cope with the run on the pound in September 1992. And I don't think Britain is the exception. In many if not all of the so-called advanced Western democracies, the list of conspicuous policy failures is long. And I haven't even begun to talk about foreign policy, where these states have been incapable or unwilling to prevent the escalation of conflicts when this would have been possible. As a result, we got an infinite number of bloodbaths, from Vietnam to Kosovo.'

Candide
'Listen, I am not going to dispute that things go wrong in the public sector, sometimes badly, and that ordinary people suffer as a result. But I think you are being overly pessimistic and to a large extent unfair to policy makers. Look at us sitting here in this pub: well fed, well dressed, quite safe from harm, comfortably sheltered from the elements with gas, electricity and water plentifully available. This may sound trivial, I know, but don't tell me that public agencies and political decision makers have nothing to do with the fact that we live so well in this part of the world. In summing up all these big disasters, you are echoing the biases of the media and pressure groups, which only pay attention to what goes wrong. Neither they nor you give sufficient credit to the day-to-day successes of public policy. And there are many such

successes, whether it is in producing or regulating infrastructures, in governing the economy, in combating the worst extremes of poverty, in creating a health care system that has raised our life expectancy dramatically, or in providing education that allows our nations to compete effectively in the world. In my view, these successes far outweigh the failures. We just don't see them in proper perspective, because we take them for granted. Well, go to Russia, look around, and you'll appreciate the difference that good public governance makes.'

Cassandra
'What you say makes some sense of course, but it is only part of the story. First of all, you may not like the reporting style of the media, but they happen to determine what we citizens get to see about our governments, and thus how we judge their performance. The fact that media and other critics are still able to come up with so many and such costly failures shows that government makes too many mistakes still. Don't blame the messenger, I'd say.'

Candide
'I am not blaming the media, I am just saying that they by their very nature tend to emphasize the sensational, the outrageous, and overlook the regular, the normal. So when reporting on governments, they focus on scandal and failure. I don't condemn them for it, but I do say that they give us an incomplete and even distorted picture of public policy.'

Cassandra
'Fair enough, but I am not just following the media here. I am simply judging policy makers by their own intentions and promises, and these have all too often proved to be too ambitious, perhaps even self-delusive.'

Candide
'Yes, but you know as well as I do that we should be very cautious in evaluating policy just by looking at its stated objectives. In a democracy, policy makers have to keep many people happy at the same time, otherwise they can't build the coalitions they need in order to govern. So they make promises and set lofty goals that have more symbolic than substantive value. Rather than looking at whether governments meet their election promises or official objectives, we should look at whether ordinary people are better off as a result of what government does. And I think the overall balance in the Western world is overwhelmingly positive.'

Cassandra
'We should not look at the past too much. Let's focus on what is happening in today's world. Things like economic globalization, mass individualism,

multiculturalism and emancipation will make it increasingly difficult for governments to identify and tackle social problems before they run out of hand. Moreover, the roots of such problems often lie far across their jurisdictional borders, and the kinds of resources needed to handle them may simply not be available to national policy makers. Look at the degradation of the environment. Sure enough we have made some of the small wins you talk about. Many citizens now select their garbage for recycling, there is more regulation of pollutant industries, and as a consequence some rivers are gradually becoming cleaner – and so on. Yet the bigger picture is one of continuing global warming, deforestation, extinction of species and water scarcity, and virtually nothing is done about it. And there are many such examples of lingering risks and crises of the post-modern society that only grow bigger: international drug trafficking, porn on the Internet, killer viruses, fraud and tax evasion. All of these present new uncertainties and new governance problems. Governments have to learn, and learn fast, how to deal with these.

And this is my next point: governments are not very good at adapting, innovating and reinventing in response to changes in their environment. Look, here in my shopping bag I have this book by Lloyd Etheredge called "Can Governments Learn?", which I just bought next door. His response to his title question is decidedly negative. He talks about how difficult politicians and senior bureaucrats find it to examine their own record critically, to redefine problems, and to break with policies they have committed themselves to. They are consumed by games of hardball politics and bureaucratic tugs of war in which what you and I would call learning is seen as blinking, as a sign of weakness. They are locked into the policies of the past, and they only really change when forced to do so by major crises. Of these we will have many, I fear, and it will be us, taxpaying citizens, who will feel the consequences.'

Candide
'Again I think you are too harsh. I happen to know Etheredge's case study, and it is about American policy towards Central America in the Cold War period. Opportunism, fanaticism and bigotry reigned, but this is hardly a representative sample. There are other, comparative, studies of learning in many different policy sectors that show a much brighter picture, even in the area of environmental policy, but also with respect to the organization and performance of government itself. I can look them up if you like and send you the references. You are of course right that there are many new policy issues out whose scale and complexity the world has never seen before. But you remain stuck in a set of expectations about what governments can and ought to do about them that is no longer realistic. Forget the idea of government as the big fixer, the all-powerful state. It has never been that way, and will be even less so in the future. Government, whether it is national or transnational is only part of the picture

at best. Capital markets, big business, the Web and mobile citizens cannot be shaped at will by policy makers. These factors and the interplay between them have become a major cause as well as part of the solution of many of the issues you mentioned. Governments can try to influence them by persuasion but cannot fully anticipate, or even monitor, let alone dictate what they do. This means we have to accept that some problems go undetected and cause us surprise, embarrassment and sometimes even serious pain. That's all in the game.

The crucial questions in assessing government performance under these circumstances must be: has it done enough to spot them and deal with them in advance, and has it organized itself properly to minimize and repair any harm done? In my view, this ever more complex world of ours will put more stress on this last bit of the equation. Modern governance should not go all out on comprehensive planning and risk prevention, because these are illusory and likely to produce serious disaffection in people such as yourself. Instead, it should go for risk management and what I would call "flexible response": creating institutions and styles of governance where unforeseen problems are not seen as occasions for political defensiveness and blaming, but as challenges for rapid learning. So you could say that I am all for governance by looking back constructively rather than by gazing forward in confusion.

But my dear Cassandra, let the problems of politics not spoil the occasion. I think we have earned ourselves another drink, don't you agree? What can I get us to top off your salad and my tasty – and forgive me my bad joke – wholesome hamburger?'

2 FROM GOVERNMENTS WHO FAIL TO POLICY MAKERS WHO SUCCEED

Candide and Cassandra were talking about one of the classic and enduring themes in the study of politics and public policy: does government as we know it serve us well, and how are we to judge if it does so or not? This question has long been debated, mostly by political philosophers, but in the twentieth century we have witnessed the development of an entire academic subdiscipline devoted to evaluating and improving what governments do. In the last five decades the policy sciences have not only produced a wide range of models and tools for supporting and upgrading public governance, they have also produced a mass of research findings showing how often, and how badly, things may go wrong in the public sector.

Beginning in the United States with the early studies of the Great Society, and more widely later with the emerging fields of policy implementation and programme evaluations, policy scientists have documented time and again that policy makers fail to accomplish their objectives; that policies can have serious unintended effects; and that efficiency is not exactly the guiding principle in many public sector programmes and organizations. A chorus of students of policy making and public service delivery in the European welfare states has subsequently echoed these findings. Often unintentionally, these studies have provided part of the impetus for the ideological swing in thinking about governments and public governance that took place throughout the West during the 1980s and into the 1990s. The Keynesianism and Enlightenment optimism which had emerged in the wake of the industrial revolution and which dominated the theory and practice of government during the early postwar decades lost their philosophical and political edge. No longer was government self-evidently granted a prominent role in society. Prompted by the countless sagas of government failure and the steadily rising costs of the welfare state in a period of economic stagnation, new ideas gained currency in the field of macroeconomics. They quickly caught on among politicians and parties at the conservative end of the political spectrum. The new ideology boiled down to a new mood of distrust of big government, and an advocacy of market-based solutions to social problems. In its wake, governments have been cutting down, privatizing and have generally found themselves on the defensive. Moreover, they found themselves being followed by a more critical media and a public opinion that was much keener than ever before to ascertain whether their tax money was being spent effectively and efficiently. And so a 'vicious circle' was emerging: more and more energy was devoted to documenting inefficiencies, disappointments, failures and scandals in the public sector, and governments were becoming more and more insecure. This picture of failure and paralysis was then widely contrasted with a more or less mythical image of the market as a naturally efficient means of allocating goods and services among the members of a community, thus deepening the critique of politics even further.

However, in keeping with the cyclical, if not dialectical, nature of public and academic debates about politics and markets, this pervasive critique of 'big government' has begun to trigger its own antithesis. Beginning in the 1980s, calls have been made for a more even-handed reassessment of the state and its bureaucracy as institutions of public governance (Goodsell, 1985). Also mixed results and accountability problems associated with the 'marketization' of state functions have weakened the neoliberal push somewhat. The proponents of the 'new public management' in Europe and the 'reinventing government' movement in the USA, among others, have made attempts at synthesis. They have tried to integrate market-oriented thinking into the organization and modus operandi of the public sector. The aim was, in a sense, to transcend the divide and have the best of both worlds: a democratically accountable public sector that was at the same time subject to the rigours of the market. Inspired by these developments, many students of government have moved from an empirical–evaluative mode of discourse to a normative–prescriptive one. Contemporary writing on what is now called 'public management' is filled with case histories about success in government, often equated with increased effectiveness and efficiency gains. These are presented as inspiring illustrations for the 'how-to' philosophy and guidelines set forth by the author. There has even been a revival of thinking positively about government ethics and accountability, spawning its own series of heroic tales and management philosophies.

And so we have come full circle. Instead of the catalogues of 'bureaucratic failures', 'planning disasters', 'limits of government', 'policy pathologies' and 'scandals' of the 1970s and 1980s (Peirce, 1981; Hall, 1982; Hood, 1976; Rose and Peters, 1978; Hogwood and Peters, 1985; Markovits and Silverstein, 1988), we are now reading about 'success stories', 'best practices', 'innovative leaders' and 'exemplary administrators' (Doig and Hargrove, 1990; Denhardt 1993; Moore, 1996).

3 FROM UNDERSTANDING FIASCOS TO EXPLAINING BOTH FAILURE AND SUCCESS

Arguably, both these approaches to public governance and policy have serious limits. They leave important questions unanswered, particularly about the factors that produce differential performance under similar conditions. Why do some policies succeed so well while others, in the same sector or in the same country, fail so dramatically? Answering this straightforward empirical question is our first aim with this book. We want to gain more systematic knowledge about why some public policies and programmes fail and others succeed.

In earlier efforts (Hogwood and Peters, 1985; Bovens and 't Hart, 1996; Gray and 't Hart, 1998) we focused mainly on policy pathologies, policy fiascos and policy disasters. In this book, we have chosen not to 'frontload' the success and failure issue. We have tried to move beyond the analysis of spectacular, but possibly atypical, single cases. Instead of focusing on already established cases of failure and success, we take as our starting point a number of concrete types of challenges to governance, irrespective of the outcomes of the attempts made by particular governments to cope with these challenges. For each type, we have studied the national experiences of six countries, which has produced considerable variety in governance approaches and their outcomes. We have asked each contributor to assess these attempts, focusing on one particular governance challenge per case. Authors were invited to concentrate on one specific policy episode within the broader agenda and development of the national policy sector they were to report on. Analytically, authors have been invited to evaluate to what extent, and with respect to which criteria, governance succeeded or failed in their cases.

Because of this comparative design, which will be explained in greater detail in the next chapter, our research is less biased towards the spectacular and darker side of governance. Great planning disasters make for great reading, but they are unreliable as the sole source for a study of the general state of contemporary governance. Likewise, exemplary administrators may very well be exemplary in a normative, but not in an empirical, sense. They may be the proverbial odd men out.

A study of success and failure in governance is inevitably also a study of politics. The assessment of success and failure of particular policies or programmes is in the end a political judgment. It is political in academia, because the criteria for success and failure are in the end dependent on implicit visions of the good life and of the power of man to influence fate (Bovens and 't Hart, 1996). It is particularly political in everyday life, because political actors, such as interest groups, politicians, journalists and voters are the main judges. As we shall see, these political evaluations do not necessarily square with the actual performance of a programme or a policy. Political evaluations have their own logic and dynamics. Perception is as important for political legitimacy as is performance.

A study into the state of governance is therefore also a study in political legitimacy. It may very well be that some of the perceived crises of governance in West European states are not crises in performance, but crises of judgment. Citizens may have rising expectations about governance, the media may be far less deferential towards public authorities, and backbenchers may have become much more critical. Thus governments may very well do better, but feel worse nevertheless. Our second aim with this book, therefore, is to shed more light on the legitimacy of governance in western Europe. Do the affairs, disasters and scandals which seem ubiquitous in modern political life reflect a decrease in performance and a decrease in trust, or do they reflect a change in the rules of the game, and a change in political style?

Thirdly, our aims with regard to the nature of the knowledge we seek to produce are more ambitious than in our earlier efforts. We have tried to go beyond *understanding* success and failure conceptually, and move towards *explaining* their genesis empirically. This is crucial if we want to understand more systematically how to avoid policy failures and to promote success.

4   FROM THE STATE OF GOVERNANCE TO GOVERNANCE IN EUROPEAN STATES

Studying success and failure in governance takes us to the heart of current debates about the modern state's capacity to govern. These discussions are often conducted on a rather abstract level. Various megatrends (such as market globalization, individualization, informatization and Europeanization) are often presumed to erode the capacity of national governments to adopt and implement policies successfully. The power of national states to govern has been 'hollowed out' gradually in the past decades, so the argument goes. Likewise, many writers on policy networks, epistemic communities, autopoiesis and other forms of 'governance without government' appear to take for granted that governments have lost their ability to act more or less autonomously.

Our final aim with this book, therefore, is to examine to what extent these more general assertions are borne out in comparative empirical research. We look closely at the way a number of West European states responded to concrete, non-routine problems. We aim to detect and understand similarities and differences in the nature and results of policy responses adopted in different countries to a problem that is more or less identical in each country. Doing so for different types of problems across different policy sectors has enabled us to compare cross-nationally as well as cross-sectorally. Furthermore, we can also address more systematically the issues of national policy styles, the influence of EU policy making and the possible convergence of policy styles across countries and sectors. Although the book is primarily about governance in West European states, it is also a book about the state of European governance.

2. Analysing governance success and failure in six European states

Mark Bovens, Paul 't Hart and B. Guy Peters

1 GOVERNANCE IN EUROPEAN STATES

The public sector in many European states has become more complex and more problematic in the past decades. While governments once could be sure of being the central, or even sole, actor involved in the process of steering their societies, and could depend upon legal authority as the principal instrument for steering, both of those assumptions are now questionable. First, governments increasingly are but one of many actors involved in governing. They generally remain a central actor in governing but must bargain and cooperate with international and private sector actors (but see Pierre and Peters, 2000). Governments are now often in the unenviable position of having to bear the responsibility for failures while not having control over many of the factors that may have produced the problems.

Nor can governments rely on hierarchical authority to impose their will on other actors, as they might at one time. Governments do have authority, but have become more reluctant to manage policy problems through hierarchy alone. Rather, networks of private and public actors surround each policy area, and their interactions often are as determinate as are direct government interventions. In the policy sectors we are investigating here there are numerous private actors that have to be involved and/or placated in order to make the policy function properly. This interaction was perhaps clearest in the case of the two health areas (see below) in which powerful professional networks are central to the solution of the challenges. There were interactions in the other areas as well, so that success and failure are government problems but by no means only problems for governments.

Despite changes in the position of governments vis-à-vis other actors, we focus our analysis on government actors. This focus is maintained largely because governments bear the ultimate burden for success and, most of all, failure. It is they who must face the media to explain what went wrong, and it is ministers who must stand up in Parliament to render an account and answer questions. Further, it is governments who are often placed in the role of defining the success and failure, especially the political success or failure, of policies. The manner in which governments structure their statements of goals, and their own assessment of policy performance, give them a crucial position in defining the terms of debate concerning policy success and failure.

2 THE CAPACITY TO GOVERN: GOVERNANCE CHALLENGES AND POLICY SECTORS

To assess the governance capacities of Western European states, we have identified a number of critical cases where these capacities are challenged seriously, and in different ways. In selecting policy domains, we have taken 'incremental politics as usual' as the benchmark (Lindblom, 1979; Gregory, 1983). Incrementalism is commonly associated to be the dominant mode of policy making for more or less foreseeable problems, with a relatively short time frame, and minor if any redistributive social consequences. When faced with such issues, governments can afford to take the policies of the past as a compass, and allow for political bargaining and bureaucratic compromise formation to decide on the margins and specifics of the small (that is, incremental) adjustments that will be made to cope (Rose and Davies, 1994).

In this study, in contrast, we shall concentrate on issues and policy sectors that are more complex, ambiguous and consequential. In particular, we have identified four types of challenges to incrementalism:

- from distributive to redistributive issues: the management of decline;
- from taking the institutional structure as given to regarding the institutions themselves as part of the problem: the management of institutional reform;
- from predictable to unprecedented issues: the management of innovation;
- from relatively benign, slow-moving to malignant, fast-moving problems: the management of crisis.

We shall briefly elaborate each of these challenges, and identify an exemplary policy sector that will be studied further.

First, the *governance of decline* will be addressed through examining the ways in which governments coped with the decline in economic performance and competitiveness of the national steel industries between the mid-1970s and the early 1990s. Most European countries have seen this major industry decline in the face of competition from other materials and global competitors or as a result of an economic recession period. The task for governments has been to restructure or even terminate these activities while mitigating the social effects of this major industrial change.

Second, the *governance of reform* will be addressed by examining how governments have tried to contain the cost of health care in the 1980s and 1990s. Governments that have tried to reform the health sector have had to intervene in institutional arrangements consisting of intricate networks of professional medical associations, health insurance companies, patients' associations and hospitals. In such settings, reform requires a certain amount of deinstitutionalization and institutional reinvention, most likely in the face of stubborn resistance by coalitions of actors benefiting from the institutional status quo. The studies in this section of the project will focus specifically on attempts made by governments to reform the medical profession and to curb its political and institutional power.

Third, the *governance of innovation* will be examined by studying the ways in which governments coped with the challenges posed to the domestic banking systems by the internationalization and liberalization of the financial markets in the 1980s and 1990s. These developments were a major change over the sheltered and regulated markets of the post-World War II era and exposed banks to new risks, potentially resulting in disruptive and costly failures. Pressed by technological advances and changing global markets, states had to adapt their regulatory frameworks, not possessing full information as to how this would affect outcomes.

Finally, the *governance of crisis* is the critical challenge that governments faced in the early 1980s when they had to cope with the sudden knowledge that there was a major risk of the HIV virus spreading widely across the population through contaminated blood products and blood transfusions. This problem could not have been anticipated or controlled in advance, especially during the early days of the disease (1980–85) when the nature of the disease and its epidemiology were not fully understood. Health authorities were forced to operate with a minimum of information. They had to learn and to adapt very quickly. Governments could not, perhaps, be blamed for some of the mistakes they had made when information about the transmission of HIV was lacking or uncertain. Yet some of them did face major legitimacy questions because of what they did or neglected to do after authoritative knowledge about the role of blood in HIV contamination had become available.

This part of the research design is shown in Table 2.1. Each section of the project is devoted to one particular challenge and policy sector. The specific structure of each policy sector and the nature of its key governance challenge will be outlined in greater detail in the introductory chapters to each of the four sections of the book dealing with a particular governance challenge.

Table 2.1 Research design: governance tasks, key challenges and policy sectors

Governance task	Key challenge	Policy sector
Coping with decline	Governing sunset industries	Steel industry
Coping with reform	Governing institutional inertia	Health sector
Coping with innovation	Governing without precedents	Banking
Coping with crisis	Governing urgent threats	HIV/blood

3 NATIONAL VERSUS SECTORAL GOVERNANCE STYLES

An interesting question that arises in a project of this design is how different states handle the same governance challenge. Moreover, we may also see if there are commonalities in the ways in which different types of governance challenges are being met in a single state. Given our preoccupation with questions of success and failure, we may even ask if, on the whole, some states did better than others in conducting non-routine, non-incremental governance tasks.

A potentially useful analytical tool for addressing these issues is the concept of national policy style, introduced first by Richardson (1982; see also Vogel, 1986) and recently even expanded to the modus operandi of the European Union (Cram and Richardson, 1999). The central idea underlying this notion is that national polities have some essential structural and cultural features that predispose them to make and implement public policy in certain distinct ways. Moreover, these national styles are roughly the same irrespective of the particular characteristics of the issue and the policy sector they belong to. A policy style can be defined as a more or less stable pattern of policy making that arises from the interaction between a government's approach to problem solving and the relationships between government and other actors in the policy process (Richardson, 1982, p. 13).

These two style dimensions need some explanation. A government's approach to problem solving can be characterized as falling somewhere between the extremes of a proactive, technocratic approach and a reactive, diplomatic approach. The former feeds on an optimistic philosophy of governance, where government is held to have the ideological zeal and the analytical capabilities to foresee and possibly forestall social problems before they become critical. The reactive approach is based on what has been called a realist philosophy of governance, where public policy makers' activist inclinations are constrained by laissez-faire ideology, pervasive uncertainty about the causes of social problems and their possible remedies, as well as its own organizational complexity and value conflicts. As a consequence, it adopts a more reactive approach where it tries to cope with social problems once they have come to be seen as urgent. In reactive problem solving, the aspiration level tends to lie with reducing the urgency of problems rather than eradicating them altogether.

The second dimension focuses on the relative autonomy of the state vis-à-vis other social actors, particularly organized interests (see, for example, Schmitter, 1979; Skocpol, 1985; Hall, 1986). The key question is whether the state is able to impose its policies upon the social actors or not. On the statist end of the continuum, the state is able (or is reputed to be able) to wield sufficient power to chart its own course. A strong executive dominates public policy making and decisions are sanctioned politically by a legislature that is not coopted by clienteles and other special interest groups. At the other extreme is policy making by consensus: institutionalized concertation between state and various social actors who in effect possess veto powers (Scharpf, 1988, 1997; Pierson, 1994). This powerful position of social groups may derive from various forces: a strong presence in the political parties, incorporation in 'iron triangles' and other forms of organized consultation, or simply by virtue of being a pivotal actor in the implementation of public policies.

In combination, these variables yield four quadrants in which to place national policy styles (see Figure 2.1). We can deduce the expected style profile of individual countries on the basis of the general characteristics of their political institutions and culture. Furthermore, by undertaking cross-national, cross-

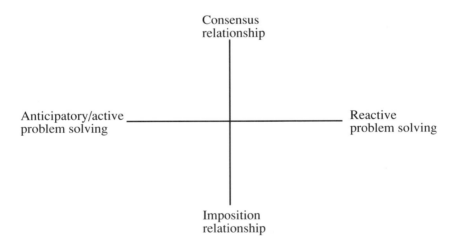

Figure 2.1   Hypothesized national policy styles

sectoral policy research we can assess empirically to what extent the predicted national policy styles are actually displayed. It is one of the main analytical objectives of this study to do so.

The notion of national policy style is not unproblematic, of course. In the original comparative volume edited by Richardson in 1982, it proved more useful as a heuristic tool to detect common trends in policy making in Western Europe than as a robust descriptor of national traditions. In particular, an important common denominator in the studies undertaken for that volume was the demise of anticipatory problem solving, under pressure from the growing complexity and interelatedness of social issues and policy domains. Also there seemed to be a trend towards a less hierarchical, more consensus-oriented style of government. Now, almost 20 years later, we observe that at least the second trend has proved to be a robust one: everywhere the state has been on the defensive, and has had to accept a renewed popularity of market-based solutions, public–private partnerships and continuing efforts at increasing accountability. Horizontalism, interactive government, corporatization and citizen empowerment have been the order of the day, at least in political rhetoric (Peters, 1996). According to some British scholars, the state has effectively been 'hollowed out' (Rhodes and Dunleavy, 1995). When it comes to the move from anticipatory to reactive modes of problem solving, that too has a continuing relevance. The information revolution that has taken place since the Richardson volume was published has further obviated national government's claims to monopolized facts and superior expertise. The increasing speed of life, the increasingly global scale of business, finance, culture and leisure, and the rapid demographic and sociocultural changes of the last 20 years have produced a paradox: although governments possess increasingly sophisticated expertise and techniques of uncertainty reduction, their ability to identify and tackle public problems proactively may well have decreased.

Notwithstanding its use in detecting these transnational trends, the basic claim of the national policy style hypothesis was not supported in the Richardson volume. The individual country studies displayed considerable intranational style variations, both across various subnational levels of government and between different policy sectors. In federal systems such as Germany, for example, the notion of 'the' government itself proved to be tenuous, since the German Länder governments play such an important role in many domestic policy domains and seem to have developed rather distinctive political cultures and policy-making routines. In Holland, the classical Lijphartian consociationalism at the political centre was under pressure from a growing 'sectorialization' of policy making in distinctive, powerful and rapidly evolving policy communities for separate fields of government activity. Moreover, in many countries it proved important to distinguish between the professed (idealised self-image) and actual (empirically discernible) ways of making public policy. For example, the common picture of 'the French state' as being a prime example of étatiste and technocratic rule becomes blurred if one looks more carefully at what actually transpires in a few cases of policy making. There appears to be much more room for give and take between state and strong business interests, and more plain 'politics' than the stereotypical French style image allows for.

Given the controversial status of the notion of national policy styles, it might be fruitful to pit it against a rival claim when examining the case study evidence. One notably different way of looking for commonalties in policy making is to emphasize the institutional features of the particular issue area or policy sector as the major explanatory factor (Weaver and Rockman, 1993). This idea lies, although sometimes implicitly, at the heart of the literature on 'iron triangles', policy communities and policy networks (Lowi, 1964; Heclo, 1978; Richardson and Jordan, 1979; Rhodes, 1990; Marsh and Rhodes, 1992; Jordan and Schubert, 1992; Kickert *et al.*, 1997; Marsh and Smith, 2000; cf. Dowding, 1995) and actor–structure accounts of public policy making (Scharpf, 1997). Without going into the intricacies of this literature here, let us take it as the basis for a counterclaim against the policy style hypothesis. The competing hypothesis is that national policy styles either do not exist or are outweighed by strong sectoral institutions and traditions of handling sectoral governance issues. These sectoral features should, in this view, operate across national boundaries. Therefore according to this hypothesis we should see roughly similar governance patterns in each of the sectors, and major differences in governance between sectors, even between cases set in the same country.

To be able to examine these competing claims, we have had to ensure not only a reasonable variation of policy sectors and governance tasks (see above), but also a proper distribution of countries with regard to the institutional features that are said to determine national policy styles. Keeping this need for variation in mind, we have selected the following countries:

Germany: Corporatist, federal system with technocratic elan, yet also strong sectoral traditions. Expected policy style (at the federal level): proactive, consensual.

Britain: Westminster, unitary system with a centralized, generalist executive under pressure from major market-oriented governance reforms. Expected policy style: moderately reactive, moderately imposed.

France: Presidential system with a centralist, technocratic bureaucracy and a political culture where 'the state' is still widely appreciated as the essential public governance mechanism. Expected policy style: proactive, strongly imposed.

Holland: Consociational system where neocorporatist bargaining (the 'polder model') has combined institutional endurance with flexible policy making. Expected policy style: moderately proactive, strongly consensual.

Sweden: Corporatist, unitary system with strong social engineering ethos, long viewed as the paradigm 'welfare state' faced with economic recession later than most other European countries. Expected policy style: strongly proactive, strongly consensual.

Spain: Federalizing state with long centralist tradition yet increasingly strong regional governments, authoritarian institutions and clientelist styles under pressure of democratization. Expected policy style: moderately reactive, weakly imposed.

Placed in the policy style matrix, this yields the style configuration that is to be tested for in the comparative case analysis (see Figure 2.2). In sum, the design of the study encompasses 24 case studies, with each of the four governance challenges being studied in each of the six countries. In the concluding part of this volume, cross-sectoral and cross-national comparisons are performed. We shall return to the issue of policy styles there.

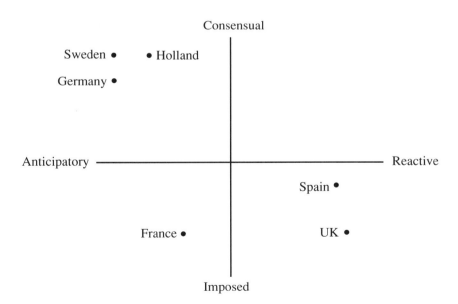

Figure 2.2   Research design: country selection and hypothesized national policy styles

4   PERFORMANCE OR PERCEPTION? PROGRAMMATIC AND POLITICAL ASSESSMENTS

The main focus of this study is not on styles but on understanding the dynamics of success and failure in policy sectors and political systems. Crucial to our project is the distinction made between the programmatic and the political dimension of success and failure in public governance. In a *programmatic* mode of assessment, the focus is on the effectiveness, efficiency and resilience of the specific policies being evaluated. The key questions asked in this dimension pertain to the classical, Lasswellian–Lindblomian view of policy making as social problem solving: does government tackle important social issues, does it deliver solutions to social problems that work, and does it do so in a sensible way (Lasswell, 1971; Lindblom, 1990)? Of course these questions involve normative and therefore inherently political judgments too (Barry and Rae, 1975), yet the focus is essentially instrumental; that is, it is on assessing the impact of policies that are designed and presented as purposeful interventions in social affairs. In our terminology, the *political* dimension of assessment refers to the way policies and policy makers become represented and evaluated in the political arena (Stone, 1997). This is the discursive world of symbols, emotions, political ideology and power relationships. It is not the social consequences of policies that count, but the political construction of these consequences, which might be driven by considerations of wholly different kinds.

Not surprisingly, there are often disparities between programme performance and political performance. Whether programmatic success is acknowledged, and how much it counts for in the overall judgment about its performance, is determined in political processes. Success and failure mean different things to different people at different times (Bovens and 't Hart, 1996). Generally, policy evaluation involves a collision between different, socially constructed frames of reference and sets of evaluation standards (Fischer, 1995). Each of these is biased, and the outcome of their collision is bound to reproduce selectively some of these biases. Assessments of success or failure in government are therefore dependent upon temporal, spatial, cultural and political factors. The dominant assessment of many conspicuous 'planning disasters' – the Sydney Opera House or the aborted London airport expansion plan of the 1960s, for example – has evolved over time, as certain issues, conflicts and consequences that were important at the time have evaporated or changed shape, and as new actors and power constellations have emerged (see Hall, 1982; cf. Bovens and 't Hart, 1996).

In this project we have taken up the challenges of studying the dynamics of policy success and failure comparatively. The study seeks to clarify the conceptual issues involved in understanding the differential nature and significance of governance success and failure in political systems. Empirically, it aims for the type of controlled research design that enables a more systematic explanatory account of the key factors that promote success and failure. In general programmatic terms, the case studies will examine whether, given a particular sectoral and issue context, governments are capable of effecting goal-directed social interventions, delivering on their promises, adapting programmes to changing circumstances and controlling costs. In parallel, we have asked the case authors to perform a 'political reality check' in each case. Indicators of political failure or success are political upheaval (press coverage, parliamentary investigations, political fatalities, litigation) or lack of it, and changes in generic patterns of political legitimacy (public satisfaction with policy or confidence in authorities and public institutions). These general criteria have formed the starting point for the analytical approach of the study. However, in each of the four sector introduction chapters, the sector editors will adapt and fine-tune these general programmatic and political assessment criteria to match the specific governance task and sectoral characteristics at hand. Table 2.2 depicts these sectoral specifications, and allows for a first comparison of the programmatic as well as political standards for evaluation used in the four sections of the project.

Table 2.2   Programmatic and political assessment criteria: an overview

Governing decline: steel sector

I. Programmatic assessment criteria:
  • The financial costs of restructuring
  • The economic viability of the industry following restructuring
  • The size of employment losses sustained
II. Political assessment criteria:
  • An absence of political crisis (conflict, elite survival, organizational survival) in the sector
  • The subsectoral and geographical distribution of the costs of restructuring
  • The political status of the sector following restructuring ('strategic industry' or not)

Governing reform: health sector

I. Programmatic assessment criteria:
  • The duration of reform episode, from first plans to actual implementation
  • The ability to achieve short-term and long-term reform ambitions
  • The reduction of professional dominance in financial, clinical and political spheres
II. Political assessment criteria:
  • The political consequences for reformist policy makers

Governing innovation: finance sector

I. Programmatic assessment criteria:
    * The number of bank failures and/or relative asset size of failed banks
    * The absolute and relative financial costs of bailouts
    * The timing of state intervention
    * The containment of the systemic impact of bank failures
    * The timing and duration of state-driven institutional changes
    * The perceived adequacy of the new financial regime
II. Political assessment criteria:
    * The judgment of official investigative bodies
    * The political consequences for financial policy makers and state institutions

---
Governing crisis: blood transfusion sector

I. Programmatic assessment criteria:
    * The introduction of effective donor selection
    * The introduction of mandatory blood tests
    * The introduction of an import stop for untreated blood products
    * The introduction of heath treatment of blood products
    * The withdrawal of untreated products from the market
II. Political assessment criteria:
    * The intensity and tone of media coverage
    * The judgment of official investigative bodies
    * The amount and nature of litigation
    * The amount of compensation paid
    * The number and nature of political casualties
    * The general sentiment in the public opinion

5 ASSESSMENT ASYMMETRIES: SOME ANALYTICAL QUESTIONS AND PROPOSITIONS

In addition to describing patterns of programmatic and political performance, this study also seeks to make a contribution to explaining them. We are particularly interested in discrepancies between programmatic and political performances. Here we shall sketch some explanatory notions we had in mind when initiating this study. In the concluding part of the study we shall revisit these notions and see how well they help us make sense of the case findings.

The Candide character from Chapter 1 would most likely expect symmetry between the programmatic and the political dimensions of performance. He would expect the mechanisms of accountability to be firmly grounded in 'reality'. Simply put, his hypothesis would be: if policies do well programmatically, this will be recognized and appreciated as such in the political domain, whereas, if policies fail to perform as expected, there will be negative feedback and political costs for the policy makers and organizations involved. Put even more simply: policy makers get what they deserve – credit where it is due, but penalties if they mess up.

Cassandra, in contrast, would take the cynical view of policy evaluation and expect a pernicious kind of asymmetry: frequent programme failures, yet much less frequent political failures. She would argue that the political imagery of success and failure has become disconnected from the real world of policy implementation, public service delivery and social outcomes of government action. Policy makers are, in this view, much better at manipulating symbols and images than at solving social problems. According to Edelman (1977) they produce 'words that succeed and policies that fail'. They are quite effective blame avoiders, increasingly aided by an entire technology of 'spin doctoring'. By playing the blame game effectively, they are often able to keep programme failures off the political agenda altogether. If not, they can try to write them off as freak incidents or bad luck. When all of this fails to work, they will try to avoid being held accountable politically by deflecting blame to 'lightning rods', that is, officials lower down the hierarchy (see Ellis, 1994) or by pointing out that the responsibility rests not just with them but with many, even countless, individuals and organizations that make up the complex machinery of government and the hybrid public–private networks in which many policies are made: the 'many hands' argument (Thompson, 1987; Hardin, 1995; Bovens, 1998).

Avoiding these extremes, a third character, Contingentia, would also expect asymmetries between programmatic and political assessments to occur, but would expect them to go both ways, and explain them differently from Cassandra. Like Cassandra, she would expect there to be instances where programmatic failure is not matched by political failure. This would not necessarily be a matter of Machiavellian manipulation, however. In many cases, besieged policy makers just get lucky: in the present era of instant news and rapidly changing soundbites, public opinion and political attention may shift away from the policy failure before the political accountability process has run its course. They get distracted by other, fresh and perhaps more shocking events. Also policy sectors differ in their symbolic content. Some sectors, such as finance and banking, are regarded as too technical and too 'boring' for general public consumption (even though, or perhaps even because, there are huge, unimaginably large sums of money involved), whereas policy failures in public health and such physical, historically rooted industries as steel, mining and shipbuilding strike an emotional chord much more easily.

Contingentia would also take into account the other type of asymmetry: policies that perform well on the programmatic side but that experience political headwinds nevertheless. She would point us to Wildavsky's (1980) paradox of health policy as an example: 'doing better, feeling worse'. Because preventive health care works so well in, for example, Germany, the people actually left in the remedial health care system are those with really serious illnesses that are more difficult to cure. This will bring down the statistics over time, and expose the system to charges of being ineffective and inefficient. More generally, public programmes that perform are easily taken for granted. They raise people's expectations and therefore unintentionally sow the seeds of their own political problems when they experience some headwinds, or when these higher expectations simply cannot be met.

Another explanation for this second type of asymmetry lies with the nature of governance. Especially when policy making is about reform, redistribution or managing crises, policy makers may be faced with 'tragic choices' where all the alternatives are painful (Calabresi and Bobbitt, 1978; Peters, 1993). Even when they operate carefully and compassionately, they may still face strong political opposition and severe criticism. Finally, the volatility of contemporary news making is such that public heroes can turn into public villains almost overnight. According to some observers, the media have evolved from watchdogs into 'junkyard dogs'. One verbal slip, one personal error may bring them on and produce a blaze of negative publicity likely to spill over into the political arena – irrespective of the fact that the person's overall record or the policy's general performance is not problematic at all.

In this study we look at our cases expecting asymmetries in the relationship between programmatic and political success. In other words we anticipate finding many cases where there is a notable politicization and depoliticization of policies, programmes and the officials involved in them. The Cassandra and Contingentia interpretations outlined above will be pitted against one another as the primary accounts of which forms of (de)politicization occur and why. The Candide interpretation will be our null hypothesis, which we regard as supported when it turns out that the number of symmetrical cases far outweighs the asymmetrical ones. We shall also check for a number of factors that we suspect influence whether in any given case (a)symmetry occurs. We have formulated them in the form of testable propositions.

- *Political structure*: the institutional make-up of a national political system and/or policy sector may encourage a more adversarial or temperate political climate. The more inclusive the policy-making structure, the lower the likelihood of an intense politicization of programme failures.
- *Political culture*: the more a sector/country is characterized by pragmatic, consensual norms and traditions of interaction between government and

private stakeholders, the lower the likelihood of an intense politicization of programme failures.

- *Policy frames*: the more the belief systems of policy stakeholders are aligned, and the more they agree on the fundamentals of the policy area at hand, the lower the likelihood of an intense politicization of policy failures.
- *Governance task*: the more redistributive the nature of the crucial governance task, the higher the likelihood of an intense politicization of policy failures.
- *Symbolic potential*: the more emotive the subject matter and the more intense the media interest in the sector as a whole, the higher the likelihood of an intense politicization of policy failures.

6   COMPARATIVE ISSUES

The data that can be derived from these 24 case studies permits us to think about comparison along three dimensions. The first, the usual scope of comparative political analysis, is to *compare across countries*. The six countries here were selected for theoretical as well as practical reasons (see above) and there does appear to be substantial variance in the ways in which they treat policy issues. Many of the stereotypical elements do emerge: for example, a tendency towards cooperative behaviour in Sweden and étatisme in France. That having been said, there will also be some findings that go against the conventional stereotypes, with German administration, for example in AIDS policy, being somewhat less legalistic than might be expected. Still, there is obvious utility in the cross-national comparison.

The second dimension of comparison is *comparison within policy areas*. Gary Freeman argued some years ago (1985) that comparative public policy studies should think carefully about comparing policies more than countries, and that policies in the same country would be more different than the same policy in different countries. Freeman's argument was that the nature of the actors involved, the technical issues considered, the basis of political coalitions and so on that surround a policy would tend to be the same in any national political setting. These 'data' provide some substantiation for Freeman's hypothesis, as they point out the extent to which the political and policy issues differed substantially across the policy areas, but had some similarities across countries. A wider sampling of issues may, we believe, demonstrate that a good deal of variance in comparative policy studies can indeed be accounted for by differences among policy areas.

The final dimension of comparison is to *compare across four policy areas*, construed as we have, as examples of decline, innovation and so on. This is a more innovative classification of policy areas than the usual functional enumeration of types of policy. Although it will emerge that this typology had its limits (see Chapter 31), it has some heuristic potential. For example, countries do seem to cope with critical developments such as the HIV issue in a more concentrated and intense manner than they deal with nagging questions such as declining steel industries and health cost containment. Again, this is a limited sample of issues in a limited range of political systems, but the general utility of schemes that focus on analytic characteristics of policy issues rather than the usual functional classifications does merit more serious consideration than it has thus far been granted. The policy analytic literature has still done little in developing schemes of this sort, so this is an important first step in further research.

7   THE DESIGN OF THE BOOK

Each of the four governance challenges is described in a separate section of the book. Each section starts with an introduction written by the sector editor, outlining the nature of the governance challenge in greater detail, specifying the sector-specific analytical framework (contextual factors, success/failure criteria, explanatory variables) and briefly placing the countries studied in the big picture of governance in that sector. The bulk of each section is taken up by the six country case studies performed by national specialists in the policy domain. Each case study has been conducted using the analytical approach outlined by the sector editor, and is reported along the same lines. Each chapter starts with a general introduction to the national problématique, followed by an overview of the key actors involved, a reconstruction of the key events of the case selected for detailed analysis, an evaluation of the programmatic and political performance of the relevant state actors and an explanation of the policy outcomes. The standardized format is part of our efforts to achieve a focused comparison (George, 1979) of national and sectoral experiences across the individual case studies.

In Chapter 31, the results of the 24 case studies will be presented. Each governance challenge will be reviewed, comparing the national experiences of the six countries in terms of their programmatic and political successes and/or failures, national policy styles and explanatory variables. In Chapter 32, we shall proceed to compare across sectors and countries, and draw some general conclusions in view of the central research questions of the overall project, as set out in the previous chapter, as well as in this one.

References to part I

Barry, B. and D.W. Rae (1975), 'Political Evaluation', in F.I. Greenstein and N.W. Polsby (eds), *Handbook of Political Science*, vol. 1, Reading, MA: Addison-Wesley, pp. 337–401.

Bovens, M. (1998), *The Quest for Responsibility: Accountability and Citizenship in Complex Organisations*, Cambridge: Cambridge University Press.

Bovens, M. and P. 't Hart (1996), *Understanding Policy Fiascoes*, New Brunswick: Transaction Publishers.

Calabresi, G. and P. Bobbit (1978), *Tragic Choices*, New York: W.W. Norton.

Cram, L. and J. Richardson (1999), *Policy Styles in the European Union*, London: Routledge.

Denhardt, R. (1993), *The Pursuit of Significance*, Belmont: Wadsworth Publishing Company.

Doig, J.W. and E.C. Hargrove (eds) (1990), *Leadership and Innovation: A Biographical Perspective on Entrepreneurs in Government*, Baltimore: Johns Hopkins University Press.

Dowding, K. (1995), 'Model or Mataphor? A Critical Review of the Policy Network Approach', *Political Studies*, 18, 136–58.

Edelman, M. (1977), *Political Language: Words that Succeed and Policies that Fail*, New York: Academic Press.

Ellis, R.J. (1994), *Presidential Lightning Rods: Politics of Blame Avoidance*, Lawrence: University Press of Kansas.

Fischer, F. (1995), *Evaluating Public Policy*, Chicago: Nelson-Hall.

Freeman, G.P. (1985), 'National Styles and Policy Sectors: Explaining Structured Variation', *Journal of Public Policy*, 5 (4), 467–96.

George, A.L. (1979), 'Case Studies and Theory Development: The Method of Structured, Focused Comparison', in P.G. Lauren (ed.), *Diplomacy*, New York: The Free Press, pp. 43–68.

Goodsell, C. (1985), *The Case for Bureaucracy*, Chatham: Chatham House.

Gray, P.D. and P. 't Hart (eds) (1998), *Public Policy Disasters in Europe*, London: Routledge.

Gregory, R. (1983), 'Political Rationality or Incrementalism?', *Policy and Politics*, 17, 139–53.

Hall, P.A. (1982), *Great Planning Disasters*, Berkeley: University of California Press.

Hall, P.A. (1986), *Governing the Economy: The Politics of State Intervention in Britain and France*, Oxford: Polity Press.

Hardin, R. (1995), *One for All: The Logic of Group Conflict*, Princeton: Princeton University Press.

Heclo, H. (1978), 'Issue Networks and the Executive Establishment', in A. King (ed.), *The New American Political System*, Washington, DC: American Enterprise Institute for Public Policy Research.

Hogwood, B.D. and B.G. Peters (1985), *The Pathology of Public Policy*, Oxford: Oxford University Press.

Hood, C.C. (1976), *The Tools of Government*, London: Wiley.

Jordan, G. and K. Schubert (eds) (1992), *Policy Networks*, Dordrecht: Kluwer.

Kickert, W.J.M., E.-H. Klijn and J.F.M. Koppenjan (eds) (1997), *Managing Complex Networks: Strategies for the Public Sector*, London: Sage.

Lasswell, H. (1971), *A Pre-View of Policy Science*, New York: Elsevier.

Lindblom, C.E. (1979), 'Still Muddling Not Yet Through', *Public Administration Review*, 39 (6), 517–23.

Lindblom, C.E. (1990), *Inquiry and Change: The Troubled Attempt to Understand and Shape Society*, New Haven: Yale University Press.

Lowi, T.J. (1964), 'American Business, Public Policy, Case Studies and Political Theory', *World Politics*, 16, 676–715.

Markovits, A.S. and M. Silverstein (eds) (1988), *The Politics of Scandal: Power and Process in Liberal Democracies*, New York: Holmes and Maier.

Marsh, D. and R.A.W. Rhodes (eds) (1992), *Policy Networks in British Government*, Oxford: Clarendon.

Marsh, D. and M. Smith (2000), 'Understanding Policy Networks: Towards a Dialectical Approach', *Political Studies*, 48 (1) 4–21.

Moore, M.H. (1996), *Creating Public Value*, Cambridge, MA: Harvard University Press.

Peirce, W.C. (1981), *Bureaucratic Failure and Public Expenditure*, New York: Academic Press.

Peters, B.G. (1993), 'Tragic Choices: Administrative Rulemaking and Policy Choice', in R.A. Chapman (ed.), *Ethics in Public Service*, Edinburgh: Edinburgh University Press, pp. 43–57.

Peters, B.G. (1996), *The Future of Governing: Four Emerging Models*, Lawrence: University Press of Kansas.

Pierre, J. and B.G. Peters (2000), *Governance, Politics and the State*, New York: St Martin's Press.

Pierson, P. (1994), *Dismantling the Welfare State? Reagan, Thatcher and the Politics of Retrenchment*, Cambridge: Cambridge University Press.

Rhodes, R.A.W. (1990), 'Policy Networks: A British Perspective', *Journal of Theoretical Politics*, 2, 293–317.

Rhodes, R.A.W. and P. Dunleavy (eds) (1995), *Prime Minister, Cabinet and Core Executive*, Basingstoke: Macmillan.

Richardson, J.J. (ed.) (1982), *Policy Styles in Western Europe*, London: Allen & Unwin.

Richardson, J.J. and A.G. Jordan (1979), *Governing Under Pressure: the Policy Process in a Post-Parliamentary Democracy*, Oxford: Robertson.

Rose, R. and P.L. Davies (1994), *Inheritance in Public Policy: Change without Choice in Britain*, New Haven: Yale University Press

Rose, R. and B.G. Peters (1978), *Can Governments Go Bankrupt?*, New York: Basic Books.

Scharpf, F.W. (1988), 'The Joint-Decision Trap: Lessons form German Federalism and European Integration', *Public Administration*, 66, 239–78.

Scharpf, F.W. (1997), *Games Real Actors Play: Actor-Centered Institutionalism in Policy Research*, Boulder, CO: Westview Press.

Schmitter, P.C. (1979), 'Still the Century of Corporatism?', in P.C. Schmitter and G. Lehmbruch (eds), *Trends Toward Corporatist Intermediation*, London: Sage.

Skocpol, T. (1985), 'Bringing the State Back in: Strategies of Analysis in Current Research', in: P.B. Evans *et al.* (eds), *Bringing the State Back in*, Cambridge: Cambridge University Press.

Stone, D. (1997), *Policy Paradox: The art of political decision making*, New York: W.W. Norton.

Thompson, D.F. (1987), *Political Ethics and Public Office*, Cambridge, MA: Harvard University Press.

Vogel, D. (1986), *National Styles of Regulation: Environmental Policy in Great Britain and the United States*, Ithaca, NY: Cornell University Press.

Weaver, R.K. and B.A. Rockman (eds) (1993), *Do Institutions Matter? Government Capabilities in the United States and Abroad*, Washington, DC: The Brookings Institution.

Wildavsky, A. (1980), 'Doing Better and Feeling Worse: The Political Pathology of Health Policy', *The Art and Craft of Policy Analysis*, London: Macmillan.

PART II

Managing decline: public policy and the steel
sector

3. Managing decline: governing national steel production under economic adversity

Geoffrey Dudley and Jeremy Richardson

1 STEEL POLITICS AND THE 'NATIONAL CHAMPIONS'

The relative decline of the European steel industry programmatically and politically over the past 25 years has posed great challenges in governance at both the national and supranational levels. These challenges have been largely overcome, via a process of exogenous and endogenous change, and steel would no longer be generally regarded as a major problem for policy-making elites. The peak of the crisis occurred in the early to mid-1980s, when, unusually for the EU, a consensus within the steel sector allowed 'a period of manifest crisis' to be officially declared under the Treaty of Paris, and which entailed direct supranational governance from Brussels on output and prices. There were also supranational attempts to control the spiralling subsidies to steel in a number of countries by means of a Steel Aid Code. These controls enjoyed mixed success, but demonstrated the extent to which interventionism had become the accepted policy style within the EU at that time.

In retrospect, not only were the 1980s the high-water mark of financial crisis for steel, they also represented the peak of the interventionist style. In the 1990s, there was an apparently 'inexorable trend away from the perception of steel as a national champion' (Cohen, 1995), towards the new 'solutions' of privatization and both national and cross-national alliances. As the six national case studies illustrate, this shift in the dominant paradigms involved greater policy changes in some countries than in others.

For example, in France and Spain the 'national champion' culture was deeply embedded, and here the trend away from interventionism in the 1990s has involved quite radical changes in governance. Similarly, in Britain, the 1980s saw a sea change with the state-owned British Steel Corporation transformed from a largely production-led public corporation to a zealous private company defending free market values. In contrast, in Germany and, especially, in Holland, the changes in governance have been less marked. In Germany, the powerful tripartite alliance between government, industry and unions has largely survived the crisis years, and the largest steel companies were already in the private sector. It could be said that the modern EU policy style is now quite close to that which has pertained in Holland for many years: intervention by government only in times of crisis, otherwise a laissez-faire approach. The principal Dutch steel company, Hoogovens, has traditionally asserted its independence, and as a private sector undertaking has had less of the 'national champion' status. Significantly, Hoogovens was an early exponent of cross-national alliances when it merged with the German company Hoesch in 1972. This alliance proved abortive, but illustrates the extent to which Holland diverged from the EU norm in the decades prior to the 1990s.

Significantly, despite its relatively recent EU membership, Sweden has followed a broadly similar pattern to that found in other EU countries, with a great deal of government intervention in the 1970s and 1980s, followed by privatization as the new policy 'solution' in the 1990s. This suggests that the cross-national spread of ideas goes well beyond institutional boundaries, and involves a high degree of transnational policy learning.

This transnational learning also reflects a political paradox for steel in that, notwithstanding the 'national champion' culture, its basic character as a key component in many manufacturing processes makes it a heavily traded commodity. Politically, this has had the effect of creating serious tensions between trading blocs. For example, even now, the United States, although regarded as the stronghold of free market values, is highly suspicious of the size and source of imports. The US steel industry has a traditionally strong voice on these issues, and the government is usually prepared to listen. Thus, in 1999–2000, both South Korea and Japan successfully secured the setting up of World Trade Organisation panels to investigate US anti-dumping duties on steel imports. Similarly, early in 2000, Japan and the EU also won WTO judgments in cases they brought against a 1916 US law allowing private companies to sue importers in the US courts for damages resulting from alleged dumping. This law had been resurrected by US steel companies and used against Japanese and EU steelmakers (*Financial Times*, 21 March 2000).

Indeed, trade issues are one area where supranational governance continues within the EU. For example, there have been a number of politically delicate crises with East European steelmakers. During the 1990s, EU steel companies became increasingly concerned about what they allege to be 'dumping' by the East Europeans, resulting in over-supply and a depression in prices. This has led to duties being placed at various times on imports from a number of countries, including the Czech Republic, Hungary and Poland. The problem is exacerbated by the fact that they are applicant states. Thus, because of enlargement, the relative decline of steel continues to involve complicated questions of supranational governance.

2 NATIONAL SUCCESS AND FAILURE AND THE INFLUENCE OF SUPRANATIONAL GOVERNANCE

Perhaps more than with almost any other industrial sector, the question of programmatic and political success and failure in national steel industries is inextricably bound up in the history and institutions of the EU. Thus developments at the European level have been crucial in shaping the fate of national steel industries and policies: in the steel section the dependent variable is the same as in the other sections – national (steel) governance – but the special characteristic of steel is the prominence of supranational governance mechanisms coexisting with, but also shaping, national policies. A brief longitudinal analysis will therefore illustrate not only the delicate interrelationship between supranational and national governance, but also how the context in which exogenous circumstances have been perceived by the principal actors has affected the style of governance.

Thus institutions can enshrine certain fashionable economic ideas at the time of their inception, and carry them forward to influence future policies. In this context, Glais makes the important point that, in economic terms, the Treaty of Paris, which created the European Coal and Steel Community (ECSC) in 1951, reflected the contemporary dominance of the Keynesian model (Glais, 1995, p. 225). In the view of the promoters of the ECSC Treaty, only a supranational organization capable of coordinating the trade would be able to lead the steel industry towards a situation of equilibrium that accorded with optimization of economic welfare (ibid., p. 226). The Treaty of Paris was therefore a distinctive hybrid in which liberal principles rested somewhat uneasily against the extensive powers given to the High Authority. Quoting Hallstein, Tsoukalis and Strauss describe the system set up by the Paris Treaty as one of regulated competition, with provisions made for central crisis management (Tsoukalis and Strauss, 1987, p. 189).

From the outset, there was an ambivalence about the Treaty which allowed it to be given different interpretations at different times. In addition, there was also the endemic paradox of the need for central control in order to create a genuine common market. These twin tensions were to run like a thread through the development of the ECSC over the following five decades. For example, in addition to articles of the Paris Treaty which enshrined the objectives of a common market and apparently outlawed cartels and state aids, Article 58 allowed the High Authority (and later the Commission), with the assent of the Council of Ministers, to declare a period of manifest crisis, and establish a system of production quotas. In addition, Article 61 allowed for the fixing of minimum prices by the High Authority/Commission if it found that a manifest crisis existed or was imminent, and that such a decision was necessary to attain the objectives of the common market. In an industry such as steel, deeply susceptible to trade cycles, it was always likely that the Keynesian counter-cyclical character of the Paris Treaty would at times lead to pressure for Articles 58 and 61 to be implemented (Dudley and Richardson, 1999).

Nevertheless, it could also be said that, even more than Keynesian values, the concept of the ECSC itself rested on the idea that all means should be sought to avoid a repeat of the horror of two twentieth-century world wars. The idea of the ECSC came from France, and was largely the brainchild of Foreign Minister Robert Schuman and Jean Monnet, at that time General Commissioner of the French Plan. Monnet was a highly influential figure in this key act of policy 'framing', that is creating a perspective from which an amorphous, ill-defined problematic situation can be made sense of and acted upon (Rein and Schön, 1991, p. 263). Monnet's policy frame became the objectives of the Paris Treaty, and he himself became the first president of the High Authority of the ECSC. The drafters of the Paris Treaty hoped to minimize national opposition to the plan, while at the same time laying the foundations for further economic integration in the future, consistent with the neofunctionalist model (Tsoukalis and Strauss, 1987, pp. 188–9). In these early years, therefore, a common market became the accepted policy 'solution' within the High Authority to the 'problem' of promoting economic and political integration.

It cannot be said, however, that this era represented a success in governance. For example, Monnet himself was more interested in the High Authority as a forerunner of a federal European government than in the detailed 'nuts and bolts' issues of the coal and steel industries (Spierenburg and Poidevin, 1994, pp. 105–6). Monnet therefore set the tone for the policy style of the High Authority in the 1950s and 1960s, where the political symbolism of the High Authority as a supranational institution took precedence over the political will to assert itself in the detailed affairs of coal and steel.

In effect, despite impressive institutions (both organizations and rules) being in place at the supranational level, steel policy remained anchored at the national level. Significantly, many of the national steel industries were decidedly unsympathetic to Monnet's supranational vision. At some point, supranational policies meet (and often clash with) what Mazey terms a national policy 'hinterland' – a whole raft of national policies, styles and traditions which can, more or less, impinge on a given policy area, sometimes in unintended ways (Mazey, 1998, pp. 145–7). Paradoxically, in view of Monnet's key role, this clash was particularly evident in France where, in the early 1950s, steelmaking was still characterized by small plants, and technology from the pre-1914 period. French steel producers wanted state protection, and the steel producers' association, the Chambre Syndicale de la Sidérurgie Française (CSSF), actually opposed the state over the formation of the ECSC. Consequently, during the Paris Treaty negotiations, steelmakers had refused to open their books for Monnet on the grounds that it would be an infringement of industrial secrecy (see Daley, 1996, pp. 52–4).

The ultimate paradox of steel was that it was a 'special case' within the EU, having its own Treaty base, setting at least a symbolic example in terms of European institutional supranationalism. On the other hand, steel was far from being the ideal example of an industry amenable to the creation of a common market and supranational governance. National policy making was still the norm and both governments and steel companies valued the 'national champion' cultures. This value system clashed starkly with Monnet's deeply held commitment to transnational governance.

3   THE GOVERNANCE OF INDUSTRIAL DECLINE: THE 1970s AND 1980s

National governance appeared to work well. However, after relative stability in the 1950s and 1960s, the EU steel industry was stricken with severe programmatic failure throughout much of the 1970s and 1980s. To a significant extent, this crisis affected all countries, with the result that a new consensus emerged that supranational intervention was required. Ironically, the High Authority/Commission had been unable to impose a common market on the unwilling 'national champions', but now that their existence was at stake, both national governments and the companies themselves were anxious to seek help from Brussels. In neofunctionalist terms, certain key actors decided that supranational solutions would deliver more benefits than national solutions.

Much of the early pressure for intervention by the Commission came from France, where, despite its earlier opposition, the influential Jacques Ferry, as president of the European steelmakers' group Eurofer, demanded that 'a period of manifest crisis' under Article 58 of the Paris Treaty be declared. The call by France was echoed in a number of other EU countries, in particular Britain and Italy, where overoptimistic and expansionist capital investment plans had been implemented. In a sense, public policy failures at the national level were 'exported' to the EU level. To a significant extent, these investment crises reflected not only failures in public policy programmes, but also the developing technology of steel, and in particular the basic oxygen steel (BOS) process, which succeeded the previously widespread open hearth method. BOS allowed steel to be produced more efficiently and in greater quantities, and had been developed particularly in Japan. As BOS spread through Europe in the 1960s and 1970s, so the 'national champions' competed with each other to devise more ambitious and costly investment plans, often via public investment. Although BOS had clear technological advantages, however, it was also something of a time bomb in that, once the cyclical market downturn for steel occurred, the capital debt and over-capacity of the steel giants would leave them fatally exposed and vulnerable. This was the situation which obtained by the late 1970s. An added technological factor was a rival technology to BOS, the so-called 'mini mills', which are electric arc furnaces. Arc furnaces use scrap steel, and although the mini mills are obviously smaller than the huge BOS works, which employ iron ore as a raw material, they can be more flexible and profitable. In the EU, however, the BOS culture was dominant, and mini mills have not become a widespread technological 'solution'. (However, they can be a regional political issue, as in the Spanish case study.) The EU experience can be contrasted with that of the United States, where mini mill development is more widespread, and companies such as Nucor have emerged as serious rivals to the established giants such as US Steel. In the USA, therefore, technological change appears to be affecting market structure. Technology, like the cyclical character of steel, can therefore act as an exogenous variable to intensify crises and consequent governance responses.

By 1980, pressure from steel interests for a 'period of manifest crisis' to be declared had become overwhelming. Only West Germany, with its relative free market values, raised serious objections, but eventually it too became part of 'the grand coalition' (Sabatier, 1998, p. 119) behind a transnational solution. The regime of mandatory output and voluntary price controls was overseen by Industry Commissioner Etienne Davignon, who provided leadership from Brussels for the whole industry. Thus the so-called 'Davignon Plan' finally brought a system of supranational governance to steel, albeit in a manner hardly envisaged by Monnet.

In 1983, the Davignon regime was tightened still further, with the introduction of mandatory price controls. The industry commissioner, however, was encountering great difficulty in agreeing rationalization plans with national governments, as in most countries there was considerable discontent at the prospect of widespread steelworks closures. Supranational policy and domestic policy were working in opposite directions. In essence, the needs of international politics and domestic politics were in conflict. Davignon left the Commission in 1985, and his plan was dismantled over the next four years (the 'period of manifest crisis' was terminated in 1988). For a period, Davignon had succeeded in creating a genuine policy community in EU steel, with consensus achieved through a process of mutual adjustment and accommodation between the Commission, Eurofer and the Council of Ministers. By the late 1980s, however, this policy community was breaking up, while the 'policy frame' which sustained it was being challenged by one which espoused more free market values and the virtues of privatization.

4 BEYOND DECLINE: PRIVATIZATION, MERGERS AND FRAGMENTED GOVERNANCE

The Davignon Plan and its associated Euro-level policy community were undermined for a number of reasons. First, there were significant exogenous factors. By the late 1980s, the general European industrial climate was improving, and so the sense of deep crisis overhanging the steel companies was lifted as the market for steel improved. Companies such as BSC and Usinor Sacilor of France began to make profits after years of catastrophic losses, and so less need was seen for restructuring and price and output controls. Better market conditions reduced demands for public policy. In addition, as Hayward emphasizes, the accelerating decline of traditional industries and of defence-related industries in the context of the end of the Cold War meant that industrial patriotism exerted a declining hold on the business, bureaucratic and political decision makers. The notion of national champions had somewhat gone out of fashion. Even the idea that every state should have independent control over its national 'industrial base' seemed less compelling as commercial considerations began to predominate (Hayward, 1995, p. 350).

A more endogenous cause of change occurred within the Commission, where there was a degree of disillusionment with the obstructive attitudes of national governments and steel companies towards works closures. Quite simply, the existing policy instruments ran up against national sovereignty. Consequently, a growing determination that the industry should be left to sort out its own problems developed within the Commission. The limits of transnational public policy had been exposed. This shift was personified in the form of the competition commissioner from 1988, Sir Leon Brittan. As a former cabinet minister in the Thatcher government in Britain, Sir Leon was able to carry the Conservative government's fervour for reduced state intervention to the supra-national level. For Brittan, the style of governance symbolized by the Davignon Plan was perceived as a key 'problem', rather than a solution, which in itself was inhibiting the steel industry from making the necessary structural changes. Thus, in 1990, the Commission produced a key document, which outlined what it saw as the future of the steel industry, and was designed to act as a blueprint for policy over the next five years (EC Commission, 1990). The report declared that steel was becoming a business like any other, and that the way forward was through the free market. Emphasizing what it saw as the new European industrial culture, it claimed that there was a new dynamism on the part of steel management.

Brittan, together with sympathetic officials, nevertheless recognized steel's distinctive governance position (in the form of the Paris Treaty) within the EU. The old policy 'frame' had been embedded in the treaty and could, therefore, act as a ratchet preventing policy change. Thus, in 1990, he proposed the radical step of abolishing the Paris Treaty ahead of its expiry date in 2002. Crucially, however, the German government came out against Brittan, and abolition plans were abandoned. In the stark confrontation between the old and new policy 'frames', national governments and the majority of steel companies were still not prepared to abandon the system of governance based on steel's status as a 'special case'.

Nevertheless, even at the national level, the traditional values were beginning to erode. As the French and British case studies describe, in both of these countries during the 1990s free market values gained a much greater hold, with the result that the balance of power began to move away from those advocating the formerly dominant interventionist style. Consequently, when a new programmatic failure struck the EU in the early 1990s in the form of another recession for steel, the old policy community could not be reconstructed. Instead, a more fragmented and problematic style of government ensued in which the British, French and former West German steel companies all opposed the old subsidy system. Even though many of them were still suffering in the new recession, they had become converts to the new policy 'frame' and recognized the long-term benefits of it for them. On the other hand, steel companies from eastern Germany, Italy, Spain and Portugal sought permission from the Commission for nearly £5.33 billion in fresh subsidies, and in return were prepared to offer five million tonnes of capacity cuts. In December 1993, the Council of Ministers voted to allow the subsidies. Although strict monitoring conditions were imposed, the companies in the new 'free market' coalition were incensed. Hence the politics of the management of decline had become more complex and adversarial.

The Commission considered that EU crude steel over-capacity stood at 30 million tonnes but, as the subsidized steel-makers had only offered five million tonnes reduction, that left the unsubsidized companies to reduce their capacity by another 25 million tonnes. The Commission wished to retain an arm's-length policy on negotiating capacity cuts, and so invited a former Industry Directorate official, Fernand Braun, to consult individual steel companies on this matter. Braun, however, was unable to win the agreement of the unsubsidized companies, which left the plan in a perilous state. By now, the Commission itself was also more fragmented, and in 1994 Sir Leon Brittan forced a vote on subsidies to the Bresciani steel mills in northern Italy. The Commission voted against the subsidies by 11 votes to four, and this symbolic defeat for the interventionist style led directly to the collapse of the restructuring plan.

This governance failure proved a watershed for EU steel policy. Henceforth, restructuring was largely delegated to the national level, with privatization and company mergers and alliances the new policy 'solution'. Public policy, apart from privatization policy, also declined in importance. As the case studies in this section describe, by the end of the century all the principal EU steel companies had moved into the private sector and steel had largely lost its traditional status as a 'special case' demanding a panoply of public policies. Consequently, the 'national champion' policy was heavily diluted, and a number of cross-national mergers and takeovers took place, such as Cockerill-Sambre of Belgium and Usinor of France; Aceralia of Spain and Arbed of Luxembourg; and the merger between British Steel and the Dutch company Hoogovens to form the new company Corus.

Ultimately, therefore, successive crises and programmatic failures over three decades had led eventually to a breakdown in the interventionist style of governance and replaced it with something much more devolved, fragmented and unpredictable. However, as the German case study describes, vestiges of the old 'frame' remained, such as the takeover of the ailing Preussag company in 1998 by the government of Lower Saxony. The apparent failure and abandonment of the former system of governance was a complex process, involving both exogenous and endogenous factors, but with the Treaty of Paris due to expire in 2002, it could be said that steel's status as a 'special case', and the system of governance which represented it, are officially over. The sector is now largely private, not public; public policy is much less important; political salience is low; and the sector is characterized by the actions of profit-maximizing private actors. In that sense, the steel story is, ultimately, one of successful governance.

5   CRITERIA OF NATIONAL SUCCESS AND FAILURE

In this introductory chapter to the steel section, it has been necessary to place particular emphasis on supranational governance because the various stories of national success and failure can only be understood in the context of the evolution of EU policies and institutions. This supranational governance was of particular significance in the 1980s, but even when it has been less strong its very presence has imbued the overall policy debate with certain ideas and values. Indeed, such was the massive political significance and symbolism of the Treaty of Paris that it could do no other.

The following six chapters reflect this pervasive presence, while also setting out the separate development and eventual shift away from the 'national champion' culture. It is this endemic tension between enormously powerful supranational and national ideas and values which gives steel its particular fascination as a study of governance success and failure.

Each of the six national case studies therefore gives a longitudinal perspective of the response to crisis and decline since the early 1970s. One key example of possible shifts in governance success/failure criteria is the extent to which the core problem of the steel industry is regarded as the 'management of decline'. It could be said that there are several possible dimensions to the notion of 'decline'. For example, first there is 'decline' as measured by the economic viability of each national industry. The inherently cyclical nature of the steel industry can give 'decline' here an intensely episodic character. Thus, as the case studies illustrate, in the late 1970s and early 1980s, and again in the early 1990s, nearly all EU steel industries were in economic crisis, but nearly all of them recovered to a greater or lesser degree when demand improved.

Secondly, there is 'decline' in terms of the total capacity of each national industry. As illustrated earlier in this chapter, imposing a supranational solution on capacity cuts was one of the most intractable governance tasks faced by the EU. In fact, despite major plant closures, in the majority of EU countries a combination of new investment and improved efficiency has caused relatively small reductions in capacity. In this case, therefore, decline may not be so apparent.

Thirdly, there is 'decline' as measured by the numbers employed in each industry. It is in this category that, for many countries, the management of decline is most apparent, with in general a secular trend downwards.

Fourthly, there is 'decline' in terms of the political salience of steel. As we have seen, this is illustrated particularly at the supranational level in the move away from interventionism in the 1990s, and the imminent demise of the Treaty of Paris. This decline of steel as a 'special case' is generally mirrored at the national level with the replacement of the 'national champion' culture by privatization and cross-national alliances.

At the national level, therefore, there can be a complex interrelationship between programmatic and governance success and failure. Within each nation, however, contextual factors may vary and thus affect the timing and degree of change. These contextual factors may include technological developments such as those arising from the growth of the BOS process in the 1960s; the degree of economic crisis in the 1970s and early 1980s, and again in the early 1990s; the Europeanization of steel policy, turning steel restructuring into a two-level game; the institutionalized nature of steel policy, with strong and traditional semi-autonomous policy communities, with in some cases a powerful role for labour interests; the political–geographic structure of the national steel industry, for example steel as a regional issue in Spain and Germany, and to a lesser extent in France and Britain; and the political–administrative system of the country: unitary/federal, majoritarian/consensual, for example.

All these important contextual elements can give each national steel policy distinctive characteristics of governance success and failure. Nevertheless, as this chapter has attempted to illustrate, there are also overarching supranational and transnational ideas and values which permeate all national steel cultures, and so give a significant common 'frame' to policy change.

6 GLOSSARY

A brief glossary of the principal steel processes and technologies will assist in the understanding of the case studies.

Alloy
Any mixture of two or more metals which mix together when molten and do not separate on cooling. Steels are alloys of iron and other elements; for example, carbon steel is iron and carbon, stainless steel is iron and nickel and chromium. All commercial alloys contain at least traces of other elements which are not there intentionally.

Arc furnace (electric arc furnace)
Any electric furnace in which the heat is generated between an electrode or electrodes and the charge. The electrode may be of carbon or of the metal being melted.

Bar
Steel of circular cross-section can be a bar, a rod or a round, and there is no generally accepted firm dividing line.

Basic oxygen furnace (BOF)
Any steel furnace in which the steelmaking chemistry is basic and oxygen is blown in for refining. Derivatives: basic oxygen steel (BOS) and basic oxygen process (BOP).

Blast furnace
The commonest primary producer of iron from iron ore. It is a tall, refractory-lined stack-like furnace, mechanically charged, and fired on coke. The blast is generally heated to 1200°C.

Bloom
A semi-finished piece of rolled steel between the ingot stage and the finished product.

Direct reduction
Any one of many processes in which iron ore or steel is produced directly from the ore, as distinct from the indirect, where pig iron is first made and then purified.

Flat-rolled products
Plate, sheet and strip, the last two being either hot rolled or cold reduced.

Furnace
Any specially designed and constructed device for heating and/or melting iron or steel. It is always provided with an external source of heat, such as coal, oil, gas or electricity.

Hot metal
In iron and steelmaking the term 'hot metal' is confined to molten pig iron or blast furnace iron.

Ingot
Steel cast in a metal mould ready for rolling or forging.
Iron ore
Any one of the many oxides or carbonates of iron occurring naturally and used for smelting to iron.
Mini mill
Term used to describe steelworks employing electric arc furnace methods.
Open hearth furnace
A steelmaking furnace, fired by gas or oil, in which the charge to be melted is held in a refractory-lined bath, while the flames from the burning fuel pass over it. Process largely superseded by BOS.
Smelt
To reduce an ore to molten metal.
Special steels
Formerly used to distinguish alloy from carbon steels, but now applied to any steel which is considered to have special qualities.
Steel
A malleable alloy of iron and carbon, the carbon not exceeding about 1.7 per cent. If other elements are present in appreciable quantities, the steels are alloy steels.
Universal mill
A rolling mill, used for plate or sections in which all four sides are rolled simultaneously (several definitions adapted from Gale, 1971).

4. France and the restructuring of the steel industry: heroic policies and everyday successes

Luisa Perrotti[1]

1 INTRODUCTION

For the greater part of the crisis years, the French steel industry experienced direct or indirect state control. Countercyclical expansionary strategies, driven or supported by the government, persisted throughout the 1970s in spite of consistent signals that structural transformations in the steel market demanded dramatic policy changes. These policies have led to over-capacity and over-manning, increased the exposure of the industry to crisis management, and set the scene for a protracted process of restructuring in the following two decades. The government's provision of flanking measures to attenuate and dilute over time the social repercussions of the crisis, together with the weakness of the French labour unions when compared to other European countries, have prevented incidents of public protest from developing into full-scale political fallout. Nonetheless, the absence of conjunctures at which, during the restructuring process, the government has been forced to abandon its sectoral policies under pressure from organized labour and societal forces should not be taken to indicate a straightforward political success. In short, a trait common to several European experiences also appears to apply to French policies towards the steel industry: insofar as the industry has remained under government control it has also emerged as a sector prone to programmatic failure compounded by relative political success.

However, in the French case, it would be incorrect to infer that programmatic failures have led to unqualified policy failures, though this would be a legitimate conclusion to draw if the analysis focused on discrete stages of the industry's restructuring. The environment in which the steel industry operates has changed dramatically, inducing all the actors involved to reorient their strategies according to transformations that occurred beyond their respective spheres of control. At the domestic level, the industry has gradually regained autonomy from government in ways not apparent through a mere observation of sectoral

45

forms of government intervention. Individual stages of corporate restructuring, such as the 1987 merger between the two largest steel firms and the liberalization of financial markets, have had a larger impact on setting the conditions for the revitalization of the industry than changes in its ownership regime. Not least, domestic economic policies have become ever more constrained by budgetary and EU requirements, which have reduced the options of national governments in matters of industrial policy. These factors complicate the task of disentangling which policy concerns have most conditioned the formulation of sectoral strategies at different moments in time, and the extent to which such strategies might have been dictated by genuine market imperatives.

One possible criterion for evaluating outcomes consists in assessing whether government policies have seconded the aligning of the industry to the cyclical course of the steel market. Accordingly, recurring poor financial performance at times of market contraction but under conditions of limited or no government intervention is not taken to signal a policy failure. To the contrary, steel policies may be termed successful if evidence indicated that the industry has recovered from the crisis and 'normalized' its performance relative to the market cycle, which appears to be the case in France. However, the *process* of restructuring policies invites a qualified argument and the answer to the question underlying the present case study – 'how does a "strong" state (which France is conventionally regarded to be) cope with foreseeable but not controllable crisis in a declining sector?' – can be summarized as follows. As in other countries not usually described as 'strong states', in France remedying crisis-generating policies has exposed the industry's restructuring to politicized bargaining and costly implementation. Peculiar to this case remains the ability of government to diffuse the stakes in the industry's destiny across a number of actors in the fragmented French steel policy community, which has allowed for diluted political responsibility at crucial stages of the restructuring process.

2   STEEL POLICY IN FRANCE: RESTRUCTURING IN STAGES

Introduction

In the second half of the twentieth century, steel production in France was mostly associated with two, initially distinct, companies: on the one hand, Usinor, incorporated in 1948 as a result of the merger between the firms Forges et Aciéries du Nord et de l'Est and Hauts Fourneaux Forges et Aciéries de Denain-Anzin; on the other hand, Sacilor, established in 1973 and heir of the Sidélor-De Wendel group with its origins in the eighteenth century. Geographically, in the postwar period Usinor identified with steel production in the north of France, whilst Sacilor predecessors' largest production sites were concentrated in the east, especially in the Lorraine region and along France's borders with Belgium and Germany. This distribution began to change from the mid-1960s, when Usinor expanded its facilities in Lorraine and, overall, when both companies built new coastal facilities: Usinor by the northern town of Dunquerque, and Sacilor (at the time, Sidélor-De Wendel) at Fos-sur-Mer, in the south. Joint operations between the two firms started at the Fos plant in 1972, and consolidated in 1984, with partnerships in the engineering steels producer Ascometal, and in Unimétal, specialising in long products.

Although the industry was entirely privately owned until 1981, behind most of the above developments was the long hand of the state. In fact, the history of Usinor and Sacilor is, in its turn, associated with pervasive state interventionism in French industrial policy. This has, at different moments in time, complied with all three dominant patterns of government–business relations in France: *faire* (the state does), *faire faire* (the states incites others to do); and *laissez faire* (the state leaves it to the private sector) (Schmidt, 1996a, 1999). Also Usinor and Sacilor have been protagonists of all major shifts in France's policy making in the industrial sphere: from President de Gaulle's policy of national champions, to d'Estaing's *politique des créneaux*, combining the creation of large sector leaders with the bailout of lame-duck industries, to Mitterrand's *politique des filières*, centred upon the reorganization of nationalized industries into vertically integrated firms, increased output and low imports, through to the more recent and indirect Europeanization of industrial policy, induced by EU-driven budgetary discipline and competition rules.

Throughout the last three decades, the centrality of Usinor and Sacilor to steel production in France has been constant. However, the firms have undergone a complex process of corporate, financial and industrial restructuring underpinned by evolving patterns of state–industry relations. The four main stages of this process are examined below.

State Interventionism without Public Ownership

At the time of the inception of the crisis, in 1974, mutual dependency and mutual captivity characterized the relationship between the state and the steel industry. The origins of these patterns of state–industry relations can be traced in earlier developments. In the 1960s, the industry needed fresh capital to update obsolete technology and equipment, but the underdeveloped domestic capital market and protectionist economic policies constrained its options for access to favourable financing. The government's response to the needs of the industry combined cross-subsidization and preferential loans with active market regulation by means of authoritative fixing of prices and centralized planning, which was pre-arranged by informal contacts between government and business officials. This policy mix secured the government indirect control over investment and, overall, the acquiescence of the independent-minded but strategic steel industry in its recommended policy of industrial concentration. Financial and corporate interconnections and market-sharing agreements would have otherwise allowed for an unregulated oligopolistic behaviour of family-controlled firms.

From the mid-1960s, the 'contractualization' of state–industry relations, enshrined in the 1965 *Plan Professionnel*, added new dimensions to French steel policies. On the one hand, the state (namely, the Treasury Division of the Finance Ministry) lost control over the use of resources destined for the industry. Mediation between funding institutions and individual producers, management of and monitoring compliance with the plan were delegated to the then powerful industry's association CSSF (*Chambre Syndicale de la Sidérurgie Française*), successor of the prestigious *Comité de Forges*. On the other hand, the 'contract' between state and the industry entailed the renunciation of steel producers of autonomous decision making in matters of corporate and industrial restructuring.

The plan succeeded in enabling the government to pursue its industrial policy aims: production expanded rapidly, and rationalization and specialization agreements led to a reduction of the number of steel firms from 82 in 1967 to 66 in 1970, and of the number of steel plants from 119 to 99. However, it did not force the industry to confront its main structural problem: the need to integrate vertically downstream and into more profitable, higher-value products. More importantly, the plan had far-reaching implications for the framing of the later course of state–industry relations.

3   FROM OLIGOPOLY TO DUOPOLY

Covert and overt nationalization

Between 1974 and 1986, the wave of government-induced mergers continued and Usinor and Sacilor became the country's two largest steel producers. Crucially, it is during this period that, following the complete failure of over-investments at times of crisis, the French government gradually became the sole shareholder of both companies. The 1981 acquisition of 90 per cent of the capital of each firm through a conversion of their debts into equity evolved into the buying back of remaining publicly traded shares, in 1986. However, the de facto nationalization of Usinor and Sacilor dates back to 1978, when the conservative government headed by Raymond Barre restructured the debt and reconstructed the equity of the then nearly bankrupt companies. The plan established and reorganized debt-financing institutions operating either in the public sector or within the framework of the CSSF. These were given non-controlling stakes in the two reconstituted holdings, while 25 per cent of the firms' accumulated debt was converted into government-held debentures bearing a nominal interest. The plan also envisaged reductions of production capacity and massive redundancies, though, upon mounting opposition, generous concessions were made: lay-offs were transformed into pay-offs, and early retirement, retraining and redeployment schemes were agreed under the negotiated collective agreements named *Conventions de Protection Sociale de la Sidérurgie.*

A few months after the election of President Mitterrand, the socialist government carried out the formal nationalization of Usinor and Sacilor enshrined in the *Loi de Finances* rectificative of 27 November 1981, on which consensus was easily formed in Parliament. Significantly, at the time of voting on the law, some right-wing MPs not only supported the decision, but also advocated the need for complementary measures in favour of the industry. This position signalled a dramatic change of course compared to only four years before, when the conservative Finance, Industry and Labour ministers produced a report arguing the case against the nationalization of the steel industry (Marklew, 1995, p. 101). Under the nationalization law, the state appointed two-thirds of the board of directors, the chairman and CEO of the firms, and controlled the companies' decision making on income allocation, approval of the annual accounts and the appointment of auditors. While interference was limited to major decisions and did not affect routine activities, the socialist government pursued and amplified Barre's debt-relief undertaking, softened the job-reduction programme, and delayed any action towards industrial restructuring. Counter to the resolution that, within the EC collective management of the steel crisis, France would reduce production capacity by 5.3 million tonnes, in 1982 Mitterrand endorsed an expansionary plan envisaging production increases and fresh investments in the industry. The government later converted the firms' debts into shares and waived dividends for the foreseeable future.

Orderly retreat begins

The year 1983 marked a major turnaround in the government's policies. The rhetoric of relying on nationalized industries to promote investment and create jobs faded away and emphasis shifted towards making the industries more competitive. State aid did not disappear, and the government continued to justify the financing of nationalized firms in the name of paramount economic interests of the country. However, the political discourse began to embrace the idea that the way towards 'industrial renaissance' crossed that of opening access to the private capital market. The latter, known as the 'policy of respiration', became a qualifying element of Mitterrand's U-turn in economic policy; a large number of stakeholders and a complex tangle of debt-financing institutions reinforced the need for it in the steel sector. Moreover, steel absorbed one-third of the budget for nationalized industries, which encroached upon concomitant ambitions to support infant industries in emerging sectors. These pressures induced the president to neutralize divisions within government and undertake a new course of relations with the steel industry. This was enshrined in a steel plan providing subsidies in return for a commitment of the industry to agreed levels of spending in R&D, rationalization and a substantial reduction of financial charges in the following three years. Thereby, the industry's fate became less and less tied to the benevolent support of the state and increasingly dependent on efforts to achieve budgetary rigour. Meanwhile, the state began playing an active role in the firm's restructuring strategies. Although Mitterrand declared that the Industry minister would receive exceptional powers, ultimate decision-making authority remained with the prime minister and the president. When the 1983 plan was revised a year later, Mitterrand took the upper hand, deciding against new investment at Sacilor's Gandrange plant, which the Industry minister favoured and the prime minister opposed.

Nonetheless, the new course was undertaken in a context of deep divisions and politically risky confrontations, and at a time of market downturn and low business confidence. The anticipated political ramifications of strict austerity programmes prevented the government from carrying out a thorough restructuring, and the strategy became one of orderly retreat accompanied by income-support programmes for laid-off workers (Ross, 1996). Yet the concomitant opening of a new competitive environment and of non-governmental sources of financing, together with decreasing regulatory and financial resources of the state to persuade business to do as it wished, contributed to a gradual loosening of the relationship between the state and the industry.

From Duopoly to Quasi-monopoly

The third stage of the industry's restructuring comprises the years 1987 to 1994. Having long competed for access to government's funding, Usinor and Sacilor were merged in 1987. This step ended protracted inter-firm rivalries, allowed for the rationalization of the companies' previously overlapping activities, made Usinor Sacilor the largest European and the world's second-biggest steel producer, and enabled the newly created group to report profits for the first time in 1988 after 14 years of consecutive losses (see Figure 4.9 below). However, in contrast with the nationalization, the merger of Usinor and Sacilor was controversial. Proposed by the firms' CEOs in January 1985, its finalization was delayed by a dispute between the Industry minister, who favoured it, and Prime Minister Fabius, who, at least at first, expressed reservations. Private sector producers also opposed the merger on the grounds of its competition-distorting effects. Hesitation was resolved in 1986, when the right returned to government, inaugurating the season of French *cohabitations*. At a time when Usinor and Sacilor's balance sheet was still deeply in the red and would, under different conditions, have received a capital injection, the value of the firms' shares was written down to zero. Chirac's government also replaced the top management of Usinor and Sacilor, appointing Francis Mer at the head of both companies. Trusted for holding entrepreneurial business values, Mer was given the mandate to prepare the firms for their merger. Thereafter, Usinor Sacilor undertook an 'all steel business' strategy based on expansion in downstream activities and in high value-added products, particularly stainless and coated steels. Key to this strategy was an unprecedented policy of acquisitions both in France and abroad.

Regarding the capital structure of the firm, a significant change occurred in 1991 when Clindus, a subsidiary of the state-controlled bank Crédit Lyonnais, acquired 20 per cent of Usinor Sacilor's shares through a two-step action. First, the state increased the capital of Usinor Sacilor by FF 2.5 billion, then it increased the capital of Crédit Lyonnais by FF 3 billion through the transfer to the bank of one-fifth of Usinor Sacilor's shares. Following an expert report, the European Commission cleared the Crédit Lyonnais operation in late 1991 amidst fierce criticism from other European producers that it involved illegal state aid.

The operation also coincided with a presidential decree allowing domestic and foreign private groups to take up majority stakes in the nationalized firms. Against this background, the Crédit Lyonnais operation might suggest enduring state interventionism and even a reinforced presence of the state in Usinor Sacilor. Arguably, however, with a new actor involved in directing the firm, the link between the state and the steel industry had been weakened. Moreover, at a stage when the group needed fresh injections to pursue its policy of internationalization and vertical integration, the channel adopted by the state to restructure the capital of Usinor Sacilor was less relevant than its effect.

Privatization

The next key stage came in 1995. Following a parliamentary decree implementing the provisions of the 1993 privatization law, the government increased the group's capital by FF 5 billion before listing its shares on the Paris Bourse on 10 July 1995. Unlike the first wave of French privatizations in 1986–8, that which began with Usinor Sacilor took place in the midst of an economic recession: a factor that should be discounted when observing the initial disappointing response of investors and the later alternating course of the group's shares. In 1997, the company acquired the new/old, simplified corporate name of 'Usinor'. In 1999, its capital structure was as shown in Table 4.1.

It could be argued that, much as nationalization crystallized a previously less apparent but pervasive role of the state, privatization gave form to patterns of relations between the government and the industry that had matured over time and in a context conducive to change. In fact, from the early 1990s, government's deficit began to grow, private capital invested in Usinor Sacilor increased, and a thorough reform and deregulation of the financial system was carried out (Wright, 1998). Already in 1993, the group was on Prime Minister Balladur's privatization list, opening the way to later developments.

Table 4.1   The capital structure of Usinor, January 1999

Core shareholders	12.2%
EDF	3.7%
COGEMA	2.9%
Crédit Lyonnais	3.0%
Lucchini	0.9%
Sidergal (Air Liquide)	1.0%
Malakoff Investments	0.7%
Private individual investors	21.2%
Institutional investors	57.3%
Group employees	4.4%
Usinor (including 2.3% Treasury stocks)	4.9%

Source: Usinor (1999).

The transformation of the ownership regime of the firm was, nonetheless, significant. Corporate governance changes included a larger board of directors (19 members, 16 elected by the shareholders and three elected by the employees) which – unlike other privatization cases – endorsed the leadership of Mer. Privatization also ended the group's dependence upon a tightly regulated bond market, and prices were no longer determined in negotiation with the Industry minister (Kuhn, 1998).

The complexity of emerging from the policy frame of state interventionism should not be underestimated (Dudley and Richardson, 1999). In this respect, a propitious convergence of ambitions catalysed the group's privatization – the first undertaken under the premiership of Alain Juppé and announced soon after the presidential elections. On the one hand, the group pressurized government to carry out the flotation at a time when it anticipated encouraging profits for 1995 but also a market downturn for 1996. On the other hand, President Chirac was willing to respond to the industry's demand at a time when he needed to reassure financial markets of the viability of his agenda, which combined integrating budget revenues with financing employment schemes (*Euroweek*, various issues, June 1995).

Today, in terms of redressing the policies that had turned cyclical problems into a structural crisis, the restructuring of the steel industry has been completed. The centrality of Usinor to steel production in France persists, with the firm accounting for over 90 per cent of the country's output, the remaining 10 per cent being produced by a small number of independent companies and French subsidiaries of foreign steel firms.

4   ASSESSING POLICY OUTCOMES

A Qualified Success

Evidence indicates that, relative to challenges posed by the crisis and following a protracted restructuring process, French policies for the steel industry have, ultimately, been successful. The selection of indicators commented upon below, however, suggests qualifications. To begin with, Figure 4.1 shows the impact of the steel crisis on the French steel industry in terms of apparent steel consumption (net industry shipments deducted from the steel trade balance), which is conventionally used to illustrate the course of domestic markets. In terms of steel production, on the other hand, available data indicate that, relative

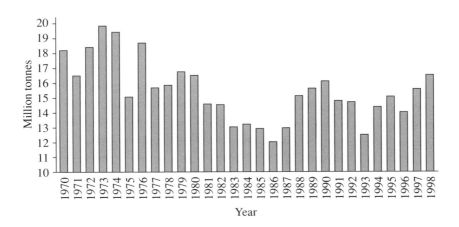

Source: OECD (1995), Usinor (1999).

Figure 4.1   Apparent steel consumption in France, 1970–98

to its main European counterparts, between 1974 and 1992, France experienced the highest contraction of crude steel production (–33 per cent against the –21.2 per cent EC average). On the other hand, steel production decreased more in the years 1974–86 than in the later phase up to 1992, suggesting that, meanwhile, the industry had improved its productivity (International Iron and Steel Institute, hereafter IISI, various years).

Workforce Reductions

The restructuring and rationalization of Usinor and Sacilor has been accompanied by massive workforce reductions: from 157 800 in 1974, to 95 200 in 1982, and 38 000 in 1998 (Figure 4.2). Relative to the political cycle and to that of the market, job losses were relatively contained between 1974 and 1981 (40 per cent), that is under conservative rule and in the first stage of the crisis, whilst they were particularly pronounced, both in absolute and in percentage terms, in the later stages of the crisis and under socialist rule. In the European context (Figure 4.3), between 1974 and 1986, job losses in France (56.7 per cent) were second only to the British steel industry (71.3 per cent) against an EC average of 50.2 per cent and lower peaks in the Netherlands (24.5 per cent) and Italy (31.4 per cent). This trend continued in later years. Between 1984 and 1992, the French steel industry lost nearly 73 per cent of the workforce: a level that was, again, second only to the UK (79 per cent) and far higher than the EC average (60 per cent).

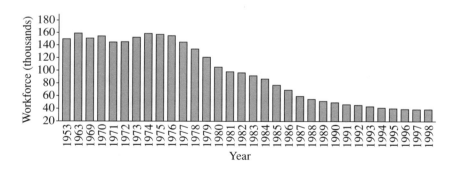

Source: IISI (various years), ILO (1997).

Figure 4.2   Employment in the steel industry in France, 1953, 1963 and 1969–98

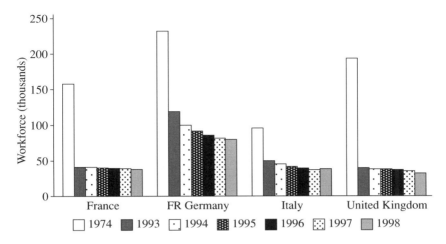

Sources: Various.

Figure 4.3   *Employment in the steel industry, selected EC countries, 1974 and 1993–8*

Regional and Subsectoral Distribution of the Pain of Restructuring

Figure 4.4 shows that production sites in the east, especially the Lorraine region, have been most affected by the industry's restructuring, both in relative and absolute terms. The industrial decay of Lorraine has its origins in the dispro-portionate loss of competitiveness of the local plants in the early 1970s compared to production sites located in the north. While the latter specialized in the relatively more profitable product range of flat steels, the former mainly produced long products. This market was particularly affected by the techno-logical change brought about by the mini-mills, which allowed contiguous countries (particularly the small-sized producers in the north of Italy) to produce at much lower costs. France, however, did not implement this production process. In this regard, it is also worth noting that Usinor has recently completely discarded production in the sector of long steels (see below).

The localized pain of restructuring has been aggravated by an unconvincing reindustrialization policy. In 1985, France and Belgium started a project aimed at creating 8000 jobs in Lorraine in 10 years, of which 5000 would be around the French town of Longwy. However, by 1997, only 3000 workers had been redeployed (*Le Monde*, various issues, September 1997). Meanwhile, Longwy and the surrounding region had been converted into a 'European development pole', receiving EU reindustrialization aid. The policy has contributed to

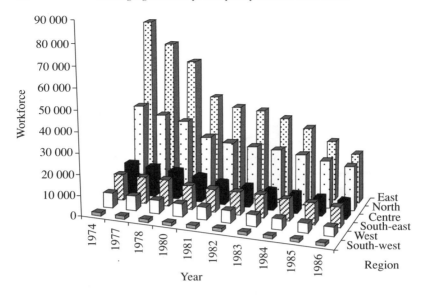

Source: CSSF-FFA (various years).

*Figure 4.4   Employment in the steel industry in France: regional breakdown,
              1974–86*

creating some new jobs, but it has not been sufficient to infuse the region with
renewed industrial vitality. On the other hand, a recent company report estimates
that, between 1991 and 1994, the group's government-sponsored subsidiary in
charge of promoting industrial redevelopment and outplacements, SODIE,
contributed to creating some 23 000 jobs (Usinor, 1999, p. 64).

Cost of Restructuring

A comprehensive estimate of the cost of the restructuring process is impossible.
At the time of the nationalization, for instance, the state's conversion of Usinor
and Sacilor's debts into equity was presented as an 'investment by the state'
which did not entail a disbursement of public finances. Moreover, the impact
of workforce reductions in the industry has been considerably attenuated by
measures including, at different moments in time, diverse combinations of pre-
and early retirement schemes, buyouts, working hours reductions, alternative
job options and so on (Mourioux and Mourioux, 1984). Between 1975 and
1983, they allowed for an average of just above 15 per cent of workers to be
actually laid off, as opposed to an EC average of 50 per cent, with peaks of 85

per cent in the UK (Houseman 1991, p. 45). Recourse to these policies was, indeed, so extensive in the steel industry that it provoked resentment among dismissed workers in other sectors, who did not have access to the same range and amount of benefits (*Wall Street Journal*, 2 April 1984). Their cumulated cost is, in any case, incalculable.

A comparable indicator of the cost of restructuring is provided by the volume of subsidies received by the industry during the crisis. In this regard, Figure 4.5 shows that, in absolute terms, France has been the third-largest recipient of subsidies in the EC after the UK and Italy. However, the above represents but one way of illustrating the volume of subsidies distributed within the EC, and the source of the data – the Association of German steel producers – is, expectedly, biased. More interestingly, EC Commission's data relative to the period 1980–85 indicate that the French industry ranks (with Italy) among the largest recipients of aid for investment, the largest of all recipients of aid for continued operation, and among the recipients of the lowest amount of aid for capacity closures (European Commission, COM (86) 235 final, 6 August 1986). Thus, at a stage of the crisis at which differences become most visible as to the orientation of governments in supporting national industries towards their restructuring, the French government emerges as still actively engaged in supporting the national steel industry, with efforts towards actual industrial restructuring being kept to a minimum.

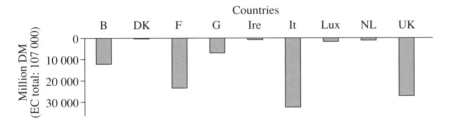

Source: Wirtschaftsvereinigung Eisen- und Stahlindustrie (1987).

Figure 4.5   Subsidies in the crisis years, 1975–85

Productivity

Productivity indicators, as applied to the steel industry, require that production techniques be taken into account with, broadly, higher productivity attributed to mini-mills. Since Usinor and Sacilor have traditionally run integrated steel plants, in order to compare the French industry with competitors facing similar difficulties during the crisis years it is preferable to rely on alternative indicators. Among these, the percentage of production obtained through a technique named

'continuous casting' – which both reduces the stages of production and makes
it possible to produce more homogeneous steel products – has increased considerably in France, and is today one of the highest in the world (IISI, 1998) (see
Figure 4.6).

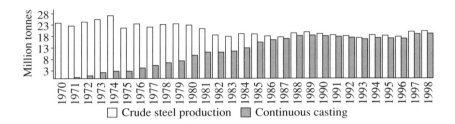

Source: OECD (1995), Usinor (1999).

*Figure 4.6   Crude steel production in France and share of production through
continuous casting, 1970–98*

As for the man-hours necessary to produce one tonne of crude steel (the higher
the figure, the lower the productivity), in 1974, a profound gap affected the
French steel industry relative to its main European counterparts. In 1976, only
the UK had a lower productivity level than France: respectively, 123 and 150
tonnes per year per worker, as opposed to 200 in Germany, 236 in the USA, 241

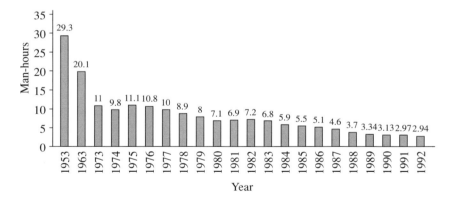

Source: CSSF-FFA (various years), Moinov (1995, p. 46).

*Figure 4.7   Man-hours per tonne of crude steel produced, 1953, 1963 and
1973–92*

in Italy and 335 in Japan. Productivity more than doubled between 1975 and 1986; that is, between the inception of the crisis and the year that preceded the merger of Usinor and Sacilor. It also almost doubled between 1986 and the beginning of the 1990s: that is, between when the firms where ready for the merger and when the path towards Usinor Sacilor's privatization began to be traced (Figure 4.7). This improvement is confirmed on the European scale: between 1982 and 1992, productivity in the French steel industry increased by 118 per cent, as opposed to the 71 per cent EC average. By 1994, Usinor was among the world's lowest cost producers in the majority of its core activities (IISI, various years).

Performance after Restructuring

After privatization, Usinor's rationalization has taken four main directions. Firstly, the company has pursued the policy of internationalization undertaken in 1988, acquiring production facilities and distribution centres in Europe, North and South America and the Far East. The volume of sales abroad confirms the international reach of the group that, in 1998, delivered 80 per cent of its products to customers outside France. Secondly, after failed attempts at three other major European takeovers, in late 1998, the firm succeeded against Germany's Thyssen in the acquisition of the Belgian Cockerill Sambre and of its German subsidiary Eko-Stahl. Thereby, the group has taken part in the wave of cross-border mergers and takeovers that, in the late 1990s, fundamentally altered the previously intensely national character of European industries. At least until the British Steel–Hoogovens partnership, in 1999, the acquisition of the Belgian firm raised Usinor to the rank of Europe's largest and world's second-biggest steel producer. Thirdly, regarding production, in 1998 the group began divesting activities in the sectors of long carbon products and speciality steels to specialize in those of carbon and stainless flat products and special plates. Fourthly, in 1999, Usinor undertook a major internal reorganization based on a condensed management structure, which is expected to substantially reduce administrative costs as well as the costs of production-support functions.

At the time of writing (December, 1999), the group's cost-reduction programme has not yet produced the expected benefits and, in September 1999, it reported losses. However, an assessment of Usinor's economic viability after restructuring based only on most recent data would be misleading. By 1994, and in spite of the adverse economic conjuncture, the company had nearly halved the level of long-term indebtedness compared to the year of the merger (about FF 16 billion compared to FF 30 billion in 1987). Also, as Figure 4.8 also highlights, after 1987, the group's performance began to develop in line with the market cycle: positive until 1990 and, again, as from 1994. On the other hand, Usinor recovered from the crisis more slowly than other European counterparts (Figure 4.9). In particular, it recovered more slowly than the UK British Steel, which was already profitable in 1986 and through to 1991, when the effects of the early 1990s downturn began to be felt.

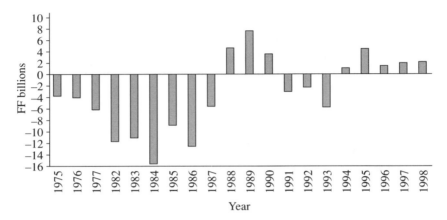

Source: Usinor (1999) and various sources.

Figure 4.8   Usinor and Sacilor (up to 1987), Usinor Sacilor (1987–97) and Usinor (1997–8): profits and losses

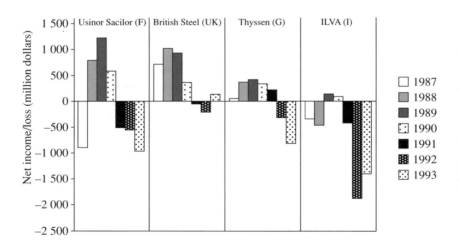

Source: Moinov (1995, p. 34).

Figure 4.9   Financial performance of some European steel firms, 1987–93

The data presented above suggest that French policies for the steel industry have entailed considerable social costs, which have been borne particularly by certain local communities rather than, in terms of their budgetary impact, by the country as a whole. These policies have, nonetheless, been successful in ensuring a steady improvement of the industry's productivity and its adaptation to the cyclical course of the steel market. More generally, it could be argued that, insofar as the industry has remained under direct or indirect state control, steel has emerged as a sector prone to programmatic failures. In the French case, the 1987 merger has contributed to redressing this propensity by ending inter-firm competition and allowing for the necessary rationalization and integration of activities. However, a belated undertaking of radical restructuring hindered the industry's opportunity to re-emerge from the crisis at the same time as some of its European counterparts.

5   EXPLAINING FRENCH STEEL POLICY: CONTEXTUAL FACTORS AND THE POLICY PROCESS

Moving on to examine a selection of factors relevant to an interpretation of the course of French policies towards the steel industry, the following appear particularly significant. Firstly, with regard to the Europeanization of steel policy, although the interests of French industrialists have traditionally been represented at the highest level within the EC, France has contributed its share in the costs of the EC collective management of the steel crisis. Secondly, in spite of the fragmented nature of the French steel policy community, overcoming opposition and consensus building on unpopular policies at the domestic level has entailed considerable costs. Thirdly, conforming to enduring patterns of the French tradition and policy-making style, change in the course of policy has been catalysed by exceptional factors, both endogenous and exogenous. These features are examined further below.

Europeanization

Three dimensions of the impact of the Europeanization of steel policy on the French case are relevant to our purposes. Firstly, France played an important role in the framing of EC interventionist policies in the 1970s and 1980s (Dudley and Richardson, 1999, p. 234), particularly among the countries that most favoured the establishment of the quota system in 1980. Moreover, throughout the crisis, the interests of French steel industrialists have been represented at the European level through highly influential channels. These included Jacques Delor – former industry minister, a prominent protagonist of the 1983 U-turn in French economic policies, and later president of the EC Commission – and Usinor Sacilor's CEO, Francis Mer, who in 1990 became president of the EC-wide umbrella organization of steel producers, Eurofer, within which framework he was determinant in the designing of the Bangemann–Van Miert plan.

Secondly, France had extensive recourse to the provisions of the steel aid codes which, between 1980 and 1986, allowed the granting of investment and operating aid to loss-making firms. Once the third steel aid code of 1985 declared operating aid illegal, Usinor and Sacilor began implementing instruments of self-financing which circumvented state aid provisions. In this respect, however, France's influential role in the conduct of EC steel policies did not prevent the Commission from declaring illegal part of the aid received by Usinor Sacilor in 1987 and – unprecedented in the steel sector – ordering its repayment to the French state in 1989.

Thereafter – the third relevant factor – French steel industrialists have fiercely opposed ongoing state aid injections by other member states in favour of domestic companies. Meanwhile, however, Usinor Sacilor became a partner in some of the widely reported regional price-fixing agreements, which have characterized steel production in Europe for most of the twentieth century: a price increase concerted with other European producers entailed, in 1998, a sanction of Ecu 3.8 million; similarly, in February 1994, Unimétal was fined Ecu 12.3 million for a price-fixing agreement concerning products supplied to the construction industry. The French case thus confirms consistent evidence that, once freed from government control and deprived of protectionist measures, the industry tends to resort to sector-specific strategies of self-protection from the full operation of market forces (Perrotti, 1995).

The Policy Community

Counter to most other European experiences, in France steel labour unions have traditionally been weak and incapable of orienting policy making: a feature that has induced some authors to consider labour as an 'outsider' to the steel policy community (Schmidt, 1996a, p. 35). Data on the membership of French unions are indicative of their weakness: in 1980, one in five employees belonged to one of the unions, a proportion that was more than halved by 1995 (*L'Année Politique, Economique, Sociale et Diplomatique*, various years). Besides membership, major sources of this weakness have been the proliferation of divisions internal to individual organizations and conflicts between them along ideological lines (Milner, 1999). Illustrative of these divisions are the violent protests originating in Longwy upon the announcement of the 1978 Barre plan. Public mobilization was impressive: 80 000 people took the streets in Metz and 100 000 in Paris. Initially, an uncharacteristic unity characterized the main labour confederations. The moderate CFDT (*Confédération Française Démo-*

cratique du Travail) unusually endorsed 'the legitimate violence of the workers', an inter-union committee was established, and efforts to mobilize media attention converged on the local radio station LCA, controlled by the oldest labour confederation, CGT (*Confédération Générale du Travail*), affiliated to the Communist Party. By acting cohesively, the unions obtained important concessions; gradually, however, they began to divide on whether to force the government into an overall revision of the plan. Internal divisions also surfaced. The bases of both CGT and CFDT and the local communities focused their protest on the steel policy issue while the CGT's Paris headquarters pressed for all-round opposition to the government, and the CFDT's leadership emphasized the need to engage in negotiations (*Le Monde Diplomatique*, October 1997). In the event, these divisions allowed the Industry minister to deal piecemeal with the unions and workers. While concessions were made concerning the number of lay-offs, in the face of government intransigence, resistance to the plan gradually faded away.

A mixed picture also emerges when examining the other camp of the policy community. Until 1987, the industry represented by the CSSF was deeply divided. Rivalries were radicalized with the consolidation of Usinor and Sacilor's duopoly. Competition over scarce resources pitted the two groups against one another and, even, within the same industrial region, one plant against the other. Rivalries were also radicalized between the public and private sector. The privileged treatment accorded to nationalized firms, in particular, exposed government to blackmail by private sector producers. In 1983–4, for instance, the private sector engineering concern Creusot-Loire, owned by the Schneider family, protested against the 'special treatment' reserved by the state to Usinor Sacilor and threatened bankruptcy and job losses in order to obtain the firm's bailout by nationalized companies and banks (*Wall Street Journal*, 15 June 1984).

It is also important to underline that, already in the 1970s, the industry attracted recruits of high calibre, often *énarques* or *polytechniciennes* (the so-called 'X's), sometimes trained in the USA, often with previous direct experience in the public sector as *inspecteurs de finance* (Cohen and Bauer, 1981). The close connection between top industry managers and government officials, with whom the former shared old school ties, membership of prestigious civil service corps and government experience, should not be under-estimated. However, while the fragmentation of the executive allowed business to play one minister against the other, ministry–industry relations remained characterized by personalistic relations rather than giving way to fully-fledged corporatism (Schmidt, 1996).

In fact, the late 1970s developments showed that the corporatist-like government–business collusion revolving around the CSSF was unstable, with the only enduring element being the exclusion of organized labour from decision making. When, in 1979, the Barre government declared that it no longer relied on the brokering role of the CSSF, it blamed the association for failing to achieve the objectives of the government's sectoral planning and for having provided overoptimistic forecasts that the crisis would not last. The CSSF's response that government aid was to be regarded as a quid pro quo for the industry's acquiescence in the policy of price control signalled that the mutual captivity of earlier state–industry relations was *not* to evolve into corporatism.

Moreover, previous delegation to the CSSF had enabled the state to externalize the tasks of resource distribution and consensus building; however, it made the executive dependent upon the association's brokering role. With the marginalization of the CSSF, the working of the interministerial committee in charge of coordinating planning and investment decisions became stymied by inter-firm conflicts as well as by clashes between the Finance and Industry ministers over spending levels. Although the incumbent prime ministers and presidents played an important role in resolving the latter conflicts, the effectiveness of government's action was undermined. Thus the state retained the authority to engage in or disengage from cooperation with the industry; however, the losses incurred by the latter did not straightforwardly result in government's gains.

Decision Makers, the Political Cycle and Policy Entrepreneurship

Whereas, elsewhere in Europe, strong and cohesive policy communities have required managing, transforming and neutralizing in order to enable restructuring to go ahead, in the French case an opposite feature emerges: the inability or unwillingness of the government fully to exploit the weaknesses of the steel policy community to push through radical restructuring plans in a timely fashion. This may be explained by a genuine interest in addressing the social repercussions of the crisis. More mundane short-termism, however, was also visible. Several prime ministers and presidents, from both ends of the political spectrum, used the political cycle. For instance, when the over-capacity crisis and falling demand began to hit the industry in 1974, the coastal plants at Fos and Dunkirk had just come on line. The industry claimed that it anticipated a short-lived crisis and continued to finance its investment through debts. Government, on the other hand, had induced Usinor to join Sacilor in the Fos operations, thereby committing them to an unsustainable project. At that stage, however, pressing electoral concerns motivated Prime Minister Chirac to announce further loans in favour of the industry in return for avoiding lay-offs, only to proclaim, soon after the elections, that more radical policies were needed. Similarly, in 1976, President D'Estaing reportedly agreed to grant stopgap measures provided rationalization was delayed until the 1978 elections. Pre-electoral concerns equally motivated Barre's covert nationalization and restructuring plan. Whilst the plan initially envisaged the granting of a FF 1.3 billion loan to enable the industry to reach a yearly level of production of 24.5 million tonnes, and would have entailed 16 000 job losses in two years, after the elections, the latter figure rose to 22 000.

The left inherited an ambiguous legacy of constraints but also of opportunities, including control over investment, production and employment decisions to be enhanced through nationalization. Actually, the potential for full-scale conflict between government and labour was at its highest during the years of socialist rule. Mitterrand's faults were aggravated by his electoral pledge to reverse the industry's long-term decline and by the worsening prospects for the regions most affected by the crisis. At this stage, however, the lack of cohesiveness of the policy community and the impact of power politics emerged in forms different from the weakness of trade unions. The highest risk of political fall-out coincided with the 1984 socialist plan, that further reinforced the measures of fiscal stringency and industrial rationalization announced a year earlier. For the first time since Mitterrand's election in 1981, the unity of the governmental alliance between the Socialist and Communist Parties was seriously called into question. Upon the announcement of the plan, three socialist members of the National Assembly and one of the Senate left their parliamentary groups in protest, and one member of the party's central committee resigned. However, the greater challenge resided in the potential reaction of the Communist Party. Although Prime Minister Mauroy's majority in the National Assembly was large enough to neutralize communist opposition to the plan, if the four communists among the 43 ministers had resigned, the Communist Party would have felt free to attack the government and mobilize opposition through the CGT and its main constituencies, which were concentrated in the regions most threatened by the government's programme. Offsetting this risk was the anticipation that the Communist Party would not have compromised participation in the government, even at the cost of muting criticism (*Wall Street Journal*, 1–2 April 1984). In the event, although the 'socialist betrayal' enhanced the frustration of the unions and Mitterrand's popularity was temporarily damaged, organized protest was too weak to induce the government to substantially modify its plan.

Policy Styles and Strategies

Policy strategies and styles have, at different moments in time, moved around all four quadrants of the model proposed by Richardson *et al.* (1982, pp. 13–14). A proactive and impositional style characterized French policies for the steel industry in the early days of the ECSC, when the government overcame the resistance of the industry to acquiesce in a sovranational system of regulation of the market by invoking the uppermost national interest in regional stability

(Lynch, 1993). Thereafter, although government leadership remained visible, as indicated by the government-induced wave of mergers and control over prices mentioned above, a more consensual pattern, built upon the close relationship between decision makers and the CSSF became prominent, culminating in the *Plan Professionnel*. From the late 1970s, on the other hand, the French policy style became more reactive and incremental, hovering between imposition, especially under the Barre premiership, and consensus building, more characteristic of Mitterrand's 'modernization *cum* solidarity' discourse, and of the policy of mutual accommodation that prevailed in state–industry relations under socialist rule.

Since the mid-1980s, however, the most prominent trait of French steel policies replicates at the sectoral level a wider change in the course of domestic economic and industrial policy: the view that it is preferable to finance unemployment and redundancy schemes than to provide artificial aid to uncompetitive firms no longer divides left and right. In its turn, this shift reflects broader contextual changes that, throughout Europe, have curtailed governments' options in sectoral industrial policy and microeconomic instruments traditionally used to ensure business compliance.

6   CONCLUSIONS

Unlike other sectors, such as agriculture, steel is perhaps not among the policy areas in which the French 'strong' state is actually very weak, allowing private interests to share in it, if not dominate it (Schmidt, 1996a). Nonetheless, the process of restructuring the steel industry conforms to broader patterns of the French 'statist' tradition of government–business relations (Schmidt, 1996a, 1996b, 1999) and 'dual style' of policy making (Hayward, 1982, pp. 114–16). In this regard, the evidence examined indicates that the state is capable of initiating policy reversals and of imposing them when deemed necessary by exploiting windows of opportunity when they emerge. This element of the statist tradition, however, does not imply that policy making is consistently characterized by a proactive approach to problem solving and by an impositional style. At the implementation stage, in particular, the constraints of pluralistic societies operate and politicians remain exposed and sensitive to the political cycle. Furthermore, at this stage (unlike that of policy formulation), consultation characterizes the relationship between government and the stakeholders in the policy. Accordingly, although the executive retains power to undertake heroic policies through unilateral action, the politics of accommodation prevails. Endogenous factors, such as the threat of disorder, as well as exogenous forces, such as the process of Europeanization, may precipitate change in the system, but the process of policy reversal remains characterized by politicized bargaining and costly implementing measures.

To conclude, the ways in which the French expansionary strategies of the 1970s and 1980s have contributed to precipitating the crisis of the steel industry and to setting the scene for a protracted restructuring process in the following two decades are not dissimilar from other European experiences. Characteristic of the French case remains the ability of government to diffuse – in different ways at different moments in time – the stakes in the destiny of the steel industry across a number of actors operating in the fragmented steel policy community. On occasions, this feature has enabled the ruling elite to exploit predictable manifestations of power politics and the political cycle to push through divisive policies. Throughout the crisis, it has allowed individual political forces to be held accountable of diluted responsibility in certain crucial steps of the restructuring process.

NOTE

1. The author wishes to acknowledge the support of Insead Recherche under research grant n. 2030-003R.

5. Success and failure in the German steel industry: crisis and consensus

Hannah Tooze

1 INTRODUCTION

Despite the implementation of continuous technological improvement and its considerable successes in improving productivity, the European steel industry is popularly considered as a declining smokestack industry. This image is explained by the reductions in the employment it provides and the declining share of European production in global steel markets. However, it conflicts with the reality of a number of highly competitive companies that have continued to sustain a significant market share, particularly in more specialized product areas. The German steel industry has been particularly successful in entering such niche markets and in improving the quality and specialization of its products to retain a competitive position in global markets. It is thus particularly suited to an analysis of policy success and failure as there is a strong requirement to make clear distinctions between the various criteria for assessment, both in terms of what success is considered to consist of and the time horizons over which it is measured.

The industry is of further interest due to its status within national economies both in providing the raw materials for key sectors of the Fordist economy and as a mass employer. These factors have provided it with a privileged position in relation to public policy in many European countries. With the transition from Fordism and the restructuring of the economies of the industrialized world that it has entailed, the steel industry has been subject to particularly dramatic change. The crises in the steel industry have consequently also had a high political status and evoked strong responses both from the public and in politics and government.

The changes in the German steel industry and the governance of this sector contrast significantly with the sector's development in its European counterparts. Indeed, the steel industry provides an especially good demonstration of both the strengths and the weaknesses of the 'German model' in adapting to economic and industrial change, and the specific German interpretation of what constitutes success in economic development.

In industrial relations the steel sector traditionally set the pattern for wage agreements across other sectors of the German economy and had the strongest determination mechanisms. Since the 1980s, however, steel has tended to become more marginalized as a leading sector in wage settlements. Here, industries such as electronics and chemicals have become more important. In terms of government intervention, although the industry has not been nationalized, as in many other European states, there has been a willingness to intervene to support restructuring processes. Compared to other sectors of the German economy such as the clothing and shipbuilding industries, which also experienced severe negative impacts of restructuring, the steel industry has been privileged in the institutional and financial support it has received. The provisions for steel may be seen as epitomizing the German model and the outcomes are also characteristic: continued high productivity and competitiveness but accompanied by severe reductions in the workforce.

This chapter is structured as follows. Section 2 briefly outlines the international context for the German steel industry: it describes the German experience of European steel crises and the effects on Germany of the EU's regulatory response. Section 3 addresses key features of the German steel industry, especially the industrial relations system, the regional distribution of the industry, its interaction with Germany's federal state structure and the policy community that has evolved around the industry and the East German experience since reunification. Section 4 sets out different interpretations of the German strategy in adapting to the steel crisis. The chapter concludes with an evaluation of the German developments according to a set of very distinct criteria.

2   THE INTERNATIONAL CONTEXT

As a relatively homogeneous product, steel is an industry that is particularly open to international competition. Furthermore, as a raw material or component for a range of industrial products, steel demand is necessarily vulnerable to the fluctuations in the international economic cycle. It is also subject to external challenge from alternative products, particularly synthetics and aluminium, that may be substituted for steel in key component areas. These factors have contributed significantly to the communication of steel crises across national borders.

The German and the Global Steel Crises

The crises in the global steel markets severely affected German steel producers as they did all European steel industries. In the initial major collapse from the fourth quarter of 1974 to the mid-1980s, German producers experienced major losses: between 1975 and 1980, German steel firms made losses of about DM7 billion, with further losses of about DM2 billion in 1980–83 (Gerstenberger *et al.*, 1985, p. 60). The crisis was the compound result of global over-capacity that was exacerbated by the entry of a number of new producers on the global markets, particularly among the newly industrialized countries, and by intense competition from Japan, and the collapse in demand with global recession. For European steel producers, rationalization responses resulted in a sharp decline in the workforce that was to start a still continuing downward trend in steel employment.

Table 5.1 sets out the substantial reductions in employment in the German iron and steel industries. The regional concentration of the steel industry (set out in section 3 for Germany) meant that this decline in employment resulted in extremely severe localized social and economic crises.

The first European steel crisis was resolved in the considerably improved global demand for steel of the mid-1980s; however, employment in the German steel industry continued to drop. This trend was to accelerate with the second steel crisis from 1989, which strengthened the tendency towards reform in the production paradigm within the steel industry. The characteristics of the second crisis and the reforms that it promoted have thus been summarized as 'radical changes in work organisation seeking functional and numerical flexibility, along with total quality management and a consequent greater commitment to training and retraining' (Morris *et al.*, 1992, p. 310). This trend has been particularly marked in the German context where it was achieved with the support of the unions who accepted continuing decline in employment numbers in return for social plans for those leaving steel employment, while actively supporting increases in the skills base and retraining of the remaining workforce. Modernization and rationalization have continued into the 1990s with the reattainment of growth in steel demand.

Table 5.1   Employment in the iron and steel industry in Germany

Year	Number employed (thousands)
1974	232
1979	205
1980	197
1983	164
1989	130
1994	96
1996	80

Source: Morris *et al.* (1992, p. 307), Iron and Steel Statistics Bureau (1999, p.v).

Current pressures on the European and US steel industry are exerted by the increasing challenge from surging imports that are lowering prices despite continued high levels of demand. This has been described by the president of US Steel as 'unique because consumption has remained extremely strong – it is the supply side that has screwed this whole thing up' (*Financial Times*, 14 May 1999). The pressure is being applied both by the mass production of countries formerly in the Eastern Bloc, now integrated into the global economy, and by a flood of cheap Asian steel that has been diverted from Asian markets as a result of their economic crises. As a result, EU steel imports rose by 50 per cent in 1998 and are set to rise further (*Financial Times*, 14 May 1999). This currently poses a clear challenge to European steel producers. It is particularly pronounced in Germany because of the geographic proximity of East European competitors and its particularly high production costs. The latter are a compound result of some of the highest tax and social contribution levels in the world, high wage levels and strict environmental standards.

European Community Regulatory Response

The German steel industry has been strongly influenced by the parameters set by EC regulation. The EC has traditionally demonstrated a dichotomy in its approach to the steel market: when there is deemed to be no crisis the liberal principle of free market competition dominates, whereas in a crisis strict regulatory parameters are enforced.

During the first steel crisis the EC invoked Article 58 of the European Coal and Steel Community Treaty and pronounced a state of 'manifest crisis'. This allowed it to impose measures for price stabilization and socially and regionally tolerable reductions in capacities by jointly imposing a regime of compulsory quotas on the 350 major European steel producers covering over 60 per cent of steel products and publishing a code on public subsidies. However, this approach failed to achieve its ends: despite the subsidy codes overall subsidies in the EC increased three times between 1980 and 1985, with the code seen as a legalization of subsidies. Furthermore, an inverse relationship became apparent with the countries receiving the most subsidy (Italy leading among these) in fact reducing their capacity the least, while the least subsidized were also closest to attaining targets for significant capacity reduction (Kerz, 1991, pp. 70–73). Here Germany was closest to achieving EC aims of the major steel-producing states: its subsidy levels were among the lowest and it achieved several times larger levels of capacity reduction.

Table 5.2 demonstrates the substantial gap between Germany and the other major European steel producers in their capacity reduction and subsidy levels. Quotas were abolished after 1988 as rising demand for steel products appeared to solve the crisis of over-capacity. The particular course of restructuring of the German steel industry that has maintained competitiveness in niche production is supported by a number of specific characteristics of the industry and its institutional arrangements. These are summarized in section 3.

Table 5.2   Subsidy receipt and capacity reduction in leading European steel-producing countries, 1980–85

Country	Subsidies received (DM billions)	Capacity reduction (million tonnes)
Italy	28.3	3.2
France	21.5	4.0
United Kingdom	13.3	4.3
West Germany	6.3	17.1

Source: Kerz (1991, p. 72).

3   THE GERMAN STEEL INDUSTRY

Industrial Relations

A highly influential parameter for developments in the German steel industry is set by its industrial relations system. Within Germany the steel industry in fact acts as the leading sector in wage settlements and is the industry in which the German system of corporatist industrial relations continues to be most pronounced. Since the 1980s steel crisis there has been some reduction in this vanguard role, but considerable significance continues to be attached to the industry's wage settlements. The primary legislative framework for industrial relations in the steel industry is provided by the law on parity codetermination set out in the *Montanmitbestimmungsgesetze* of 1951 and 1976 (Codetermination Acts of the Coal, Iron and Steel Industries) and the *Montanmitbestimmungsergänzungsgesetz* of 1956 (Supplementary Codetermination Acts of the Coal, Iron and Steel Industries). The provision for codetermination involves supervisory boards for the major steel companies that are composed of representatives selected by both the employees (both through the union and through direct selection) and management and allows a workforce veto on the company director in charge of personnel and social matters (Vitolis, 1993, p. 5).

In addition to this strong structural position that is provided for labour within the companies, the influence of the workforce is further strengthened through single union representation by the Metal Union, IG Metall. IG Metall is Germany's largest union, with a current membership of approximately 2.7

million (IG Metall, 1999). It provides a strong bargaining position for the workforce in Germany's system of collective bargaining on wages and conditions which sets industry-wide wage levels and minimum social conditions. At company and plant level works councils can further enhance the provisions gained through collective bargaining for the benefit of their workforces. Despite pressures for greater flexibility in working practices and conditions the industrial relations system continues to be particularly effective in the metal sector.

The contribution of the industrial relations system to the restructuring of the German steel industry has been summarized by Vitolis as follows:

> Industrial relations have crucially contributed to the successful restructuring of the German steel industry through the minimising of the threat of involuntary layoff (thus allowing for long-term attachment of worker to company) and by increasing the skill level and flexibility of the workforce. (Vitolis, 1993, pp. 24–5)

Regional Distribution of the Steel Industry and Relations with Political Parties

The German steel industry is strongly concentrated primarily in the Ruhr, in Saarland, in Lower Saxony and selected locations in the new Länder, including Eisenhuettenstadt. The effects of this concentration are apparent in both the social impact of restructuring and the political response. The Ruhr has suffered particularly acutely owing to the fact that the coal industry that has shared the steel crises and gone through its own equally dramatic restructuring process is also prevalent in the region. In the 1980s, the looming devastation of the Ruhr economy prompted the North Rhine–Westphalian Land government to introduce a series of measures both to promote the modernization of the coal and steel industries themselves and to encourage the diversification of the regional economy, for example the *Zukunftsinitiative Montanregion* (Initiative for the Future of Coal and Steel Regions). The success of this measure in encouraging alternative economic activity led to its extension to cover the whole Land in the *Zukunftsinitiative Nordrhein-Westfalen* (Initiative for the Future of North Rhine–Westphalia).

Both the Saarland and North Rhine–Westphalia have traditionally elected SPD governments. There is a contrast, however, between Saarland and North Rhine–Westphalia. The latter has traditionally elected SPD governments, but in the 1970s in Saarland there was a CDU/FDP government during the first major steel crisis. This government also played an integral part in the later corporatist crisis regulation made during the SPD government under LaFontaine. In contrast, the SPD held the mayorships in Neunkirchen and Saarbrucken, the leading steel locations. The party has identified these regions and the employees of their heavy industries as among its core constituencies. However, recently tensions have arisen. From within the party the increasingly centrist policies of the *Neue Mitte* (new centre) strategy pursued by the Schröder-led government have clashed with the 'old SPD' identification with core industries. This faction of the SPD had coalesced around Lafontaine, the former minister president of Saarland and initial *Finanz Minister* in the Schröder government, who resigned as tensions rose between the two groupings within the SPD. Secondly, pressures have been exerted by the *Bündniss 90 die Grünen* (Green Party), the SPD's coalition party in government, who have pushed for the introduction of environmental taxation. The industry has challenged the measure, claiming that it would cost them an extra DM625 million a year (*Steel Times*, 226 (12), 1998, p. 434).

East Germany and Steel

The East German steel industry has followed a very different development path from its West German counterpart. The economy of the German Democratic Republic was characterized by industrial monostructures. This also applied to the steel sector, which was particularly concentrated in the town of Eisenhuettenstadt. It is located in a landlocked position and the development of steel production in the area was a product of integration into Comecon (Council for Mutual Economic Assistance), the Eastern Bloc trading zone, as steel production at Eisenhuettenstadt was fed by Soviet iron ore and Polish coal. Since reunification the East German steel industry has been hit by the pressures of adaptation to global markets and the restructuring process that is occurring in all steel industries across Europe, but which was postponed in the context of Eastern Bloc isolation. In areas like Eisenhuettenstadt the impact has been devastating. Employment in steel in Eisenhuettenstadt declined by over a half to less than 6000 by 1994 (Owen Smith, 1994, pp. 41–2). Since privatization, steel employment in the town has sunk further to 2400 in 1997 (see *http://www.virtualsteel.com*).

In contrast to numerous industrial sectors, notably car production, where Volkswagen took over key Trabant works, West German steel producers did not become actively involved in purchasing East German steel production facilities. This reflects their priorities in improving production technologies rather than increasing capacity. The primitive facilities of East Germany had little to offer West German firms with these strategic goals. In terms of entering East European markets, West German facilities had adequate capacity and proximity to supply the demand. The result has been that East German steel production has been bought by a foreign steel conglomerate, whereas in the west steel production has remained dominated by traditional German companies.

The major investment in the Eisenhuettenstadt plants came from Cockerill Sambre, the Belgian conglomerate, which purchased a majority stake in 1994. It bought the remaining 40 per cent from the residual privatization agency in 1998. In the same year the French steel company USINOR in turn purchased a majority stake in Cockerill Sambre, so that EKO Stahl, as the Eisenhuettenstadt works has been named, now belongs to one of the largest global steel producers.

By 1998, combined public and private investment in the plant amounted to DM1.1 billion. This has allowed the construction of new facilities and extensive modernization. Considerable progress has been made in closing the productivity gap between East and West German steel producers. Productivity in all East German metal industries lies at 75 per cent of West German levels, while wage levels stand at 66 per cent (IG Metall Press Release, 4 June 1999). However, it is doubtful whether such investment would have gone ahead without substantial public subsidies. These subsidies should be seen in the context of the high levels of public financial support that were provided for many, though not all, branches of East German industry, rather than as an aspect of a steel-specific public policy. So, for example, high levels of subsidy were also provided for the chemical works of the Halle area, while the mechanical engineering plants in Magdeburg were not given similar subsidies. The choice of which branches and locations were subsidized was the result of a constellation of interests rather than a systematic rationale. These included the capacity of local and regional interests to assert themselves, the hostility of West German producers to the subsidy of potential East German rivals and their own willingness to invest in the east.

Demand for East German steel was initially promoted by the building boom that followed reunification. However, as this boom has slowed to more normal rates of construction, demand has declined. As for West Germany, the industry faces a future of strong competition and is likely to need to continue modernizing if it is to sustain a competitive position. The situation of the East German steel industry and responses in the public and private sector to it are not characteristic of the German policy community for steel. This policy community and public sector initiative are considered below.

The German Policy Community and Public Sector Initiative for the Steel Industry

In significant contrast to most other European countries, the German steel industry has at no stage been nationalized on any significant scale. This has meant that there has been no national concept for restructuring the industry. As a result the steps towards restructuring that have occurred since 1975 have included decisive input from all of the corporatist partners, while national governments have 'generally shied away from direct government involvement in economic restructuring such as nationalisations and direct subsidies; rather, the tendency has been to support private restructuring plans' (Vitolis, 1993, p. 41). After 1980, German national efforts centred around support for the European concept.

There are several notable exceptions to this pattern of low concerted public sector involvement. In the second half of the 1970s, the Saarland-based companies which had not engaged in the rationalization wave that had spread across the Ruhr in the early 1970s were particularly badly affected and turned to the public sector for support. The government first attempted to find a Ruhr-based company to take over the smaller Saarland companies, but the former showed no interest. It then found a more willing candidate in Arbed, a Luxembourg concern, which was prepared to take over the Saar companies with significant government subsidies. These included DM900 million in bank guarantees, later to be tripled by the Land government, DM224 million conditionally repayable for new investments and DM480 million cash for immediate social measures. In addition the state government was required to pay DM120 million for construction of a new foundry, while banks were pressurized into writing off DM60 million of outstanding debt (Esser and Fach, 1989, p. 225). As a result of the restructuring achieved with these measures, steel employment in Saarland was reduced by over 50 per cent from 30 000 to 14 000, by the mid-1980s (ibid., p. 223); however the Saar steel industry continues to be among the least profitable branches of German steel production.

A further example of unusual public sector involvement in the industry was provided in 1982–3, when the federal government proposed a plan to restructure the steel industry to form two major cartels, the Ruhr Group, to consist of Thyssen and Krupp, and the Rhine Group, to consist of Hoesch, Klöckner and Salzgitter. The government was to provide substantial subsidies to help finance the consolidation. However, the proposal was basically flawed, as it was also clear from the outset that, while the Ruhr group around the giant Thyssen was likely to achieve international competitiveness, this could not be foreseen for the smaller Rhine group. The plan also altogether neglected the most problematic company, the Saarland's Arbed. The plan failed in the face of opposition from the disadvantaged firms, some local Land government intervention and the unions, who had been altogether marginalized in the development of the proposals.

A final example of the pragmatism and periodic willingness for direct involvement in the steel industry of the German public sector has been provided more recently by the Preussag case. Preussag, a predominantly engineering-based company, announced that it wanted to sell its steel-making business centred in Lower Saxony. Interest was shown by British Steel and Voest Alpine, the latter being already involved in a joint venture with Preussag Stahl.

However, at the last moment the government of Lower Saxony and its regional bank, the NordLB, intervened under the leadership of the then premier of Lower Saxony, Gerhard Schröder. Voicing fears of the possible impact of foreign ownership on employment, the government effectively prevented the sale of the steel subsidiary to Voest Alpine (an Austrian company) which had offered over £439 million. The Lower Saxony government and NordLB paid £358 million for a 51 per cent stake in Preussag Stahl, the remaining 49 per cent being retained by the Preussag group (*Steel Times*, 226 (3), 1998, p. 434). 'The move was widely seen as a way of protecting the jobs of the 9,000 strong workforce prior to elections' (*Steel Times*, 226 (3), 1998, p. 434). Although the Lower Saxony government has since sold 49 per cent of its shares, it retains a decisive 25.5 per cent stake in the company. The case represents the willingness of the German public sector to become pragmatically involved in specific instances in order to protect employment and political interests.

Despite its lack of a strategic input into the development of the steel industry, the German public sector has been continuously involved in the process of restructuring, not least through the extensive subsidies and programmatic payments in which it has been involved, particularly in crisis years. In addition to these direct payments the industry benefits from the extensive public research infrastructure. Of particular significance is the Max Planck Institute for Iron Research which performs interdisciplinary basic research on iron, steel and related materials and is supported equally by the publicly funded Max Planck Society and the German Iron and Steel Institute. 'The research aims at a better understanding of the basic phenomena as a starting point for the improvement of materials, their properties and applicability' (*Steel Times*, 227 (8), 1999, p. 304). It is an example of the German state's willingness to invest in research with direct industrial applicability and Germany's more intimate relations between the academic and research establishment and the business sector.

In addition to this specific public sector role, Germany has also differed from other European countries in the relative lack of concentration in its steel industry, although this has more recently been subject to major change. It traditionally had three major steel corporations: Thyssen, Krupp and Hoesch (formerly divided into the crude steel producer Thyssen Stahl and refined steel producer Thyssen Edelstahl) all with factories located in the Ruhr. In 1990, these accounted for about 70 per cent of West German crude steel production (Vitolis, 1993, p. 16). Several further smaller companies include Klöckner in Bremen, Salzgitter in the former border region with the GDR and Saarstahl, formerly owned by Arbed and considered above. All of these companies were members of the industry association.

The 1990s have seen a major shake-up in this traditional formation of German steel companies. In 1992, Krupp acquired a majority share holding in Hoesch, merging to form Hoesch–Krupp in December of that year (Krupp, 1999). In a more ground-breaking move, Krupp then launched a hostile takeover bid for the far larger company, Thyssen. This has been described as 'an un-German act of aggression' (*Economist*, 1998) but was eventually resolved in negotiations between the two companies returning to the more conciliatory style of inter-sectoral firm relations that is characteristic of German business. In March 1999, this resulted in a merger to form Thyssen Krupp AG 'with around DM 68.8 billion sales, 173,000 employees and core competencies in technologies, materials and services' (Krupp and Thyssen, 1999). (A key factor in the governance of the Krupp–Thyssen merger was the role played by the SPD-led government in North Rhine–Westphalia in moderating the dispute between the two firms.) The merger has paved the way to extensive rationalization with the closure of a number of major facilities in Dortmund (*Steel Times*, 227 (8), 1999, p. 306).

In addition to the public sector support for the steel industry it has also enjoyed the willing financial backing of the German banking community. Indeed, in the recession of the late 1970s when European steel industries were forced into major restructuring drives, instead of tightening the financial require-ments German banks increased their lending to the sector. This allowed German companies to engage in active restructuring policies while releasing the public sector from some of the burden of high-level subsidy requirements. The influence of the banking sector was particularly clear in the case of Kloeckner, Germany's third-largest steel group at the time, which was experiencing par-ticularly heavy losses. Its capital reorganization was the initiative of the deputy chairman on its supervisory board whose full-time employment was membership of the management board of the Deutsche Bank (see Owen Smith, 1994, pp. 363–4): 60 per cent of Koeckner's debt was simply cancelled – the equivalent of a major subsidy from the banking system.

The German steel policy community thus has three key characteristics. First, the highly structured industrial relations and strong union representation which enforce consensus on approaches to restructuring and involve a corporatist basis to any change. Secondly, the role of the public sector, apart from a few exceptions, appears pragmatic, and is generally restricted to the payment of large subsidies to sustain production and promote modernization while preventing the complete collapse of individual firms. It only once attempted to provide more strategic leadership, the plan of 1982–3, which failed as the corporatist model reasserted itself. The public sector role is reinforced by the active support of German banks in the capital management of the steel companies and their willingness to be actively involved in supporting the sector, as demonstrated by their writing off of debts at times of acute crisis in the steel industry. Thirdly, in terms of the relations between the steel companies themselves, there are low levels of aggressive competition or aggressive acquisition policy. The one example of such an approach, while achieving the ultimate end of a merger, returned to the more typically German consensual approach in its achievement. Esser and Fach summarize the outcome of such a policy community as 'consensual modernisation' (Esser and Fach, 1989, p. 235).

4 INTERPRETING THE GERMAN STRATEGY TOWARDS STEEL RESTRUCTURING

Unlike the nationalized steel industries of many European countries, the independent German steel producers have had the opportunity to diversify their activities significantly, while maintaining their bulk production of basic steel in their favourable location at the centre of Europe. However, although diversification has sustained high profitability for the steel companies, it has also imposed costs on the steel-producing regions as these profits have been largely invested in southern Germany and abroad, and in the 'industries of the future' rather than in the steel regions and core steel production (see Esser and Fach, 1989, pp. 227–8). This fact demonstrates that, despite the consensus that the Germany corporatist relations achieve, basic differences in the interests of the social partners remain. A steel company's success is not necessarily analogous to the success of a steel region or the steel workforce.

However, German companies have also repositioned themselves successfully within the market: for example, Thyssen shifted from mild to zinc-coated steel production for car bodies during the 1980s. Companies have also engaged in vertical integration, for example, 80 per cent of the German stockholder market is controlled by steel manufacturers. Thus Hudson (1992, p. 8) summarizes the company response to restructuring as:

- repositioning within the market,
- selective mergers,
- vertical integration,
- seeking comparative advantage through technical innovation,
- and diversification out of steel.

Further interpretations of the German strategy have chosen to highlight different aspects of the industry's response. Despite their scepticism about some more specific aspects of the restructuring process, Esser and Fach offer an overall positive assessment of the German strategy, summarizing it as rationalization, technological modernization and product diversification and the fact that 'social costs have been transformed into economic competence' (Esser and Fach, 1989, p. 226). This approach is shared by Vitolis who, though differing in some details, also stresses the role of corporatist industrial relations in allowing companies to improve their skill base and modernize while effectively cushioning the social costs. He summarizes the resulting key features of the strategy that could be successfully achieved with low levels of industrial conflict:

- reduction in capacity,
- the concentration of production on sites with good transport links,
- the shift in production from lower to higher value added,
- selective product specialization,
- computerization allowing increasing control,
- increased emphasis on research and customer relationships,
- and increased emphasis on later, higher value-added stages of production (Vitolis, 1993, pp. 16–17).

Germany has been subject to the same competitive challenges in global steel markets as other European nations. However, unlike other European countries, its private firm structure, in combination with its formalized and strongly binding industrial relations structures and the willingness of its public sector to provide financial and institutional backing, have allowed it to engage in active modernization strategies. Although the workforce has been sharply reduced the extensive use of social plans and schemes for regional economic diversification, retraining and so on have alleviated the social costs of these modernization and rationalization strategies. The willingness of the public sector even to engage in the temporary nationalization of specific firms, such as in the case of Preussag, demonstrates the considerable significance that is attached to achieving such a socially tolerable course in the German assessment of the success of a restructuring process.

5   EVALUATING GERMAN STEEL POLICY

Profitability and Output

German steel companies have successfully turned around the losses of the late 1970s and early 1980s crisis years. Through diversification strategies their susceptibility to crises in demand for German steel has been reduced. Krupp Thyssen, the dominant conglomerate, now functions through five divisions: steel, automotive industries, general industrial, engineering and materials and services. The corporation enjoys strong profitability. In the first six months of 1998, Thyssen alone made a profit of DM411 million (£149.5 million) (*Steel Times*, 226 (12), 1998, p. 434). Steel is still the major source of profit as the merged steel branch of the group, Thyssen-Krupp, accounted for £138.2 million of profit in the same period (ibid.).

Such profit rates have allowed Germany to sustain its leading position in European steel production. As Table 5.3 demonstrates, despite the strategy to invest increasingly in the production of specialized steel, Germany continues to be Europe's major producer of crude steel.

Table 5.3   European crude steel production, April 1997–April 1999: monthly averages (million tonnes)

Country	April 1997	April 1998	April 1999
Germany	3.855	3.830	3.474
Italy	2.225	2.320	1.946
France	1.712	1.769	1.725
United Kingdom	1.598	1.511	1.473

Source: *Steel Times* (225 (7), 1997, p. 268; 226 (7), 1998, p. 243; 227 (7), 1999, p. 269).

Employment

In terms of securing employment there has been an evident failure of German policy for the steel industry. As demonstrated by Table 5.1, there has been a steady decline in German steel employment. However, the German steel industry has successfully combined the reductions in the workforce with increases in the skill level of the workforce and its more flexible deployment. This has allowed the introduction of new technologies and a considerable extension of the use of computers that have improved the overall competitiveness of the sector.

Consensus

Consensus has been a key feature of the German system and has contributed to the smooth achievement of reductions in the workforce and improvement in skill levels and practices, as outlined above. In addition to the structurally strong position of the workforce and unions, German steel workers have also shown their willingness to strike where they consider their interests to be at risk. For example, the plans of the Krupp management to close its Rheinhausen factory in Duisburg in 1987 led to immense popular protests, including a Steel Action Day. More recently, the merger of Krupp-Hoesch and Thyssen resulted in a wave of street protests and strikes as workers feared the merger would result in massive job cuts brought about by internal company rationalization. However, union cooperation was eventually achieved for the merger. In comparison to the experiences in other European countries, where restructuring has been marked either by sustained industrial conflict or the virtual disenfranchisement of labour representation (as in the UK), Germany has achieved high and sustained consensus, with unions cooperating both in the specific design of lay-offs and helping an improved skills base and process modernization.

Cost and Public Sector Initiative

Policy for the German steel industry has been successful in sustaining its position as the major European steel producer. It has done so without major public sector strategic input, but there has been substantial public subsidy. Between 1975 and 1983, the German steel industry received DM3 billion of subsidies, as reported to the ECSC, of which DM825 million provided investment grants to steel companies, DM600 million subsidized research projects and the majority of the rest went to the Saarland (Vitolis, 1993, p. 43). In a more comprehensive definition, the *Deutsches Institut für Wirtschaft* (German Economics Institute) estimated that there was a very substantial rise in the amount of subsidies between 1980 and 1985, but that this was followed by a decrease (ibid., p. 44).

The modernization of the German steel industry has thus been achieved at considerable cost to the public purse. This contrasts with a number of other sectors similarly affected by restructuring pressures that have not benefited from such extensive public financial commitment, for example textiles and shipbuilding. The success in modernizing the steel industry in a socially tolerable manner sustaining regional core production may thus, in the context of the limited availability of public funding, be seen as in part having taken place at the expense of other sectors that have suffered a more brutal restructuring process. For steel the cost is justified in that the future competitiveness of the German steel industry appears secured.

6   CONCLUSIONS

Germany maintained its leading position as Europe's largest steel producer into the 1990s and continued to enjoy a positive trade balance in steel throughout the 1990s. Table 5.4 demonstrates Germany's major share of European crude steel production that has been sustained through both steel crises. Table 5.5 demonstrates Germany's positive trade balance in steel products despite the threat of cheap imports that has grown during the 1990s. This position has been achieved through corporatist industrial relations that have achieved extensive workforce reductions in association with an increase in skills and flexibility and the introduction of new technologies and production processes.

Table 5.4 German output as a percentage of total EU crude steel production and annual output (thousand tonnes)

	1980	1985	1990	1993	1994	1995	1996	1997	1998
% of EU Total	28.6	27.5	25.9	26.1	26.9	27.0	27.1	28.1	27.5
output	43 838	40 497	38 434	37 625	40 837	42 051	39 793	45 007	44 046

Source: Iron and Steel Statistics Bureau (1999, p. iv).

Table 5.5 German trade balance in steel products (thousand tonnes)

	1994	1995	1996	1997	1998
Imports	13 603	15 141	12 497	14 213	15 239
Exports	15 355	16 082	16 704	19 221	22 400
Balance +/−	+ 1 752	+ 941	+ 4 207	+ 5 008	+ 7 161

Source: Iron and Steel Statistics Bureau (1999, p. v).

Despite continued competitive pressures, the German steel industry appears to have stabilized in terms of its trade balance, market share and the volume of output. Sustaining this situation will depend on the continued modernization of the industry and willingness of the public sector to continue engaging in its supporting functions in terms of the pragmatic issuing of subsidies and continuing infrastructural and research support.

Further rationalization of German steel production is likely to continue to create regionally specific pockets of high unemployment despite social plans and public measures. This pattern is not specific to the steel industry but is characteristic of the wider post-Fordist economy. Germany's federalized state structure allows the stronger voicing of regional concerns and significant public sector compensatory measures are thus likely to continue.

6. A 'Dutch miracle' in steel policy? Laissez-faire intervention, wage restraint and the evolution of Hoogovens

Hans Schenk[1]

1 INTRODUCTION

Just before the turn of the century, British Steel acquired one of the best performing European steel producers of the late 1990s, Hoogovens of the Netherlands. While only less than half its size in terms of sales, and only slightly larger than a third in terms of steel production, Hoogovens realized net returns of DGL415 million as against DGL697 million for British Steel (BS) in 1998 (for some basic indicators on Hoogovens, see Appendix, Table 6A.1).[2] Preliminary figures on the first six months of 1999 indicate that BS even suffered a loss of DGL600 million, while Hoogovens made profits of DGL200 million. Provided that the newly formed firm will be able to derive synergy from the merger, which in view of the generally negative performance of large mergers is far from certain (see Schenk, 2001), BS may well have executed a move that will strengthen its position within the industry as the new firm, now listed under the name of Corus, has cornered Europe's no. 1 and the world's no. 3 spot (see Table 6.1).

The fact that Hoogovens is virtually synonymous with Dutch steel offers a unique opportunity to discover the extent to which its relative success in weathering the sector's decline can be explained either by the Dutch government's policies or by firm-specific causes such as 'quality of management'.[3] In other words, is steel governance another example of the much-acclaimed 'Polder Model' or 'Dutch miracle' of tripartite consensual governance (cf. Visser and Hemerijck, 1997)? This chapter will not be able to address this question in full. However, it will examine parts of the evidence by discussing several competencies of Hoogovens as a firm and by reviewing elements of Dutch industrial policy in general as well as that pertaining to steel.[4] The following section discusses the industrial policy setting in order

Table 6.1   Top 10 and selected largest steel producers, 1998

World rank		Production (mn tonnes)	World rank		Production (mn tonnes)
1	Posco (Rep. of Korea)	25.6	15	Bethlehem Steel (USA)	9.6
2	Nippon Steel (Japan)	25.1	18	Nucor (USA)	8.8
3	Corus (UK)	23.0	19	Cherepovets (Russia)	8.5
4	Arbed (Luxembourg)	20.1	23	Magnitogorsk (Russia)	7.7
5	Usinor (France)[a]	18.9	24	LTV (USA)	7.4
6	LNM (UK)	17.1	25	Cockerill Sambre (Belgium)[a]	6.7
(6)	British Steel (UK)	16.3	(25)	Hoogovens (Netherlands)	6.7
7	Thyssen Krupp (Germany)	14.8	26	Novolipetsk (Russia)	6.6
8	Riva (Italy)	13.3	40	Mariupol (Ukraine)	4.3
9	NKK (Japan)	11.5	44	Huta Katowice (Poland)	4.1
10	USX (USA)	11.0	56	SSAB (Sweden)	3.4

Note: [a] Cockerill 75% owned by Usinor since late 1998.

Sources: IISI; Hoogovens; British Steel.

to establish what the Dutch type of steel governance entails. The two subsequent sections will be more directly focused on Hoogovens itself. In the longitudinal perspective taken, 1982 has been chosen as a cut-off point as Hoogovens abandoned its merger with Hoesch and had to make a new start as an independent firm in that year. The chapter concludes with a preliminary assessment of the role that governance played in Hoogovens's success and therefore amounts to an assessment of success or failure in Dutch governance.

2   INDUSTRIAL POLICY SETTING

The Netherlands has a tradition of economic liberalism that goes back as far as the late-sixteenth and seventeenth century when this country, following its dependence on international trade with its colonies, established itself as arguably the most liberal country of Europe (Van Zanden, 1999).[5] Throughout the second half of the twentieth century, this liberal orientation survived, although the government at times was willing enough to lend support to certain firms. A rather peculiar characteristic of the Dutch model of liberal governance was the gradual increase of tripartite consultations and a deliberate and government-led focus on wage restraint, culminating in the by now rather famous Wassenaar agreement of 1982 (Visser and Hemerijck, 1997). Tripartite consensus building only decreased in importance during the late 1980s and 1990s, when the economy appeared to be on a steady growth trajectory again and new-economy individualism began to manifest itself.

Prewar Origins

The economic crisis of the 1930s had initiated the first steps towards what was to become a more intimate government involvement with industry during the post-World War II industrialization process. The crisis also challenged the labour movement to initiate alternative ideas on development. Unions began to collaborate with regional and local governments in order to foster and guide industrial development, partly by helping to set up semi-public industrial banks and so-called 'Economic–Technological Institutes' that were to map the routes of industrialization. These initiatives were all grounded in what was called 'engineer's socialism', the idea that smart engineers would be able to select and/or develop projects that were financially feasible if only their social returns were included in investment calculations. Ultimately, however, these initiatives were quite unsuccessful as the government hesitated to proceed to full-fledged support for fear of being accused of preferential treatments (Tellegen and Brouwer, 1998). Yet this involvement of labour unions in industrial development sowed the first seeds of post-World War II industrial policy corporatism by making the unions an accepted party to industrial policy consultations.

Postwar Industrialization, 1940s–1960s

Following World War II, the government, while formally retaining a non-interventionist approach, laid down several policy papers in which it was announced that the industrialization of the Netherlands should be pursued with determination and led by the development of basic industries such as chemicals and steel. A policy of guided wages was initiated immediately after the war. It was to be effective almost unopposed and without significant changes until 1959, and it has been observed that no other system of administered wage determination did as well for an equally long period of time (Windmuller, 1969). In 1960, wages were an estimated 20 to 25 per cent below those in Germany and Belgium. However, the guided wage policy's very success in terms of continuity during the 1950s became its undoing in the 1960s, when wages exploded in order to make up for lost purchasing power.

The industrialization targets that were put forward were to be realized by means of self-serving and independent business firms. The government was not to interfere with private considerations, certainly not in terms of selective (specific) intervention. However, some experiments in industrial policy were undertaken, according to Van Zanden (1999) probably only because schemes for future spending had to be presented in order to qualify for Marshall Aid funds. Apart from the usual generic tax facilities, substantial financial support was granted to such firms as AKZO's predecessor, Koninklijke Zout, the chemical divisions of DSM, Shell's Pernis refinery and also Hoogovens. Today, all these firms are still major players in the Dutch economy. A Reconstruction Bank (*Herstelbank*), with the government as the majority shareholder, was set up to channel parts of this support. Private shareholders, mainly banks and institutional investors, were to obtain a government-guaranteed return of 3.5 per cent on their investments. Occasionally, the state took part in private firms, but such stakes remained quite small. Industrialization as such, however, was high on the agenda of Dutch politics. Together with full-fledged promotion campaigns and government-enforced wage restraints, this pointed the Dutch economy in a direction that was to benefit Hoogovens, as this firm was increasingly focusing on export markets.

Specific state intervention only started to become more apparent by the end of the 1960s, when several industries as well as large firms turned into decline and certain regions in the country proved unable to follow the pace of economic development in the heartland. One such region was the north-east of the Netherlands. It was here that Hoogovens participated in a joint venture to set up an aluminium industry backed by long-term government guarantees of low-cost supply of energy (see futher below). In 1967, similar facilities had been granted to the French aluminium firm Péchiney in order to persuade it to set up smelter facilities in the relatively backward south-west coastal region. Together, these two firms eventually made the Netherlands into Europe's largest exporter of this non-ferrous metal.

The 1970s and 1980s

As in other countries, Dutch industrial policy during the 1970s and early 1980s came to focus more heavily on the support of declining industries and particularly of individual so-called 'leading' firms. Its aims and instruments were similar (Schenk, 1987) and showed inherent weaknesses. First, financial support was only rarely conditional on strategic restructuring and replacements of incumbent management teams. Thus decline was almost exclusively seen as an inevitable consequence of unfavourable economic circumstances, in spite of abundant evidence of management failure and inadequate managerial practices. Consequently, 'temporary' support by means of subsidies meant to bridge the difficult times was legitimate. Secondly, Dutch industrial policy sought to improve the fate of declining firms and industries by pressing for mergers and acquisitions. Vested beliefs in economies of scale led to the creation, in 1972, of a Restructuring Corporation (*Nehem*, similar to the IRC in Great Britain) which was given the explicit task of forging mergers and acquisitions among medium-sized firms. Owing to insufficient follow-up support, the *Nehem* largely remained ineffectual.

Large-scale concentrations were more directly encouraged (or even concocted) by the Ministry of Economic Affairs – sometimes producing disastrous effects. Billions of public money were spent on firms that eventually went bankrupt (or almost so). RSV Shipbuilders became a landmark case of misguided industrial policy (Wassenberg, 1983). Encouraged by the government, several shipbuilders merged to become RSV in 1971. RSV was granted more than DGL2.5 billion in subsidies during the following 10 years, despite its woefully inadequate management practices. After several phases of demerger, and a suspension of all payments in 1983, the firm was finally liquidated in 1993. The RSV case became the standard 'proof' of the impossibility of specific industrial policy and was invoked time and again to criticize current, or to preclude requested, support measures. It never occurred to the policy makers that, in fact, the rescue operation failed because it was sought via merger. However, in some important cases public funds did allow firms to overcome cyclical downturns, among them Hoogovens (Dercksen and Schenk, 1982).

Meanwhile, a tightly knit corporatist network had evolved on the basis of the postwar cohabitation of market and planning ideologies. Thus, when unions and employers, watched over closely by the government, concluded the wage-restraint-in-return-for-work agreement of Wassenaar in 1982, generally seen as the 'official' beginnings of the Polder Model, the same parties had already met to discuss the implications of a novel approach to industrial policy that had just been advocated by an authoritative advisory committee (WRR, 1980; see below).

For the moment, Dutch industrial policy did not strive for some strategic industry blueprint. The institutions of industrial policy were mainly meant to offer financial backing against unfavourable conditions. This could take the form of government subsidies, small state holdings or government-backed loans.

The more it became evident that many firms, including several of the biggest multinationals, were not able to manage themselves through adverse economic conditions, the more the role of government increased. The late 1970s and early 1980s became the high point of government subsidies to industry. Remarkably, government support did not coincide with a substantial increase of government control over firm decision making.

The use of these subsidies was not uncontroversial. The debate was basically between those who argued that subsidies were given to the wrong firms, and those who argued against government subsidies *tout court*, as those subsidies prevented the rigours of the market from operating fully. The first argument was most forcefully put forward by an advisory committee of the independent WRR think-tank, led by a social-democratic professor of economics, Arie van der Zwan (WRR, 1980).[6] According to the WRR, support should be given to selected sunrise industries and firms, instead of sunset, smokestack industries. Since the latter largely coincided with low value-added industrial activities, the WRR also argued for turning around those manufacturing firms that were focusing on basic product markets.

The WRR suggestions became effectively buried when the government appointed an assessment committee in which business interests were overrepresented. Although the importance of moving the Dutch economy into high-tech industries was upheld, the committee, led by a former Shell CEO, again stressed the importance of wage restraint and free markets. The committee's report changed most of what was to remain of industrial policy into technology policy, mostly amounting to relatively small-scale support programmes. It also started to lead the Dutch away from the traditional corporatist way of consensus building, and towards the Anglo-Saxon veneration of deregulation and privatization (see Hulsink and Schenk, 1998). Interestingly, this did not eliminate the granting of large-scale financial support to a handful of large firms that were perceived as strategic actors in the Dutch economy. One of those firms was Hoogovens. Others were Philips, Volvo, Daf-Trucks and Fokker.[7] The interventionist, subsidy-focused part of the Dutch governance model did not recede until the economic boom of the 1990s appeared to be persistent, and further government support became superfluous.

As Table 6.2 demonstrates, the Wassenaar agreement was quite effective in slowing down wage growth. For almost any year, standard disposable income growth trailed productivity increases. While real productivity increased by 3.8 per cent in 1994, standard disposable income even decreased by 0.4 per cent. During 1984–96, the real costs of labour in the private sector grew by only a meagre 0.8 per cent annually. Table 6.3 demonstrates that the Dutch policy of wage restraint indeed caused wages to increase much less than in other countries.

Table 6.2 Income, wages and labour costs in the Netherlands, 1984–96 (percentage growth)

	1984	1985	1986	1987	1988	1989	1990	1991	1992	1993	1994	1995	1996
GDP	4.9	4.9	2.8	0.7	3.9	5.9	6.6	5.0	4.2	2.8	5.3	3.9	4.1
Real national income	2.7	3.7	3.3	-0.2	2.5	5.6	4.4	1.9	1.0	0.9	3.8	2.3	3.1
Standard purchasing power	-1.1	1.5	2.4	1.5	1.1	2.1	2.4	0.2	0.5	0.6	-0.4	0.9	0.2
Standard gross wage	0.3	1.1	1.2	0.8	0.8	1.4	2.9	3.5	4.3	3.1	1.8	1.4	1.6
Real labour costs	0.7	0.2	-0.7	0.7	-0.7	-0.9	1.8	2.8	2.7	1.6	0.9	1.0	0.6

Source: Van Witteloostuijn (1999) from CPB.

Table 6.3   Development of wages in selected OECD countries, 1986–90

Country	Average annual wage increase	Country	Average annual wage increase
Austria	5.0	Italy	6.1
Belgium	3.0	Japan	3.7
Denmark	6.0	Netherlands	1.7
Finland	8.2	Norway	8.7
France	3.7	Spain	8.2
Germany	4.2	Sweden	8.2
Greece	16.0	UK	8.5
Ireland	5.6	USA	2.6

Source: OECD (1993).

The Dutch Approach: Governance at a Distance

The first 35 years of post-World War II Dutch governance were characterized by the gradual emergence of a corporatist system whose foundations had been laid during the prewar years. Apart from a wage explosion during the 1960s, the government consistently and successfully compelled and later encouraged unions and employers to moderate wages. Investment of the proceeds was thought to result in a strengthening of the industrial base. Firms were encouraged to attain a larger scale by means of mergers and acquisitions, while the government at the same time tolerated or even triggered the rise of many cartel-like arrangements (De Jong, 1990). The cycle of subsidies to industry in the Netherlands was not much different from that in other EU (or even OECD) countries. However, the extent to which subsidies were used has always been moderate in a comparative sense (Schenk, 1993).

During this period, the Dutch model of industrial policy boiled down to an idiosyncratic mixture of (rather limited) financial support for specific firms, non-interference with business decision making, and general wage restraint. These were achieved in an institutional context characterized by consensus making rather than fierce competition. The Dutch approach is best captured by the somewhat paradoxical phrase 'laissez-faire intervention'. Its policy imperatives were to grant subsidies when large firms are in trouble (specific intervention), but not to interfere with managerial practices (non-intervention), and, for the remainder, to trust that wage restraint policies will do the job (generic intervention). More generally, the corporatist form of governance also produced a system of welfare benefits that allowed firms to shed thousands of workers without causing large-scale labour unrest.

3   PRE-1982 STEEL POLICY: THE CASE OF HOOGOVENS (I)

Hoogovens (in full: *Koninklijke Nederlandsche Hoogovens en Staalfabrieken* or, in English, Royal Dutch Blast Furnaces and Steel Plants) was established in the aftermath of World War I when Dutch industrialists wished to decrease their almost total dependence on foreign imports of steel. Production began in 1924, backed by the Dutch government, which took a 25 per cent stake and gave its promise to provide Hoogovens with cheap coal from its own mines, together with the City of Amsterdam, which took a 17 per cent stake in return for Hoogovens's decision to locate in a coastal site near IJmuiden (close to Amsterdam), and banks that were rather suddenly developing a taste for industrial finance (see, further, Table 6A.2).

As we have seen, the industrialization plans that were made following World War II defined steel as a strategic industry and therefore Hoogovens as a strategic firm. Helped by Marshall funds and funds provided by the *Herstelbank*, Hoogovens was meant to become an important supplier of steel to Dutch industry, especially shipbuilding. Government support was so extensive that the state would have obtained a majority stake in Hoogovens if the funds had gone straight into the firm. In order to prevent this, it was decided to set up a separate firm, *Breedband*, which would be almost fully owned by the state, yet in keeping with its non-interventionist ideology the government delegated managerial authority to Hoogovens management. *Breedband* would be inextricably part of the Hoogovens production process at its IJmuiden works. This solution was extraordinary, even for the Netherlands. It symbolized the governance model of laissez-faire intervention, a form of governance in which financial support was granted to strategic firms without a corresponding degree of government control over their decisions.

The *Breedband* 'division' proved very successful. Demand for its flat-rolled products was so high that by the 1960s Hoogovens felt it wanted to add another, similar rolling mill in the near future (Dankers and Verheul, 1993). However, this would further complicate the intricate *Breedband*–state–Hoogovens construction. Consequently, Hoogovens opened negotiations for taking over *Breedband* in 1960. The acquisition went ahead in 1964. To the Dutch state, the *Breedband* sell-off turned out to be rather profitable. It managed to negotiate a price that was more than five times the original investment (during the preceding years, it had also received substantial dividends). As part of the deal, the government also saw its stake in Hoogovens increase to 30 per cent.

Breedband's production capacity exceeded the domestic consumption of its products and so Hoogovens turned to foreign markets. This was successful, as there was a growing demand for flat products and coated steel (especially tin plate) throughout the developed economies. During this period, Hoogovens became perhaps the most internationalized steel manufacturer of the EC (see Table 6A.3). This development had several enduring effects. First, Hoogovens became accustomed to selling at world market prices, which forced it to stress productive efficiency and product quality at a relatively early stage. Secondly, the firm became a relative outsider to European policy cabals, which explains why Hoogovens could consistently maintain that survival in the European steel industry should be more a matter of productive efficiency than of national predilections. Finally, supplying many different export markets made Hoogovens less vulnerable to regional problems of excess capacity.

Another decision that was to determine much of Hoogovens's future was taken in the early 1960s, that is, soon after huge natural gas reserves had been discovered in the relatively backward north-eastern part of the country. Having learned that Billiton, a Dutch firm active in the mining of bauxite in the Dutch colony of Surinam, was expecting to obtain energy supplies at discount prices in return for setting up a new aluminium smelter in the north-east, Hoogovens offered its technological expertise and investment strength in a joint venture. After the government had, indeed, agreed to an especially attractive pricing scheme for the supply of energy, Hoogovens and Billiton teamed up with Alusuisse, which contributed both technological and marketing knowledge to establish Aldel in 1964. With a 50 per cent stake, Hoogovens became the dominant party. It proved the first step on the road that would lead to Hoogovens becoming, next to Japan's Kobe Steel, one of only two steel firms in the world with substantial interests in the production of aluminium.

The acquisition of an aluminium branch seemed a clever decision at the time as new production techniques in major steel-consuming industries were rapidly transforming input requirements. For example, in a typical 1985 US car, 44 per cent less steel and 65 per cent less iron were used than in its precursor of 1975, but 81 per cent more aluminium (see Table 6.4). More generally, the 1970s saw a departure from the long-term growth trend that could not be attributed to cyclical factors. Between 1973 and 1980, consumption of steel in advanced market economies fell by 13 per cent, despite GNP and industrial production rises of about 15 per cent (Ballance and Sinclair, 1983).

Other than several of its bigger competitors, such as British Steel, Hoogovens seems to have anticipated these structural changes rather well. Or was it just luck, triggered by the availability of huge natural gas reserves, and an industrial policy that wished to use these reserves in part for the benefit of the relatively backward region where they were found? According to De Voogd (1993), referring to an interview with former Hoogovens CEO J.D. Hooglandt (member of the board from 1970 to 1988), Hoogovens did not understand the structural changes until the mid-1970s. On the other hand, this was at least several years earlier than the industry's International Iron and Steel Institute, that kept on forecasting a growth of demand for well into the 1980s. In any event, Hoogovens appeared to be well-equipped to confront the coming changes. Evidently, this would increase the chances for laissez-faire intervention.

Table 6.4   Inputs of materials for US-built cars, 1975–85 (in pounds)

	1975	1980	1985	% change 1975–85
Steel	2 420	1 834	1 356	−44
Iron	626	458	216	−65
Plastics	168	184	252	+50
Rubber	160	124	180	+13
Aluminium	86	124	156	+81
Glass	94	80	72	−22
All others	416	276	168	−60
Total car weight	3 970	3 080	2 400	−40

Source: Ballance and Sinclair (1983) from Arthur Andersen & Co; *Business Week*, 15 June 1981.

Unfortunately, this potential advantage appeared to be compromised significantly in another area of the firm's pursuits. In 1972, Hoogovens merged with Germany's Hoesch to form Estel. On paper, as with most mergers, the logic seemed impeccable at first. Following negotiations with the American and British occupational forces, in 1953 Hoogovens had managed to convert its prewar stake in Germany's Phoenix steel works into a substantial minority stake in Dortmund-Hörde-Hüttenunion (DHHU), one of the larger German steel firms that was created after the split-up of Vereinigte Stahlwerke. This participation had proved to be problematic (see Dankers and Verheul, 1993). When Hoesch, also located in Dortmund, proposed to take over DHHU via an exchange of shares it enabled the company to rationalize the Dortmund locations, thereby solving a problem for Hoogovens which would still obtain part of any potential proceeds. Thus, in 1966, it agreed on the condition that the deal would also entail productive rationalization among Hoesch and Hoogovens. It was intended that Hoesch's inland site would specialize in the manufacture of downstream steel products, whereas Hoogovens's coastal site would focus on the production of semi-finished steel. The ECSC's approval for the pseudo-cartel was obtained by invoking scale economy and rationalization arguments, yet it is quite remarkable that such arguments were hardly ever used in internal Hoogovens documents (Dankers and Verheul, 1993), apparently because the Hoogovens management was not so certain that the predicted effects would really be forthcoming. It was perhaps not too surprising that the arrangement hardly materialized.

The third merger wave of the century, peaking in the USA around 1969, suggested the ultimate – but in fact mostly illusory – solution to the typical problems of coordination in alliances. Thus, in 1972, Hoogovens and Hoesch proceeded to form the first truly international steel firm. By size, the firms suddenly jumped to third place in Europe, and it was believed that this would strengthen their position within EC negotiation processes considerably. While this may have been true, it could not, of course, solve the major problem of oligopolistic competition in capital-intensive industries, which is the preemptive creation of excess capacity (see, for example, Cowling, 1982). Moreover, it only made things worse, as teaming up with a German major sucked Hoogovens into the coordination problems that were manifest in the largest steel market in Europe. On top of this there were problems with diverging management styles. These were not very different from those encountered by other merged firms, but they were more visible since Hoesch and Hoogovens never formally integrated, but built an intermediate holding instead. This implied that strategic decisions still required the consent on equal terms of the non-executive boards of both firms, despite the fact that Hoogovens had a factual majority share in Estel, as a result of the minority stake in Hoesch which it had negotiated as part of the DHHU deal. Although at the time this was regarded as a serious failure (Dankers and Verheul, 1993), with hindsight it can only be concluded that it eventually proved fortunate for Hoogovens, as it was now easier to break up the merger.

As soon as the tide turned against expansive capacity investments during the steel crisis of the second half of the 1970s, and even before the expensive new headquarters could be inaugurated, the Estel merger started to show signs of fatigue. The tensions between the constituent parts, which had never fully disappeared as each continued to operate as an individual profit centre, now increased as tough decisions had to be made about lay-offs and closures instead of growth and new investments. Evidently, Hoogovens was the more modern subsidiary, but Hoesch was more closely linked to major markets, especially the car industry. A pivotal question was which location should undergo surgery? Probably the most delicate conflict concerned the significant losses incurred by Hoesch. According to the merger arrangement, Estel was to cover these losses, which in effect meant that Hoogovens had to take the burden. During 1981, Estel could no longer carry the losses and applied for government support. The Dutch government was willing to support Estel, but only on the condition that the German government would match it. The Germans were only prepared to do so if the Estel restructuring would be part of a larger restructuring of the German steel industry, in particular intensified collaboration with Krupp. This would draw Hoogovens even further into the loss-making parts of German steel.

Faced with this prospect, and under pressure from its Dutch banks, Hoogovens eventually decided to extricate itself from Estel. The Dutch government tried to save the merger, but its efforts were later widely interpreted as token gestures aimed at preventing high indemnity claims from the German side, which undoubtedly would have been issued if it had become clear that Hoogovens and the Dutch government had in fact been plotting the break-up of the merger. Since Hoogovens also succeeded in leaving Hoesch to carry the can, Estel was dissolved by mutual consent in 1982, exactly 10 years after it had been established.

In sum, while the state had been instrumental in getting Hoogovens on the map, and in re-establishing the firm after World War II, in part by taking large minority stakes, it had refrained from substantive interference with decision making. Nevertheless, its indirect and strategic support was substantial throughout the first 35 or so years following World War II, probably even crucial when it was needed most, that is, when a tough power game had to be played in the break-up of Estel. This game was played well by the Dutch side with tight coordination between the government and Hoogovens's executive as well as non-executive board.

Throughout this era, government support in terms of direct subsidies remained comparatively small, especially when expressed in terms of installed capacity (see Table 6.5). For example, during the 1975–9 period, the Dutch steel industry (that is, Hoogovens) received the smallest amount of government subsidies in the European Community. As Table 6.5 also demonstrates, this was due to change significantly during the 1980s, although financial state support still remained minor in a comparative sense.

4   POST-1982 STEEL POLICY: THE CASE OF HOOGOVENS (II)

Following the break-up of Estel, a substantial restructuring of Hoogovens was to correct what was called the 'imbalance' that had been created in the IJmuiden works. Thus Hoogovens and Hoesch had decided to concentrate the initial stages of production in IJmuiden, and the later stages of steel production and finishing in Dortmund. A DGL2.7 billion investment plan was presented to the Ministry of Economic Affairs, of which the government pledged to finance almost a third by means of (a) a subsidy of DGL195 million meant to undertake 'strategic' investments in IJmuiden; (b) a subordinated loan of DGL570 million, on favourable terms, which was to be used to bridge the debts from the Estel demerger; and (c) an addition to equity of DGL130 million, unless the capital market would be able to carry an offering to this amount (Dankers and Verheul,

Table 6.5   Subsidies to the steel industry in selected EU countries, 1975–85*

	1975–1979			1980–1985			1975–1985
	Average installed capacity (1000 tons)	Average annual subsidy (mn DM)	Average annual subsidy per 1000 tons installed capacity (DM)	Average installed capacity (1000 tons)	Average annual subsidy (mn DM)	Average annual subsidy per 1000 tons installed capacity (DM)	Average annual subsidy per 1000 tons installed capacity (DM)
Ireland	107	15.2	142 056	267	103.5	387 641	276 012
United Kingdom	28 396	2 770.4	97 563	25 035	2 212.5	88 376	92 552
Italy	34 636	865.4	24 985	38 943	4 719.5	121 193	77 462
France	32 930	412.0	12 511	29 249	3 585.8	122 598	72 559
Belgium	19 300	545.0	28 238	17 138	1 669.5	97 415	65 971
Denmark	1 097	23.0	20 966	1 067	31.8	29 844	25 809
Luxembourg	7 764	6.6	850	6 238	247.5	39 674	22 027
Netherlands	7 787	4.4	565	8 272	178.8	21 620	12 050
Germany	66 812	184.0	2 754	60 743	1 053.3	17 340	10 710
Total	198 811	4 826.4	24 276	189 550	13 802.3	72 816	50 752

Note: * ranked by position in last column.

Source: Own calculations from *Wirtschaftsvereinigung Eisen- und Stahlindustrie* (1986, 1987, 1990).

1993). In addition to this, the Dutch government set apart an amount of DGL150 million as a contingency loan to be used in case this was 'deemed necessary'.

The arrangement signalled a much increased role of the government in Hoogovens decision making. First, the government's right to information was stepped up substantially. Second, it obtained the possibility to veto important decisions. Hoogovens was required to report to the ministry on a monthly basis, and was not allowed to take certain decisions (ranging from lay-offs to executive pay) without government consent. Nevertheless, the laissez-faire tradition was not fully abandoned; for instance, the ministry never made use of its (heavily contested) right to appoint an observer to the firm's board in addition to the existing two government representatives, both high-ranking civil servants, on the non-executive board. Moreover, the government never really blocked proposals from the firm.

Meanwhile, the Ministry of Finance started complaining about the favourable energy deal that had been arranged earlier between Aldel and the Ministry of Economic Affairs. The Finance ministry argued that the support measures that had been taken in the aftermath of the Estel break-up had been so generous that it was time to redress the energy support arrangement, which it estimated at DGL150 million annually. To Hoogovens this was unacceptable. It replied that it was prepared to abandon its aluminium business if the Finance ministry were to get its way. Obviously, to the Ministry of Economic Affairs such an outcome would mean both a loss of interdepartmental prestige and a possible setback to its regional policy for the north-east, with the result that it continued to back Hoogovens in the dispute. By intervention of the prime minister, a deal was struck that implied the energy price support would be adapted (downward) to the prices paid by Aldel's foreign competitors, especially Péchiney. Since this latter firm was profiting enormously from heavily subsidized nuclear power in its home country, both Hoogovens and the Economics ministry could trust that they had concluded a clever arrangement.

As if to prove the Ministry of Economic Affairs right, Hoogovens's performance improved so much during the following years that a public offering in 1984 was successful. As Table 6A.1 demonstrates, 1984 was the first of three consecutive years during which Hoogovens produced positive net returns, while cash flows had already improved substantially. Consequently, the government did not need to fully implement its pledge of equity support, nor was it necessary for Hoogovens to break into the promised contingency loan. In accordance with the then current privatization policy, the state even sold off a substantial part of its stake in Hoogovens in 1986, thus reducing its ownership to 15 per cent. By the end of that year, state ownership was effectively at 13.5 per cent (see Table 6A.2).

Part of the improved performance was due to the fact that Hoogovens had introduced the more efficient method of continuous casting which had been in use in other countries since the 1970s. This late adoption allowed Hoogovens to comply rather painlessly with the EC's capacity reduction demands, as it simply closed down several of its outdated facilities. Besides, being relatively late in one respect normally creates a chance to reap first-mover advantages in another when technological development has continued. Indeed, Hoogovens became the first steel manufacturer to successfully introduce computer-integrated manufacturing (Dankers and Verheul, 1993). Consequently, a smaller but state-of-the-art steel works was born.

Hoogovens thus succeeded in improving its performance considerably at the same time that Europe was going through a severe steel crisis. While government support was crucial at the time that Hoogovens wished to give up its merger with Hoesch, much of the improvement was the result of internal restructuring. As can be seen from Table 6A.1, the restructuring of Hoogovens – rather than the steel crisis of the early 1980s as such – took its toll on labour. Between 1982 and 1986, approximately 3000 jobs were shed in Hoogovens's steel division, while production volumes declined substantially only from 1981 to 1982. This reduction in employment of approximately 14 per cent was almost fully realized without forced dismissals. Sheltered by the Polder Model's corporatist agreement structure, special redundancy and early retirement schemes were set up that softened the pain. During the second half of the 1980s similar redundancy packages were agreed which allowed Hoogovens to axe another 2000 jobs in a further drive to increase productivity. Throughout steel production volumes remained almost stable.

Hoogovens's policy of diversification into high value-added markets was probably not much different from its rivals' so that it is unlikely to have contributed to the firm's relatively good performance. Moreover, it was partly abandoned when an opportunity arose to acquire Kaiser's European aluminium businesses from its troubled US parent in 1987. While aluminium had remained a secondary activity for a long time, especially during the Estel troubles, Hoogovens jumped at the chance to become a major player – only a few years after it had declared its preparedness to sell off its aluminium activities altogether (see above). Together with the modernization and extension of its own facilities (such as those at its Sidal subsidiary in Belgium), the acquisition of Kaiser Europe made Hoogovens the fourth largest aluminium producer in Europe. Total production increased twofold and in 1988 Hoogovens's aluminium activities made up slightly less than 35 per cent of total sales. Hoogovens therefore more or less stumbled into a so-called 'two-metals strategy' which, however, served it well, at least until the early 1990s.

The largest lay-offs occurred during the steel crisis of the early 1990s. About 4000 steel jobs were lost before employment picked up again in 1995 (this was, however, partly the result of changes in internal reporting). Paradoxi-cally, however, Hoogovens' steel production volumes increased throughout the crisis years. Thus the lay-offs were obviously a result of intensified 'downsizing' and rationalization efforts. Again, the Polder Model proved its effectiveness for Hoogovens, as the state and society as a whole carried large parts of the burden by absorbing many of the redundant employees in generous social welfare arrangements.

5   STEEL GOVERNANCE IN HOLLAND: AN ASSESSMENT

The Dutch model of industrial governance during the second half of the twentieth century consisted of specific support, both financial and strategic, to several large firms deemed to be important to the Dutch economy. Such support was not accompanied by a concomitant share of government in firm decision making and can therefore be classified as 'laissez-faire intervention'. This governance style did not entail development programmes based on industrial grand designs, but left firms to decide whether to expand or contract. Firm decision making was, however, buttressed by government policies that stressed the importance of international competitiveness. Since the Dutch economy was (and is) heavily dependent on exports, wage restraint was self-evidently an important policy goal. More generally, the Dutch approach began with guided wage policies and evolved into implicit or even explicit agreements under which labour and employers agreed on wage restraint in return for jobs and attractive welfare arrangements. In terms of policy style over time, the Dutch moved further along on the imposition–consultation continuum.

In the case of Dutch steel, this type of governance was able to cope successfully with decline. Although Hoogovens right from its beginnings has been partially owned by the Dutch state, it has always been allowed to behave as if it were a fully private company, apart from a brief period during the first half of the 1980s, when it had to recuperate from its broken-up merger with Hoesch. The government studiously avoided obtaining a majority stake. Still, it was evident to all parties concerned that Hoogovens could always count on government support, in terms of subsidies but perhaps especially in terms of strategic and negotiation support, as was the case during the break-up of Estel and the cheap-energy dispute with the Ministry of Finance. Although not insignificant, state financial support remained comparatively small.

More generally, Hoogovens benefited from the Dutch approach to industrial governance in two respects. First, wage restraint allowed the firm to offer its output abroad at relatively attractive prices. Second, it allowed Hoogovens to axe several thousands of jobs without causing serious labour unrest. In fact, forced dismissals were only necessary during the steel crisis of the early 1990s, but by that time the imminent economic boom did not require special arrangements to manage decline in terms of employment. In terms of steel output, there hardly ever was a decline to begin with.

When seen from a broader macroeconomic perspective, however, there are downsides to this governance style. First, wage restraints can lead to intermittent wage adaptations (so-called 'explosions') which firms may find it difficult to cope with. What happened to the Dutch economy during the 1960s serves as a textbook case in this respect. Second, as Kleinknecht (1998) has argued, one of the probable effects of the Dutch emphasis on wage restraint has been that innovation has remained lacklustre as firms were not sufficiently encouraged to find new means of increasing productivity. By implication, this must have slowed down the modernization of the Dutch economy. In the case of Hoogovens, we have indeed observed that the continuous casting innovation was introduced relatively late. Also, since purchasing power increased only slightly, consumers were also slack in adopting new products, which had a discouraging effect on the introduction of new products and services. Likewise, the presence of many cartels and semi-cartels may have reduced incentives to improve technologies and services even further. When added to the penchant of industrial policies for sunset industries and firms, the combined retardation effects may have been quite significant. Perhaps this explains why it took so long before the Dutch economy as a whole got back on a growth trajectory.

Third, the success of laissez-faire intervention heavily relies on the presence of 'competent' management in the firms that receive support. Since formal, ex ante assessments of management quality and firm policies remain rare, it follows that 'chance' becomes a crucial determinant of policy success in the Dutch approach. Indeed, while several other similarly supported firms folded (such as RSV shipbuilders, and Fokker Aircraft Manufacturers in the 1990s, both eminent examples of bad management), state support for Hoogovens turned out to be a success only because this particular firm happened to make several 'right' policy choices, albeit partly forced by circumstances (export focus and break-up of Estel) and partly by accident (continued involvement in the aluminium industry). It could easily have been otherwise.

NOTES

1. The author would like to thank the participants at the 1999 Governance Workshop at Nuffield College (Oxford University), and particularly Paul 't Hart, for suggestions and comments; Yvo Nelissen provided preparatory assistance while Pieter Van Der Hoeven suggested a few corrections. The usual disclaimer applies. Contact: E.J.J.Schenk@kub.nl
2. At the time of writing, DGL 1 ≈ Euro 0.5.
3. To be more precise, there is one other steel firm in the Netherlands, Nedstaal. Established in 1938, it was taken over by Thyssen of Germany but regained its independence in 1998. Total production of Nedstaal is estimated at about 3–6 per cent of Hoogovens's. Its main input is

scrap steel. Demka, the first Dutch commercial manufacturer of steel (founded in 1915) became a fully owned Hoogovens susbsidiary in 1964, but its mills were closed down in 1983. In addition, one of the largest and most acquisitive steel makers in the world, Ispat International, is incorporated in Amsterdam and quoted on the Amsterdam Stock Exchange as well as Wall Street, but it has no operating subsidiaries in the Netherlands. Ispat is a subsidiary of LNM Group, headquartered in the UK.

4. Large parts of Hoogovens's history as a firm have been documented exhaustively; see De Vries (1968) and especially Dankers and Verheul (1993). Since the latter overlaps the former, I was able to rely on the latter only; see the appropriate references in the text. Information concerning Hoogovens that has no reference is taken from the steel archives of GRASP Research (Erasmus University Rotterdam) that mainly consist of newspaper clippings from *NRC Handelsblad*, *de Volkskrant*, *het Financieele Dagblad*, *Financial Times* and *The Economist*.

5. The term 'liberal' is used in its European meaning; that is, as an ideology that is definitely in favour of free markets.

6. The 'Wetenschappelijke Raad voor het Regeringsbeleid' (literally: Scientific Advisory Council on Government Policy) was formed in 1972. Though initiated by the government, and founded by a royal decree (enforced by law in 1976), it is an independent advisory body with a relatively small staff but ample opportunities to recruit ad hoc experts. Its task is to focus especially on long-term developments by means of applied research. Together with the SER (Social and Economic Council, a tripartite advisory body founded in 1950) and the Centraal Planbureau (CPB), founded in 1945 to develop forecasts and plans on the basis of large econometric models of the Dutch economy, now a more general bureau for economic policy analysis, it is one of the most highly regarded and important advisory bodies in the Netherlands.

7. In the 1990s the Dutch government came up with a quite innovative solution for channelling funds into private firms, the so-called technolease scheme (see Hulsink and Schenk, 1998). This facility was applied most conspicuously, though at first secretively, in the Fokker drama (1994) and as an emergency backing for Philips (1993). Under this scheme, which is equivalent to the sale-and-lease-back schemes which are widely used for tangible assets, a firm sells (part of) its as yet undepreciated know-how to another firm, usually a bank, upon which it is leased from this other firm. The latter enjoys considerable tax benefits as the purchasing costs can be deducted from profits, while the former immediately receives a substantial cash flow. Evidently, the scheme is most attractive if the former firm's profits are not sufficient to allow full depreciation while the latter firm's profits are. The indirect state subsidy amounts to the opportunity loss as a result of lower and/or postponed tax collections. The gross cash flows for the two firms mentioned alone amounted to at least one billion euro and perhaps to as much as 1.7 billion euro, whereas the attendant risks were largely covered by complex vice-versa payments and put option clauses. The facility became subject to controversy between the European Commission and the Dutch government, but was found acceptable in 1999.

APPENDIX:

Table 6A.1   Basic indicators, Hoogovens

	Employees, steel division	Employees, aluminium division	Steel production (1000 tonnes)	Net revenue (million DGL)	Cash flow (million DGL)	Net return (million DGL)
1980	n.a.	n.a.	4 953	5 743	237	−274
1981	n.a.	n.a.	5 178	6 451	151	−394
1982	20 655	n.a.	4 122	5 943	365	−106
1983	20 080	n.a.	4 277	6 048	315	−38
1984	19 379	n.a.	5 532	7 259	867	207
1985	19 214	n.a.	5 302	7 465	688	279
1986	17 569	3 604	5 052	6 093	628	155
1987	16 988	6 831	4 836	5 848	416	−76
1988	16 632	7 116	5 260	7 868	963	301
1989	16 307	6 607	5 419	9 011	1 718	751
1990	15 687	6 713	5 180	8 429	867	298
1991	15 074	6 490	4 943	8 095	551	−51
1992	14 215	5 994	5 197	7 722	476	−595
1993	12 092	4 535	5 812	7 219	474	−234
1994	11 601	4 591	5 949	7 934	786	354
1995	12 714	4 556	6 149	8 100	1 173	507
1996	12 234	4 975	6 171	7 933	812	326
1997	15 912	5 161	6 674	9 996	647	498
1998	15 631	5 283	6 725	10 811	1 117	415

Note: Employee figures exclude non-steel and non-aluminium employees (on average 2250 employees during 1994–8); increase in 1997 largely the result of take-over of Hille and Müller and consolidation of Boël of Belgium.

Source: Annual reports, Hoogovens.

Table 6A.2 Government ownership of Hoogovens (years during which mutations occurred)

	1924	1961	1964	1979	1984	1986	1987	1990	1993	1994	1995	1997	1998
Stake (%)	25	27	30	29	29	13.5	14	12.3	15.5	15.3	13	10.2	10
Paid value (mn DGL)	7.5	n.a.	n.a.	74.3	92.4	54.0	54.0	55.0	97.5	97.5	97.5	97.5	97.5

Note: When Hoogovens was founded, the City of Amsterdam also held a significant (17%) share of Hoogovens's stock (see text) but this was gradually reduced to approx. 8.5% in 1982 and further to 5% just before it was sold off in 1993.

Source: Dutch Ministry of Finance.

Table 6A.3 Steel exports as a percentage of steel production

	1982	1983	1984	1985	1986	1987	1988	1989	1990	1991
EU[a]	39	40	42	44	43	43	41	43	43	44
Hoogovens[b]	75	77	81	81	83	82	82	80	82	83

Notes:
a EU: extra-EU exports plus intra-EU imports as a percentage of total ferrous metals production expressed in current prices.
b Hoogovens: exports as a percentage of total production expressed in tonnes.

Source: Own calculations from CEC (1993); Dankers and Verheul (1993).

7. Steel restructuring in Spain, 1979–95: the attrition game

Gabriel Saro Jauregui and
Mikel Navarro Arancegui

1 STEEL POLICY IN SPAIN: GOVERNANCE CHALLENGES AND KEY ACTORS

In October 1982, the Spanish Socialist Party won the general elections by a landslide; one year later, local elections gave them control over Spain's most important cities. For more than a decade this party was to enjoy an unrivalled political power in Spanish democratic history. The Socialists' reforming platform, focused on the idea of *el cambio* (change), had gained the support of a wide coalition of workers and urban middle classes. The party's modernizing ambition sat squarely within a classic social-democrat programme: democracy consolidation, accession to the EEC, enlargement of the welfare state and economic restructuring (Maravall, 1991).

The new government was acutely aware of the urgencies of the economic situation, particularly throughout manufacturing. By the early 1980s, on top of energetic crisis and inflation, common to the rest of Europe, the Spanish case showed some peculiarities that aggravated the industrial problem.

First, the political transition that was going on rendered extremely difficult any process of industrial adjustment, given its corollary in terms of lay-offs and plant closures. Besides, the Spanish union movement had just been legalized and it was rebuilding its structures; in that context, militancy was widespread and union leaders were reluctant to engage themselves in such an unpopular programme as industrial adjustment. Finally, any adjustment would have a clear territorial impact, for the endangered manufacturing sectors were concentrated in such 'sensitive' regions as the Basque Country and Asturias.

Secondly, Spain's political and economic élites were committed to a rapid process of accession to the EEC. 'Europe' was presented as a haven of political stability and economic welfare, overlooking the impact of a scenario of trade liberalization – a dire impact, because Spanish industrial development had relied so far on trade protection and subsidized official credit, which favoured over-specialization in those very sectors – textiles and heavy industry – that were to be decimated in the following two decades. In sum, adjustment requirements under the twin effects of regime change and trade liberalization were more demanding in Spain than across the EEC.

The preceding centrist governments (1979–82) had devoted most of their efforts to carrying out the political transition, so in the industrial policy area they had been unable to strike an agreement with unions and managers over how the sacrifices were to be shared; in addition, government's ascendancy over the social partners receded rapidly after 1980, as crisis grew and party unity crumbled. Consequently, the steps taken consisted largely in the rescue of several – (politically relevant) firms and other 'ad hoc' measures aimed at buying time while the regime change was completed. In a context of unprecedented recession, this attitude promoted the extension of the malaise to whole manufacturing sectors.

The new Socialist government considered industrial restructuring, to be known as *Reconversión Industrial* (RI), as one of the pillars of its economic agenda. For almost two decades, RI was to monopolize the debate in this policy area and to absorb three-quarters of the Department of Industry's budget. By early 1983, the government had designed an ambitious programme which encompassed 12 manufacturing sectors, with an annual turnover of 850 bn pta (1 euro = 166.38 pta) and 280 000 employees. It was a costly programme that consumed over 4 000 bn pta (24.1 bn euros) in the period 1982–93. Labour adjustment and financial reparations accounted for the bulk of the programme while capital investment totalled 20 per cent.

Steel, shipbuilding and white goods constituted the 'hard core' of the programme, that is, where the fight between government and the unions was to take place. By 1982, steel employed some 80 000 workers in Spain and it was deemed a 'strategic' sector by the government: second in exports and fourth in terms of contribution to the GDP. In fact, integrated steel firms received up to 55 per cent of all the funds devoted to the RI.

Steel has been traditionally divided into three subsectors: integrated steel, speciality (alloyed) steels and common steels (see Table 7.1). Although all three were grossly non-competitive in Spain, challenges were distinct and their reform followed parallel but different paths. For instance, capacity excess and fragmented ownership posed a great obstacle to adjustment in the speciality and common subsectors but not in integrated steel, given the traditional deficit in flat products. On the other hand, while the former included a bunch of competitive firms, cost inefficiency and low added value plagued the whole integrated sector.

Contrary to the northern European model, electric steel production in countries like Spain or Italy has been relatively more important than the integrated one; small but aggressive commercially, they kept an agenda distinct

Table 7.1   The Spanish steel sector, 1982 and 1997

	Production (million tonnes)	Turnover (million pta)	Employees	Firms Integrated	Firms Speciality	Firms Common
1982	Int: 6.47 Spec: 1.35 Com: 4.49	Int: 233 635 Spec: 59 800 Com: 149 581	Int: 38 010 Spec: 11 744 Com: 10 088	AHM, AHV, Ensidesa	12	17
1997	Int: 4.8 Spec: 1.1 Com: 6.07	Int: 270 040 Spec: 110 473 Com: 313 813	Int: 12 225 Spec: 3 399 Com: 5 300	Aceralia	Sidenor, GSB, Olarra	6

107

from that of the integrated producers. If in the early 1980s there was an equilibrium between both methods in Spain, it tilted progressively in favour of electric steels, so now the rate is 2:1; it produces 11.6 per cent of ECSC crude steel but up to 20 per cent of long steels.

Regarding ownership, there were three integrated steel firms: Ensidesa was located in Asturias, AHM in Valencia and AHV in the Basque Country. The territorial connection is very important in this type of sector, where firms are deeply rooted in their local communities' history and economy. Besides, this political dimension was even clearer given that, by the late 1970s, all three companies survived on state's subsidies. Ownership fragmentation was greater in the other two subsectors, which had about 20 firms each. They could be classified into three groups:

- obsolete and small firms, that were quickly closed down;
- those which had invested heavily – thanks to state grants – in enlarging capacity. Most of these (including Acenor and Nervacero) were so heavily indebted to the state that, like AHV, they were private only in a formal sense;
- companies that strived to remain free from public moneys (and directives) such as Acerinox, M.Ucín or Aristrain. Contrary to the previous ones, they had largely financed their own plant modernization, so indebtedness was not high. In most cases, the founding family had retained power.

2   THE POLITICAL AND INSTITUTIONAL CONTEXT OF STEEL RESTRUCTURING

The Spanish adjustment programme evolved around sector-based plans. Formally, each one was to be agreed within the sector-based policy communities. These communities had been set up under the centrist government in an attempt to 'share sacrifices' and the socialist government reinforced their role by agreeing to work through them. Three were the insiders in the steel restructuring process: politicians–officials, firm managers and unions leaders.

First, *central government*'s role was crucial as both owner, financier and even midwife of the sectoral plans. In practice, its representative was a 'troika' constituted by the 'directores generales' (first-rank political appointees in the ministry) of Industry, Employment and the Treasury. Agreements then passed to the main cabinet's economic committee (CDGAE), which would sanction their implementation. Prime ministerial interventions or even open cabinet discussions were limited to some crisis points of high political visibility. These three departments assumed their classic roles, in the sense that Industry's metal and shipbuilding division adopted a more accommodating stance ('friend in court') towards managers' and unions' demands. Meanwhile, Treasury officials fought a rearguard battle to minimize the amount of funds devoted to restructuring, maintaining that a case-by-case approach was both cheaper and less risky in political terms. Employment's role was limited to fine-tuning the labour agreements.

Trade unions were the adjustment's second actor. The so-called 'class unions' (UGT, CC.OO and ELA) held a solid position throughout heavy industry, where they enjoyed a disciplined militancy and experienced officers. In fact, they had achieved during political transition veto power over the most important decisions, at least at a plant level. UGT and CC.OO, as main Spanish national unions, were the government's preferred partners for bargaining over adjustment; ELA (a Basque nationalist union) held key positions in some manufacturing sectors such as speciality or common steels. By the early 1980s, their relationship with political parties was close and in fact double affiliation between the UGT and the Socialist Party, and between CC.OO and the communists was common. This political connection loomed large over both unions' strategy. Thus, while the former was prepared to help the Socialist government to implement the restructuring, CC.OO adopted the Communist Party's strategy of frontal opposition, in an attempt to destabilize the cabinet's whole economic programme. However, power distribution within the three steel policy communities must be understood in dynamic terms and, as the decade passed, several factors (high redundancies, vanishing influence of UGT over the executive and increased EEC influence on policy making) forced unions into an increasingly outsider role, detached from the *inner core* of the steel policy community.

Thirdly, the *industry's management* was a key actor. In the beginning it was quite a heterogeneous group, including senior bureaucrats in the nationalized companies, owners ready to sell facilities and, finally, managers committed to the future of their companies. As time passed, the divide between 'nationalized' and private managers grew wider, both in operational and strategic terms. Clashes were frequent, to the point that independent producers – a majority only in common steels – abandoned the steel business association (Unesid) in 1981 to form Siderinsa. The latter was to be vocal in its opposition to further state aid for integrated producers and it became a thorn in the government's side. In contrast, managers in the state-owned industries were used to play a much more political game, trying to maximize public funds; in order to achieve this objective they often resorted to building up coalitions with local unions and territorial interests.

Territorial interests – no matter what their multi-faceted nature – should not be overlooked in any account of Spanish steel restructuring. Analytically, we can differentiate between locally based coalitions and regional governments. The former were built around an endangered plant and usually comprised plant unions, local politicians and social movements; they were particularly powerful around the big plants of the integrated subsector. However, they were clearly outsiders to decision making and their internal heterogeneity prevented their going beyond defensive actions or unilateral proposals.

In contrast, regional governments represent a much more respectable actor in the Spanish political scenario. Over the last two decades, the country has undergone a decentralization process unparalleled in Europe that has transformed a centralist state into a quasi-federal one (by the late 1990s, regional governements account for almost a third of total public expenditure). Those governments endowed with a distinct political status and a stake in the future of the steel industry, such as the Basque one, enjoyed a 'de facto' veto power over the sectoral plans. All this being true, mistrust has been endemic between the two administrations: the former complained of not being informed and the central executive regarded them as 'parochial interests' (Malaret, 1991). For instance, authority over speciality steels has been a matter of contention between Basque and Spanish authorities for almost 15 years.

3   THE RESTRUCTURING PROCESS

'The Classic RI'

The first Socialist cabinet in 50 years adopted an industrial strategy which pivoted around the adjustment programme, the Reconversión Industrial (RI). In its 1983 White Book (MINER, 1983) Industry declared that a pure market adjustment would destroy most of the manufacturing sectors, so the state had to step in to strike an equilibrium between competitiveness and social sacrifices. In a classic social-democrat style the programme aimed at combining rigour and solidarity (Bermeo, 1994, p. 39). RI was to be developed in two phases: it would begin by restructuring these endangered sectors so their public resources could then be devoted to the promotion of 'sunrise sectors' such as electronics or telecommunications. Although the plan comprised several schemes to attract private financial institutions, Spanish banks were eager to get rid of their ruinous participation in those sectors and they refused to participate in the programme (Buesa and Molero, 1998). For instance, in integrated steel, non-guaranteed private funds constituted hardly 10 per cent of total funds. The rest was provided by the central administration and in particular by Industry, either through direct aid or official credits (BCI); the Department of Employment funded part of the labour adjustment. In fact, Spanish banks were one of the main beneficiaries of the RI, for most of their bad debt was taken on by the government.

Cabinet's desire to implement adjustment through agreements at the sectoral policy community levels was in line with the consensual tradition forged in the Spanish transition and with previous measures adopted in the area of industrial policy. The government shared the principle that each plan should be able to muster a 'reasonable support' in each of the three or four parts concerned: government, unions, managers and territorial interests. This procedural ambition led to an extremely complex and time-consuming process that required nearly a year and a half of constant meetings.

Bargaining took place simultaneously at two levels: at the 'higher' level, the broad lines of the RI were negotiated and, in the 'lower', sectoral plans. Both levels were closely connected and, in fact, deadlocks over sensitive issues in the political table were broken at the sectoral level where the 'real fight' took place. Steel and shipbuilding were to set the pace of the whole process and measures adopted there were then exported to less sensitive sectors.

In a context marked by an unprecedented economic recession and with unemployment levels over 20 per cent, the Socialist government faced a stronger social opposition than expected, which extended from the local communities menaced by redundancies and plant closures to whole regions. The process assumed fearsome proportions in the north, the cradle of Spanish heavy industry. These deep social and territorial connections explain the high level of media attention received by the RI, in spite of accounting for just 10 per cent of the million jobs lost in Spanish manufacturing in the period 1979–84.

Eventually, the Socialist administration got away with the adjustment plans thanks, to a great extent, to the support received from the UGT, which, although limiting itself to signing the labour side of the agreements, achieved a degree of 'tacit tolerance' of the RI at the plant level. Given the limited resources allocated to the whole programme, these social concessions augmented the share going to labour adjustment to a third of total costs, reducing the amount devoted to financial debt and industrial investment. The most relevant concessions UGT extracted from the government were the following:

1. *Un ajuste laboral no traumático.* That is, labour adjustment would be completed only through early retirement and voluntary redundancies. In this sense, there was a management attempt in the speciality subsector in January 1984 to enforce lay-offs, but union opposition gathered such a momentum that President Gonzalez intervened and accepted UGT's demands, despite the fact that Industry and Treasury secretaries had publicly supported lay-offs. To meet the redundancy requirements the *Fondos de Promoción de Empleo* were set up: for three years, workers ascribed to these funds were to receive training and a top-up to the unemployment benefit that would almost equal previous income. Meanwhile, they would find another job or reach the age of early retirement (60 years). Given their huge

cost, funds were only set up in the sensitive sectors: speciality, integrated steel or shipbuilding.

2. *Un ajuste equilibrado territorialmente*. Those areas most affected by the adjustment achieved a privileged status as *Zonas de Urgente Reindustrialización*. Capital investment and job creation in these zones would benefit from a wide array of incentives (including grants and tax breaks); however, the scheme performed poorly in the areas most badly affected, such as Asturias or the Basque Country.

In the steel sector, the existing excess capacity ensured that restructuring entailed a zero-sum game, for the plans had to allocate investment and at the same time decide which plants had to be closed down – a delicate issue which caused great strain within the unions and greatly weakened their ability to modify Industry's proposals as, both in integrated and in speciality steels, workers often broke ranks and allied with managers to assure their own plant's future. On the part of the management, the possibility of striking a deal was not greater, given the traditional rivalry between firms: Ensidesa and AHV, Ensidesa and common steels, and so on.

Insiders' internal divisions and the government's role as sole financier eventually reinforced the government's position. However, it did not exploit the 'divide and rule' card and most sector plans were bargained in quite a consensual way: months of continuous tripartite meetings followed by 'firm' public statements and fierce behind-doors horse trading. Typically, the final scheme would have been 'cooked up' between Industry–Treasury officials and firms' managers and it would strike a delicate balance between competitiveness and social–territorial acceptability. As far as the labour package was concerned, the government's stance was more compromising and real consensus was achieved with unions. However, no matter how 'realistic, flexible and prudent' the plans, this style of problem managing produced blueprints that were economically suboptimal and which did not solve economic problems.

As far as steel is concerned, the common subsector's economic situation was not desperate by 1983 (it received aid totalling 'only' 56 bn pta), so plans concerned only the integrated and the speciality subsectors. Regarding the former, the aid package totalled around 500 billion pta (3 bn euros) with the objective of regaining competitiveness by 1989. The hard fight over which plant was to receive the bulk of investments was resolved by a 'Salomonic' decision in favour of both Ensidesa and AHV that made AHM the 'odd man out'; within the policy community its position was weaker because it lacked key support at both the government and the union leadership levels. Thus, in spite of a year's resistance by the local community, its heavy end was closed in 1984. The economic rationale of the plan has been a matter of great contention and many analysts (Navarro, 1989) considered then that the revamping of

AHV's heavy end was hopeless – as proved to be the case. In fact, the decision should be understood largely as a political measure aimed at reducing social unrest in the Basque Country, where a cascade of plant closures had created deep resentment in such a politically sensitive part of the country. On top of that, we have to take into account that AHV enjoyed close links both with UGT-Metal's leadership and with Industry bureaucrats.

This consensus-seeking procedural ambition respected the status quo in terms of ownership, so AHV remained formally private. It was officially considered that a private–public competition would discipline the whole sector, but spurious competition went on with the government as lender of last resort, a situation that fostered both firms' parochialism and managers' unaccountability. Anyway, this middle-of-the road decision failed to produce real debt reduction, for AHV kept on being overburdened with official credit and the state-owned Ensidesa received insufficient funds in order to avoid criticisms of 'unfair competition' from AHV quarters. Months after AHM's closure, the RI process acquired legal status by the enactment of the *'Ley de Reconversión y Reindustrialización'* (LRR 27/84) which established the global framework for the rest of the sectors (Malaret, 1991).

Regarding speciality steels, in a critical position too, ownership fragmentation was somehow reduced by covert nationalization of those firms unable to honour their debts into a 'restructuring society' called Aceriales. Only those firms that had maintained financial orthodoxy – Afora and P.Echeverría – were able to remain aloof from a scheme that contemplated 45 bn pta in state aid. Again the most pressing problem, that is too much capacity in too many plants, was solved only partially, for there were few closures and the modernization of facilities ended in augmentation of real capacity.

As far as the total bill is concerned, although there are no official figures, the overall process absorbed a minimum figure of 12 billion euros for the period 1980–89, three-quarters going to steel and shipbuilding (Navarro, 1989). RI absorbed all the attention at Industry's headquarters and horizontal measures, such as promotion of R&D or SME policy, suffered from a dearth of funds.

Simultaneously, the government was completing the negotiation of the Accession Treaty to the EEC, a cherished and long overdue ambition among Spanish elites. The process had been going on for almost a decade and only once the new socialist government showed its moderate credentials (at the Stuttgart summit at the end of 1983), was there political will on the part of the EEC. Steel was one of the contentious chapters, for the European producers strongly lobbied the European Commission – and their own governments – to adopt an uncompromising stance on state aid and capacity reduction. They saw the Spanish market as an outlet to domestic over-production and weak prices, so they pressed heavily for shorter transition periods. Finally, a three-year period was agreed (five was common for industrial goods) and the Spanish delegation accepted a reduction of three million tonnes per year in finished capacity (–15 per cent). Trade dismantling was to take place gradually, and in January 1989 the Spanish steel industry became a full member of the ECSC, which had just agreed its own plan of adjustment and banned state aid beyond 1986.

These terms provoked a fierce argument in Spanish quarters. Steel producers accused the government of having sacrificed the steel sector to obtain advantages in other areas and CC.OO said that Commission officials were behind the 1984 adjustment plan. In fact, in a context of economic recession, the Spanish bargaining position was weak, for accession was deemed urgent by both the government and the economic élites. On the other hand, we have to accept that overall reduction was in line with the EEC average; even more – as happened in the Italian case – it was painless, for Spanish steel producers had previously 'inflated' their maximum output capacity: they honoured the plan with only a few real closures in the common steel subsector. Regarding the role played by the Commission on the 1984 plan, it surely transmitted its concern over the level of state aid to Industry officials, a concern that anyway was shared by the Spanish government. As happened then across the ECSC, the pace and timing of steel adjustment was still governed by domestic agendas.

A Second Round

Politically speaking, the mid-1980s saw the consolidation of the Socialist project and the widening of its political margin of manoeuvre thanks to widespread economic recovery. Years of austerity and structural reforms had succeeded in taming inflation and public deficits, though at a great cost in terms of unemployment. After its landslide in 1986, the government considered that time had come to implement more positive programmes that would allow economic growth and the enlargement of the welfare state. The term 'reconversión' was to be replaced by *ajuste permanente* and connected with more positive soundbites such as the promotion of research/investment or territorial regeneration.

However, some unsolved problems were to dent this objective. Across Europe, falling oil prices and a weak dollar fostered steel demand from key customers such as the car industry, white goods and construction, but for Spanish heavy industry, recovery was years away because the Accession Treaty had left 'open' the issue of trade flows. While Spanish steel exports to the ECSC were limited to 0.7 per cent of the EC market, European flows were vaguely limited to 'traditional levels'. Incredibly enough, the designers of 1984 steel plans had forecast a scenario of equilibrium with the ECSC, notwithstanding higher domestic prices. In sum, European producers were the main beneficiaries of the stronger Spanish demand in 1986–7 and their competitive products stormed the market to the extent that, in March 1986, the Spanish government had to ask the Commission for safeguarding clauses: the steel export/import ratio for Spain–ECSC fell from 1.5 in 1976 to 0.43 in 1987. This inflow frustrated the recovery in speciality steel and integrated and also put the export-driven common steels in a delicate position. The 1984 plans proved utterly optimistic, so further labour adjustment and financial aid were necessary in order to achieve the objective of stand-alone competitiveness by the year 1989. Several reports underscored the negative effects of Ensidesa–AHV's vicious rivalry in integrated steels and the excessive number of plants in speciality steels. The latter's public image as an efficient private producer was deeply tarnished.

In spite of the cabinet's reluctance to get enmeshed in another unpopular struggle with unions and territorial interests, Industry obtained in 1987 a one-year mandate to bargain a second round of aid for sectors such as steel and shipbuilding (Navarro, 1990, p. 240). No matter the mandate, the government wanted to avoid both the 'demonstration effect' and the open clash with the trade unions which happened in 1983–4, so Industry officials tried to keep a low profile and plans were to be designed individually by firms. This being true, bargaining took place under a different scenario to that of 1983.

1. Steel policy's *communitarization*. The ECSC reduction agreements signed in late 1983 sanctioned the state members' agreement to let the European Commission conduct an 'ordered' European steel adjustment; the outcome was that the centre of policy making moved irrevocably to Brussels, where conflict around capacity reductions and state aid rolled on between national governments and steel firms. As market recovery and firms' internal clashes allowed the Commission to scrap production quotas in December 1988, the Spanish steel industry entered the ECSC at a moment when public protection was waning and liberal opinions were riding high.
2. *The end of social agreement*. The relationship between the UGT and the government became increasingly strained once the austerity years were over. The union demanded more public spending in social areas, which was rejected by the cabinet's economic team. In a process that combined ideological, strategic and personal factors, crisis degenerated into an open clash that ended a period of Spanish neocorporatist agreements and paved the way for a joint UGT–CC.OO strategy. UGT's executive purged the union of pro-government elements – notably in the Metal branch – so plan bargaining became increasingly difficult in steel and in shipbuilding.

Industry policy makers were conscious that any plan containing more state aid had to include a 'compensation' to the Commission in terms of further capacity reduction. After some months of tough bargaining in Brussels, the latter accepted an aid package totalling 185.9 bn pta for integrated steels, 40 bn for speciality steels and, finally, 58 bn pta for the common subsector (which also provided the majority of the additional reduction – two million tonnes per year).

Regarding speciality steels, the package was subject to the firms' formal merger into one corporation (Acenor). Integrated steels continued to be a much more complex affair and there was no merger or change of ownership: fierce lobbying by AHV and the Basque lobby was aided by the negative experience of previous mergers between state-owned enterprises. In spite of the successful French example (Usinor–Sacilor), Industry considered finally that merging two less than profitable firms would only create more problems. There were just a few vague recommendations for closer coordination that came to nothing.

Despite the rosier economic scenario and low-key strategy, labour turmoil was rampant and the government got as deeply involved as four years before, while the RI kept its politicized nature. In this sense, resources allocated to 'sunrise sectors' or to horizontal measures were clawed back in order to manage this heavy inheritance that continued to absorb up to 70 per cent of Industry's investment. Only in common steels could the government maintain a lower profile, given the existence of some well-run firms (Celsa, M.Ucín and Aristrain); Industry gave them political and financial support to lead sector concentration through acquisitions and closures.

This being true, procedures did change because both Industry and Treasury officials had grown increasingly frustrated at the unaccountability of some steel 'private' managers in spite of huge public funds. Concretely, loyal men were placed at the helm of Acenor and AHV, where the state obtained a majority on the board, and finally an organism was set up (*Gerencia Siderúrgica*) with the mission of controlling the use of funds. It was increasingly clear that central government held the reins within the community, for the rest of the insiders were totally dependent on state funding.

At the same time, Industry was moving its focus away from steel, whose long-term viability was increasingly in doubt; for instance, its metal division was submerged in a greater one, so steel producers lost an important lobbying venue. More or less consciously, the government accepted the 'politics of pessimism' and limited itself to reducing the problem's dimension. So, as soon as strong domestic demand and rising prices improved results and integrated steel produced its first profits in 15 years, Industry moved its attention to more positive issues: R&D, 'sunrise' sectors and so on. These 'lost years' were to be ruefully missed when the next crisis arrived.

A New Recession: 1992–4

In macroeconomic terms, increasing public expenditure – and deficits – in the late 1980s in areas such as welfare or capital investment was to take its toll once the Spanish economy entered recession and overheating gave way to a crash landing scenario. In an attempt to keep inflation under control and to shore up its orthodox credentials, the Spanish government had entered the European Monetary System in 1989; however, the peseta's overvalued rate combined with high interest rates to play havoc with the country's manufacturing.

Regarding steel, the end of the economic cycle and the Gulf War caused demand stagnation in Europe as early as 1990. Weak prices were aggravated by increasing imports into the ECSC from eastern Europe: in 1993, price levels were only two-thirds those of 1989 and the European steel industry was 'in the middle of its worst recession in at least 50 years' (*Financial Times*, 30 June 1992). Logically, non-competitive producers were most affected, particularly the Spanish ones who had enjoyed only two years of high demand and prices. In fact, AHV, Ensidesa and Acenor were by 1992 close to bankruptcy.

Meanwhile, in Brussels, pro-market views were dominant and even the DGIII maintained that sectoral measures only delayed the adoption of necessary adjustment; thus – unlike what happened in 1980 – the Commission rejected unions' and some producers' demands to re-establish a sort of the Davignon system. Backed by their governments, disputes between competitive and subsidized steel firms over state aid flared up. When, in April 1992, the AHV–Ensidesa adjustment plan arrived to Brussels including state aid of almost 1 bn pta (6 bn euros), there was frontal opposition from both the competitive producers and the DGIV.

Plan-making in 1992 built on the tendencies observed in 1987. On the one hand, Industry showed an arm's-length attitude towards the sector, giving full powers to firm management; on the other, unions were progressively marginalized from policy-making; finally, the government discourse focused on 'competitiveness' and away from non-economic considerations (social/territorial equilibra). In general terms, the spirit of the integrated steel's plan was more entrepreneurial and client-focused than previous ones: it contemplated acquisitions downstream (stockholders), upgrading of the added value mix and the merger into a corporation called CSI (CSI, 1993). Regarding speciality steels, its plan also fostered concentration by creating Sidenor to replace the previous holding.

Plan makers had forecast a ratio of aid/capacity reduction that was in line with other precedents (Italsider) in order to be accepted by the DGIV. Preliminary projects offered a 20 per cent reduction in crude steel production (1.5 million tonnes per year) and a 1997 deadline for stand-alone profitability. This meant further closures: two of the five Sidenor plants (a third to be sold) and AHV's heavy end. The new CSI was to concentrate the assets of the two firms while liabilities were externalized to allow the firm a clean start.

It seemed that, after 15 years, AHV's saga would come to an end. It was not to be so, for one of the outstanding features of the CSI plan was the construction on the same site of a 'thin slab casting' mill, only four years after Nucor's pioneer plant in Indiana. It was said that this rather new technology would increase operational flexibility and provide CSI with a competitive edge vis-à-vis other integrated producers (CSI, 1993). On the other hand, it would certainly sweeten the pill in the Basque Country; in fact, its regional government was the mill's main supporter and lobbied Brussels in parallel with the Spanish administration. As Asturias was to receive the bulk of CSI's investment, opposition there was muted.

Facing a plan comprising closures and a 40 per cent loss in employment (10 400), union opposition was massive. The fact that CSI, after keeping them in the dark, presented a 'closed plan' did not help to make the meetings a success: unions' demands were rejected out of hand; management said quite clearly that this was the 'lesser evil' option and the only plan that would be acceptable to Brussels. Unions and local movements resorted to marches and social mobilization, taking advantage of harsh economic conditions throughout the north; again, protest in speciality steels degenerated into serious public disorder. Despite all this, by then industrial adjustment had come to be socially accepted in those territories through a mixture of resignation and fatalism. The problem's sheer dimensions had been greatly reduced and part of public opinion began to point out the privileges achieved by these workers in each adjustment round, far away from the redundancy conditions in the private sector.

The outcome was that social opposition was increasingly localized and feeble. On top of that, regional governments, the 'rising stars' in the area of industrial policy, were more interested in sunrise activities than in defending heavy industry. So, when in the summer of 1992 Sidenor workers voted for the plan against their unions' wishes, UGT and ELA gave in and signed up to CSI's labour package.

Steel managers (backed by the government) had overcome social and territorial opposition, but their bargaining position in Brussels was weaker. As the required unanimity in the Industry Council was not forthcoming, both Spanish plans were blocked in the midst of a harsh debate between liberalizers and supporters of another 'ordered adjustment'. On the one hand, British and Dutch representatives considered unacceptable the existing level of state aid and, on the other hand, German or Italian representatives wanted to delay approval while they were finishing their own 'dossiers'. In this situation, the Commission's support was fundamental to break the deadlock, so the Spanish delegations had to ease their stance over the integrated plan by offering earlier closures and the compromise that the new mill would have a private majority. An agreement was reached in December 1992: Ecus 2.817 mn would go to CSI between 1994 and 2001 in return of net reduction of capacity totalling 2.3 million tonnes; finally, 485 mn went to Sidenor (reduction of 0.44 million tonnes). In this way, the Commission achieved unanimity. In return, the

Commission assured unanimity in the Industry Council for a steel aid package including CSI and six other steel firms.

Epilogue: Out of the Public Realm

These plans left Sidenor and CSI with relatively modern facilities, a reduced payroll and liability-free books. These assets, combined with booming domestic markets and currency devaluation, set them solidly on the path of profitability, away from decades of despair and losses; in fact, they were definitively out of the red in 1995–6. In 1994, CSI was the seventh-largest European steel producer, with a turnover of 300 bn pta (1.9 bn euros), 75 per cent of debt/equity ratio and 11 773 employees.

The 1993 agreements included a tacit compromise on medium-term *privatization*. To implement this, it was believed that CSI and Sidenor required an alliance with a 'respectable' producer that could provide further technological and managerial skills. Given its minor dimension and the existence of two bids with an important Spanish participation, denationalization proved to be easier and Sidenor was eventually sold in late 1995 to an Italian–Spanish consortium (Digeco-Roda).

CSI was a more intractable an issue than Sidenor. Regarding the former, Industry considered that the likeliest scenario was simple absorption by Usinor–Sacilor, which coveted CSI's control of domestic markets (50 per cent). To avoid a foreign firm benefiting from all the public moneys invested, officials opted for selling separately CSI's flat and long divisions; negotiations were called off when a general election was announced for March 1996. This acceptance of internationalization is more relevant if we take into account that previous attempts to sell AHV or Aristrain to foreign firms had been vetoed by Industry. It showed the waning support that the idea of a powerful state-owned industrial corporation enjoyed within the Socialists' economic team. The process of financial liberalization in Spain and the Commission's stringent attitude on state aid favoured the process. All over Europe, the steel industry was losing its strong 'national' features and cross-border deals were becoming increasingly common.

The Conservative government that came to power in 1996 was to delve into the liberal agenda embraced by the last Socialist administration. Unlike the Socialists, they were outspoken in favour of privatization. The Industry secretary quickly announced the objective of selling all state-owned firms (except coalmining) by the year 2000, including 'difficult' cases such as integrated steel. It was clear for CSI unions that there was no other alternative to liquidation, so they did not put up a great fight; the management even got away with the principle of decentralized bargaining. The acute sense of escaping annihilation, shared by workers and managers, is facilitating a change in the corporate culture away for bureaucratic attitudes.

CSI's privatization was designed as a three-step process. First, an 'industrial partner' would buy a third of CSI equity, subject to a compromise over the fulfilment of the investment programme; surprisingly, a Benelux producer, Arbed, won the tender auction, mainly because it showed a greater commitment to CSI's investment plan than Usinor. Then the government tried hard to get some Spanish steel producers on board; after some cajoling, Aristrain agreed to merge into the new concern, renamed as Aceralia. Finally, in December 1998, 50 per cent of the shares went public in what constituted a remarkable success for Spanish stock markets; its shares have underperformed the (bullish) Madrid market, but they stay in line with other European steel firms.

In fact, since privatization, 'pessimism' or 'decline' soundbites have been replaced by a much more upbeat discourse, to the extent that the steel issue has disappeared from the political agenda. Profits have come on top of solid demand growth – particularly in the construction and automotive industries – peaceful labour relations and Arbed's ambitious investment plans which include a great deal of investment in Spain; in fact, with the integration of Aristrain and M.Ucín in the Aceralia project a big electrical–integrated concern has been created in Spain, an objective that evaded successive governments for decades. In sum, it has been an optimum scenario for the government, which seems all too happy to see off steel politics; in any case, Arbed being a foreign producer reduces the government's political responsibilities.

4 OUTCOME ASSESSMENT: PROGRAMMATIC FAILURE AND POLITICAL SUCCESS?

Programmatic Failure

Success or failure should be assessed in regard to the fulfilment of the programme's objectives. However, public policies are complex packages with multiple and evolving objectives, not all of them being public. Although we can differentiate between political, economic and social objectives, it is difficult to draw the line between official objectives, privately-held ones, by-products and post hoc rationalizations.

In economic terms, the whole industrial adjustment of the period 1980–93 should be considered a failure, steel being in this sense archetypal. On the one hand, whole industries were gradually decimated while competitiveness was regained only partially: common steels and white goods were the exception to the rule. On the other, the process proved to be hugely expensive: in order to obtain social non-belligerence, a generous redundancy mechanism was set up, followed by a fair deal of wishful investment – an 'error' rather common throughout European steel. Decision making was tortuous and deadlines were systematically extended: it has taken more than 20 years to restructure Spanish steel, a time only surpassed by Italy; moreover, the public funds devoted in the 1980s to steel restructuring in Spain (over 2 500 bn pta; 15 bn euros) largely surpassed the European average (Buesa and Molero, 1998). The successful privatization of Aceralia and Sidenor should not then lead us to overlook a saga of closures and failed expectations: the state got back no more than 15 per cent of the absorbed public funds.

Political Success

However, it would be naïve to consider the RI as a strictly economic programme, for Spanish industrial adjustment (of which steel is a paramount case) has been *a politically managed process*. It has been primarily oriented to mitigate social and territorial consequences and only secondly to deliver firm competitiveness. In this sense, our assessment of the case should be altogether different, for serious social and inter-territorial conflict was prevented or at least localized: a political victory, remarkable given the initial stakes. In this sense, the Socialist Party won handsomely the 1986 and 1989 general elections, retaining its solid electoral support among manufacturing workers. Unions did not get a raw deal either, quite the contrary, for employees obtained a much better path to retirement than their counterparts in the private sector or in other countries. In sum, it was a plan carefully designed to avert full-blown opposition from either territorial or labour quarters.

Insiders may have got a fair deal but, as we have mentioned, governance has changed beyond recognition. As old interdependencies were severed and consensus over values and policy objectives waned, the steel policy community was deprived of most its policy contents by the government. Beyond rhetoric and much-trumpeted tripartite meetings at crisis points, there are no 'self-organizing interorganizational networks' left, at least at the Spanish level. Issues regarding heavy industry monopolized the policy debate for most of the 1980s, but now they hardly catch any headline, even in regional newspapers.

In fact, if we take a long-term perspective, this political success should be qualified. In spite of the fact that consensual restructuring avoided short-term social disorder and the delegitimation of the young Spanish democracy, it left long-term scars in the area of industrial policy. Meagre results fostered the rejection of the whole policy paradigm of state activism in this area, to the extent that the problem has been *reframed* and privatized: now industrial adjustment is considered either as an enterprise affair or as a social (*asistencial*) policy. The sentiment that public intervention would nilly-willy degenerate into costly, inefficient and socially unfair programmes extended from government ranks to mainstream public opinion. The backlash is such that, in the mid-1990s, Spain comes second only to the UK in the bottom of an EU-wide league in terms of state aids, well below countries such as Germany or Italy.

Incidentally, RI's tarnished image as a national programme has helped the decentralization of industrial policy, in the sense that it has provided regional governments with the means to grab most competencies in the area of industrial policy. By the late 1990s, industrial promotion in Spain was an area increasingly controlled by regional authorities. 'Controlled' is not the same as exercised, for only a few regions – the Basque Country or Valencia – have developed a clear industrial programme beyond scrambling for EU aid.

5 SPANISH STEEL POLICY: ANALYSING THE PROCESS

Factors such as technological developments, the excess of steel supply and the Europeanization of the policy area have affected the Spanish steel sector in a similar way to the rest of the EU, so we have decided to focus on those aspects which departed from the norm.

Contextual Factors

First, we must take into account that industrial policy in Spain has been traditionally a low-key affair, lacking a clear strategy for most of the twentieth century (Fraile, 1992). State intervention in industrial matters has been largely a reaction to the demands of several interest groups, whether firm owners or workers. Consequently, measures frequently benefited these groups at taxpayers' expense.

Although we maintain a sceptical attitude towards 'national policy styles', we shall mention some policy features shared by the three steel sectors (and many other Spanish policy areas) that could be candidates for 'standard operating procedures'.

- *Lack of transparency in policy making.* Agreements were done typically by élites behind closed doors and practices inside the policy community differed remarkably from policy discourse issued for public consumption. Social mobilization did take place, but in parallel with bargaining and influencing decision making only on critical points (Subirats and Gomá, 1998).
- *Consensus seeking as a procedural ambition,* in our case to the point of sacrificing economic efficiency. During the double process of political transition and decentralization, the prevailing spirit of consensus among

political élites favoured the creation of policy communities and even neo-corporatist mechanisms, inclusiveness that included, notably, trade unions and territorial interests.

- *A narrow view of the competitiveness problem*, that tended to accommodate insiders' interests. On the one hand, steel managers blamed the excess of employees and, on the other, unions complained about dearth of investments. Thus steel policies were focused on upgrading facilities and managing redundancies, while key aspects such as marketing, the quality of management or industrial relations were overlooked.
- On top of these features came the *dispersion of political resources and legitimacy among the community's main actors*. Several decades of authoritarian rule had reduced both the state's and employers' legitimacy to impose policies once in a democracy, particularly in the face of 'rising stars' such as unions as regional interests. In our case, fragmentation was aggravated by the endemic strife between common steel producers (mostly private-oriented) and the integrated ones, greatly dependent on public funds.

Process Dynamics

In Spain, policy communities remained for more than a decade 'the lesser evil option' in implementing adjustments, and policy discourse reflected this 'community of interest' between the government, managers and union leaders.

However, from that rather neocorporatist environment, Spanish adjustment policies have evolved towards a depoliticized and 'privatized' model. This evolution was largely a consequence of a change in strategy and values on the part of Industry decision makers in the late 1980s: as time passed, government remained as the only actor endowed with enough resources to keep integrated steel alive. In this sense, the ups and downs of plan bargaining constitutes a vantage point for analysing the community's increasing asymmetry. Government's *policy learning* derived in our opinion from three factors: frustration over results, the 'EU factor' and a more market-minded paradigm shared by industrial policy makers.

First, the politics of pessimism gained ground in the government from the late 1980s onwards as steel firms' economic performance remained poor. The 1983 White Book's main objective of providing a new start for these sectors while avoiding serious social disruption gave way to increasing frustration and reluctance to get enmeshed in these 'intractable problems'. This, combined with steel's diminishing importance, paved the way for implementing an attritional game (the 'salami approach'): beyond official discourse, voluntarism was replaced by 'managing the decline'. Thus the adjustment problem was to be managed – not solved – through several (three or four) crisis plans that would adjust 'as far as possible' while maintaining a certain degree of consensus within the community.

Secondly, the requirement of 'competing in Europe' was a paramount policy excuse for the whole period. Accession to the EEC marked a watershed in Spanish politics and of course in the industrial area, accounting for trade liberalization and a decreasing margin of manoeuvre for state intervention. Both aspects came to strengthen the position of those politicians–officials favouring a detachment strategy. We have mentioned that 'Brussels' both reduced government's responsibility and strengthened its bargaining position vis-à-vis the rest of the community: in return for less autonomy in policy making, it increased its isolation from national actors (Subirats and Gomá, 1998, p. 34).

Finally, the government was not aloof from the paradigm policy change towards a more liberal agenda in industrial issues. From the start, the members of the Socialist economic team were no *nationalizers*: its first solution to crisis was to cajole employers, employees – and regional interests – into bilateral agreements, with the promise of public funds as a facilitating factor (De la Dehesa, 1993). Once it was clear that 'voluntary' agreements were not forthcoming, they would use competitive private producers as the instrument to consolidate the sector rather than fully-fledged nationalization; this was the case in common steels. In their absence, the last option was full and public nationalization, as happened in integrated and speciality steels.

As far as Spain is concerned, new ideas entered pragmatically as old recipes proved unable to check decline (see Rose, 1993). Of course, this policy learning is common to most European countries and notably to social-democratic governments, but the frustration caused by failed experiences in public policy is often overlooked, with all attention focused on some mega-trends (globalization, orthodox fiscal policies and so on). Privatization appeared by the early 1990s as the definitive solution to this trade-off and to the related problem of how to deal with state-owned enterprises in Spain. Now public authorities seem quite happy to replace past redistributive or clientelistic policies with a more regulatory approach, centred on promotion and acting as 'travelling salesman' abroad (Wright, 1994); horizontal measures are considered to be more efficient and less market-disruptive. Actually, the 'rediscovery of the firm' as *the* engine of economic development is most remarkable in a country where capitalism and liberalism have traditionally lacked social support.

In sum, years of losses and successive failed plans had starkly displayed a trade-off between achieving competitiveness and meeting social demands. Industry wanted to place competitiveness as the overriding policy objective and for that purpose the governance in the integrated steel community had to be changed. The combination of a fragmented policy community and consensus-prone strategies had produced an extremely complex and time-consuming decision-making process. This was quite suboptimal in economic terms, for on top of 'possibilistic' adjustment plans that fell short of the competitiveness requirements, implementation delays meant that high-price periods passed by with Spanish steel firms still undergoing adjustment.

Increasing power asymmetry helped the government in its purpose and, as in other countries, the alliance between frustrated politicians and market-oriented steel managers proved unbeatable. For instance, in common steels the central executive could adopt a problem-solving approach through the political and financial support given to Celsa, M.Ucín or Aristrain to lead a process of firm concentration; restructuring there was quite successful: short, not very expensive and it delivered a competitive subsector. In contrast, this type of manager was scarce in heavy industry, owing to absence of a deep cultural reform across the Spanish state-owned sector; there privatization broke the political gridlock, by reducing state responsibility and allowing for the entry of new managers.

6   CONCLUSIONS

Power dispersion within the Spanish steel policy communities and consensual procedures were the two main characteristics of the 'classic' RI. The adjustment took place via successive crisis plans: each one meant a step further towards a private, market-oriented view of the problem, reflecting the Spanish government's own ideological evolution in economic issues. As time passed by without profits, the central executive concentrated resources, and older interdependencies were replaced by its hegemony. Eventually, its option for privatizing the issue of industrial adjustment hollowed out these policy communities. Three factors have to be taken into account for that evolution: failed experiences, 'competing in the EU' and the influence of the liberal policy paradigm.

In sum, we find two models in Spanish industrial adjustment: the state-run and the sector-driven. In most cases, the central government had to lead the process, fostering politicization and multiple objectives, while varying coalitions of managers, unions leaders and territorial interests scrambled for protection and public funds. As a result the economic outcomes were poor but the social impact of restructuring was kept limited. On the other hand, we have RI's only two success stories (common steels and white goods) where a number of well-run firms were able to lead adjustment and firm concentration in a process that was quicker and cheaper, at least from the perspective of the state.

8. Restructuring the Swedish steel industry: learning through path dependency?

Jon Pierre

1 INTRODUCTION

The overarching problem addressed in this chapter is to what extent the configuration and objectives of the governance in the Swedish steel sector were conducive to a relatively smooth process of industrial restructuring. The governance of the Swedish steel industry shares some features with that of other countries, but, as will be described in greater detail later, the Swedish political economy has some characteristics which probably set it apart from that of most other national contexts.

Thus the broader, theoretical issue here is the extent to which the outcome of a governance process can be related to the configuration of that governance, that is, the degree of institutionalization and the composition of actors involved in the governance. The governance configuration is also important for defining the goals and objectives of governance because different groups of actors bring different types of resources to the table. Restructuring an industrial sector requires a wide variety of resources of which capital is but one. Generally speaking, industrial restructuring appears to be one of the few stages of industrial development where industrialists see a distinct role for the state. Most countries have experienced a governance of the steel sector in which the role of the state has been highly fluid and contextual (O'Brien, 1994; Howel *et al.*, 1988; McConnel, 1963). What explains the changes in the role of the state: is this role primarily defined by the state itself, by other actors in the steel governance, or by some third party in society? And to what extent can we relate the model of governance which evolved during the critical years to the outcome of the restructuring process?

The second question, more closely related to the general theme of this volume, is whether Sweden was successful in managing the decline of steel, and whether its distinctive patterns of governance are as successful in decline as they had been in expanding the welfare state. The close link of state and society found in Sweden and other 'corporatist' political systems can be argued to be an excellent mechanism for distributing an expanding resource base, but to be less amenable to managing a situation in which there is an inherent redistribution between winners and losers. As in most other countries, managing the steel industry has meant making decisions about who loses how much, and where those losses will be concentrated geographically. This in turn leads to a distinct possibility of programmatic success and political failure.

To address these questions we must first trace the process of restructuring, something which, in turn, leads us to assess the long-term development both of the Swedish industry *tout court* and of the steel industry more closely. Here we will map the structure of the steel sector itself, in terms of number of steel mills, ownership structure, union involvement and so on. Following that, the chapter focuses on changes in the patterns of governance pertaining to the steel sector over the last several decades. The perspective on governance advanced in the chapter is rather state-centric. There are several reasons for that. First, although the chapter addresses governance in a corporate sector, or a market, the Swedish state has nearly always been a predominant player, whether it has been as a party in tripartite arrangements of interest representation and mediation, or as a dominant political force voicing the interest of the working-class constituency. Most importantly, however, in a society with the biggest public sector in the world, historically speaking, it would be erroneous not to assume that the state has been an integral part of the governance of core sectors of the industry.

This chapter first walks the reader quickly through the Swedish political economy during the postwar period. The main purpose here – apart from taking the analysis beyond the many stereotypes which Sweden has given birth to in these respects such as 'the mixed economy' or, even worse, 'socialism with a human face' – is to outline the main characteristics of the industrial policy terrain and patterns of governance in the Swedish economy and the role of government herein. Following that, the chapter describes the restructuring process of the Swedish steel industry and, in section 4, conducts a more analytical discussion about the patterns of governance which have been observed in that process. A concluding section ends the chapter, pointing to the success and failures of this exercise in managing decline in a corporatist welfare state.

2   CONTEXT: DEVELOPMENTS IN SWEDISH INDUSTRY AND INDUSTRIAL POLICY

The trajectory of the Swedish industry probably differs from that of most other countries. While much of the steel industry in Europe was devastated after

World War II, the Swedish steel industry was intact. Given the tremendous demand for steel to reconstruct infrastructure in Europe, Swedish steel producers could sell steel at good prices with only limited international competition. Since this situation applied not just to the steel industry but to most of the manufacturing industry in Sweden, most of the 1950s and the 1960s witnessed a sustained boom in the Swedish economy.

However, economic booms tend to entail complacency. One of the perils of an economic boom is that it conceals the need to upgrade technology and production processes. This was very much the case with several industrial sectors in Sweden. Thus by the mid-1960s, Swedish industry rather suddenly began facing increasing competition from the reconstructed and technologically superior European and Asian industries. Interestingly, the international exposure which had been critical to the previous industrial expansion and which clearly had played an integral role in increasing returns and profits, now suddenly worked against the Swedish industry (Henning, 1987; Katzenstein, 1985; Kuuse, 1986).

The growing international competition in the mid-1960s uncovered a massive need for structural change and technological upgrading in the Swedish industry. However, industrial policy at this time was a neglected and insignificant policy sector with limited state spending, diffuse and vague policy objectives and a poor institutional capacity. Indeed, it is safe to say that neither the Social Democrats nor the non-socialist opposition parties at this time had a clear industrial policy agenda. With regard to the governance of the economy, the traditional Swedish policy style since the early 1960s had been to rely on an active labour market policy coupled with a macroeconomic policy characterized by a high level of public spending and gradually increasing taxes. Given the high growth in the economy during the 1950s and early 1960s, maintaining a budgetary balance was not a very big problem.

The Social Democrats incurred a significant setback in the 1966 general elections, something which the party leadership attributed to increasing unemployment, plant closures and an overall growing insecurity concerning jobs and economic development in its core constituency. This triggered an intensive intraparty policy-formulating process which resulted in the so-called 'industrial policy offensive', launched at an extra party conference in 1967 (Pierre, 1986). The tenor of the 'offensive' was that the state should take a higher profile on industrial policy matters, compensate for market failures such as shortage of investment capital and low levels of investment in future-oriented sectors, develop its institutional capacity to increase spending on research and development and link industrial policy to regional policy.

In addition to these objectives, the Social Democrats also wanted to bring together a small group of state-owned companies under the umbrella of a new state-owned company, Statsföretag AB, which was to function as somewhat of a holding company for state-owned companies. Part of the reason for this was that the Social Democrats were leaning towards a philosophy according to which the state – more on an ad hoc basis than as a matter of policy – should acquire companies in distress with strategic importance in terms of job provision in lagging regions. The underlying logic was that this would save the state money; even if the companies were operating at a negative profit level, covering that loss would still be less expensive than bringing in labour market support should the company fold. Thus what was not economical from the point of view of an individual company could often be economically justified at a societal level.

The programme was successful in restoring some of the lost faith in the party; the Social Democrats did very well indeed in the 1968 general election. Now was the time to implement this far-reaching strategy for industrial and economic development. In the late 1960s and early 1970s a number of institutional changes in the industrial policy sector were executed; an agency for industrial development (SIND, later to become part of a new agency for economic and industrial development, NUTEK) was created, as well as an agency for research and development (STU, later merged with SIND and the National Agency for Energy Policy into NUTEK) and a state-owned bank (*Investeringsbanken*) geared to provide investment capital in projects and sectors where private capital thought the risks of investing were too high.

Alongside these institutional changes, and to some extent propelled by these new institutions, the early 1970s witnessed a rapidly increasing number of specific support programmes which served to encourage structural change in Swedish industry: what Henning (1987) aptly refers to as the 'support structure'. While many of these support programmes looked good on paper, the imple-mentation of the programmes was frequently distorted by regional or local considerations (Pierre, 1995). Thus financial resources designated to help private industry through the structural change period were frequently allocated according to other criteria, including bailing out companies in distress (Krauss and Pierre, 1993).

The 1970s were a turbulent decade for Swedish industry. Industry and the economy more generally experienced a deep recession in the early 1970s. When the economy eventually picked up, the oil-price shock, coupled with high nominal wage increases, threw the economy right back into recession. This recession and the decreasing competitiveness of the Swedish industry in inter-national markets triggered a series of structural crises in industrial sectors such as shipbuilding, steel and the manufacturing industry. This in turn confronted the state with a need to manage declining industries and to do so while minimizing its political costs.

In the political arena, the Social Democrats in 1976 lost an election for the first time in more than 40 years and were replaced by a non-socialist coalition government. The incoming government obviously lacked any experience in running the machinery of government and was determined not to allow the industrial crisis to prove the Social Democrats right: that only they could guarantee a high level of employment (cf. Rydén, 1983). The paradoxical outcome of this situation was that the non-socialist, conservative-dominated, coalition government interfered more in the ownership structure of the industry than had been done in 44 years of Social Democratic rule. The non-socialists, in a surprisingly pragmatic style, believed that the best way to attack the structural crisis was to bring the distressed industries under state control. Thus a number of shipyards which faced close-down and massive lay-offs of labour were simply acquired by the state at a token price as a first step towards helping the distressed city and region to reconstruct its industry. Cities like Malmö, Landskrona and Uddevalla were offered 'packages' consisting of labour market support, retraining programmes and venture capital to help bring in new industrial concepts. Also the government negotiated agreements with companies such as SAAB and Volvo to invest in the city in order to absorb parts of the laid-off labour (Henning, 1987; Pierre, 1989). The restructuring policy for steel followed a slightly different path, as the next section will show.

3   RESTRUCTURING THE STEEL INDUSTRY: THE POLICY PROCESS

Together with mining, pulp and paper and forestry, steel has historically been thought of as part of the core industrial sectors in Sweden. The steel industry has not just been an industrial sector capitalizing on the country's wealth of ore and hydro-electrical power; it provided for a long period of time much of the raw material for the car industry, the shipbuilding industry and the bearing production by SKF, one of the country's key multinational companies. In addition, the rapid development of an important segment of the industry, specialized steel, put Sweden in the forefront of knowledge-intensive steel production for a considerable time. Steel was thought of as one of Sweden's basic industries (*basnäringar*).

To some extent, however, this account of the Swedish steel industry is more image than reality. The steel industry has never been one of the dominant sectors of Swedish industry in terms of employment. Between 1950 and 1980, only some 5 per cent of the Swedish workforce were employed in the steel industry (Kuuse, 1986, p. 100). The structural crisis facing the steel industry had a disproportionately high saliency because the impact of the crisis has been most strongly felt in small one-company towns with a massive Social Democratic constituency. The steel industry has a distinct relation to place, or, more correctly, the vertical integration of production coupled with a vast accumulation of employment have accorded steel mills a dominant role in the places where they have been located (Markusen, 1987). Most industrial countries have witnessed how the decline of the steel industry has devastated the social fabric of the locality that hosted the once prosperous steel mills, as eloquently described by Hoerr in his account of how the steel crisis in the United States affected Pittsburgh and the communities in the surrounding river valleys (Hoerr, 1988). In Sweden, steel has a strong connotation of the small one-company town in mid-Sweden (*brukssamhälle*) where the daily life of the populace was completely centred upon the mill; the steel company owned not just the mill but also most of the food stores in the town and provided much of the housing. This geographical concentration of the industry sets the stage for possible major failures, both programmatic (massive unemployment in a region) and political (reactions to that unemployment).

Even if mass production of steel has never been a big industry in Sweden, there are upscale, high-technology segments of the steel industry and the international steel market in which Swedish specialized steel has had a strong position and which could be seen as vital to Swedish export revenues (Sölvell *et al.*, 1991). Together, these local and national interests probably explain the readiness of the SAP government – and to a great extent also the post-1976 non-socialist government – to ameliorate the structural crisis. Again, this was necessary to attempt to avert both industrial and political problems.

However, while there is a high degree of similarity in terms of the impact of structural change in different national contexts, the political assessment and saliency of the crisis differ substantively. In Sweden, the predominance of the Social Democratic Party throughout most of the postwar period – SAP was in office from 1932 to 1976, and from 1982 to 1991, and has been again since the 1994 general elections – has meant that industrial structural crises and their impact on the labour constituency has been high on the political agenda. There has, for most of the postwar period, been a strong political and institutional inclination to intervene in the process of decline to ensure that it does not generate mass unemployment. Certainly, there have been exceptions to this rule, most notably the SAP's proposal, propelled by the LO, the Confederation of Labour, to launch a proposal for so-called 'wage-earners' funds' in the late 1970s.[1] The Swedish postwar political economy has often been referred to as a 'mixed economy' with a huge public sector embedded in a capitalist economy. That analogy is appropriate as long as the notion of mix does not indicate a true blending of the two components. The strong labour constituencies embedded in a capitalist economy are features of the Swedish postwar economy which help explain much of the nature of the industrial restructuring during the 1970s and 1980s because they point to a governance which seeks to accommodate both capital and labour and where the state plays a critical role also in the market but does so in what Weaver (1985) aptly refers to as a 'market-conforming' fashion.

The structural problem in the steel sector emerged in the middle of the 1970s alongside similar problems in the shipyard sector. In February 1976, the Industry Minister appointed a Royal Commission to investigate 'the future development and structure of the Swedish steel industry' (SOU 1977:15, p. 3).[2] The Commission had a total of eight members, of which five represented the steel industry, one represented the unions, one (the chairman) was an economist and one represented the Ministry of Industry. It is no exaggeration to say that the Commission was effectively controlled by the steel industry itself. The composition of the Commission is worth noting, for here is a textbook case of an industrial sector governing itself. Equally important, by conducting the inquiry as a Royal Commission the proposals could easily tap into state resources, both in terms of capital and labour market resources, and could be implemented in the form of public policy, yet the proposals voiced the interests and objectives of the steel industry.[3] Perhaps the most accurate label for the process would be self-governance under state auspices.

The Commission's proposals rested on a comprehensive analysis of the Swedish steel industry and the international steel market. The Commission chose to see the steel sector as 'an entity' (ibid., p. 77), which is not the expected approach, given the fairly fragmented ownership structure of the 10 or so steel mills in the country at the time. However, the approach was strategically chosen because only in that perspective could the Commission conduct an analysis which could identify steel mills with growth potential and steel mills where productivity was low and technology was obsolete. Thus, somewhat paradoxically, perhaps, the holistic perspective allowed the Commission to target its proposals to a much greater extent than any other approach would have facilitated.

The Commission's proposals can be summarized in two general ideas. First, the Commission suggested that steel production be concentrated in a limited number of state-of-the-art, technologically updated steel mills and that steel production be discontinued in a couple of the older steel mills. The analysis is conducted less on a mill-by-mill basis but more on a product-by-product basis. This helps fend off any critique that the Commission catered to the interests of some locales more than others. That having been said, it remains sensational that a Royal Commission put forward proposals that privately owned steel mills be shut down. With regard to the more specific proposals, perhaps the most surprising one was the idea that nearly all the steel production at the Domnarvet should be discontinued, a proposal which was later implemented in full. Domnarvet was at the time one of the three biggest steel producers in the country, with some 6000 employees.

In terms of employment, the suggested restructuring would reduce the number of jobs from about 20 000 to some 15 000, a 25 per cent reduction. As tends to be the case with structural changes in the steel industry, this strategy would hit several smaller, steel-dominated towns terribly hard. Given the political saliency of labour-related issues during the 1970s, decline was assessed primarily in terms of jobs lost, although one might suspect that for the steel industry itself, cutbacks in the number of jobs was a means of enhancing the competitiveness of the industry.

Secondly, the Commission also put forward the idea that the steel mills be brought together under an umbrella company, Svenskt Stål AB (SSAB). The company was to be owned jointly by private owners and the state through Stats-företag AB on a 50–50 basis. To some extent, this idea reflects the *Zeitgeist* of the 1970s in Sweden, with a strong reliance on the state and collective solutions to most salient problems in society and the economy (Richardson, 1982). The steel industry's interest in moving closer to the state and an indirect significant state ownership is proof of the grave concerns that were felt among the industrialists that the challenge of the structural crisis was too overwhelming for them, not least financially, to solve alone. By setting up the SSAB, a whole new governance structure was created, and we will later discuss the broader consequences of this. Here suffice it to say that the SSAB, in addition to institutionalizing the governance of the steel sector, also provided a gateway to the state, which meant that the industrial restructuring now could be conducted with the understanding that the state would be much more willing to offer labour market, retraining and other types of support measures for the laid-off labour.

Most of the Commission's proposals were implemented after a Government Bill and a Parliamentary decision had reiterated most of the perspectives suggested in the Commission's report. Several smaller steel mills were closed down, as was the larger steel facility in Domnarvet. Also, in 1978, SSAB was set up with an ownership structure and assignment very similar to the ones suggested by the Commission.

It appears to be beyond doubt that the restructuring was successful on a programmatic basis, if by 'success' we mean the consolidation of the industry and the creation of steel facilities that could confront international competition. Concentrating the industry on fewer but larger and more technologically advanced steel plants, specializing in knowledge-intensive products, was a formula that helped create an internationally competitive steel industry. Today SSAB has affiliates in more than 25 countries worldwide and is clearly a player in the international steel market.

SSAB was privatized in a two-step process, with stocks made available to the public first in 1989, then in 1992. In 1989, and consistent with a Government Bill on the privatization of state-owned companies (Government Bill 1991/92: 69), 23 per cent of the company's shares were made available for private interests on the stock market. In 1992, the remainder of the state-controlled shares were sold to private interests.[4] The larger context of the Swedish privatization programme at this time was the notion that the state should resort to its core societal functions, and owning companies was not believed to be part of those core functions. Also introducing SSAB onto the stock market through a privatization was a way for the state to generate funds to help cover its huge budgetary deficits, and also for the company itself to generate investment capital. Presumably, there was also a belief that the company was more likely to strengthen its competitiveness if it operated under private auspices than under state ownership and control; privatization would expose the company to market pressures which would force it to enhance its efficiency.

In retrospect, one might think that this completes a very logical and idealized model of state presence in industrial structural change. According to this model, the state plays a fairly passive role while the industry is doing well, but offers to participate in the restructuring process by temporarily accommodating private companies under its protection and to enforce a restructuring policy laid down by the industry itself, and then to hand over the successfully restructured and competitive companies to the market again. It is clearly an attractive model of state–market exchange and the role of the state in resolving market failure which should be palatable to most political constituencies. It accords a clear primacy to the market but allows for the state to cover the costs associated with the management of decline. The only problem with this picture is that it is wrong, as we will discuss in the next section.

4   ANALYSING STEEL RESTRUCTURING IN SWEDEN

Before we look more closely at the governance patterns that characterized the steel restructuring in Sweden, we should be aware of two important distinctions. First, it is important not to assume the existence of governance as a given. What might at first glance appear to be a case of failure in governance could well be a case of non-existent or poor governance. One could assume that the steel industry with few, big facilities should be more easily governed than industrial sectors with a large number of smaller companies, but even so the existence of governance should probably be subject to research rather than take for granted.

Secondly, we must be aware of the important distinction between the governance of decline, however defined and measured, and the governance of restructuring. Although they may be linked, public policy aiming at restructuring the steel industry – upgrading technology, changing ownership structure, redefining the structure of the industry – draws on a different type of governance process than a policy aiming at managing the decline of the industry, primarily the closure of steel mills. It must also be remembered that, although processes of managing decline and processes aiming at industrial restructuring frequently tend to occur side by side – and there is much to suggest that a successful restructuring requires that the two strategies be implemented simultaneously – they address different types of problems and will set off different reactions from different constituencies and interests.

The governance of decline in the Swedish case saw a complex network of actors coming together around the locales hit by the structural crisis in the steel industry: political institutions from all tiers of government, the distressed company itself, and to some extent also unions. The more future-oriented process also highlighted, as we have seen, the state through Statsföretag and SSAB and also several steel mills. Thus the governance of the decline process had primarily a focus on place whereas the governance of restructuring focused on the industry. The two parallel governance processes thus addressed related but intrinsically different political problems posing different challenges to governance; they draw to some extent on different casts of actors, serve different objectives, draw on funding from different types of sources, and should be assessed according to different criteria.

The basic problem explored in the chapter is to what extent the increasing role of the state in the restructuring process of the Swedish steel sector was an efficient and successful model of governance. The strategy of conducting the restructuring under state auspices was a path-dependent solution; a similar model had been employed in the shipbuilding sector with some degree of success (Pierre, 1989). The overarching problem was to conduct the restructuring in such a way that it accommodated the redundant labour while at the same time creating viable, competitive and up-to-date steel plants. The governance of the Swedish steel sector prior to the restructuring had probably not been very effective; the steel industry was dispersed over several competing 'spheres of industry' (that is, competing groups of owners and stockholders). Furthermore, the restructuring occurred at a time when the predominant policy style was still to look to the state for guidance and financial support. Also, as the Commission pointed out, there was a growing gap between a limited number of competitive steel plants and a fairly large number of smaller, less up-to-date steel production facilities.

Against this backdrop, it made sense to initiate a process which aimed at allowing the larger, competitive mills to increase production while smaller and less competitive mills should leave the market. One of the main problems in executing such a strategy appears to have been that the self-governing process in the steel industry lacked the leverage and integrity necessary to implement a plan which distinctly picks winners and losers and which then is capable of enforcing that strategy. The only structure in society with such institutional leverage, integrity and legitimacy was the state. Equally important, by bringing the state into the governance of the steel industry, companies could tap into a wide variety of resources controlled by the state: financial resources to find concrete restructuring projects, labour market support, retraining programmes, early retirement programmes and trade policy measures which could protect the industry from international competition during the reconstruction. Indeed, so present was the role of the state in the steel industry during the 1980s that the United States and other countries raised tariffs against Swedish steel on the grounds that it was produced under massive state subsidies (Mény and Wright, 1987).

Although the restructuring strategy chosen was clearly path-dependent, it became more successful in many ways compared to the shipyard sector restructuring. The Swedish steel sector was better able to capitalize on high levels of technology and expertise and could position itself successfully in the special steel and stainless steel markets. Furthermore, as the state withdrew its coordinating role, Swedish steel companies secured international partners to help cut costs and sustain market positions. Also there appears to have been a broader understanding of the collective interests among the steel plants than among the shipyards, who entered a quasi-competition for state rescue, whereas the steel mills acted more in concert. Thus the steel restructuring process refined the methods and strategies employed in the restructuring of the shipbuilding sector. Ironically, however, the steel sector was the last sector in which the state took a high profile in the restructuring; once the policy instrument was fully developed it was also abandoned.

Understanding industrial restructuring, which in Sweden was the case to a greater extent than merely managing decline and closedown, is to a large extent a matter of interpreting the combined outcome of measures employed to mitigate decline on the one hand and the efficiency of future-oriented measures on the other. The Swedish case conveys a very clear image of a management of decline coupled with a coordinated strategy to bring up-to-date technology into the steel industry. Further, it points to the political power of conceptualizing a policy that may have some negative consequences, such as closing mills, with the more positive label of restructuring.

One of the key problems in the present analysis is to distinguish between different, sometimes competing, patterns of governance. There are frequently competing governance processes, pursuing competing goals and displaying competing casts or actors present during industrial restructuring. One governance process is defined by the industrial sector while another governance process is situated in the institutional, intergovernmental arrangements of the state, and yet another governance process is defined spatially, that is, by the territory within which individual restructuring shipyards, or steel mills or plants, are situated. What makes industrial restructuring so complex in a governance perspective is that sector and region tend to overlap (Markusen, 1987) and that an acute crisis brings new actors onto the stage and/or changes the relationship between actors.

Given the complexity in these governance processes, it is perhaps no great surprise that the learning process in governance was quite complicated in the declining industrial sectors. The fairly dramatic and rapid decline in the Swedish shipbuilding industry was not handled efficiently or appropriately, as the long-term outcome shows (Pierre, 1989). These problems were exacerbated by two circumstances: the declining industries were labour-intensive and the structural crisis had a distinct spatial dimension. The labour intensity of the declining industries forced the state to inject substantive financial resources into the restructuring process to accommodate the laid-off labour through retraining or other means. On the whole, the geographical dimension of the restructuring was probably conducive to efficient governance; it helped bring together a wide variety of actors and to mobilize local and regional resources. Also the state's strategy of supporting localities and regions, not companies in distress, served to strengthen the networks among public and private actors.

We mentioned earlier that the idealized model of state presence in processes of industrial restructuring was incorrect. Certainly, the initial phase did portray a role for the state which comes close to an ideal model of state action in the resolution of market failure. However, the second phase, returning success-fully restructured companies to the market and private ownership, was more the result of political coincidences than one of intentions formulated early on in the process. There is nothing in the Commission's analysis which implies that they (that is, the industry itself) saw the growing presence of the state in the steel sector as a temporary phenomenon. The privatization of SSAB in 1989 and 1992 was part and parcel of a larger privatization project in which most state-owned companies were sold off to private interests. This project, in turn, could be seen as part of a larger political project aiming at reducing the size of the public sector, to bring in market mechanisms into many areas which had previously been subject to political control, and later also a project of 'purification' of the state's activities, that is to say a focus on traditional state roles and a hiving off of activities which cannot be directly related to that role (Pierre, 2000).

Coming back to a point made earlier in this chapter, that steel was thought of as part of the core industrial sectors in Sweden, this shift in the political perspective on steel should be noted. While the Social Democrats in the late 1980s and early 1990s still relied heavily on the electoral support of the blue-collar constituency, the 1980s had seen the state redefine its responsibility for ensuring employment throughout the country, a responsibility which was clearly felt – and expected – in the 1970s (Henning, 1987). The policy pattern which had evolved during the 1970s, that the state should come to the aid of distressed cities, regions and companies, was replaced by a rather firm policy stance according to which companies had a responsibility for the municipality where they had been located and also that municipalities themselves had to develop a strategy of local mobilization of resources in times of plant closures. This policy shift was in part driven by fiscal necessity – the state simply did not have the financial means to sustain any number of such rescue operations – and partly by an insight that supporting declining industries or regions is often a matter of throwing good money after bad. Thus, during the 1980s, there was a clear increase in the relative amount of state financial resources that were allocated to offensive, future-oriented purposes and an decreasing relative amount of state money spent on defensive, 'bailing out' operations (ibid.).

Today, SSAB is an internationally competitive steel company with a global network of facilities. Assessing the strength of the company is to some extent complicated by the instability of the international steel markets. The year 1998 was a tough one for the steel producers, what with the Asian crisis and falling prices and decreasing demand (SSAB, 1998, pp. 4–5).

5   CONCLUSIONS: A QUALIFIED SUCCESS

This chapter has looked at the politics of industrial restructuring perhaps to a larger extent than most other accounts of similar processes covered in this project. However, in Sweden the policy style was such that almost any industrial crisis during the 1960s and 1970s was a political issue, where state actions and non-actions were believed to be essential to the success of the restructuring process. Also the steel industry underwent its most profound restructuring in a politically volatile period in Sweden, what with a change in government for the first time in more than four decades. It is a historical irony that the incoming non-socialist government appeared to be just as firmly committed to Social Democratic industrial policy and labour market policy as were ever the Social Democrats themselves. The fact that the Royal Commission which outlined the future structure of the steel industry was appointed by a Social Democratic minister of industry but reported to a non-socialist minister, apparently with no significant alterations in its proposals, is proof of the non-socialists' belief in the way their predecessors had run the labour market policy. It is probably also proof of the industry's determination to have a strong say on how it should restructure itself.

The issue of success and failure in governance in the case of Swedish steel restructuring is intriguing. First of all, was the decline in the Swedish steel sector, or the early responses to the crisis, the result of governance failure? The answer here is probably 'no'; the crisis was precipitated by a combination of factors most of which were beyond the control of individual companies or the sector as a whole, as with the oil price crisis in the early 1970s and high wage increases across the board in 1974–5. Secondly, to what extent can the relative success in restructuring be attributed to appropriate forms and strategies of governance? The answer here is probably 'to a significant extent'; the steel industry's strategy to seek to bring in the state was highly appropriate. Conducting structural change under state auspices neutralizes the issue in terms of owner–union friction and the presence of the state brings with it financial support to cushion close-downs and strategies aiming at bringing in new industrial ventures.

This observation, in turn, highlights the fact that ownership is integral to the governance of industrial change. There are several reasons for this. First, ownership defines to a very large extent the constituent interests of the governance process. Secondly, the ownership structure defines much of the definition of constituent interests (states being more closely associated with some constituencies than with others); given the long tenure of the Social Democrats in Sweden, state ownership structure defines a very clear constituency, labour. Finally, ownership is critical to define most of the key variables in the economics of restructuring. A quick comparison between the United States and Sweden suggests that ownership in the USA defines the quarterly dividend as a key variable for assessment, whereas in Sweden as in most of Europe (Albert, 1993) factors such as employment carry much more weight. This has a particular significance in the steel sector where plants can be run for an extended period of time with little or no capital investment in upgrading to maximize the returns until closure is inevitable.

If thus ownership is a critical factor in the governance of industrial structural change, what role has privatization had on SSAB's development since it was privatized? The point here is that state ownership was a decisive factor for the governance of a complex restructuring of the Swedish steel sector; it could be argued that ownership is more important during such transformation processes than in more stable time periods. As was suggested early on in this chapter, the governance of industrial restructuring is a different governance challenge from the governance of a stable market or industrial sector.

Given the size and significance of the manufacturing sector of the economy, Sweden faced a series of structural crises during the late 1960s, the 1970s and the 1980s. It is fair to say that, over time, some degree of expertise in handling such crises has been built up in the government. The Commission outlining the restructuring of the steel industry was a path-dependent solution to the structural crisis; a similar approach had been employed in other industrial sectors and, historically, Sweden has relied on committees of this sort to manage difficult policy questions. What is particularly intriguing about the restructuring of the steel sector is the firm reliance on key players in the sector; the restructuring was to a large part a process of self-governance, with the government and its financial and other resources waiting in the wings, a factor that may have contributed to the relative political as well as programmatic success of the restructuring. The Commission could rely both on some support from the state and on a considerable legitimacy and support from the industry itself, given the dominance of industrialists serving on the Commission.

The long-term success or failure of this strategy of industrial restructuring is obviously difficult to assess. What does seem clear, however, is that SSAB today is internationally competitive and that there is little or nothing in its current performance which would suggest that it is in any way impaired by the way the industry was restructured. Indeed, there is probably more support for the opposite statement: that the restructuring process helped create a competitive steel industry. The accommodation of labour during the restructuring, to give but one example, was considerably eased by the presence of the state in the process. Thus the corporatist structures common in Swedish politics in this case helped to create a positive outcome for the policy process. The political consequences are, however, somewhat more ambiguous, although the ability to depoliticize the decision to some extent softened any political fallout, even for the SAP governments that were involved in a part of the process.

Another circumstance which may or may not have an impact on the Swedish steel industry is Sweden's joining the European Union. The distinct presence of the state in the steel industry which was a feature of the late 1970s and 1980s clearly does not conform to EU policy in these respects. However, fortunately for the Swedish steel industry, perhaps, the privatization of the SSAB was completed well before Sweden joined the Union. Indeed, the type of restructuring which we have here described might not have been possible had Sweden been a member of the EU during the structural crisis. Currently, the SSAB is no more subject to EU regulations than any other privately owned companies in any member state.

NOTES

1. The wage-earners' funds were an attempt to give local unions access to 'excessive' profits in individual companies to purchase shares in that company, a system which theoretically over time would make the local union the chief stockholder. However, the system has thresholds that would ensure that there never was a union takeover. The system, drastically redesigned and moderated, was eventually launched in the early 1980s, only to be abolished by the next non-socialist government.
2. 'Steel' here referred to 'commercial steel' or specialized steel, that is, high-quality, mass-produced steel. This type of steel was the predominant type of steel produced in Sweden at the time, accounting for more than 70 per cent of the steel produced (SOU 1977:15, p. 21) or 40 per cent of the total number of employees in the steel industry.
3. The pattern is highly similar to the way in which the Japanese steel industry conducted its production cuts in the 1980s.
4. For a detailed account of the 1989 and 1992 reforms, see Riksgäldskontoret (1992).

9. British Steel and the British government: problematic learning as a policy style

Geoffrey Dudley and Jeremy Richardson[1]

1 GOVERNANCE SUCCESS AND FAILURE

A longitudinal analysis of the relationship between the British steel industry and government over the past quarter of a century provides a good example of the potentially highly unpredictable and problematic character of policy learning. The essence of this particular form of governance rests on a perpetual state of tension between the two sides, but the form of that tension has varied considerably over the years. In essence, it could be said that, in the days of nationalization of the British steel industry (1967–88), often horrendous financial problems were managed with ultimate success by the relationship between the industry and government. Since privatization in 1988, the industry has enjoyed much greater financial success, but even the remnants of the system of public governance have broken down.

The character of this governance pattern has reflected not only institutional modalities, but also prevailing ideas and values. It would therefore be an over-simplification to regard the system of governance simply as the management of decline. For example, even before privatization, the British Steel Corporation (BSC) placed great emphasis on achieving the goal of becoming one of the world's most efficient steel companies. Since privatization, British Steel (BS) has sought to develop a globalized strategy which, although it has met with mixed success, does not particularly reflect the politics of decline. In fact, on several occasions during the 1990s BS has made large profits (for example, £578 million in 1994–5, £1102 million in 1995–6 and £451 million in 1996–7). Steel deliveries have also remained relatively stable (for example, 12.1 million tonnes in 1987–8, 14.4 million tonnes in 1998–9). Similarly, the period of nationalization saw a massive decrease in the numbers employed, from 253 000 in 1968 to 51 000 in 1988. In 1999, however, numbers employed by the company (including overseas) totalled just over 44 000.

Ironically, therefore, it could be said that in the 1990s the chief evidence of decline has been in the system of governance itself. The globalized strategy of BS, combined with the reluctance of government to regard steel as a 'special case' (in contrast to the days of nationalization), has caused the two sides to drift apart, and even at times to become quite adversarial. Only in the late 1990s is some sort of network being reconstructed (Dudley, 1999a).

In the 1970s and 1980s, therefore, massive financial, economic and employment problems (the politics of decline) were dealt with by problematic policy learning but in a relatively stable political structure. In the 1990s, decline is less evident but the governance structure is dominated by the politics of uncertainty.

2   FINANCIAL CRISIS AND GOVERNANCE SUCCESS

In 1967, the 14 major steel companies in Britain were nationalized to form the BSC. Prior to that time, since 1945 steel policy may be characterized as a classic example of the adversary politics which some writers (such as Finer, 1975) saw as being typical of the British policy process as a whole, with each of the two main political parties seemingly determined to reverse the other's policies.

After nationalization, a large element of the adversarial approach went out of steel policy, and by the early 1970s it could be described as typifying the more normal policy style of that time (Richardson, 1982) of consensual politics (Dudley and Richardson, 1990). Conservative and Labour governments agreed that a unified and state-owned British steel industry was required in order to implement large investment and rationalization plans, and so obtain economies of scale. For the next decade and a half the crucial question of governance became the appropriate relationship between the BSC and government, rather than state ownership itself. Officially, this relationship rested on the arm's-length principle whereby government determined the overall strategy for the industry, but the BSC was in charge of day-to-day management. In reality, ministers and officials lacked the expertise to direct the BSC, and so corporation management determined the strategy. This was typical of the relationships in many of the nationalized industries (see, for example, Foster, 1971; Hannah, 1982).

For a decade, from the mid-1970s to the mid-1980s, the BSC, like many European steel industries, fell into a state of deep financial depression. This put great political strains on the system of governance, which could be described as a typical policy community, with decision making taking place within an enclosed circle (Richardson and Jordan, 1979). Even the Thatcher government, with its powerful advocacy of the free market, recognized the political and social limitations of these principles, and heavily subsidized the BSC in order to maintain the continued existence of the UK steel industry (at the time of privatization over £8 billion was effectively written off). Consequently, huge sums of public money were poured in to keep the BSC in existence, and so prevent the corporation, with its 'national champion' image, from falling into a state of total collapse (Ovenden, 1978; Bryer *et al.*, 1982; Abromeit, 1986; Dudley and Richardson, 1990). Thus steel was treated politically as a 'special case' which had massive political salience.

From the mid-1980s, however, the BSC began to make profits once more (for example, from a loss of £1784 million in 1979–80, a profit of £178 million was made in 1986–7), and to this extent it could be said that the system of governance achieved its objectives and proved a success. Thus the government began to seriously contemplate the ultimate privatization of the industry. The dynamics of the relationship between BSC and government were also deeply affected by a culture shift within the BSC itself. In the 1970s, considerations of long-term planning and investment had dominated, but now commercial efficiency and profit became the salient goals.

3   FINANCIAL SUCCESS AND GOVERNANCE FAILURE

When the government decided to privatize the BSC after lengthy pressure from senior management, it appeared to represent another huge political and financial gamble. After privatization of state assets such as British Telecommunications (BT), British Gas (BG) and British Airways (BA), the commitment to sell off the BSC contained a high degree of political symbolism. In effect, it proclaimed a watershed in the prevailing policy style, so that, henceforth, government was prepared to sever its close connections with 'national champion' basic industries such as steel, and undertakings previously considered exempt from privatization (such as British Rail, British Coal and the Rover car company) could expect to be sold off at the appropriate time.

Given the crisis-ridden history of the BSC, it might have been anticipated that, although government had nominally cut its connections with the steel industry, residual networks would remain, and that any future financial crises for BS would be met by the steel industry and government resuming their traditionally close relationship. In the event, almost the exact opposite has occurred. Financially BS, perhaps surprisingly, has maintained a relatively stable state of equilibrium (particularly when compared with the BSC), despite periods of recession in the early and late 1990s. Politically, however, the relationship between BS and government has frequently been strained and, on occasions, openly hostile.

Since privatization, therefore, it could be said that, although BS has made a reasonable success of its affairs financially, politically the dynamics of the company represent a failure in governance. The use of the word 'governance' here is equated with Osborne and Gaebler's assertion that the transformation of the public sector involves 'less government' (or rowing) but 'more governance' (or steering) (Osborne and Gaebler, 1992, p. 34). As Richardson argues, in reality governments operating the principles of governance may find themselves 'doing less by doing more' in order to make new modalities work effectively (Richardson, 1994). In the case of BS and government, however, it has been more a case of the two sides holding separate policy 'frames'. In this case, different actors construct a view of social reality through a complementary process of naming and framing. They select for attention a few salient features and relations from what would otherwise be an overwhelming complex reality. They give these elements a coherent organization, and they describe what is wrong with the present situation in such a way as to set the direction for its future transformation (Schön and Rein, 1994, p. 26). Schön and Rein, argue that the general relevance of frame-reflective policy inquiry is constructed around the central idea of a reflective policy conversation. Participants in such a conversation must be able to put themselves in the shoes of other actors in the environment, and they must have a complementary ability to consider how their own action frames may contribute to the problematic situations in which they find themselves (ibid., p. 187).

For BS and government, occupying separate 'frames' has led to a discourse in which neither side has generally been prepared to put itself in the shoes of the other. A cognitive gap emerges in which they occupy separate 'orders of comprehension' (Dunsire, 1978, p. 158). This separate policy 'framing' has manifested itself particularly in BS adopting a global strategy, in which it has sought to construct alliances with a number of steel companies in Europe, the USA and Asia. This quest by BS for a more global identity has met with mixed success, but it has had the effect generally of separating itself from the UK government, rooted more in domestic and EU institutional policy agendas.

This globalization strategy diluted the image of BS as a 'national champion', culminating in its 1999 merger with the Dutch company Hoogovens. In addition, the company's free market values, with an emphasis on efficiency, cost containment and profits, also placed strains on its relationship with government in the EU arena. Here, although the UK government ostensibly opposed subsidies to ailing national steel industries, political circumstances on occasions caused it to vote in favour of state aid in the Council of Ministers, a strategy which infuriated BS.

4   GOVERNANCE AS PROBLEMATIC LEARNING

Governance as 'steering' has become particularly identified with a 'hollowing out of the state', which, in addition to privatization, includes the loss of functions by central and local government departments to alternative delivery systems (such as agencies); the loss of functions by British government to European Union institutions; and limits set to the discretion of public servants through the new public management, with its emphasis on managerial accountability, and clearer political control through a sharper distinction between politics and administration (Rhodes, 1996, p. 666). Governance is therefore broader than government, covering non-state actors. Changing the boundaries of the state means that the boundaries between public, private and voluntary sectors become shifting and opaque. Continuing interactions occur between network members, but the state can only indirectly and imperfectly steer networks (ibid., p. 660).

Implicit also in a system of governance, however, is a process of learning, with problematic outcomes. The political and financial resource dependencies which buttressed the UK steel policy community during the period of nationalization have fallen away, and with these fundamental institutional changes the formerly strong policy community has been destroyed (Dudley, 1999a). It has been replaced by a process of problematic learning in which 'puzzling' is more important than 'powering' (Heclo, 1974). In fact, it could be said that a process of unpredictable and problematic learning has become the new dominant policy style of the UK steel sector. Thus it may be more appropriate to employ the word 'governance' as applying to the actual dynamics of government and formerly state-owned industries exploring new modalities, rather than to particular network structures or policy outcomes (Dudley, 1999b).

In this context, Rhodes defines governance as referring to self-organizing interorganizational networks. He correctly identifies a key characteristic of this process as a significant degree of autonomy from the state, with networks not accountable to the state and self-organizing (Rhodes, 1996, p. 660). At the same time, if resource dependencies no longer exist, and interests hold separate policy 'frames', then the dynamics of governance may also involve the collapse and disappearance of networks, or at best produce networks greatly transformed and loosely connected. As Jacobs argues in the context of subnational government, the dynamics of network transformation require a new theoretical assessment which emphasizes the importance of networks, but places greater stress upon organizational complexity, political competition, ambiguity and fragmentation (Jacobs, 1997, pp. 40–41).

One feature which remains constant during the days of both nationalization and privatization, however, is the dominance of the BSC and then BS within the UK steel sector. Traditionally, the steel unions have a fragmented structure, and are relatively moderate and collaborative in their relationships with the steel companies. Brannen *et al.* see the relatively high wages and the small working group as prime factors in shaping union attitudes. They also stress the importance of the widespread use within the industry of conciliation boards, which in many cases were well established by the turn of the century (Brannen *et al.*, 1976, p. 73). At the same time, Vaizey also stresses the importance of deeply ingrained cultural institutional factors, illustrated by union leaders being prepared to identify themselves with the objectives of management, even in the case of policies which appeared to be detrimental to the interests of their members (Vaizey, 1974, p. 28). This means that, despite the existence in the 1990s of a BS European Consultative Council (required by the EU), the unions continue to have little direct input into BS strategy.

Since privatization, the relationship between BS and the unions has also become more problematic and fragmented, with greater emphasis on performance-related pay, tightened employment conditions and shifts in the timing of settlements (Upham, 1997, p. 223). In addition, in a capital-intensive industry, labour is a diminishing cost (ibid., p. 241) and the increasing internationalization of BS has also caused tension with the unions. For example, in 1991 the Annual Delegate Conference of the largest steel union, the Iron and Steel Trades Confederation (ISTC), called on the government to use its golden share 'to prevent denationalised companies investing abroad to the detriment of the industry in Britain' (ibid., p. 242). In the late 1990s, the relationship between BS and the unions has taken on yet another fresh complexion with the proposed introduction of teamworking. This policy initiative by the company, an idea learned chiefly from its dealings with Japanese-owned motor manufacturers in the UK, emphasizes that traditional working practices and inter-union relationships in the steel industry are also entering uncharted waters.

By the end of the century, therefore, the BS company culture, and its relationships with government, were almost unrecognizable from those which had obtained 30 years earlier, at the time of nationalization. Although the management of the politics of decline has played a large role in explaining subsequent events, particularly in the 1970s and early 1980s, it is by no means the whole story. New ideas about the relationship between industry and the state, the fashion for globalization and EU institutional factors have also made a highly significant contribution. Nevertheless, the policy dynamics and problems of governance for the privatized BS have their roots in the company's experience, and its relationship with government, during the days of nationalization.

5   THE POLICY PROCESS (I): FROM STATE SUBSIDIES TO PRIVATIZATION

Notwithstanding its traditional economic and political status as a basic industry, steel suffers from an apparently endemic cyclical character which makes it particularly prone to periods of crisis and depression. In the 1970s, however, a period of recession was overlaid with a crisis caused by an overambitious investment strategy. In 1973, the government produced a White Paper, *Steel. British Steel Corporation: Ten Year Development Strategy* (Cmnd 5226) which announced that the BSC would require a programme of investment amounting to £3000 million. The plan involved a major development of the five main coastal Heritage sites and of special steel plants in the Sheffield–Rotherham area, in addition to the development of a major new steel complex. It was also expected that two 'mini' electric arc furnace plants would be constructed in Scotland. In 1972, BSC production totalled 22.9 million tonnes, but the BSC and government were now planning for a corporation capacity in 1980 of 28 to 36 million tonnes. The decision to accept the BSC's strategy represented a great act of faith by the government, thereby supporting the corporation's contention that the future demand for steel would justify such large-scale expansion (Dudley and Richardson, 1990, p. 52).

In the event, this wildly overoptimistic investment strategy proved to be a policy fiasco of the first magnitude. As Bovens and 't Hart observe, however, the wisdom-after-the-event trap makes one aware of the limited validity of deterministic and monocausal explanations of the evolution of policy episodes, including policy fiascos. The fact that these policy episodes have unfolded in the ways they did does not mean they were inevitable (Bovens and 't Hart, 1996, p. 9). In the case of the BSC, it was not just the commitment to a risky investment strategy which posed the problem, but a range of difficulties which needed to be solved if disaster was to be avoided. For example, experience of steel should have suggested to the government that there were powerful internal factors – such as trade union structure, attitudes towards changes in work practice and quality of management – which if not tackled would ensure that the UK steel industry would indeed find difficulty in 'securing maximum output from new equipment' (Dudley and Richardson, 1990, p. 53).

When these problems were added to a recession in steel demand from the mid-1970s, and the fact that several countries were already well ahead of Britain in terms of modern investment, it quickly became obvious that the BSC was in a state of potentially terminal crisis. Instead of the hoped for 28–36 million tonnes, in 1979–80 BSC crude steel production totalled 14.1 million tonnes, and the corporation made a loss after tax of over £1.7 billion. Consequently, in 1978, the Labour government published a new White Paper, *The Road to Viability* (Cmnd 7149) in which for the first time it was accepted that the decline in demand for steel was of a long-term nature and that some markets might be lost forever. Some development projects were 'deferred' in favour of a 'step-by-step' approach which would retain the flexibility to adapt to unexpected changes in the situation (ibid., para. 12). Henceforth, therefore, it was officially acknowledged that the politics of pessimism would pertain in the affairs of the

British steel industry, and in fact that the management of decline had become the dominant policy objective.

The BSC took full advantage of the new political climate, and from the late 1970s embarked on a ruthless series of plant closures. The political commitment of government to the corporation meant that relatively high redundancy payments could be offered, and nearly all the closures were implemented peacefully. In other words, the steel policy community remained intact, with the appropriate resource dependencies. The BSC required the government for the necessary financial and political support, but the government needed the BSC to implement a strategy which would ensure the survival of a national basic industry.

The strength and depth of these dependencies were well illustrated in the early 1980s in the aftermath of a damaging three-month national steel strike. Officially, this was over the question of a pay award, but it could also be seen as the union's one great symbolic protest against the massive restructuring of the industry. In June 1980, the chairman of the BSC wrote to the Industry secretary in the Thatcher Conservative government explicitly stating that, unless drastic action was taken, the corporation would be forced into liquidation. For a government ideologically committed to free market values, this would have been the opportunity for ministers to make an example of the steel industry and to shut it down. Instead, the Industry secretary announced to the House of Commons that the BSC would continue trading as an on-going business. In the last resort the government would have to ensure that the creditors of the corporation had their claims met in full (HC Debs. 26:6:80, col. 755). The government was finally admitting that it was not politically feasible to close down the BSC, and so a blank cheque was to be issued in order to cover losses (Dudley and Richardson, 1990, p. 151).

The government's interventionist approach was further indicated by its support in 1980 for a 'period of manifest crisis' to be declared within the European Coal and Steel Community. The so-called Davignon Plan, named after the Industry commissioner chiefly responsible for its creation and implementation, continued until 1988 and involved a complex package of output, price and trade controls. Even in the depths of recession, however, and despite being keen supporters of the Davignon Plan, British ministers were lending their support to an alternative policy 'frame'. This long-term goal was reflected at the BSC through two chairmen in particular: first, Sir Ian MacGregor, chairman from 1980 to 1983, second, and more significantly, Sir Robert Scholey, chairman from 1986 to 1992, also president of the EU steelmakers' trade association Eurofer from 1985 to 1990. He became the dominant figure in British steel policy in the 1980s, and increasingly espoused Thatcherite principles (his principal aim was to return the BSC to the private sector) (Dudley and Richardson, 1999, p. 235).

Even in the early 1980s, the BSC was involved in a process of partial privatization when a series of so-called 'Phoenix' projects involved the hiving-off of a number of businesses, although in the majority of these the BSC retained a significant shareholding. From 1985–6, however, the corporation returned to profit, after a decade of heavy losses, and privatization of the whole organization became a viable option. In order to maximize the receipts from a sale, the government bowed to pressure from the BSC and agreed to privatize the corporation as an entity, and in 1988 shares were sold which valued the BSC at £2.5 billion.

The traumatic experiences during public ownership, however, were to have profound effects on the behaviour of both BS and government in the decade after privatization. This legacy took several forms. First, BS made a virtue out of what had been a necessity during the years of crisis. Hence the company identified efficiency and cost containment as an absolute policy priority. BS took particular pride in making itself one of the most efficient steel companies in the world, and did everything in its power to maintain this status. It could be said that there was a significant degree of symbolism here, mixed with an element of insecurity: the company was anxious to destroy its former image as a 'lame duck', while also fearing the consequences of another financial crisis. Second, the company generally adopted a conservative investment strategy. Even when reserves were available for this purpose, there was little inclination to return to the days of radical investment strategies.

Third, with all the enthusiasm of the convert, BS became zealous in its advocacy of free markets. To a significant extent, this represented the ideology of senior managers such as Sir Robert Scholey, but it could also be argued again that there was an anxiety to prove that the company was no longer dependent on state aid. Fourth, the company also had an ideological commitment to almost completely sever its connections with government. Thus the policy community which had preserved the BSC was almost immediately destroyed after privatization, with BS senior management making a point of not lobbying or consulting ministers on any matter at all (by the mid-1990s, BS had come to realize that this policy was an over-reaction, and sought to construct new networks with government: Dudley, 1999a).

Fifth, for its part government ceased to regard steel as a 'special case'. It had neither the political commitment nor the resources to intervene on matters of investment or rationalization, and generally restricted itself to assisting the industry on such matters as trade promotion and benchmarking. Sixth, BS took privatization as a signal to change its image as a 'national champion', and instead sought alliances and new investment opportunities wherever in the world they might occur.

To a great extent, therefore, the policies of both government and BS after privatization can be interpreted as a direct reaction against the events of the nationalization period. New governance ideas about 'enabling' and 'steering' government appeared to chime in well with this scenario. At the same time, there was also an underlying tension bequeathed by the years of crisis and the resource dependencies of the policy community. Such a legacy was perhaps not the best foundation on which to build a successful new system of governance.

6   THE POLICY PROCESS (II): THE POST-PRIVATIZA-TION BREAKDOWN IN GOVERNANCE

If the essence of the policy style between BS and government has been one of policy learning, then as a test of governance it has largely been a failure. On most issues, the two sides hold separate policy 'frames', particularly on matters such as globalization, the regional consequences of plant closures and an EU institutional agenda. At the same time, it could also be said that each side accepted the fact of privatization, and the ideology which underpinned it. Hence the new policy style implied that, for steel, management of the politics of decline was over, and that the former resource dependencies had dropped away. Under the new regime, it was mutually accepted that BS could no longer rely on steel being treated as a 'special case' by government, and that the company would operate autonomously. On the other hand, it had not been anticipated that the relationship would become so adversarial.

The nub of the problem was that neither side truly understood the political implications of steel privatization. The industry might indeed have been no longer a 'special case' to the same degree as formerly, and the policy community would not be reconstructed, but salient political issues with regard to steel continued to occur, and the sector lacked a mechanism or forum for discussing or negotiating these issues. Instead, the total breakdown of the network produced a series of ad hoc confrontations. Thus government still had political and institutional responsibilities for steel, but appeared surprised to discover that the industry could not be dismissed from its calculations.

For its part, BS was anxious to shed its 'national champion' image, but discovered not only that in many other countries steel retained its national prestige, but also that it was consistently brought back to domestic political and economic considerations.

BS and the Frustrations of Globalization

After privatization, BS chairman Sir Robert Scholey took the initiative in seeking to buy into a number of EU and US steel companies. This BS strategy was derived from a policy 'frame' which envisaged a set of multinational steel companies operating in a free market. Scholey had a particular ambition for BS expansion into Europe, not only in terms of physical assets, but also exporting what he considered to be the company's distinctive brand of US-style liberal capitalism (interview, 4 November 1996). The steel industry, however, like airlines, is one where the 'national champion' culture is traditionally strong. Even in the case of BS itself, for five years after privatization government held a 'golden' share which restricted the size of individual share holdings to 15 per cent of the equity. In the case of many other EU countries, governments had an even more protective attitude to their 'national champion' steel companies, and were not willing to see policy through the same 'frame' as BS (Dudley, 1999a).

On the other hand, it could be said that the BS globalization strategy at least allowed the company to break free from its 'lame duck' image and the politics of decline. Even if the strategy was for several years not especially successful, it announced to the world that BS was no longer living in the shadow of government, and was seeking to expand rather than contract. In this context, globalization offered a particular policy 'solution' to a BS policy 'problem' (Kingdon, 1995).

The limitations of the strategy, however, were exemplified by BS's attempts in 1990 to purchase the Aristrain company in Spain. At the prospect of this, the state-owned Ensidesa company became alarmed at the prospect of BS gaining control of another Spanish company, and together with another Spanish steel company launched a counterbid. Eventually, the Spanish government itself expressed concern about the BS bid, and the company withdrew its bid.

Scholey experienced similar frustrations in the USA, where he proposed a joint venture in 1991 with the Bethlehem steel company. Here union opposition eventually vetoed the deal. BS experienced little more success in Germany in gaining major inroads. For example, in 1990, BS began preliminary negotiations with the Hoesch company, but in 1991, with the encouragement of the German government, Krupp launched a friendly takeover of Hoesch. Similarly, in 1998, when BS made tentative overtures for the Preussag company, the government of Lower Saxony stepped in and took over the company. Scholey's successor as BS chairman, Sir Brian Moffat, has tended to adopt a more conservative strategy, but has sought to develop some joint ventures in the Far East. These are relatively small-scale so far, however, and have also been limited by the financial crises in that region of the world in recent years.

BS has enjoyed some success in developing overseas ventures, but again on a relatively small scale. These include purchasing the small Troisdorf plant in Germany, the Tuscaloosa mill in Alabama in the USA, and a joint venture (Trico) with US and Japanese companies to build a flat product mini mill. In 1999, BS's newly appointed chief executive declared an intention for the company to adopt a more aggressive strategy of overseas expansion. This includes the possibility of greater involvement in stockholding ventures. At least in the EU, by the late 1990s all the principal national steel companies were in the private sector, but politically, as the Preussag example illustrated, the impression remained that, when the moment of truth arrived, national or regional governments would generally protect their 'national champions' in steel.

As the 1990s progressed, therefore, BS consolidated its domestic position and its existing interests. For example, a large joint venture with Sweden was Avesta Sheffield AB, formed by the merger of Avesta AB and BS's stainless steel interests to become one of the world's largest manufacturers of stainless steel products. In 1995, BS increased its shareholding in Avesta from 49.9 per cent to a controlling 51 per cent. Also in 1995, BS significantly consolidated its UK interests by paying GKN £93 million for its share in UES Holdings. Ironically, UES had been created in 1986 and split off from the BSC as part of the Phoenix privatization programme.

Finally, at the end of the 1990s, BS achieved its aim of a major overseas alliance. During the previous two years, consolidation of the European industry had accelerated, with Cockerill Sambre of Belgium falling to Usinor of France, Aceralia of Spain to Arbed of Luxembourg (a 35.8 per cent share) and Krupp of Germany to the largest German company, Thyssen. There was some irony in that BS, which had been at the forefront of this trend, appeared to find itself excluded from the outcome. In 1999, however, a merger was announced between BS and Hoogovens, the largest Dutch steelmaker. The new company (known as Corus) became the world's third-largest steelmaker after Nippon Steel of Japan and Posco of South Korea.

The merged group has a market capitalization of £2.9 billion after deducting a payment of £694 million to BS shareholders. About 61.7 per cent of the shares will be held by BS shareholders and 38.3 per cent by Hoogovens shareholders. Within Dutch circles there was some scepticism about this merger, for in 1972 Hoogovens had merged with Hoesch of Germany, but the deal was undone 10 years later. Nevertheless, for BS the deal finally marked the company's end as a 'national champion'. It also suggested still more complex problems of governance, for henceforth major investment and rationalization decisions would cross national borders.

Ravenscraig and Separate Policy 'Frames'

BS's at least attempted globalized strategy symbolized politically that the company was no longer restricted to the domestic political agenda. The case of the closure of the Ravenscraig steelworks, however, demonstrated more starkly the problems in governance caused by privatization. The Ravenscraig works in Scotland had long been a delicate political problem. Although one of the BSC's five major coastal works, the original decision to construct it in the 1950s was a political decision to split investment between Scotland and Wales. When the BSC crisis began to bite in the late 1970s, the corporation pressed the government for approval to close the plant. On two occasions, however, in 1982 and 1985, the government vetoed the BSC's plans and guaranteed Ravenscraig's survival. In 1986, however, the BSC was allowed to close the Gartcosh hot steel mill, a decision which was widely regarded in Scotland as the thin end of the wedge which would eventually see off Ravenscraig, as Gartcosh took one-third of Ravenscraig's hot mill steel.

Nevertheless, prior to privatization, the BSC was compelled by government to make a commitment that Ravenscraig would remain in operation for at least another seven years, subject to market conditions. After privatization, however, events moved towards the final resolution of the politics of Ravenscraig, and emphasized the extent to which BS and government held separate policy 'frames'.

In 1990, BS announced that the Ravenscraig hot strip mill would close in 1991. The Scottish Secretary, Malcolm Rifkind, immediately declared that he deplored the decision, which he found arbitrary and unreasonable. He added that BS might have to be pressured to sell the plant to a competitor in order to retain the Scottish steel industry. To Rifkind's disappointment, however, it became clear that, unlike the situation a decade earlier, ministers were sensitive about challenging Scholey and BS. Privatization had been promoted by the government as a means of freeing the industry from political interference, and so there would be considerable political embarrassment in now challenging the BS 'frame'. Ministers might hold a different 'frame', but now lacked the authority to impose their will on BS management.

In view of the lack of support from other ministers, Rifkind backtracked somewhat from his initial stance, and said that BS's investment and operational decisions were a matter for the commercial judgment of the company, although he hoped the company would reconsider its decision (*Financial Times*, 22 May 1990). Not surprisingly, BS had no intention of reconsidering, and the final closure of Ravenscraig took place in 1992, with BS pointing out that its 1987 commitment to keep the works open for at least another seven years had been made subject to 'market considerations'. On this occasion, the BS 'frame' had prevailed, but in other arenas it would find government a more formidable adversary.

The EU Arena and a Breakdown in Governance

In the European arena, steel has long held a status as a 'special case', due to the foundation of the European Coal and Steel Community (ECSC) and the signing of the Treaty of Paris in 1951. The key role of the steel industry in the foundation of the European institutions, together with its traditional status as a strategic industry, has allowed it to be given particular attention by the European Commission, and for national governments and the steel companies themselves to believe that, in times of crisis, a pan-European solution is required (Dudley and Richardson, 1999).

In the 1990s, however, EU steel policy drove a wedge between BS and the British government. First, there was the ultimate failure of a Commission-led pan-European solution to a fresh crisis in the steel industry in the early 1990s. As part of this plan, steel companies from eastern Germany, Italy, Spain and Portugal sought permission for nearly £5.33 billion in fresh subsidies, and in return were prepared to offer five million tonnes of capacity cuts. BS was totally opposed to the payment of these subsidies, and sought assistance in its campaign from French and former West German steel companies. Article 95 of the Treaty of Paris allowed a loophole for the subsidies to be paid, but a unanimous vote was required in the Council of Ministers. The British government was not willing to be isolated on this issue, and in December 1993 agreed to the payment of the subsidies in return for strict monitoring conditions. BS considered that it had been deserted by its own government, and called the package 'a compromise driven by political expedience' (*Financial Times*, 18 December 1993), but the British government had been forced to concede a deal under heavy pressure from other industry ministers and the Commission. BS refused to let the matter rest, however, and in 1994 took the matter to the European Court, maintaining that the subsidies granted to Ilva of Italy and CSI of Spain fell outside the State Aid Code agreed in 1985 by the Council of Ministers (in 1997, the European Court came down in favour of the Commission, although BS appealed). The company argued that it could not operate in a Single European Market in which different cultures existed. Where BS had developed a strong corporate culture which depended on a free market 'frame', the British government took a more pragmatic approach (Dudley, 1999a).

Secondly, in 1995 the Irish government wished to inject £39 million into Irish Steel prior to its privatization, but BS argued that this subsidy would threaten the continued existence of its own Shelton plant, and would once again breach the Steel Aid Code. For a period in late 1995, the British government held out within the Council of Ministers, but then withdrew its opposition. There were strong suggestions that the government feared continued opposition would endanger the Northern Ireland peace process, which was then gaining momentum. The government therefore had its own distinctive 'frame' and priorities, and some issues constituted more of a 'special case' than others. BS, however, once more took its case to the European Court on the grounds of illegal state aid.

In 1995, a joint group had been set up between BS, the British government and the British Iron and Steel Producers Association (BISPA) (the trade group dominated by BS) to monitor state aid within the EU, but the separate 'frames' of BS and government resulted in a breakdown in governance on these issues.

Reconstructing Governance

As the 1990s progressed, BS came to the realization that its initial policy of divorcing itself from the British government had been a mistake. Consequently, there was a recognition that it still needed to influence government on such matters as state aid, exchange rates and environmental regulations. In 1993, the company appointed a senior manager as Director of Commercial and International Affairs, with responsibilities including relations with government and the EU Commission, assisting in the organization of the steel producers' group Eurofer, and monitoring regulatory matters which concern the company.

BS has thus sought to gain a more sympathetic understanding of the government's 'frame', particularly through a greater appreciation of the mechanics of government. For example, BS places great emphasis now on understanding the relationship between the Department of Trade and Industry and the Treasury, and in reading the minds of key officials. The company has also singled out for special attention advisers in the prime minister's Policy Unit. During 1997–8, BS put this strategy to use on the key issue of the high value of the pound, which has an adverse effect on the company's terms of trade. On this issue, however, the 'hollowing out of the state' was evident in 1997 when the new Labour government handed over to the Bank of England the responsibility for setting interest rates. Consequently, BS has also set about the task of cultivating relationships with the Bank, and understanding the minds of its key individuals.

For government, on the other hand, there is no longer the sense of responsibility for the welfare of the industry to be found in the days of nationalization, and consequently the need for frame reflection is lower. On such matters as the value of the pound, although BS is listened to by government, its input is only one amongst many interests. In addition, the greatly reduced political salience of steel is reflected institutionally. In the days of nationalization, Iron and Steel occupied a whole division within the Department of Trade and Industry. Now steel matters are dealt with by one of five sections within the Metals, Minerals and Shipbuilding Directorate. Officially, the policy objectives of the DTI are to promote the interests and improve the competitiveness of the steel industry (Dudley, 1999a). The merger between BS and Hoogovens is likely to make relations between steel and national government still more problematic.

A further illustration of the problematic relationship is the fate of the Steel Round Table. Largely on the initiative of the unions and sponsored MPs, it was suggested that a round table be set up involving BS, government and the unions to meet periodically to discuss matters of mutual concern. The government was neutral on this proposal, but BS has refused to cooperate, arguing that its global identity prohibits such a body. Once again, therefore, we see a failure to construct a new system of governance.

7   THE PENALTIES AND RISKS OF PROBLEMATIC LEARNING

The evidence of the relationship between BS and government illustrates that a heavy price can be paid in destroying an established policy community and attempting to set up a system of governance which relies on a policy style of problematic policy learning. For BS, the major institutional change of privatization also created a political opportunity to speedily develop its new policy 'frame' and cut itself off from government. For government itself, although ministers and officials did not have the same motivation to destroy the policy community as BS senior management, there was nevertheless a general relief at relinquishing responsibility for steel, and little stomach for the political risks involved in even attempting to undertake government by 'steering'.

Although it could be said, therefore, that the initial trigger for the failure in governance came from institutional change, it was a change in the prevailing policy style which produced the divorce between government and BS: that is, the destruction of the policy community was not an inevitable effect of privatization.

Once the policy style of problematic policy learning was embarked upon, in the case of steel there was perhaps almost an inevitability that relationships would be aggravated. Steel may have lost some of its political salience, but the industry still produces delicate political questions which must be resolved. This was particularly illustrated by events in the EU arena. In addition, the policy style itself obviously increases uncertainty and unpredictability: unstructured policy learning will almost inevitably produce some policy discontinuity and failures. Unlike the situation in a policy community, where disputes can be negotiated on behind closed doors by a process of accommodation, unstructured policy learning produces politically embarrassing public disputes without the means to settle matters by a process of 'giving reason' to different policy 'frames'. The failure to set up a Steel Round Table is a symptom of these separate 'frames'.

Yet it cannot be assumed that network reconstruction is naturally the appropriate policy style. Problematic policy learning may have damaged the political credibility of steel, but it could also be argued that it fairly reflected the attitudes of the principal interests in the 1990s. In the years immediately after privatization, it was unlikely that BS would have accepted a process of 'giving reason', particularly on issues such as Ravenscraig. In other words, at least highly uncertain and problematic policy learning reflected the prevailing values. Here uncertainty and experiencing painful lessons may be the inevitable price to be paid for problematic policy learning.

8 CONCLUSION: PROGRAMMATIC AND POLITICAL SUCCESS AND FAILURE

As illustrated in the first section, the concept of 'decline' in the British steel industry as applied to the criteria of programmatic and governance success and failure is complex and far from uniform and linear. In the 1970s and early 1980s, for example, the BSC suffered appalling losses, but from the mid-1980s the position stabilized, and in the 1990s the privatized BS has generally been profitable.

On capacity, a totally overambitious investment plan in the 1970s envisaged demand as high as 36 million tonnes, but from the mid-1980s output stabilized and has not fluctuated greatly since. It is in numbers employed where the decline from the 1960s and 1970s is most evident. Even here, however, the shifts in the size of the workforce since privatization in 1988 have been much less than in earlier years, although to some extent this is accounted for by new cross-national ventures.

It could be argued that it is in the criteria of political salience that 'decline' is particularly evident. Indeed, here 'decline' has two particular dimensions. First, there is 'decline' as measured by steel's loss of status as a 'special case'. Secondly, however, there is 'decline' represented by the disintegration of the steel community after privatization, and its replacement by a much more problematic and adversarial relationship between industry and government. It is this paradox of programmatic failure and governance success, followed by relative programmatic success and governance failure, which gives steel in Britain a distinctive character.

Exogenous forces have played a significant part in the evolution of these phonomena. For example, over-reliance on new technology helped to exacerbate the crisis of the 1970s, while Europeanization has assisted in aggravating the governance problems of the 1990s. Nevertheless, endogenous 'framing' is at the heart of the more recent adversarial conditions. Thus both BS and government deliberately abandoned steel's former status as a 'special case' and chose to 'frame' policy in a much more commercial and market-led manner. Once this historically important step had been taken, there was an air of inevitability about the eventual adversarial clashes, regardless of the programmatic successes enjoyed by BS.

NOTE

1. We wish to acknowledge the support of the Economic and Social Research Council under grant number R000236193.

Bibliography to part II

Abromeit, H. (1986), *British Steel*, Leamington: Berg.

Albert, M. (1993), *Capitalism Against Capitalism*, London: Whurr.

Ballance, R.H. and S.W. Sinclair (1983), *Collapse and Survival: Industry Strategies in a Changing World*, London: Allen & Unwin.

Bermeo, Nancy (1994), 'The Political Economy of Structural Adjustment in New Democracies: The Case of Spain', manuscript.

Bohlin, J. (1989), '*Svensk Varvsindustri 1920–1975*', Göteborg: Meddelanden från Ekonomisk–historiska institutionen vid Göteborgs Universitet, no. 59, stencil.

Bovens, M. and P. 't Hart (1996), *Understanding Policy Fiascoes*, New Brunswick: Transaction Publishers.

Brannen, P., E. Batstone, D. Fatchett and W. White (1976), *The Worker Directors: A Sociology of Participation*, London: Hutchinson.

Bryer, R.A., T.J. Brignall and AR. Maunders (1982), *Accounting for British Steel*, London: Gower.

Buesa, M. and J. Molero (1998), *Economía Industrial de España: Organización, Tecnologiá*, Madrid: Civitas.

Carlsson, B. (1981), 'Structure and Performance in the West European Steel Industry: A Historical Perspective' in H.W. de Jong (ed.), *The Structure of European Industry*, The Hague: Martinus Nyhoff Publishers, pp. 125–58.

CEC, Commission of the European Communities (1993), *Panorama of EC Industry 93*, Luxembourg: Office for Official Publications of the European Communities.

Chambre Syndicale de la Sidérurgie Française (CSSF) – Fédération Française de l'Acier (FFA) (various years), *La Sidérurgie Française*, Paris.

Cmnd 5226 (1973), *Steel: British Steel Corporation: Ten Year Development Strategy*, London: HMSO.

Cmnd. 7149 (1978), *British Steel Corporation: The Road to Viability*, London: HMSO.

Cohen, E. (1995), 'France: National Champion in Search of a Mission', in J. Hayward (ed.), *Industrial Enterprise and European Integration: From National to International Champions in Western Europe*, Oxford: Oxford University Press, pp. 23–47.

Cohen, Elie and Michel Bauer (1981), *Qui Gouverne le Groupe Industriel? Essai sur l'Exercice du Pouvoir du et dans le Groupe Industriel*, Paris: Seuil.

Corporación de la Siderurgia Integral (CSI) (1993), *Plan de Competitividad Conjunto de AHV-Ensidesa: presentación a los sindicatos*, Madrid, 13 April.

Cowling, K. (1982), *Monopoly Capitalism*, London: Macmillan.

Daley, Anthony (1996), *Steel, State and Labour Mobilization and Adjustment in France*, Pittsburgh: Pittsburgh University Press.

Dankers, J.J. and J. Verheul (1993), *Hoogovens 1945–1993. From steelworks to two-metal provider: A study in industrial strategy* (in Dutch), The Hague: SDU Publishers.

De Bruin, J.A. (1990), *Economische Zaken en economische subsidies*, The Hague: VUGA.

De Jong, H.W. (1990), 'The Netherlands: a European Paradise for Trust-Mongers?' (in Dutch), *Economisch Statistische Berichten*, 73, (14 March), 244–8.

De Jong, H.W. (ed.) (1993), *The Structure of European Industry*, 3rd rev. edn, Dordrecht: Kluwer Academic.

De la Dehesa, Guillermo (1993), *Political and Economic Reform in Contemporary Spain*, Conference 'The Political Economy of Policy Reform', organised by the Institute of International Economics, Washington, DC, January.

De Voogd, C. (1993), *The decline of shipbuilding and other manufacturing industries* (in Dutch), Vlissingen: Den Boer/De Ruiter.

De Vries, J. (1968), *Hoogovens IJmuiden 1918–1968. Rise and development of a basic industry* (in Dutch), IJmuiden: Hoogovens.

Dercksen, W. and H. Schenk (1982), 'Industrial policy as the captive of international rivalry' (in Dutch), *Tijdschrift voor Politieke Ekonomie*, 6 (1)5 129–50.

Dudley, G. (1999a), 'British Steel and Government since Privatisation: Policy "Framing" and the Transformation of Policy Networks', *Public Administration*, 77 (1), 51–71.

Dudley, G. (1999b), 'Transplanting Ideas in Policy Networks: Reinventing Local Government and the Case of Steel Action', *Local Government Studies*, 25 (35), 76–89.

Dudley, G. and J. Richardson (1990), *Politics and Steel in Britain 1967–1988*, Aldershot: Dartmouth.

Dudley, G. and J. Richardson (1999), 'Competing Advocacy Coalitions and the Process of "Frame Reflection": A Longitudinal Analysis of EU Steel Policy', *Journal of European Public Policy*, 6 (2), 225–48.

Dunsire, A. (1978), *Implementation in a Bureaucracy*, Oxford: Martin Robertson.

EC Commission (1990), *General Objectives for Steel 1995*, COM (90), 201.

Economist (1998), 'Restructuring Corporate Germany', 21 November.

Eisenhammer, John (1987), 'Longwy and Bagnoli: A Comparative Study of Trade Union Response to the Steel Crisis in France and Italy', in Y. Mény and V. Wright (eds), *The Politics of Steel: Western Europe and the Steel Industry in the Crisis Years (1974–1984)*, New York: Walter de Gruyter, pp. 593–622.

EKO Stahl (1999), 'Firmengeschichte', *http://www.eko-stahl.de/deu/de3news/ nfraineseet.htm*.

Esser, J. and W. Fach (1989), 'Crisis Management "Made in Germany": The Steel Industry', in P.J. Katzenstein (ed.), *Industry and Politics in West Germany Towards the Third Republic*, New York: Cornell University Press, pp. 221–48.

Financial Times (1999), 'World Steel Industry Survey', 14 May.

Finer, S.E. (1975), *Adversary Politics*, London: Wigram.

Foreman-Peck, J. and G. Federico (eds) (1999), *European Industrial Policy: The Twentieth-Century Experience*, Oxford: Oxford University Press.

Foster, C.D. (1971), *Politics, Finance and the Role of Economics*, London: Allen & Unwin.

Fraile Balbín, Pedro (1992), *Interés Público y captura del Estado: la empresa pública siderúrgica en España: 1941–81*, FIES, Documento de Trabajo no. 9203.

Gale, W.K.V. (1971), *The Iron and Steel Industry: A Dictionary of Terms*, Newton Abbott: David and Charles.

Gerstenberger, W. (1985), *Subventionen in Europa – Konzequenzen einer Laissez-Faire Politik am Beispiel der deutschen Stahlindustrie*, Institut für Wirtschaftsforschung e.V. München, Studien zur Industriewirtschaft, no. 29.

Glais, M. (1995), 'Steel Industry', in P. Buigues, A. Jacquemin and A. Sapir (eds), *European Policies on Competition, Trade and Industry: Conflict and Complementarities*, Aldershot: Edward Elgar, pp. 219–59.

Hall, Peter A. (1986), *Governing the Economy: The Politics of State Intervention in Britain and France*, Oxford: Oxford University Press.

Hall, Peter A. (1994), 'Pluralism and Pressure Politics' and 'The State and the Market', in P.A. Hall, J. Hayward and H. Machin (eds), *Developments in French Politics*, 2nd edn, London: Macmillan, pp. 77–92 and 171–87.

Hannah, L. (1982), *Engineers, Managers and Politicians*, London: Macmillan.

Hayward, J. (1995), 'International Industrial Champions', in J. Hayward and E.C. Page (eds), *Governing the New Europe*, Cambridge: Polity Press, pp. 346–73.

Hayward, Jack E.S. (1982), 'Mobilising Private Interests in the Service of Public Ambitions: The Salient Element in the Dual French Policy Style?', in J. Richardson (ed.), *Policy Styles in Western Europe*, London: Allen & Unwin, pp. 111–40.

Hayward, Jack E.S. (1986), *The State and the Market Economy: Industrial Patriotism and Economic Intervention in France*, Brighton: Wheatsheaf Books.

Hayward, Jack E.S. (1987), 'The Nemesis of Industrial Patriotism: The French Response to the Steel Crisis', in Y. Mény and V. Wright (eds), *The Politics of Steel: Western Europe and the Steel Industry in the Crisis Years (1974–1984)*, New York: Walter de Gruyter, pp. 502–33.

Heclo, H. (1974), *Modern Social Politics in Britain and Sweden*, New Haven: Yale University Press.

Henning, R. (1987), *Näringspolitik i Obalans*, Stockholm: Allmänna Förlaget/Publica.

Hoerr, J.P. (1988), *And the Wolf Finally Came*, Pittsburgh: University of Pittsburgh Press.

Hoffmann-Martinot, Vincent and Pierre Sadran (1987), 'The Local Implementation of France's National Strategy', in Y. Mény and V. Wright (eds), *The Politics of Steel: Western Europe and the Steel Industry in the Crisis Years (1974–1984)*, New York: Walter de Gruyter, pp. 534–92.

Hogan, W.T. (1983), *World Steel in the 1980s: A Case of Survival*, Lexington, MA: D.C. Heath and Company/Lexington Books.

Hollingsworth, J.R., P.C. Schmitter and W. Streek (eds) (1994), *Governing Capitalist Economies*, Oxford: Oxford University Press.

Hood, Christopher (1994), *Explaining Economic Policy Reversals*, Buckingham: Open University Press.

Houseman, Susan (1991), *Industrial Restructuring with Job Security: The Case of European Steel*, Cambridge, MA: Harvard University Press.

Howel, T.R., W.A. Noellert, J.G. Kreier and A.W. Wolff (1988), *Steel and the State*, Boulder, CO: Westview Press.

Hudson, R. (1992), *Restructuring the West European Steel Industry: Social, Spatial and Technical Changes in Production*, Durham University, Centre of European Studies, Working Paper, no. 3.

Hudson, R. and D. Sadler (1989), *The International Steel Industry: Restructuring, State Policies and Localities*, London: Routledge.

Hufen, J.A.M. (1990), *Instrumenten in het technologiebeleid*, PhD dissertation, Leiden University.

Hulsink, W. and H. Schenk (1998), 'Privatisation and deregulation in the Netherlands', in D. Parker (ed.) *Privatisation in the European Union: Theory and Policy Persectives*, London: Routledge, pp. 242–57.

IG Metall (1999), *Website*, http://www.igmetall.de.

International Iron and Steel Institute (IISI) (various years), *World Steel in Figures*, Brussels.

International Labour Office (ILO) (1997), *The Iron and Steel Workforce of the Twenty-first Century: What it will be Like and How it will Work*, Geneva.

Iron and Steel Statistics Bureau (1999), *International Steel Statistics, Country Book Series: Germany*, London.

Jacobs, B. (1997), 'Networks, Partnerships and European Union Regional Economic Development, Initiatives in the West Midlands', *Policy and Politics*, 25 (1), 39–50.

Jänicke, M. (1990), *State Failure: The Impotence of Politics in Industrial Society*, University Park, PA: The Pennsylvania State University Press.

Katzenstein, P.J. (1984), *Corporatism and Change*, Ithaca: Cornell University Press.

Katzenstein, P.J. (1985), *Small States in World Markets*, Ithaca: Cornell University Press.

Kerz, S. (1991), *Bewältigung der Stahlkrisen in den USA, Japan und der Europäischen Gemeinschaft, insbesondere in der Bundesrepublik Deutschland*, Göttingen: Vandenhoeck und Ruprecht.

Kingdon, J.W. (1995), *Agendas, Alternatives and Public Policies*, 2nd edn, New York: Harper Collins.

Kleinknecht, A. (1998), 'Is labour market flexibility harmful to innovation?', *Cambridge Journal of Economics*, 22 (3), 387–96.

Krauss, E.S. and J. Pierre (1993), 'Targeting Resources for Industrial Change', in B.A. Rockman and R.K. Weaver (eds), *Do Institutions Matter? Government Capabilities in the United States and Abroad*, Washington, DC: The Brookings Institution, pp. 151–86.

Krupp (1999), 'Krupp: A Brief History', *http://www.krupp.com/gb98/eng/ueber.htm*.

Krupp and Thyssen (1999), 'Krupp and Thyssen: a future together', *http://www.krupp.com/gb98/eng/fusion.htm*.

Kuhn, Nicole (1998), 'Le rôle du gouvemement lors des privatisations', *Revue du Trésor*, 6, 307–20.

Kuuse, J. (1986), *Strukturomvandlingen och Arbetsmarknadens Organisering* (The Structural Change and the Organization of the Labour Market), Stockholm: Svenska Arbetsgivareföreningen.

L'Année Politique, Economique, Sociale et Diplomatique (various years), Paris: Editeur du Moniteur.

Lundgren, N. and I. Ståhl (1981), *Industripolitikens Spelregler* (The Rules of the Game in Industrial Policy), Stockholm: Industriförbundets Förlag.

Lynch, F.M.B. (1993), 'Restoring France: The Road to Integration', in A.S. Milward, F.M.B. Lynch, F. Romero, R. Ranieri and V. Sorensen, *The Frontiers of National Sovereignty. History and Theory 1945–1992*, London: Routledge, pp. 59–87.

Malaret i García, Elisenda (1991), *Régimen Juridico-Administrativo de la Reconversión Industrial*, Madrid: Civitas.

Maravall, José Mª. (1991), 'Democracia y social-democracia. Quince años de politica en España', *Sistema*, no. 900.

Marklew, V. (1995), 'The French Steel Industry', *Cash, Crisis and Corporate Governance: The Role of National Financial Systems in Industrial Restructuring*, Ann Arbour: University of Michigan Press, pp. 85–112.

Markusen, A. (1987), *Regions: The Economics and Politics of Territory*, Totowa, NJ: Rowman & Littlefield Publishers.

Mazey, S. (1998), 'The European Union and Women's Rights: From the Europeanisation of National Agendas to the Nationalisation of a European Agenda?', *Journal of European Public Policy*, 5 (1), 131–52.

Mboweni, T. (ed.) (1993), *Antitrust, Monopolies and Mergers*, Johannesburg: UWC Press.

McConnel, G. (1963), *Steel and the Presidency, 1962*, New York: W.W. Norton.

Mény, I. and V. Wright (eds) (1987), *The Politics of Steel: Western Europe and the Steel Industry in the Crisis Years: (1974–1984)*, New York: Walter de Gruyter.

Milner, Susan (1999), 'Trade Unions', in M. Cook and G. Davies (eds), *Modern France: Society in Transition*, London: Routledge, pp. 132–50.

Moinov, Stephan (1995), *Privatization in the Iron and Steel Industry*, Working Paper SAP 2.47/WP.93, ILO: Geneva.

Morris, Jonathan and Paul Blyton, Nick Bacon and Hans-Werner Franz (1992), 'Beyond survival: The implementation of new forms of work organisation in the UK and German steel industries', *International Journal of Human Resources*, 3 (2), 307–29.

Mourioux, Marie-Françoise and Rend Mourioux (1984), 'Unemployment Policy in France 1976–1982', in J. Richardson and R. Henning (eds), *Unemployment: Policy Responses of Western Democracies*, London: Sage, pp. 148–66.

Navarro, Mikel (1989), *Crisis y Reconversión de la Siderurgia Española: 1978–88*, Junta del Puerto de Pasajes, MOPU.

Oberender, P. and G. Rütger (1993), 'The Steel Industry: A Crisis of Adaptation' in H.W. de Jong (ed.), *The Structure of European Industry*, Dordrecht: Kluwer Academic, pp. 65–90.

O'Brien, P. (1994), 'Governance Systems in Steel: The American and Japanese Experiences', in J.R. Hollingsworth, P.C. Schmitter and W. Streek (eds), *Governing Capitalist Economies*, Oxford: Oxford University Press, pp. 43–71.

OECD (1993), *Economic Surveys: Netherlands 1992–1993*, Paris.

OECD (1995), *World Steel Trade Developments: A Statistical Analysis*, Paris.

Osborne, D. and T. Gaebler (1992), *Reinventing Government*, Reading, MA: Addison-Wesley.

Ovenden, K. (1978), *The Politics of Steel*, London: Macmillan.

Owen Smith, E. (1994), *The German Economy*, London: Routledge.

Padioleau, Jean Gustave (1981), *Quand la France s'Enferre: la Politique Sidérurgique de la France depuis 1945*, Paris: Presses Universitaires de France.

Parker, D. (ed.) (1998), *Privatisation in the European Union: Theory and Policy Perspectives*, London: Routledge.

Perrotti, Assunta Luisa (1995), 'La Gestione Comunitaria della Crisi della Siderurgia', in E.V. Heyden (ed.), *Administration Publique et Crise Éonomique*: *Yearbook of European Administrative History*, vol. 7, pp. 251–81

Pierre, J. (1986), *Partikongresser och Regeringspolitik* (Party Conferences and Public Policy), Lund: Kommunfakta Förlag.

Pierre, J. (1989), 'Public–Private Partnerships in Industrial Structural Change: The Case of Shipyard Closures in Sweden', *Statsvetenskaplig Tidskrift*, 200–209.

Pierre, J. (1995), 'Policy Diffused, Policy Confused?: The Politics of Regional Economic Development in Sweden', *Regional and Federal Studies*, 5, 173–97.

Pierre, J. (forthcoming), 'From Managing the State to Managing Contingencies: Changing Roles of the Senior Civil Service in Sweden', in E. Page and V. Wright (eds), *The Role of Senior Officials in the Modern State*, Oxford: Oxford University Press.

Rein, M. and D. Schön (1991), 'Frame-Reflective Policy Discourse', in P. Wagner, C.H. Weiss, B. Wittrock and H. Wollman (eds), *Social Sciences and Modern States: National Experiences and Theoretical Crossroads*, Cambridge: Cambridge University Press, pp. 262–89.

Rhodes, R.A.W. (1996), 'The New Governance: Governing Without Government', *Political Studies*, 44 (4), 652–67.

Richardson, J. (ed.) (1982), *Policy Styles in Western Europe*, London: Allen & Unwin.

Richardson, J. (1994), 'Doing Less by Doing More? British Government, 1979–1994', *West European Politics*, 17 (3).

Richardson, J. and A.G. Jordan (1979), *Governing Under Pressure*, Oxford: Martin Robertson.

Richardson, Jeremy, Gunnel Gustafflon and A. Grant Jordan (1982) 'The Concept of Policy Style', in J. Richardson (ed.), *Policy Styles in Western Europe*, London: Allen & Unwin, pp. 1–16.

Riksgäldskontoret (1992), *Invitation to acquire bonds in the Swedish Government Bond Loan nr 2001 and purchase rights in SSAB Swedish Steel Limited*, Stockholm: National Swedish Debt Office.

Rose, R. (1993), *Lesson-Drawing in Public Policy*, Chatham: Chatham House.

Ross, George (1996),'The Limits of Political Economy: Mitterrand and the Crisis of the French Left', in A. Daley (ed.), *The Mitterrand Era: Policy Alternatives and Political Mobilization in France*, New York: Macmillan, pp. 33–55.

Rydén, B. (ed.) (1983), *Power and Powerlessness*, Stockholm: SNS Förlag.

Sabatier, P.A. (1998), 'The Advocacy Coalition Framework: Revisions and Relevance for Europe', *Journal of European Public Policy*, 5 (1), 98–130.

Schenk, H. (ed.) (1987), *Industrial and Technology Policy: Analysis and Perspectives* (in Dutch), Groningen: Wolters-Noordhoff.

Schenk, H. (1993), 'West-European Industrial and Competition Policies: Content and Assessment', in T. Mboweni (ed.), *Antitrust, Monopolies and Mergers*, Johannesburg: UWC Press, pp. 1–37.

Schenk, H. (2001), *Mergers, Efficient Choice and International Competitiveness*, Cheltenham: Edward Elgar. (forthcoming).

Schmidt, Vivien Ann (1996a), *From State to Market? The Transformation of French Business and Government*, Cambridge: Cambridge University Press.

Schmidt, Vivien Ann (1996b), 'An End to French Economic Exceptionalism? The Transformation of Business under Mitterrand', in A. Daley (ed.), *The Mitterrand Era: Policy Alternatives and Political Mobilization in France*, New York: Macmillan, pp. 117–40.

Schmidt, Vivien Ann (1999), 'La France entre l'Europe et le Monde. Le Cas des Politiques Économiques Nationales', *Revue Française de Science Politique*, 49 (1), 51–78.

Schön, D.A. and M. Rein (1994), *Frame Reflection: Toward the Resolution of Intractable Policy Controversies*, New York: Basic Books.

Smith, W. Rand (1996), 'The Left's Response to Industrial Crisis: Restructuring in the Steel and Automobile Industries', in A. Daley (ed.), *The Mitterrand Era: Policy Alternatives and Political Mobilization in France*, New York: Macmillan, pp. 97–113.

Sölvell, Ö., I. Zander and M.E. Porter (1991), *Advantage Sweden*, Stockholm: Norstedts.

SOU 1977:15, *Handelsstålsindustrin inför 1980-talet*, Report from a Royal Commission.

Spierenburg, D. and R. Poidevin, (1994), *The History of the High Authority of the European Coal and Steel Community: Supranationality in Operation*, London: Weidenfeld & Nicolson.

SSAB (1998), *Årsredovisning 1998* (Annual Report 1998), Stockholm: SSAB.

Steel Times (1997–99), various articles.

Subirats, Joan and Ricard Gomá (1998), *Políticas Públicas en España*, Barcelona: Ariel.

Tellegen, J.W. and M. Brouwer (1998), *Industrial Policy* (in Dutch), The Hague: Welboom.

Thyssen (1999), *Geschichte des Unternehmens Thyssen*, http://www.thyssen.com/deutsch/thyssen/geschich/i-gesc4.htm.

Tsoukalis, L. and R. Strauss (1987), 'Community Policies on Steel, 1974–82: A Case of Collective Management', in Y. Mény and V. Wright (eds), *The Politics of Steel: Western Europe and the Steel Industry in the Crisis Years (1974–84)*, New York: Walter de Gruyter, pp. 186–221.

Upham, M. (1997), *Tempered Not Quenched: The History of the ISTC 1951–97*, London: Lawrence & Wishart.

Usinor Consultants (1995), *Le Secteur Sidérurgigue*, manuscript.

Usinor (1999), *Rapport Annuel 1998*, Paris.

Vaizey, J. (1974), *The History of British Steel*, London: Weidenfeld & Nicolson.

Van Witteloostuijn, A. (1999), *Anorexia Management: A critical analysis of downsizing* (in Dutch), Amsterdam: Arbeiderspers.

Van Zanden, Jan Luiten (1999), 'The Netherlands: the history of an empty box?' in J. Foreman-Peck and G. Federico (eds), *European Industrial Policy: the Twentieth Century Experiences*, Oxford: Oxford University Press, pp. 177–93.

Visser, J. and A. Hemerijck (1997), *'A Dutch Miracle': Job Growth, Welfare Reform and Corporatism in the Netherlands*, Amsterdam: Amsterdam University Press.

Vitols, S. (1993), *Industrial Relations and Restructuring in the German Steel Industry*, Social Science Research Centre Berlin Working Paper, FSI 93–302.

Wassenberg, A. (1983), *Dossier RSV: Diversions of Industrial Policy* (in Dutch), Leiden: Stenfert Kroese.

Weaver, R.K. (1985), *The Politics of Industrial Change*, Washington, DC: The Brookings Institution.

Weiss, L. (1998), *The Myth of the Powerless State*, Cambridge: Cambridge University Press.

Windmuller, J.P. (1969), *Labor Relations in the Netherlands*, Ithaca, NY: Cornell University Press.

Wirtschaftsvereiniging Eisen- und Stahlindustrie (1986), *Statistisches Jahrbuch der Eisen- und Stahlindustrie 1986*, Düsseldorf.

Wirtschaftsvereinigung Eisen- und Stahlindustrie (1987), *Flankenschutz durch die Politik bleibt unverzichtbar*, Düsseldorf.

Wirtschaftsvereiniging Eisen- und Stahlindustrie (1990), *Statistisches Jahrbuch der Eisen- und Stahlindustrie 1990*, Düsseldorf.

Wright, Vincent (1984), 'Industrial Policy-Making under the Mitterrand Presidency', *Government and Opposition*, 13 (3), 290–93.

Wright, Vincent (1990), 'The Nationalization and Privatization of French Public Enterprises, 1981–1988: Radical Ambitions, Diluted Programmes and Limited Impact', *Staatswissenschaften und Staatpraxis*, 2 (2), 176–201.

Wright, Vincent (1994), 'Reshaping the State: The Implications for Public Administration', *West European Politics*, 17 (3), 103–38.
Wright, Vincent (1998), 'La Fine del Dirigismo? La Francia negli Anni '90', *Stato e Mercato*, 54 (3), 51–387.
WRR, Wetenschappelijke Raad voor het Regeringsbeleid (1980), *Present position and future of Dutch industry* (in Dutch), The Hague: Staatsuitgeverij.

PART III

Managing reform: public policy and the health sector

10. Managing reform: controlling the medical profession in an era of austerity

Michael Moran

1   THE NATURE OF THE REFORM

Managing health care policy is a major concern of the modern state. For the states that are the subject of this book the reasons are encapsulated in Tables 10.1 and 10.2 below. The first table indicates the very substantial commitment of resources to health care made by all six nations in the 1990s and also the scale of growth in those commitments in the last generation. Not all these commitments involve state spending by any means, but states have assumed the dominant role in the management of health care systems. Table 10.2 provides a summary indicator of the scale of public commitment to health care provision and it explains as well as any summary measure can why states are so important: it shows that, by the late 1990s, the overwhelming proportion of populations in our states (and in a wide range of others, for that matter) were covered by government assured systems of health insurance. In summary: health care is big business and states are major players in the business.

Table 10.1 *The growth of health care spending since 1960 (% of GDP spent on health in the six country cases)*

	1960	1990	1997
France	4.2	8.9	9.6
Germany	4.8	8.7	10.4
Netherlands	3.8	8.3	8.6
Spain	1.5	6.9	7.4
Sweden	4.7	8.8	8.6
United Kingdom	3.9	6.0	6.7

Source: Anderson and Poullier (1999, p. 179).

Table 10.2 *Percentage of populations with government assured health insurance in the six country cases*

	1960	1997
France	76.3	99.5
Germany	85.0	92.2
Netherlands	71.0	72.0
Spain	54.0	99.8
Sweden	100.0	100.0
United Kingdom	100.0	100.0

Source: Anderson and Poullier (1999, p. 181).

But the significance of health care transcends even these impressive indicators of scale. In every one of the nations considered in this volume health care is a highly valued and expensive social good. Consequently, the political process in health care is a perpetual distributive struggle over the terms of access and the terms of funding. States provide the most important arenas where those struggles take place. The state's key role is magnified by another feature: the historically deep-rooted role of states, not only in the financing of health care services, but in their regulation and structuring. There are some obvious and striking indicators of the deep roots of this role. Modern health care systems are systems for the delivery of specialized personal services, and professions heavily dominate the institutions of delivery. Many of these professions (notably the most important of all, doctors, to whom we turn later) exist as professional configurations because occupational groups have formed distinctive relationships with states, and the changing fortune of those professions is in part a function of the changing historical character of that role. In short, the regulation of medical professionalism is a responsibility of states that transcends any financial responsibilities which states may have for the financing or the delivery of health care.

The origins of the development of health care as a valued consumption good lie in changes that came over medicine about a century ago. The application of knowledge generated by laboratory sciences and the use of the artefacts of modern technology produced a revolution in the therapeutic efficacy of medicine. Until about 100 years ago it was positively dangerous for most sick people to consult physicians; but the rise of modern scientific medicine changed that state of affairs. Medicine actually started to benefit the sick. The modern health care system differs greatly from its historical antecedent in the nineteenth century, which focused on *public* health rather than the treatment of individual complaints, and was closely tied to disciplines like civil engineering in its concerns with the regulation of public sanitation (De Swaan, 1988). The characteristic features of modern medicine – a concern with cure through science, and technology-based treatment – are the result of intellectual and social revolutions in which states played a key part. The most obvious example of this is the central role played by states in the historical emergence of medical technology industries (Foote, 1992), in particular as the result of the involvement of states in war, especially World War II. This historical turn has drawn states into health care systems in two ways: often as the promoters of innovation in medical care and, more often still, as regulators of medical technology in the interests of safety, medical efficacy, cost containment and the promotion of domestic medical technology industries.

These brief sketches are intended to highlight an outstandingly important feature of modern health care systems, one that makes the case of health care central to this book: health care institutions and the institutions of the state are bound together in a symbiotic relationship across the advanced industrial world. States have major policy-making responsibilities as the sources of finance, as the regulators of the key occupational groups that deliver health care and as the regulators of the scientific and technological infrastructure which underpins modern medicine.

The links between states and health care systems are historically deeply rooted, but the significance of those links has become greater over the epoch since the close of World War II. The reasons are again well known. The '30 glorious years' of growth in the advanced capitalist economies that soon followed the end of war also funded other kinds of growth, notably a great expansion in the scale of publicly funded welfare services. This was the golden age of the welfare state and, by extension, of the 'health care state' (Moran, 1999). In those decades most states constructed, or extended, schemes to provide universal, or near universal, coverage of their populations by a range of welfare services, of which health care services were central. The cost of this was paid, in the last analysis, from the proceeds of the '30 glorious years' – from the long boom in the capitalist economies which lasted more or less uninterrupted until the recession precipitated by the sharp rise in world oil prices following the Yom Kippur War in the autumn of 1973. In health care, states either paid for the cost of these expanded entitlements direct from the public purse, or else mandated the extraction of the cost from workers and employers through some systems of compulsory insurance. In the case of health care, resource commitments had, and continue to have, a sort of unstoppable momentum: demographic factors, such as the ageing of populations, advances in medical technology and the rising expectations of populations about what health care should deliver, all inexorably combine to push up the resource demands.

An obvious question arises: what happened when the 'thirty glorious years' came to an end, and states entered colder economic climates? This question lies at the root of the problématique examined in these chapters.

2   THE PROBLÉMATIQUE

In Bovens and 't Hart's original study of policy fiascoes the 'problématique' did not consist of some straightforward set of phenomena – fiascoes – which could be unambiguously identified by the observer as objective phenomena. The problématique was itself a kind of discursive construction: 'the interrelated crises of policymaking and policy science, as dramatized especially by the stream of widely publicized and recurrent instances of major government failures' (Bovens and 't Hart, 1996, p. 3). The problématique in the health care sector shares some of these complex characteristics: 'real' problems, arising out of objectively measurable resource constraints, subjected to a complex process of definition and redefinition by competing social interests. The starting point is one of the most influential of all discursive constructions of recent decades, the crisis of the welfare state. After the great shock of the end of the long boom in the 1970s, a large and influential literature developed which represented 'the welfare state in crisis' (reviewed in Moran, 1988). More than two decades later on we can see that part of the function of this literature of crisis was exactly that identified by Alford (1975) in his account of the function of 'crises' in struggles over health care policy: as a rhetorical construction intended to dramatize problems, and thus to be used as a resource by competing interests. One of the major sets of beneficiaries of the episode of 'crisis construction' in the welfare state were neoliberal critics of state intervention, who were able to represent welfare states as crisis-ridden because they were supposedly caught between contradictory imperatives – for instance, between those of economic efficiency and funding entitlements. Health care was particularly vulnerable to these neoliberal constructions of crisis, for the policy innovations of the long boom had in numerous instances converted health care into a free, or nearly free, service, whose consumption could be represented as unimpeded by any budget constraint on the part of the individual patient.

The complex interrelationship between the construction of 'crisis' and the progress of policy is well illustrated by the history of health care reform. Outside the United States – a health care system unique in its organization and in its problems – the years after the end of the long boom were actually years of comparative policy success. The leading health care systems of western Europe, far from being trapped in a crisis of consumption caused by the 'free' character of health care as a service, actually developed remarkably successful modes of cost containment, though naturally there were variations in the amount of success enjoyed.

Yet the language of crisis did not die away. Instead, the development of policy exhibited a superficially odd feature: as health care systems evolved mechanisms (notably various kinds of global budgets) successfully to cope with problems of cost containment, the pressure to reform actually intensified. The more apparently successful did policy systems become in coping with resource scarcity, the more the sense of crisis and the felt need for radical reform persisted: as the country case studies in the following chapters show, some of the critical reform episodes actually occurred in the later 1980s and 1990s, and some of the most dramatic reforms have been in systems (Britain is the outstanding example) which already seemed to be very well adjusted to living in a cold economic climate. What is more, although certainly not disconnected from issues of cost containment, the focus of these reform initiatives has been other than on the raw issue of containing costs.

That focus is reflected in the central theme that joins all the chapters on health policy: a concern with reforming the medical profession. Why has the 'problématique' taken this form? Or, to put it in other words, why has the construction of the problems of reforming health care systems so often turned, in whole or in part, into the problem of controlling doctors more effectively?

Some of the answers are obvious, and appear at the forefront of the policy narratives in the succeeding chapters. The development of comparatively successful mechanisms of cost containment did not mean that resource constraints disappeared: an international economy marked by increasingly globalized competition meant that the pressure on individual nations to search for macro and micro efficiency became increasingly intense. In the search to manage resources more effectively, doctors were in the front line, for reasons to do with features noted earlier, notably the central role historically occupied by the medical profession in health care services. Doctors are central to the management of resources for two linked reasons. First, as the profession that has historically been at the apex of health care systems, doctors are major direct consumers of resources; but, second, this has only been a part of the resource consumption picture, and in many respects the less important part, for the importance of doctors lies not primarily in what and how they are paid, but in the fact that their institutional and cultural dominance of health care institutions has given them the largest say in the allocation of resources. The centrality of doctors to resource allocation means that any serious attempt at reform of health care services must in the process tackle the question of the role to be occupied by doctors in health care institutions. Starr has eloquently described the general importance of the medical profession in his famous study of the United States:

The medical profession has an especially persuasive claim to authority. Unlike the law and clergy, it enjoys close bonds with modern science, and at least for most of the last century, scientific knowledge has held a privileged status in the hierarchy of belief. Even among the sciences, medicine occupies a special position. Its practitioners come into direct and intimate contact with people in their daily lives; they are present at the critical transitional moments of existence. They serve as intermediaries between science and private experience, interpreting personal troubles in the abstract language of scientific knowledge. (Starr, 1982, p. 4)

Thus far, the problématique is capable of construction in terms of a fairly simple policy chain: policy is focused on more effective control of resources at both the macro and the micro level; doctors are the single most important group in allocating resources; the effort to control resources by states soon leads to efforts to reform the medical profession. But the policy narratives that follow suggest concerns well beyond resource allocation, something particularly noticeable in the British and German cases. In other words, the forces driving reform of the medical profession are something more than an immediate concern on the part of states to exert more control over resources. The particular character of those forces best emerges in the individual chapters, but one common structural feature of the medical profession should be highlighted. The central, dominant role of the medical profession in the health care systems examined here is, we saw earlier, a historically engrained feature. Indeed, the dominion of medicine over other health care actors – including citizens and patients – is in large measure a pre-democratic creation. Part of the pressure for reform experienced by doctors is a reflection of the stress between interests consolidated under oligarchic systems of politics and the workings of more modern democratic systems of politics (an argument elaborated in Moran, 1999).

The 'problématique' in the case of the health care sector is therefore complex: born out of conceptions of health care as a manifestation of a wider 'crisis' of the welfare state, it has fixed on the reform of the medical profession long after the immediate moment of crisis has passed by. That is why, in the following cases, the critical question, irrespective of the objective condition of health care systems, is: what did the policy episode do to the medical profession?

3   THE CASES

The authors of these chapters were asked to focus on a key episode in the reform of the medical profession since the end of the 'long boom', to narrate that episode, to explain its outcome and to offer some assessment of the extent to which the episode had been accompanied by political or programmatic success. The particular episodes, therefore, were chosen by the authors themselves and represent the best estimate by country specialists of the episodes most worth concentrating upon. The *countries*, by contrast, were chosen by criteria outside the particular sphere of health care, representing the wider research design of the project reported in this book – a design outlined earlier by the editors. The mix of cases, however, represents most of the important types of health care system now existent in Europe. Three particularly important kinds are represented here:

1. *Mature tax-based national health services*, represented in the present mix by the United Kingdom and Sweden. Although the United Kingdom and Sweden differ markedly in their degree of geographic centralization (with the United Kingdom showing markedly more central control) they nevertheless constitute a distinct type. Resources are overwhelmingly raised through species of general taxation; entitlements, though not necessarily expressed in a formal language of citizenship, are in practice an outcome of citizenship rather than of either market power or occupational location. Just as resources are raised by administrative means, so the allocation of resources is heavily influenced by administrative modes of allocation. Indeed, so distinctive has this administrative mode been that some observers (Saltman and von Otter, 1992) have dubbed these 'command and control' systems. Some ancillary features further support this characterization – notably the extent to which the 'means of medical production' are publicly owned and controlled. However, under democratic politics such systems run the risk of openly politicizing the process of resource allocation and facing politicians with electorally explosive rationing choices. Thus there has been extensive reliance on a division of labour between the state and medical profession, in which states retain control over global resource allocation but delegate authority over clinical decisions (and thus everyday rationing) to doctors. An important subtext in the reform of the medical profession in these systems, therefore, concerns what is to happen to the division of labour between doctors and states over the rationing process.

2. Germany, the Netherlands and France represent *compulsory health insurance systems*, in varying forms. The institutional features of these three systems vary greatly: the Dutch system, as Trappenburg and De Groot's chapter shows, is a complex mosaic involving both public and private institutions; the French system is highly centralized, or at least nationalized; and the German system is marked by a high degree of territorial decentralization. But all three systems share key characteristics, of which two should be highlighted. First, financing is linked, via various forms of payroll taxes, to the occupational system, and to that degree reflects the stratification features of the occupational system. Second, non-state institutions, among both providers and financiers, have been historically dominant in the system. The prototypical example is Germany, the largest health care system in

Europe, where the Federal Republic that existed after 1949 for much of its history had only a residual regulatory role. In questions of reform, therefore, the critical issue has been how far some institutions of the state can acquire the capacity to assert authority over other historically entrenched institutions.

3. *Late developing national health service systems*, represented here by Spain, but arguably characterizing the wider family of Mediterranean health care systems in Europe (Ferrera, 1996). The Spanish system is to some degree consciously modelled on north European national health services, in some instances (for example, in the explicitness with which citizenship entitlements are spelt out) advancing on them (Guillén and Cabiedes, 1997). But two features obstruct the extent to which north European arrangements can be replicated, both connected to the late development of these systems. The first is obvious: the extension of health care entitlements in the British case took place at the very dawn of the '30 glorious years', and when harder times came from the middle of the 1970s the NHS was institutionalized; there existed a substantial public clientele; it was deeply embedded in the state machine; and it was connected to powerful professional and industrial interests. The inauguration of the Spanish system coincided, on the other hand, precisely with the more austere economic climate that succeeded the end of the long boom. But late development was also significant in a second sense: whereas the National Health Service systems of northern Europe had succeeded in displacing, or marginalizing, a range of private interests, such as doctors with extensive private practices, late developers have had to learn to live with these entrenched interests. Part of the story unfolding in our Spanish case study is about this latter consequence of late development.

Even these simple sketches alert us to a key feature of the policy processes described in the succeeding chapters: both the measure of success and failure, and the explanation of success and failure, have a highly contingent character, because the institutional and historical matrices within which reform efforts take place are very dependent on individual national context. The matter of success and failure is examined next.

4   MEASURING SUCCESS AND FAILURE

Perhaps more than in any other sector examined in this book, 'success' or 'failure' in the health sector involves a highly contingent set of judgments. Our authors, while working with the established distinction between *political* and *programmatic* success, have been obliged to fashion their own measures. The reasons for this may be summarized under three headings, and they all spring from the highly individual contexts examined here:

1. The time frames examined here are very different, in the sense both that the particular periods are often very different and that the amount of time which has elapsed since reform efforts were initiated is very different: they vary from the British case, where we have virtually a decade of experience to witness policy outcomes, to the Spanish case where much of the story is still unfolding. Yet notoriously, as the original study of policy fiascos showed, judgments about success and failure are highly sensitive to the moment when we make the judgment (Bovens and 't Hart, 1996, p. 21).

2. The policy objectives examined here are highly variable both in the degree to which they are explicit and in the degree to which they are ambitious. Some are explicitly focused on inducing identifiable changes in the condition of the medical profession – the particular instance with which the Dutch case opens being a good instance. In other cases (the German is the best example) reforms in the medical profession are part of a larger complex package aimed at wholesale restructuring of the wider health care system. In the British case complexity is greater still: not only are the episodes recounted by Harrison part of a long story of struggles for control over health care resources stretching back to the 1970s, but also the central episode – the reform following *Working for Patients* in 1989 – is inseparable from wider aspects of the Thatcherite reconstruction of interests in British society.

3. The resources and skills of the actors vary greatly between different national settings. Although these variations can in principle be incorporated into explanations of success and failure, they immensely complicate any attempt to arrive at any estimate of the contribution of different institutional settings or the skills of individuals to policy outcomes. To put the point a little starkly: both the British reforms and the German reforms can be interpreted as 'victories' for public policy makers over (at least sections of) the medical profession. But any policy maker attempting to confront the medical profession starts from very different points in the two systems. The establishment of the National Health Service in 1948, although it left doctors in positions of comparative power and privilege, nevertheless established the central state as the dominant actor in health care policy. By contrast, at just about the period when the NHS was being constructed, the postwar reconstruction of the German system was recreating arrangements which entrenched doctors, especially doctors in ambulatory practice, as the dominant actors in the system. German reformers faced a much more politically formidable opponent in the medical profession than did British reformers. The Seehofer reforms of the 1990s, discussed in Chapter 12,

amount to a much less comprehensive institutional reconstruction than was achieved in the decade in Britain; but in terms of moving successfully against a powerful medical profession, Seehofer's is arguably a more impressive achievement.

5   EXPLAINING SUCCESS AND FAILURE

If success and failure are 'malleable', explaining the two also involves highly contingent judgments. If explanations involve bias (as they surely do) all the explanations offered in these case studies across the different sectors exhibit different biases. Inevitably, specialists in health care policy are likely to fix on factors different from those invoked, even at a high level of generality, by students of, for instance, financial reform. What matters most to the project of which the health studies are only a part is the general conceptualization of the sources of success and failure. All that is possible, and probably desirable, in reviewing the health sector cases, is to anatomize the main explanatory accounts that recur. They may be summarized as follows:

- *Structural accounts*, which lay emphasis on the way policy is a more or less compelled response to structural forces driving health systems, notably forces (like demographic change) driving policy makers to search for solutions to problems such as resource scarcity. Every one of the cases examined here has these structural forces at least as an important background feature.
- *Agency-centred accounts*, which lay emphasis on the creative role, in particular, of elite individuals (or groups) with a strategic vision of change. Elements of such accounts come out of almost all the health policy narratives (which must of necessity describe what key individuals did at key moments) and in part out of the attempt to explain sudden and unexpected turns in policy outcomes, such as the apparent reversal of the German system's history of reform immobility in the Seehofer reforms.
- *Institutional accounts,* which tie success and failure to key organizational features of both the health care system and the wider state system. Wilsford, in Chapter 11, faced with a choice of explanatory possibilities, most obviously opts for a bias in favour of this sort of institutional account of policy outcomes.
- *Cultural accounts,* which rest heavily on identifiable aspects of national policy 'style'. This explanatory bias is particularly evident in Trappenburg and De Groot's policy history of the Dutch case, where the evolution of reform attempts is seen as highly constrained by the search for consensual solutions, and where the final evaluation of success or failure is also

conditioned by a (critical) judgment about the adequacy of this policy style as a means of bringing about significant structural reforms.

Harrison provides the fitting epilogue at the start of his chapter on Britain: 'The terms "success" and "failure" have rationalistic overtones; their usage is relative to the *intention* of an identifiable policy actor.' The intentions of the policy actors in the health sector of the different countries examined were obviously very diverse. Nevertheless, the history of health care policy had backed all into the same, or a similar, corner. To do anything serious by way of reform they had, in some way or another, to confront and face down the medical profession.

6   GLOSSARY

Admitting privileges
A system where selected doctors have entitlement to admit patients to institutional care.
Ambulatory care
Medical care of patients who do not require confinement – literally, care of the walking wounded.
Basic health care package
A pre-defined package of medical treatments identifying the boundaries of care covered by insurance systems.
Bed mountain
Colloquial description of the surplus of beds that exists in many health care systems.
Capitation payment
Payment per head per patient; a common alternative to fee-for-service (qv).
Clinical autonomy
The doctrine that doctors should enjoy freedom from external control in medical decision making.
Command and control
A summary description of health care systems that extract resources using state power and distribute resources by administrative decree.
Compulsory health insurance
Health funding from compulsory levies imposed, usually, on workers and employers (*see also* payroll taxes).
Co-payments
Contributions by patients to part of the cost of medical treatment.
Cost containment
The movement to restrict cost growth that has dominated health policy in all advanced industrial nations for 30 years.

Diagnosis-related groups
Classification of treatment procedures for purposes of establishing pre-set prices for reimbursement.

Fee-for-service
A payment system under which doctors bill for each separate medical procedure or service they perform on a patient.

Gatekeepers
Medical personnel who control access to specialist and hospital care; *see also* referral systems and general practitioner.

General practitioner
A physician, usually operating in the community, who cares for the general health of patients and who acts as a point of referral to specialists and hospitals.

Global budgets
Spending limits set in advance for all, or a specified part, of the health sector.

Health care state
A shorthand expression for the modern intertwining of state structures and health care systems.

Managed competition
The practice of simulating market competition in the supply of health care by establishing regulated contracts between purchasers and providers.

Medical technology industries
The industrial system that provides the physical artifacts for scientific medicine (qv).

National health service
A health care system defined by reliance on general taxation as the main source of funding.

Office doctors
Physicians who practise from their own surgeries (offices) in the community; *see also* solo practitioners.

Output pricing
System allocating fixed prices, for reimbursement, to all distinguished medical procedures.

Payroll taxes
Health insurance levies on individual workers, normally imposed by law and normally shared between individual workers and employers.

Primary care
Literally the first level of care; normally shorthand for medical care to patients beyond hospitals.

Private practice
Shorthand for forms of doctor practice organization where the physician operates as a private entrepreneur.

Purchaser–provider split

A system for separating purchase and provision of health care by obliging purchasers to negotiate contracts for health care delivery with providers.

Referral systems

Systems for referring patients from their first medical consultation to specialists and/or hospitals; *see also* gatekeepers.

Scientific medicine

The style of medicine that developed out of advances in laboratory medicine in the last quarter of the nineteenth century.

Solo practitioners

Doctors who operate their practices as single entrepreneurs.

Utilization review

A set of procedures for measuring and comparing the resource outcomes of clinical decisions.

11. Paradoxes of health care reform in France: state autonomy and policy paralysis

David Wilsford

1   INTRODUCTION

As in many developed countries, economic pressures have been bearing in on French health care policy makers for many years and, recently, increasingly so. In the health care domain, the apparent autonomy of the French state's structures and institutions ought to give it great leverage over reform. But it will be argued below that, in spite of apparent autonomy, the imperatives imbedded within the policy arena make the state's current structures very sticky indeed. That is, they are highly inelastic and therefore substantial reform is quite difficult to achieve. In health care, governance has failed in France.

If this first paradox is striking, that the strong Jacobin state in France is capable of only weak, ineffectual policy responses in health care, then it is also underlaid by a second paradox: underlying clear policy failure is a different bedrock of stability and success – all in all, a paradox upon a paradox. Stability lies in the consistent and persistent configuration of interests at play in the policy sector: doctors, patients, ancillary providers and drug companies. Stable too is the universe of comprehensive, ready and fairly high quality care, this over a relatively great period of time, most of the postwar period. The great reforms of the 1950s succeeded. The only problem is the cost!

2   STATE STRUCTURES AND ACTORS

In France, the main contours of the current health system were put into place in the period from 1945 to 1950, when national health insurance was extensively reformed and generalized. After the war, the ordinance of 19 October 1945 instituted a new and expanded social security system in three parts: retirement, family allowances and sickness. This ordinance completely replaced the significantly less extensive social security system that had been established in 1930 during the inter-war period.

Key decisions were made during this conjunctural moment that would affect the functioning and dysfunctioning of the system for many years to come. These decisions set the French health care system off upon its particular postwar policy path. Unlike the British, who established a national health service to be financed directly from tax revenues, the French chose to base their system on obligatory employer–employee contributory insurance. Unlike the British, who national-ized the whole of the medical corps, the French left private practitioners in place. And unlike the British, who established a strict hierarchical referral system between general practitioners who delivered ambulatory care and hospital-based specialists who delivered non-ambulatory care, the French left in place the generalist–specialist overlap in ambulatory care, just as they left in place the uncoordinated links between the ambulatory and hospital sectors.

These structures are still in place today. For ambulatory care, patients in France choose their physician freely (and may change as often as they wish), may seek care directly from general practitioners or specialists, and are reimbursed at fairly generous specified levels for payment of physician fees and for the cost of laboratory tests and prescription drugs. The physician, for her or his part, is free to prescribe any treatment she or he deems medically suitable. However, fee levels are strictly regulated through regular fee agreements that physician unions negotiate with the sickness funds. Rodwin (1982), in particular, has been quite critical of the suboptimality of this system.

Unlike the free market place of ambulatory care (which does *not* lead to effi-ciencies), the French national hospital system is centrally directed from the ministry of health in Paris. 'Private' practitioners (all those in the ambulatory sector) do not enjoy admitting privileges to French hospitals as their American counterparts do in the United States. When patients are admitted for hospital care, the medical dossier passes from the private practitioner – generalist or specialist – to the full-time hospital medical staff. These hospital doctors are paid on a salaried basis and are considered professional civil servants of the French state. Hospital budgets are fixed by the ministry of health on a prospective global envelope basis with little connection to the type or quantity of services that a given hospital medical staff might think it medically appropriate to deliver in any given case.

Clearly, therefore, in the ambulatory sector – unlike the hospital sector – there are few if any incentives to economize, as there are no central controls on patients or doctors. One persistent subtext to the French story is that it is sub-optimally user-driven in the ambulatory sector.

By contrast, there are strong incentives to economize in the hospital sector under the centrally directed global budget procedure. Since that procedure was adopted in 1983, growth rates of hospital expenditures have stabilized and even dropped significantly. In 1992, hospital expenditures as a percentage of total health care expenditures in France had dropped from 51.8 per cent to 46 per cent (a decrease of 11.2 per cent). Ambulatory care expenditures, however, as a percentage of the total had increased by 16.8 per cent from 24.7 per cent of the total to 28.8 per cent, and pharmaceutical expenditures had increased from 17.3 per cent to 17.8 per cent of the total. Overall during this period from 1983 to 1992, total French health care expenditures increased from 7.4 per cent of GDP to 9.1 per cent, putting France in a middle-range category for OECD countries, doing a little worse than the Germans (8.5 per cent), a little better than the Canadians (10.0), much better than the Americans (13.4), but much worse than the British and the Japanese (both spending 6.6 per cent of GDP on health care) (CREDES, 1993; OECD, 1993).

The Focal Point: The Sickness Fund

The administrative focal point of the whole French health care system under national health insurance is the national sickness fund (*Caisse nationale d'assurance maladie des travailleurs salariés*, or CNAMTS). This fund does not alone comprise the whole system. A separate fund for agricultural workers and others for the independent professions, government employees, the merchant marine and so on cover altogether perhaps 20 per cent of the French population. But, since it alone covers 80 per cent, the national sickness fund is clearly the dominant player and sets the tone for the other funds in negotiations with providers, in particular. Virtually the entire population of France, over 99 per cent, is covered by national health insurance in one form or another.

Traditionally, the national sickness fund fixes all general policy – often at the direction of the central government – regarding levels of contribution, levels of reimbursement and levels of charges and fees. It also generally oversees the administration of the system. The national sickness fund is also responsible for the general financial equilibrium of the system, a task that has become increasingly difficult with each year. Given that French health care is an employer-based insurance system, revenues are generated by employer and employee payroll taxes which are determined as a proportion of salaries. In 1994, the levels of payroll withholding (*cotisation*) for national health insurance were respectively 12.8 per cent of the salary from the employer and 6.8 per cent from the employee. Retirees are subject to lower levels of withholding on their pensions. Overall, national health insurance directly covers about three-quarters of personal health expenditures in France.

This sickness fund is considered a quasi-public agency, as opposed to an integrated organ of the state, as it is governed by a board composed equally of elected representatives of labour and management in France. In truth, all the laws framing the sickness funds' operations reserve ultimate authority to the French state, which increasingly intervenes in the funds' decision making.

'Autonomous' State Structures

While the administrative focal point of the French system is the national sickness fund, the decisional focal point is not. Rather, the centralized French bureaucracy continues to exert almost total control over each key aspect of the health care system. In this, the French state acts principally through two ministries, social affairs (which includes health) and finance.

In France, the state structures that govern the health care sector are relatively homogeneous, with clearly defined agendas. They also benefit from clear, effective policy instruments which give them a certain number of 'tactical advantages' against actors from society, especially organized medicine (cf. Wilsford, 1988, 1989). By contrast, state structures in a country such as the United States are much more dispersed, heterogeneous and operate upon less well-defined policy agendas. Also broad consensus over the health care agenda has been far clearer in France than in the United States. French state institutions in health care are therefore clearly characterized by what Atkinson and Coleman (1989, p. 52) have called state autonomy at the sectoral level.

The whole French health care system is, at least in theory, quite rationally organized with elaborate hierarchical structures, deliberate planning procedures and clear lines of responsibility and mission. Formally, the central government assumes responsibility for general public health, such as prevention, planning and preparedness, and the fight against widespread sociomedical problems (for example, drug addiction or alcoholism). It organizes the training of health care personnel, participates in the regulation of their practice conditions and serves as a watchdog over the norms of quality and security of health care establishments and pharmaceutical production. It also ensures that health care services, including prevention, are adequate to need and regulates the volume of available health care services: personnel, establishments, medical equipment and marketing authorization for drugs. Of utmost importance here, the state exercises regulatory authority over social protection, intervening actively in the means and methods of finance (assessment and rates of contribution), in the rules that govern the coverage available to the population, in its relations with the producers of health care services, in the levels of coverage of health care services (prices and levels of reimbursement) and tries to ensure the equilibrium of social welfare programmes (cf. Duriez and Sandier, 1994).

At the national level, the ministry for social affairs and health is the most important government actor in the health care system. But other French ministries also regularly intervene in health care. The ministry of finance is of primary and regular importance when the budget is being drawn up and when social security deficits are being confronted. The ministry of national education controls medical training, including the number of physicians permitted to graduate from French medical schools and in what specialities. The ministry of industry plays an important role in setting drug prices.

This description of the French state in the health policy domain clearly points to a state whose structures are strong, whose mandate and agenda are clear, and whose civil servants pursue their mission with zeal and coherence. This pattern remarkably resembles what Atkinson and Coleman (1989, p. 59) defined as the 'state-directed' policy network. In this network,

> with little warning and sometimes with little explanation, the state embarks upon economic projects that have serious repercussions for the investment decisions of business. Business is typically divided and, in any event, considered untrustworthy by officials. Politicians and bureaucrats are often self-righteous and manipulative. Officials are not in the mood for concertation, and they are by no means neutral with respect to outcomes and instrumentalities. The political–administrative style is one of managerial directive followed by a polite briefing. Business–state relations are barely cordial.

Nonetheless, we will see that these state structures, autonomous as they may be, are definitely not omnipotent. In particular, historically fundamental policy decisions have laid out suboptimal structural arrangements that constitute a powerful drag on reform efforts that attempt to lay out new, more optimal policy paths.

3   SOCIETAL INTERESTS AT PLAY

As with any issue, the state and its institutions interact more or less aggressively with interests from society, who more or less effectively press their policy demands upon the state. From the society end of the equation, we will concentrate on the providers of health care services – physicians and hospitals – and the consumers, the French public.

Doctors as Medical Corps: Heterogeneous and Poorly Organized, but Definitely Entrenched

As in any developed country characterized by increasingly complex and sophisticated health care systems, the medical profession in France has evolved into a highly heterogeneous mix of private practitioners, specialists and generalists, civil service hospital staff, biomedical researchers, older and younger generations and increasing numbers of women. In general, French medical doctors, like other French workers, are not highly unionized. Most are apathetic to political organizing, although, like most French, this does not mean that they do not hold highly distinct political opinions quite deeply.

Doctors as Organized Medicine: Highly Divided and Divisive

Abetting the state's dominance in making health care policy in France is the historical weakness of organized medicine as a political force. It has been weak since the earliest days of the nineteenth century because medicine has, except for the occasional moment, been deeply fragmented organizationally and poorly mobilized politically. These organizational variables cut across the generic imperatives imbedded within the 'professions,' such as technical expertise, which establishes the doctor as the strategically key figure in the health care system. Organizational variables are particularly important when professionals must mobilize politically and especially in the face of strong, focused opposition. Therefore, in the French case, fragmentation and poor mobilization have weakened the influence of organized medicine, and by extension the profession as a whole, in the health policy universe. What is worse, organized medicine in France is riven by internal conflicts that manifest themselves in *competing* professional associations that are in turn plagued by very low membership levels.

Both division and divisiveness, we will see, are deeply rooted in the history of the medical profession in France. These two dimensions will be referred to together under the rubric of 'interest mobilization.' To what extent are the interests in the sector under study characterized by unitary organization ('peak association'?), high rate of membership, sufficient resources for collecting and analysing political and technical information, and the ability of the organization to speak authoritatively with the government on behalf of its members? This last characteristic means that the association can negotiate effectively with the government because it can ensure the cooperation of members in implementing any accord that it reaches with the state authorities (cf. Atkinson and Coleman, 1989).

Along these dimensions, the fragmentation of the French medical profession and its organizational weakness are striking. The first form this fragmentation takes is a splintering of organized medicine into competing medical *unions,* as well as into functional divisions. There are today three major medical unions that compete with each other to represent private practitioners, both generalists and specialists. A number of minor unions exist as well. In addition, there are a number of other unions representing the hospital and salaried sectors, often in competition with each other.

The oldest and largest medical association representing private practitioners in France is the Confédération des Syndicats Médicaux Français (CSMF). It was founded in 1928 and had momentarily consolidated a tenuous pre-eminence by 1930. One of the most persistent problematics facing the CSMF is how to handle the competing pressures, both internally and externally, of union forces within the medical profession that compete against it. By the 1980s, the CSMF had managed to consolidate a truce of sorts with its main rival, the Fédération des Médecins de France (FMF), enabling it to cooperate, or at least coordinate its activities, with the rival group. Yet, by the end of the 1980s, an antagonistic sentiment among general practitioners within the CSMF had grown so strong that a new rival union split off and regrouped under the label MG France, for *médecins généralistes de France*. This group began in a small number of provincial departments and within two or three years had gathered great strength and was represented in most departments nationally. In the universe of medical profession forces, MG France was considerably reinforced when in 1989 the minister of social affairs designated it a 'representative' union, that is, granted it official status for fee negotiations.

In France, there are additional dimensions of fragmentation that character-ize the medical corps as well. The first is common to all advanced health systems, the segmentation of the medical corps into general practitioners, the various and diverse medical specialities, hospital staff and the biomedical research community. This functional segmentation is one centrifugal force damaging to the unity of the medical corps. In some countries, such as Germany, Japan or the United States, the profession's political structures have done a better, but not perfect, job of containing these centrifugal forces. In France, they have not.

Moreover, the French medical profession is also fragmented demographi-cally in the face of a very high supply of physicians. Generational fragmentation (young versus old) pits older, more established doctors against young, struggling doctors in a resource environment characterized by extreme scarcity. Young doctors in France face great difficulties establishing a practice. Further, all doctors, young and old, compete with each other for patients who are perfectly willing to 'shop around'. The shopping takes the form of seeking the physician who will provide the desired treatment: the right prescription drugs, the authorized medical leave from work, the better bedside manner, and so forth. French physicians also operate within a fee-for-service structure characterized by very low fees, but without limits on the number of services delivered for which they may charge these fees.

Local Interests and the Hospitals

Other structural interests at play clearly work against the collective rationality of the French health care system in spite of its highly rational structure as outlined theoretically. In particular, while in theory the hospital system is centrally directed from the ministry of health in Paris, in reality each individual hospital also occupies the corner of an iron triangle which includes the local municipality (usually through the mayor) and the electoral–bureaucratic pork barrel process in Paris. This triangle often works to protect the interests of the hospital in the individual locality, even when the collective interest is not served, especially through bed or medical equipment over-capacity. Frequently, the mayor or his agent chairs the local hospital's administrative council (*conseil d'administration*). This mayor is also often a deputy or senator in Parliament, especially if it is a medium or large city. Longstanding, complex patterns of patronage work to shore up the local hospital's position vis-à-vis the health bureaucrats in Paris, who might otherwise wish to not favour that local hospital in terms of beds or physical or technological infrastructure.

The French Public: Consumers of Health Care

Finally, as we have indicated above, the French health care system awards a remarkable degree of freedom of choice to patients regarding ambulatory and hospital care – between doctors, between generalists and specialists, between the ambulatory sector and the hospital sector, between hospitals overall, between public hospitals and private hospitals.

   In such a system, there are no controls over the amount of health care services that are consumed, much less over the level of services that is medically appropriate. From 1981 to 1991, the number of office and home visits per capita per year increased from 5.5 to 8.0. From 1983 to 1989, the number of pathological and biological tests performed per capita increased from 78.8 to 145.4. And from 1982 to 1990, the amount of prescription drugs consumed per capita rose from 29 units to 38 (OECD, 1993).

4   STICKY STRUCTURES: PATH DEPENDENCY IN THE ABSENCE OF CONJUNCTURE

Wilsford (1995) explored cross-nationally the path-dependent character of most policy making in health care (and indeed in other policy domains). A path-dependent sequence of political changes is one that is tied to previous decisions and the existing institutions that these decisions have put into place. In path dependency, structural forces dominate, therefore policy movement is most likely to be incremental. Strong conjunctural forces are required to move policy further away from the existing path onto any new trajectory. It is the combination of path-dependent limits along with occasional windows of exceptional opportunity, or conjunctures, that determines the ways, small or big, in which a political system responds to policy imperatives.

In economics, the notion describes the interaction of state-dependent individual decision making in a decentralized decision-making network that leads to path-dependent collective decision outcomes. Individual decision making early on in the path may lead to 'lock-in' of a pattern that is collectively suboptimal. Each decision-making moment constitutes a powerful focusing device for subsequent decision making. As time unfolds, clearly, the probability of continuing along the same path increases, while the probability of significantly deviating from the established path, or even striking out upon a new path entirely, decreases (David, 1985, 1989).

The notion of path dependency is especially suitable for explaining long periods of essentially non-incremental policy making, or policy making without big change. On the other hand, path dependency explanations of policy evolution can obviously not accommodate the occasional occurrence of rather big changes from the established policy path, which are often associated with seemingly unpredictable contingencies in the policy environment. The key lies in the interplay of on-going, long-term institutions with conjunctures. These are the distinctive short-term mixes of fluid contingencies with sticky structures.

Conjunctures are the fleeting coming together of a number of diverse elements into a new, single combination. Being fleeting, in the grand scheme of history, conjunctures may change quite rapidly. By the same token, while the effects of structures are more predictable (given their long-term character), the effects of conjunctures are very unpredictable. The actual coming together of a propitious conjuncture in itself is perhaps the most highly unpredictable element of all – both as to when it will occur (timing) and as to whether it will occur at all (actuality) (cf. Wilsford, 1985). As yet, there is no theory of conjuncture.

Put another way, structures are the institutions and processes that form the infrastructural framework for policy (decisions) within which dynamic events unfold over time. This may be thought of as an endogenous universe, one characterized by sticky stasis, which then may be subject to exogenous shocks that suddenly introduce dynamic fluidity; that is, conjunctures (either positive or negative) that comprise distinctive mixes of contingencies and structures. These conjunctures may or may not provide opportunites for big change.

History of French Health Care Structures

We may divide the postwar history of French health care policy making into two periods. In the first, from the 1950s to the early 1960s, the state established and reinforced its dominance (cf. Wilsford, 1992). In the second period, from roughly the 1970s to the present, the state's attempts to reform structures and processes (in order to control expenditures and the medical decisions that ultimately determine expenditure) have been largely stymied. This period is characterized by persistent suboptimality, especially in ambulatory care: no gatekeeping to control access to the more expensive specialists, continued reliance on a fee-for-service system to remunerate private practice doctors, high levels of prescription drug consumption, and multiplication of consultations, tests and other fee-for-service acts. In short, during this second period, policy rationality has been in short supply, but not through lack of trying.

For many years, French governments of both the left and the right have grappled with the vexing problems of health care reform. In 1983, for example, the socialist government proposed the Plan Bérégovoy which froze physician fees and pharmaceutical prices and put into place the global budgeting method for hospital financing. In 1986, the Plan Séguin instituted a variety of measures mostly designed to exact more co-payments (*tickets modérateurs*) from patients for hospital stays and drug reimbursements. (It also eliminated the franking privilege that all French citizens enjoyed when sending in reimbursement forms to the sickness fund!) And throughout the 1980s and 1990s, the sickness fund has been extremely stingy with fee increases for private practitioners, who work on a fee-for-service basis, and the government has been equally stingly regarding approved prices for prescription drugs. Yet year after year, after momentary stability, high growth in total expenditures resumes and the social security accounts dive back into the red.

The results of reform have been so poor in France because most reform has been tied closely to the habitual path of French health policy, where the structures of the system allow uncontrolled use of the system, leading in turn to higher, uncontrollable expenditures. These structures have proved highly inelastic. In the ambulatory sector every reform effort left intact, for example, the fee-for-service system of physician remuneration. And while, indeed, the sickness fund has been stingy with increases, the medical corps has responded by multiplying the number of services rendered, as we have seen above. Equally important, there is no gatekeeping of use in the ambulatory sector. French citizens are free to consult with any and as many doctors as they wish. In all this, the patient has the legal right to be reimbursed at the specified levels for each and every consultation and for all the drugs prescribed.

The 1984 Reform of Hospital Financing

However, in all this, one example of truly big change within the French system was the reform of hospital financing in 1984, and it was the only one able to meet the goals set out for it: stabilization of hospital expenditures. What enabled this non-incremental reform to set hospital financing onto a trajectory far from its habitual path, overcoming the inelasticity of sticky structures?

Here, precisely, the crucial variable was conjunctural. Social security deficits were nothing new, but became a particularly salient target when the leftist government in power executed an economic policy U-turn in 1983. After two years of disastrous experimentation, when France tried to spend its way alone out of an American-led global recession, the government announced a severe new austerity policy. Within the social security system, the health accounts constitute by far the largest component, and they typically run in the red far more than the other social security accounts (pensions, unemployment and family allowances). Within the health accounts, the hospital sector presents a particularly inviting target. Hospital financing is centrally controlled by the ministry of health (under the watchful eye of the finance ministry); in the early 1980s, hospital expenditures had been growing at a particularly alarming rate under a per bed, per day financing mechanism (wherein the incentives clearly drive hospitals and their doctors to fill as many beds as possible with as many patients as possible for as long as possible). In the period from 1975 to 1982, French hospital expenditures as a percentage of total medical consumption had risen from 46.0 per cent to 51.8 per cent.

At the time of the 1983 austerity policy, a new director of hospitals was also named by the government. Jean de Kervasdoué, a civil administrator sympathetic to the socialists, took over the post from a communist, Jack Ralite. Kervasdoué proved to be an especially tenacious reformer. Completely revamping the hospital financing system, he instituted a system of anticipatory global budgeting: Each hospital was given an 'envelope' for the year, a fixed lump sum out of which it had to pay all of its operating and capital expenses.

The hue-and-cry from the largely conservative hospital medical corps was loud and long. But with the unwavering support of a socialist government (which did not care much for conservative doctors anyway) preoccupied with digging the country out of near financial ruin (therefore willing to be severe with measures that would reduce and control expenditures), Kervasdoué succeeded where others had feared to tread. In this story of successful departure from a traditional but suboptimal path, Kervasdoué benefited from a favourable conjuncture and was smart enough to make the most of his structurally strategic position at the head of the centralized national hospital system (cf. Wilsford, 1995). The results were impressive: from 1984 to 1988, French hospital expenditures as a percentage of total medical consumption fell from 50.8 per cent to 46.9 per cent. From 1988 to 1992, they continued to decline slightly, from 46.9 per cent to 46.0 per cent (CREDES, 1993).

But unlike hospitals in France, the ambulatory care system is neither centralized nor hierarchically structured.

5   THE POLICY PROGNOSIS: RESULTS OR NON-RESULTS

Since the mid-1970s, France, like many other countries, has experienced a slowing of economic growth and an increase in levels of unemployment and, until very recently, it was largely left out of the economic boom originating in the United States that dates from 1995. Both phenomena have affected the contributions to the social security system because these are based on workers' incomes. Assuring the financial equilibrium of the various health care regimes is therefore a primary preoccupation of the public authorities. The various reform attempts made up to the present have so far done little to introduce major changes in the organization of health care in France. This is because, in fact, these measures have heretofore only touched on the margins of the fundamental elements of the system: the preponderant role of national health insurance, the coexistence of public and private sectors, widespread private practice medicine, the patient's freedom of choice and the doctor's freedom of treatment without restraint in the ambulatory sector (clinical autonomy).

Other policies have reduced the level of collective coverage for different areas of medical consumption. These measures aim to slow the demand for health care services by increasing the financial participation of the patient. Among these measures are the increase in co-payments for certain pharmaceutical products, for physical therapy and for laboratory tests, the implementation of a hospital day charge to be paid by the patient, the extension of fee exemptions to private practitioners in Sector 2 (not subject to the negotiated fee schedules) and a limiting of special illnesses that qualify for 100 per cent coverage. It is, however, impossible to quantify the exact impact of these various policies or to estimate whether or not they have worked to avoid unnecessary medical consumption without, at the same time, limiting access to care which is justifiable. Anecdotal evidence indicates clearly that medical consumption has not diminished at all; neither has access to care.

Other policies have also had mixed results. For example, the adoption of the global budget system for public hospitals has greatly slowed the growth in hospital expenditures. Negotiations between national health insurance officials and representatives from the health care professions have limited the growth in medical fees to the levels of general inflation, but aggregate remuneration of the medical corps as a whole has risen as a result of the multiplication of acts. Likewise, pharmaceutical prices in France have been kept very low, but overall pharmaceutical consumption is up. Agreements for 'moderation' have been signed with nurses, biological laboratories and private clinics, but enforcement of moderation is not specified. Recent national agreements (*conventions*) have also set annual targets for medical services. If these targets are exceeded, the agreements provide for reimbursement to the national health insurance system or for downward adjustments in fees charged, a very substantial reform. But these agreements were declared void by the French courts.

Nonetheless, in spite of all these measures, the financial difficulties of the national health insurance system that result from the poor economic situation remain. Yet another significant attempt at reform was undertaken in 1993–4 that contained three significant new provisions, although in the event they proved highly problematic:

1. the application of utilization guidelines (*références médicales*) to a disease, a technique or a treatment, aiming to help the physician use the most appropriate health care services. But these guidelines remained indicative, not mandatory;
2. the creation of a permanent patient file, to be carried on a credit card-sized health card containing a computer chip, was to permit the treating physician to avoid contradictory or redundant prescriptions. But this measure fell foul of public hostility to 'authoritarian' government oversight;
3. the setting of a preliminary annual target (an increase of 3.4 per cent for 1994) for the growth in total private practice fees and prescriptions. But in practice these targets have been regularly exceeded.

6   AUTONOMY VERSUS PARALYSIS: STICKY STRUCTURES TRIUMPH OVER POLICY IMPERATIVES

Clearly, structural changes in the delivery of ambulatory care services are the most pressing need in France. Unrestricted freedom of choice for the patient and unrestricted freedom of prescription for the doctor (clinical autonomy) mean that a third of total expenditures escape any regulation or control whatsoever. The entrenched character of the ambulatory sector (widely supported by both patients and doctors) weighs very heavily against non-incremental reform efforts, in spite of a virtual consensus among bureaucratic elites that non-incremental change is very long overdue.

Let us define the optimal policy solution in health care to be one which works more or less to assure (a) relatively high access to (b) fairly comprehensive coverage while (c) not breaking the bank. For the OECD countries, generally, this constitutes (a) covering about all of the population with (b) major ambulatory, hospital and prescription drug benefits, while (c) spending about 6 to 9 per cent of GDP on health care with (d) rates of growth in expenditure that are fairly flat as percentages of GDP.

In France, in the absence of a powerful, compelling conjuncture, private practitioners are still paid on a hopelessly suboptimal fee-for-service basis. Worse, there is still no gatekeeping of patients seeking treatment and there is still no overall coordination of treatment patterns for ambulatory medicine. Even in the highly centralized French system, where strategically placed bureaucrats execute their health care mission with great determination and zeal, the hand of history is noticeable and makes a difference.

What conjuncture might come together to permit non-incremental change in the ambulatory sector and among hospital structural relationships? Clearly, for big change in the face of widespread support for the current system among both patients and doctors, the French government must invest a great amount of political capital in order to achieve health care reform.

In 1995, Jacques Chirac won the French presidency at the close of 14 long years of François Mitterrand's reign. Would conjunctural conditions now prove sufficiently different to provide Chirac with fresh, strong leverage for a fundamental overhaul of the system? Upon assuming office in May 1995, Chirac appointed Alain Juppé, a long-time confidant and 'politico-technocrat', to the prime ministership. In the autumn of 1995, Juppé unveiled a proposal for vast reform of the social welfare system. In addition to seeking health care reform, he also proposed to rein in the very generous retirement benefits of public sector workers. This latter proposal ignited a dramatic three-week period of strikes throughout France in December 1995, especially concentrated in the transport sector, paralysing Paris and some other major regional centres.

The Juppé government backed down on pension reform, but held firm to the health care proposals, which were passed into law in April 1996. They called for the total social security budget to be fixed in advance annually by parliamentary vote, removing this prerogative from the sickness funds. In the ambulatory sector, patients who accepted new gatekeeping powers of their general practitioner would be reimbursed at higher levels than those that went directly to specialists or that changed GPs frequently. And, for private practitioners, financial penalties would be imposed if overall spending targets were exceeded in a given year.

Three of the main doctors' unions, the CSMF and the FMF among them, opposed the government's reforms and organized a number of public demonstrations and even a 'strike' in April 1996 – to little apparent avail, for the major union representing general practitioners, MG France, pointedly supported the government, for it had long been militating for measures increasing general practitioners' influence in the health care system. Furthermore, French public opinion showed little support for the medical unions opposing the reforms.

Juppé's structural reforms in ambulatory care were greater than any ever attempted before, but they foundered in the face of highly imperfect implementation and the unfavourable conjuncture of the disastrous results of the May 1997 snap legislative elections. The Juppé government was replaced by a socialist one led by Lionel Jospin. As Juppé had intended, ceilings of future health care expenditures were indeed fixed by the Parliament, but these remained indicative not mandatory. GP gatekeeping measures were not implemented and financial penalties were not imposed on spendthrift doctors.

In the Jospin government, Martine Aubry was given the health care porfolio (along with social affairs and employment) and she set out to grapple with the same intractable policy problems. Similar solutions were proposed; no progress has been made. All this, in a policy environment of 'dérapage de dépenses' in spite of efforts to assume greater and greater direct control from the centre, imposing measures designed to rein in health care spending while not having nearly the desired effect.

In the case of Mme Aubry, it is singularly remarkable that she was able to impose a 35-hour working week upon extremely hostile private sector employers, and with little help from decidedly lukewarm labour unions. But that policy effectiveness has proved lacking in health care, just as it was to her predecessors. In employment policy, both she and the government chose to invest tremendous political capital in the 35-hour working week.

It would therefore be mistaken to speak of 'policy paralysis' in the industrial and employment policy domains, but the term describes accurately the state of affairs in health policy, despite powerful efforts to the contrary. This represents the ultimate paradox of French policy making in health care.

In the French health care policy arena, the state is theoretically powerful, but paradoxically ineffective. It is ineffective because, in spite of its political powers, the state is tied to path dependency, especially when powerful social interests get involved. Equally paradoxical, organized medicine is politically weak when it comes to improving its own economic lot, while it is at the same time structurally powerful in defending the status quo of clinical autonomy and its traditional fee-for-service remuneration system.

The structures are very sticky and no encompassing conjuncture has yet crystallized to enable non-incremental reform to triumph over them. Governance in the French health care domain has therefore failed.

12. Medical reform in Germany: the 1993 health care legislation as an impromptu success

Viola Burau

1 INTRODUCTION

In the case of Germany, health policy since the end of the long boom (Moran, 1990) has been characterized by a succession of health care reforms aimed at cost containment.[1] However, these policy initiatives have largely been perceived as a failure, considering that their programmatic success has only been short-term and that they lacked 'structural reform'.[2] Health policy appeared to be locked into 'reform blockades' (cf. Rosewitz and Webber, 1992). These were seen to originate from the institutional characteristics of health governance. As decision-making powers are dispersed among a multitude of mainly non-state actors across different levels, federal government has little direct influence on health care. Moreover, through the joint self-administration with the insurance funds, doctors are at the heart of the governance of health care. Thus it is difficult to address the relationship between economic and medical rationality in the context of reform.

Against this background the 1993 health care legislation, the so-called *Gesundheitsstrukturgesetz*, came as something of a surprise. The policy process was speedy, and succeeded at establishing and maintaining a cross-party consensus, while excluding organized interests. The structural reform itself was widely heralded as a success (cf. Bandelow, 1994; Reiners, 1993). In political terms it was seen to have re-established the ability of government to act, in spite of the opposition by the medical profession. This was also reflected in programmatic terms in that the reform combined temporary measures of cost containment with structural changes, such as limiting the number of office-based doctors or introducing diagnosis-related payments for hospital services. While many of these measures built on previous policies or debates about reform, their scope was significant and new. As such they were part of a gradual move from macro measures to restrict expenditure, to micro measures which aim to influence the practice of doctors itself. The prima facie success of this reform stands in marked contrast to the previous reform initiatives, and as such the 1993 structural reform provides an interesting episode when exploring the success and failure in the governance of German health care.

2　THE ACTORS IN HEALTH CARE

The actors central to health care in Germany are the state, insurance funds as the third-party payers of health care and doctors themselves. This section outlines how they are organized, while the following analyses the institutional context of health care governance in which they operate.

The state primarily comprises the federal government and more specifically the federal ministry of health (*Bundesministerium für Gesundheit*). Its role is largely regulatory in nature and it provides the statutory framework in which insurance funds and providers operate.[3] The limited role of government is a corollary of the fact that health care is financed by statutory but independent insurance funds, and that the governance of health care is dominated by different forms of self-administration (*Selbstverwaltung*).[4] However, the legitimacy of a more interventionist role of the federal government increases if the institutions of self-administration are seen to fail. The continuing concern for cost containment since the late 1970s has provided such a condition. More specifically, Döhler and Manow-Borgwardt (1992b) suggest that the 1980s have seen a gradual expansion of self-administration. But, significantly, this has been accompanied by stronger hierarchical elements. These include tighter deadlines for implementation and threats of sanctions. As a result state interventions have become not only more legitimate, but also more feasible in structural terms (Bieback, 1992).

The structure of the statutory health insurance (*Gesetzliche Krankenversicherung*) is highly heterogeneous in that it consists of over 1300 individual insurance funds (*Krankenkassen*) (Schulenburg, 1994, p. 1473).[5] However, these largely operate through peak associations at state and federal level. The insurance funds fall into two groups: basic insurance funds (*Primärkassen*) and substitute funds (*Ersatzkassen*). While this distinction largely reflects historical legacies, there is a certain degree of competition between the two, particularly over voluntary members and in the context of negotiations with providers. However, this is changing, not only as the room for financial manoeuvre has become smaller, but also as a result of health care reforms in the 1980s (cf. Alber, 1992). These have extended the scope of the joint self-administration of insurance funds and doctors at federal level. As a result fewer issues are subject to the (sole) responsibility of doctors or subfederal tiers of the insurance funds.[6] The statutory health insurance, then, has become more centralized and standardized. Its political influence has also benefited from the fact that it has become the 'natural ally' of the state in its attempt to contain health care expenditure (ibid., p. 168).

Finally, with regard to doctors a distinction can be drawn between office-based doctors (*niedergelassene Ärzte*) who work in practices outside hospitals acting as gatekeepers, and hospital doctors who are salaried employees. The interests of both groups are represented by a wide range of professional organizations. The majority of these are academic in nature and are concerned with specialists areas in medicine, while only a few explicitly focus on 'professional politics'.[7] For office-based doctors these are the *Hartmannbund* and the *Verband der niedergelassenen Ärzte Deutschlands* which operate as parallel organizations. Moreover, in order for office-based doctors to provide services under the statutory health insurance, they have to become members of one of the regional associations of insurance doctors (*Kassenärztliche Vereinigung*). These assume an intermediate position between professions and state: on the one hand they represent doctors' interests, for example in negotiations with insurance funds over pay, and on the other they have statutory responsibilities such as organizing the remuneration of their membership (Webber, 1992a, pp. 214ff). Interestingly their statutory role strengthens their position as an interest organization: as only a few can afford to rely entirely on private practice, almost all office-based doctors are registered as insurance doctors (*Kassenärzte*). This makes the *Kassenärztliche Bundesvereinigung*, which is the peak association at federal level, an important and reliable negotiating partner for the state and insurance funds (Rosewitz and Webber, 1992, p. 313).

These different types of interest representation have tended to complement each other (Webber, 1992a, pp. 254ff): whereas the federal association of insurance doctors assumes a moderate stance, having to maintain contact with the state and the insurance funds, the professional organizations can hold more radical views and thereby provide 'ideological backing'. However, as a result of cost containment measures and rising number of doctors, distributional conflicts among doctors have increased, and the associations of insurance doctors find it more difficult to integrate the conflicting interests of their membership. This has weakened their negotiating position (Wanek and Lehnhardt, 1989, pp. 6f).

In hospital care, by comparison, organized interests are weak, which reflects the heterogeneous provision of secondary care (Alber, 1992, p. 79). There are no statutory bodies and hospital doctors are represented by 'private' interest groups instead. The most important of these is the *Marbuger Bund*, which acts as both a professional organization and as the recognized trade union of salaried doctors.

3   THE INSTITUTIONAL CONTEXT OF HEALTH CARE

The German health system is based on a compulsory insurance model: it is financed equally by employer and employee contributions which are paid on monthly earnings. The contributions are set by individual insurance funds and are adjusted to meet changing expenditure levels. The statutory health insurance is thus administered by self-governing, non-profit, statutory insurance funds. These also negotiate contracts and pay with providers, that is the regional associations of insurance doctors at state level, and hospitals at local level. The control over financial resources and health care expenditure is therefore fragmented. However, insurance funds have to follow the principle of an income-related expenditure policy (*einkommensorientierte Ausgabenpolitik*). This means that the rise in expenditure must not exceed the rise in wages so that insurance contributions remain stable.

As health care is largely defined as medical care, doctors play a dominant role in the provision of health care. Office-based doctors are self-employed and comprise generalists (*Allgemeinärzte*) and specialists (*Fachärzte*). Over the last decades the ratio between the two has continuously changed in favour of the latter (Alber, 1992, p. 69). Patients have to register with an office-based doctor for a minimum period of three months, but as referrals are merely a formality, patients in effect have direct and unlimited access to any kind of office-based doctor. At the same time, however, there is a clear separation between ambulatory care and hospital services as office-based doctors have a 'gatekeeping' function. Office-based doctors are paid on a fee-for-service basis: each medical treatment is assigned a certain number of points. The value of each point is determined by the volume of funding and the volume of services provided by doctors. Consequently, the more services are provided, the lower the point value and the lower the income of doctors.[8] In contrast, the provision of hospital care is heterogeneous and is divided more or less equally between public, non-profit and private hospitals (ibid., p. 78). While investments are financed by state governments, insurance funds pay for the operating costs of hospitals. The financing of hospitals follows a cost–price system (*Selbstkostendeckungsprinzip*) whereby all expenditure is met by the insurance funds. In practice hospitals are paid a fixed rate per day and occupied bed. This so-called '*Pflegesatz*' has an inbuilt incentive to prolong the length of stay in hospitals. Moreover, it allows hospital doctors considerable autonomy as 'the treatment of patients and the relationship between the patient and doctors in the hospital [are] not influenced by economic considerations, as all expenses [are] paid by the sickness funds' (Greiner and Schulenburg, 1997, p. 89).

These structural features result in a large number of actors, which is also reflected at the level of regulation. Here negotiations and collective bargaining prevail within a general framework of corporatism. It is institutionalized in different forms of sectoral self-administration (Alber, 1992, pp. 157f): first, insurance funds and associations of insurance doctors as independent statutory associations exercise 'self-regulation'. This takes the form of insurance funds setting their own contribution rates or of associations of insurance doctors remunerating their members. Second, there are 'interorganizational negotiations' between associations of insurance funds and providers. As these deal with contracts setting terms and conditions as well as expenditure levels they tend to be confrontational in nature. In contrast, third, the style of 'collective bargaining' at federal level is more consensus-oriented as both sides are more remote from their membership.

The institutional context of the governance of health care in Germany therefore appears decentralized, if not fragmented, as power is scattered between multiple actors and arenas of decision making across different levels. Moran (1994, p. 94) thus characterizes German health policy as a 'search for control'. However, there are different factors which promote institutional coordination and integration. Wilsford (1994, p. 259), for example, points to the importance of 'coordinating umbrella organizations that work to centralize a good bit of the policy process'. At the same time all decision making ultimately takes place within the framework set by federal law. This is strengthened by the strongly legalistic nature of governance in Germany (Dyson, 1992). Integration is also promoted by the basic principles underpinning the German model of health care, such as solidarity and self-administration. These serve as a common cognitive frame of reference for the different actors involved in health governance (Döhler and Manow-Borgwardt, 1992b, p. 67).

4   THE *GESUNDHEITSSTRUKTURGESETZ*: POLICY PROCESS AND REFORMS

The Pressures of a Failed Reform

The initial pressures for reform originated from the perceived failure of the 1989 health care reform act, the *Gesundheitsreformgesetz*, which had been envisaged as the first of a series of health care reforms. It had only short-term success in programmatic terms: the implementation of its measures which mainly lay in the hands of the joint self-administration had only progressed slowly, or had not proved as effective as expected (Zipperer, 1993, p. 25). At the same time the expenditure of the statutory health insurance was again rising faster than wages from the second half of 1990. This trend continued in 1991 when expenditure rose twice as much as wages, which resulted in a deficit of DM5.6 billion (ibid., p. 25). At the beginning of 1992 the first insurance funds had to increase their premiums. It was estimated that, if this trend continued, the deficit of the statutory health insurance would add up to DM10 billion by 1992 (Müller, 1992). A further rise of insurance contributions would also be inevitable.

The financial development of the statutory health insurance was particularly problematic under the economic circumstances at the time: the German economy was not only confronted by the pressures of a recession and increasing international competition, but also had to bear considerable burdens as a result of the costs of unification. The government wanted to avoid a further increase of insurance premiums also in view of the general election in 1994. Higher premiums would not only result in greater burdens for employers and employees but would also slow down the rise of pensions as these were linked to employees' net income.

Consequently, the prospect of rising health insurance premiums put the government under considerable pressure to take action (Lindenberg, 1992). However, it was evident that any deliberations of the governing coalition parties, the Christian and Liberal Democrats, were unlikely to begin before two state elections in April 1992.[9] At the same time, any reform would have to pass Parliament before the end of 1992 to avoid any disrupting overlaps with the election campaign. These two dates set the timetable for the policy process (elaborated in Box 12.1).

Testing the Ground: Preliminary Proposals for Reform

In spring 1992, several discussion papers were circulated, written by health policy experts of the main political parties and the federal ministry of health. These initiated the debate about the priorities for the 'second stage' of health care reform. At the same time they also provided an opportunity for actors to outline their views and as such had an important role in preparing the subsequent policy process.

The discussion paper by Rudolf Dressler (Dressler, 1991), the vice-chairperson of the parliamentary group of the Social Democrats, mainly reflected the longstanding reform priorities of his party. Nevertheless, it was influential in the later negotiations with the governing coalition parties. With regard to doctors it demanded readdressing the imbalance between insurance funds and providers. More specifically, this included stricter limits on the number of office-based doctors and alternatives to fee-for-service payments. Similarly, for hospital services, it was proposed to replace the cost–price system with more differentiated forms of remuneration, based, for example, on diagnosis-related groups.

In comparison the discussion paper by Paul Hoffacker (1992), who was a senior health policy expert of the governing Christian Democrats, included

BOX 12.1 POLICY PROCESS LEADING TO RESTRUCTURAL HEALTH REFORM (*GESUNDHEITSSTRUKTURGESETZ*)

Spring 1992	Discussion papers by health policy experts of Social Democrats, Christian Democrats and the federal ministry of health outlining the 'second stage' of health care reform.
May 1992	Talks between the governing coalition parties in Nürburg, setting the framework for the 'second stage' of health care reform.
August 1992	Publication of draft legislation of the structural health care reform.
September 1992	Minister of health offers the Social Democrats joint talks.
October 1992	Talks between the coalition parties and the Social Democrats in Lahnstein about joint draft legislation.
November 1992	Publication of joint draft legislation of the structural health care reform.
January 1993	The *Gesundheitsstrukturgesetz* becomes law.

additional proposals for reform such as budgets for pharmaceuticals. It also suggested that doctors should be held financially responsible if budgets were exceeded. While it was unclear whether Hoffacker had sought the approval of his party and its coalition partner, the discussion paper was important in two respects: not only did it reflect the feelings and views widespread among political actors at the time, but, coming from a member of the governing coalition, it also acted as a 'predecessor to reform' testing the reactions of the public and organized interests (Oldiges, 1992b, p. 287).

In contrast, the position of the federal ministry of health remained unclear. This reflected the weak standing of the then minister of health, Gerda Hasselfeld, who had lost the reform initiative to parts of the governing coalition parties. Ironically, the final discussion paper written under her auspices was dated the same day as her letter of resignation. Nevertheless, it provided the basic framework for the subsequent discussions both within the coalition parties and with the Social Democrats (Zipperer, 1993, p. 26). It called for regional budgets for ambulatory care services and drugs (including sanctions) and for stricter limits on the number of office-based doctors, which would include reassessing the relationship between general and specialist medical services.

In the context of hospital care it was proposed to change the mode of paying hospitals and to subject hospitals to tighter efficiency controls (Clade, 1992, pp. B-1114f).

In summary, while the views of the main political parties differed on the issues of co-payments and the reform of the statutory health insurance, there was general agreement about the reforms of physician services. Even the Liberal Democrats, who had traditionally defended the interests of the medical profession, supported the proposed reforms (Cronenberg, 1992, pp. 46ff). Although the fate of the overall reform project remained uncertain, the emerging party consensus at this early stage weakened the political influence of doctors on the subsequent policy process. This is significant as the infighting of coalition governments has been described as one of the central blockades of reform (Webber, 1991, pp. 51f).

Moreover, against the background of the projected increase in the statutory health insurance the trade unions and employers' organizations broadly supported the reforms.[10] Thus doctors were relatively isolated in their opposition: while the federal association of insurance doctors, for example, was prepared in principle to cooperate on issues of 'structural reform', it rejected the introduction budgets for ambulatory care services and drugs, especially any sanctions. The federal association of insurance doctors was also critical of the strengthening of general, as opposed to specialist, ambulatory care services.[11] Similarly, the *Marburger Bund*, which primarily represents hospital doctors, rejected any budgeting of hospital expenditure as well as the introduction of diagnosis-related payments, arguing that these might encourage 'cream skimming'.[12]

Formulating the Health Care Reform: The Nürburg Talks

The broad framework of the subsequent policy process, then, had already been set in terms of both the substance of reform of medical practice and the relationship between the central actors. The beginning of the core stages of the policy process was marked by the resignation of the then minister of health, Gerda Hasselfeld in April 1992. She was replaced by Horst Seehofer, whose conditions of office were more favourable (Clade, 1992, p. B-1113): as a junior minister in the federal ministry of labour and social affairs (*Bundesministerium für Arbeit und Soziales*), he had gained expertise in health policy.[13] Moreover, the initial stages of reorganizing the newly-created ministry of health had been completed. The appointment of Horst Seehofer therefore cleared the way for 'serious' discussions about health care reform. Beyond that, his expertise and skills in steering the policy process proved to be central for the subsequent course of events (Wilsford, 1994, p. 260).

Only a month after his appointment, the minister of health announced that the coalition parties would determine the core elements of the second stage of health care reform in a series of internal discussions.[14] Considering the strong opposition by the medical profession in particular, the exclusive nature of the discussions was not surprising. However, it stands in contrast to the many 'windows of influence' lobbyists had been granted in the running-up to the preceding health care reform. It also set the tone for the style of decision making which became characteristic of the policy process as a whole.

The discussions took place in Nürburg at the end of May. After these had ended, lobbyists, among them representatives of various doctors' associations, were invited to talks. Here the participants were informed of the government's reform intentions and were given the opportunity to voice their concerns (Oesingmann, 1992, p. B1861). These events were later referred to as 'non-talks': while the government wanted to benefit from the expertise of organized interests, these were denied influence on the substance of the proposed reform. Thus politics had more or less autonomously set the framework for reform and the scope for the medical profession to exert influence was very limited.

While the Nürburg agreement provided the basis for the subsequent draft legislation, the scope of the reform was considerably extended. The so-called *Gesundheitsstrukturgesetz* (Deutscher Bundestag, 1992a) was published in August and some of its measures were particularly relevant for the medical profession (see Box 12.2).

Discussing the Reform: The Reactions of the Actors

In the discussion of the initial Nürburg agreement the Social Democrats rejected the government's reform proposals, although not on the grounds of the suggested reforms of physician services. They argued that the increase in co-payments would be socially unacceptable and that important structural reforms were missing, notably that of the organization of the statutory health insurance.[15] The stance of the opposition party was crucial as the health reform legislation required the assent of the second chamber of Parliament (*Bundesrat*), in which the Social Democrats held the majority. As a result of this unusual balance of power between government and opposition, the focus of the negotiations shifted from the coalition parties, as in the context of the previous reform, to the con-frontation between the governing parties and the Social Democrats (Döhler, 1993, p. 10). But with view to the general elections in 1994, neither side wanted the reform initiative to fail (Reiners, 1993, p. 24). Against this background the negotiations between the governing coalition parties and the main opposition party became a central element of the subsequent stages of the policy process.

The federal associations of the insurance funds, the trade unions and the employers' associations broadly supported the proposed reforms of ambulatory and hospital care services. The insurance funds, however, were highly critical

---

BOX 12.2   *GESUNDHEITSSTRUKTURGESETZ*: DRAFT LEGISLATION PROPOSED BY GOVERNMENT (AUGUST 1992)

Ambulatory care
- Expenditure is limited by budget between 1993 and 1995.
- The number of additional office-based doctors is gradually limited and from 1999 onwards only a certain number of doctors are allowed to work in any one district.
- Introduction of retirement age for doctors.
- The position of generalist (as opposed to specialist) medical practitioners is strengthened by the introduction of a post-graduate qualification in general practice.

Pharmaceuticals
- Expenditure is limited by regional budgets between 1992 and 1995.
- After 1995, the regional drug budgets are replaced by stricter controls of cost efficiency (*Wirtschaftlichkeitsprüfungen*) and indicative drug budgets (*Richtgrößen*).

Hospital care
- Expenditure is limited by budget between 1992 and 1995.
- The fixed rate per day and occupied bed is replaced by payments based on diagnosis-related groups.

---

of some procedural aspects which were seen to limit the scope of the self-administration.[16] These included the requirement that agreements over doctors' pay would need external approval, and that the ministry of health would impose its own provisions if the self-government failed to implement the reform measures.

The reaction of the medical profession varied: while the stance of the federal association of insurance doctors changed and was characterized by increasing willingness to compromise, some of the professional organizations stuck to their outright rejection of the reforms. Similarly, the *Marburger Bund*, which mainly represents hospital doctors, broadened its critique.

Initially, the federal association of insurance doctors rejected all reform measures except for the introduction of a postgraduate qualification in general practice and general limits on the number of doctors (Kassenärztliche Bundesvereinigung, 1993, pp. 39–83). But at the same time the Nürburg talks had already demonstrated that the core aspects of the reform were not subject to negotiation. This was unlikely to change in view of the problematic financial situation of the insurance funds and the broad consensus among the key actors, especially concerning the controversial reforms of ambulatory care services. Thus the scope for negotiation had already been defined and was restricted to details (Maus, 1992). A prominent example of such a strategy of 'success in detail' is the so-called *Malus-Regelung*, which represented one of the most controversial reform measures.[17] The Nürburg agreement had envisaged that the income of individual office-based doctors was to be reduced if the regional budgets for drugs had been exceeded. However, in talks with the minister of health, the federal association of insurance doctors managed to change this, so that now the associations of insurance doctors would be collectively responsible for any compensation (Hess, 1992, p. B1744). Moreover, after two years, instead of three, the budget could be replaced by tighter efficiency controls and indicative drug budgets. This version of the socalled *Malus-Regelung* was included in the draft legislation.

The strategy underlying the subsequent reform proposals by the federal association of insurance doctors, which it had already pursued in the context of previous reforms, was to accept short-term financial restrictions on pay and drug prescriptions in order to prevent more substantial state interventions in ambulatory care (Kassenärztliche Bundesvereinigung, 1993, pp. 87–115). However, while from the early stages of the policy process the leadership had been aware of the limited political influence of doctors and the need to make constructive criticism as well as to compromise, it had difficulties winning over its membership. This was an early indication of the ensuing division among doctors which became more apparent in the following stages of the policy process.

In contrast, the professional organizations played a subordinate role in the policy process. While the federal association of insurance doctors was the preferred point of contact of the government, some of the professional organizations also isolated themselves politically as well as within the medical profession by their strong opposition to the draft legislation. This is particularly true of the *Hartmannbund* (Schmidt, 1992), which represents office-based doctors.[18] Thus, far from strengthening the position of the federal association, this constellation largely highlighted the deep divisions within the medical profession. These were exacerbated in the course of the policy process especially as a result of the proposed separation of general and specialist ambulatory care services. The federal association then found it increasingly difficult to integrate different camps and further lost ground among office-based doctors. The situation was further complicated by the stance of hospital doctors: while the reform of hospital services was controversial, their criticism mainly focused on ambulatory care services, especially the proposed plan to limit the number of office-based doctors. It was argued that this would seriously constrain the job opportunities of specialists as well as newly qualified doctors.[19]

The Coalition of Reason: The Lahnstein Talks

Since the success of any new health care legislation depended on the support of the main opposition party, in early September of the same year the minister of health offered the Social Democrats joint negotiations. While they accepted the offer, they stressed that any agreement was predicated on certain conditions. At the same time, however, there was already a tacit consensus about the reforms of physician services.

In early October representatives of the coalition parties, the Social Democrats and the federal ministry of health met for talks in Lahnstein to discuss joint draft legislation. Again lobbyists were not involved which, in contrast to the Nürburg talks, was seen as unusual (interview material).[20] However, this certainly helped the negotiating parties to reach an agreement (Döhler, 1993, p. 11). Moreover, the 'grand coalition' across party lines made it easier to overcome opposition from within the parties themselves to certain measures (Perschke-Hartmann, 1994, p. 266). The final agreement was a conglomeration of almost all reform proposals of the governing coalition and the Social Democrats, including the reform of the statutory health insurance. As there had already been general agreement before the Lahnstein talks only minor changes were made to the reform of physician services initially outlined in the government's draft legislation. These are shown in Box 12.3.

The insurance funds welcomed the reforms of physician services and were only divided on the issue of aligning substitute and basic funds. In contrast, the federal association of insurance doctors rejected the proposed reform measures, reiterating its previous criticism (Kassenärztliche Bundesvereinigung, 1993, pp. 121–47). This was surprising: not only had its stance been more positive before but some of its views such as on the age limit for the retirement of office-based doctors had also been included in the draft legislation. However, it might have been a reaction to the increasingly open divisions among its membership, especially over the division of ambulatory care services into general and specialist services. The specialists in particular feared serious disadvantages in terms of both pay and entry into ambulatory care services.[21] This concern was echoed by the concerns of hospital doctors for whom specialist ambulatory care provides an important career opportunity. The coalition parties and the Social Democrats celebrated the Lahnstein agreement as an indication that, if politics was determined and united, they were able to act, even against the strong opposition of powerful interest groups (Deutscher Bundestag, 1992c, pp. 9920f, 9936). The consensus among the main political parties was crucial as it marked the beginning of the final stage of the policy process. As such it also considerably reduced the scope for lobbyists to exert political influence. The passage of the act through Parliament was relatively smooth. As the health committee

BOX 12.3   *GESUNDHEITSSTRUKTURGESETZ*:
CHANGES AND AMENDMENTS
COMPARED TO THE INITIAL
GOVERNMENT DRAFT LEGISLATION
(NOVEMBER 1992)

Ambulatory care
- Clearer distinction between generalists and specialists to be reflected at the level of remuneration: capitation payment is introduced for general medical services while the individual fees of specialist services are grouped together.
- The primary and substitute funds negotiate the pay of office-based doctors at the same, that is, state level.
- Regulations of the substitute funds on ambulatory care services are brought into line with those of the basic insurance funds.

Pharmaceuticals
- If the budgets for prescriptions are overspent, the state associations of insurance doctors have to pay financial compensation to insurance funds; the pharmaceutical industry pays compensation for any overspending exceeding a certain limit.
- Introduction of a list of pharmaceuticals that are reimbursed by insurance funds.

Hospitals
- No significant changes.

made only minor amendments, the act passed almost unchanged in the middle of December. It came into force on 1 January 1993.

Beyond the Policy Process

The policy process leading to the reform and the reform itself can be regarded as a success story in political and programmatic terms. Nevertheless, there was the question whether the 'double success' of the reform episode could be sustained in the medium term.

While many measures of the *Gesundheitsstrukturgesetz* had provoked considerable controversy within the arena of health care, this was likely to increase with the third stage of health care reform. It was expected (cf. Döhler, 1993, pp. 13f) that it would challenge the very foundations of the statutory health insurance by addressing issues such as a distinction between core and optional services. As any (cross-party) consensus would be difficult to achieve, the minister of health not only allowed considerable time for the formulation of the reform but also involved the Social Democrats and key actors of the health care arena in the process, by way of a series of joint talks in 1995. This strategy of seeking broad support for the reform differed markedly from the style of the previous reform episode. By spring 1996, however, it became clear that there was little chance of a renewed consensus (Hoffacker, 1996) and government and opposition submitted separate draft legislation on health care reform (Orde, 1996a, p. 46).

The developments at the level of politics were mirrored in the finances of the statutory health insurance (cf. Schmaus, 1997): in 1992, the expected rise in expenditure and premiums was avoided and, in 1993 and 1994, insurance funds even managed to make savings and to lower marginally their contribution rates. Also the accumulated deficit of around DM8–10 billion in 1995 and 1996 could be attributed to falling income, rather than rising costs. Regardless of the external nature of these factors, the government was coming under increasing pressure to act while the chances for finding support for another 'structural reform' were low.

Unlike the previous reform initiative, health policy from spring 1996 was characterized by a mixture of short-term cost containment measures and attempts to get through the third stage of reform. The first type of policies included the extension of hospital budgets until the end of 1996, the so-called *Krankenhaus-Stabilisierungsgesetz* (Fink, 1996). Moreover, as part of a broader set of measures of economic growth and employment, the statutory health insurance was required to lower its contribution rates by 0.4 percentage points from January 1997 by way of cutting expenditure, for example through the increase of co-payments (Orde, 1996b). In terms of the second type of policies, by late summer of 1996 it was clear that the government's draft legislation on further structural reforms would not pass Parliament. The government had failed to secure the support of the Social Democrats. Subsequent discussions focused on those reform measures which would not need the assent of the second chamber. These cumulated in a twofold reform (*Erstes und Zweites GKV Neuordnungsgesetz*) which became law in July 1997.[22] Doctors were particularly affected by the following changes: hospitals have to expand flat rates per case and lump-sum payments; the expenditure for ambulatory and hospital services as well as drugs is limited by indicative budgets, which take the speciality of the physician as well as the type and number of cases into account; the scope of the self-administration, for example in the context of contracts, is expanded.

5   ASSESSING SUCCESS AND FAILURE

The *Gesundheitsstrukturgesetz* was heralded as a success by political actors and policy analysts alike. The main political parties which had played a crucial role in the policy process pointed to the regained ability of politics to act as well as to the structural nature of many reform measures. This view was shared by the other actors in health care, reflected either in their overall support for the reform (as in the case of the insurance funds) or in their opposition to it (as in the case of the medical profession). Similarly, policy analysts characterized the reforms as 'historic' (Reiners, 1993).[23] Considering that reform blockades had long been regarded as the central feature of German health policy after the end of the 'long boom', these enthusiastic reactions were not surprising. Moreover, as the policy process had been shielded from the influence of the other actors, particularly the medical profession, the legislation contained many far-reaching reform measures. These either had long been part of the discourse about health care reform or had not been implemented as part of previous legislation, as with the limits on the number of office-based doctors and the restrictions on drug prescriptions.

In the short term the reform was a political success in that it further challenged the prevailing understanding of health governance. As discussed earlier, it is dominated by different forms of self-administration, particularly between insurance funds and the associations of insurance doctors. The nature of self-administration, though, is ambivalent: although purchasers and providers largely 'govern themselves', self-administration ultimately is granted by the state. It contains elements of both negotiation and hierarchy and over time it is likely to oscillate between the two (Döhler and Manow-Borgwardt, 1992a, 1992b). While self-administration had long been defined as more or less autonomous negotiations, the successive attempts to contain health care expenditure have called this interpretation into question. At the same time this also gave greater legitimacy to more direct state intervention. The *Gesundheitsstrukturgesetz* confirmed and even strengthened a more hierarchical, that is state-centred, form of health care governance.[24] In the short term it did so in two ways: the policy process leading to the legislation demonstrated the ability of government in collaboration with the opposition to set the political agenda. Thereby the influence of other actors was considerably limited. This style of decision making was also reflected in the reform measures themselves. They set any future action by self-administration explicit terms and conditions and limited their room for manoeuvre: not only were temporary budgets introduced for drugs, ambulatory and hospital services, but the implementation of the other reform measures was also subject to a strict timetable. It was accompanied by the provision that, if the self-administration failed to meet the deadlines, the ministry of health would intervene in the implementation.

Nevertheless, the question remains as to whether a more hierarchical mode of health care governance was sustainable in the medium term. In terms of the decision-making style, the *Gesundheitsstrukturgesetz* was unusual and largely reflected extremely favourable circumstances. As such it did not necessarily establish a new style of decision making. This was confirmed by the policy process leading to the 1997 reform which was much closer to the legacy of lengthy decision making and lack of (cross-party) consensus. Nevertheless, the health policy initiatives since 1993 have confirmed the hierarchical style of governance. As part of the 1997 health care reform, insurance funds and providers negotiate prospective budgets within the overall framework of income-related expenditure policies. But again the expansion of self-administration is hierarchically contained by the provision that any expenditure exceeding the budgets is only partially reimbursed. However, it might be difficult to uphold the hierarchical version of self-administration: while state interventions in health care have become more acceptable as well as feasible, they might threaten the legitimacy of government in the long term. The more government gets involved, the more it will be held responsible for the 'state of health'; the fiercer the distributional conflicts, the less likely government is to succeed (Alber, 1992, p. 169).

In programmatic terms, the *Gesundheitsstrukturgesetz* aimed at stabilizing insurance contributions. It combined structural changes with short-term measures of cost containment. By their nature these budgets almost guarantee success for the time they are in place, especially as they tend to deter excessive spending. This was reflected in the expenditure of the statutory health insurance between 1993 and 1994. The exception was hospital spending, which considerably exceeded the budgets (Orde, 1996a, p. 47). This, together with an externally induced fall in income, led to deficits in 1995 and 1996. In contrast, the implementation and effectiveness of structural reforms are more uncertain. While many changes were implemented, other important ones, such as the positive list for pharmaceuticals (Gerlinger and Schönwälder, 1996), the list of pharmaceuticals that are reimbursed by insurance funds, were not.

6   EXPLAINING SUCCESS AND FAILURE

The *Gesundheitsstrukturgesetz*, then, was a political and programmatic success in the first years after its enactment, whereas its medium-term effects point to both success and failure. The success/failure of the reform episode can be attributed to a combination of structural factors, that is cost pressures, and institutional factors reflecting the characteristics of health governance. In addition agent-centred factors played an important role in the context of the initial success of the reform, notably the determination of the new minister of health, Seehofer. However, it was further strengthened by specific conjunctural factors.

In the literature there is widespread agreement that particularly favourable circumstances largely contributed to the success of the reform.[25] While the political pressure of rising health care expenditure was not unusual, it was exacerbated by the already high financial burden of unification and the downturn of the German economy. Moreover, owing to the unusual balance of power between government and opposition in the two chambers of Parliament, health care legislation could only be passed if it had the support of the Social Democrats as the main opposition party. This provided the initial basis for the negotiations and also helped to unite the main political parties against internal/external opposition from early on. This made it possible to exclude the medical profession from the crucial stages of the decision-making process. The latter's influence was also weakened by the outbreak of deep internal divisions which made it difficult for the peak associations to integrate the interests of their membership. The opportunities to exert influence were further curtailed by the sheer speed of the policy process. In part this reflected the tight timetable set by election dates but here the clever manoeuvring of the minister of health also came into play. Beyond these immediate economic and political circumstances, Perschke-Hartmann (1994, p. 275) also points to the importance of policy learning. The 1989 health care reform in particular served as a 'negative blueprint'. It was perceived as a dramatic failure as it has been watered down by lobbyists even before it became law.

But even if taken together, these conjunctural, structural and agent-centred explanations cannot fully account for the political and programmatic success of the reform. Although the *Gesundheitsstrukturgesetz* represents the unusual case of 'big reform' (Wilsford, 1994) it did not come 'out of the blue'. Adopting a wider time frame, Döhler (1993, 1995) points to institutional explanations. He argues that the success was also due to the reform's consistency with previous reform initiatives which paved the way for the 1993 structural reform. The success reflected policy learning accompanied by an incremental growth of the institutional capacities of the state. While the previous reforms had failed politically as well as programatically in the short term, they gradually altered the institutional landscape of health governance and the balance of power between its central actors.[26] The succession of cost containment measures highlighted the weak position of the insurance funds vis-à-vis the providers of health care. In attempts to readdress the balance of power, the structure of the statutory health insurance was standardized and centralized. Thus the differences between basic and substitute funds were reduced and the importance of the peak associations at federal level was increased. At the same time the scope of the joint self-administration, especially at federal level, was increased so that fewer issues fell into the sole responsibility of the associations of insurance doctors. Similarly, hospitals lost the backing of the states as their financial situation deteriorated (Döhler, 1995, p. 394). Significantly, this increased the ability of the federal government to assume a more interventionist role in the governance of health care. Thus the meaning of self-administration gradually changed and the system of negotiations was increasingly accompanied by elements of hierarchy. While this strategy of 'corporatization' (Döhler and Manow-Borgwardt, 1992b) originated in ambulatory care, it has 'spilled over' into other sectors of health care, which highlights its importance for German health governance more generally.

The notion of continuity can also explain the medium-term success of the *Gesundheitsstrukturgesetz*. In contrast, its partial failure reflects altered political and economic circumstances and also points to the limits of health governance. In political terms, the decision-making style of the 1993 structural reform was difficult to sustain as the issues of future reform concerned the very foundations of the statutory health insurance. While the consultative style of policy formulation potentially increased the chances of consensus, it reduced the likelihood of a speedy policy process which would lead to substantive reform. In part the programmatic failure of the reform can be explained by the falling income of the statutory health insurance which was both politically and economically induced. This reflected high unemployment, low wage rises and a shift of financial burdens from the other parts of the social insurance to the health insurance (Orde, 1996a, p. 47). But at the same time, and despite strict timetables and threats of state intervention, the self-administration lagged behind in terms of reform implementation. This points to the limits of the prevailing mode of health governance: increasing distributional conflicts constrain the effectiveness of self-administration while at the same time government does not necessarily have adequate resources and expertise to intervene.

7   REFORM AND THE POWER OF DOCTORS

With its measures of cost containment and structural reform, German health policy has challenged the power of doctors since the 'end of the long boom'. This can be defined broadly as the exercise of professional autonomy. Here a distinction can be made between economic autonomy understood as the ability to determine the terms of practice at the macro level (for example, pay) and clinical autonomy understood as the freedom of clinical practice (Freidson, 1970). In the past doctors often succeeded in preserving their clinical autonomy by accepting limits to their economic autonomy, for example in the form of pay restraint (Döhler, 1989). However, this has become more difficult as the 'politics of health care reform' has moved from macro measures of cost containment which aim at revenue control rather than at limiting services, to micro measures which affect the clinical practice of doctors more directly (Abholz, 1990). The *Gesundheitsstrukturgesetz* illustrates this trend (Grisewell, 1993): the temporary drug budgets, for example, were replaced by indicative, physician-specific budgets, and hospitals saw the introduction of fixed diagnosis-related and lump-sum payments. Both measures not only require doctors to make their practice more transparent but also force them to take economic as well as medical considerations into account.

While these measures concern the power of individual doctors, the collective power of the medical profession has also been challenged. In part its influence on the policy process has been weakened as a result of increasing distributional struggles within the medical profession itself. In the *Gesundheitsstrukturgesetz* this manifested itself in the conflict over the introduction of a distinction between general and specialist services and the emerging divisions among office-based doctors. This made it more difficult for the peak associations, especially the associations of insurance doctors, to integrate these diverging interests. Moreover, the collective power of doctors has also been weakened as the position of the insurance funds has become stronger and as the state has taken a more active role in defining the scope of self-administration.

NOTES

1. In the German context, successful cost containment tends to be defined in terms of stable insurance contributions where the rise in health care expenditure does not exceed the rise in wages. While Germany has been relatively successful by international comparison (cf. Schulenburg, 1994, p. 1476) cost containment has remained the primary focus of health policy. Possible explanations are that cost containment has only been achieved by a succession of reforms (ibid., p. 1478) and that health care expenditure is more transparent as it is financed out of a separate, quasi tax (Moran, 1994, p. 95).
2. Webber (1991, p. 50) defines structural reforms as government initiatives 'which redistribute responsibilities or competencies with regard to funding, providing or regulating health care'.
3. In contrast, state governments approve federal legislation in the second chamber (*Bundesrat*) and are responsible for hospital planning and investment as well as for the regulation of medical education (OECD, 1992, p. 63). Owing to their vested interests as providers they have long exercised considerable veto power in the context of hospital reform.
4. Webber (1992b, p. 210) summarizes the role of federal government by arguing that it is engaged in 'procedural' rather than 'substantive' regulation: while the former is concerned with 'the stipulation of the "rules of the game", which lay down how decisions are to be reached in the sector' substantive regulation describes 'the making and implementation of the concrete decisions concerning the funding and the delivery of health care'.
5. Following the 1993 health care reform this number has fallen considerably as many insurance funds have merged and now mainly operate at state level.

6.	The remit of the federal committee of doctors and insurance funds (*Bundesausschuß der Ärzte und Krankenkassen*), for example, has been extended and its recommendations have become binding (cf. Abholz, 1990, pp. 9f; Heinze, 1990, p. 174).

7.	For an overview, see Schulenburg (1984).

8.	However, Schulenburg (1992, p. 728) points out that the 'German system of remunerating physicians employs the positive incentives of a fee-for-service scheme but guarantees cost containment, so that expenditures do not increase faster than wages.'

9.	See 'Sparsame Strukturen schaffen. Gesundheitsminister Seehofer vor großen Herausforderungen', *Die Ortskrankenkasse*, 74, 320.

10.	Cf. Engelen-Kefer (1992), Fiedler (1992), Murmann (1992), Oldiges (1992a).

11.	See 'Dr. Ulrich Oesingmann: Bericht zur Lage. "Einseitige Maßnahmen werden auf den entschiedenen Widerstand der Kassenärzte stoßen."', *Deutsches Ärzteblatt*, 89, 1992, B-1175–1182.

12.	See 'Kassenärzte kündigen Seehofer "erbitterten Widerstand" an', *dpa Sozialpolitische Nachrichten*, no. 22/92, 25.5.1992, 12f.

13.	Before a separate ministry of health was created in 1991, the ministry of labour and social affairs was responsible for health policy.

14.	See 'Thomae: Fahrplan steht', *Tagesdienst der FDP Bundestagsfraktion*, no. 1011, 2.6.1992.

15.	See 'SPD Präsidium lehnt Seehofers Sparpläne ab', *dpa Sozialpolitische Nachrichten*, no. 27/92, 29.6.1992, 15–16.

16.	See 'Stellungnahme der Spitzenverbände der gesetzlichen Krankenversicherung zum "Gesundheitsstrukturgesetz 1992" anläßlich der Sondersitzung der Konzertierten Aktion im Gesundheitswesen am 16. Juni 1992 in Bonn', *Die Ortskrankenkasse*, 74, 1992, 447–9.

17.	See 'Durch die Bank: Kassenärzte lehnen Seehofer-Malus rigoros ab', *Deutsches Ärzteblatt*, 89, 1992, B-1633.

18.	In contrast, the *Verband niedergelassener Ärzte Deutschlands* adopted a more moderate stance which was largely in line with the position of the federal association of insurance doctors (NAV-Virchowbund, 1992, pp. 3–6). This can be seen as an attempt to distance itself from the *Hartmannbund*.

19.	See 'Marburger Bund will gegen Zulassungssperren in Karlsruhe klagen', *dpa Sozialpolitische Nachrichten*, no. 35/92, 24.8.1992, 7–8.

20.	The opportunities to exert political influence were further curtailed by the fact that the offer of joint negotiations and the Lahnstein talks were only three weeks apart (interview material).

21.	See 'Keine Kapitulation vor dem Gesundheits-Strukturgesetz', *Deutsches Ärzteblatt*, 89, 1992, B-2769–B2772.

22.	For an overview, see Kamke (1998).

23.	Similarly, Bandelow (1994), Perschke-Hartmann (1993), Wilsford (1994).

24.	See Greiner and Schulenburg (1997), Schwartz and Busse (1997).

25.	Cf. Bandelow (1994), Döhler (1994), Perschke-Hartmann (1993), Reiners (1993), Wilsford (1994).

26.	As Döhler (1995, p. 32) summarizes: 'The implicit "everything now" yardstick for measuring political success typically leads to an underestimation of policies which proceed on a circuitous route.'

13. Controlling medical specialists in the Netherlands: delegating the dirty work

Margo Trappenburg and Mariska de Groot

1 INTRODUCTION

On 10 June 1997, the Dutch Order for Medical Specialists addressed a large newspaper-reading audience with a page-wide dramatic message. A very dangerous new law was in the making. Should this law be accepted by Parliament, patients would fall prey to heartless accountants and uncaring hospital managers. Medical specialists would no longer be in a position to defend their patients' interests, since they would have to answer (financially and otherwise) to the aforementioned accountants and managers.

In December 1998, the law on the integration of medical specialist care was accepted by the Senate.[1] The law came into force in February 2000. The newspaper-reading audience has not been further informed about impending chaos and disaster. Apparently, most hospital administrations, hospital associations, medical specialists and their secretaries are busy implementing a new administrative structure. In the future medical specialists will send bills regarding patients who are enrolled in sickness funds to the hospital and no longer directly to the insurer. The Order for Medical Specialists will advise its members to follow a similar billing system for privately insured patients. This might mean that those patients will no longer have to pay two separate bills for one hospital visit, as they have done in the past: one for the hospital (including services such as laboratory research, nursing care, use of the operation room and equipment, bandages and so on) and the other for the medical specialist's performances. It is not quite clear what the new law will do to the medical specialists' position in the hospital and otherwise. They have to do business with hospital managers instead of dealing directly with patients and their insurers. That much is certain. This does not mean the end of professional autonomy as they know it. They will still be bound to deliver medical services according to standards upheld by their profession, and if they fail to do so they may have to answer to a disciplinary court (Roscam Abbing, 1998). It seems unlikely that hospital managers can boss their medical specialists around in the near future, although they may and almost certainly will invite them to share some of the responsibility for the total hospital budget. The department of health, welfare and sport has assured medical specialists that they will retain the privileged status of private entrepreneur, with its accompanying tax benefits, despite the new law. Medical specialists will not become ordinary employees with a salary paid by the hospital. However, no one knows for sure whether tax inspectors and the minister of finance will share this view when push comes to shove (Orde van Medisch Specialisten, 1998, p. 1238; *Ordenieuws*, 1998).

The law on the integration of medical specialist care seems to be the final episode in a protracted struggle between the Dutch government and the medical profession about health care costs and doctors' incomes. After years of bitter fighting in which Dutch medical specialists felt compelled to go on strike a couple of times, and years of endless discussion about major changes in the health care system which were never implemented in the end, in 1998 things seemed to have quietened down.

What has happened in the Dutch health care system? Should we qualify the law on the integration of medical specialist care as an outright victory for the department of health? Did the government finally manage to get a firm grip on the medical profession? In this chapter we will try to evaluate the success of the new law by putting it in a wider context. We will take a closer look at the Dutch health care system and reflect on the possibilities and impossibilities for reform inherent in this institutional structure. We will try to formulate a couple of 'do's and don't's' for governmental authorities who have to work within a setting such as the Dutch health care system. From this perspective we will characterize the law on the integration of medical specialist care as a successful attempt to control the medical profession. The present minister of health has carefully steered within the do's and don'ts structure of the health care system. However, the do's and don'ts structure is such that accepting it as a given instead of trying to change it also means accepting a number of consequences that are considered undesirable by almost everybody and from almost every point of view. Hence we cannot conclude that the introduction of the law on the integration of medical specialist care was an unqualified success.

2   UTTER COMPLEXITY

The Dutch health care system is extremely complex in every respect. It is generally characterized as corporatist (Okma, 1997, p. 9) or neocorporatist (Van der Grinten, 1997, pp. 163–4). There are a large number of interest groups, scientific councils, advisory boards, private or semi-public institutions dealing with prices, budgets, provisions, tariffs, ethical issues, building and extension permissions, hospital regulations and so on, even after a wave of reforms has been launched in the sector in order to weed it. In this chapter we will try to give a broad picture of the most important actors and their function in the Dutch health care system.

Insurers

The Dutch health insurance system is layered. The first layer consists of a social insurance for so-called uninsurable risks: long-term hospital care, nursing home care, institutions for the physically and/or mentally retarded and the like. The general law on exceptional sickness costs (AWBZ) includes the whole population.

The second layer is supposed to cover normal sickness costs (short-term hospital care, visits to one's general practitioner, (complicated) dental care, prenatal care and so forth). This layer takes a different shape for different sections of the population. Low-income employees and their families (about two-thirds of the population) are socially insured through sickness funds; they pay income-related premiums. High-income employees and their families (almost one-third of the population) are privately insured. Their premiums vary with age, health status and the amount of risk they are willing to take. These premiums are not income-related. However, privately insured citizens have to pay a law-based supplement on top of their premiums so as to enable their insurers to offer a reasonably priced standard health care package to high-risk individuals (the elderly and people with chronic conditions) who have to buy private insurance. (Before 1986, high-risk individuals could opt for a voluntary sickness fund insurance.) A number of civil servants working for local and regional government and members of the police force have an insurance package and premium based on administrative law (about 6 per cent of the population).

The third insurance layer covers luxurious medical provisions (such as certain forms of cosmetic surgery) and consists of private insurance or is paid for by patients themselves. Given this complicated insurance system it will come as no surprise that there are sickness funds, private insurers, apex organizations of private insurers, a sickness funds council consisting of various representatives (representatives of employers and unions among others), organizations speaking on behalf of the public insurance for civil servants and organizations of both private insurers and sickness funds.

Providers

The Dutch system of health care provisions is layered, too, though the layers do not correspond to the stratification structure of the insurance system. The first layer consists of so-called 'extramural', out-of-hospital care: general practitioners, physiotherapists, social workers and midwives. All Dutch citizens have a general practitioner, who functions as a gatekeeper to the hospital system: in principle, patients cannot enter the second layer (the hospital system) without a letter of referral by a general practitioner or other first layer/first line medical provider.[2] General practitioners receive a fixed price per month for patients who are enrolled in a sickness fund. There is a fee-for-service system for privately insured patients.

Hospital doctors (medical specialists) come in two varieties. A minority (paediatricians, nursing home doctors and medical specialists working in university hospitals) are simply employed by the hospital. They receive a flat salary which does not relate to the number of patients, services or treatments. The vast majority of medical specialists are private entrepreneurs. They have purchased a private practice in a hospital for a price usually referred to as 'goodwill', equal to approximately one year annual sales. The goodwill money serves as some sort of pension plan for retiring medical specialists. Thus every new specialist starts with a large debt and has to make quite a lot of money to pay for his investment. Entrepreneur medical specialists negotiate or do business with patients or their insurers directly. They are paid on a fee-for-service basis which means that they can raise their own income by performing extra services. In view of the goodwill debt (and, maybe, a general fondness for money) medical specialists are inclined to do as much as possible. Both the goodwill payments and the fee-for-service system have been heavily criticized for years.

Health care providers in general and medical doctors in particular have organized themselves in an impressive number of organizations. Almost all doctors are members of the Royal Dutch Association for the Advancement of Medicine (the KNMG), a professional–scientific organization. General practitioners have a professional–scientific organization of their own: the Dutch General Practitioners Society (NHG). General practitioners and medical specialists have their own unions (respectively the LHV and the Order for Medical Specialists[3]). Medical specialists usually also belong to associations related to their own specialism (internal medicine, surgery, radiology, gynaecology and so on). The medical specialists have seen their former organization (the National Specialists' Association, LSV) split into three parts when some members thought that their union was being too tough on the government whereas others thought that the union was being too soft. The hardliners (usually belonging to high-income specialisms) organized themselves in the Dutch Federation of Specialists (NSF) and the more tender-hearted members (usually belonging to the lower income specialisms) founded the Dutch Specialists Society (NSG), which has developed into something similar to the Dutch General Practitioners Society.

Hospitals have their own apex organization, the Dutch Association for Hospitals (NVZ). This association was founded in 1993. Before 1993, hospitals were organized in an even larger apex organization together with nursing homes and institutions for the mentally disabled (the National Hospitals Council, NZR). The Dutch Association for Hospitals chose to become independent because it wanted to function as a proper 'branch organization' without having to reckon with other interests. Since 1998, the NVZ makes its own contracts with unions of nurses and other hospital personnel.

The Government

The Dutch health care system is steered by a department that has changed names and been reshuffled three times during the last 20 years (public health and environment, 1971–82; welfare, public health and culture, 1982–94; public health, welfare and sport, 1994 until the present). Depending on the outcome of coalition agreements public health is attributed to a deputy minister or to the minister of the department him or herself.

There are quite a number of quango-like organizations in the health care system. The most important one for our story is the CTG, formerly the COTG, an institution set up in 1982 to deal with hospital costs and tariffs for medical specialist care. Its members are appointed by the government,[4] but are mostly somewhat sympathetic towards providers (Okma, 1997, p. 92).

3   CONTROLLING HEALTH CARE COSTS

Budgeting Hospital Care

During the 1970s a certain planning optimism had dominated the Dutch government's vision on the health care sector. In 1974, deputy minister Hendriks (a Christian Democrat[5]) published a report on the future structure of the Dutch health care system with a very ambitious legislative programme. However, this reform programme slowly faded away in the complexities of the Dutch health care system. Hendriks's most important law, a planning law on health care provisions (the WVG) never came into force and was eventually withdrawn in 1996. By the end of the 1970s the planning optimism had disappeared as well. The government's main concern then was to cut back expenses, firstly on welfare state provisions such as disability allowances and unemployment benefits, but secondly also on health care.

In 1983, the government decided to abolish the open-ended financing of hospital care[6] and introduce a budgeting system. Part of the hospital budget is fixed and based on a set of parameters (number of inhabitants in the adjacent area, number of medical specialists in the hospital, number of hospital beds, and so on). The rest of the budget is negotiable and depends on hospital production. Hospitals and insurers negotiate, with luck reach an agreement and then submit this agreement to the CTG for approval. If no agreement is reached, the CTG can determine the budget itself (Okma, 1997, p. 92). The hospital budget system functioned reasonably well. However, there were two disadvantages visible from the beginning.

Firstly, the hospital budget did not include medical specialists' fees and hospital managers had no means to influence medical specialists' behaviour (Van Kemenade and Van der Velde, 1996, p. 32). Practical problems arose: for example, what will happen if there is no budget left for certain forms of surgery, but a medical specialist still deems this type of surgery necessary for his patients? The surgical performance itself is not budgeted, but the accompanying nursing care is, as well as the use of the operating room and certain hospital instruments. Who is to decide what happens and who is going to pay the bill? In accounting practice this dilemma was solved as follows. The hospital budget is fixed in advance. Most services have fixed prices. The price of one day's hospital care varies and will be determined after the budget year. So, if a hospital spends more on surgery or other performances than contracted with the insurers, the CTG will adjust the price of one day's hospital care in such a way that the hospital will receive its fixed budget and no more than that. This procedure has led to resentment between hospital directors and medical specialists. Medical specialists had the power to order whatever performances they thought were necessary (and they had a financial interest of their own in doing as much as possible), while hospital directors had to make do with a shrinking budget.

Secondly, many health care workers felt that they could not stay within a given budget just by working more efficiently. Fixing the hospital budget meant that choices would have to be made. Somewhere along the line, someone would have to choose between patients or between treatments. Health care workers in general and medical doctors in particular found that they could not make that type of choice. Their professional ethic compelled them to give the best possible care to each individual patient. This could never be reconciled with choosing between patients or withholding certain treatments for budgetary reasons. If the government wanted a budgeting system, then the government should make the accompanying choices.

This call for political intervention was reinforced because of another development. During the 1970s and the early 1980s private health insurers had gradually changed their policy. One of the bigger insurance companies had started to offer cheap insurance policies to students, thus breaking the existing gentlemen's agreement between private insurers not to charge risk-related premiums. Following this first breach of the moral code other insurance companies also offered low-premium packages for low-risk individuals (Okma, 1997, p. 105). High-risk individuals (the elderly, people with chronic conditions) were either refused by private insurers or had to pay excessively high premiums.

Many of these high-risk individuals opted for the then existing voluntary sickness fund insurance instead. Consequently, the voluntary sickness fund, having to cater for a growing high-risk clientele, ran into ever deeper trouble and was continually on the verge of bankruptcy (Van der Made and Maarse, 1995, p. 81).

The first difficulty (the problem of medical specialist care) coincided with a then existing and quite frustrating policy trajectory to control medical specialists' incomes. The second problem seemed more fundamental and called for both immediate action and long-term reflection.

A Decent Income for Medical Specialists[7]

By the end of the 1970s, the Dutch government thought that entrepreneur medical specialists were making far too much money compared to other professionals. The government wanted a well-balanced income policy and decided to intervene. The minister for economic affairs used the law on prices (*Prijzenwet*) to lower the tariffs of those medical specialists who seemed to make too much money. The union for medical specialists went to court to fight the price measures. The judge argued that the law on prices was meant to fight inflation and should not be used for income policy; he ruled in favour of the medical specialists.

The government then decided to take other actions. It proposed to regulate medical specialists' incomes by means of a specific law on the incomes of free entrepreneur professionals. The government undertook two attempts to make such a law. Both laws required cooperation by the free entrepreneur professionals whose incomes were supposed to be regulated. General practitioners and medical specialists would have to make an elaborate job description so as to enable the government to compare their workload and responsibilities with those of other professionals (medical doctors working in university hospitals and civil servants working at a government department). The government would then determine a reasonable salary and instruct the CTG to adjust the tariffs in such a way as to guarantee free entrepreneur doctors an income according to standard, but preferably not much more than that.

The general practitioners cooperated with the government, providing it with an accurate job description. The government turned a sympathetic ear to their profession, since it was government policy to strengthen first-line health care provisions. There was some extra money to gild these intentions. Moreover, general practitioners were not making very much money to begin with: compared to their hospital colleagues they had moderate incomes.

Having reached an agreement with the general practitioners the government then tried to use their income as a norm for the medical profession as a whole. (see Box 13.1) Medical specialists argued that their jobs were much more complicated than general practitioners' and that they should be entitled to much more money consequently. They chose the most prestigious of medical specialists' positions and presented those functions as points of reference for a job description. When the government refused to accept this the medical specialists refused further cooperation. Thereupon government unilaterally determined a decent income and tried to enforce this by means of a tariff decree by the CTG. The medical specialists went to court and fought each and every government move. They convened special meetings and finally decided to go on strike: that is, not to do anything other than emergency medicine (so-called 'Sunday rosters').

BOX 13.1   INCOME POLICY FOR MEDICAL SPECIALISTS

1979   Measures based on the law on prices. The judge disapproves.

1981   Temporary law on the incomes of free entrepreneur professionals.
          General practitioners cooperate with the government.
          Medical specialists oppose the government.

1985–87   Heightened conflict between government and medical specialists.
          One-sided tariff decrees by the government. Strikes, legal actions and protest meetings by medical specialists.

1987   Law on the incomes of free entrepreneur professionals.

1989–92   Five Party Agreement between insurers, the hospital association and the medical specialists (*Vijf partijen akkoord*).

1992–94   New tariff decrees by the government

During this war between the government and the medical specialists the hospital budgeting process took shape. Hospital managers, other hospital personnel and hospital organizations were confronted by the conflict in several ways. Firstly, they had to cope with the specialists' actions, in particular the Sunday rosters. They had to tell their patients that specialist X or Y had gone on strike and would not be available in the near future. Secondly, it was generally assumed that lowering specialists' tariffs increased the number of medical performances. After all, the only way specialists could maintain their old income was to compensate for lower tariffs by doing more. This was very frustrating for hospital managers who had to guard the hospital budget.

By 1989, governmental policy (intentionally or not) seemed to have resulted in a transformation of the battlefield in the health care system. Owing to the budgeting system, hospital managers, who had traditionally sided with medical specialists, now seemed to be much more inclined to side with insurers or even the government (Harrison and Lieverdink, forthcoming). Patients and patient associations disapproved of the specialists' Sunday rosters. So did the judge when the matter was taken to court. So did the media. In effect, medical specialists had been isolated and had managed to isolate themselves even further (Lieverdink, 1999, p. 87). Thus cornered, the specialists were willing to cooperate with hospitals and insurers and co-sign what became known as the Five Party Agreement, a covenant between three insurers' organizations, the apex hospital organization and the medical specialists' union. The agreement was meant to install a budget ceiling for medical specialist care alongside the hospital budget. The specialists were willing to sign provided the government would withdraw its law on income regulation and refrain from tariff reductions in the near future.

Another carrot that was used to win the majority of medical specialists over was income harmonization. Even among free entrepreneur specialists there are huge income differences in the Netherlands; many lower-earning medical specialists turned a favourable eye on the Five Party Agreement because it set out to bring their incomes more in line with those of the high-income specialisms (radiology, radiodiagnostics and heart surgery, to name a few of the most notorious culprits) (Lieverdink, 1999, pp. 94–100) The Five Party Agreement was signed, but it turned out to be extremely difficult to put it into a suitable legislative framework. In fact many arrangements agreed on were never implemented (Lieverdink and Maarse, 1995). In 1992, the government once again decided to intervene directly and adjust the specialists' tariffs.

Though the Five Party Agreement period did not come to much good, its indirect effect was a further transformation of the battlefield. Owing to the continuing discussions about income harmonization the medical specialists were no longer able to close ranks entirely. Their organization was split up into quarreling factions and, although the specialists managed to reorganize members of the competing factions in one new organization in 1997, this organization would never be quite as powerful as the old specialists' union used to be. This may have prepared the ground for later policy measures such as the law on the integration of medical specialist care (Lieverdink and Maarse, 1995, p. 92; Harrison and Lieverdink, forthcoming).

Changing the Insurance System

The call for political choices in health care which had followed the hospital budgeting process and the trouble with private insurers, entailed the revival of an ancient debate in the Netherlands: the health care insurance debate. The Dutch health care system is an uneasy compromise between the major political parties. The Dutch Social Democrats Party (PvdA) favours a social insurance system for the whole population or, alternatively, a tax-based national health service. The Christian Democrats (CDA) also prefer some sort of social insurance system, but they are traditionally very friendly towards societal interest groups, corporatist organizations and other civil society actors. They would be reluctant to advocate a system which would decrease the influence of corporatist civil society in one way or another. The conservative liberals (VVD) would like to abolish the sickness funds and let everybody buy private insurance. For the lowest income groups who cannot afford private insurance premiums there should be some kind of governmental support. Given these party preferences, and given the fact that no party in the Netherlands has ever had a majority of seats in Parliament, reforming the insurance system in any direction is a major challenge.

In the mid-1980s the government decided to take immediate action concerning the voluntary sickness fund. The fund was dissolved and its clientele was transferred to the private insurance market. A new law obliged private insurers to offer a standard insurance package at a fixed price to high-risk individuals. Many high-risk individuals would need much more care than their premiums could pay for. Therefore private insurers could charge their other clients with a solidarity bonus on top of their premiums, which could be used to pay medical treatments for the standard package clientele. This operation became known as the 'small change of the insurance system' (*kleine stelselwijziging*).

Meanwhile the government installed a special committee chaired by retired captain of industry Wisse Dekker to think about a new insurance system for the long run. The Dekker committee published its report in 1987. Dekker advocated a uniform two-layer insurance system. The first layer would be a basic package of essential medical provisions, covering about 85 per cent of the existing range of treatments. This standard package was to be a non-competition zone and should be financed by income-dependent social insurance premiums. Insurers would have to compete for clients to sell the remaining 15 per cent of medical treatments. They could choose to compete in a number of ways: by contracting with cheap (or cost-efficient) providers only, by offering sharp prices, or by offering extended packages or extra services. The Dekker committee also proposed to terminate a large number of corporatist organizations and advisory councils in the health care system (Okma, 1997. pp. 95–6).

The cabinet (a coalition of Christian Democrats and Liberals) embraced the Dekker proposals and embarked on a major project for legislative reform. Apart from the insurance laws (the law on the sickness funds and the general law for exceptional sickness costs) a number of other laws would have to be changed. For example, so far insurers had been legally obliged to have contracts with all providers in the adjacent area. The Dekker proposals would make these contracts optional. Henceforth insurers could choose not to make a contract with certain providers (ibid., p. 95). And of course the termination of a large number of law-based advisory bodies required a number of legislative changes.

In 1989, the cabinet was brought down as a result of a conflict with the Liberal Party in Parliament on a minor issue totally unrelated to health care (the tax deductibility of travel expenses). The new cabinet (again chaired by the Christian Democrat Lubbers) was a coalition of Christian Democrats and Social Democrats. Whereas the former deputy minister for health, Dees, was a liberal, the new deputy minister was a social democrat and an ambitious one to boot. He decided to accept the Dekker inheritance but to make a number of important changes in the proposals so as to make the plans more acceptable for his own party. The proportion between the basic health provisions package and the optional extras (85 versus 15 per cent) was changed drastically. In the new plans of deputy minister Simons the basic package would include 95 per cent of all health care provisions leaving only 5 per cent for the non-income-related package of optional extras. Simons intended to extend the range of provisions covered by the general law on exceptional sickness costs gradually, so that it would turn into a near total social insurance for health care in due course. To make his plan acceptable for non-Social Democrats he had engineered some carefully managed elements of market competition between insurers in the system (Van der Made and Maarse, 1995, p. 83).

However, the tide seemed to have turned. The Dekker plan of the previous cabinet had met some opposition and some support. The resistance came from societal groups (mostly from patients and providers who were afraid that the Dekker proposals would lead to risk selection between insurers). The support was mostly political; the cabinet seemed determined to lead the way, to change the system and control health care costs. The revised Simons plans, however, seemed to meet fierce resistance and only lukewarm political support. Private insurers correctly interpreted the plans as the end of private health insurance (Okma, 1997, p. 100). Employers foresaw that the plan would entail more income solidarity and, thus, higher health care premiums for higher-income groups. Moreover, they feared that the Simons plans did not contain any impetus towards cost-efficient behaviour by patients, since in the new system virtually everything would be covered by the standard health insurance (ibid., p. 99). The Simons plans would be largely financially neutral towards medical providers but, of course, every change of system would mean extra administrative efforts. Thus providers did not offer much resistance, but neither did they show much enthusiasm. The political enthusiasm for the Simons plans decreased over time. The second chamber (the Dutch House of Commons) demanded that every single step of the system change should be put before Parliament for explicit approval. Simons met even more opposition in the

Senate, where members of different parties had connections with private insurers in one way or another.

With the benefit of hindsight one might wonder whether it was a good idea to realize the small change of the insurance system separately. Choosing to solve the most pressing issue incrementally may have reduced the support for a major system change. In terms of policy scientists one might say that the small change in the insurance system had left the window of opportunity for the Dekker committee only slightly ajar. When Simons took over and decided to rewrite the Dekker plans the window was closed.

While the Simons plans slowly faded away, new reports on choices in health care were published, some requested by the government, others initiated by organizations in the health care system. A specially installed committee on choices in health care chaired by cardiologist Ad Dunning reported in 1991. Dunning's 'community-oriented approach' to choices in health care, which entailed citizens (or their political representatives) having to decide which medical treatments were necessary in order to function as a member of the political community, was widely discussed both in the Netherlands and abroad. *Choices in Health Care* did not lead to any real policy measures, though. Much more influential was *Medical Practice at the Crossroads*, by the Health Council (1991).[8] The Health Council had interviewed a large number of doctors, both general practitioners and medical specialists. The Council found that doctors ordered different treatments and different diagnostic tests for the same condition, that some treatments were controversial and were practised by a minority of doctors, that some treatments and tests were practised for mere financial reasons, and that communication between medical specialists and general practitioners was not always optimal. The Council concluded that there ought to be many more guidelines and standards to regulate medical professional behaviour.

Deputy minister Simons installed another special committee chaired by former prime minister Biesheuvel, to develop plans to improve medical practice (Elsinga, 1996, p. 52). This committee reported in 1994. The Biesheuvel committee was very critical about the fee-for-service system for medical specialists. It proposed to abolish the goodwill system and suggested different ways to integrate medical specialist care in the hospital budget.

Combining Two Trajectories

After the general elections in 1994 a new cabinet took office. The health care portfolio was attributed to a proper minister, E. Borst-Eilers, a member of D66 (the Social Liberal Party), but more importantly, a minister who knew the health care system through and through. Borst-Eilers is a medical doctor. Before she became minister of health, welfare and sport she had been medical director of Utrecht University Hospital and she had served on the Health Council as vice-president. Actors in the health care system knew her and trusted her. Her policy was generally considered much more successful than the policy approach of her predecessors. Borst-Eilers decided not to proceed with the Dekker–Simons plans to change the insurance system. Given the fact that the new coalition consisted of social democrats and liberal conservatives, whose respective ideas on the insurance system were irreconcilable, chances of success in this respect were virtually nil (Coalition agreement Cabinet-Kok I, appendix 1). This decision entailed the government abandoning one possible way of cost containment in health care, namely cutting back expenses by making political choices regarding the contents of a basic health care package. Without ever saying this in so many words, Borst-Eilers delegated the whole problem of choices and cost containment (the dirty work) to the health care system.

- Sickness funds and insurers were instructed that they had to 'converge', to grow towards one another. If they were unwilling to do so, the minister would take legislative action to ensure 'convergence'.[9]
- General practitioners and medical specialists were encouraged to make up guidelines and standards for medical treatment, following the recommendations of the Health Council and the Biesheuvel committee.[10]
- Following the recommendations of the Biesheuvel committee, the minister decided to orchestrate a large number of local hospital experiments. Medical specialists, insurers and hospitals had to reach agreement on a hospital budget including medical specialist care. Medical specialists who were willing to cooperate in such an experiment would not have to cope with tariff reductions (Elsinga, 1996).

These local experiments were very successful. Participating in these experiments gradually lured medical specialists into some sort of employment relation with the hospital, to be instituted by means of the law on the integration of medical specialist care in 1998. Medical specialists hoped that they could avert this danger by cooperating with hospital managers in the development of a system of so-called output pricing, which was also recommended by the Biesheuvel committee (*Gedeelde zorg, betere zorg* 1994, pp. 51–2). Output pricing was supposed to provide a better view on hospital production. The idea is to put one price ticket on elements of hospital production, as in one appendectomy is 1000 guilders (instead of saying, the treatment of A consisted of two days of hospital care costing so much, one surgical procedure costing so much, the use of the operation room costing so much and so on). Output pricing may improve the budgeting process, since it will enable insurers to demand a given production (so many appendectomies) for a certain price. Medical specialists hoped that implementing this system could persuade the minister to withdraw her law on the integration of medical specialist care (*Annual report*,

Order for Medical Specialists, May 1996). However, the medical specialists' cooperation in developing the system of output pricing has been very much appreciated but has not led to the withdrawal of the abhorred law. The minister can have her cake and eat it too. Of course we should realize that the cake did not come cheap. The enrolment of medical specialists in the local budgeting experiments has been 'bought'. The introduction of the law on the integration of medical specialist care will cost her too. If the law is to function as something more than an administrative measure, if it is to be the legislative framework for a (quasi) employment contract between hospitals and medical specialists, then at some point or other the medical specialists' goodwill system will have to be dissolved. This means that some kind of fund will have to be created to compensate the specialists' costs. The cabinet has stated that it does not feel responsible for the financial problems caused by the elimination of the goodwill system, since, after all, this system was created and kept alive by the medical profession itself.[11] However, this position may be characterized as idle day dreaming. Medical specialists will never abolish the goodwill system without such a fund, if only because general practitioners did receive a substantial sum from the government when they abolished their goodwill system. Box 13.2 provides a summary of the above developments.

4   ASSESSING AND EXPLAINING SUCCESS AND FAILURE

Controlling Medical Specialists

Can we call Borst-Eilers's approach successful? That depends on what we consider to be the chosen objectives. If we look at her strategy as merely a means to control the medical profession we will come up with a rather positive answer. If we look at the strategy from a broader perspective (is this incrementalist approach the right way to manage institutional change?) our answer will be less positive.

Let us first try to evaluate Borst's attempt to control the medical specialists. Compared to the income policy measures drawn up by her predecessors in the 1980s (the laws on the incomes of free entrepreneur professionals) the law on the integration of medical specialist care seems an important step forward. The medical specialists have been set on the road towards an employment relationship with the hospitals from which there seems to be no turning back. However, it remains to be seen whether they will march ahead on this road. After all, the law does not amount to more than an integrated billing system for hospital patients; if it is to become more than an administrative system,

BOX 13.2   CONTROLLING HEALTH CARE COSTS

1982–6   **Lubbers I cabinet** (Christian Democrats and Liberals). Junior minister for health: J.P. van der Reijden (Christian Democrat).
1983   Introduction of hospital budget system.

1986–9   **Lubbers II cabinet** (Christian Democrats and Liberals). Deputy minister for health: D.J. Dees (Liberal).
1986   'Small change of the insurance system'.
1987   Dekker committee, *Willingness to Change*.
1988   Cabinet adopts Dekker proposals.

1989–94 **Lubbers III cabinet** (Christian Democrats and Social Democrats). Deputy minister for health: H.J. Simons (Social Democrat).
1990   New cabinet changes Dekker proposals.
1991   Dunning committee, *Choices in Health Care*.
1991   Health Council, *Medical Practice at the Crossroads*.

1994–8   **Kok I cabinet** (Social Democrats, Liberals and Social Liberals). Minister for health: E. Borst-Eilers (Social Liberal).
1994   Biesheuvel committee, *Shared Care: Better Care*.
1995   Cabinet adopts Biesheuvel proposals. Budgeting experiments for medical specialists in a majority of hospitals.

1998–present   **Kok II cabinet** (Social Democrats, Liberals and Social Liberals). Minister for health: E. Borst-Eilers (Social Liberal).
1998   Law on the integration of medical specialist care accepted by Parliament.

further cooperation by all the relevant parties, including the medical specialists themselves, will be necessary. Still, it seems fair to call the law on the integration of medical specialist care a moderate success even at this early stage. Several factors seem to have contributed to this success:

- The continual struggle in the 1980s had weakened the medical specialists' organization. Minister Borst could take advantage of this.
- Orchestrating budgeting experiments at the hospital level may have strengthened the bonds between medical specialists and their hospital and

at the same time weakened the bond between medical specialists and their organization.

- Unlike the unfortunate laws on the incomes of free entrepreneur professionals, Borst's hospital experiments did not require the cooperation of the medical specialists' organization. The minister could do business with hospital authorities and small groups of specialists, thus bypassing the specialists' organization which had been such a formidable opponent in the past.

- With regard to powerful groups such as medical specialists and private insurers, it is probably more effective to lure them into a seemingly innocent experiment than to force them into a new, law-based institutional structure.

- Borst-Eilers's background as a medical doctor, former vice-president of the Health Council and former hospital director created a lot of goodwill in the health care sector when she first took office in 1994. Borst probably gained some extra popularity by stating repeatedly that the Dutch health care system was doing an excellent job and did not need much change or government intervention. After years of being bombarded with major blueprints for change, the sector was relieved to be left in peace for a while.

Controlling Health Care Costs

Compared to the income policy measures for medical specialists enacted by her predecessors, minister Borst's strategy was quite successful. How does her strategy compare to the major plans to change the system, such as the ones initiated by Dees and Simons? The law on the integration of medical specialist care can play a certain role in controlling health care costs. Before the introduction of this law the government could influence the volume of hospital care and the tariffs for medical specialist care, but it could not influence the volume of medical specialist care, which diminished the effectiveness of budgeting hopitals. The law on the integration of medical specialist care will change that. If the minister manages to stay friends with (or at least control) the relevant actors she may end up with a system that can be used to regulate the volume of hospital care, including medical specialist care – or, more precisely, a system that allows health care providers and insurers to do the government's dirty work; that is, to make choices in health care within a given macro budget. The minister's policy measures to promote professional guidelines, standardized treatment and evidence-based medicine, as well as her instructions to insurers and sickness funds (thou shalt converge), can also be seen as instruments that should stimulate the sector to guard the health care budget one way or another.

The Dekker and Simons plans have been set in motion and subsequently turned back. Hence they may be characterized as clear-cut cases of governmental failure. Can we call Borst's 'cost containment through self-regulation' strategy a success? We do not think so. At present everything in the Dutch health care system that can be budgeted has been budgeted. Consequently, the demand for health care systematically exceeds the health care budget. There are waiting lists for many types of medical specialist care (ophthalmologists, orthopaedists, cosmetic surgeons, cardiologists). There are waiting lists for places in institutions for the mentally handicapped and for geriatric patients. Hospital managers and insurers are tempted to think of ways to bypass their budget and thus solve their waiting list problem. Every once in a while they come up with ideas to do this. Some of them have proposed to help rich patients in private clinics and thus to make profits, and subsequently use these profits to increase the hospital budget. Others wanted to strike deals with employers who want to buy preferential treatment for their workers. Minister Borst does not like these initiatives. She has argued time and again that patients should be treated according to medical need, and that entrance to the medical system should not be easier for certain sections of the population. However, as Theo van Berkestijn, secretary-general of the Royal Dutch Association for the Advancement of Medical Care, once noted, the health care system has been manoeuvred in a frustrating situation. They have been ordered to solve the waiting list problem and most actors are willing to do just that. But they have to make do with a limited public budget and any attempt to raise money in another way is forbidden or prevented (Van Berkestijn and Van der Werf, 1997).

The dominant government view during most of the Borst-Eilers era seemed to be that waiting list problems had to be solved by working more efficiently and it seems reasonable to assume that after years of cost containment there was not very much 'waste' left in the system. Moreover, the waiting list problems will not very likely disappear in the future: the Dutch population is getting older and will need ever more medical care. In 1997, the Scientific Council for Government Policy argued that the government should reconsider the plans for a uniform insurance system and a uniform basic health care package, since the country cannot afford to postpone political choices in health care forever. If politicians cannot change the health care system on time, the waiting lists will grow longer and longer and there will come a time when the government can no longer forbid preferential treatment for special groups.

The first steps in this direction are visible already. Private clinics operate in the shadow of the law and in the shadows of the regular health care system. Certain forms of preferential treatment have crept into the system and do not seem to be rooted out again (WRR, 1997). Sticking with self-regulation and an incrementalist approach means not investing in a timely system change and thus having to accept preferential treatment in health care in the long run. At present the government tries to avert this danger by installing waiting list funds which are meant to solve the most urgent problems. But this is a luxury which the government can afford because the economy is thriving and it seems very likely that the economic tide will change sooner or later. When that happens we will be confronted with choices in health care that are basically market-driven. A government or a minister committed to preventing this should rearrange the system in such a way that other choices can be made.

At the beginning of 2000, minister Borst seemed to acknowledge this fact. She announced that she wanted to introduce a basic health insurance for all. Somehow the timing for this announcement was perfect. The quarrelling actors who had prevented the implementation of the Simons plans seemed willing to compromise now. The conservative liberals (the VVD) made known that they would no longer oppose a basic health insurance for all, provided the standard package was limited. The Social Democrats declared that they were willing to discuss a reduction of the present sickness fund package. Important private insurers announced that they were no longer against a basic health insurance. It remains to be seen whether this mood of general benevolence and willingness to compromise will last and whether minister Borst will manage to make the most of it.[12]

5   CONCLUSION

Evaluating the health care policy adventures described above, we may draw a conclusion along the following lines. A complex, corporatist institutional structure cannot easily be steered and managed by politicians and policy makers. It is usually more effective to let such a system manage itself. Policy makers may help the system evolve smoothly in the direction they prefer, by trying to regroup the parties on the battlefield, by providing financial incentives and threatening new legislation. They should ask different actors in the system to work out plans for change, encourage them to take responsibility, help them implement their own plans where necessary and applaud their efforts. Politicians and policy makers who abide by these guidelines will go a long way.

However, there are limits to what can be accomplished by this type of self-regulation. Neither health care professionals nor other actors in a health care system (hospital managers, private insurers) are able and willing to make political choices. Health care professionals are inclined to distribute medical services according to medical need; they may be willing to reconsider the appropriateness of certain treatments for certain diseases, but they will not be able to refuse treatment for non-medical reasons. If they are put in a situation of induced scarcity, this will lead to waiting lists. Hospital managers and insurers will try to find creative solutions for waiting lists and these solutions will, almost by definition, make use of some sort of market mechanism. If a government wants a limited health care budget and to uphold social solidarity at the same time, it must ensure that it will be able to make political decisions concerning the distribution of medical care.

NOTES

1. Law of 24 12 1998, *Staatsblad*, 1999, no. 16.
2. Social workers may refer their patients to hospital psychiatrists and midwives may refer them to gynaecologists. One of the weaknesses of the system is that, although there is efficient control on entering the hospital system, there is no similar rule regulating the way out. General practitioners complain that they do not receive adequate information about what happens to their patients in the hospital system. Medical specialists often benefit financially when they keep patients in the second layer (*Gedeelde zorg: betere zorg*, 1994, p. 28).
3. The Order for Medical Specialists came into being in January 1997 as the result of a merger of four organizations: the regular medical specialists organization (LSV), the federation for medical specialists (NSF), the organization for doctors working in university hospitals (ASV) and the apex organization for scientific medical societies.
4. Before 1997, the CTG was a larger body. Some of its members were appointed after consultation with relevant interest groups: unions, employers, hospitals, insurers (Boot and Knapen, 1996, p. 388).
5. Technically, Hendriks was not a Christian Democrat but a member of the KVP, one of the parties that merged into the Dutch Christian Democratic Party.
6. See, for details on the open-ended financing before 1983, Lieverdink (1999).
7. This section is largely based on G. Scholten, '*De omsingeling van medische specialisten. Een organisatie-sociologisch onderzoek naar de relatie tussen de overheid en de medische specialisten, 1979–1989*', PhD thesis, Erasmus University, Rotterdam, 1994.
8. This report by the Health Council was requested by deputy minister Dees in 1989. It was written by a Health Council committee chaired by Els Borst-Eilers, vice-president of the Health Council. She became minister for health, welfare and sport in 1994.
9. The coalition agreement explicitly mentions a law on convergence, but so far no such law has been submitted to Parliament.
10. Cf. Annual report, Order for Medical Specialists, September 1996: Tk 1994–1995 23 619, nos. 3–4, Standpunt op het advies van de Commissie modernisering curatieve zorg.
11. TK 1994–1995 23 619 nos. 3–4, Standpunt op het advies van de Commissie modernisering curatieve zorg.
12. Cf. Frits van Veen, 'Basisstelsel ziektekosten komt nabij door ommezwaai VVD', *de Volkskrant*, 1–3–2000, 3; 'PvdA zint op inperking ziekenfonds', *de Volkskrant*, 14–2–2000, 1; 'Ziekteverzekeraars zijn niet meer tegen basisverzekering', *de Volkskrant*, 20–4–2000, 3.

14. The Spanish state and the medical profession in primary health care: doctors, veto points and reform attempts

Ana Rico, Marc Balaguer and Pablo González Alvarez

1 INTRODUCTION

What is the medical profession's impact on the state's success in reforming health care in Spain? To answer this question, we have selected the case of primary care reform, which is particularly relevant for two reasons. First, successful implementation of primary care reform requires that doctors are willing to accept a marked change in their working and salary conditions within the public sector, which clearly goes against their interests. Second, a reformed, effective public network of general practices would surely decrease demand for private primary care, by far the most profitable sector in Spain. As a result, primary health care reform represents one of the most important attempts of the Spanish state to regulate the medical profession.

Given the deep regional political decentralization launched since the late 1970s, it is important to consider the relationship between the state and the professionals at the regional level, which forces us to consider a second research question: does political decentralization alter the state's capacity to regulate the medical profession?

There is already some evidence of this from the case of Galicia (González, 1999; Rico, Fraile and González, 1998; Rico, González and Fraile, 1998), one of the most backward of Spanish regions, and the one that achieved the highest degree of failure implementing reforms. Qualitative analysis suggested that the power of the medical profession to resist state mandates was a crucial explanatory variable for the low degree of implementation. However, there are other potential explanations which cannot be excluded in this case, such as very low economic development and social capital levels, below-average health care resources, delayed health care transfers, and shared rule of central and regional authorities during the previous period, 1984–90. In order to control for those factors, we explicitly undertake a comparative study, which applies the logic of 'the most different cases'. To this end, the case of Catalonia is especially pertinent: it is a highly developed region, with high levels of social capital, above-average health care resources and full health care transfers since 1981. However, in spite of this, Catalonia achieved the lowest implementation rate after Galicia.

2   THE POLITICAL ACTORS: DOCTORS AND STATE AUTHORITIES IN THE PROCESS OF HEALTH CARE REFORM

The role of doctors in health care policy making has been limited in Spain mainly owing to the long period of authoritarian rule following General Franco's coup (1939–77). Francoism prohibited associations and imposed strong state control over the medical profession. The only institutions which survived during this time, the Provincial Colleges of Physicians, were integrated into a vertical centralized structure, the General Council of Medical Colleges. These institutions were represented within a national political organization, the *Organización Médica Colegial* (literally, Organization of Medical Colleges, OMC), following the traditional, authoritarian pattern of state corporatism (Rodríguez, 1992; Guillén, 1996).

At the advent of democracy, the situation of the medical profession has been described as follows (Rodríguez, 1992, p. 22):

> The francoist inheritance for the medical profession meant its political weakness and its almost complete dependence on the State. The first democratic decade was characterized by the attempts of the profession to strengthen itself politically and to obtain independence from the State. The high level of authoritarianism of the official organizations (mainly controlled by the professional right) favoured the appearance of alternative professional organizations (syndicalist, political, ideological), which rivalled the official organizations for the representation of the profession. The political division of the profession negatively affected its political and bargaining power.

Regarding primary care reform, the medical profession can be politically divided into two fronts. On the one hand, there were the traditional, middle-aged general practitioners (GPs) working within the old primary care network who strongly opposed state reforms. Their interests were represented by the conservative OMC and its trade union branch CESM (the 'official organizations' in the above paragraph). On the other hand, there was a generation of young communist and socialist doctors who participated in the design of primary health care reform from below.

From the mid-1980s, as primary care reform proceeded, new generations of family doctors entered the public system who were the natural allies of state reformers. Generally speaking, their interests were defended by a scientific association, the Spanish Society of Family and Community Medicine (*Sociedad Española de Medicina Familiar y Comunitaria*). In addition, the socialist and communist trade unions (UGT and CCOO), in spite of their very limited power within the medical profession, were also important political actors during the process of implementation, especially at the central level.

The relevant state actors are represented by three political parties. First is the Socialist Party, PSOE, which was in office at the central level between 1982 and 1996. PSOE launched primary health care reform between 1984 and 1986. Second is the conservative Popular Party, which at the start of democracy had an open pro-francoist profile. The party occupied the Galician regional government during most of the democratic period. Over the years, it renewed itself, firmly established its democratic standing, attracted a new elite group of young professional politicians, and moved to the centre-right. In 1996, it won the general elections, and came to hold office at the central level.

The third party is the Catalan nationalist centre-right coalition Convergencia i Unió (CiU), which won the Catalan elections in 1981, and has stayed in office ever since. As regards the Catalan public health care sector, an important fact to note is that two-thirds of public hospital services are provided by private non-profit hospitals, which have deep historical roots, related to the strong Catalan tradition of civil society mutualism. They are politically organized into two powerful associations, CHC and UCH. This situation stands in stark contrast with the rest of Spain, within which private hospitals hold a fairly marginal status both as providers and as political actors.

3   HEALTH CARE GOVERNANCE IN SPAIN

The development of an extensive publicly owned hospital network within a Social Security model of insurance can be considered the main distinctive feature of the Spanish health care sector as it emerged from the francoist period. Since the mid-1960s, the state has owned 70 per cent of the available hospital beds and employed between 70 per cent and 80 per cent of doctors (Guillén, 1996), while public providers spent 75–85 per cent of the public health care budget during the period 1975–95 (Coll, 1980; Lopez Casasnovas, 1993). In the primary care field, public provision completely dominates the scene, with GPs having the status of part-time civil servants. In addition, city and provincial governments held (somewhat overlapping) responsibilities for health prevention and promotion as well as rural primary health care. The 1977 Constitution partly transferred such local government powers to the 17 Spanish regions.

Power sharing among regional and central government tiers is rather unusual in Spain. The 1977 Constitution distinguishes between 'special' and 'ordinary' regions. In the field of health care, the special regions have almost full legislative and implementation power, only curtailed by central basic legislation. In the ordinary regions, health care is governed through regional bilateral committees which formally concede equal representation to the regions and the central state. In practice, the balance of power clearly favours central state authorities. In short, it can be said that regional governments basically retain the capacity of vetoing implementation of a limited range of policies, which include primary care reforms.

In 1982, the Socialist Party, PSOE, won the general elections with a majority of votes and obtained 58 per cent of the seats in the central Parliament. A few months later, the ministry of health publicly presented the first package of reforms (Lluch, 1983), articulated around the transition from the francoist Social Security system to a National Health Service model (universal access, tax financing, full public provision). As regards the centre–periphery balance of power, it was soon clear that the ministry intended to reinforce central power up to the maximum levels permitted by the constitutional framework.

Unsurprisingly, the project of reinforcing centralized steering soon encountered strong resistance from the Basque and Catalan governments. Throughout the first socialist term, elected representatives from these governments found an open negotiating attitude on the part of the ministerial team, presided over by the Catalan socialist minister, Ernest Lluch. The ability of the special regions to block central legislation by appealing to the constitutional court, as well as their proven political mobilization capacities, should be stressed here.

An additional significant fact is that, during these early years, the first socialist ministers introduced a new confrontational style in their relationships with traditional lobby groups, by closing the informal channels established by the previous centre-right government (Rodríguez, 1992). The closure of channels of communication also affected the rightist opposition parties, which openly defended the interests of the medical profession in Parliament during that period (Rico, 1998a). On a different front, the socialists' expansionist plans were not supported by the majority of the medical profession: only 25 per cent of doctors favoured the complete socialization of health care services (Servicio de Estudios Sociológicos del IESS, 1979). As we will see in the next section, the professionals' rejection of public provision was especially significant in the field of primary care.

4   REFORMING PRIMARY CARE IN SPAIN

In 1979, a series of surveys conducted by central state authorities revealed that there was general agreement on the need for a deep structural reform of the health care system. The specific content of the reform package, however, was not so widely shared. Regarding the survey question which asked respondents to opt between socialized and liberal medicine, barely 10 per cent chose the latter model. The other responses revealed important differences of opinion among health care professions and the general population: complete socialization was favoured by two-thirds of the general population (valid responses), while the same proportion of doctors supported a mixed model instead (Servicio de Estudios Sociológicos del IESS, 1979).

By health care subsector, the situation was as follows. Of the sample of 3000 medical professionals included in the study, 85 per cent declared that the quality of primary care was clearly unsatisfactory, an opinion shared by two-thirds of the general population. In contrast, just 15 per cent of doctors, together with 40 per cent of the general population, were dissatisfied with public hospital care. Unsurprisingly, the public network of general medicine was seen by the majority of survey respondents as the first priority for government reform (ibid.).

The Battlefield: Institutional Weaknesses of the Primary Health Care Sector in Spain

Dissatisfaction with primary care can be directly traced to its institutional features. General medicine emerged from the francoist period as a residual programme in terms of budget, infrastructure and manpower, especially in contrast with the extensive, modern public hospital network developed during the 1960s and 1970s. At the political level, primary care governance was a highly fragmented task, divided among largely uncoordinated state authorities. Health promotion and prevention, together with basic primary care for the poor, were initially in the hands of local councils and, from 1986 on, partly transferred to the regions. From 1942 on, with the inception of the Social Security system, rural ambulatory care for insured, low-salary workers was also included in this local network. Solo practitioners working in small villages and towns retained their status as part-time employees of local councils, but the network of rural practices itself was formally in the hands of the centralized Social Security administration. Their responsibilities were basically restricted to attending to appointments for two and a half hours a day, and to covering emergency home visits during normal working hours. In practice, however, rural practitioners also covered, on a private basis, (a) after-hour and weekend emergencies, (b) non-emergency appointments outside their two and a half hour working day, as well as (c) primary care for the affluent, non-insured sectors of the population.

Generally speaking, the significant increase in Social Security coverage during the 1960s and 1970s, together with the inclusion of after-hours and weekend emergency in-home visits within the public health care services, gradually transformed such private activity into an increasingly marginal source of income. However, in some rural, underdeveloped areas, such as Galicia, the pace of change was slower and, accordingly, private arrangements (*igualas*) between GPs and Social Security patients to cover additional appointments and emergency care were common up to the 1980s and early 1990s.

In urban settings, ambulatory care was part of a separate, distinctive subsystem, with GPs holding the formal status of part-time Social Security employees. Their duties and salaries were similar to those of their rural counterparts. Work after hours and weekend emergencies were covered by a parallel network of basic emergency services. Other shared features of rural and urban GPs were the following. Each doctor worked on his/her own, without direct contact with other colleagues. Administrative and diagnostic support was almost completely absent. Lack of time for appropiate care fostered a prescription drug-oriented style of medicine. In fact, almost 40 per cent of visits to traditional GPs were just bureaucratic, to obtain or renew prescriptions or sick leave (MSC, 1992).

The Fight: Doctors against the State in the Primary Care Field

In this context, the socialist reform package was as follows: development of an extensive network of publicly owned primary care practices; introduction of team work, full-time dedication by professionals and fixed salary remuneration schemes; integration of preventive and health promotion activities; reinforcement of administrative and social services support; investment in new technology (diagnosis, minor surgery) and site facilities; and introduction of a new style of practice which included individualized patient records and clinical guidelines. The centre-right Unión de Centro Democrático (UCD) governments in office between 1977 and 1982 had already paved the way for improving professional practice by developing postgraduate training in a new specialism (family and community medicine), compulsory for becoming a public primary care doctor.

It is important to note that there were early divisions within the socialist block on primary care. The reform model described, which promoted an enlarged public health care sector, was basically designed and supported by a small group of socialist and communist doctors working from within the system. These groups gathered together a series of innovative experiences and proposals developed by some teams of public doctors working in collaboration with the recently created university departments of family and community medicine (Villalbí and Farrés, 1998). Their proposals were broadly supported by the middle-rank experts and bureaucrats responsible for primary care at both the regional and central levels of government.

The minister himself, a liberal social democrat, favoured a mixed model of care instead. In sum, it can be said that his views were predominant within the socialist government, but were not shared by members of the party itself, a majority of whom supported full public provision. As mentioned above, this latter view was also the dominant position among the general population. In addition, it should be noted that primary care was hardly a priority within the minister's reform plans, as was reflected in the first ministerial reform report (Lluch, 1983).

Regarding the medical profession, opinions were as follows. According to survey data, in 1983, 30 per cent of doctors agreed with full public provision, while an additional 10 per cent did not answer the question. The remaining 60 per cent were opposed (Rodríguez, 1987). The model of reform favoured by this group was closer to traditional liberal medicine (Vila, 1979): introduction of sizeable user co-payments in primary care, free choice of general doctors by patients, and flexible labour contracts compatible with private practice. Their opinions were represented by the conservative OMC, the political organization of the National Council of the Colleges of Physicians, which soon launched a violent campaign of opposition to the reform plans. The dynamics and outcome of the fight had been described as follows:

> The political battle between the Consejo General-OMC and the socialist government during the first socialist term (1982–1986) is possibly one of the most interesting political phenomena of the Spanish new democracy. Both sides used a wide range of political artillery: insults, lobbying, public campaigns, sanctions, demonstrations, strikes and so on.... The political battle defeated two leaders: Ramiro Rivera quit after his term in office and Ernest Lluch was one of the very few Ministers replaced at the end of the first socialist term.... The profession suffered a devaluation of political and social prestige, and the government suffered an important political erosion (reflected in electoral punishment in the 1987 local [and Autonomic] elections). (Rodríguez, 1992, p. 30)

As a result of the struggle, the socialist reform package was considerably modified, although not much beyond the limits already foreseen by the government. With regard to primary care, the first version of the reform proposal was approved through government decrees between 1984 and 1985. Nearly the same terms were later included in the text of the General Health Care Act approved by Parliament in 1986. The main change consisted of introducing the possibility for doctors to opt for voluntary integration into the new reformed network (under changed working conditions) or for preserving their old status.

An additional modification, forced through by Catalan and Basque regional government representatives, was the suppression of many of the articles of the law dedicated to primary care, with the exception of the core reforms. Although these regional governments were still forced by central legislation to implement reforms, they obtained the freedom to decide on the pace of the implementation process as well as on many institutional details of the model of provision. This represented a very substantial achievement, providing regional governments with a considerable capacity to block reforms.

The Implementation Process at the Central Level and the Role of Unions

One of the main advantages of primary care from a practical point of view is that there are clear indicators of the degree of success or failure achieved in the implementation of reforms, most notably the percentage of the population covered by the newly reformed primary health care network. Until 1990, implementation progress directly depended on the percentage of doctors who opted for voluntary integration. In addition, from 1990, specific incentives and labour negotiations were used by central state and special regional authorities to promote integration into the new working scheme. This was partly the result of pressure exerted by the socialist and communist unions on the central state in order to accelerate the pace of changes in the sector. The role of the class-based unions at the central level has to be understood in the context of their previous relationships with the government.

In short, throughout their first term in office, the socialists progressively moderated their former programmatic proposals for improving and enlarging public welfare provision. This was partly the result of an intended political strategy. However, the shift was also an unintended result of the confrontational political style chosen to defend the core socialist credo about the role of the public sector. Soon a strong, open opposition arose from traditional powers such as the Church, banks and insurance companies, or doctors themselves. As a result, by the end of the first socialist term in 1986, some of the reforms were set aside, and implementation of the rest came to depend on a pragmatic, selective, moderate strategy of advancing along the lines of less resistance.

This moderate strategy ended up leading to open opposition of the class unions and the communist party (PCE), which launched a campaign against the socialists. A year later, survey data reflected an important decrease in the population's satisfaction with government's welfare policies. In 1988, the socialist union (UGT) announced their official break with the Socialist Party, and joined the communist union (CCOO) to launch a political strike against the government, focused on social policy vindications. The socialists' response made clear that the government's first priority was to avoid open political confrontations with organized interests. From 1989, welfare expenditure significantly increased, and several agreements were reached with the unions to accelerate implementation of formerly approved reforms.

In the primary care field, the main pacts were signed in 1990, 1992 and 1993. Although there are no reliable data for the years prior to 1992, the evolution from this date to 1994 is considerable, with public coverage by the new reformed system increasing from one-half to two-thirds of the population. This crude indicator seems to reflect considerable success in the implementation of primary health care reform, in spite of the 10-year period required to reach the 1994 levels. The microinstitutional regulations included in the agreements with the unions help to explain the expansion of the reform beginning in 1990.

The first socialist legislative pieces guiding the implementation process included a remuneration system which did not provide incentives for primary care doctors' voluntary integration in the new schemes, reflecting the half-hearted attitude of the socialists towards the reforms. In particular, two aspects merit special attention. First, to enter the new, reformed network, doctors had to multiply their daily working hours by three, but their salary was not proportionally increased. Moreover, the new timetable was a serious obstacle for the practice of private medicine. In 1979, each doctor working for the public sector held two jobs on average (Servicio de Estudios Sociológicos del IESS, 1979); in 1983, 50 per cent of them declared (Rodriguez, 1987) that they had an additional job in the private sector. Second, the reform involved a shift from a remuneration scheme based on a sizeable capitation supplement to a new fixed salary system.

The regulation agreed upon by the government and the unions between 1990 and 1993, on the other hand, included a series of measures to foster the implementation process, among them the reintroduction of the capitation supplement, rationalization of emergency care and home visits, the establishment of a maximum number of patients per doctor and the promotion of temporary personnel to the status of civil servants. Among the negative incentives for doctors refusing integration, the agreements included possible forced early retirement and involuntary geographic relocation.

If we shift from the central government scenario to the regional level, as shown in Figure 14.1, the persistently low figures for Galicia and Catalonia are puzzling. On the one hand, Galician health care services were under the rule of the central state until 1991, which is when the central government transferred the Social Security health care network to regional authorities, and when Galicia obtained in practice the powers reserved for special regions. Why then was the implementation process delayed in Galicia during the period 1984–91, and not in the rest of the Autonomous Communities subject to central rule? On the other hand, Catalonia, the first Autonomous Community to obtain access to full health care power, had shown an important capacity for innovative leadership in the regulation and management of the health care sector during 10 years of regional rule (Rico, Fraile and González, 1998). Why was the pioneering, efficient Catalan government so slow in launching reforms in the primary care field? To answer these questions, we will first describe the political dynamics of the process of reform in both regions. Then we will attempt to build a theoretical explanation for the facts described below.

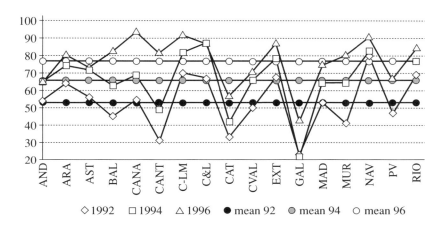

Figure 14.1   Percentage of population covered by the reformed primary care network

Galicia: Rural Doctors against the State

The first factor that merits attention in the Galician case, in contrast with other regions, is that its rural network of health care was double the size of its urban one. This implied a numerical predominance of old GPs over young hospital doctors. As survey data from the late 1970s and early 1980s reflect, agreement with the socialist reforms was highest among young hospital doctors and lowest among middle-aged primary care professionals (Servicio de Estudios Socio-lógicos del IESS, 1979; Rodríguez, 1987, 1992). The opposite is true regarding the position of both groups with respect to the Colleges of Physicians and its central political organization, the OMC. This helps us to understand the second peculiarity of Galicia: the central role of the colleges themselves within the regional health care governance system. The close sociological and political connections of rural, traditional doctors with a regional government dominated by local *notables* contributed to explaining this fact. Unsurprisingly, 1984–91 constitutes a period of strong resistance to central state mandates by a coalition formed by the regional government and the provincial colleges. As a result, the regional government put forth six appeals to the Constitutional Court to block attempts of central state authorities to implement reforms within the Galician territory. At the central level, the OMC put forth parallel judicial appeals against all the legislative pieces related to primary health care reform.

Devolution of full health powers in 1991 considerably changed the scenario. Between 1991 and 1993 the regional government, now fully accountable for health care, shifted its position in relation to primary health care reform, moving from a consensual to a confrontational style in their relationship with doctors. Several factors may help to explain this change.

First, from 1986 onwards, the Popular Party suffered several internal crises that ended in the party's expulsion from the regional government during the period 1987–9. This came about through a censorship vote in the Galician Parliament promoted by the socialists, who accused the PP of colluding with vested interest groups to block welfare policies. The party reacted by starting a conscious move to the centre-right in order to occupy the gap left by the breakdown of the former centre-right party, UCD. The strategy soon reaped its rewards: from 1990, it came to occupy the role of the main opposition party at the central level, with real chances of getting access to central government, and in the same year it won the regional elections in Galicia. To reinforce this move, the third Galician popular government showed a clearly renewed profile: the old

Table 14.1   Doctors integrated into the new primary care network by 1996

Districts	No. of centres	Voluntary Incorporations Total: 75 GPs By previous network			Promoted by Incentives Total: 195 GPs By previous network			Total	% of total public GPs
		Local[a]	SS[b]	ISM[c]	Local[a]	SS[b]	ISM[c]		
A Coruña	10	1	9	2	1	23	2	38	2.6
Ferrol	3	2	2	0	1	11	1	17	1.2
Santiago	11	4	8	4	2	9	1	28	1.9
Lugo	8	0	3	0	6	15	1	25	1.7
Orense	46	0	4	0	30	27	0	61	4.1
Pontevedra	18	4	13	8	5	18	3	51	3.5
Vigo	16	5	3	3	3	29	7	50	4.0
Galicia	112	16	42	17	48	132	15	270	18.9

Notes:
[a]   Local GPs, contractually linked with regional administration.
[b]   Social Security GPs, contractually linked to central administration.
[c]   Instituto Social de la Marina (Navy's Social Institute) GPs, contractually linked to central administration.

middle-aged, conservative members were replaced by young, well-trained professionals who had no sociological or political connections with the traditional vested interest groups of the region.

These changes were also reflected in programmatic terms. The regional government, in its new commitment to the reform, launched an integration plan to foster primary health care reform. Regional state officials introduced, as did their central counterparts, a package of positive incentives to encourage old-system members to join. However, such a strategy was a relative failure (Table 14.1). In spite of this, however, the increase in the number of doctors integrated within the new system resulted in an unintended, self-reinforcing effect on the process of implementation of the reform, by changing the composition of the medical colleges and reducing the intensity of resistance through increased contact with the new model. Former strong resistance to the reforms was thus progressively eroded (Table 14.2).

Table 14.2   Distribution of primary care doctors by 1998

District	Old network	%	New network	%	Total
Coruña-Ferrol	194	59.3	133	40.7	327
Santiago de Compostela	95	56.2	74	43.8	169
Lugo	189	66.5	95	33.5	284
Orense	91	37.0	155	63.0	246
Pontevedra-Vigo	181	39.6	276	60.4	457
Total	750	50.6	733	49.4	1483

Source: X.M. Segade Buceta, J. Combarro Mato and M.J. Cerecedo Perez (1998), 'Desenvolvemento do Novo Modelo de Atención Primaria en Galicia', *Cadernos de Atencion Primaria*, 5 (3), 138.

Catalan Primary Care: The Power of the Hospital and Private Sectors

In contrast with Galicia, the key actors for understanding the long blockage of reforms in Catalonia are not rural GPs or the provincial colleges, but rather a group of affluent urban private doctors together with the powerful Catalan associations of private hospital providers, CHC and UCH. They both hold strong sociological and political connections with the regional government, made up of young, well-trained professionals from the private management sector (Matas, 1995).

A further difference from Galicia is the open (although half-hearted) agreement of the Catalan centre-right government with the core of the socialist reform proposals. A relevant factor for understanding the position of the Catalan party in office, CiU, is the relative strength of the Socialist Party in Catalonia, which, since the inception of the Catalan democratic institutions, has been the main opposition party at the regional level, and controls the city council of Barcelona, the capital of Catalonia. Another important fact to highlight is the prominent role played by Catalan socialist and communist primary care doctors in promoting primary care reform at both the regional and central levels. In addition, from the mid-1980s to the mid-1990s, there was a general consensus among most health professionals in the region on the need for implementing primary health care reform. In particular, the Catalan College of Physicians openly supported the socialist reform model throughout the period, in contrast with most of their Spanish counterparts.

In 1987, the regional government formally initiated the implementation process by promoting a sophisticated package of positive labour incentives to promote integration into the new system, which included weighted capitation funding based on the health needs and the demographic structure of the assigned population, concentrated seven-hour timetables (which left either the morning or the afternoon and evening free to exercise private practice) as well as specific bonuses to compensate rural doctors who decided to enter the reformed network. The package, however, was not sufficient to reach the average implementation levels nationwide.

Opposition came from three sides. First, policy makers probably underestimated the volume of private business obtained by urban public doctors in Barcelona, one of the most affluent cities in Spain, with a strong tradition of high-quality private medicine. The most prestigious professionals, in addition, tended to be concentrated in the wealthier districts, in which the official number of public patients on their lists was considerably smaller than the real one, given the strength of the private market. This fact made the capitation supplement even more sizeable, while sharply decreasing average workload levels. Thus it is not surprising that urban public doctors opposed a remuneration system which would drastically reduce the size of capitation payments, together with a threefold increase in working hours.

In spite of the fact that Catalonia received an above-average share of the Spanish health care budget, the second problem came from the resources side. During the early 1980s, the Catalan government launched an extensive programme of investment in local general hospitals in order to cover the more isolated areas of the country. The initial plans included progressively closing some of Barcelona's oldest hospitals, in order to rationalize the historical pattern of over-concentration of hospital resources in the capital. Unsurprisingly, problems appeared precisely on this front, consisting of mounting pressure from the private, contracted-out, not-for-profit hospitals, which managed to block the planned closures. In this, as in other confrontations (most notably those related to the vindication of increased wages to meet public salary levels), the power of private provider associations to increase their share of public resources at the expense of primary care was clear.

Third, the socialist council of Barcelona blocked the transfer of the local government network of health care centres and manpower for several years, which further delayed implementation. The conflict began to be resolved from the late 1980s onwards, through the creation of a public partnership between both levels of government, as a way of sharing control over the council health care network. In turn, this fact, together with shared nationalistic feelings, fostered a certain collusion between the two main Catalan parties which was not restricted to the issue of primary health care reform. This probably helps to explain why a coalition of doctors and politicians who favoured acceleration of the implementation process did not materialize.

5   PRIMARY CARE: A STORY WITH A HAPPY ENDING?

The previous paragraphs underline how the incentives provided by the institutional framework interplayed with the rational calculations of actors. The cultural dimension of institutions may also play a role here. In this vein, an additional, deeply rooted factor that may help to understand the Catalan puzzle is the existence of a strong historical tradition of civil society mutualism, paralleled by an extensive network of emblematic not-for-profit hospitals. Accordingly, mixed models of health care provision were deeply entrenched within Catalan culture, cutting across party lines. This may explain why the idea of a fully publicly owned network of GP practices staffed by civil servants seems to have only attracted half-hearted support by many of the actors involved, contributing to the weakness of the coalition favouring the reform, facilitating collusion between government and opposition, demobilizing the medical college and helping public hospital providers and affluent urban doctors to flourish.

In fact, the evolution of the reform process in Catalonia from the mid-1990s seems to confirm this insight, at least partially. The internal market reforms approved in 1990 allowed the Catalan government to adapt the socialists' primary care model to the Catalan culture. In particular, integrated private management of both primary and specialized care was introduced into the system, together with the possibility for public primary care centres to opt out of the public sector and turn themselves into private enterprises contracted out to the public system. These developments helped to foster the extension of the new primary health care network, although under a different structure of provision. In fact, in the mid-to-late 1990s, some 10 per cent of the population was covered by these new, private primary health care providers. This implies that the introduction of new organizational forms does not fully account for the significant, twofold increase in the percentage of the population covered by the reformed network experienced between 1994 and 1998, which rose from 40 per cent to 70 per cent (Table 14.3). In contrast with Galicia, the reasons for this late expansion remain relatively unclear, although they may have to do with financial increases linked to the changes introduced in the resource allocation system from 1994 onwards, as well as with the desire of the Catalan government to compensate the potential adverse political effects of the increased recourse to private contracted-out providers.

Table 14.3   The reformed primary care network in Catalonia, 1998

Health Region	Population covered by the new network	Total population	% of population covered by the new network
Lleida	267 337	340 960	78.,4
Tarragona	334 755	438 735	76.3
Tortosa	133 228	133 228	100
Girona	343 315	519 387	66.1
Costa de Ponent	923 254	1 154 068	80.0
Barcelonès Nord	415 202	687 421	60.4
Centre	946 508	1 309 140	72.3
Barcelona	699 801	1 508 192	48.4
Catalonia	4 063 400	6 092 054	66.7

Primary care reform in Spain may thus look like a story with a happy ending. Nonetheless, the evidence only allows mixed conclusions. From the mid-1980s to the late 1990s, the implementation of primary care reforms at the central level can be considered a success story: by 1998, almost 90 per cent of the population was covered by a new network of brand new health centres characterized by teamwork, extended working hours, diagnostic and minor surgery facilities, and increased administrative support. In addition, there is evidence suggesting that some of the programmatic goals may also have been achieved (Larizgoitia and Starfield, 1997; Ortún and Gèrvas, 1996): the time dedicated to each visit seems to have increased, as well as the cost-effectiveness of pharmaceutical prescription patterns and some aspects of accessibility, while referrals to specialist care and overall costs per patient seem to have decreased. From the point of view of equity, there is evidence that the poor and the needy use the services more (Urbanos, 1999) and show higher satisfaction levels than the rest of the population.

In global terms, the percentage of the population satisfied with primary care increased from 40 per cent in 1985 to nearly 80 per cent in 1995 (Rico and

Pérez-Nievas, 1999). From the macro perspective of the health care system, the reform seems to have increased quality of care at a relatively low cost: the percentage of the total health care budget dedicated to primary care has remained the same over the period, while the utilization of private primary care services has increased throughout the period.

At the regional level, however, the cases of Galicia and Catalonia show that the story of primary care reform has not been fully successful in Spain. Long-enduring political blockage of reforms account for consistently below-average implementation figures, which can be considered a partial failure. From the mid-1990s, these differences are apparently being resolved, partly owing to the political costs of the implementation gap. The electoral defeat of the Galician government in the late 1980s, and the consistently below-average satisfaction rates of the Galician population with primary care seem to point in this direction. In Catalonia, such political costs may have been avoided, partly through the existing collusion with the socialist parliamentary opposition and partly through the over-concentration of the new network of care in the most disadvantaged areas of the region, which is reflected in below-average satisfaction levels among the low to middle social classes (which represent the bulk of the electorate and of public sector users) and below-average ones among the upper classes (which mostly opt out of the public sector) (Rico, 1998b). The latter comprise many of government's loyal voters, who might however hold ideological and vested interest in the sort of modern means-tested primary care network that emerged from the first stage of reforms. In turn, this would help to explain the low electoral costs registered in this front. In any case, the final results of the reform process in Catalonia, as in Galicia, are still uncertain.

6   MAKING SENSE OF THE CASE STUDY: THE POWER OF INTEREST GROUPS IN DECENTRALIZED STATES

As for our initial research question, we may safely conclude that both professional and private provider associations in Spain have at least managed to delay reforms over a considerable period of time. The political means used to do so included demonstrations, strikes and judicial appeals, as well as personal, clientelistic connections among politicians and vested interest groups. On an individual basis, professional resistance has been reflected in the reluctance of a sizeable number of public GPs to integrate into the new network of care.

Our second research question relates to the effects of the quasi-federal structure of the Spanish state: did federalism activate the existing barriers to primary care reforms? Established knowledge on the consequences of decentralization mainly emphasizes that federalism tends to hinder welfare state development (Rico, 1997, 2000). Recent work by Pierson (1994, 1998) offers a useful summary of the potential causal mechanisms involved. First, the power-sharing schemes prevalent in federal states generally hinder accountability (through reduced visibility of those responsible for each decision, and decreased control of central government over regions). Lower accountability discourages popular policies (such as the one we are discussing) by increasing the difficulties of claiming the electoral credit for successful reforms, and by reducing the political costs of governmental non-compliance with citizens' wishes. Second, federal institutions always increase veto points, in the following sense. Multi-tiered government structures imply that each reform package has to obtain the approval of many additional decision bodies (such as the Senate, regional parliaments, regional governments and bureaucracies). This offers more institutional points of access to different internal and external vested interests, thus increasing their ability to block reforms by imposing their formal or informal veto power.

However, the reform process in Spain support these theoretical arguments only partially, in view of the different results obtained by Spanish autonomous regions. In particular, some of the regions with full autonomy seem to be high performers in the primary care field, as in the case of Navarra (see Figure 14.1). Much seems to depend, therefore, on the territorial configuration of preferences and power. In fact, in the reminder of this chapter, we try to use the empirical evidence for the Spanish case to suggest the potential causal pathways mediating the impact of federalism on the relationships between interest groups and the state.

Veto Points and Pressure Groups in Decentralized States

First, increased veto points seem to contribute to policy blockage only in the presence of a dominant coalition of powerful interest groups opposing the reform, and capable of actually vetoing policies. As regards welfare reforms this may crucially depend on *the size of the private sector*, and on the strength of the corresponding coalition of provider and professional associations opposing welfare state expansion policies. Their relatively high pressure power, as well as the prevalence of private care, seem to be associated with a historically under-developed public sector in the cases of both Galicia and Catalonia. In turn, the weaknesses of the public system may stem either from a strong tradition of civic society mutualism combined with an affluent private health care market (as in Catalonia) or from the prevalence of informal, precarious private arrangements and under-the-table payments between doctors and patients in rural, economically underdeveloped areas (as in Galicia). In both cases, such weaknesses seem to create a sort of reinforcing mechanism by simultaneously decreasing the power and strength of public providers and users associations.

Second, federalism may strengthen some interest groups and weaken others, depending on the nature of their *organizational structure prior to decentralization*. Unions, for instance, may be better prepared to exert coordinated pressure at the central level, and less suited to diversify their vindications and strategies regionally. In contrast, professional associations may be stronger at the regional level if, as in the case of Spain, they have traditionally been organized and self-governed at the subcentral level. The same is true with regard to providers' associations, which may operate under widely different regional conditions of oligopoly and monopoly, and thus enjoy different degrees of market power. In the same vein, the ability of interest groups to exploit increased veto points to their advantage seems to depend critically on the nature and strength of their links with the government in office at each territorial level.

Power Sharing and Accountability

Third, the effects of federalism on political accountability seem to depend on *the specific power-sharing schemes prevalent in each decentralized state*. The relevant question here refers to the extent to which federal structures hinder the due translation of consistent majority preferences into public policy. The distinction between marble-cake (Germany) and layer-cake (USA) federalism should be recalled here. Under the former scheme, most policy decisions are shared among two or possibly three levels of government. This is probably the type of federalism Pierson has in mind when arguing that federalism hiders political accountability. Typically, political power is divided in each policy sector between the central government (in charge of policy formulation) and the regions (which implement policy). In addition, joint decision making is the rule, either in the form of parallel decision bodies at each territorial level (Congress and Senate, central and regional parliaments and cabinets) or in the form of bilateral or multilateral committees including representatives from both levels of government (as in the case of Spanish ordinary regions).

The consequences of this type of federalism have been widely discussed. First, as pointed out by Scharpf (1988) it tends to reduce the efficiency of the decision-making process. This is due to what has been termed *the joint-decision trap* (ibid.): unanimity informally becomes the prevalent decision rule, sharply increasing transaction costs and delaying or blocking most policy decisions. The concept of accountability, as introduced in the debate by Pierson (1994) and Banting (1987), captures, in turn, the dimension of democratic quality and equity of political decisions. As the authors have rightly emphasized, a decision system such as the one described above surely contributes to decreased accountability. Unless a significant investment is made, through a research and diffusion process, in clarifying which are the dynamics of political negotiations and pacts reached within the complicated and sometimes obscure web of committees which characterizes marble-cake federalism, the decision-making system harms account-ability mainly by decreasing the visibility of the policy process (Sartori, 1987).

In contrast, under layer-cake federalism (prevalent in the Spanish special regions), each level of government retains almost full powers over the policy sectors which are attributed to them by the Constitution. This power-sharing scheme allows for clearer political accountability, in two senses: on the one hand, with respect to marble-cake schemes, as the case of Galicia from 1991 on emphasizes; on the other hand, as regards the degree of accountability prevalent in a centralized state, contrary to what Pierson (1994) argues. Why? Regional governments are closer to citizens, which decreases information asymmetries and may lower the costs of political mobilization and collective action against government. In addition, regional authorities have a more limited package of policies under their responsibility, which might simplify the task of punishing them through elections for their poorer performance in a particular policy field.

Institutions, however, constrain or expand the opportunities for citizens to control state actions, but do not automatically guarantee that such control is actually exerted. The extent to which those improved opportunities are fully exploited depends on the *relationships between citizens and the state*: that is, on the eagerness of the population to obtain information on government policies, on the transparency and visibility surrounding political decisions, and on the local capabilities for collective action and political mobilization – or, in other words, on the regional level of social capital (Putnam *et al.*, 1993). Other significant political actors here are mass media, political opposition and other political associations like unions and users associations. The extent to which those actors are truly independent from regional governments and vested interests, responsive to citizens' preferences and active in their intermediating role is crucial to fostering improved levels of accountability in a federal state.

More concretely, the impact of federalism on accountability seems to depend on the level of government at which civil society is more democratic and active. In principle, the regional level apparently offers improved conditions of scale and cultural homogeneity that may contribute to its development. Nonetheless, and at least during the transition period, historical traditions of centralization usually account for a central level with more organizational, associational and informational muscle. The final answer, however, is likely to vary from country to country and from region to region. It remains, therefore, an empirical question, as the Spanish case exemplifies.

Policy Failures: The Way Out

The final question raised throughout the case study is a critical one. How can policy blockage be sorted out? In other words, under which circumstances might governance failure evolve into reform success? The dynamics of policy implementation in primary care at the central level give us some clues about an apparently successful strategy, which combines a particular policy style with a specific institutional development scheme. As regards *the policy style*, the first lesson from the Spanish case is to avoid open confrontation with interest groups at the macro political level in the initial stages of the reform process, even at the cost of modifying programmatic content during the formulation process. The strategy followed by Spanish central government (eliminating compulsory integration of doctors, and softening implementation obligations for regions) clearly exemplifies this. The second, crucial lesson is to proceed cautiously, incrementally, at the micro institutional level, by combining general consensual strategies (such as negotiations with the unions and correctly designed positive incentives to integrate) with selective confrontational strategies (such as negative incentives for those doctors who are not willing to integrate). The lower political visibility of the micro level, together with the reduced group to which selective negative incentives apply, sharply decreased the potential electoral costs of the fight against powerful, respectful interest groups which developed in the Spanish primary care field.

The *institutional development scheme* which helped to clear political blockage in Spain is as follows. It simply consists of progressively increasing the size and quality of public primary care manpower and infrastructure, which had two important political consequences. First, it allowed for the entrance into the system of new generations of young, better trained GPs, with vested interests in the success of welfare expansion reforms. This, in turn, fostered a demographic change in the prevalent political coalitions within the sector. In fact, this constitutes one of the main strategies to sort out political blockage, as pointed out by established organizational theory (Cyert and March, 1963). Second, it seems reasonable to assume that popular support for welfare expansion policies will depend on the percentage of the population actually using public health care services and, therefore, on the very quality and strength of the public sector vis-à-vis the private one. As remarked elsewhere, both effects may develop through the dynamics described by Schelling (1978) as *threshold models*: as the public primary care sector progressively expanded, the number of GPs and citizens who favour welfare expansion increased, up to a point (or threshold) at which they became the majority within the sector, thus cleaning out policy blockage.

7   THE LANDSCAPE AFTER THE BATTLE: CONCLUDING REMARKS

The evidence examined for the case of Spain points to the following conclusions. The medical profession has played a significant political role in the process of decision making and implementation of primary care reforms.

Both as individual players and as collective political actors, conservative doctors with strong links to the private sector have contributed to delaying and sometimes blocking implementation at the central and regional levels of government. There are apparent differences, however, in the strength of their effects across government tiers. In particular, the prolonged policy blockage in Galicia and Catalonia contrasts with the almost full implementation achieved at the central level.

Does this means that decentralization increases the probabilities of collusion between government and interest groups, and thus of policy blockage? The answer seems to be yes and no at the same time. It is yes in the sense of improved institutional access of interest groups to the state, due to multiplied veto points which characterize federal or quasi-federal decision systems. It is no if power-sharing schemes are correctly designed so as to minimize decision costs and maximize accountability, and if an active, democratic civil society exists to counterbalance the pressures of vested interests.

More specifically, federalism seems to hinder welfare state development under the following circumstances: unclearly allocated political responsibilities; low political consensus and intensity of preferences for the reform by the main political actors; existence of strong interest groups opposed to the reform, which are better organized at the regional level, and hold sociological and personal connections with the government in office; insufficiently mobilized regional civil societies; and prevalence of opposition parties which are either inefficient or uneager to play the role of agents of citizens' preferences.

In programmatic terms, the evidence examined underlines that the development of an extensive, reformed public health care sector can constitute a considerable political success even in times of cost containment and pre-dominance of market-led political ideologies. Politicians faced with an underdeveloped public welfare sector, and wanting to improve on it, may well decide to start by expanding public provision instead of contracting out to the private sector from the beginning. The advantages of doing so, at least in the primary care sector, seem to be as follows. First, it is a cheap way of guaranteeing homogeneous quality of provision through public training of doctors and infrastructure development, especially in developing countries in which the private sector may be as weak as the public one. Second, it strengthens the political power of state authorities vis-à-vis interests groups, via reduced dependence on powerful private providers, and increased support by public GPs and users. After expanding public provision, market-led reforms might be more safely introduced through the promotion of opting-out strategies for public providers trained within the public sector, who are more likely to be loyal to and cooperative with state authorities. Such a strategy will have the additional advantage of guaranteeing more efficient subsequent state regulation of the private sector, due to reduced informational asymmetries between purchasers and providers, and a more powerful position of state authorities.

15. Making health policy in Sweden: the rise and fall of the 1994 family doctor scheme

Peter Garpenby

1 INTRODUCTION

Sweden is often described as a nation in which comprehensive health services occupy a central position in the welfare state that was built up after World War II (Ham, 1992b). During the three decades immediately following the war, Sweden was able to allocate an increasing proportion of its national resources to welfare services, not the least of which went to a greatly expanding health care sector focused on hospital services. From 1950 until 1980, total health care spending, expressed as a percentage of GNP, increased in Sweden from 3.5 per cent to 9 per cent.[1] During the 1980s and to an even greater extent during the 1990s, health care, like other publicly financed services in Sweden, experienced economic constraints as a result of limited economic growth and shrinking revenue from taxation. At the same time, interest in shifting the balance between hospitals and primary health care increased, and the latter became attractive not only from an ideological but also from an economic point of view.

During the first part of the twentieth century health care services located outside large institutions were of low priority in Sweden. Around 1970, a new concept of primary health care (PHC) was presented based on public health care centres with population responsibility (*Socialstyrelsen*, 1968). The initiative did not come from the medical profession, but was instead a product of political–administrative deliberation. A new type of general practitioner was to be trained for service in PHC. Doctors were not to be predominant, however, as the organization was to be based on multiprofessional teamwork with strong ties to social services. From the beginning, the role of the new general practitioner was not clear in relation to other professional groups in PHC and to hospital doctors. The result was long-term difficulties in filling general practitioner positions in PHC. The general public, which was used to seeking care

259

directly from hospital outpatient clinics, also had difficulty in accepting PHC as the point of entry to the health care system.

The family doctor scheme of 1994 (*Husläkarreformen*) was an attempt to make PHC more attractive both to doctors and to the general public. The doctors' role was to be emphasized and the doctor–patient relationship strengthened by making it possible for people to freely choose a personal family doctor. The scheme was quickly introduced by the non-socialist coalition government that took office in 1991, and the plan was for the new system to be implemented throughout the country during 1994. Through its trade union, the Swedish Medical Association, the medical profession had supported the main direction of the scheme, but the organized medical profession had difficulty handling the practical consequences.

When the Social Democrats regained power in 1994, the law requiring county councils to implement the family doctor scheme was repealed. Elements of the scheme have survived, but the structure of PHC has become more pluralistic during the remainder of the 1990s. The problem of making PHC more attractive to the medical profession remains.

This chapter intends to show how the 1994 family doctor scheme can be understood as a challenge to both institutional and political interests. The scheme infringed upon the ideologically charged concept of population responsibility that had long been a guide for PHC. Since according to legislation the scheme was to be implemented in a similar way throughout the country, it also violated the sector-specific policy style that had been established in Swedish health care.

2   THE MAIN ACTORS IN SWEDISH HEALTH CARE

The key actors in the Swedish health policy arena are the central, regional and local governments, their representatives at the national level, for example public authorities and interest organizations, and various professional associations.

In contrast to many other countries the governmental departments in Sweden are quite small and have rather weak administrative capacity. The ministry of health and social affairs (*Socialdepartementet*) is mainly occupied with broad policy making, including the preparation of legislation, but must also take on issues in need of urgent political consideration. For detailed policy formulation in health care, and particularly with respect to implementation of policy, the ministry relies on a number of state agencies.

At the national level, the National Board of Health and Welfare (NBHW) is the authority that is responsible, under the ministry of health and social affairs, for monitoring, follow-up and evaluation of health care. To some extent the government controls the NBHW's activities by means of standing instructions and annual assignments. Like other Swedish state agencies, however, the NBHW (*Socialstyrelsen*) has a large amount of freedom regarding the implementation of mandates. Ministries in Sweden have neither the constitutional nor the practical possibility of directing the agencies in detail.

According to the Health and Medical Care Act of 1983 (HSL) the main responsibility for providing preventive and curative care to the population rests with regional and local government.[2] During the 1980s and much of the 1990s, health care providers consisted of 26 regional and local government units (23 county councils and three municipalities).[3] They are directly elected bodies with their own right of taxation. In the 1990s, the local government level in Sweden – the municipalities – took over responsibility for health services, especially to the elderly part of the population.

The regional and local government providers of health services have some powerful representatives at the national level that look after their interests. The Federation of County Councils (FCC) was established in the 1920s as an employers' organization when regional and local government wanted to act collectively towards health service unions. The FCC (*Landstingsförbundet*) is consequently not an agency, but is instead an employers' and interest organization (its members are the county councils and municipalities responsible for health care provision in Sweden). The FCC still has an important role as an employers' organization, but since the mid-1970s it has increasingly become a key actor on the national scene and an intermediator in contacts between the government and the county councils. During the 1990s, the Federation of Municipalities (*Kommunförbundet*) has increased its role as the voice of the 289 municipalities in issues related to health policy. Nevertheless, this organization is less important than the FCC with respect to health policy issues.

There is a multitude of professional associations on the national scene, but in this context we focus only upon those bodies representing the medical profession. The two main professional branches have different responsibilities, and with respect to health and medical policy issues they can sometimes end up in a competitive situation in relationship to the state.

The Swedish Medical Association (SMA), which organizes well over 90 per cent of the medical profession in Sweden, is built up as a strictly democratic organization. Influence by the membership is canalized through seven professional associations and 28 local bodies. This means that the numerical size of the different professional associations is important. The largest is the Swedish Association of Senior Hospital Physicians (*Överläkarföreningen*), followed by the Swedish Junior Hospital Physicians Association (SYLF). There is also a branch for general practitioners working in primary care, the District Physicians Association (*Distriktsläkarföreningen*, DLF). Since the SMA (*Läkarförbun-*

det) is a trade union as well as a professional association, it has extensive contacts with the FCC concerning terms and service and continuing education of physicians in the public sector, but the organization also has contacts with the ministry of health and social affairs. The SMA usually represents the profession when the government appoints consultation committees to consider health policy issues.

Within the Swedish Society of Medicine (SSM) the university medical faculties have a strong position, and the interest of the organization is largely directed towards issues involving education, research and the standard of medicine. The national body of the SSM (*Läkaresällskapet*), which has approximately 60–70 per cent of the profession as members, arranges symposiums and conferences, provides funding for research and publishes literature. However, the real power is vested in the slightly more than 60 speciality associations, which have a very independent position in the SSM. The degree of activity within the different speciality associations varies, as do their organizational forms (number of work groups and so on). The largest speciality associations represent general practice, general surgery and internal medicine.

3   THE POLITICAL AND INSTITUTIONAL CONTEXTS OF SWEDISH HEALTH CARE

From the 1960s to the 1990s, increasingly more responsibility for both funding of health care and the actual provision of services was transferred to regional and local government, while the central government withdrew from the role of care provider, concentrating instead on broad policy making and supervision. At the beginning of the 1990s, 80 per cent of public health care was financed by means of regional and local government taxes, 10 per cent through state grants, and 10 per cent through other sources of revenue such as patient co-payment. This shift in responsibility is not unique to health care, but part of a general trend in Swedish society (Premfors, 1998).

During the 1970s, the county councils strengthened their political and administrative capacity, and through the FCC, their interest organization, they challenged the NBHW and the detailed control of the health care sector (Garpenby, 1995). During the first part of the 1990s, when the family doctor scheme was initiated, the central government had access to a limited number of policy instruments for influencing health care. Over and above financial instruments, which are powerful but blunt, the central government had to rely mainly on dialogue with regional government providers and solutions reached through negotiation. Health care providers, on the other hand, had been accustomed since the 1970s to a situation in which they themselves could make decisions concerning organizational solutions in health care, and elements of detailed legislation – other than regulations about purely medical issues – were minimal. It can thereby be contended that the sector-specific policy style concerning health care had shifted since the 1970s. Policy style, as defined by Richardson *et al.* (1982), stands for 'standard operating procedures for handling issues, which arrive on the political agenda'. The concept of policy style consists of two aspects: (a) a government's approach to problem solving and (b) a government's relationship to other actors. In both respects a functional division had developed among central, regional and local government. Intervention via legislation from the national level in the organization of health care could not be understood as anything less than violation of an established order.

After World War II the relationship between the state and the medical profession in Sweden changed dramatically, owing above all to the successively introduced, all-inclusive, publicly financed health care system, where terms increasingly came under the control of political decision makers. In the late 1940s and 1950s, the SMA made fruitless attempts on behalf of the medical profession to uphold the role of doctors as constituting an independent profession (Heidenheimer, 1980). However, the Swedish medical profession, with a very long tradition of cooperation with the state, was ill-suited for taking up a militant fight. Through negotiations, and in certain cases in combination with economic compensation, the right of hospital doctors to collect fees directly from patients was restricted, and by means of the so-called 'Seven Crowns' reform in 1970 an all-inclusive salary system for doctors was introduced in public service (Garpenby 1989). To simplify somewhat, it can be maintained that regulation of the Swedish medical profession was concluded in the mid-1970s when private doctors affiliated with the national health insurance (NHI) had their fees regulated. The medical profession was thereby positioned totally within a politically controlled health care system. This process, which was under way from the end of World War II until the mid-1970s, can be interpreted in terms of professional regulation activities (Moran and Wood, 1993). The activities in Sweden (executed through negotiation and legislation) concerned both *payment regulation* for doctors (for example, the Seven Crowns reform) and the *regulation of market structures* (where the private activities of doctors were limited).[4] Governments of different political colour thereafter imposed marginal changes on doctors by, for example, allowing or prohibiting publicly employed doctors from having a private practice in addition to their public positions. On the whole, however, the regulative measures of the 1970s still apply to Swedish doctors.

4   THE FAMILY DOCTOR SCHEME OF 1994: AN INSTITUTIONAL AND POLITICAL CHALLENGE

Restoration of Primary Health Care: A Political Project

Towards the end of the 1940s, Sweden stood at a crossroad with respect to the design of the health care system. As was the case in the UK – which carried out great changes at this time through the introduction of the National Health Service (NHS) – Swedish health care was relatively 'run-down', and the pressure for 'modernization' was great. An essential difference compared with the UK was that the totally dominant public health care in Sweden, with emphasis on hospital care, was bound by close ties to regional and local government, and no change in this regard was of interest. Another difference compared with the UK was the modest role played by general practice outside of hospitals. To be sure, there was an old ambulatory care system operated by the central government – the district medical service – but it had become stagnant and was not attractive to either doctors or the general public. At the end of the 1940s, parts of the central health care administration launched plans for a new organization for primary health care based on public health care centres staffed with salaried general practitioners (the *Höjer* Plan). At this time, however, there was strong opposition to such a development on the part of the medical establishment, regional government health care providers, the leading trade unions and vital sections of national political actors. During the following decades Sweden therefore modernized its health care, with strong emphasis on hospital service. The public obtained direct access to outpatient clinics at hospitals, and the district medical organization never got the role of gatekeeper. At this time, the 1950s and 1960s, jobs at hospitals were those that attracted the medical profession, and interest in working in primary care was weak. As a result, public outpatient care outside the hospital degenerated further through vacancies in doctors' positions (Garpenby, 1989). In an attempt to improve the situation, the regional government, at the initiative of the central government, took over responsibility in 1963 for the district medical service. This was already in disrepute, and the county councils were totally focused on the continued expansion of hospitals.

Around 1970, a new concept was presented for primary health care in Sweden that was based on public health care centres with population responsibility (*Socialstyrelsen*, 1968). The initiative did not come from the medical profession, but from political–administrative circles around the ministry of health and social affairs and the NBHW. Two strong arguments were presented for revitalizing PHC: that developments in medical technology made it possible to move activities out of hospitals, and that developments within society motivated a decentralized organization for cooperation between medicine and social services. In the background, economic arguments also advocated an expansion of PHC, although at this time these were not as prominent as two decades later (Skånér, 1993). A new type of general practitioner (*allmänläkare*) was to be trained to work in PHC. Nevertheless, this role was rather diffuse in the beginning, as medical aspects were toned down and the social dimension was emphasized (Haglund, 1992). The new PHC was to be based on multiprofessional teamwork, where the doctors' role was not pre-eminent (Krakau, 1995).

Despite attempts with carrots (favourable working conditions) and sticks (control of educational appointments) in order to induce future doctors to choose a career in PHC, expansion went very slowly. During the 1970s and 1980s, Sweden had a lower proportion of general practitioners than any other European country. In 1973, there were 1250 positions for publicly employed GPs in Sweden, 35 per cent of which were not permanently filled (*BRA Gruppen*, 1974). At the end of the 1980s, there were approximately 3000 general practitioners in Sweden, which can be compared to the planned number of 4500. Many new doctors quit the GP training programme, and a significant number changed specialisms later (*Sveriges Läkarförbund*, 1988). The problems originated in difficulties in giving general practitioners a clear identity in the political project constituted by the new primary health care. The county councils also had trouble challenging the dominant hospital establishment in favour of PHC, and met resistance both from the medical profession and from the general public. When the need for economic restrictions in health care became urgent during the 1980s, primary health care became more attractive to politicians on the national and regional levels. However, advocates of the population-based primary health care had difficulty at the beginning of the 1990s in finding appropriate forms by which to regenerate PHC and make it more attractive to doctors.

Post-1991 Top-down Reforms ('the Family Doctor Scheme')

Under the non-socialist coalition government that ruled Sweden between 1991 and 1994, sweeping changes in primary health care were initiated. The family doctor scheme (*Husläkarreformen*), which was to be launched in 1994, can be viewed as the single most ambitious attempt to reform the medical profession since 1975, although it was directed towards only one part of the health care system. The aim of the reform was to upgrade the role of PHC in the health care system, increase its role as gatekeeper and make it more attractive to both doctors and patients.

When the non-socialist coalition took over the government in Stockholm in the autumn of 1991, civil servants in the ministry of health and social affairs, who were controlled by the Liberal Party, were given the task of working out the details as fast as possible for a reorganization of PHC. To be sure, the Liberal

Party had long advocated a reorganization of primary health care, but there was no prepared plan when the new government took office. In March of 1992, the new minister of health, Bo Könberg, commissioned a work group within the ministry to formulate a detailed proposal for a family doctor scheme. The group completed the assignment in May of the same year, and the report was then sent in usual Swedish fashion to the authorities and organizations concerned for their consideration (the so-called 'remiss system').

What the work group presented was a national scheme to be carried out in a uniform way throughout the whole country. The principal idea was that the public would obtain a fixed point in the large and chaotic health care apparatus through the free choice of a family doctor. This doctor was to stand for continuity and was to send the patient onward to the correct level of care. The scheme was also intended to give general practitioners greater influence over their own work situation and thereby make PHC more attractive (*Socialdepartementet*, 1992a). The need for better doctor continuity had long been discussed and was not in itself controversial. Other components of the proposal were all the more controversial, however. The free choice of a doctor was emphasized and was manifested in the individual's right to choose among general practitioners irrespective of previous geographic affiliation. The work group proposed that those who did not actively choose a doctor could be assigned to a particular doctor by the county council. The individual would have the right to change the family doctor after six months. The ambitions of the non-socialist government were clearly reflected in the fact that general practitioners were offered the right to establish a private practice in whatever form they chose. In other words the doctor could choose whether he or she wanted to be employed by the county council (the predominant system) or by a company, or to work in a staff cooperative, as a part-owner of a group practice, or as a self-employed doctor. The proposal emphasized that remuneration for the doctors was to be provider-neutral; that is, preferential treatment would not be given to any particular provider. Capitation fees – a fixed, age-related remuneration per listed person – were to comprise 70–80 per cent of the total remuneration. Capitation fees were something totally new in Sweden and had never before been tested in health care. Exactly how capitation fees would be weighted, however, was not clear when the first proposal was presented in the spring of 1992.

The proposal created strong feelings in many parts of the Swedish health care sector, and the ministry received approximately 150 commentaries from authorities, organizations, trade unions, health care personnel and individuals (*Socialdepartementet*, 1992b). The aim was to begin to implement the family doctor scheme during 1993, but the proposal had to be reworked and the proposition was not submitted to the Parliament until early 1993 (Proposition 1992/93, 160).

In the Bill the government pointed out that PHC had been the subject of discussion and policy statements for close to 20 years, and the scheme was presented as a further development of a process that had already begun within PHC. The minister of health explained this in the following way:

> The system I am proposing does not follow any already-existing system. My aspiration has been to utilize experience, both international and domestic, and adapt it to Swedish developments and our current circumstances. I have also taken into consideration the opinions of the bodies to which the proposal was referred for consideration. (Proposition 1992/93: 160, p. 29)

Many influential bodies had criticized the idea that the work of family doctors should be regulated by law – a common view was that this should be left to the county councils. An important exception in this regard was the organized medical profession, which wanted a national standardization (see further below). The government chose to back down on this point and allow room for local variations, but explained that a minimum standard had to be stipulated by law. Included in this would be the doctor's obligation to have round-the-clock responsibility for the individual patient and to coordinate the medical measures needed by the patient. The family doctor's activities were to comprise between 1000 and 3000 patients. However, each county council got the right to set the level for capitation fees, which would constitute the largest proportion of the doctors' remuneration. The motive behind this was that the costs in PHC, even the costs for salaries, varied throughout the country. In order to be eligible for remuneration, the doctor who wanted to work as a family doctor had to be able to show after 12 months that at least 1000 patients had signed up with him or her. By way of exception, in rural areas the county councils could grant fees for doctors with whom fewer patients had signed up. Among the bodies to which the proposal had been submitted for consideration, there was no great enthusiasm about the right to establish a private practice. Only four county councils accepted this principle, but the minister insisted that free establishment of a practice was one of the cornerstones of the scheme, as was the aim for the system to be neutral regarding providers and competition.

Instead of emphasizing the collective element and the social dimension, such as teamwork, as the basis of PHC, as previous governments had done, the coalition government thought that PHC had much to gain by having family doctors compete for patients. Consequently, totally new terms were advanced in PHC: the free choice of a doctor where the general public could change doctors at intervals, the free establishment of practices, which opened the way for private practice in a health care system that had previously been dominated totally by public providers, and remuneration for doctors through capitation fees, all of which set the stage for competition. In time, the possibility existed that a doctor who did not succeed in attracting patients would lose the right to remuneration – a totally new situation in Swedish health care, where for over 20 years doctors had had full-time employment for life. Under protest from the opposition parties to the left, the Swedish Parliament passed the proposal for the family doctor scheme during the autumn of 1993.

The Partisan Dimension of the Reform

The family doctor scheme contains a party-political dimension without which its rapid introduction and abrupt downfall cannot be understood. The primary care that emerged in Sweden after 1970 was formulated to a great extent in accordance with a social democratic view of what constitutes good health care. To a greater degree than was the case for hospital-based health care, primary health care was a political project whose design the Social Democrats, by virtue of having long been in control of the government, could influence. The possibility of people choosing was of subordinate importance, and the model was based on doctors having responsibility for a geographic area; thus population responsibility was emphasized rather than the general practitioner's responsibility for individual patients.

The main advocate of the family doctor scheme was the Liberal Party (*Folkpartiet Liberalerna*). During the late 1940s and the early 1950s, the Liberal Party had been the dominant non-socialist opposition party in Sweden, with over 20 per cent of the voters supporting it in the *Riksdag*, but thereafter the party had lost voter support. To be sure, in the 1985 *Riksdag* election the Liberal Party temporarily succeeded in interrupting a downward trend when it obtained 14 per cent of the votes, but in the following general election in 1988 it again lost votes. Its weakened position in Swedish politics and the increased demand for media attention in election campaigns meant that the Liberal Party was to a very great extent forced to search for new profile issues by which to attract flexible voters with non-socialist sympathies. A subject area which had attracted increasingly great interest among the Swedish electorate since the 1970s was social politics and health care (Gilljam and Holmberg, 1990). During the 1980s, the Liberal Party made recurrent attempts to introduce health care as a profile area, where the party wanted to combine elements of greater freedom of choice for the population with safeguarding resources for the welfare sector.

At the end of the 1980s, several political parties in Sweden directed their attention to the issue of freedom of choice in health care for the population and the need for greater continuity in the doctor–patient relationship. Even the Social Democrats began to acknowledge the value of giving the individual a greater possibility of choosing a health care provider. The Liberal Party was alone, however, in focusing on primary health care and in introducing its own concept for remodelling the area – the family doctor. As early as the mid-1970s, the party submitted a proposal along these lines to the *Riksdag* for a reorganization of primary health care. During the 1980s it was quiet on the national political scene regarding the family doctor issue; primary health care was expanded according to the population responsibility model (Krakau, 1995). Within the Liberal Party, however, the idea continued to live on, and it was awakened once again prior to the 1991 general election. In that election, when the non-socialist parties together succeeded in defeating the Social Democrats, the Liberal Party continued to lose voters. Nevertheless, in the political platform (*regeringsförklaringen*) of the coalition government the party succeeded in getting a section included on a family doctor scheme. The coalition government promised to 'press on' in order to make it possible for everyone to have a freely chosen family doctor. Since the Liberal Party wanted to create an image for itself regarding social issues and health care issues, the party demanded control of the ministry of health and social affairs. Bo Könberg, the new minister of health, had been a county council politician and was an ardent supporter of the family doctor concept.

The Reaction to the Reform Proposal

The central medical administration (the NBHW)

In its response to the ministry regarding the proposed measure, the NBHW showed great independence and presented serious objections to the proposal. The NBHW was of the opinion that the proposal did not show how the general public's free choice would increase access to the GPs, or how the changeover to a family doctor scheme would even out differences in geographic access to doctors. The state authority pointed out that existing labour market legislation would make it difficult to attain provider neutrality between publicly employed and private family doctors. The state authority was doubtful about a special law for PHC and thought that the government should instead consider an amendment to the 1983 Health and Medical Care Act (*Socialdepartementet*, 1992b).

The regional government representatives

The family doctor scheme meant that the government intervened at a level of detail not seen after the introduction of the 1983 Health and Medical Care Act. It was thus expected that the county councils and their representative at the national level, the FCC, would react very negatively to the sections of the reform that involved regulatory intervention by the central government. However, the government got the support of the FCC concerning the fundamental principle of the family doctor scheme: the free choice of a doctor. This was not particularly controversial at the beginning of the 1990s, when most parties in the *Riksdag* accepted a development that involved greater freedom of choice in health care for the public. With respect to the proposal for the right of family doctors to open a private practice, there was strong opposition from the county councils. The FCC emphasized that the reform had to take local circumstances into consideration and provide room for local decisions, that is to say within the county councils. Hence the majority of county councils objected to those parts of the proposal that involved a uniform contract for the family doctor, imposed by the government (*Socialdepartementet*, 1992b).

The medical profession

As is the case in other countries, the medical profession in Sweden is not a homogeneous group, but instead consists of different segments representing various interests, and they act accordingly. Within the SMA, general practitioners constitute a minority, and hospital-based doctors have long dominated the association. The doctors' professional and trade union organization had earlier claimed that PHC needed to be strengthened and that working conditions for general practitioners needed to be improved, but the SMA had hesitated to present a proposal that would involve a reallocation of resources from hospitals to PHC, which could provoke large groups of hospital doctors. At the end of the 1980s, the SMA defended the geographic population responsibility that publicly employed general practitioners had, and the proposal for reorganization of PHC that was presented was based on the existing organization (*Sveriges läkarförbund*, 1988). The new leadership of the SMA that took over at the beginning of the 1990s was, however, open to more radical reforms in Swedish health care. A work group developed a proposal for a totally new organization and financing of primary health care (*Piff*). According to this, PHC would be financed through national health insurance (a solution advocated at the political level only by the Conservative Party) and different types of providers were recommended: doctors employed at health care centres, in private group practice and in individual practices. The work group recommended a multitude of solutions to stimulate development of a stagnant PHC. Doctors would be remunerated by means of capitation and fees for visits. The main features of the proposal, with the exception of financing, resembled those of the family doctor scheme introduced by the non-socialist government. An important difference, however, was that the county councils had a subordinate role as care providers in the SMA proposal. The intention was that monitoring of activities would be carried out by state authorities and by the profession itself (peer review) (*Sveriges läkarförbund*, 1991). It is difficult to say how well anchored the proposal (or 'draft', which was the exact term used) was within the association. The leadership claimed that the proposal was discussed in all important meetings and that a majority backed it (Milton, 1992a, 1992b).

When the non-socialist government presented its first outline of the family doctor scheme in the spring of 1992 (*Socialdepartementet*, 1992a), the SMA was disappointed at the fact that the government was forced to compromise and leave decisions on matters of detail to the county councils. With respect to free choice by the population, the association noted that popular and well-known doctors risked being 'overburdened' by care-demanding patients. The organization therefore wanted an additional report on the model for choosing one's own family doctor. The SMA did not say anything, however, about the risk that less popular doctors would fail to register a sufficient number of individuals (which had consequences later for the association; see below). The opinion of the SMA was that capitation would have to be set high so that doctors would not be forced to provide 'unnecessary' visits (*Läkartidningen*, 1992). The chairman of the SMA complained about the fact that the county councils received the right to determine the size of the capitation fees. In that way PHC would also to be in the hands of local politicians in the future (Johnson, 1993). The SMA was cautious, however, about touching on the issue of competition among doctors – for which the reform paved the way. Instead, it was the trade union of the publicly employed general practitioners (the DLF, which is part of the SMA) that emphasized in a more forceful way the risks entailed by the government proposal. Against the background of the intention for family doctors to have 24-hour responsibility for patients, the DLF wondered if this was compatible with the Restriction of Working Hours Act and the Occupational Safety and Health Act. The association did not oppose the free choice of a doctor, but wanted population responsibility to live on in some form. The general practitioners' professional association within the SSM, the SFAM, was protective to an even greater extent concerning the established structure of PHC. It was totally against the possibility of family doctors establishing private practices and upheld teamwork in PHC. As the umbrella organization, the SSM emphasized that the reform could not take resources away from hospitals and it wished, among other things, that specialists other than general practitioners could become family doctors (*Läkartidningen*, 1992; *Överläkaren*, 1992). Consequently, there was much mixed reaction to the proposal within the bodies representing the organized medical profession.

The nursing profession

As there was a lack of general practitioners when the new PHC was introduced in the 1970s, it was in many cases the nursing staff who actually shouldered the activities. The community nurse (*distriktssköterskan*) was dominant in the geographic teams that were organized, and because of the vacancies in doctors' jobs consequently got a very prominent position, which was also recognized by the political decision makers. The family doctor scheme was perceived as a threat to the community nurse's position in the organization, as the proposal placed the doctor in a central position and the principles of geographic population responsibility and teamwork were done away with. Over the long run the general public's free choice of a family doctor could involve a difficult organizational adjustment for the community nurse, who was used to working with a particular GP in a stable geographic district. In its commentary to the non-socialist government's proposal for a family doctor scheme, the nurses' trade union, the SHSTF, rejected the idea of national legislation. The SHSTF declared that there was a risk that the proposal would divide and threaten preventive efforts in the existing population-based model and break up an organization that in many places was functioning well (*Socialdepartementet*, 1992b). In August 1992, the county division of the SHSTF in Stockholm arranged a demonstration against the family doctor scheme (Nyman, 1992).

A Dilemma for the SMA: Remuneration of the Unattractive Doctor

During the first part of 1994, when the family doctor scheme began to be implemented, the SMA ended up in a dilemma regarding the balance between being a professional association advocating radical reforms in health care and the trade union that safeguards the narrow interests of its members. One effect of the free choice of a doctor was that certain family doctors did not succeed in having a sufficient number of patients sign up with them, and this caused problems, especially in public health care. In their role as employers, the county councils demanded that the patients' choice of a doctor should have priority over the Security of Employment Act of 1974 (which stipulates that no one can be fired without objective reasons, and that the principle that the last person hired is the first to be fired is in effect when there is a scarcity of work). In addition, it was the wish of the FCC that the number of patients doctors had on their lists would affect the salaries of the publicly employed GPs in accordance with provisions for private family doctors. The SMA was unable to accept these principles and demanded complete employment security for all GPs in public employment, with no change in salaries. During a three-week period in the spring of 1994, the SMA ordered doctors in hospitals and health care centres in four county councils to take strike action as a result both of these issues and of other salary and employment questions. With respect to employment security, which is regulated by law, the county councils were forced to yield, and on the issue of the family doctors' salaries there was a compromise: the parties agreed to a local revision of salaries according to the size of the doctors' lists, although this was not binding. The conflict showed that as a trade union the SMA found it very difficult to accept in practice the consequences of the population's free choice within the framework of the family doctor scheme – a principle which the association officially went along with. For many decades Swedish health care had been totally covered by labour market legislation, and publicly employed doctors had adapted to this. When it was seen that some doctors were more popular than others and that some doctors were unable to attract a sufficient number of patients, the SMA in its trade union capacity also had to take action for these members: the fact that patients were voting with their feet was then of secondary importance.

The Repeal of the National Reform

Back in 1992, when the non-socialist government first introduced the family doctor scheme, the Social Democrats opposed national legislation. The official view of the party was that the reform would destroy a functioning primary health care and that there was a risk that it would be detrimental to the teamwork that had long characterized PHC (Motion, 1993/4: s15004pa). When the proposal for legislation was dealt with in Parliament, the Social Democratic representatives in the standing committee on social affairs rejected the intro-duction of the family doctor scheme. They felt that it would have a negative effect on the chances of establishing equally good and equitable health care throughout the country, and pointed out that the legislation would involve a serious encroachment on regional government autonomy (*Socialutskottet*, 1992/3). When the Social Democrats regained governmental power in 1994, they took the initiative in repealing the family doctor scheme. The national law ceased to exist at the end of 1995. Implementation of the law varied greatly throughout the country. Some county councils had rapidly tried to put the scheme into effect, while others delayed in implementing it in expectation of a change of government.

Since 1995, PHC has taken different directions throughout the country; some county councils have reverted totally to the old principle of geographic population responsibility, where people are assigned a doctor on the basis of where they live, while other county councils have retained elements of the family doctor scheme. In this regard the county council of *Västmanland* constitutes an extreme: signing up with a particular doctor is still practised there, and the GPs are remunerated by means of capitation fees. Of the family doctors in *Västmanland*, 60 per cent are publicly employed, while 40 per cent are private contractors to the county council (Pineus, 1999).

5 ASSESSING THE CASE

One aim of the family doctor scheme was to even out access to doctors throughout the country; the northern parts of Sweden had traditionally experienced difficulty in recruiting GPs. Approximately 4000 doctors joined the scheme, and slightly over 700 intended to work in the private sector. In Gothenburg, for example, 40 per cent of the family doctors worked in the private sector, while in the far north (*Norrbotten*) there were no doctors who voiced an interest in private practice. About 20 per cent of the private family doctors had left positions with the county councils, while the others were former company doctors or private practitioners affiliated to the national health insurance. In this respect the scheme did not succeed in contributing to a change in access to doctors, and the regional differences remained (Rehnberg and Garpenby, 1995). In defence it can be said that the scheme was in effect for only a limited period of time, so that any long-term influence was not seen.

Primary health care received a great deal of attention through the introduction of the family doctor scheme, but positive effects on the recruitment of GPs were limited. By allowing exceptions from the rule that all family doctors working under the scheme should have a specialist licence in general practice it was hoped that the scheme would attract doctors in other parts of the health service. The fact that only 200 doctors applied for and obtained dispensation was considered a fiasco by the NBHW. In 1998, the NBHW reported that more than 500 doctors were still needed within PHC before the stated goal of 2000 people per GP was attained (*Socialstyrelsen*, 1998). Interest in training to be a GP continues to be limited in Sweden. As late as 1999, a report issued by the NBHW warned of the risk of a serious lack of general practitioners in the future, despite the political attention that has long been focused on PHC (*Socialstyrelsen*, 1999).

In political terms the scheme can be interpreted as a confirmation that the central government in Sweden has obvious difficulty in intervening in order to make changes in health care at the level of detail represented by the family doctor scheme. The legitimacy of the government's measures – legislating alongside the 1983 Act – was also questioned by regional government politicians who were positive towards the content of the reform. On the whole, the political parties forming the non-socialist coalition government from 1991 to 1994 had difficulty in finding a uniform line to follow in reforming health care (Garpenby, 1995). Owing to the disjointed political management of PHC during the early 1990s, the element of disillusion among those working in this area of the health care sector was also intensified. PHC received a great deal of attention, but the results were quite meagre.

The Liberal Party was the loser, as it did not succeed in profiting at all from the public discontent with the condition of Swedish health care at the beginning of the 1990s. It was found that reforming PHC in the direction advocated by the liberals did not engage the public to the extent imagined by the party. A poll taken after the 1994 general election showed that only 37 per cent of the voters with non-socialist sympathies regretted that the family doctor scheme had been repealed. There was little support for the scheme among voters with socialist sympathies (Österman, 1995). In the 1991 general election the liberals had 9 per cent of the voters behind them, but in the 1994 election they continued to lose support and won only 7 per cent of the votes.

6 CONCLUSION

How should the origins of the 1994 family doctor scheme, as well as the outcome of this reform, be understood? The fact that Swedish health care was 'out of balance' was observed as early as the 1950s, with massive expansion of hospital services and a stagnant primary health care. From 1970, the central government took an interest in this lack of balance, which became more pressing when control of costs in health care became a political issue in the 1980s. Consequently, there was strong political support at the national level for the expansion of PHC, and it was hardly provocative to recommend reforms in order to increase its importance in the health care system. The way in which the reform got onto the policy agenda can be explained partly by the idea that an expanded PHC encourages monitoring of costs in health care (structural accounts), but also by ambitions within the Liberal Party to create an image by means of this issue (agent-centred accounts).

Which factors were decisive regarding the chances the reform had to be a success or a failure? Of greatest significance in this connection was the fact that it broke so obviously with the sector-specific policy style that had been established within health care. The aspect of 'top-down' implementation was a challenge to the autonomy of the county councils. This resulted in the fact that even the non-socialist governed county councils, which were positive towards the fundamental features of the family doctor scheme, reacted negatively.

The reform also risked upsetting established institutional interests in PHC: the multiprofessional team. By placing doctors in the centre, the ministry of health and social affairs caused other health care workers to go against it, especially the nurses' professional and trade union organizations.

Considering the position of the Swedish medical profession, the 1994 family doctor scheme can be regarded as the most revolutionary reform since 1975. By making possible a large-scale transition from public employment to the role of private contractors, the scheme could have meant a new situation for the profession. Family doctors could have become self-employed and employers of other professional groups instead of being part of a team within the public sector-dominated primary health care. On the other hand the scheme did not reflect any ambition on the part of the state to deregulate the medical profession. On the contrary, it constitutes an example of the way the state, with the help of new incentives, sought to change the profession's terms, in this case changes in *the regulation of market structures* (Moran and Wood, 1993). With the aim of attaining the desired effects, the government was prepared to give general practitioners greater opportunity to establish private practices, but on the other hand the doctors were required to expand their commitment to patients and to be prepared to compete for patients.

In the early 1990s, the Swedish Medical Association (SMA) demanded, in its capacity as the most vociferous part of the organized medical profession, increased professional freedom for doctors. On the rhetorical level the association was prepared to go even further than the non-socialist government with respect to making the Swedish medical profession self-employed. In its final form the scheme was a disappointment to the SMA, as it allowed the county councils free range in influencing the terms of the relationship with the doctors. But since a large majority of the profession were in salaried service, the SMA was unable in practice to accept all the consequences of changed terms of employment for the doctors. Reactions to the scheme also showed that the majority of the Swedish medical profession had adapted to being a salaried professional group working under the protection of labour market legislation, and they were protective of employment security. Owing to this, the organization's actions were contradictory, which did not promote its credibility. If anything, the collective voice of the profession was weaker at the end of the 1990s than it was at the beginning of the decade.

NOTES

1. It is difficult to make comparisons of total spending for health care over time owing to changes in definitions, but the rate of increase was nevertheless real during the period reported upon. At the beginning of the 1990s the definition of health care services was changed in Swedish general statistics, which also meant that the percentage of the GNP fell markedly, but there were also other reasons such as that the municipalities took over large parts of elderly care from the county councils.
2. For the sake of clarity both the regional and local government health care providers, responsible for health care provision under the 1983 Act, will be referred to as 'health care providers' or 'county councils'.
3. Since 1 January 1999, there have been only 21 health care providers in Sweden (18 county councils and two regions – comprising amalgamated county councils and municipalities in southern and western Sweden – and one municipality).
4. The extensive regulation affected the collective and individual autonomy of the doctors. With respect to clinical autonomy the Swedish doctor enjoyed great freedom, at least up to the 1990s when attempts to influence clinical management (for example, clinical guidelines) were introduced in Sweden, as was the case in many other countries; but that is another story.

16. Reforming the medical profession in the United Kingdom, 1989–97: structural interests in health care

Stephen Harrison[1]

1 INTRODUCTION

The terms 'success' and 'failure' have rationalistic overtones; their usage is relative to the *intention* of an identifiable policy actor. Yet there is a substantial strand in the literature of policy analysis which questions whether such a perspective is ever capable of approaching the complexity of real-world policy making and implementation. It occupies a spectrum running from the recognition that problems do not arrive pre-defined on the governmental agenda (Kingdon, 1984), through the notion that policy and action cannot be distinguished analytically (Barrett and Fudge, 1981), to complete non-rationality (Cohen *et al.*, 1972). It is not necessary to adopt a precise position in relation to this literature in order to concede that the specific case which is described here cannot be straightforwardly interpreted as an intention to reform the UK medical profession in a specific way.[2] There has been a succession of policy measures, by a succession of governments, begun for a variety of reasons including the trivial and accidental; it is 'a chain of successive policy choices made up to the present' (Lindblom, 1959, p. 88). Attempts to reform the medical profession have continued under the post-1997 Labour government; although the central focus of this chapter is upon the policies of Conservative governments in the period 1989 to 1997, the concluding section alludes to the way in which the latter have contributed to what has been practicable for the former.

The absence of explicit policy objectives does not prevent the identification of an underlying agenda for these reform attempts; in this case that agenda is cost containment (Harrison and Moran, 2000) though UK governments have gone to great rhetorical lengths to deny it (Harrison and Hunter, 1994; Harrison and Ferguson, forthcoming). It is important therefore to be clear that the analysis which follows rests significantly on an 'ideal-regarding' (rather than 'want-regarding') concept of actors' agendas and interests (Fishkin, 1979). The content of 'reform' thus cannot be specified in terms employed by the actors themselves;

rather it must be specified by the analyst. In this chapter, 'successful reform of the medical profession' is taken to mean a significant reduction in what Alford (1975) has termed the 'professional monopoly' of doctors. It follows that the term 'reform' has no normative content in this context.

2   ACTORS AND 'STRUCTURAL INTERESTS' IN THE UK HEALTH CARE CONTEXT

Historical Background

Almost 25 years ago, the American political sociologist Robert Alford published his study of health care politics in New York (Alford, 1975), in which he introduced the concept of 'structural interests'. These were to be defined in terms of the extent to which their 'interests [are] served or not served by the way in which they "fit" into the basic logic and principles by which the institutions of society operate.' Three types of structural interest were distinguished in an analysis which owed a good deal to contemporary elite theories. 'Dominant' structural interests were those 'served by the structure of social, economic and political institutions as they exist at any given time. Precisely because of this, [they] do not continuously have to organise and act to defend their interests.' 'Challenging' interests were 'those being created by the changing structure of society', whilst 'repressed' interests were 'the opposite of the dominant ones ... the nature of institutions guarantees that they will *not* be served unless extra-ordinary political energies are mobilised' (p. 14, original emphasis). Structural interests thus were to be distinguished from pressure groups which organize to represent their interests, and the possibility of conflict within a structural interest was not ruled out.

In the context of New York in the early 1970s, Alford identified the dominant interest as the 'professional monopolists': 'medicine is a classic case of social organisation of production but the private appropriation of powers and benefits. [It] has maintained control of the supply of physicians, the distribution and cost of services and the rules governing hospitals' (p. 14). However, the dominant interest was currently under challenge from the corporate 'rationalisers', created by 'changing technology and division of labour in health care production and distribution, and the shifting rewards to social groups and classes. Bureaucratic organisations, mainly the hospitals, are the principal agents potentially available to organise this complex technology... . Hospital administrators, medical schools [and] government health planners ... share a common relationship to the underlying changes in the technology and organisation of health care. This ... generates their developing structural interest in breaking the monopoly of physicians over the production and distribution of health care' (p. 15). 'Repressed interests' (which are outside the scope of this chapter) were the 'community population', including poor people and members of the middle class with incomes marginally too high to qualify for state-funded medical care.

Alford's schema has been influential as a fairly crude categorization in brief textbook analyses of possible shifts in the power relationships between doctors and NHS managers (see, for instance, Baggott, 1998; Allsop, 1995; Mohan, 1995; Ham, 1992a; Harrison *et al.*, 1990), though it cannot be applied uncritically to the UK. An obvious difference between the UK and the United States is that health care in the former is almost entirely publicly funded; 'corporate rationalisers' in the UK are therefore likely to be predominantly agents of the state (most obviously NHS managers: Harrison, 1988a, pp. 118–25) rather than employees of private corporate organizations.[3] Moreover, the most important policy development described below, general practice fundholding, is difficult to accommodate within Alford's theory (North, 1995), a matter which is addressed in the concluding section. The following subsections provide background concerning, respectively, the state's relationship to the NHS and the UK medical profession.

The State and Health Care in Britain

The tax-financed NHS, introduced in 1948, currently accounts for some 85 per cent of UK health care expenditure (or about 5.9 per cent of gross domestic product) despite the uneven growth of private insurance since the 1970s (Office of Health Economics, 1997). UK citizens have formal access to a comprehensive range of services (mainly without user charges), though legally the NHS is founded on a central government *duty* to provide services rather than on citizen *rights* to receive them. This enables governments to 'cash-limit' (that is, cap) increasing proportions of the annual NHS budget; total UK health expenditure thus remains at 6.7 per cent of GDP, modest by the standard of OECD comparators. Yet public preferences, at least as revealed by opinion polls, are for more health expenditure; a time series of polls from 1984 to 1990 never shows less than 47 per cent of respondents identifying health as their 'first priority for additional government spending', with the second-ranked preference (education) never securing more than 27 per cent of responses (Jowell *et al.*, 1995) and other poll evidence is consistent with this. The NHS is the most popular sector of the UK welfare state, and perhaps of government endeavour more generally. Despite initial Conservative opposition to the precise form taken by the NHS in 1948 (Webster, 1998), successive governments since that time have been well aware of the political capital to be made or lost in their handling of it (Klein, 1983).

The continued development of new medical technologies and the continued ageing of the population have added to the pressure of rising demand to be expected in any system of third party payment for health care (Harrison and Moran, 2000). Since the 1970s, governments of both main parties have faced this rising demand alongside the economic pressures resulting from the end of the 'long boom' in the postwar West with a macroeconomic orthodoxy in favour of reducing public expenditure (Donaldson and Farquhar, 1988). This is not to imply that determinism is at work here; there is no simple relationship between (for instance) fluctuations in the UK budget deficit and the measures chosen to match supply of and demand for health care. Controlling medical professionals through rationalization of their work is certainly one such measure which might be chosen, but numerous other approaches exist and indeed have coexisted with it (Harrison and Pollitt, 1994; Harrison and Moran, 2000).

The State and the Medical Profession in Britain

There have always been conflicts within British medicine or between the state and medicine, not least at the creation of the NHS in the 1940s (Webster, 1998). At times since then, there has been considerable tension between specialists and junior doctors in training (Harrison *et al.*, 1990, ch. 4) and between specialists and general practitioners (GPs), whilst doctors' pay has been a source of recurring friction with governments (Seifert, 1992). Nevertheless, there are several features of the medical profession[4] in Britain that can be employed to support the claim that (in Alford's terms) it is an interest 'served by the structure of social, economic and political institutions as they exist at [a] given time'. One such feature is the pervasiveness of the so-called 'medical model', that is the view that ill-health equals individual pathology, and that medical interventions are individual ones. It is clear that such an ideology did not simply occur autonomously; Colwill (1998) has shown how the possibility of a NHS centred upon a broader public health approach was rejected in the early 1940s by medical interests in alliance with civil servants.

A second such feature is the close corporatist relationship between the profession as embodied in the British Medical Association (BMA) and medical royal colleges, and the department of health.[5] At national level, this resulted in workforce planning practices very much in the profession's interests (Harrison, 1981; Harrison *et al.*, 1990, ch. 4; see also Groenewegan and Calnan, 1995; Döhler, 1989) as well as parallel medical administrative hierarchies within the department. The impact of this relationship has however been at least as great at local level, since many aspects of the NHS's formal organization have long been constructed in a way which serves medical interests. Thus GPs have the status of self-employed business persons under a rather vaguely worded contract for services to the NHS; 'A doctor shall render to his [*sic*] patients all necessary and appropriate personal medical services of the kind usually provided by general medical practitioners' (Ellis and Chisholm, 1993, p. 12). Until 1991, GPs were entitled to refer patients to any specialist in any hospital anywhere in the UK, and (subject to administrative intervention in only the most extreme cases) to prescribe from the pharmacopoeia in whatever quantities they chose. Until 1984, doctors (especially hospital specialists) dominated the management of the NHS, not in the sense of being formally responsible for it, but in the sense of having an entrenched and effective veto. Thus until 1974 the local statutory bodies which ran the NHS had large numbers of doctors in membership (Ham, 1981), after which (until 1984) the local NHS was managed by multidisciplinary consensus decision-making teams in which doctors, each with the power of veto, held half the membership (Harrison, 1982). Until the 1990s, consultants' (that is, specialists') contracts of employment were carefully insulated from managerial discretion by being held at the regional, rather than operational, level of organization and included a number of unilaterally exercisable rights, including private practice and appeal to the Secretary of State against dismissal. A proportion of consultants was able to receive substantial 'distinction awards' in addition to their salary; these awards were unilaterally, and secretly, determined within the profession.

Third, despite their dependence on the state, doctors enjoyed considerable clinical autonomy, that is freedom to accept patients, control over diagnosis and treatment, control over evaluation of care and control over other professions (Schulz and Harrison, 1986). This implies considerable freedom from being managed. Commitment to clinical autonomy for doctors figured prominently in the official pronouncements of governments from before the creation of the NHS until the 1980s. A wartime coalition government's 1944 White Paper stated that 'whatever the organisation, the doctors taking part must remain free to direct their clinical knowledge and personal skill for the benefit of their patients in the way which they feel to be best' (Ministry of Health, 1944). These sentiments were subsequently echoed on several occasions by Aneurin Bevan, the Minister of Health who presided over the inception of the NHS (Allsop, 1995; Watkin, 1975). The same view was manifested by both main political parties in the preparations for the first reorganization of the NHS in 1974; Labour policy was that 'the Service should provide full clinical freedom to the doctors working in it' (DHSS, 1970), whilst the Conservative line specified that 'professional workers will retain their clinical freedom ... to do as they think best for their patients' (DHSS, 1972a), noting in a subsequent document that 'management plays only a subsidiary part ... [it] can help or hinder the people who play the primary part' (DHSS, 1972b). In 1979, it was stated (by the then newly-elected Conservative government) that 'It is doctors ... who provide the care and cure of patients and promote the health of the people. It is the purpose of management to support them' (DHSS and Welsh Office, 1979, pp. 1–2). The picture implied by these policy pronouncements is fleshed out in a number of empirical research studies conducted between 1966 and 1982; NHS managers possessed little influence relative to doctors and indeed were very much focused on responding to the organizational problems raised by them, with the result that organizational change tended to be incremental (Harrison, 1988a).

Policy as Blueprint

In the 1960s and 1970s, the prevailing style of policy making in respect of the NHS was consonant with the then received wisdom in other policy sectors. Thus, for instance, the design of the 1974 reorganisation had been carefully developed over a period of several years. The process of its development included extensive consultation via two 'Green Papers' (Ministry of Health, 1968; DHSS, 1970), both of which discussed organizational design and the various functions of each tier in some detail, and an equally detailed White Paper (DHSS, 1972a). The reorganization was preceded by several years of design work by management consultants and academics, which produced rather distinctive formal organizational arrangements (see, for instance, Rowbottom *et al.*, 1973; Jaques, 1978). The plans which took shape over this period survived changes of government from Labour to Conservative in 1970, and back in January 1974, with only minor changes such as the Conservatives' even more explicit emphasis on management (Klein, 1983, p. 91). They were promulgated to the NHS in a document which became known as the 'Grey Book' (DHSS, 1972b), a detailed and densely packed nationally uniform organizational prescription of structures, and institutional, managerial and professional roles and relationships, including elaborate consultative mechanisms and formal powers of veto.

3   REFORMING THE UK MEDICAL PROFESSION

1982–8: The Introduction of 'General Management'

The introduction in 1984 of individual general managers (later 'chief executives') in place of the system of consensus team decision making described above was almost accidental (Harrison, 1994), and certainly not foreseen when the government attempted in 1982 to commission an inquiry into NHS 'manpower'. The person offered its chair declined the offer. Ministers and officials did not have an immediate substitute in mind and sought advice from a number of industrial *confidants*; Roy Griffiths, managing director of a supermarket chain, was proposed and was subsequently offered the role.

Griffiths accepted only when the government conceded that the terms of reference should be changed to focus upon NHS *management*. The eventual policy recommendations were radical but also vague; the report (NHS Management Inquiry, 1983) took the form of a letter from Griffiths to the Secretary of State containing only the sketchiest account of his proposals. Of these, the proposal to appoint general managers met a good deal of resistance from the medical profession over a prolonged period; the British Medical Association wrote to the Secretary of State in the following terms:

> It could be interpreted from the [Griffiths] report that a somewhat autocratic 'executive' manager would be appointed with significant delegated powers, who would – in the interests of 'good management' – be able to make major decisions against the advice of the profession.... it should be clearly understood that the profession would neither accept nor cooperate with any such arrangement – particularly where the interests of patients are concerned. (Quoted in *British Medical Journal*, 288, 14 January 1984, p. 165)

Despite this and some diffidence by the Secretary of State, the new arrangements were accepted by the government when it became clear that they had the Prime Minister's support. Thus the roles of the new general managers and the shape of local organizational structures were left to emerge.

Although these reforms clearly offered something of a challenge to clinical autonomy, a review of empirical research carried out between 1984 and 1990 concluded that, despite defeats over the form of the Griffiths innovations, the medical profession had experienced little resulting loss of autonomy (Harrison *et al.*, 1992, ch. 4). However, managers had become increasingly compelled to respond to governmental agendas and consequently less able to respond to internal professional agendas (Flynn, 1988). Hospitals also began to develop decentralized budgetary systems and corresponding internal organizational structures which reflected medical workload (Packwood *et al.*, 1991, 1992). By 1985, there was no longer any pressure for a return to consensus team management; general managers had achieved legitimacy if not substantial influence.

1989–97: The 'Purchaser–Provider Split'

Prior to 1991, the NHS was organized primarily through health authorities (HAs) whose functions included both the local allocation of health care resources and the actual provision of local services in publicly owned hospitals, clinics and domiciliary settings. GPs were self-employed contractors to the NHS, remunerated through capitation fees, fees for service and various allowances, and were somewhat insulated from the remainder of the NHS, their contracts being held by separate public bodies. However, they were able to refer their patients freely to NHS hospitals and other services, the financial consequences of such decisions falling upon the hospitals and the HAs who governed them. Although the early 1980s saw the withdrawal from NHS prescription of a number of preparations, GPs were also able freely to prescribe drugs within the wide-ranging NHS pharmacopoeia without financial implications for themselves. The 1991 reorganization represented a major departure from this by providing an institutional structure radically different from that which preceded it; the policy process by which the purchaser–provider split arrived also differed from what had gone before.

Like the Griffiths report that preceded it, there were elements of accident in the inception of the prime ministerial review of the NHS, which led in turn to the purchaser–provider split (Harrison, 1994, pp. 92–5). This review was the product of widespread concern about the level of NHS funding during the second half of 1987. This reflected the disappointment of health authorities at their budget allocations and decisions by several major interest groups (including the National Association of Health Authorities, and a combination of the BMA, Royal College of Nursing and Institute of Health Services Management) to commence their own enquiries into NHS funding. The same concerns came to be reflected in Parliament, especially after substantial media coverage had been given to reports of delays in urgently needed treatment of some children's cardiac conditions. The predominant mood was crystallized at the end of the year in a statement by the presidents of the Royal Colleges of Physicians, Surgeons, and Obstetricians and Gynaecologists, calling in the strongest language for more funds (Leathard, 1990, p. 129). Despite early indications that the government was prepared to 'tough it out' even to the point of a media battle with the BMA, the Prime Minister (without having previously informed Parliament) announced on television that a review of NHS funding would be conducted. Although the review had been established in response to issues about the *amount* of NHS funding, media analysts were quick to assume that funding *methods* would be the prime focus; in the event the recommendations were for yet another reorganization, into what became called the 'purchaser–provider split' (see below). As with the Griffiths reforms, the government faced a good deal of opposition from the BMA:

> [BMA Council] does not believe ... that the changes proposed would achieve [the government's stated] aims. Indeed, it is convinced that many of the proposals would cause serious damage to NHS patient care, lead to a fragmented service and destroy the comprehensive nature of the existing service. The Government's main proposals would appear to be to contain and reduce the level of public expenditure devoted to health care. The proposals would undoubtedly increase substantially the administrative and accountancy costs of the service, and they ignore the rising costs of providing services for the elderly and of medical advances. In the absence of any additional

funding the proposals would inevitably reduce the standards of NHS patient care. (British Medical Association, 1989, p. 2)

By mid-1989 there was a widespread perception that the government was losing political ground on the issue, circumstantial evidence of which continued to be apparent in opinion polls throughout 1990 and 1991, but the government persisted with the necessary legislation, and in June 1992 the BMA formally ended its campaign against the changes.

The process by which the new arrangements emerged can be described as representing a shift from policy based on blueprint (which characterized the 1960s and 1970s, exemplified by the 1974 reorganization referred to above) to policy based on 'bright ideas' (Harrison and Wood, 1999): a deliberate eschewing of blueprints in favour of the promulgation, in vague terms, of a core set of ideas combined with an invitation to relevant actors (which they could not easily refuse) to constitute the formal institutions which would embody these ideas. The key characteristics of the new process were as follows. First, the process of initial design of the reforms was short and closed. The review which led to the reorganization was conducted informally, largely in secret and uninformed by expert opinion from the field (Lee-Potter, 1997), all but one of the review team members being politicians. Second, the White Paper *Working for Patients* (Secretaries of State, 1989) contained only the barest account of the purchaser–provider split and the roles of its key institutions (see below). It promised further details in a forthcoming series of working papers on organizational and financial matters. As Klein has summarized it, 'the white paper's proposals were little more than outline sketches, even when supplemented by a series of working papers' (1995, p. 198).

Third, even by the formal implementation date of April 1991 aspects of the reorganization fundamental to the purchaser–provider split, not least the contracting process, had not been thought through. Relationships between institutions were adapted as perceived to be necessary and some of these amounted to far more than minor adjustments in government thinking; for instance, the relative importance given to competition and cooperation, the importance of GP fundholding rather than health authority purchasing, and the ideal service configuration for trusts (that is, whether acute and non-acute services should be combined in one institution) all varied substantially between 1991 and 1996. Finally, the implementation arrangements for the new organization structure were not uniform, but rather centred upon a process of annual waves of volunteers for reformed status. The criteria for admission of volunteers to this were developed in parallel with the application process. This allowed continuing adjustments; thus initial criteria for acceptance of volunteers were relaxed over time to ensure the apparent success in implementation terms of the approach. Indeed, there were incentives for managers and senior professionals not only to acquiesce in the innovations, but to volunteer to participate in their development; for instance, trusts were freed from a number of policy constraints, including national pay scales, and might aspire to accumulating financial surpluses with which to develop services. It is such incentives that underpin the description of the process as 'manipulated emergence' (Harrison and Wood, 1999).

In substance, the purchaser–provider split took two, not entirely compatible, forms, HA purchasing and GP fundholding (GPFH), both centred on the notion that the actual provision of services should be the function of NHS trusts, independent of direct HA control, but in a quasi-contractual relationship with both them and GPFH for the supply of patient services. In the first model of purchasing, HAs became financially responsible for health care for their geographically defined resident populations, being expected to purchase this from hospitals and community service providers which progressively attained the status of NHS trusts. Although GPs remained self-employed, this entailed a potential reduction in their freedom to refer, since referrals normally had to fall within the contractual arrangements made by the patient's home HA. Empirical evidence about the outcomes of HA purchasing (Flynn and Williams, 1997; Robinson and Le Grand, 1993) attributes little impact to any provider competition that may have occurred, but it seems likely that the *possibility* of such competition helped to change medical/managerial relationships within hospitals (Harrison and Wistow, 1992; Harrison and Pollitt, 1994, ch. 5). Thus cost pressures and the necessity to calculate the price of services made medical activity more transparent, whilst the newly acquired mutual interests of managers and doctors in ensuring the survival and prosperity of their institution rendered unwise any medical strategy which ignored institutional interests. Moreover, doctors' employment contracts were now held locally by the trust, and their rights publicly to criticize developments in the NHS thus somewhat curtailed; they subsequently lost their rights of appeal to the Secretary of State. In many cases, the local process of securing trust status entailed managerial outmanoeuvring of opposed physicians (Peck, 1991; Harrison *et al.*, 1994).

The second model of purchasing owed a clear intellectual debt to the US concept of the health maintenance organization; like trust status, GPFH was introduced on a voluntary basis and the population coverage of fundholding increased over time as more and more volunteers came forward. By 1996, over 30 per cent of general practices were involved (Audit Commission, 1996). The central feature of the scheme was the allocation to GPFHs of a budget to purchase specified secondary care services from NHS trusts or perhaps from the private sector. The specified services were redefined and expanded over time, but the largest components were elective surgery, directly access diagnostic and therapeutic services (such as pathology, radiology and physiotherapy), most specialist outpatient services and (within certain restrictions) domiciliary nursing. GPFHs also received a prescribing budget and one for ancillary staffing; although these three budgets were calculated and allocated separately, GPFHs were able to reallocate ('vire') money between them. The greater freedoms of GPFHs were themselves an incentive to participate, as was the provision that budget underspendings could be retained for reinvestment in the business. Empirical evidence about the impact of GPFH has been reviewed by several authors (Petchey, 1995; Dixon and Glennerster, 1995; Harrison and Choudhry, 1996; Goodwin, 1995). The actual impact of fundholding on referral behaviour, prescribing and relationships with patients is unclear, but there is quite strong qualitative evidence that GPFHs were willing and able to shift some specialist clinics into a primary care setting. It also seems clear that GP fundholding led to changed relationships with trust providers and therefore with hospital specialists. Threats to reallocate referrals led to concessions in terms of such matters as turnround of pathology results, more prompt patient discharge reporting and the reduction of waiting lists.

A number of further measures which affected doctors were associated with the 1991 reforms. Some of these related to employment status. Consultants became employees of local trusts (rather than of the more remote regional authorities) and thus fell more clearly within the authority of local managers. Managers also acquired a role in the allocation to doctors of the distinction awards previously wholly controlled by the profession. Other measures related to clinical practice. An NHS research and development strategy was introduced (Baker and Kirk, 1996), linked to so-called 'evidence-based medicine', the normative doctrine that professional clinical practice ought to be based upon sound biomedical research evidence about the effectiveness of each diagnostic or therapeutic procedure promulgated to professionals via 'clinical guidelines' (Harrison, 1998, p. 15). Clinical audit became a compulsory activity for doctors. Although these latter measures had little immediate effect on medical practice, they proved to have some political significance, as will be seen below.

4   ASSESSING SUCCESS AND FAILURE

Assessing the success and/or failure of policy requires two sorts of analysis. The first is the equation or otherwise of the outcome with the apparent intentions of policy makers: programmatic outcomes. In the present case, this is not straightforward. It has been seen that reforming the UK medical profession has been more of a sporadic long-term 'project' than a programme; moreover, it is a project whose existence is inferred by observers from government actions rather than announced as government intentions. Second, political success or failure is in principle distinguishable from programmatic outcomes (Bovens and 't Hart, 1996); it is possible, as it were, to win the battle while losing the war, or vice versa. In the present case, there again are difficulties since political and programmatic outcomes are not clearly distinguishable. If a weakening of medical dominance is the outcome under examination, the fact (or otherwise) of such weakening is itself intimately connected with the distribution or redistribution of legitimacy between government and its agents, on the one hand, and the medical profession, on the other. The assessment of success or failure must therefore be approached with these qualifications in mind.

Has Medical Dominance been Weakened?

In order to assess the programmatic outcome of the project described in this chapter, it is necessary to return to the institutions which were identified above as the basis of professional monopoly in Britain; in Alford's terms, are medical interests less well served by these than before? The first such institution is the 'medical model' of health and illness; it is clear that this remained the pervasive ideological basis of UK health policy in the 1990s. Thus the purchaser–provider split could only function on the assumption that health care was a commodity consisting of discrete interventions by health professionals. In parallel with this both government and opposition chose to make hospital waiting lists the salient political issue, also very much in conformity with the medical model. A further manifestation of the present robustness of the medical model was the continued assumption of the various forms of GP fundholding that doctors are the ex officio leaders of clinical teams.

The second institutional source of medical dominance is the corporatist inclusion of the 'peak associations' of medicine, particularly the BMA and the medical royal colleges, in government decision making about health policy, along with a pervasive influence on local institutions. In contrast to the durability of the medical model, it seems clear that the 'insider' role of medicine in government has been weakened. This is observable in the changed position of doctors in the civil service hierarchy, their reduced role on NHS governing bodies and gradual managerial encroachment on the allocation of distinction awards. Its most obvious manifestation, however, is the series of defeats which the profession incurred with respect to NHS organization. It resisted the introduction of both general managers and the purchaser–provider split, and the latter can be interpreted as government retaliation for professional temerity in the form of the Royal College presidents' demands for more NHS resources. In the classic neocorporatist account of liberal democracies (Schmitter, 1974, p. 96) the medical profession is a state-licensed elite which has been granted a representational monopoly in return for observing certain controls on the behaviour of its members. One interpretation of the events described here is that a state may be strong enough to terminate or at least attenuate a corporatist relationship which is not seen to be delivering the required controls of the rank and file.

The third institutional source of medical dominance is the professional autonomy of individual clinicians. This was weakened as a result of two aspects of the 1991 reforms; not only did the possibility of competition between trusts create an incentive for doctors to collaborate with managers in order to manage their new organizational environment, but medical conditions of employment were changed so that doctors became trust employees. The purchaser–provider split meant that non-fundholding GPs lost some of their freedom of referral of patients. Fundholders, however acquired an ambiguous status as providers of primary care but purchasers of secondary care; in Alfordian terms they were both professional monopolists and corporate rationalizers (North, 1995). Fundholders were able to employ their new financial influence to change some aspects of the behaviour of hospital specialists; it is likely that much of this influence was applied via trust managers.

In summary, although there were attempts from the mid-1960s onwards to draw it into the management of the NHS (Harrison, 1988a, ch. 2), there was little attempt to control the UK medical profession until the late 1980s. Given the structure of institutions at that time, medicine could justifiably be regarded as the dominant structural interest and, moreover, one which was unchallenged; comtemporary research clearly shows the role of NHS managers to have been subordinate to, and supportive of doctors. The Griffiths and related changes can be seen as the beginnings of a challenging structural interest; this period saw both the translation of managers from agents of medicine into agents of government and the legislation of the managerial function. The 1990s, the period of the purchaser–provider split, created new institutions which served and strengthened this challenging interest, though without the latter achieving dominance. This period also created a new interest group, GP fundholders, who were in the fortunate position of being served both by the pre-existing structures of medicine and by the new structures of management.

Political Outcomes

Despite the political popularity of the NHS, and the high level of occupational esteem accorded to doctors (Harrison, 1988a), governments have successfully weakened professional dominance without this of itself having adverse political consequences. Some of the means employed to do so have, however, damaged the government's own legitimacy. It is clear, for instance, that neither the purchaser–provider split nor Conservative health policy more generally had much public support and this is likely to have contributed to the size of New Labour's massive election victory of May 1997. The new government has not only retained Conservative institutions such as trusts and many of the features of fundholding,[6] but has adopted new health policies aimed at reforming the medical profession (NHS Executive, 1998) and has done so more vigorously than its predecessors.

A central concept is that of 'clinical governance' under which NHS managers will become responsible for clinical quality. This new responsibility will be largely defined by the activities of the National Institute for Clinical Excellence (NICE), which undertakes evidence-based appraisals of new or existing clinical interventions. Such appraisals may result in the production of clinical guidelines for the management of relevant medical conditions, or in recommendations to the Department of Health that particular treatments require further trials or, indeed, cannot be afforded by the NHS. In addition to this central specification of *clinical* models, there is to be central specification of *service* models; 'National Service Frameworks' (NSFs) will be developed as a means of defining the pathway through primary, secondary and tertiary care which a particular type of patient will be expected to follow. Finally, the Commission for Health Improvement (CHI) will review local compliance with clinical guidelines and NSFs. The advent of the Labour government has also created potential challenges to the 'medical model' in the form of new institutions (such as Health Action Zones and Health Improvement Programmes) predicated on assumptions that ill-health should be seen partly as a social phenomenon which can be addressed by multi-agency, multiprofessional measures.

The main political legacy of Conservative reforms of the medical profession has been a platform upon which a rival political party has built its own reforms. This is an ironic sort of success.

Explaining the Outcome

The problem to which reform of the UK medical profession has been addressed is substantially structural in the sense that pressures of rising demand are an inherent feature of third party payment. The content of policy, that is the choice of medical reform as a solution to the problem, is of course not structurally determined; there are policy alternatives (Harrison and Moran, 2000). But it is significant that most obvious alternatives have been attempted in the UK, so that there have certainly been structural constraints on policy choice. Other factors, however, have been important in determining policy outcomes.

The institutional framework of the NHS within UK government was certainly a key factor in facilitating the outcome. Specifically, the combination of its tax-financed, budget-capped, central government-controlled character with its position as the dominant provider of medical care means that (despite ostensible managerial decentralization and the delivery of services through local institutions) government has levers which would not exist in a more pluralist system. This is not to say that the NHS is a command-and-control system in which the reforms were simply decreed, but rather that there is little by way of an 'exit' option (Hirschman, 1970) for doctors; although the private medical sector represents some 15 per cent of the whole, virtually all doctors practising in that sector are also NHS employees. As has been noted, the medical profession was ready enough to employ the alternative option of 'voice'; central government's answer to this was indeed to use its extensive powers to introduce the reforms in a formal sense. But the formal existence of a policy does not constitute its implementation (Hogwood and Gunn, 1984) and it is in this respect that a number of aspects of policy-making style also made a difference.

First was political opportunism: the Conservatives succeeded in exploiting (albeit after some delay) Griffiths' demand for changes in his terms of reference, and the public perception of an NHS funding crisis in 1987. In Alford's analysis, the manufacture of 'crises' is a tactic commonly adopted by groups 'seeking to make political capital out of a situation that has existed for many years and will continue to exist after the "crisis" has disappeared from public view' (1975, p. xi); 'responses to [these] take the form of symbolically reassuring investigations, whose reports call for new administrative devices' (p. xiv). For Alford, the implication is that nothing of substance will result, since such symbolic politics 'serves simultaneously to provide tangible benefits to various elites and symbolic benefits to mass publics ... blurring the true allocation of rewards' (p. ix).[7] But in this case, something of substance has occurred, albeit in the relationship between two elites.[8]

Second, government chose to exploit the historically rather loose coupling between the medical profession as represented by its peak associations and individual practitioners at local level. Until the 1980s, this frequently worked against government, as national agreements were simply not delivered locally (Harrison *et al.*, 1990, ch. 4), but governments were subsequently to turn this to their own advantage and into a 'collective action problem' (Olson, 1965) for medicine. Thus 'manipulated emergence' was possible because (for instance) some GPs did seek greater influence and with suitable incentives were prepared to volunteer for fundholding status. 'Manipulated emergence' turned out not merely to be possible but to be highly successful as an implementation strategy for the reforms. The absence of a blueprint allowed unannounced policy adjustment to emerge when deemed necessary and blunted potential opposition to the reforms by making it difficult for opponents to seize on concrete proposals to criticize; the volunteer arrangements allowed time for the reluctant both to become used to the idea of the new status (of trust or fundholder) and to feel that nothing was compulsory. Most importantly, a 'bandwagon effect' was rapidly created.

Finally, a certain antipathy to the medical profession, which Prime Minister Thatcher notoriously regarded as indistinguishable from a trade union (Wilding, 1997, p. 718), may well have contributed to government ability to face down medical opposition to the implementation of both the Griffiths reforms (Harrison, 1994) and the purchaser–provider split.

5   CONCLUDING COMMENTS

Evaluations of policy outcomes often have insufficient concern for establishment of the counterfactual: that the outcome would not have occurred without the policy (Pollitt *et al.*, 1990). This clear example of medical resistance having been overcome therefore contributes to the plausibility of the general claim that government made a difference in this policy field, though in political terms not only the one intended. Nevertheless, choices of implementation strategy which took advantage of pre-existing institutional characteristics were not the least important determinant of the outcome. Taken in isolation from other policy fields and from post-1997 developments in health policy making (see Harrison and Wood, 1999), the events described in this chapter can be seen as representing a shift along one of Richardson's (1982, p. 13) dimensions of policy style: from one which seeks consensus with interest groups towards one more inclined to impose policy.

NOTES

1. This chapter would not have been possible without the award to the author by the University of Manchester of a Hallsworth Research Fellowship in the Department of Government during 1997–8. The analysis has benefited from discussions with Bruce Wood and Mick Moran.
2. Strictly, the United Kingdom has not one National Health Service (NHS) but four: one for each constituent country. Though in practice health policy tends to be led from England, there are some important differences of organization and many differences in terminology. For simplicity, all terminology employed in this chapter relates to England, though the general thrust of the analysis is valid for the UK.
3. The term has been retained in this chapter both for clarity and because, in NHS management jargon, 'corporate' is employed to refer to the institution which employs the speaker.
4. This chapter does not attempt a contribution to the theory of professions (as opposed to any other sort of occupation); see Freidson (1983, pp. 25–6).
5. In 1988, the Department of Health and Social Security had its functions divided, the NHS becoming the responsibility of the new Department of Health. For simplicity, the latter term is used throughout this chapter, even where strictly anachronistic.
6. 'Primary Care Groups' of GPs hold capped budgets for the purchase of secondary care for their patients.
7. Alford is here drawing on the formulation of Edelman (1964, 1971), originator of the notion of 'symbolic politics'.
8. Despite considerable rhetoric of consumerism and public involvement, there is little evidence of much influence on the part of non-elites (Harrison and Mort, 1998).

Bibliography to part III

Abholz, Heinz-Harald (1990), 'Steuerung und Kontrolle ärztlichen Handelns auf der Basis des "Gesundheitsreformgesetzes"', *Jahrbuch für Kritische Medizin*, 15, 7–15.

Alber, Jens (1992), *Das Gesundheitswesen der Bundesrepublik Deutschland: Entwicklung, Struktur und Funktionsweise*, Frankfurt am Main: Campus.

Alford, R. (1975), *Health Care Politics: Ideological and Interest Group Barriers to Reform*, Chicago: University of Chicago Press.

Allsop, J. (1995), *Health Policy and the National Health Service*, London: Longman.

Anderson, G. and J.-R Poullier (1999), 'Health Spending, Access and Outcomes: Trends In Industrialized Countries', *Health Affairs*, 18(3), 178–92.

Atkinson, M.M. and W.D. Coleman (1989), 'Strong States and Weak States: Sectoral Policy Networks in Advanced Capitalist Economies,' *British Journal of Political Science*, 19 (1), 47–67.

Audit Commission (1996), *What the Doctor Ordered: A Study of GP Fundholders in England and Wales*, London: HMSO.

Baggott, R. (1998), *Health and Health Care in Britain*, 2nd edn, London: Macmillan.

Baker, M. R. and S. Kirk (eds) (1996), *Research and Development for the NHS: Evidence, Evaluation and Effectiveness*, Oxford: Radcliffe Medical Press.

Bandelow, Nils (1994), 'Ist Politik wieder autonom? Das Beispiel Gesundheitsreform', *Gegenwartskunde*, 43, 445–56.

Banting, K. (1987), *The Welfare State and Canadian Federalism*, Kingston: McGill-Queen's University Press.

Barrett, S. and C. Fudge (eds) (1981), *Policy and Action*, London: Methuen.

Bieback, Karl-Jürgen (1992), 'Regulierungskonzepte und Regulierungsprobleme des Gesundheits-Reformgesetzes', in Karl-Jürgen Bieback (ed.), *Das GRG – eine gescheiterte Reform der GKV?*, Sankt Augustin: Asgard, pp. 21–38.

Boot, J.M. and M.H.J.M. Knapen (1996), *De Nederlandse Gezondheidszorg*, Utrecht: Het Spectrum.

Bovens, M. and Paul 't Hart (1996), *Understanding Policy Fiascoes*, New Brunswick: Transaction Publishers.

Bra Gruppen (1974), *Det Behövs Fler Allmänläkare*, Stockholm: Social-styrelsen, *Landstingsförbundet*, Sveriges läkarförbund.

British Medical Association (1989), *Special Report of the Council of the British Medical Association on the Government's White Paper 'Working for Patients'*, London: British Medical Association.

Burau, Viola (1994), *'Ansätze und Instrumente zur politischen Steuerung niedergelassener Ärzte: Eine vergleichende Analyse am Beispiel der letzten Reformen des britischen und deutschen Gesundheitssystems'*, MA dissertation, Ruhr-Universität Bochum, Fakultät für Sozialwissenschaften.

Choices in Health Care, Report by the Government Committee on Choices in Health Care, The Netherlands (1992) (the Dutch version of the report, entitled *Kiezen en delen*, was published in 1991).

Clade, Harald (1992), 'Seehofer geht mit Hypotheken ins Rennen. Ein CSU-Sparpapier als Richtung für die alte/neue Gesundheitspolitik', *Deutsches Ärzteblatt*, 89, B-1113–15.

Cohen, M.D., J.G. March and J.P. Olsen (1972), 'A garbage can model of organisational choice', *Administrative Science Quarterly*, 72 (1), 1–25.

Coll, P. (1980), 'Problemática actual de los conciertos con instituciones sanitarias', *Revista de Seguridad Social*, 6, 185–213.

Colwill, J. (1998), 'Professionalism and control in health care provision: Some lessons from the health service in Britain', *Journal of Contemporary Health*, 7, 71–6.

CREDES (1993), *Eco-Santé France*, Paris: CREDES.

Cronenberg, Dieter-Julius (1992), 'Kostendämpfung durch Marktwirtschaft', *Gesellschaftspolitische Kommentare*, special issue 1/1992, 45–8.

Cyert, R.M. and LG. March (1963), *A Behavioural Theory of the Firm*, Englewood Cliffs, NJ: Prentice-Hall.

David, P.A. (1985), 'Clio and the Economics of QWERTY,' *American Economic Review*, 75, 332–7.

David, P.A. (1989), *A Paradigm for Historical Economics: Path Dependence and Predictability in Dynamic Systems with Local Network Externalities*, Stanford, CA: Center for Economic Policy Research, Stanford University.

Department of Health and Social Security (1970), *The Future Structure of the National Health Service*, London: HMSO.

Department of Health and Social Security (1972a), *National Health Service Reorganisation: England*, Cmnd 5055, London: HMSO.

Department of Health and Social Security (1972b), *Management Arrangements for the Reorganised National Health Service*, London: HMSO.

Department of Health and Social Security, and Welsh Office (1979), *Patients First: Consultative Paper on the Structure and Management of the National Health Service in England and Wales*, London: HMSO.

Deutscher Bundestag (1992a), *Gesetzentwurf der Bundesregierung: Entwurf eines Gesetzes zur Sicherung und Strukturverbesserung der gesetzlichen Krankenversicherung (Gesundheits-Strukturgesetz 1993): Vom 7.9.1992*, BT-Drs. 12/3209, Bonn: Deutscher Bundestag.

Deutscher Bundestag (1992b), *Gesetzentwurf der Fraktionen der CDU/CSU, SPD und F.D.P. Entwurf eines Gesetzes zur Sichertme und Strukturverbesserung der gesetzlichen Krankenversicherune (Gesundheits-Strukturgesetz): Vom 5.11.1992*, BT-Drs. 12/3608, Bonn: Deutscher Bundestag.

Deutscher Bundestag (1992c), 'Erste Beratung des von den Fraktionen der CDU/CSU, SPD and F.D.P. eingebrachten Entwurfes eines Gesundheitsstrukturgesetzes: 117. Sitzung des Deutschen Bundestages (5.11.1992)', in Deutscher Bundestag (ed.) *Stenographische Protokolle der Verhandlungen des Deutschen Bundestages* (volume 164), Bonn: Deutscher Bundestag, pp. 9918–43.

Dixon, J. and H. Glennerster (1995), 'What do we know about fundholding in general practice?', *British Medical Journal*, 311, 727–30.

Döhler, Marian (1989), 'Physicians' professional autonomy in the welfare state: endangered or preserved?', in Giorgio Freddi and James Warner Björkman (eds), *Controlling Medical Professionas: The Comparative Politics of Health Governance*, London: Sage, pp. 178–97.

Döhler, Marian (1993), *Ist das Gesundheitswesen reformierbar? Einige Überlegungen aus politikwissenschaftlicher Sicht*, Vortrag für die AOK-Geschäftsführung am 11.5.1993, mimeo.

Döhler, Marian (1995) 'The state as architect of political order: policy dynamics in German health care', *Governance*, 8 (3), 380–404.

Döhler, Marian and Philip Manow-Borgwardt (1992a), *Gesundheitspolitische Steuerung zwischen Hierarchie und Verhandlung*, MFG discussion papers, 92/7, Cologne: Max-Planck-Institut für Gesellschaftsforschung.

Döhler, Marian and Philip Manow-Borgwardt (1992b) 'Korporatisierung als gesundheitspolitische Strategie', *Staatswissenschaften und Staatspraxis*, 3 (1), 64–106.

Donaldson, P. and J. Farquhar (1988), *Understanding the British Economy*, London: Penguin.

Dressler, Rudolf (1991), *Zur Lage im Gesundheitswesen*. Bonn, 19.12.1991, mimeo.

'Dr. Ulrich Oesingmann: Bericht zur Lage. "Einseitige Maßnahmen werden auf den entschiedenen Widerstand der Kassenärzte stoßen"', *Deutsches Ärzteblatt*, 89 (1992), B-1175–82.

'Durch die Bank: Kassenärzte lehnen Seehofer-Malus rigoros ab', *Deutsches Ärzteblatt*, 89 (1992), B-1633–4.

Duriez, M. and S. Sandier (1994), *The French Health Care System: Organization and Functioning* (in French), Paris: Ministry of Health.

Dyson, Kenneth (1992), 'Theories of regulation and the case of Germany: a model of regulatory change', *The Politics of German Regulation*, Aldershot: Dartmouth, pp. 1–28.

Edelman, M. (1964), *The Symbolic Uses of Politics*, Urbana, IL: University of Chicago Press.

Edelman, M. (1971), *Politics as Symbolic Action: Mass Arousal and Quiescence*, Chicago, IL: Markham Publishing.

Ellis, N.D. and J. Chisholm (1993), *Making Sense of the Red Book*, Oxford: Radcliffe Medical Press,

Elola, J. (199 1), *Crisis y Reforma de la Asistencia Sanitaria Pública en España*, Madrid: Fondo de Investigaciones Sanitarias.

Elsinga, E. (1996), 'De Commissie-Biesheuvel', in Y.W. van Kemenade and K.C.N.M. Bakx (eds), *Medische Specialisten Gehonoreerd?*, Utrecht: De Tijdstroom, pp. 5159.

Engelen-Kefer, Ursula (1992), 'Die Nachfragemacht der Kassen stärken: Kurzfristige und mittelfristige Reformen', *Gesellschaftspolitische Kommentare*, special issue 1/1992, 56–8.

Ferrera, M. (1996), 'The "southern model" of welfare in social Europe', *Journal of European Social Policy*, 6 (1), 17–37.

Fiedler, Eckhart (1992), 'Weitere Struktureingriffe erforderlich: Die Maßnahmen des Gesundheitsreformgesetzes reichen nicht aus', *Gesellschaftspolitische Kornmentare*, special issue 1/1992, 59–62.

Fink, Gabriele (1996), 'Stabilisierungsgesetz 1996: Kurzfristige Notbremsung im Krankenhausbereich', *Die Betriebskrankenkasse*, 84, 428–32.

Fishkin, LS. (1979) *Tyranny and Legitimacy: A Critique of Political Theories*, Baltimore, MD: Johns Hopkins University Press

Flynn, R. (1988), *Cutback Management in Health Services*, Salford: University of Salford Department of Sociology and Anthropology.

Flynn, R. and G. Williams (eds) (1997), *Contracting for Health: Quasi-markets and the National Health Service*, Oxford: Oxford University Press.

Foote, S. (1992), *Managing the Medical Arms Race: public poligy and medical device innovation*, Berkeley: University of California Press.

Freidson, Elliot (1970), *Professions of medicine: A study in the sociology of applied knowledge*, New York: Dodd, Mead.

Freidson, E. (1983), 'The theory of professions: State of the art', in R. Dingwall and P. Lewis (eds), *The Sociology of the Professions: Lawyers, Doctors and Others*, London: Macmillan.

Garpenby, Peter (1989), *The State and the Medical Profession: A Cross-National Comparison of the Health Policy Arena in the United Kingdom and Sweden 1945–1985*, Linköping: Linköping University.

Garpenby, P. (1995), 'Health Care Reform in Sweden in the 1990s: Local Pluralism Versus National Coordination', *Journal of Health Politics, Policy and Law*, 20 (3), 695–717.

Gedeelde zorg, betere zorg (1994), Report by the Commissie modernisering curatieve zorg, department of WVC, Zoetermeer.

Gerlinger, Thomas and Thomas Schönwälder (1996), 'Die dritte Stufe der Gesundheitsreform: Das GKV Weiterentwicklungsgesetz', *Soziale Sicherung*, 45, 125–30.

Gilljam, Mikael and Sören Holmberg (1990), *Rött, Blått, Grönt: En bok om 1988-års Riksdagsval*, Stockholm: Bonniers.

González, P. (1999), *Descentralización, benestar e rendimento institucional: a atención primaria en Galicia*, Santiago de Compostela: EGAP.

Goodwin, N. (1995), 'GP fundholding: A review of the evidence', *Health Care UK 1995–96*, 116–30.

Greiner, Wolfgang and J.-Matthias Schulenburg (1997), 'The health system of Germany', in Marshall W.Raffel (ed.), *Health Care and Health Care Reform in Industrialized Countries*, University Park: Pennsylvania State University Press, pp. 76–104.

Grisewell, Gunnar (1993), 'Durchsetzung und Umsetzung: Das Gesund-heitsstrukturgesetz im Spannungsfeld der Interessenpolitik', *Die Ortskrankenkasse*, 75, 39–48.

Groenewegen, P.P. and M. Calnan (1995), 'Changes in the control of health care systems in Europe: implications for professional autonomy', *European Journal of Public Health*, 5 (4), 240–4.

Guillén, A.M. (1996), *Politicas de reforma sanitaria en España: de la restauración a la democracia*, PhD dissertations series, Madrid: Fundación Juan March.

Guillén, A.M. and L. Cabiedes (1997), 'Towards a National Health Service in Spain: the search for equity and efficiency', *Journal of European Social Policy*, 7 (4), 319–36.

Haglund, G. (1992), 'Från provinsialläkare till distriktsläkare', *Socialmedicinsk Tidskrift*, 3–4, 137–9.

Ham, C.J. (1981), *Policy Making in the National Health Service*, London: Macmillan.

Ham, C.J. (1992a), *Health Policy in Britain*, London: Macmillan.

Ham, C.J. (1992b), 'Reforming the Swedish health services: The international context', *Health Policy*, 21 (2), 129–41.

Harrison, M.I. and H. Lieverdink, 'Controlling Medical Specialists: Hospital Reforms in the Netherlands', forthcoming in *Research in the Sociology of Health Care*.

Harrison, S. (1981), 'The Politics of Health Manpower', in A.F. Long and G. Mercer (eds), *Manpower Planning in the National Health Service*, Farnborough: Gower.

Harrison, S. (1982), 'Consensus Decisionmaking in the National Health Service: A Review', *Journal of Management Studies*, 19 (4), 377–94.

Harrison, S. (1988a), *Managing the National Health Service: Shifting the Frontier?*, London: Chapman & Hall.

Harrison, S. (1988b), 'The workforce and the new managerialism', in R. Maxwell (ed.), *Reshaping the National Health Service*, Hermitage: Policy Journals.

Harrison, S. (1994), *Managing the National Health Service in the 1980s: Policymaking on the Hoof?*, Aldershot: Avebury.

Harrison, S. (1998), 'The politics of evidence-based medicine in the UK', *Policy and Politics*, 26 (1), 15–31.

Harrison, S. and N. Chouffiry (1996), 'General practice fundholding in the UK National Health Service: evidence to date', *Journal of Public Health Policy*, 17 (3), 331–46.

Harrison, S. and D.J. Hunter (1994), *Rationing Health Care*, London: Institute for Public Policy Research.

Harrison, S. and M. Moran (2000), 'Resources and Rationing: Managing Supply and Demand in Health Care', in G. Albrecht, R. Fitzpatrick and S. Scrimshaw (eds), *The Handbook of Social Studies in Health and Medicine*, New York: Sage

Harrison, S. and M. Mort (1998), 'Which champions, which people? Public and user involvement as a technology of legitimation', *Social Policy and Administration*, 32 (1), 60–70.

Harrison, S. and C.J. Pollitt (1994), *Controlling Medical Professionals*, Buckingham: Open University Press.

Harrison, S. and G. Wistow (1992), 'The purchaser/provider split in English health care: towards explicit rationing?', *Policy and Politics*, 20 (2), 123–30.

Harrison, S. and B. Wood (1999), 'Designing health service organisation in the UK, 1968 to 1998: from blueprint to bright idea and "manipulated emergence"', *Public Administration*, 77 (4), 751–68.

Harrison, S., D.J. Hunter and C. Pollitt (1990), *The Dynamics of British Health Policy*, London: Routledge.

Harrison, S., N. Small and M.R. Baker (1994), 'The wrong kind of chaos? The early days of a National Health Service hospital trust', *Public Money and Management*, 14 (1), 39–46.

Harrison, S. David Hunter and Gordon Marnoch (1992), *Just Managing: Power and Culture in the National Health Service*, London: Macmillan.

Heidenheimer, Arnold J. (1980), 'Conflict and Compromises Between Professional and Bureaucratic Health Interests 1947–72', in Nils Elvander and

Arnold J. Heidenheimer (eds), *The Shaping of the Swedish Health System*, London: Croom Helm, pp. 119–41.

Heinze, Meinhard (1990), 'Die Vertragsstrukturen des SGB V', *Sozialgerichtsbarkeit*, 37, 173–8.

Hess, Rainer (1992), 'KBV zum Streit um die Malus-Regelung: Gespräche – aber keine Zugeständnisse an Seehofer', *Deutsches Ärzteblatt*, 89, B-1745.

Hirschman, A. (1970), *Exit, Voice and Loyalty*, Cambridge, MA: Harvard University Press.

Hoffacker, Paul (1992), 'Mehr marktwirtschaftliche Steuerungsinstrumente für das Gesundheitswesen', mimeo.

Hoffacker, Paul (1996), 'Gesundheitsreform – 3. Stufe: Unüberbrückbare Gegensätze zwischen Koalitionsentwurf und Oppositionsentwurf: Behandlung der Entwürfe im parlamentarischen Verfahren', *Arbeit und Sozialpolitik*, 50 (1), 24–8.

Hogwood, B.W. and L.A. Gunn (1984), *Policy Analysis for the Real World*, Oxford: Oxford University Press.

Jaques, E. (ed.) (1978), *Health Services: Their Nature and Organisation and the Role of Patients, Doctors and the Health Professions*, London: Heinemann.

Johnson, K. (1993), 'Robert Leth: Problem att husläkarlagen inte ger enhetligt system', *Läkartidningen*, 90, 4174, 4179.

Jowell, R., J. Curtice, A. Park, L. Brook and D. Ahrendt (1995), *British Social Attitudes: The 12th Report*, Aldershot: Dartmouth.

Kamke, Kerstin (1998), 'The German health care system and health care reform', *Health Policy*, 43 (2), 171–94.

'Kassenärzte kündigen Seehofer "erbitterten Widerstand" an', *dpa Sozialpolitische Nachrichten*, no. 22/92, 25.5.1992, 12–13.

Kassenärztliche Bundesvereinigung (1993), *Tätigkeitsbericht der Kassenärztlichen Bundesvereinigung 1992: Für die Zeit vom 1.1.1992 bis zum 21.12.1992*, Cologne: Deutscher Ärzteverlag.

'Keine Kapitulation vor dem Gesundheits-Strukturgesetz', *Deutsches Ärzteblatt*, 89 (1992), B-2769–72.

Kingdon, J.W. (1984), *Agendas, Alternatives and Public Policy*, Boston, MA: Little, Brown.

Klein, R.E. (1983), *The Politics of the National Health Service*, London: Longman.

Klein, R.E. (1995), *The New Politics of the National Health Service*, London: Longman.

Krakau, I. (1995), 'Primärvårdens utveckling', *Socialmedicinsk tidskrift*, 4–5, 145–52.

Läkartidningen (1992), 'SFAM Gruppläkarverksamhet bör uppmuntras, Läkaresällskapet: Förslaget ofullständigt, DLF förordar förtur för närboende', *Läkartidningen*, 89, 2812–13.

Larizgoitia, I. and B. Starfield (1997), 'Reform of primary care: The case of Spain, *Health Policy*, 41, 121–37.

Leathard, A. (1990), *Health Care Provision: Past, Present and Future*, London: Chapman & Hall.

Lee-Potter, J. (1997), *A Damn Bad Business: The NHS Deformed*, London: Gollancz.

Lieverdink, H. and H. Maarse (1995), 'Negotiating Fees for Medical Specialists in the Netherlands', *Health Policy*, 31 (2): 81–101

Lieverdink, H. (1999), *Collectieve besluiten, belangen en wetgeving. De totstandkoming van tarieven voor medisch specialisten in Nederland tussen 1986 en 1992*, PhD thesis, Maastricht: Rijksuniversiteit Limburg.

Lindblom, C.E. (1959), 'The science of muddling through' *Public Administration Review* 19 (1): 79–88.

Lindenberg, Ruth (1992), 'Wahljahr 1994 setzt Koalition bei Gesundheitskosten unter Druck', *dpa Sozialpolitische Nachrichten*, no. 21/92, 18.5.1992, 5–6.

Lluch, E. (1983), *Política General del Ministerio de Sanidad y Consumo*, Madrid: Ministerio de Sanidad y Consumo

'Marburger Bund will gegen Zulassungssperren in Karlsruhe klagen', *dpa Sozialpoltische Nachrichten*, no. 35/92, 24.8.1992, 7–8.

Matas, J. (1995), *Public administration and the recruitment of political elites: formal and material politicization in Catalonia*, Working Paper no. 18, Barcelona: Institut de Ciències Polítiques i Socials.

Maus, Josef (1992), 'Vertreterversammlung der Kassenärztlichen Bundesverinigung: Keine Kapitulation vor dem Gesundheits-Strukturgesetz', *Deutsches Ärzteblatt*, 89, B-2769–72.

Milton, A. (1992a), 'Järhult glömmer grundläggande faktum', *Läkartidningen*, 89, 99.

Milton, A.(1992b), 'Frågor och svar om husläkarförslagen: Kan Piff-förslaget alltjämt försvaras?', *Läkartidningen*, 89, 2804–6.

Ministerio de Sanidad y Consurno (1992), *Estudio sobre la satisfacción de la población con la atención primaria en el territorio INSALUD*, mimeo, Madrid: Ministerio de Sanidad y Consumo.

Ministry of Health (1968), *National Health Service: The Administrative Structure of the Medical and Related Services in England and Wales*, London: HMSO.

Ministry of Health and Department of Health for Scotland (1944), *A National Health Service*, Cmnd 6502, London: HMSO.

Mohan, J. (1995), *A National Health Service? The Restructuring of Health Care in Britain Since 1979*, London: Macmillan.

Moran, M. (1988), 'Crises of the Welfare State', *British Journal of Political Science*, 18 (3), 397–414.

Moran, M. (1999), *Governing the Health Care State*, Manchester: Manchester University Press.

Moran, Michael (1990), *European Health Care Policy Since the End of the Long Boom*, paper presented at the planning session on 'The welfare state: autonomy and integration on the EEC', 18th Joint Sessions of the European Consortium of Political Research, University of Bochum, 2–7 April.

Moran, Michael (1994), 'Health care policy', in Jochen Clasen and Richard Freeman (eds), *Social Policy in Germany*, Hemel Hempstead: Harvester Wheatsheaf, 83–101.

Moran, Michael and Bruce Wood (1993), *States, Regulation and the Medical Profession*, Buckingham: Open University Press

Müller, Joachim (1992), 'Finanzentwicklung der GKV 1992: Unterschiedliche Trends in den alten und neuen Bundesländern', *Die Ersatzkasse*, 72, 175–9.

Murmann, Klaus (1992), 'Selbstbeteiligung kein Tabu: Gegen eine Überforderung der Solidargemeinschaft', *Gesellschaftspolitische Kornmentare*, special issue 1/1992, 54–6.

National Health Service Management Inquiry (1983), *Report*, London: Department of Health and Social Security.

NAV-Virchowbund (1992), *Stellungnahme zum I. Entwurf eines Gesetzes zur Sicherung und Strukturverbesserung der Gesetzlichen Krankenversicherung, II. Entwurf eines Dritten Gesetzes zur Änderung des Fünften Sozialgesetzbuches*, mimeo.

NHS Executive (1998), *A First Class Service: Quality in the New NHS*, London: Department of Health.

North, N. (1995), 'Alford revisited: The professional monopolisers, corporate rationalisers, community and markets', *Policy and Politics*, 23 (2), 115–25.

Nyman, K. (1992), 'Intensivt fackligt arbete för att stoppa Stockholms husläkarförslag', *Vårdfacket*, 14, 8–9.

OECD (1992), *Reform of health care: A comparative analysis of seven OECD countries*, Paris: OECD.

OECD (1993), *OECD Health Data*, Paris: OECD.

Oesingmann, Ulrich (1992), 'Oesingmann: Fakten gegen Gerüchte und Unterstellungen', *Deutsches Ärzteblatt*, 89, B-1861.

Office of Health Economics (1997), *Compendium of Statistics*, 10th edn, London: Office of Health Economics.

Okma, G.H. (1997), *Studies on Dutch Health Politics, Policies and Law*, PhD thesis, Utrecht: Utrecht University.

Oldiges, Franz (1992a) 'Dynamische Faktoren beeinflußen: Ohne Reform keine längerfristige Beitragsstabilität', *Gesellschaftspolitische Kornmentare*, special issue 1/1992, 63–5.

Oldiges, Franz (1992), 'Entwicklungen in der GKV: Gesundheitsreform Teil 2: Zur Diskussion aktueller Vorschläge kostendämpfender Maßnahmen', *Die Ortskrankenkasse*, 74, 287–92.

Olson, M. (1965), *The Logic of Collective Action*, Cambridge, MA: Harvard University Press.

Orde, Bettina am (1996a), 'Die sogenannte "Dritte Stufe der Gesundheitsreform"', *Soziale Sicherheit*, 45, 46–51.

Orde, Bettina am (1996b), 'Gesundheitspolitik vor dem Aus? Die 3. Stufe der Gesundheitsreform, das Beitragsentlastungsgesetz', *Soziale Sicherheit*, 45, 292–8.

Orde van Medisch Specialisten, *Jaarverslag 1996–1997*, Utrecht 1998.

Orde van Medisch Specialisten (1998), 'Wat regelt het wetsvoorstel wel en wat niet?', *Medisch Contact*, 53 (39), 1237–8.

Ordenieuws (1998), speciale editie, (2) 11.

Ortún, V. and J. Gèrvas (1996), 'Fundamentos y eficiencia de la atención médica primaria', *Medicina. Clinica*, 106, 97–102.

Österman, Torsten (1995), *Vitbok över Riksdagsvalet 1994. En Långtidsstudie*, Stockholm: Tidens Förlag.

Överläkaren (1992), Remissyttrande: Läkarförbundet om husläkarförslaget, *Överläkaren*, 4, 19–21.

Packwood, T., J. Keen and M. Buxton (1991), *Hospitals in Transition: The Resource Management Experiment*, Milton Keynes: Open University Press.

Packwood, T., J. Keen and M. Buxton (1992), 'Process and structure: resource management and the development of sub-unit organisational structure', *Health Services Management Research*, 5 (1), 66–76.

Peck, E. (1991), 'Power in the National Health Service: a case study of a unit considering Trust status', *Health Services Management Research*, 4(2), 120–30.

Perschke-Hartmann, Christiane (1994), *Die doppelte Reform: Gesundheitspolitik von Blüm zu Seehofer*, Opladen: Leske & Budrich.

Petchey, R. (1995), 'General practitioner fundholding: Weighing the evidence', *The Lancet*, 346, 1139–42.

Pettigrew, A.M., E. Ferlie and L. McKee (1982), *Shaping Strategic Change: Making Change in Large Organisations: the Case of the NHS in the 1980s*, London: Sage.

Pierson, P. (1994), 'The new politics of the Welfare State', *World Politics*, 48 (2), 143–79.

Pierson, P. (1998), 'Irresistible forces, inamovable objects: Post-industrial welfare states confront permanent austerity', *Journal of European Public Policy*, 5, 539–60.

Pineus, I. (1999), 'Västmanland ses som förebild: Lika villkor för alla mottagningar – 40 procent drivs i privat regi', *Dagens Medicin*, 35, 7.

Pollitt, C.J., S. Harrison, D.J. Hunter, G. Marnoch (1990), 'No hiding place: On the discomforts of researching the contemporary policy process', *Journal of Social Policy* 19 (2), 169–90.

Premfors, R. (1998), 'Reshaping the democratic state: Swedish experiences in a comparative perspective', *Public Administration*, 76, 141–59.

Putnam, Robert D. (1995), 'Turning in, turning out: The strange disappearance of social capital in America', *Political Science and Politics*, 28 (4), 664–83.

Putnam, R., R. Leonardi and R. Nanetti (1993), *Making Democracy Work*, Princeton: Princeton University Press

Rehnberg, Clas and Peter Garpenby (1995), Privata Aktörer i Svensk Sjukyård, Stockhom: SNS Förlag.

Reiners, Hartmut (1993), *Das Gesundheitsstrukturgesetz – Ein 'Hauch von Sozialgeschichte'? Werkstattbericht über eine gesundheitspolitische Weichenstellung*, WZB discussion paper, P93–210, Berlin: Wissenschaffizentrum Berlin für Sozialforschung.

Richardson, J. (ed.) (1982), *Policy Styles in Western Europe*, London: Allen & Unwin.

Richardson, Jeremy, Gunnel Gustafsson and A. Grant Jordan (1982), 'The Concept of Policy Style', in J. Richardson (ed.), *Policy Styles in Western Europe*, London: Allen & Unwin, pp. 1–16.

Rico, A. (1997), '¿Es la descentralización sanitaria una reforma deseable? Expectativas teóricas y experiencia comparada', *Reformas Sanitarias y Equidad*, Madrid: Fundación Argentaria and Ed. Visor.

Rico, A. (1998a), *Descentralización y Reforma Sanitaria en España (1976–1996)*, PhD dissertations series, Madrid: Fundación Juan March.

Rico, A. (1998b), '*Las Políticas Sanitarias Redistributivas: Universalización y Atención Primaria*', paper presented to the 'I Sessions on social inequalities in Catalonia', organized by the Fundación Bofill, Barcelona, 17–18 December.

Rico, A. (2001), '*Federalism vs. Welfare State?*', working paper, Madrid: Centro de Estudios Avanzados en Ciencias Sociales.

Rico, A. and S. Pérez-Nievas (1999), 'La satisfacción de los ciudadanos con los servicios sanitarios públicos en Andalucía, Cataluña, País Vasco e INSALUD', in G. López (ed.), *Evaluación de las Politicas Sanitarias Autonómicas*, Barcelona: Institut d'Estudis Autonòmics.

Rico, A., M. Fraile and P. González (1998), 'Social capital does not tell the whole story: Regional decentralization of health policy in Spain', *West European Politics*, Special Issue on 'Politics and policy in democratic Spain: No longer different?', 21(4), 180–200.

Rico, A., P. González and M. Fraile (1998), 'La descentralización sanitaria en España: Autonomía política y equidad social', *Politicas de Bienestary Desempleo*, Madrid: Fundación Argentaria and Ed. Visor.

Robinson, R. and J. Le Grand (eds) (1993), *Evaluating the NHS Reforms*, London: King's Fund.

Rodriguez, J.A. (1987), 'La rebelión de los médicos: Análisis sociológico de las actitudes de la profesión médica ante la organización de la sanidad en España, *Sistema*, 78, 69–100.

Rodriguez, J.A. (1992), 'Struggle and revolt in the Spanish health policy process: The changing role of the medical profession', *International Journal of Health Services*, 22 (1), 19–44.

Rodwin, V.G. (1982), 'Management without Objectives: The French Health Policy Gamble,' in Gordon McLachlan and Alan Maynard (eds), *The Public/Private Mix for Health*, London: The Nuffield Provincial Hospitals Trust.

Roscam Abbing, H.D.C. (1998), 'De nota van de medisch specialist: Het wetsvoorstel integratie medisch-specialistische zorg', *Medisch Contact*, 53 (35), 1088–1089.

Rosewitz, Bernd and Douglas Webber (1992), *Reformversuche und Reformblockaden im deutschen Gesundheitswesen*, Frankfurt am Main: Campus.

Rowbottom, Ralph (ed.) with Jeanne Balle et al. (1973), *Hospital Organisation: A Progress Report on the Brunel Health Service Organisation project*, London: Heinemann.

Saltman, R. and C. von Otter (1992), *Planned Markets and Public Competition: Strategic Reform in Northern European Health Systems*, Buckingham: Open University Press.

Sartori, G. (1987), *Theory of Democracy Revisited*, New Jersey: Chatham House.

Scharpf, F. (1988), 'The joint-decision trap: Lessons from German federalism and European integration', *Public Policy and Administration*, 66, 239–78.

Schelling, T.C. (1978), *Micromotives and Macrobehaviour*, New York: W.W. Norton.

Schmaus, Herbert (1997), 'Droht dem Gesundheitswesen die Rationalisierung?', *Die Ortskrankenkasse*, 79, 19–25.

Schmid, Klaus (1992), 'Hartmannbund: Ein unheimlich schwacher Abgang', *Der Kassenarzt*, 32, 16–18.

Schmitter, P.C. (1974), 'Still the century of corporatism?', *Review of Politics*, 36 (1): 85–131.

Scholten, G. (1994), *De Omsingeling van Medische Specialisten: Een Organisatie-Sociologisch Onderzoek naar de Relatie tussen de Overheid en de medische specialisten, 1979–1989*, PhD thesis, Rotterdam: Erasmus University.

Schulenburg, J.-Matthias (1984), *Selbstregulierung durch Berufsverbände: eine Studie am Beispiel des Gesundheitswesens*, WZB discussion paper, IM/84–30, Berlin: Wissenschaftszentrum Berlin für Sozialforschung.

Schulenburg, J.-Matthias (1992), 'Germany: Solidarity at a price', *Journal of Health Politics, Policy and Law*, 17, 715–38.

Schulenburg J.-Matthias (1994), 'Forming and reforming the market for third-party purchasing of health care: A German perspective', *Social Science and Medicine*, 39, 1473–81.

Schulz, R.I. and S. Harrison (1986), 'Physician autonomy in the Federal Republic of Germany, Great Britain and the United States', *International Journal of Health Planning and Management*, 1 (5), 335–55.

Schwartz, Friedrich W. and Reinhard Busse (1997), 'Germany', in Chris Ham (ed.), *Health Care Reform. Learning from International Experience*, Buckingham: Open University Press, 104–18.

Secretaries of State for Health, Wales and Scotland (1989), *Working for Patients*, Cmnd 555, London: HMSO.

Seifert, R. (1992), *Industrial Relations in the NHS*, London: Chapman & Hall.

Servicio de Estudios Sociológicos del IESS (1979), 'Estudio comparativo sobre profesionales sanitarios y opinión pública sobre organización y reforma sanitaria', *Revista Española de Seguridad Social*, 3, 113–40.

Skånér,Y. (1993), 'Rationaliseringsvinster, folkhälsa, helhetssyn: Argument för utbyggnad av primärvården 1934–1968', *Läkartidningen*, 90, 3098–3100.

Social Services Committee (1984), *First Report, Session 1983–4: Griffiths NHS Management Inquiry Report*, HC209, London: House of Commons/HMSO.

Socialdepartementet (1992a), *Husläkare: för Kontinuitet och Trygghet i Vården*, DS 1992: 41, Stockholm: Socialdepartementet.

Socialdepartementet (1992b), *Sammanställning av Remissyttranden över Departementspromemoria med Förslag om Husläkarsystem*, DS 1992: 113, Stockholm: Socialdepartementet.

Socialdepartementet (1992/3), Om husläkare m.m., Regeringens proposition 1992/3:160, Stockholm: Socialdepartementet.

Socialstyrelsen (1968), *Ett Principprogram om Öppen Vård*, Stockholm: Socialstyrelsen.

Socialstyrelsen (1998), *Från Slitna Honnörsord till Praktisk Verklighet*, Stockholm: Socialstyrelsen.

Socialstyrelsen (1999), 'Allmänläkare i primärvården', *Socialstyrelsens Meddelandeblad*, (11), 1–12.

Socialutskottet (1992/3) *Husläkare m.m.*, Socialutskottets betänkande, 1992/93:SoU22, Stockholm: Riksdagen.

'Sparsame Strukturen schaffen: Gesundheitsminister Seehofer vor großen Herausforderungen', *Die Ortskrankenkasse*, 74, 320–21.

'SPD Präsidium lehnt Seehofers Sparpläne ab', *dpa Sozialpolitische Nachrichten*, no. 27/92, 29.6.1992, 15–16.

Starr, P. (1982), *The Social Transformation of American Medicine*, New York: Basic Books.

'Stellungnahme der Spitzenverbände der gesetzlichen Krankenversicherung zum "Gesundheitsstrukturgesetz 1992" anläßlich der Sondersitzung der Konzertierten Aktion im Gesundheitswesen am 16. Juni 1992 in Bonn', *Die Ortskrankenkasse*, 74, 1992, 447–9.

Sveriges läkarförbund (1988), *Rekrytering av Distriktsläkare i Allmänmedicin: Rapport med Förslag till Åtgärder*, Stockholm: Sveriges läkarförbund.

Sveriges läkarförbund (1991), *En ny primärvård – idéskiss från läkarförbundet*, Stockholm: Sveriges läkarförbund

Swaan, A. de (1988), *In Care of the State*, Cambridge: Polity Press.

'Thomae: Fahrplan steht', *Tagesdienst der FDP Bundestagsfraktion*, no. 1011, 2.6.1992.

Urbanos, R. (1999), '¿Es realmente redistributivo el gasto sanitario público?', in *Necesidad Sanitaria, Demanda y Utilización*, XIX Jornadas de Economía de la Salud, Barcelona: Asociación de Economía de la Salud.

Van Berkestijn, Th.M.G. and W.T.P.F. van der Werf (1997), 'Het perspectief van de artsen', in: E. Elsinga and Y.W. van Kemenade (eds), *Van Revolutie naar Evolutie. Tien Jaar Stelselwijziging in de Nederlandse Gezondheidszorg*, Utrecht: De Tijdstroom, pp. 125–43.

Van Kemenade, Y.W. and L.J.K. van der Velde (1996), 'Het Huidige stelsel', in: Y.W. van Kemenade and K.C.N.M. Bakx (eds), *Medisch specialisten gehonoreerd?*, Utrecht: De Tijdstroom, pp. 15–37.

Van Veen, F., 'Basisstelsel ziektekosten komt nabij door ommezwaai VVD', *de Volkskrant*, 1 March 2000, p. 3.

Van Veen, F. 'PvdA zint op inperking ziekenfonds', *de Volkskrant*, 14 February 2000, p. 1.

Van Veen, F. 'Ziekteverzekeraars zijn niet meer tegen basisverzekering', *de Volkskrant*, 20 April 2000, p. 3.

Van der Grinten, T.E.D. (1997), 'Tien jaar hervormingsbeleid. Pendelen tussen overheid, markt en middenveld', in: E. Elsinga and Y.W. van Kemenade (eds), *Van Revolutie naar Evolutie. Tien Jaar Stelselwijziging in de Nederlandse Gezondheidszorg*, Utrecht: De Tijdstroom, pp. 162–78.

Van der Made, J.H. and J.A.M. Maarse (1995), 'Het plan-Simons. Een blindganger in de gezondheidszorg', *Bestuurskunde*, 4 (2), 80–88.

Vila, Luis (1979), 'Posición tradicional de los Colegios de médicos sobre el tema de la liberalización de la profesión médica', *Revista de Seguridad Social*, 3, 199–218.

Villalbí, J.R. and J. Farrés (1998), 'La reforma de la atención primaria de salud: una valoración critica', *Quadern CAPS*, 27, 14–22.

Wanek, Volker and Uwe Lehnhardt (1989), 'Dämmerung der Expertenmacht? Krise in der ambulanten Medizin', *Jahrbuch für kritische Medizin*, 14, 6–23.

Watkin, B. (1975), *Documents on Health and Social Services: 1834 to the Present Day*, London: Methuen.

Webber, Douglas (1991), 'Health policy and the Christian–liberal coalition in West Germany: the conflicts over the health insurance reform, 1987–8', in Christa Altenstetter (ed.), *Comparative Health Policy and the New Right. From Rhetoric to Reality*, London: Macmillan, pp. 49–90.

Webber, Douglas (1992a), 'Die kassenärztlichen Vereinigungen zwischen Mitgliederinteressen und Gemeinwohl', in Renate Mayntz (ed.), *Verbände zwischen Mitgliederinteressen und Gemeinwohl*, Gütersloh: Bertelsmann, pp. 211–73.

Webber, Douglas (1992b), 'The politics of regulatory change in the German health sector', in Kenneth Dyson (ed.), *The Politics of German Regulation*, Aldershot: Dartmouth, pp. 209–34.

Webster, C. (1998), *The National Health Service: A Political History*, Oxford: Oxford University Press.

Wetenschappelijke Raad voor het Regeringsfeleid (WRR) (1997), *Volksgezondheidszorg*, Den Haag: SDU.

Wilding, P. (1997), 'The welfare state and the Conservatives', *Political Studies*, 45 (4), 716–26.

Wilsford, D. (1985), 'The *conjoncture* of ideas and interests,' *Comparative Political Studies*, 18 (3), 357–72.

Wilsford, D. (1991), *Doctors and the State: The Politics of Health Care in France and the United States*, Durham NC: Duke University Press.

Wilsford, D. (1993), 'The Medical Profession in France,' in F. W. Hafferty and J. B. McKinlay (eds), *The Changing Medical Profession: An International Perspective*, New York: Oxford University Press.

Wilsford, David (1994), 'Path dependency, or why history makes it difficult but not impossible to reform health care systems in a big way', *Journal of Public Policy*, 14 (3), 251–4.

Wilsford, D. (1995), 'States facing interests: Struggles over health care policy in advanced, industrial democracies,' *Journal of Health Politics, Policy and Law*, 20 (3), 571–614.

Zipperer, Manfred (1993), 'Gesundheitsstrukturgesetz stellt neue Weichen in der Gesundheitspolitik', *Die Ortskrankenkasse*, 75, 3–14.

PART IV

Managing innovation: public policy and
the financial sector

17. Managing innovation: regulating the banking sector in a rapidly changing environment

Andreas Busch

1   BANKING: A SPECIAL SECTOR

Nowadays, everybody has come to rely on banks.[1] While four or five decades ago, the possession and use of a bank account were still restricted to the wealthier parts of the population, today, in an increasingly cashless economy, almost every citizen has and uses a bank account to pay their bills, receive their salary and manage their money. This is especially true in (but not exclusive to) the industrialized democracies. As a consequence, the safety of these deposits is a matter of the greatest political and economic importance, requiring that the state have a close eye on the banking industry.

But even apart from such – electoral – considerations, regulation of the banking industry is important, because banking is a special sector. Among the various sectors of an economy, it occupies a distinguished position. In the first place, it makes credit available to all the other sectors in the economy and to consumers; a well-functioning banking sector is thus a vital prerequisite for a well-functioning economy as a whole. Secondly, it is particularly vulnerable: the failure of a bank can have distinctly different consequences from the failure of a business in another sector of the economy and threaten the viability of the whole banking sector. The reason for this is as follows: if a normal business fails, it is very likely that a competitor will step in and take over the failed firm's business. In the banking sector, however, such a failure could lead to contagion effects, either because other banks are affected by the failure and become insolvent, or because the public, unable to distinguish between sound banks and the failed bank, loses faith. A *bank run* might ensue, with unforeseeable consequences for other banks which are in principle economically sound, endangering the payment system as a whole, with negative consequences for other economic sectors and generally high social costs.

As a consequence, banking is historically something most states have paid particular attention to. They have taken action primarily in two ways which are related to the points mentioned above. On the one hand, they have tried to put the banking system to use for purposes of economic and structural policy. This can be done by influencing the allocation of credit and channelling resources into preferred sectors and tasks – a task made easier if the state owns significant parts of the banking system. On the other hand, they have tried to ensure the safety of deposits through regulation, with a view to securing the viability of the banking system as a whole – avoiding systemic risk – and the protection of individual deposits.

There are a number of ways in which a state can try to achieve these various aims, such as the following:

* taking over the whole or part of the banking system, allocating resources to preferred uses and implicitly guaranteeing the deposits;
* issuing legal directives or using other mechanisms to influence the allocation of credit;
* imposing capital controls to ensure the functioning of such directives;
* imposing a separation of activities between commercial banks and investment banks to limit risk;
* leaving banking in the private sector, but limiting competition through cartelization or the imposition of caps and limits on deposit and lending rates;
* setting up a mandatory system of deposit insurance financed by contributions from all banks which will pay out depositors in the case of a bank failure.

States have historically mixed these ingredients in different ways and to a different extent, reflecting different political preferences and motives for regulation, which created specific national systems of banking regulation. While for some of them macroeconomic considerations were the main reason for intervention – using it as an instrument in a Keynesian strategy or to influence the transmission of monetary policy – other countries' situations reflected specific historical experiences such as severe banking crises (or the absence thereof) or social policy concerns about the safety of small depositors' deposits.

All these interventions, however, also incur costs which can take on various forms: a decrease in economic efficiency in the case of socialization of the banking industry due to the – intended – limitation of competition; similar effects in the case of regulation of deposit and lending rates; and the danger of unintended consequences as a reaction to regulation. The latter can most evidently result in the case of deposit insurance: as the protection of deposits is ultimately provided by a bank's competitors, each bank has an incentive to commit 'moral hazard'. This is done by offering higher interest rates to its depositors, thus extending its share of the market, but requires on the other hand higher interest income from loans, which can only be obtained by increasing the risk portfolio. Thus deposit insurance can lead to a changed situation in the market place and an accumulation of risks in certain banks.

2   CHALLENGES

Most of the aforementioned national systems were constructed in the time after World War II. This was a time when economic policy in most countries consciously imposed capital controls in order to control interest rates and thus manage the domestic economy as well as protect the new welfare state from capital flight induced by the burdens of social legislation (Helleiner, 1994, pp. 33ff). This situation hardly changed in the 1950s and 1960s, but was massively challenged in the following decades. It has been said that the 'internationalization and integration of capital markets has been the most significant change in the political economy of the industrialized countries over the past three decades. [...] No other area of the economy has been so thoroughly internationalized as swiftly as have capital markets since the 1970s' (Simmons, 1999, p. 36). After 1973, the breakdown of the system of fixed exchange rates – the system of Bretton Woods – altered conditions in international markets fundamentally. At the same time, the oil shocks of 1973–4 and 1978–9 plunged economies into recession and put enormous strain on the international financial system, while liberalization tried to lower the barriers to international exchange. Countries started to abolish the capital controls which had relied on the logic of a system of fixed exchange rates. While some started this process earlier than others, by the mid-1990s almost all OECD countries had completely removed all controls on capital movements (see the data in Simmons, 1999, p. 42; Freitag, 1999, p. 159). As a consequence, international bank lending – which had been low in the predominantly national financial systems – increased nearly twentyfold in the two decades after 1973 (Herring and Litan, 1995, p. 26). In the 1980s and 1990s, these developments were reinforced by the effects of computerization, the telecommunications revolution, the development of ever more sophisticated new financial instruments and increasing disintermediation.

As a result, the rules for conducting business, especially in financial markets, changed dramatically. New opportunities sprang up, but new risks as well. Competition in the banking industry increased, and at the same time margins in banking decreased. This was a major challenge for established systems of banking regulation in all countries to adjust to new circumstances. Given that by now most citizens – and no longer only the wealthy – held most of their assets in bank accounts and were threatened with bankruptcy in the case of failure, the situation also led to growing concerns about depositor protection (Gardener, 1992, p. 156). Liberalization brought new opportunities for bank business which could increase their risk markedly. If banking supervision failed, bank failures and lost deposits could be the consequence. Thus the issues of financial liberalization and of banking supervision and regulation were directly linked, and if bank failures were to be avoided, the new risks demanded the finding of new ways of regulating banking (Franke, 1998, p. 293). What precisely these new ways would have to be, however, was uncertain. While change in the sector was *foreseeable*, its precise nature was unknown, making it *not controllable*.

Assessing the degree to which national systems of banking regulation managed to cope with the challenges just mentioned is the underlying question of the contributions in this part of the volume. Did the adjustment process succeed, or did it fail?

Clearly, not all countries in the world managed to meet the new challenges. In many of them, banking failures and crises ensued. The IMF has reported that no fewer than two-thirds of its 181 member countries have suffered from some kind of banking crisis in the period since 1980 (Lindgren *et al.*, 1996). These failures and crises have differed substantially in their severity, but some of them became very costly indeed.[2] The crisis of the savings and loans system in the United States, for example, cost approximately $160bn, of which some $130bn had to be borne by the taxpayer (Federal Deposit Insurance Corporation, 1997, p. 39). As a proportion of GDP, crises in some other countries were even costlier, as Table 17.1 demonstrates. This indicates that avoiding such costs may be a strong incentive for a country to get its regulatory system in order. But it also makes clear that the transition from an almost exclusively domestically oriented, strongly regulated financial system to one existing in an internationally oriented, deregulated system clearly had a distributive side to it as well. It was by no means only a technicality. Besides the bailout costs in case of failure mentioned above, there were consequences for borrowers and consumers, for example through the switch from fixed- to variable-rate loans and mortgages. Especially under conditions of high and variable inflation such as were prevalent in the 1970s and early 1980s, risk-averse borrowers could be adamantly opposed to such a change. This opposition could be picked up by interest groups and political parties and thus influence the political process shaping the transition.

Table 17.1   Costs of banking crises as a percentage of GDP

USA	3.2
Finland	9.9
Spain	15.0
Chile	33.0

Source: Dziobek and Pazarbaşioğlu (1998, p. 4).

3   THE CASES UNDER CONSIDERATION

This section will try to give an overview of fundamental characteristics of the banking and financial systems in the countries under consideration in this study. This is done in a comprehensive manner in this place mainly in order to save space in each individual contribution, but also to facilitate comparison between the national systems.

We will first look at the characteristics of the banking systems, before assessing differences in the regulatory systems and then discussing the differences.

Types of Banking Systems

In the literature, a number of attempts to classify national financial systems exist. Most of them agree on a main distinction between *capital market*-based and *bank*-based systems according to the main source of finance for enterprises (for example, Zysman 1983; Cox, 1986; Story and Walter, 1997). With respect to the latter category, an additional distinction is often made relating to the role the state plays in the price-setting process. Among the countries covered in this study, only the United Kingdom can be classified as a capital market-based system, while Germany and France are counted among the bank-based systems (with the state playing an important role in the latter), along with the other continental European systems. Furthermore, banking systems are usually classified according to the sort of business they are allowed to take on. Here the main distinction is between a *universal bank* and a *specialized bank* (cf. Canals, 1997). The reason for such specialization can lie either in legal regulation (as in the United States) or in historical development, as is the case in the United Kingdom, where a banking system characterized by a clear functional differentiation primarily between commercial and investment banks has emerged as a product of self-imposed constraints and restrictive practices (cf. Llewellyn, 1992). The banking systems of France, Germany, the Netherlands, Spain and Sweden, can be classified as universal banking systems where banks may conduct business that can include deposit, lending, discount, securities, guarantee and checking activities. Only in the case of Sweden are there some regulations limiting banks' business concerning the areas of real estate business and investments in non-financial firms (Barth *et al.*, 1997, Table 5).

On theoretical grounds, the literature seems inconclusive on whether a universal bank system or a specialized bank system is preferable with respect to risk and safety of deposits. On the one hand, it is argued that universal banks may be less efficient than their specialized counterparts, thus increasing the risk of failure and therefore default. Furthermore, circumstances can be modelled where universal banks are particularly prone to moral hazard which may increase the obligations of deposit insurance in the case of failure over those incurred in a specialized banking system (Canals, 1997, pp. 127–32; Boyd *et al.*, 1998). On the other hand, specialized banks may run an inherently greater risk of default because their revenues are less diversified than those of universal banks, either sectorally or geographically, posing a threat to them in the case of a recession. Since an optimal allocation of risk is impossible, they run a higher risk of failure (Canals, 1997, pp. 127–32; Herring and Litan, 1995, pp. 52–61). Unfortunately, empirical examples can be found for both positions, so that no general statement seems possible in this respect.

It has to be stressed that these classifications have to be treated with some degree of caution anyway, for most of the data on which the above-mentioned classifications rest are somewhat dated, so that their merits are probably open to some debate. Also, they do not take into account historical developments and change. But above all, as was stressed before, the whole banking industry has been in a process of considerable structural change, which ultimately may well render some of those distinctions negligble. As will be seen in more detail in the studies that follow, some states have made considerable attempts at strengthening the role capital markets play in their economy. The French state, for example, in the 1980s very actively tried to overcome the system of specialized banks imposed originally by the Banking Act of 1941 and create a system of universal banks. As a result, it can be classified as a universal bank system, but only since 1984. Over the same period, France has seen the – previously dominant – share of credit provided by the banks decrease substantially owing to a process of disintermediation, moving it away from the bank-based type (see Coleman, Chapter 18, below, and Klein, 1991, p. 37). In addition, more detailed empirical research indicates that classification on the national level hardly seems appropriate since it neglects the substantial differences existing within countries, such as between firms of different sizes (Sauvé and Scheuer, 1999). Thus the classifications summarized in Table 17.2 can only serve as a very rough guide to distinguish the systems.

Institutions of Banking Supervision

Contrary to financial systems, no attempts have been made so far to classify regulatory systems. It used to be possible to distinguish broadly between two groups of countries (cf. Pecchioli, 1989, p. 45), namely those where banking supervision was conducted in an informal way and essentially without legal regulations, and those with a formal system of banking supervision with detailed legal regulations.

While the former group comprised countries such as Australia, Canada, New Zealand and the United Kingdom, the latter consisted of Japan, the countries of continental Europe and the United States. Factors such as the nature of the

Table 17.2   Characteristics of financial and banking systems

	FRA	GER	NL	SPA	SWE	UK
Financial system type	bank	bank	bank	bank	bank	capital mkt
Banking system type	universal	universal	universal	universal	(universal)	specialized
Market concentration	69.9%	18.4%	74.4%	56.8%	n.a.	38.4%

Note: Market concentration measured in percentage of client deposits in top five banks, 1989.

Source: Valdez (1993).

Table 17.3   Characteristics of supervisory systems

	FRA	GER	NL	SPA	SWE	UK
Agency in charge	Commission bancaire	FBSO, Central bank	Central bank	Central bank, treasury	FSA	Central bank
Deposit insurance established	compulsory 1980	voluntary 1966	compulsory 1979	compulsory 1977	compulsory 1974	compulsory 1982
run by	industry	industry	government/industry	government/industry	government	government
Coverage (in 1995 US$)	80 000	30% of bank's equity	25 000	12 000	35 000	28 000

Source: Barth *et al.* (1997).

legal system, the number of banks and the degree of concentration of the banking system played a role in structuring the regulatory system. Over the last two decades, however, most countries have switched to a more formalized mode of conducting banking regulation. Nevertheless, there are still substantial differences between the national systems, both with respect to institutional factors and to the way in which legal regulations are being handled. An overview is given in Table 17.3.[3]

The institutionalization of banking regulation in the countries considered seems to differ most prominently with respect to the role played by the central bank. It is either exclusively in charge (Netherlands and United Kingdom), shares responsibility with another agency (Germany, Spain and France) or is not involved at all (Sweden). Since the demands of monetary policy may conflict with those of banking regulation (for example, if raising interest rates is avoided because that might negatively influence the viability of a number of banks; or if the pursuit of tight monetary policy causes banks to fail), this might be an important aspect and, as the cases of Sweden and Spain in this sector show, it indeed is.

Different Approaches to Economic Policy

While we have so far primarily looked at institutional characteristics, it may be much more helpful to distinguish between two kinds of concerns driving the behaviour of public officials and policy makers: those focused on *macroeconomic* objectives and those concerned with the *microeconomic* characteristics of financial markets. The experiences described in the case studies may be classified as falling somewhere on a continuum with those dominated by macroeconomic problems and dynamics at one end and those driven primarily by microeconomic dynamics at the other. Such an approach not only highlights an important dimension in the changes experienced by national financial systems, but also helps to explain the differing perspectives taken in the individual contributions.

The cases of *Sweden* and *Spain* are located at the *macro* end of that scale. They are similar in that they both originally had banking systems which were instrumentalized by the state to achieve goals of macroeconomic policy. In Sweden, the state also owned significant parts of the banking system, which was an additional help. In both cases, attempts were made to reform this system for reasons of improved control over monetary policy – and it comes as little surprise that in both cases the respective central banks were the driving force behind the reforms. In either case, the macroeconomic strategy changed: in Spain, to shed the legacy of the Franco era and prepare the country to profit from the integrated European financial market; in Sweden, to turn a highly regulated and largely isolated financial system into a liberal and open system.

As a result, the two case studies adopt a macro-oriented perspective and a systemic approach, which is fitting, because the problems that arise in both cases are of a systemic kind as well.

France probably has to be positioned somewhere in the middle of the continuum, for here sectoral considerations drove state activity (with a view to positioning French banks in the coming European financial market). But the French macroeconomic policy machine had already been reformed before: the banking sector played no important role, and capital and credit controls had been lifted. Accordingly, the problems encountered were not of a system-wide nature, but surfaced at Crédit Lyonnais, the state-owned bank that was instrumentalized to push the strategy.

The Dutch case is similar to the French in that the government tried to influence and encourage the consolidation of the banking industry by means of structural policy. It refrained, however, from detailed intervention, not least because it lacked the means, like a bank comparable to Crédit Lyonnais. But it was also spared comparable disasters.

The *United Kingdom* had been a case on the *macro-oriented* end of the spectrum until the 1970s. But already in the early 1970s, it pursued a change of strategy by deregulating its banking sector – interest rates – and abolished all capital controls in 1979 (Vogel, 1996, p. 66). It thus underwent a change during an early phase, which was completed and codified in the 1979 Banking Act. While some problems occurred after 1973 (the 'Secondary Banking crisis'), they were of a minor character. Since then, the UK has been a liberal system forgoing capital and credit controls, in which the banking system was not instrumentalized for macroeconomic purposes.

In *Germany*, such an attempt had never been made since World War II. Germany had already abolished all capital and interest regulations by the late 1960s. It has thus to be placed at the *micro-oriented* end of the spectrum from the beginning. In both the latter cases, the perspective adopted by the contributors is one focusing not on the banking system, but on individual cases of failing banks and the way the political system coped with this failure.

4   ASSESSING SUCCESS AND FAILURE

Since the individual chapters will have to assess success or failure of the policy episodes under consideration, there are obviously common indicators needed. These indicators have to be of a nature compatible with the widely varying institutional and other characteristics of the systems under consideration. Three main indicators have been suggested to the authors of the case studies to assess the *programmatic* dimension of success or failure: (a) bank failures (both the number of failed banks and their assets in proportion to those of the whole banking system), (b) costs of bailing out (both in absolute terms and as a percentage of GDP), and (c) the time point of state intervention (early or late intervention).

There are some ambiguities with these indicators, however. With respect to bank failures, there is a problem if a bank does not openly fail, but is being taken over by or merged with a competitor. It can be argued, however, that the latter case does not constitute failure with respect to governance, since market exit is a common – and necessary – feature in market economies. Thus a bank failure is determined only when a bank crashes with losses to one or several parties, not in the case of a merger which saves a bank which would otherwise have failed.

With respect to the costs of bailing out, the problem is that they may be hard to find out in cases where deposit insurance is organized along private lines and not by the state – as in the German case. It should, however, be possible to assess whether substantial costs have been incurred, for example by looking at the premia banks have to pay for deposit insurance.

A further word of caution is necessary. While such indicators may help to structure the assessment, the concrete case studies demonstrate that the authors must be given considerable latitude in rating their cases. Failure does not show up in each of the indicators alike as they may pick up different variants of crisis. In the Swedish case, for example, no bank failed, owing to state aid, which on the other hand proved very costly, causing the author to rate it as failure.

In assessing the *political* dimension of success or failure, the authors will look at such things as ministerial resignations, official inquiries, public trials and the like. While these are obviously only relevant in the case of programmatic failure, we find an obvious asymmetry here between losses in terms of money and political consequences. As was demonstrated above and is shown in more detail in the respective case studies, very considerable costs had to be borne by the public sector in the cases of Spain, Sweden and France.[4] But, in spite of that, no substantial political fall-out was noted apart from a number of public reports (in the case of France, not even that). In terms of political victims per public money lost, this certainly begs explanation. The reason, I would suggest, can be found in the low degree of politicization of the financial sector. This is a policy area that is commonly held to be very 'technical', accessible only to 'experts' and thus lacking in transparency. Since programmatic measures in such fields are usually uncontested because of their technical nature, they are unlikely to become the subject of political controversy after the fact. In addition, politicians are often shielded from having to accept responsibility because that is delegated to subordinated authorities which can be blamed in the case of failure. Often, however, as the case studies show, there is little public interest even in an inquiry about the reasons for the failure. It may be that the characteristics of the field are such that there are simply no 'frames' (Schön and Rein, 1994) available to politicize it.[5] On the other hand, the fact that a small policy community dominates the field may also play a role, for the people that perform the post mortem, conduct the inquiries and write the reports are often close to or even the same people that initiated the failed reforms in the first place (particularly evident in the cases of Britain, France and Spain). Dealing with failure is also made easy if 'rogue traders' can be singled out that have overstepped their brief or acted in a fraudulent manner, as occurred in the (much more limited) failures in the German and British cases: if these individuals can be blamed, then no systemic and political questions need to be asked. Lastly, it should not be forgotten that, even if losses had to be covered, it was precisely in the nature of deposit insurance that potential political crises were diffused: the depositors were more or less completely covered and the – often substantial – amounts were spread very evenly and non-transparently over time and over the electorate.

5   EXPLAINING SUCCESS AND FAILURE

In a way, it is much easier to explain failure, not only because there is a substantial literature on it (see Bovens and 't Hart, 1996; Bovens *et al.*, 1998), but also because the degree of change and innovation in the field was so enormous that failure seems in a way natural. But why then did some countries *not* fail? In the literature on financial regulation, it is readily admitted that description and analysis of the processes and consequences of liberalization 'are in their infancy' (Quinn, 1997, p. 531).[6] But we can offer some speculations. On the basis of the studies in this section, it seems that the probability of failure increases with the degree and speed with which the parameters of the environment changed. This was particularly strongly the case in Sweden and Spain and to some extent in France, where changing conceptions of policy multiplied the shocks coming from a changing international environment. The addition of both effects was apparently more innovation than the systems could handle properly. In the British and German cases, the systems could concentrate on the external challenges, leaving more time and capacity to cope with them.

Evidently, there is also a correlation between the *micro–macro* classification proposed above and the 'success' rate of the cases: the failures tend to lie in the macro cases, the successes in the micro cases, with France falling in between in both aspects. The macro cases can also be described as the 'latecomers' to the consensus that has emerged with respect to the conduct of macroeconomic policy, and it comes as little surprise that adaptation proved costly.

In terms of the relevant policy actors, another interesting distinction emerges. Here it seems that the number of relevant policy actors is inversely correlated to the probability of failure. In Sweden and Spain, the reforms were initiated and pushed through by the respective central banks,[7] who pursued their goal of increasing control over monetary policy without much concern for side-effects and possible collateral damage. Central banks have been identified in the literature as the typical 'epistemic communities' prompting ideational change in economic policy (cf. Haas, 1992), and it therefore comes as little surprise that they would be the agents to implement the emerging macroeconomic consensus in their countries. In contrast, the successful cases of Germany and Britain (and to a degree France) are characterized by policy networks which have been described as (meso-) corporatist, where a greater number of actors – such as industry associations – are involved in policy formulation and often implementation. In addition to the fact that there was less 'to reform' in these countries, innovation was easier to handle and progressed at a slower pace. Finally, it should be noted that, even in the cases classified here as failures, there were no policy reversals.

A final remark concerns the role of the European Union. Contrary to the case studies in, for example, the steel sector, the EU (or its predecessor, the EC) has not played a very prominent and active role in these sectoral studies. Why is this? I would argue that the major challenges in this sector came up at an early stage, before European institutions started playing an important role in this field (which arguably was the case with the Second Banking Directive of 1989). Prior to this, interaction in this field was primarily of an intergovernmental character with little influence from the Commission, and countries had to cope with their problems themselves. Indirectly, however, European integration played an important role by favouring liberalization and shifting the objectives that inspired state authorities, most clearly in the French and Spanish cases, where the impending integrated financial market prompted reforms, and probably also in the Swedish case, although here internationalization may better characterize the driving force than Europeanization. In addition, it becomes clear that, even after the adoption of the Second Banking Directive, we have not seen the abolishment of nationally specific institutional set-ups of banking supervision, because harmonization of regulatory content does not necessarily need harmonization of institutional structures. Whether we will see it in the future remains open. While the European Central Bank was not given specific tasks in banking supervision in the Maastricht Treaty, the argument for a single bank supervisor in the Eurozone can still be made. Furthermore, national central banks such as the Bundesbank, bereft of their powers in the field of monetary policy, may be looking for new tasks in the field of supervision. It will thus certainly be interesting to watch developments in this area in the future.

6 GLOSSARY

Capital controls
Limitations on the free movement of capital across borders. Originally imposed in many countries as a reaction to collapsing financial markets to stabilize currencies and prevent capital flight in the early 1930s, they were kept in place in the Bretton Woods system to facilitate management of the domestic economy and the exchange rate. The collapse of the system of fixed exchange rates and the growth of offshore markets led to the gradual abandonment of capital controls from the mid-1970s. Today, almost no capital controls exist in OECD countries.

Derivative
An asset or security whose value is derived from another basic variable which is called the basis. The basis can, for example, be a stock or commodity price, an index or an interest or exchange rate. The value of the basis at a particular point in time determines the value of its derivative products which have names such as options, forwards, futures, swaps or warrants. Ever more sophisticated and complicated derivatives have been developed over the last two decades in financial markets with the main aim of managing risk.

Disintermediation
Change in financial relationships characterized by decline of the role of banks (intermediaries) and an increase in the direct relationship between the ultimate suppliers and users of financing. An example would be companies lending funds directly to each other or issuing bonds and selling them directly to savers. The likelihood of further disintermediation may impose limits on authorities' abilities to impose controls and regulations on financial intermediaries.

Macroeconomic policy
Economic policy aimed at influencing economic aggregates such as the rate of growth or inflation or the level of unemployment.

Microeconomic policy
Economic policy aimed at influencing the efficiency of certain markets in an economy, for example by altering regulations.

Monetary tightening
A move towards a more restrictive monetary policy by the central bank, generally by raising interest rates. This may put a squeeze on banks' profits, as market conditions may force them to raise the rate they pay to their depositors, while their income from outstanding loans remains constant.

Moral hazard
The presence of incentives for individuals to act in ways which maximize their own utility while incurring costs that they do not have to bear. For example, the owner of a car that is insured against theft has less incentive to be careful to protect it. In case of a theft, the costs are borne by the insurance community.

Oligopsony

A market which is dominated by a few large buyers with consequently great influence on the setting of market conditions such as price. It is the demand-side equivalent of an oligopoly and thus another deviation from perfect competition.

Regulation

Governmental actions to control price, sales and production decisions in order to protect the public interest. Measures include, for example, the required certification or licensing of products, the setting of safety or environmental standards and the provision of antitrust laws.

Second banking directive

A European Community directive of 1989 which is part of the Single Market (1992) programme. It introduced the 'single passport' principle, which meant that all banks licensed to do business in one country of the EC could do business in any other member country. Banks are supervised according to the 'home country control' principle, which required further harmonization such as the own funds directive and the solvency directive to make regulation comparable across the EC.

Self-regulation

Execution of regulatory tasks by producers of goods or services themselves, often to prevent the imposition of regulation by state authorities.

Specialized banking system

A system in which individual banks specialize in certain banking activities and do not offer the full range of them. In the Anglo-Saxon tradition, for example, investment banks and brokerage firms deal with stocks and securities, while deposit taking and lending is performed by retail banks. Such a specialization can either develop historically, as in Britain, or be imposed by law, as in the United States.

Universal banking system

The opposite of a specialized banking system where individual banks engage in all sorts of banking business, from deposit taking to brokerage. Such banking systems are traditionally found in continental Europe, most notably in Germany and Switzerland.

NOTES

1. I would like to thank the authors of the sectoral case studies, the general editors of the project and the other participants of the workshop on 'Success and Failure in Governance' at Nuffield College in September 1999 for important input and comments on an earlier draft of this chapter. The usual disclaimer applies.
2. Comparative data on banking crises can be found in Caprio and Klingebiel (1996), Dziobek and Pazarbaşioğlu (1998) and Goodhart *et al.* (1998, ch. 1).

3. The information given here relates to the time covered in the contributions in Part IV of this volume, namely the mid-1970s until the mid-1990s. It should be noted, however, that in the meantime changes have occurred in some countries, most notably in the UK, where responsibility for banking supervision was transferred from the Bank of England to the new Financial Services Authority (FSA) in 1997.
4. In the British and German cases, no public money had to be paid and no deposits were lost.
5. An interesting counterexample is provided by the case of 'Black Wednesday' (October 1992), when the British pound had to leave the ERM: while the technical details of exchange rate policy are just as arcane as those of banking supervision, this case was politically disastrous. Of course, sterling's membership in the ERM was hotly contested, and currency policy, with its association with national sovereignty, is 'high politics'.
6. The analysis of Demirgüç-Kunt and Detragiache (1998) which claims to give answers is in fact of little help, as it suffers from simplistic operationalization of variables and evident selection bias.
7. This is, by the way, an interesting contrast to the British case mentioned above, where policy change was to a considerable degree prompted from outside, through the IMF in 1976.

18. Governing French banking: regulatory reform and the Crédit Lyonnais fiasco

William D. Coleman[1]

1   INTRODUCTION

Like many other democracies with advanced market economies, France began to experience increasing pressures to reform its banking sector in the 1970s and 1980s. The pressures for reform had diverse sources. Domestically, the tight management of credit and the reliance on bank loans rather than financial markets for meeting industrial investment needs were producing inefficient investment on the one side and stifling innovation and growth in the banking sector on the other. On the European level, the EEC had agreed to the First Credit Directive in 1977, which initiated a push towards the liberalizing of financial services markets within the regional area. The European push, in turn, represented a response to changing financial markets in the United States where deregulation was already under way and to the competition from growing global or Eurocurrency markets in bank lending, short-term money market securities and bonds. These markets tended to be centred in London, a long-standing rival of the French financial capital in Paris.

By 1989, when the important Second Credit Directive of the EC became law, French financial services policy had undergone a wholesale reform that enabled indigenous financial services firms to take full advantage of opportunities for growth in domestic, European and global markets. These reforms have had remarkable staying power. Unlike those that began with the deregulation of banking in 1979 and of securities with the Big Bang in 1986 in the UK, the French changes have proved solid and workable. In contrast, the regulation of British financial services has undergone virtually constant change since the mid-1970s.

These regulatory reforms, however, encouraged a dynamic in the French banking sector that was to take on the form of a dream gone mad. One of the objectives of the financial market reforms in France was to open the door fully to the universal bank model of banking. In this model, a bank engages not only in the traditional deposit-taking and lending activities, but also in new issue securities markets, secondary securities markets, the provision of brokerage services and the selling of such investment services as trusts and estates management, portfolio management and investment advice (Coleman, 1996, p. 21). The architects of the new French regulatory system also emulated part of the German approach to universal banking; regulatory reforms made it easier for French banks to take equity positions in industrial and commercial corporations.

Almost as soon as the final set of reforms was in place, Crédit Lyonnais, one of the country's three largest commercial banks and also a bank owned by the state, embarked on an ambitious plan of growth and expansion. This plan included the taking on of a large portfolio of equity positions in a host of French and offshore companies. After some initial successes, however, the expansion began to give way to a series of financial problems. By 1993, the French government was forced to initiate the first in a series of bailout plans. Three years later, the total amount of bad debts had reached 24.22 billion dollars and the government was desperately looking for a means to hive off the bad debts and to privatize the remaining assets of the bank.

The Crédit Lyonnais débâcle comes close to the concept of a policy fiasco elaborated by Bovens and 't Hart (1996, p. 15). A socially and politically significant group in French society perceives the bank's rapid decline to be at least partially caused by avoidable and blameworthy mistakes made by policy makers. Public recognition of blame admittedly has been slow to come, but parliamentary inquiries and changes in government have gradually shed some light on the problems of the bank: sufficient light for the government to have contemplated criminal proceedings. The issues at the centre of the fiasco reach deep into the heart of the French state. Not only was Crédit Lyonnais the last of the three largest commercial banks still to be owned by the state, but also its president during this period of rapid growth and decline was a former Directeur du Trésor, the most prestigious post in the French finance ministry, and the very architect of the successful reform of banking and financial market regulation in the 1980s. Accordingly, this fiasco has raised questions about state ownership and the system of *pantouflage* whereby senior civil servants move into positions in the public corporate sector following their careers with the state.

The fact that the French state would be effective in designing new structures on the one side, while experiencing a fiasco in working with these structures on the other, is not completely a surprise. In his examination of the strengths and weaknesses of the French administrative apparatus, Rouban (1990) argues that the institutions developed under the Fifth Republic gave priority to conception and formulation of policy and taking decisions over the implementation and evaluation of policies. With the state giving priority to technical expertise over social expertise, the dominant public figure became the senior career official. Information flows were much stronger going down to society than returning from society to the state.

Generally speaking, Rouban adds, reforms like those of financial services that were carried out in the 1980s were intended to give more emphasis to strengthening policy implementation. In seeking to enhance programme delivery, the French state had more recourse to independent administrative authorities and opened the door to more direct involvement in policy making by societal actors. In this process, however, the public agenda became much more fragmented and the state ran a greater risk of becoming clientelized by societal groups.

This analysis is instructive for our purposes because the conception and formulation of financial services reforms and the efficiency of the state in taking decisions on those reforms conform closely to Rouban's expectations. Policy objectives were clearly specified, appropriate policy instruments designed, and decisions were made over a rather short period between 1980 and 1987. Certainly, if one were to contrast this process with the protracted reform sequences in the USA or the UK, the comprehensiveness and efficiency of the French changes would seem to be a significant achievement. Where the state seemed to have much less success, however, was in creating the necessary boundaries between public authority and private actors critical to effective implementation of regulatory policy. The corporatist framework put in place was vulnerable to reckless banking behaviour, with the Crédit Lyonnais fiasco being an unfortunate consequence. Such vulnerability was to prove highly consequential as Europeanization and globalization of banking put their own constraints on the tools available to national regulatory authorities.

This argument is developed in the following steps. First, the particular challenge to French financial services from the growing globalization of markets is outlined. The chapter then notes the main actors in the French policy-making regime and describes their place in the wider context of banking regulation in France. Next we turn to examine the design and passage into law of significant reforms to banking and financial markets regulation, taking particular note of the way these changes also facilitated French participation in reforms at the EU level. With this understanding of the new regulatory apparatus, we examine the policy fiasco that arose out of the adventurism of Crédit Lyonnais. The chapter concludes with an examination of the factors apparently responsible for the inability of regulatory institutions to prevent one of the most significant banking failures in French financial history.

2 INTERNATIONAL CHALLENGES TO FRENCH BANKING AND SECURITIES REGULATION

The growing interdependence of domestic financial services markets that began developing as long ago as the 1960s, the growth of distinct global markets for bank lending and short-term and long-term securities in the 1960s and 1970s, and the emergence of innovative global markets for equities and derivatives in the late 1970s posed challenges for longstanding market segmentation in financial services. Once non-financial firms could begin to substitute international loans for loans raised on domestic markets, or short-term securities for bank loans, traditional approaches to segmenting and protecting markets began to feel more like straitjackets for many financial firms.

Although common to all OECD countries, such market segmentation was especially deep in France. Commercial banks operated under different rules than did merchant banks, savings banks and financial cooperatives. The latter, in turn, were further segmented to serve distinct markets including agriculture, artisans, small business and housing. Finance houses were reserved for consumer lending markets and securities transactions were the monopoly of stock exchange brokers (*agents de change*). French segmentation also assumed that smaller savers would not be borrowers. Accordingly, the savings banks system (*caisses d'épargne*) had restricted lending powers and funnelled savers' assets to a state body, the *Caisse des dépôts et consignations*, that, in turn, functioned to finance the state's industrial policy objectives. Reinforcing market segmentation were distinct regulatory systems, each with its own and different set of rules and with its own approach to supervision.

This segmentation of banking markets allowed considerable state 'guidance' in directing bank credit to investment needs deemed important by the state (Zysman, 1983). French firms tended to rely strongly on bank lending for meeting their investment needs, while securities markets were relatively underdeveloped. As international markets for bank lending and for short- and long-term securities began to open up, French firms began to have an option for satisfying capital needs that lay beyond the control of the state. Firms were likely to be tempted to look for such alternative sources of capital because a highly intricate system of credit allocation and capital controls overlaid the deeply segmented banking markets and the small securities markets (Loriaux, 1991). Not only did this system of controls restrict competition and thus innovation among financial services firms, but also it began to create inflexibilities for industrial firms as they sought to gain access to needed capital.

Perhaps even more importantly, the various systems of controls over credit created increasing problems for macroeconomic policy. Loriaux (1991) develops a convincing argument that the movement towards flexible exchange rates in the international monetary system set in motion a series of effects that put intense pressure on France's approach to macroeconomic policy. He suggests that French companies, particularly those in favoured sectors, had an assurance that they could borrow from public or parapublic lenders, even in times of financial difficulty. This assurance fortified their ability to resist policies of monetary stabilization and weakened the power of the French finance ministry to control monetary growth, using internal policy instruments. Loriaux demonstrates that liberalization of financial markets offered the prospect to the French state of more control over its monetary and exchange rate policy. In short, the French state had its own interests in liberalization, given growing incompatibilities between floating exchange rates in the international monetary system and quota-based allocation of credit in the real domestic economy.

A final challenge to French financial services regulatory policy arose in the late 1970s, when the European Economic Community was beginning to consider how financial services might be liberalized in the Community. The First Credit Directive agreed to in 1977 set up common criteria for the licensing of banking firms, stipulated that the home country of a bank was responsible for supervising all its operations, and set up the Banking Advisory Committee, a permanent grouping of national regulators and supervisors with a specific mandate to harmonize regulatory policies. Would the deep segmentation of French markets inhibit French firms from gaining a strong market presence in the soon to emerge European financial area?

3   THE FRENCH POLICY-MAKING SYSTEM

Historically, three principal actors are at the centre of the financial services policy community: the finance ministry, the central bank and the principal representative bodies of the firms in the sector. The *Ministère de l'Économie, des Finances et du Budget* (MEF) has an encompassing mandate that includes oversight of the functioning of the financial system as a whole and responsibility for the overall health of the economy. Vested with responsibility for oversight of the financial system within the department is the *Direction du Trésor*. Although relatively small, the Trésor embodies Rouban's characterization of the strength of the French state because it has often been remarkably good at identifying problems, conceiving solutions and then bringing about the policy changes necessary to make implementation possible. Branches within the Trésor have acted as guardians, regulators and supervisors of securities markets, guardian of all banking firms, and manager of government shares in nationalized banks. To these ends, the ministry would appoint representatives to sit on boards of directors of all public financial services firms including the nationalized banks, the central organizations of the savings banks and oversight bodies of securities exchanges.

Central to its success as the conceptual leader in the reform process has been the relatively high proportion of graduates of the *École nationale d'administration* (ENA), the elite school specializing in the area of economics, whose top graduates make a career at the Trésor. Many of these, in turn, are members of the *grand corps* called the *Inspection générale des finances*. Members of this body will often begin their careers at middle levels in the MEF, move up the ministerial ladder, with some time spent in the minister's *cabinet*, and then eventually leave in their early 40s for a position in one of the nationalized banks or parastate institutions active in the financial sector (Suleiman, 1978). As we shall see below, this career path comes into serious question following the Crédit Lyonnais fiasco.

During the period when the reforms took place and of the subsequent rapid expansion of the assets of Crédit Lyonnais, the second principal player, the Banque de France, was not yet independent of the finance ministry. Independence was to come only in 1993. In its advisory role to the minister of finance on monetary policy, the central bank was given responsibility for the proper functioning of the banking system. It also had direct jurisdiction over short- and medium-term securities markets, including inter-bank dealers. For these reasons, prior to the reforms, the Banque de France chaired the agency responsible for banking supervision, the *Commission de Contrôle des Banques* (CCB), whose staff in turn were central bank employees.

Emerging out of a corporatist system set up under the Vichy regime during World War II were two compulsory, monopolistic associations designated as representatives of the banking sector (Coleman, 1993, pp. 126–9). The *Association professionnelle des banques* represented all of the commercial banks while the *Association professionnelle des établissements financiers* spoke for other registered financial services firms. The Law of 2 December 1945 set out the organizational structure of these two groups and gave them a defined public status. They were given the right to speak on the advisability of the registration of any new firm in their respective domains and to be consulted on any general policy decisions taken by the government. They also had the responsibility to communicate government directives and decisions to their constituent members.

French thinking on the relationships among these three players emphasized first of all balance and collaboration between the finance ministry and the central bank. Thus the body formally responsible for policy formulation in the postwar system, the *Conseil national du crédit*, was chaired by the minister of finance, with the governor of the central bank acting as its vice-chair. Conversely, the central bank governor chaired the CCB, the principal agency responsible for supervision, while the finance ministry occupied the vice-chair role. The idea here was to ensure that the finance ministry and the central bank discuss and agree upon policy change before proceeding further. Because the two associations representing the banking firms were represented on both of these bodies, played an active role in their working committees and had a right by law to be consulted, the system also ensured that the finance ministry and the central bank would also need significant support from the sector itself before proceeding with change. For these reasons, this policy network has been described as a corporatist one (Coleman, 1993).

4 MODERNIZING BANKING REGULATION IN THE 1980s

Planning to carry out a reform of the banking system began in the latter stages of Giscard d'Estaing's presidency. In 1980, Jean-Yves Habérer, then Directeur of the Trésor, commissioned a member of his staff to draw up a document indicating lines of possible changes. After a year of consultation involving the staff in the Trésor, the central bank and the banking profession, a final document was prepared and presented to Jacques Delors, the finance minister for the new socialist government and a former employee of the Banque de France. Delors completed work first on a new set of bank nationalizations, a socialist priority, and then proceeded with the reforms of the banking law. They were debated in the Assemblée Nationale in 1983 and passed into law on 24 January 1984.

The important changes in the legislation can be divided into three groups. First, the government modernized regulatory structures. The government sought to rationalize drastically the number of agencies involved in the policy process, while building on the idea of a balance among the finance ministry, the central bank and the banking sector. Responsibility for policy making was transferred to a new body, the *Comité de la réglementation bancaire* (CRB). This agency was assigned powers over regulatory policy governing commercial banks, savings banks, financial cooperatives and finance houses, powers previously scattered across a variety of different bureaus. It is chaired by the minister of finance, with the governor of the central bank acting as vice-chair. Its members included representatives of the banking sector, bank employees and two outside experts in recognition of the increased complexity of banking matters.

Responsibility for implementing policy was given over to another new agency, the *Commission bancaire* (CB). Like the CRB, the CB has a collegial structure that encourages the balancing of the views of the finance ministry and the central bank. The central bank governor chairs the commission with the finance minister acting as vice-chair, with some outside experts in banking issues rounding out the members. Distinct from its predecessor body, the CCB, the CB does not include representatives of the banking sector, such a step now being perceived as a conflict of interest.

Committed to systematic policy collaboration with the banking sector itself, the government also took steps to rationalize the old corporatist policy network to fit the wider scope of the new law. Section 23 of the Banking Act directed all credit institutions to belong to a professional association or central organization which, in turn, is required to belong to a new peak association, the *Association française des établissements de crédit* (AFEC). In effect, AFEC is a compulsory, monopolistic peak association covering the whole of the financial services sector: commercial banks, savings banks, financial cooperatives, finance houses and self-regulatory arms of the stock and derivatives exchanges. Thus AFEC is the official representative of the sector on the CRB, the government channels its communications to the sector through AFEC, and the sector's firms are expected to communicate their opinions on matters of common concern using AFEC.

Consistent with the rationalization of the regulatory system, the second component of the reforms sought to break down the many barriers between market segments that had come to plague the system. Thus the law gathered within one framework deposit banks, merchant banks, savings banks, financial cooperatives, financial holding companies, inter-bank money market brokers, finance houses and securities firms. Providing a very broad definition of banking, the law then said that any firm engaging in any of the activities embraced by this definition would be defined as a 'credit institution' and would be governed by the law. The government thus set out to harmonize the diverse and not necessarily consistent rules and regulations spread across the previously separate groupings of firms. It anticipated common rules for management, solvency, liquidity and risk assessment.

Other changes outside the banking law complemented this desegmentation process. In 1983, the Trésor initiated a series of changes to the savings bank system in anticipation of their moving beyond the traditional function of taking in savings to include lending and related activities. Previously specific market privileges enjoyed by particular segments were also ended. Thus subsidized lending to agriculture was put up for bid to all banks rather than being controlled by *Crédit Agricole*. Similarly, the *banques populaires* lost their monopoly over subsidized lending to small business and artisans.

Third, these reforms had at their heart the fostering of the universal bank as the preferred structure for financial services. The various reforms anticipated that financial services firms would engage in a broad range of activities from deposit taking and lending to securities underwriting and investment services. The new legislation also anticipated closer equity ties between banks and industrial corporations along the lines of the German-style universal bank. Section 6 of the Banking Act provided explicitly for credit institutions to take and hold equity positions in existing or new enterprises. As we shall see, Crédit Lyonnais was to take swift advantage of this provision of the law.

Thus, by the end of the 1980s, French financial services had undergone a dramatic change. No other country in the OECD removed institutional segmentation of markets as quickly as did France. Nor did any other country, with the exception of Germany, succeed in bringing all credit establishments under a single regulatory system with a harmonized system of rules. Financial markets grew rapidly under a new liberal regulatory approach. Previously fragmented money markets were sufficiently unified for the central bank to be able to use them in place of credit controls to orchestrate monetary policy. All of these accomplishments are testament to the strength of the French state in conception and passage into law of policy changes under the Fifth Republic.

Moreover, these reforms proved to be highly functional for subsequent negotiations on creating an internal market in financial services in the EC. We have already noted that the strong presence of graduates of ENA and of members of the *grands corps*, the *Inspection générale des finances* (IGF) in the finance ministry (and we might add at the head of the central bank) facilitated greatly the strategic policy capacity of the French state. It also made building understanding between the state and representatives of the banking sector easier. Josselin (1997, p. 64) surveyed the background of the directors of financial services professional associations in 1990. She found that 19.3 per cent had attended ENA, including the chairs of AFEC, and of each of AFEC's member groups representing commercial banks, finance houses, stock exchange firms and the stock exchanges themselves. If one expands the elite schools to include the *École Polytechnique* and the *Institut d'Études politiques*, the number of directors with 'elite' ties grows considerably. In addition, Josselin found that 12 board members had previously worked for MEF or for the IGF, including the five chairs of key associations noted above. Josselin (ibid., p. 65) concludes: 'the majority of French professional organizations in the sector of financial services were headed by former bureaucrats – and what's more issued from the same prestigious department (MEF), which did not comprise more than 200 top civil servants in the 1980s'.

The 1984 reforms ensured that France would come to EC negotiations on realization of a single financial market with a unified voice. One department was in charge, the MEF, and that department had a collegial policy-making forum, the CRB, whose structure encouraged concertation or collaboration among the department's senior officials, the central bank and the sector itself. The structure of chair and vice-chairs of the CRB and the CB ensured that strategic concerns of the finance ministry about the competitiveness of French financial services firms in a globalizing economy would be balanced by prudential considerations of safety and soundness on the part of the central bank. Josselin (ibid., p. 146) notes that this centralization, joined with the elite school ties permeating the policy network, provided France with a definite asset in the Second Credit Directive negotiations.

At the European level, the key forum for preliminary consultation on banking policy directives had been the Banking Advisory Committee. Here was where first drafts of directives were vetted and technical questions considered. France has three representatives on the Committee: the secretary-general of the CRB, the head of the CB and a senior Trésor official. The collegial structures of the CRB and the CB helped ensure that the finance ministry, the central bank and the sector itself would work out a unified position before France began negotiations at Brussels.

Such unity also brought France some notable successes in the negotiations of the Second Credit Directive and its companion directives on Own Funds and Solvency. The approach to universal banking adopted at the EC level was very close to the conception in the 1984 French banking law. After a difficult fight, France was also able to secure a tougher reciprocity provision for non-EC countries than had been demanded by the UK and Germany. If we extend our purview to the negotiations over the directive on investment services, France's principles favouring selling and trading on open, regulated exchanges were given recognition, thereby ensuring a continued competitive place for France's Paris-based financial centre (Coleman and Underhill, 1998). Each of these examples suggests that the reform of the French banking law not only brought about more sweeping change than could be achieved by most of its OECD counterparts at the time, but also equipped it very well to negotiate and bargain over policy changes at the regional level in the EC.

5   THE CRÉDIT LYONNAIS FIASCO

At the time when the present phase of financial services globalization began in the early 1970s, the Crédit Lyonnais bank was one of the 'big three' commercial banks in France. Like its sister institutions, the Banque Nationale de Paris and the Société Générale, the bank was owned by the government of France, following a series of nationalizations after World War II. Following the victory of the right in the legislative elections of 1986, moves began to privatize the other two banks, leaving Crédit Lyonnais the principal large commercial bank in government hands in the 1990s. In 1987, Jean-Yves Habérer, graduate of ÉNA, member of the *Inspection générale des finances*, former director of the Trésor in the finance ministry, and architect of the reforms to the banking system, was appointed president of the bank, consistent with the tradition of *pantouflage* noted above.

Assessing the Failure: How Bad is Bad?

Six years later, when Habérer was replaced by a fellow *énarque*, Jean Peyrevelade, the bank was said to have lost FF25 billion. Two years later, the losses were estimated to be FF50 billion, a total larger than the bank's capital base (Verkhovskoy, 1995, p. 22). By 1998, the total losses had reached FF190 billion or US$31.8 billion. Based on this amount, the collapse of Crédit Lyonnais was the largest single commercial bank failure in the postwar period in the OECD. When the difficulties of the bank first became known in 1993 and 1994, the finance minister, Édouard Alphandéry, had stated that the bank would be rescued without French taxpayers having to contribute a centime to its support. By 1998, however, it had become evident that French taxpayers would be on the hook for a minimum of US$20 billion. Such a figure would indicate that only the bailout of the savings and loans system in the United States in the late 1980s put a higher cost on taxpayers when it came to banking failures in OECD countries in the postwar period.

The fiasco had two other dimensions. First, from 1993 to 1998, addressing the bank's financial problems required three separate rescue plans. Once it became clear that substantial financial assistance from the state would be involved in these plans, the French government was also required to negotiate with the European Commission to ensure that rules of competition in the single financial market were not violated. The final set of these negotiations did not conclude until May 1998, some five years after the resignation of Habérer and almost a full decade after the first signs of problems emerged. It has gradually become clear that the steps taken by the government between 1993 and 1995 in an attempt to rescue the bank probably worsened the situation. Particularly crucial here were the decision to create a 'bad bank' to hold the worst assets of Crédit Lyonnais and the conditions the government put on the relationship between the remaining good bank (Crédit Lyonnais) and this institution (Andrew, 1998, pp. 25–6). In short, the government of France did not manage well the process of rescue.

Second, by 1998, there were also 75 different judicial inquiries under way examining allegations of fraud, corruption, political party financing and relations with such controversial figures as the French entrepreneur and friend of the Socialist Party, Bernard Tapie, and the Italian Gianfranco Parretti, a controversial businessman convicted of fraud in his home country in 1990. The French finance minister had also initiated criminal proceedings, giving further indication not only of financial mismanagement, but also of illegal practices involving senior bank officials.

Identifying Agents: Who or What Brought this Failure About?

As in all instances of policy fiasco, no single source or agent was involved in the failure of Crédit Lyonnais. The actions of four different persons and organizations would appear to be contributors. First, the government of France took several steps that contributed to the failure. When a government owns a bank, it may adopt one of two rather different attitudes to its ownership: (a) it can legislate a mandate for the bank, ensure that the enterprise has in place the management tools and personnel to carry out the mandate, require the bank to follow the usual rules of prudential behaviour under watchful supervision, and then leave it alone to fulfil its mandate; or (b) it can take a more directive position, leave the mandate of the institution rather vague, and draw on the bank to address various public policy objectives as they arise.

In the late 1980s, the French government took a position closer to the latter one. Worried about the growing financial strength of Germany and particularly about the expansion of its large commercial banks such as the Deutsche Bank, François Mitterrand, the president, urged Crédit Lyonnais to expand in ways to match and counter the German institutions (Fitchett, 1996). Such a route, of course, was now possible with the reformed banking laws, which had set the German version of the universal bank as the French model as well. In his testimony to a parliamentary hearing in 1994, Habérer noted the importance of government direction in his decisions as president of the bank. He explained that the government had asked Crédit Lyonnais to expand its investment abroad and to assist various state-owned, industrial firms as they too sought to compete in the global economy.

In giving this informal mandate to Crédit Lyonnais the government also trusted its senior managers to act prudently. It did not take a great interest in the bank's management arrangements, nor did it construct a board of directors that might conduct the normal kind of oversight that would normally occur with a private firm. Habérer and his senior managers were basically left to their own devices in carrying out the general wishes of the government.

Finally, the government took steps in 1994 and 1995 that also contributed to the crisis. For political reasons, when announcing both the first and the second rescue plans for the bank, the finance minister sought to assure the French public that no taxpayers' funds would be required to return Crédit Lyonnais to a healthy position. In order to help fulfil this promise, the minister directed the bank to make a substantial loan at below market rates to the *Consortium de Réalisation* (CDR), the so-called 'bad bank' created in 1995 to relieve Crédit Lyonnais of its bad debts (Anonymous, *The Economist*, 1997). The government also required Crédit Lyonnais management to provide the CDR with various good assets to ensure that the CDR would be sufficiently viable to carry out the required sell-offs. These two decisions, however, tied Crédit Lyonnais hands to the point that it ran into further trouble in 1996, precipitating a third and final rescue plan.

Jean-Yves Habérer is a second contributor to the fiasco. All the evidence suggests that he took up with relish the government's charge to create a suitable competitor to Deutsche Bank. By 1990, Crédit Lyonnais had already become the largest non-Japanese commercial bank in the world (McClintick, 1997, p.

36). Habérer brought to his position a majestic style, building a 'floating floor' in the bank's headquarters so that it would not be disturbed by outside traffic, and adopting a hierarchical management style that discouraged upward communication in the organization. Known as the *Napoléon de la banque* (Warde, 1994), Habérer was an inconsistent manager. He left his senior lieutenants considerable scope for action, even though he had been personally warned by the Dutch central bank of improper behaviour on their part as early as 1988 (McClintick, 1996). When it became clear that some rather improper banking practices would be needed to finalize the purchase of MGM by Parretti in 1990, he became directly involved (Fitchett, 1996). Clearly, then, a third set of contributors to the failure included other senior managers of Crédit Lyonnais. McClintick's (1996) exposure of the bank identified Georges Vigon, head of Crédit Lyonnaise's Dutch subsidiary, plus several other senior officials, as receiving bribes and engaging in imprudent, if not illegal, banking practices.

Finally, the *Commission bancaire* (CB), the new supervisory organization created under the banking reforms of the 1980s, and its parent organization, the Banque de France, must be identified as contributors. As the supervisory bodies in the home country of Crédit Lyonnais, they had responsibility for oversight of all of the bank's operations, both at home and abroad, and the duty to work in concert with supervisors in all countries where the bank was economically active. Consistent with this division of labour, the Dutch central bank informed both the CB and the Banque de France of the dangerous lending practices of Crédit Lyonnaise's subsidiary in the Netherlands as early as 1989 (McClintick, 1996). The Dutch supervisor took this step after an initial letter to Habérer about these problems had gone unanswered. There is no evidence that the CB took any action at this time. Nor is there any evidence that the CB or the Banque de France intervened in the operations of Crédit Lyonnais as the evidence began to mount of financial difficulties in 1990 and after. In fact, the CB did not issue any statement on its role in the affair until 1995, well after the damage had occurred (Brankin, 1995). Nor did either the CB or the Banque de France conduct any public inquiry into the affair. This silence stands in sharp contrast to the inquiries commissioned by the Bank of England and the British government following the failures of both Bank of Commerce and Credit International and Barings Bank, and of congressional investigation of the savings and loans fiasco in the USA.

What Prompted the Actions of those Contributing to the Fiasco?

The French government's desire to strengthen and to build up Crédit Lyonnais represented a response to growing regionalization and globalization. With the completion of the Second Credit Directive and its associated capital adequacy and solvency directives looming following the Single European Act, the prospect of a single financial services market increased significantly in the late 1980s. To the extent that such a market developed, banks would be better placed to compete the more they had operations throughout the EC. Germany's banks had recognized this challenge and begun to develop a stronger position in London, still the financial centre of Europe and a major global player. Deutsche Bank acquired the British investment bank, Morgan Grenfell, a clear indicator to its competitors of its intentions to compete strongly in the European financial area. With Crédit Lyonnais still under government control, an attempt to push France's competitive position by encouraging the growth of the bank was quite consistent with longstanding *dirigiste* practices by the French state.

Not only was the government concerned about the regional European market, but also it recognized the growing globalization of financial services. Rapid innovation in short-term securities instruments, in Eurobonds and similar longer-term securities, and in derivatives, indicated the importance of global markets, less tied to physical location and national spaces. It was also evident that the firms that would dominate these markets would themselves be global corporations, with major investment activities in all three of the world's principal financial areas, Europe, the USA and East and South-east Asia. The rise of global financial markets also had implications for financial centres such as Paris. To the extent that such centres could not keep up with the innovations, a condition partially dependent upon having important global firms active on site, the prospect of being relegated to a third-rate financial power loomed larger. Evidence that these concerns were operating in France came in various ways. For example, when France's other commercial banks criticized the government's rescue plans in 1994 and 1995, the government and Crédit Lyonnais responded by accusing them of acting against the interests of the *Place de Paris* as a world financial centre (de Quillac, 1995).

The government's desire to provide a bailout without drawing on taxpayers was consistent with another keystone of the French approach to banking regulation, the private character of depositor protection. Unlike the USA and, to a lesser extent the UK, France preferred to rely on informal consultations with the banks themselves to deal with banking failures (Coleman, 1996). No formal depositor protection scheme existed. Such an approach worked well when it came to difficulties with smaller banks, but was clearly inadequate when a very large bank began to fail. Crédit Lyonnais was too big a player in French and European financial markets and too visible politically to be permitted to fail. Unfortunately, the French government lacked the tools of formal depositor protection insurance to cushion the fall. The initial decision not to engage taxpayers' money was thus consistent with earlier practice. Unfortunately, it prevented the government from acting sufficiently quickly and with enough funds to prevent the bank's condition from worsening further.

Finally, a number of commentators have raised the possibility that the unique elite networks that dominate senior positions in the French state and the economy help explain aspects of the fiasco (de Quillac, 1995; Warde, 1994; Fitchett, 1996; Anonymous, *The Economist*, 1997). As de Quillac (1995, p. 22) notes, 'the state's rescue of France's largest commercial bank has opened a bigger debate on what many people see as the bigger scandal: a system where a caste of elite civil servants, apparently accountable to no one and rarely punished, play monopoly with the French economy'. The author adds that 12 of the 15 top industrial companies in France were headed by persons drawn from this civil service elite, as were two-thirds of the state-owned enterprises privatized since 1986 (ibid., p. 23). The issue then is whether there is a kind of code of silence within these elite circles that fosters deference to the best and the brightest such as Habérer. Was it such deference or the implicit trust among members of this elite that led senior officials at the *Commission bancaire* to concentrate their efforts on supervising the smaller banks, while leaving the larger banks more to their own devices (Fitchett, 1996)? Would a decision to allow Crédit Lyonnais to fail rather than being rescued have exposed certain elements of the elite networks at the pinnacle of the French state and the economy, thereby undermining the very legitimacy of the French state?

Who is to Blame?

In his Bastille Day address of 1996, Jacques Chirac, president of the republic, deplored publicly the fact that the finance ministry, specifically the Direction du Trésor, and the central bank had not 'well exercised' their responsibility over Crédit Lyonnais and another state financial institution, Crédit Foncier (Anonymous, *The Banker*, 1996). He added, 'I take note of the fact that nobody is trying to find out who is responsible for such financial disasters.' In its commentary in July 1997, *The Economist* refers to megalomania and misman-agement, thereby fingering Jean-Yves Habérer, his senior vice-presidents and the French government officials responsible for banking supervision. McClintick (1996) in his *Fortune* magazine exposé of the fiasco points his finger directly at Habérer and especially at several of his senior deputies. In taking an ever greater interest in the difficulties of Crédit Lyonnais and the attempts by the French government to use state subsidies to right the bank, the European Commission seemed to express some concern about the general approach of the French state to banking, especially its continued reliance on state ownership. In short, both within and without France, observers can be found who would place the blame on one or more of each of the major players discussed in this chapter.

The problem that arises out of trying to place blame on any of these agents is that it fails to take sufficient account of the changing market situation and rapid innovations taking place in financial services. Is it fair to fault the government of France for seeking to ensure that French banks would be prepared to compete in the highly innovative and emerging globalizing markets? Is it humanly possible for banking regulators and supervisors to know and understand all of the innovations taking place in financial markets, given the speed at which changes have been taking place? If so, one would need to extend the blame to their regulatory colleagues in the UK because of the failures of Barings and the Bank of Commerce and Credit International, to those in the USA because of the savings and loans disaster, and still later in the decade to the Japanese regulators as some of that country's largest banks teetered on the edge. The venality of Habérer's senior managers is hardly exceptional in the banking world and Habérer's personal *hauteur* is scarcely uncommon among the world's leading bank executives. Is the institutionalized elitism in France all that different from the informal class relations that are prominent in the British banking sector (Moran, 1986) or the old school ties so important in the upper reaches of the Japanese public and private sectors?

Accordingly, placing blame in these circumstances may be easy to do, but difficult to sustain. Crédit Lyonnais is hardly the first large commercial bank that governments and other banks have thought too large to fail. Once this type of decision is made, managing such a financial crisis is a very difficult task, one whose complexity has increased exponentially with the regionalization and globalization of financial markets. The failure of a large transnational bank like Crédit Lyonnais leaches very quickly into the global financial space, where it becomes very difficult for national regulators to contain, let alone control. What is to be regretted, however, is the failure of the French government or the banking supervisory authorities to conduct a full, open and transparent investigation of the Crédit Lyonnais fiasco. In the absence of such an investigation, it is not clear that the policy learning that could arise out of close study of the crisis will ever take place. Without such learning, other governments in different parts of the world, as well as the French government, may not act as effectively as possible when they are faced with a similar disaster. What is certain is that the difficulties of Crédit Lyonnais will not be the last to occur in world banking circles.

6   CONCLUSIONS

In the introduction to this chapter, following Rouban (1990), it was observed that the institutions of the Fifth Republic in France appear to be well adapted to the agenda-setting and policy design phases of the policy process, but less suited for the policy implementation and evaluation phases. The examination of financial services presented in this chapter appears to fit these observations well. The French state took the lead at a crucial moment and developed a design for reforming banking regulation that was executed remarkably quickly and required relatively little subsequent reconfiguration, at least when put in a comparative context. The same state working through some of the institutions at the heart of the banking reforms helped to exacerbate a crisis in one of its largest financial institutions. Indeed, some would suggest that, if it had acted with the same alacrity and foresight when faced with a failing bank as it did when reforming the banking system, Crédit Lyonnais would not have become the single largest bank failure in an OECD country in the postwar period.

It would be a mistake, however, to ascribe the failure to prevent the Crédit Lyonnais crisis only to a traditional weakness of French political institutions or to a *dirigiste* French policy style. The very reforms of banking regulation initiated in the early 1980s were a response to changing and globalizing financial services markets. By the time the reforms were in place and Crédit Lyonnais had embarked upon its expansion plans, the context of financial services policy making had itself changed. The political geography of the nation-state no longer fitted the economic geography of regional and global financial services markets. Faced with such a disjuncture, Reinicke (1998) suggests, one needs to work towards a 'global public policy'. Such a policy involves nation-states working together in a collaborative way to pool their authority so as to provide rules and ensure soundness of the new, more globally expansive financial markets. Such collaboration requires a learning process and the development of working relationships at the inter-state level that are time consuming. Not enough time had elapsed when the difficulties of Crédit Lyonnais had emerged and not enough lessons had been learned from failures in other countries for France to engage its partners in an effective policy of crisis prevention. No longer can one say that the institutions of France or the style of its policy makers are at fault. The largest banks in the world's financial system are now a global responsibility.

NOTE

1. The author would like to thank Andreas Busch for his comments on an earlier version of this chapter.

19. Banking supervision and deposit insurance in Germany, 1974–84: keeping the state at arm's length

Andreas Busch

1 INTRODUCTION

This chapter is about whether or not the German political system coped with the challenges posed by the momentous changes of world financial markets in the last 25 years.[1] The policy episode chosen is the time between 1974 and 1984, which covers the collapse of Herstatt Bank in 1974, arguably the most important event in this policy field in Germany in the last 65 years. This period of crisis (in which two other banks from the public sector also came close to collapse) had the potential to alter the sectoral regime of regulation and the distribution of power between government and private actors in the field fundamentally. However, while the breakdown of Herstatt Bank did have important institutional consequences internationally by leading to the creation of the Basle Committee, which paved the way towards a regime of cooperative banking supervision (Dale, 1992, p. 320; Kapstein, 1994, p. 42), interestingly enough, as we shall see, the institutional domestic consequences of the crisis have been much less momentous, at least seen from today's perspective.

A main argument of this chapter is that there was relatively little change in the sectoral governance mechanism which had to deal with the challenges. Its main characteristics (a small number of cooperative actors both on the state and on the industry side, a 'hands off' approach to banking supervision, institutionalized involvement of industry associations in policy formulation and implementation) have been preserved. That does not mean that there was no change. But the banking industry managed to fend off substantially increased state involvement: it managed to keep the state at arm's length.

The remainder of this chapter will first give a brief account of the structure of the German banking industry, the historical development of banking supervision in Germany and of the institutions involved in banking policy. The main focus will then be on the policy episode between 1974 and 1984, first outlining the challenges stemming from changes in the international framework and culminating in the collapse of Herstatt Bank, then describing the policy response to this. In the next two sections, an assessment of success or failure and an analysis of the policy episode will be undertaken, before some further remarks conclude the chapter.

2   HISTORICAL DEVELOPMENT AND INSTITUTIONS INVOLVED

Historically, banking supervision in Germany is a twentieth-century invention. The nineteenth century was, as in most other European countries, an epoch of 'free banking'. In spite of several debates about banking supervision and deposit protection in the 1890s and 1900s, the governing principle remained that of *Gewerbefreiheit* (freedom of trade) (Niethammer, 1990, pp. 41ff).

First restrictions on that principle were imposed during the course of World War I, but real change only came about with the banking crisis of 1931.[2] The breakdown of Darmstädter-und Nationalbank, in spite of the state's swiftly guaranteeing that bank's deposits, triggered a general bank run and the collapse of the German banking system. A moratorium on payments had to be imposed, and further guarantees be made. As a result, the Reich ended up in possession of a third to half of the shares in the three 'big banks', and practically put large parts of the banking system into public ownership.

Having bailed out the banks, the state then moved to impose substantial regulation on the whole credit sector. The path chosen differed markedly from that in the United States, which underwent a widespread banking crisis at about the same time: while there the solution was seen in the creation of a state-run deposit insurance system with mandatory membership which should protect depositors from losses (Kareken, 1992, p. 315), the approach in Germany centred on protection through limitation of competition in the credit system and a stabilization of banks' profits, both reached through a comprehensive cartel.

After considering the report of a Commission on the Structure of the Banking System, the Banking Act of 1934 (*Kreditwesen-Gesetz* or KWG) laid down a general framework for the industry. It codified the regulations from the emergency measures and introduced caps for loans as well as regulations on liquidity requirements and equity capital. A concession was now needed for banking, and the authorities had substantial latitude in granting it, for example by assessing the 'need' for a new bank or branch. In the following years, the regulatory structure was further centralized, while at the same time the big banks were reprivatized between 1933 and 1936.

After World War II, the authority for supervision came to lie with the Länder (the regional governments). Although they soon started to coordinate their actions, this decentralization fitted well with attempts by the occupying powers to decentralize the German banking system. But this policy ended in 1957 with the re-emergence of the three big banks. It was followed by a recentralization of banking supervision through the Banking Act of 1961. This more or less brought back the situation existing before 1939, retaining detailed powers concerning regulations of book-keeping, caps for loans and liquidity requirements for the new *Bundesaufsichtsamt für das Kreditwesen* (BAKred).

This authority, located in Berlin (but moved to Bonn in spring 2000), is the only one of the three institutions involved in banking supervision which deals exclusively with this issue. It has the primary responsibility for issuing orders, regulations and written opinions on banking issues, and only it can issue or repeal bank licences and take other direct supervisory actions against a bank.[3] Although charged with a number of important tasks, the BAKred is a comparatively small authority, employing only 520 officials to supervise some 3500 credit institutions and 4500 financial services institutions. But on the one hand it is not concerned with the day-to-day decisions of single banks, it rather sees as its primary task to put into place a framework of rules within which banks can conduct their business. It thus primarily deals with legal tasks, employing many lawyers, although economists also play a role on its staff. On the other hand, it can rely on its cooperation with the Bundesbank (and external auditors) for tasks such as the collection of economic data and information from the banks. One reason for this is that the BAKred's legal status as a national administrative body according to Article 87 of the German Constitution requires it to have no subsidiaries.[4] In the conduct of its business, the BAKred is relatively autonomous, but subject to directives from the ministry of finance (Fischer, 1997b, p. 3725; Coleman, 1996, p. 75).

The *ministry of finance* (BMF), located in Bonn, does not play a major task in the day-to-day business of banking supervision. Its main task is the development of laws which codify the field. This is, of course, an eminently important task when it comes to setting the long-term direction and is especially crucial in the case of challenges and reforms. As will be seen below, the BMF did indeed play a crucial role in the 1974–84 policy episode.

The *Bundesbank*, the country's central bank, located in Frankfurt, is the third federal institution involved in banking supervision in Germany. Its constituent parts, the state central banks (*Landeszentralbanken*), collect and analyse most of the data and information from the credit institutions that are used for banking supervision. Thus the Bundesbank is well-informed about the situation in the banking industry. Bundesbank and BAKred are required by law to communicate to each other any observations and findings that may be relevant for carrying out their respective functions.[5] As a result of all these factors, the Bundesbank's opinion on matters of banking supervision carries a great weight with the BAKred and, although it does not have a formal veto, the BAKred has never issued regulations with which the Bundesbank strongly disagreed (General Accounting Office, 1994, p. 20).

The German banking policy network, as far as state institutions are concerned, thus combines a regard for the perspective of general economic policy (BMF) with the more technical perspective which views the practical considerations of banking supervision (BAKred) and the aspects of the banking system as a whole and monetary policy (Bundesbank). All three institutions, moreover, share a perception of their role which does not advocate strong state intervention, although the institutional set-up facilitates high state capacity (Coleman, 1996, pp. 75, 133). Cooperation between the BAKred and the Bundesbank is relatively frictionless, which is certainly as much a result of the facts just mentioned as of its being enshrined in legislation.

On the industry side, conditions are also favourable for concertation. As the introductory chapter to Part IV demonstrates, the German banking system is characterized by being a *universal banking system* which has *a large public sector*.[6] Three main sectors can be distinguished, and they have roughly maintained their relative strength in terms of market share over the last decades: the public law banks (that is, the approximately 600 savings banks and the 13 Central Giro Banks)[7] are the biggest group with more than a third of the market, followed by the 320 commercial banks with about a quarter of it. Of this share, the three 'big banks' (Deutsche Bank, Dresdner Bank and Commerzbank) account for roughly 50 per cent, which is approximately the size of the whole third, the cooperative sector. The latter, with around 2400 credit cooperatives, is the most numerous, and it has managed to increase its market share considerably over the last decades. Although market shares have remained relatively stable, the postwar banking industry has undergone substantial change, marked by concentration and an extension of bank branches. While in 1957 there were 13 359 banks, their number had by 1997 shrunk to 3577, mainly accounted for by the number of credit cooperatives declining from more than 11 570 to 2400. At the same time, the number of bank branches has doubled: from some 25 000 to 50 000.

Peak-level associations exist that are organized according to private or public law status and according to the type of institution. The most important ones are the peak associations of the commercial banking sector (*Bundesverband deutscher Banken* or BdB); the savings banks (*Deutscher Sparkassen- und Giroverband* or DSGV); the cooperatives (*Bundesverband der deutschen Volksbanken und Raiffeisenbanken* or BVR); and the publicly owned banks (*Verband öffentlicher Banken*). All four associations are members of the *Zentraler Kreditausschuß* (ZKA) which has been in existence since the 1930s and serves as a forum for coordination between the different sectors of the banking industry. Conditions for this are, as already mentioned, good, because the associations each represent important sectors of the industry and do not compete for membership.[8] They also have 'a place at the table' in state policy making, since section 10 of the KWG gives them the right to a hearing before regulations concerning liable capital (the main instrument of banking regulation in Germany) are changed.

The German banking policy network has thus been categorized as a highly corporatist one, with associations being horizontally and vertically integrated, and being involved regularly and in an institutionalized manner in both policy formulation and policy implementation (Coleman, 1996, p. 82).

3 COPING WITH NEW CHALLENGES AND CRISIS, 1974–84

In the early 1970s, a number of structural changes occurred that altered profoundly the conditions under which – among others – banks worldwide conducted their business. This could not fail to have an impact on German banks as well, and on the regulation of banking. Although liberalization in itself was foreseeable, how exactly it would proceed and what the national consequences would be were unforeseeable. Not just the banks came 'under stress' (OECD, 1992), but also their national systems of regulation. This latent crisis was in Germany turned into acute crisis with the collapse of Herstatt Bank in 1974. The problem of protecting deposits in an era of increasing financial internationalization and volatility, and of maintaining trust in the safety of deposits that is vital for the financial system, was suddenly brought to the centre stage of politics.

This situation brought about the opportunity of a complete overhaul of the sectoral regulatory system (which had so far widely relied on self-regulation) and a change in the power relations between state and banks. The policy episode described in the following pages lasts from the onset of the crisis in 1974 to the Third Amendment of the Banking Act in 1984.

The Challenges

As mentioned above, the early 1970s saw a number of fundamental changes in the world economy. Among them were the breakdown of the system of fixed exchange rates that had been in operation for nearly three decades and the oil price shock of 1973–4, which caused recessions and inflation in many countries. Together, they ushered in an era of economic instability. Banks responded to this by diversifying their assets and liabilities on a global scale.

Besides these systemic and general economic challenges, countries faced specific political challenges of their own. In the case of Germany, these included challenges to the established system of universal banking from forces both on the left and on the liberal side of the political spectrum. In addition, the political struggle over how to protect depositors from the consequences of increased deregulation of the banking system had been going on for well over a decade, when the collapse of the Herstatt Bank from misspeculation in foreign exchange trading not only had severe consequences for payments systems abroad (Kapstein, 1994, pp. 39f), but also threatened a repetition of the breakdown of the whole German banking system, as had happened in 1931.

Liberalization and depositor protection

When the KWG was passed in 1961, it provided for regulation of interest rates, which (as in many other countries) was seen as an appropriate means of protecting both banks from excessive competition and small consumers from being overcharged on loans. The enforcement of the respective regulations, however, was lacking and in fact higher interest rates were being paid (Franke, 1998, pp. 296f). As a result, in 1967 the federal economics ministry announced the lifting of the interest rate decree. This was a further step towards financial liberalization.[9] But already in March 1961, while passing the Banking Act, the Bundestag had been concerned about possible negative effects of liberalization with respect to the safety of deposits. It had therefore asked the government to compile a report on competitive changes in the banking sector and the necessity and desirability of a general deposit insurance system (Ronge, 1979, p. 98).

In June 1966, the peak association of the private banking sector, the *Bundesverband deutscher Banken* (BdB), established a voluntary fund to help banks which had become insolvent. This was portrayed as a confidence-building measure on the part of the banking industry and a reaction to the broad guarantees of the public law savings banks and the credit associations (Landesbank Rheinland-Pfalz, 1983, p. 195). The latter had set up deposit protection schemes as early as in the 1930s (Coleman, 1996, p. 125).

The government report was published in November 1968.[10] The report stated an increased need for deposit protection since competition in the banking industry had increased for a number of reasons: the traditional division of labour between locally oriented savings and cooperative banks on the one hand and (especially the bigger) commercial banks on the other had gradually dissolved as the former offered a full range of services; the number of bank branches had increased markedly after the 'necessity check' had been abolished; business conditions and interest rates now varied after state regulation of interest rates had been done away with; and the lifting of the regulation on advertising saw banks increase their attempts to win new customers.[11] By introducing deposit protection, the report concluded, the banking system would be protected from bank failures, which might in the future lead to renewed calls for state limits on competition. Seen from that perspective, such a system would serve a double purpose: it would preserve a market order based on competition and would curb the safety advantage the publicly owned banks enjoyed. The report concluded that attempts made by the banking industry so far were insufficient, and that a legal solution would have to be found if there was no marked improvement in this situation. A general deposit insurance system, run by the government, might have to be instated.

Again this caused a reaction from the private banking industry (Landesbank Rheinland-Pfalz, 1983, p. 196). Its fund was changed in 1969 to now guarantee individual savings deposits in member banks up to DM10 000 per person.[12] While admitting that it was doing so at the government's suggestion, the BdB stressed the voluntary and private character of the enterprise (Bundesverband Deutscher Banken, 1975, p. 17).

The 'power of banks' under fire

The issue of deposit insurance was not the only political debate at that time that involved the banking industry. In the early-to-mid-1970s, there was a much more fundamental argument going on about the 'power of the banks', deemed excessive in Germany. Interestingly, the criticisms came from two different parts of the political spectrum: market-liberal and leftist forces criticized similar aspects of the existing system, such as banks' influence on non-financial firms via equity ownership, proxy votes and seats on supervisory boards (although they offered rather different remedies).

The liberal critique focused especially on the three big banks and argued that they received inside knowledge which provided them with a lead on information over other firms. Since, in addition, banks were often involved with firms that competed against each other in the market place, a conflict of interest might evolve.[13] Such concentration of power might also cause disadvantages for customers who would be charged higher prices than under full competition. Banks, in this view, should only offer bank services and not get involved with other things. Their investment in non-financial firms should therefore be limited to 5 per cent in order not to become dominant (Monopolkommission, 1976, pp. 296f.; see also Eckstein, 1980).

The leftist critique also focused on the concentration of power from an antitrust point of view, but its solution included a much more active role for the state vis-à-vis the banks. It is probably most explicitly argued in the 1975 medium-term programme of the SPD (Sozialdemokratische Partei Deutschlands, 1976, pp. 75, 83ff, 125) which calls for the abolishment of the universal bank system, a restructuring 'separating credit and investment business', an instrumentalization of banks for 'investment steerage' with investments being 'subject to registration and permission, such permission being revocable'. The repeated reference to the *Godesberg Programme* and its statement about the appropriateness and necessity of public ownership 'when economic power relations cannot be guaranteed by other means' was a thinly disguised threat to the commercial banking industry in the case of non-compliance with these plans.

While the commercial banking industry engaged in the public debate and argued their case, it must have remained clear to them that the threat of fundamental change was real. The liberal and leftist critics were influential – their parties, after all, formed the SPD/FDP government at the time.

The Herstatt crisis

It was against this background that the most important bank failure of the previous 40 years in Germany happened, in June 1974. The reasons for it stemmed largely from the drastically changed circumstances after the end of the Bretton Woods system which made possible both huge profits and huge losses in a very short time. Together with Franklin National Bank in New York, the collapse of Herstatt Bank was one of the great bank failures in the 1970s, attributable to losses in forward exchange deals (Kapstein, 1994, pp. 31, 39f).

These losses eventually amounted to DM1.2 billion. After an attempt by the Bundesbank to mount a rescue operation had failed, the BAKred closed Herstatt Bank on 26 June 1974. Although Herstatt Bank was only number 80 among the German banks in terms of size, the effects were dramatic. The deposit protection fund run by the banking association so far had had to spend only DM7 million in the five years it existed. Now more than DM100 million were needed just for Herstatt Bank (Bundesverband Deutscher Banken, 1974, pp. 14ff). Although the money was put forward by the participating banks within a couple of days in what the BdB called a 'remarkable demonstration of solidarity' (ibid.)[14] and the more than 30 000 depositors received their money, a major crisis in the viability of the banking system ensued. Deposits were withdrawn from private banks on a major scale, with insurance agencies and public law institutions being among the most prominent actors. As the crisis of confidence spread throughout the banking system and threatened to turn into one of liquidity, the Bundesbank had to increase the refinancing opportunities for banks and remove the cap from its Lombard credit line (Franke, 1998, pp. 297f).

It thus became clear that even banks without any problems of their own came to suffer severely from the indirect consequences in the event of a single bank in the system failing, forcing the Bundesbank to act as a lender of last resort. And the event demonstrated that the existing deposit protection scheme which guaranteed deposits up to DM20 000 per person[15] could not prevent a bank run (ibid.).

The case of Herstatt Bank clearly brought the issue of deposit insurance back onto the agenda. This was exacerbated by the fact that two of the major public banks, Westdeutsche Landesbank (West LB) and Hessische Landesbank, had in the same year suffered major losses as well, and for the same reason. In the case of *Hessische Landesbank* (HeLaBa), DM2 billion were needed to put it on its feet again, 50 per cent of which had to be borne by the state of Hesse, which had to pass an additional budget to fulfil its duty (Ronge, 1979, pp. 86f). As the municipalities of Hesse were struggling to carry the rest of the load, political pressure was mounting to solve the problem of deposit insurance in a comprehensive way.

Tactics, Solidarity and Procrastination: Adapting the Existing System

In the political process to cope with the challenges and to adjust the existing system to them, three phases can be distinguished:

- the immediate reaction, in which emergency measures were taken and the scene was set for the following phases. This phase took about six months, lasting until the end of 1974;
- the main phase, in which the new settlement was hammered out and agreed between the parties involved. Its end is marked by the passage of the 'emergency amendment' to the KWG in March 1976;
- the last phase, up to the Third Amendment of the KWG in 1984. In it, the initial settlement was supposed to be reconsidered, but for a number of reasons no further changes took place.

Thus, overall the policy episode under consideration lasted some 10 years. In reality, as we will see, decisions were made much more quickly: the outlines of a comprehensive settlement were visible less than a year after the start of the Herstatt crisis, and they were not changed subsequently.

Initially, however, emergency measures topped the agenda. Immediately after the Herstatt collapse, the BdB set up a 'liquidity consortium' consisting of 15 big banks, regional banks and private bankers whose task it was to supply banks with short-term loans in the event of a liquidity crisis (Wagner, 1976, p. 99).[16] In September 1974, the consortium was extended and further formalized: in cooperation with the Bundesbank (which played a major role in thinking up this concept: cf. Franke 1998, p. 298) and the other branches of the credit industry, the *Liquiditäts-Konsortialbank GmbH* (LiKo-Bank) was set up, thus providing a broader base for future interventions. Its aim was similar to its predecessor institution, namely to help banks which had liquidity problems in order to secure the domestic and international payments system. The new bank (which would not take on any other business) was to have an equity capital of DM250 million, and there was an obligation to make additional contributions, if needed, up to DM750 million. The shares in the bank were held as follows: BdB 30 per cent, Bundesbank 30 per cent, DSGV 26.5 per cent, BVR 11 per cent; in addition, 1.5 per cent were held by the small association of 'Gemeinwirtschaftliche Geschäftsbanken' and 1 per cent by a trust fund of the instalment finance banks (Wagner, 1976, p. 99). The institution thus encompassed members from the different sectors of the commercial banking industry; the burden was not shouldered solely by the 'big three', but they were joined by regional and small banks. This 'inclusiveness' was to become a characteristic of actions on behalf of the commercial banking industry, and indeed of the banking industry as a whole.

Turning up the heat: political initiatives

The German government also moved quickly to reassure the public (Knapp, 1976, pp. 100f., Wagner, 1976). By the end of August 1974, wide-ranging proposals to change the KWG and other regulations were ready. On 3 September 1974, the minister of finance, Hans Apel (SPD), held a press conference to outline the government's plans:

1. A number of proposals for amending the KWG should be passed as quickly as possible. They contained increased powers for the BAKred and regulations to diminish the risks both in the deposit and the lending business of banks, such as putting a cap on the maximum size of loans.
2. A comprehensive system of deposit insurance, encompassing all branches of the credit industry, should be set up by law, and it should be designed to offer complete protection of all deposits (thus removing any reason for bank runs). It would have the additional advantage of levelling the playing field between private and public law institutions.
3. A commission of experts should be asked to review 'fundamental questions of the credit system' and make proposals for reforming it.

These proposals threatened to alter substantially the existing system of banking supervision and, if carried out, would have done so in favour of direct government involvement. The introduction of a mandatory system of deposit insurance, run by the state, would have reversed the result of 15 years of lobbying and attempts by the banks to keep this in their own domain. The expert commission's report could potentially serve as an opportunity for a shake-up of the whole system of the universal bank and the tight linkages between industry and banks. It might even – if the leftist critique were to dominate it – be an excuse to transfer parts of the commercial banking system into public ownership, as had been the case in 1931, or in neighbouring countries such as Austria and France.

Quick action to avoid further damage: the banking industry

For the private banking industry, the issue of deposit insurance became one of overriding importance in the wake of the Herstatt Bank collapse. It was no longer only one of directly protecting deposits, but of remaining competitive overall as the issue gained a hitherto unknown importance for banks' customers, as the BdB acknowledged (Bundesverband Deutscher Banken, 1975, pp. 17f). The latter issue was especially pressing since in the savings and cooperative banks' sectors of the German credit industry comprehensive protection measures were already in place. Consequently, these sectors protested strongly against being forced to participate in an industry-wide deposit insurance fund. They feared that they would have to cover their commercial competitors' losses and pointed to their own well-functioning deposit protection schemes (Deutsche Bundesbank, 1976, p. 22; Ronge, 1979, p. 124). The BdB, however, (which stood to profit from an industry-wide protection scheme) was in favour of it and had been prepared to accept such a system since 1969 (Wagner, 1976, p. 101).

A formidable collective action problem within the overall banking industry arose. If the banking industry as a whole wanted to have a chance of fending off the governments proposals, it first had to achieve internal unity. As a result, intense negotiations were going on in the following months. The obstacles were substantial: any voluntary scheme would compel a bank to open up its books to its competitors; a mechanism had to be found to intervene against banks deviating from prudent behaviour; and comprehensive membership had to be secured, preventing 'outsiders' from gaining business advantages by not having to contribute to the deposit protection fund.

Faced with the prospect of state intervention, the BdB managed to agree among its members on a model which would be voluntarily organized by the commercial banking industry and run by the BdB. It would offer substantial improvement in terms of protection for the individual depositor, extending the protection to *all* kinds of non-banks' deposits up to 30 per cent of a bank's equity capital. Furthermore, even deposits higher than this threshold should now (contrary to previous practice) be protected up to that level. This meant that practically *all* deposits would henceforth be protected, even in smaller banks, at a level far surpassing past systems or systems in other countries.[17]

With this proposal, the commercial banking industry managed to gain the acceptance of the other branches of the banking industry which could now present a united front against the government proposal. It became clear that the private banking industry preferred restriction through 'associational authority' to that of 'state authority'.

The settlement: voluntary and group-specific instead of state-run insurance

In the political discussion, a similar proposal had been made to the effect that the government's encompassing system of deposit protection should be replaced by sector- or group-specific protection schemes. The idea had first been advocated by the opposition in the Bundestag, the CDU/CSU in November 1974, but in December 1974, the FDP (a part of the governing coalition) made it clear that it also favoured a group-specific and voluntary solution (Ronge, 1979, pp. 124f). The Bundesbank, however, expressed its preference for a legally constituted, comprehensive system of deposit insurance that would create equal conditions across the whole industry and sufficient depositor protection (Deutsche Bundesbank, 1976, p. 22). The government was meanwhile negotiating with the BdB behind the scenes, and as a consequence did not include regulations about a deposit insurance scheme in the proposed amendment of the KWG which was passed by the cabinet in December 1974.

In April 1975, the BdB finally presented its proposals for a voluntary deposit protection scheme along industry-sector lines. It contained the elements outlined above. As a countermove, a number of important elements had been agreed with the government that would make the model more functional. These included the following:

- a duty for all deposit-taking institutions irrespective of their size to publish an annual report and the amount of equity capital;
- the right of the respective peak association to obtain a hearing before the BAKred licenses a new bank;
- and, most importantly, changes to some procedures in commercial law: the BAKred was empowered to impose a moratorium on any payments that a bank in trouble could make, and the authority to open bankruptcy proceedings was exclusively vested into the BAKred. Both regulations aimed at saving troubled institutions time and allowing attempts at restructuring and rescuing them (Deutsche Bundesbank, 1976, pp. 22f).

When the Bundesrat criticized the absence of a mandatory deposit protection scheme, the government declared its preference for the compromise reached by basically stating that such a system had become unnecessary.[18] Both the peak associations of the savings banks and the credit cooperatives had increased their protection funds to DM500 million and DM350 million, respectively. Furthermore, in both sectors no deposit had ever been lost through insolvencies in the member institutions. The BdB proposals promised to offer better protection for individual depositors than could likely be achieved through a state-regulated system without substantial financial contributions on the part of the state.

In the bill's first reading, the minister of finance assured the Bundestag that 'if these regulations enter into force, Ladies and Gentlemen, there will be a level of depositor protection in the Federal Republic enjoyed nowhere else in the world'.[19] He also indicated that the compromise reached with the banks was to a significant extent the result of threatening them with a 'very detailed legal solution of deposit protection'. He repeated, however, his preference for the solution that had been found. In the second reading of the bill, the interpretation of the initial proposal as a mainly tactical device was seconded when a speaker from the SPD described it as 'throwing a big stone into the water to make something happen'.[20] He called the ensuing cooperation of government, Parliament and interest groups 'exemplary' and 'productive'. In addition, the compromise had advantages such as speed (since the problems inherent in the legal construction of a state-run deposit insurance scheme would have been considerable[21]); the absence of costs for the state; and the compatibility with the existing economic system which valued highly the principle of *subsidiarity*.[22]

All is well that ends well: the Commission on the Credit System
The third element in the finance minister's initial response to the Herstatt Bank crisis was the setting up of a commission that should report on 'fundamental questions of the credit system' and make proposals for reforming it. The *Studienkommission 'Grundsatzfragen der Kreditwirtschaft'* was set up in November 1974, still in the phase of immediate reaction to the crisis. As indicated above, this commission was a potentially threatening device, and there are signs that the banking industry saw it as such. In its annual report that year, the BdB expressed hope that the commission would be manned by 'true experts' and promised to answer all questions and provide all information demanded from it. It went on to praise the German system of the universal bank as highly efficient and expressed the wish that the commission might provide clarification in the public debate concerning the 'alleged "power of banks"' (Bundesverband Deutscher Banken, 1974, p. 16).

The commission was asked to investigate three main issues:

1. the merits of a universal banking system versus separation between deposit and credit business on the one hand and securities business on the other;
2. aspects of concentration of power in certain banks, especially the principal questions of bank share holdings in industry and commerce, voting by proxy and domination of the securities markets;
3. the policy instruments of the KWG, especially concerning equity capital and liquidity.

When its members were appointed in November 1974, the government was already negotiating with the banking industry. That may be one reason why it chose to comply with the wish for 'true experts'. The commission had 11 members – government officials, banking sector representatives and academics – none of which had the characteristics of a potential revolutionary (Studienkommission Grundsatzfragen der Kreditwirtschaft, 1979, pp. 2f).[23]

Initially, the commission was expected to deliver its report after two years, in the spring of 1977. The commission, however, did not report until May 1979. The result was unspectacular. It was greeted with relief by the BdB and with a certain amount of sarcasm in the financial press. While acknowledging some problems, the commission saw no need for substantial change: 'The universal bank system has overall proven itself; alleged or existing shortcomings of the present system give no sufficient reason for a systems change.' (ibid., p. 26).

The commission amassed a lot of detailed information, but it made only a few policy recommendations. Among them were a restriction of bank share holdings in non-financial enterprises to 25 per cent plus one share, and a reform of the system of proxy voting. Such a result did not merit or demand quick action. Procrastination was driven to the extreme first by ministerial change and then by a change in government. Thus the planned amendment of the KWG did not take place until 1984. And when it finally did, 10 years after the commission had been set up and five years after it had reported, the recommendations of the commission were not incorporated into the KWG (Deutsche Bundesbank, 1985, p. 38).

In terms of policy change, therefore, the commission was not very effective. One may speculate that, similar to the initial proposals about deposit insurance, its inception was mainly a tactical device and that, after the successful compromise about the problem had been reached, the commission's work was put on the back-burner. As no further problems had arisen in this domain in the meantime, none of the actors could have an interest in questioning old settlements. In addition, it had become clear that a systemic change would have consumed immense political, legal and economic resources.

4   ADAPTING THE SYSTEM: SUCCESS OR FAILURE?

Programmatic Assessment

As we have seen, the policy episode was characterized not by a radical change in the existing system of sectoral governance, but by an adaptation of it. Core characteristics of the system, such as an approach to banking supervision which focuses on setting a legal frame, and the involvement of banking associations in the formulation and implementation of policy, have been retained. Also retained was the character of deposit insurance as a voluntary, privately organized programme with which the state is not involved and in which it does not function as a guarantor.

Other parameters of the regime, however, have been changed. In the field of regulation and supervision, they included regulations on the size of large-scale loans a bank could make as well as the inclusion of banks' open positions in the foreign exchange market under the BAKred's *Principle 1a* (issued in October 1974), which treated such positions like loans. Banks were also required to give the BAKred more information.

The main change, however, was the drastic extension of deposit insurance. Protection was increased to offer the highest level of safety for deposits anywhere in the world: up to 30 per cent of a bank's equity capital for *each* individual non-bank depositor. While some observers were initially worried that in the event of the collapse of a major bank this guarantee could not be kept, a first test in 1976 (when the *Pfalz-Kredit-Bank* was closed) showed the positive impact of the new regulations: there was no run comparable to the Herstatt case by the bank's customers, let alone the public at large. Evidently public trust in the German financial system had been restored. And the banking industry demonstrated its commitment: although the amended KWG and the new deposit insurance fund had not yet entered into force, Pfalz-Kredit-Bank's depositors were refunded according to its principles (Knapp, 1976, p. 874).

Of course even the new regulations did not prevent occasional bank failures. In a market economy, this is very unlikely ever to be achieved, and it is unclear whether this would be a desirable goal, given the function of market exit. Compared with other countries, however, the German banking system seems to have posed particularly few problems. Taking the number of bank failures as an indicator, the following picture emerges: in the savings banks' and cooperative banks' sectors, as was mentioned above, the protection systems aim at protecting the solvency of the institutions, which gives an indirect deposit protection. As a consequence, none of these institutions failed. In the third sector, the commercial banking industry, there were 37 bank failures in the period between the beginning of 1973 and 1997, 25 of which took place after 1976. None of them was a major bank; in fact, Herstatt Bank, although comparatively small, remained by far the largest bank to collapse in the whole period.[24]

In terms of failed assets, 1974 marks the high point, with DM2885 million. Put in relation to the DM291 678 million in assets in the commercial banking industry in that year, however, this represented slightly less than 1 per cent. When in 1995 the sum of failed assets amounted to the second-highest value in the period under consideration, DM2619 million, this merely amounted to some 0.1 per cent of the assets of an immensely bigger industry. On average, the commercial banking industry had failed assets which amounted to DM267 million annually in the period between 1977 and 1997. If one takes 1987 as the middle year, with an industry volume of DM805 936 million, this amounts to only 0.03 per cent of the assets per year. On the same basis, the *sum* of the failed assets after 1977 represents only 0.7 per cent of the commercial banks' assets in 1987.[25]

In the United States, as a comparison, 1617 banks were closed in the period between 1980 and 1994. This represented 9.14 per cent of the banks licensed in 1979. The failed banks represented 8.98 per cent of all bank assets, indicating that not only small banks had collapsed (Federal Deposit Insurance Corporation, 1997, pp. 13f). Indeed, the failed Continental Illinois bank, for example, was number nine in terms of size in the industry (Edey and Hviding, 1995, p. 54).

Contrary to the situation in the United States, however, in Germany it is very difficult to estimate the costs for the bailouts of the banks. The reason is institutional: while the state-run deposit insurance in the United States (the Federal Deposit Insurance Corporation) collects and publishes these data, the German system is privately run and refuses to publish figures.[26] The only comparison that can meaningfully be made is with the costs that the contributing banks have to make towards the fund, whether state- or privately run, for (at least in the long run) these contributions have to cover the costs from bailouts. Here figures show elements of what could be called a virtuous circle, for, as a result of fewer bank failures in Germany, contributions to the fund are lower and as a consequence German banks have to pay less. The Bundesbank states that annual contributions in Germany amount to 0.03 per cent of assets,[27] while in the United States they amount to 0.23 per cent, or *seven times* the German rate (Deutsche Bundesbank, 1992, p. 35).

Political Assessment

It has become clear in the preceding section that the policy response to the challenges faced in the case of adapting the German system of banking supervision and deposit insurance was successful. This was the case both in terms of the programmatic measures taken and in terms of political measures taken.

In the case of trust in the viability of the financial system, the two are probably hard to disentangle anyway, for, if the programmatic measures are judged to be insufficient by the public, it is unlikely that any amount of political measures can stop bank runs, for example, from occurring. On the other hand, if programmatic measures are considered sufficient, there is little or no need for political measures.

In the case of *restoring* lost trust, political measures may have a place. As could be seen above, the German government acted swiftly and promised decisive measures. As later bank failures showed, trust was indeed restored, and as a consequence the turmoil following the closing of Herstatt Bank, not to mention the bank runs and domino effects that had characterized the German banking system in the crisis of 1931, could be avoided. As a consequence, the issue did not gain further salience and was soon relegated to the status of an unimportant technicality with little appeal to arouse political or programmatic passion.

5 EXPLAINING THE RESILIENCE OF THE GERMAN BANKING SYSTEM

On the state side, the character of the institutional framework played an important part in the successful response to the policy challenges. There were few actors involved, which is, as comparative research shows, not necessarily the case in federal political systems (Lehner *et al.*, 1983; Coleman, 1996). In the German case, however, the Länder had in 1962 lost their battle to play a role in banking regulation before the Federal Constitutional Court. This was an important precondition for the course of action that was followed after the crisis broke out: one of a highly tactical nature.

The federal government clearly dominated the initial phase. With the idea of a state-run deposit insurance scheme it put forward a proposal which was at odds with the preferences of the other two actors on the state side, the BAKred and the Bundesbank. However, by acting swiftly and making the proposal publicly, it managed to extract substantial concessions from the commercial banking industry.

The commercial banking industry felt sufficiently threatened not to try to call what might well have been a government bluff, given the problems inherent in the proposal. On the other hand, it felt under great competitive pressure from the savings and cooperative banks which had functioning and proven systems of deposit insurance which had resulted in no lost deposits for decades.

The commercial banking industry managed to react to the government proposal in a remarkably well coordinated manner. It quickly overcame any inherent collective action problems and offered a constructive counterproposal. The high level of coordination within the German banking industry has featured prominently in many studies of the system (Ronge, 1979; Lehner *et al.*, 1983; Coleman, 1996). What is remarkable is the extent to which the industry adopted uniform preferences and explicitly declared the preservation of a varied banking landscape with small, medium-sized and big banks to be among its main goals (Bundesverband Deutscher Banken, 1975, p. 18). Another approach might well have been detrimental to the smaller banks, and especially the 'big three' might have stood to profit from this. Nevertheless, a united front was kept, and the 'inertia' of the status quo preferred to a more risky shake-up of the banking industry with uncertain outcomes.

Through its constructive counterproposal, the industry managed to avert the introduction of a state-run deposit insurance scheme and keep the state at arm's length, as had been the tradition in the German system of banking regulation and supervision. It thus retained a substantial degree of autonomy and the opportunity for the banking industry to sort its problems out itself. Even in crises, as experience has shown, the state regulators rely on and even pressure the banking associations to resolve a bank's problem, rather than step in (General Accounting Office, 1994, p. 30).

The nature of the political discourse concerning banking at the time of the crisis also had an impact on the solution that was found. The recurring debates from both the political left and the right about the 'power of banks' and potential public ownership of the sector helped bring about an agreement which was characterized by a particularly *low* level of state interference. Anticipation by the banks that the consequence of a 'non-solution' or a long-drawn-out struggle might be very serious indeed provided an incentive for making quick and substantial concessions.

6   CONCLUDING REMARKS

This policy episode is perhaps best summarized as 'early crisis, successful solution'. The structure of the sectoral regime was left largely unchanged, because the German banking policy network was capable of finding a successful solution relatively quickly. It thus supports the categorization of the German political system as one which tends to act in an active and anticipatory manner (Richardson, 1982, pp. 100, 120), at least when compared to other European countries, most of which only set up systems of depositor protection much later (Barth *et al.*, 1997, Table 10). Once the initial deal had been struck, none of the relevant actors had an interest in shaking that consensus. The balance between industry and the state was therefore not changed; things remained broadly as they had been before. The industry managed to avert an extension of intervention, which would have tilted that balance in favour of the state. The state, on the other hand, forwent the potentially costly engagement in deposit insurance and detailed intervention in banking business. As an aside, it should be noted that the relatively high degree of independence and self-regulation on the part of the banking industry, as well as the low level of detailed state intervention and the conscious confinement to the setting of a framework of regulation, seems to contradict today's often repeated conventional wisdom which views Germany as a system with a high degree of 'state-interventionism', for which the 'social market economy' is allegedly to blame. Perhaps conventional wisdom should take a second, closer look.

Finally, in spite of the successful management of the challenges described in this chapter, this cannot simply be projected into the future. It has been argued that the high degree of self-regulation is costly insofar as it keeps the German state from developing powerful institutions and bureaucracies in that field, which is a disadvantage when it comes to international negotiations (Coleman, 1996, p. 135). Similarly, it may cause a relatively high level of 'ignorance on the part of the state about the "inner life" of banks and their business problems'

(Lütz, 1999, p. 9). With the structural changes in financial markets now increasingly turning the regulation of risks into a problem of *knowledge*, the German regulatory structure – the 'arm's length' approach, so to speak, with its emphasis on *rules* – may not be particularly well equipped to cope. The development of complex, computerized models of risk assessment at the level of individual banks may demand more 'on-site' inspections which may better suit the regulatory structure and tradition of the British or the American system (ibid., p. 16). It remains to be seen, however, whether this new mode of regulation will really be widely adopted throughout the various sectors of the German banking system and whether the new challenge to the German regulatory system that Lütz predicts will really become a fundamental one.

One may also speculate about the durability of the balance of power within the German banking industry. An explicit wish to preserve a multifaceted landscape consisting of small, medium-sized and big banks was behind the compromise on deposit insurance, as was demonstrated above. Twenty five years later, as the big commercial banks in Germany aspire to be 'global players', there are signs that they may consider the present model a subsidization of their small competitors which they are unwilling to continue. At the same time, the advent of European monetary union calls all national solutions to the problem of deposit insurance into question anyway. Thus major changes in the field may be ahead.

NOTES

1. I would like to thank Sofia Perez, Adam Tickell and Bent Sofus Tranøy for helpful comments on earlier versions of this chapter. All errors and omissions, however, remain the author's.
2. The following description draws on Ronge (1979, pp. 69–81), Niethammer (1990, pp. 45ff), Wagner (1976, pp. 34–46), Alsheimer (1997) and Fischer (1997a, pp. 3721).
3. For a description of the tasks of the BAKred see, for example, General Accounting Office (1994, pp. 16f), Becker (1998) and Bundesaufsichtsamt für das Kreditwesen (1998).
4. Arcane though this aspect may seem, it is important because it was the subject of an (unsuccessful) lawsuit before the Federal Constitutional Court with which the Länder tried to have the KWG declared unconstitutional. In that event, banking supervision would have remained decentralized and in the domain of the Länder. See BVerfGE, 14: 197–221, July 1962.
5. Cf. section 7 KWG.
6. These two features become especially evident in international comparison (see, for example, the data given in Coleman, 1996, p. 28). See also Pozdena and Alexander (1992).
7. All data in this section are from Deutsche Bundesbank (1988, p. 179; 1999, p. 104).
8. This does not exclude the possibility of fierce and continuing fights between the different groups of industry. One example is the campaign against the perceived privileges of the public banks sector which has been going on for decades and has been supported by the commercial banks' association.
9. The banking industry, incidentally, was rather sceptical about the lifting of regulations and refused further steps (Landesbank Rheinland-Pfalz, 1983, p. 195).
10. Deutscher Bundestag, Drucksache V/3500, 18.11.1968.
11. See pp. x and 138ff of the report, and Ronge (1979, pp. 98f).

12. Other kinds of deposits were not protected.
13. Former Deutsche Bank CEO Abs, for example, was famous for sitting on more than 20 supervisory boards. When an amendment of the respective law limited this to 10 seats in 1965, it was dubbed 'lex Abs'.
14. All translations from German language sources are by the author.
15. The amount had been doubled from the previous sum of DM10 000 in January 1974 through voluntary action by the BdB in agreement with the BMF and BAKred (Bundesverband Deutscher Banken, 1974, p. 14).
16. The 'liquidity consortium' proved to be a timely invention: when in August 1974 three small banks collapsed, it was able to pay out the depositors.
17. Data on protection levels in OECD countries can be found in Deutsche Bundesbank (1992, p. 36).
18. The system is described in great detail in Burghof and Rudolph (1996, pp. 73–9) and Deutsche Bundesbank (1992). See Deutscher Bundestag, Drucksache 7/3657, Anlage 3, S. 23
19. Deutscher Bundestag, Stenographische Berichte, 7/176. Sitzung, S. 12357f.
20. Deutscher Bundestag, Stenographische Berichte, 7/219. Sitzung, S. 15248.
21. The ministry of justice had even brought forward serious legal reservations about such a scheme. Cf. Deutsche Bundesbank (1992, pp. 31f). The BAKred also was not in favour (Franke, 1998, p. 298).
22. Deutscher Bundestag, Stenographische Berichte, 7/219. Sitzung, S. 15252; Ronge (1979, pp. 134f).
23. Coleman (1996, pp. 135f) thus overestimates the extent to which members of the banking industry, especially the private commercial banks, managed to 'capture' the commission. Given that some of the commission's recommendations – such as the one on the maximum level of shares a bank could own in a non-financial enterprise – were made with the slimmest of majorities (six to five: cf. Studienkommission Grundsatzfragen der Kreditwirtschaft, 1979, pp. 282f), it is important to stress that banking representatives did *not* have a majority of their own on the commission.
24. Communication from the Bundesbank to the author, 22 February 1999.
25. Author's calculations after Bundesbank communications (see above), Deutsche Bundesbank (1988, p. 180) and Deutsche Bundesbank (1999, p. 107).
26. Private communication to the author from the deposit insurance funds of BdB, DSGV and BVR, February 1999.
27. This is exactly the amount calculated above as the average loss of the whole commercial banking system per year.

20. Structural regulation of the banking industry in the Netherlands: a shift of power, 1980–95

Leo A. van Eerden[1]

1 INTRODUCTION

The Netherlands has a long history of trade in commodities and financial instruments. The Amsterdam Stock Exchange, the first regular exchange, was established in 1611. Closely linked to its trading activities, the international presence of Dutch banks can be traced back for far more than a century.

In the development of exchange economies, financial regulation has always been of fundamental importance. Basically, this type of economy is money-based, and so the circulation and value of money have to be guaranteed and regulated. This has been done in various ways in different countries, in accordance with their particular histories and economic and political power configurations. Generally, a triadic relationship between the state, the central bank and private banks exists. In this triad, according to De Cecco (1987, p. 4), large banks dominate the banking system. However, for each country the specific configuration of this triad is based on a multiplicity of economic and political relations and interactions. In practice, however, there are often well-established broad policy communities (Story and Walter, 1997). The central and unifying element in these communities is a shared set of beliefs about the proper management and control of finance. Historically, these policy communities, and the triads embedded in them, have always had a predominantly national character. Nowadays, the globalization of finance and the growing importance of capital market financing have weakened these (national) communities (Van Eerden and Graafsma, 1998).

During the last two decades, the financial services industry has been subject to a historically unprecedented process of financial innovation. The use of new financial information and communication technologies, the development of a wide range of new financial products, the entrance of new non-bank and non-financial market players, liberalization of capital flows, and, not least, deregulation have been responsible for the emergence of a new type of financial market place. As a consequence, the historical dominance of general banks as the main providers of credit to the private sector and to the state has eroded. These innovations, combined with a continuing process of internationalization of financial activities, have raised competitive pressures on the banking industry. This has been true for the Netherlands as much as for any other advanced economy.

In response to these competitive pressures Dutch banks have engaged in an almost frantic series of mergers and acquisitions in recent years. One of the striking features of this development has been the national concentration of financial institutions: big financial conglomerates were created which engaged in universal banking as well as insurance activities. This transformation of the Dutch financial landscape could not have been accomplished without the active or passive support of the regulatory bodies. In this case study, we shall analyse the success and failures of the postwar financial structure policies of regulatory agencies vis-à-vis the banking industry in the Netherlands, with special emphasis on the crucial period between 1980 and 1995.

2   BANK REGULATION IN THE NETHERLANDS: HISTORICAL PATTERNS

The Dutch financial system consists of supervisors, different financial markets and a myriad of institutions (see Figure 20.1). According to an estimation of Van Ewijk and Scholtens (1999) the balance sheet total of supervisors and financial institutions is about DFL3500 billion. Approximately 45 per cent of this amount rests with banks. Pension funds and life insurance companies cover almost 35 per cent of the general balance sheet total.[2] In the Netherlands, two supervisory institutions control the industry. *De Nederlandsche Bank* (hereafter DNB) is responsible for bank supervision, security-credit institutions, mortgage banks, special financial institutions, participation and investment companies. The *Verzekeringskamer* controls life insurance companies, pension funds and property insurance companies. In order to understand the major transformations in Dutch banking policies of the 1980s and 1990s, we should first retrace the historical roots of banking regulation in the Netherlands.

De Nederlandsche Bank

DNB was originally founded on 1 April 1814 after the foundation of the Kingdom of the Netherlands.[3] The initiative was taken directly by King William I, without prior consultation of Parliament. The bank began as a circulation bank. Because of the king's role in setting it up, it soon acquired the label of a

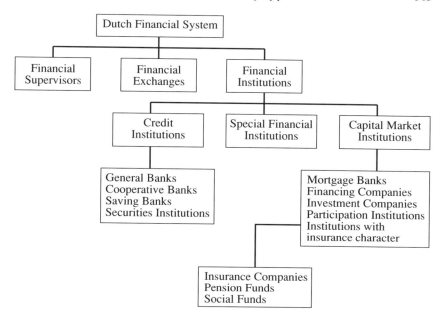

Figure 20.1   Dutch financial system

national institution. During this period, the 'national' or 'public' character of the bank was of great importance. In general, the existing money and banking systems did not fit the spread of different 'national 'capitalisms' and there was a particular problem with the institutionalization of money circulation in these old economies. At the time, two of Holland's competitors in Europe were not very successful with the implementation of this circulation function. The Banque de France (founded 1800) had to suspend the exchangeability of money bills twice. The Bank of England had been forbidden, since 1797, to change money notes for gold. Nevertheless, the close relation between ruler and national bank seems to be important for the development of the national economy.[4] In the Netherlands, the private actors were not able to construct a stable exchange and circulation bank by themselves.

In the period between 1814 and 1948, DNB's position was changed profoundly by the growing acceptance of banking notes as means of payment, the expanding international presence of Dutch business and the problems in the international monetary relations in the inter-war and war period. As a result of the expansion of the private credit business, the development of fiduciary money and the concentration in banking, DNB became more and more a 'bankers' bank' (Van Wijk, 1988). As such it provided liquidity in the form of credit to the banking system. During the 1930s the private banking community began to report its credit business information, voluntarily and informally, to DNB (Touw, 1997). These years also saw the birth of a close relationship between these two pillars of the national economy. In the Banking Act of 1948, DNB became a public limited liability company owned by the state, and took its present shape as the central bank of the Netherlands.

Postwar Reconstruction

For the Netherlands, World War II ended with an urgent need for economic reconstruction. At the end of the war, about 30 per cent of the capital stock had disappeared. The stocks in trade and industry had been diminished by 94 per cent. At the end of 1945, labour productivity stood at a mere 68 per cent of the 1938 level (Knoester, 1989, p. 69). From an economic point of view, there was also a fundamental need to organize the postwar business system.

Something had to be done to uplift the economy. The end of World War II thus marked a new phase in the social–economic development of the Netherlands. Prewar laissez-faire notions were replaced by Keynesian approaches to state-regulated economic development. Beside being a period of speedy reconstruction, the early postwar years were also of crucial importance for the renewal of the institutions of financial regulation and supervision for economic reconstruction; state institutions had to be freed from their wartime organization and management. For both dimensions of reconstruction, politics became the driving and crucial force. The fragile political environment made this a delicate task. The government had been in exile and the political parties, if they had not gone underground altogether, had been toothless throughout the German occupation. Moreover, radical political parties and trade unions enjoyed considerable popular support in the early postwar years.

From 1945 to 1958, the Netherlands had six different governments, all comprising coalitions of Labour Party (PvdA), Catholic (KVP) and Protestant (ARP) ministers. During their tenure economic reconstruction was accomplished and the country was made ready to face international competition and expansion. From an economic point of view, these governments had two main objectives. First of all, they had to facilitate the restarting of national production. Secondly, they needed to create and implement a macroeconomic policy framework. In the first postwar government, the Labour Party was in charge of economic management, holding the three crucial portfolios of economic affairs, social affairs and finance. The labour ministers were strong advocates of more planning in the economy.[5] At the same time, just like labour, the Christian political parties focused on social issues, and especially on mitigating industrial conflicts between employers and employees.

The Labour and Christian Parties became the leading advocates of Dutch corporatism, that is, the so-called public–statutory industrial organizations (PBO, or *Publiekrechtelijke Bedrijfsorganisatie*). The PBO system revolved around the tripartite power relationship between state, employers and employees. The PBO were responsible for engineering and consolidating binding agreements on all social and economic issues that might occur in a particular branch of trade and industry. The most successful PBO operated in the agricultural industry and, to a lesser extent, in trade and retailing. Central coordination at the national level was provided by the tripartite Social Economic Council (SER). Later on, strong opposition from the Liberal Party reduced the SER's mandate primarily to policy advice to the government instead of coordinating policy by itself.

A central pillar in early Dutch corporatism has been the wish to manage the economic crisis by means of close cooperation between the social partners (Keman *et al.*, 1985). The willingness to institutionalize corporatist structures provided the backbone of the consensual management of social conflict in the Netherlands. The recent performance successes of the Dutch economy have often been viewed as an achievement of this Dutch brand of consensualism, the so-called 'Polder Model'. There is one common element in this modern 'Polder Model' and postwar neocorporatism: the commitment of socially antagonistic groups to (temporary) consensus and pragmatic partnership.[6] However, there is also a major difference between the early corporatism and the present-day Polder Model: the new consensus management system now operates without a major influence of Christian politics. It originates in the economic crisis of the 1980s and is aimed at linking the 'modernization'of Dutch social and labour relations to greater flexibility in the national economy (Visser and Hemerijck, 1998).

Employers were very cautious about the organization of Dutch business in the immediate postwar period. There was generally common fear of strong government influence on business. Industry representatives regarded the tripartite PBO as a means to circumvent central government power. In fact, the strongest opposition to these postwar reconstruction concepts came from the Dutch banking community. The bankers were strongly against any form of PBO. Bankers were particularly reluctant to accept any employee participation at the industry level (Van den Brink, 1989). For the bankers it was simply unacceptable to join a discussion table with employees and strong government delegations.

This opposition meant that older structures, in particular those erected during World War II, endured for some time. Shortly after the 1940 invasion, the German authorities and Dutch senior civil servants forced the banks to join a newly created body, the Banks Group (*Hoofdgroep Banken*), encompassing different financial industry groups. State intervention was direct: the secretary-general of special economic affairs was given far-reaching competence in the field of bank regulation and supervision. The concrete supervision of banks was delegated to DNB. At the time, the bankers did not oppose these changes and it is remarkable to see that this management structure was virtually replicated in the Banking Act of 1948 and the Supervision of the Credit System Act of 1952 (Wijnvliet, 1989, p. 22). In this Hoofdgroep Banken, bankers opposed employee representation in the industry, and rejected joint responsibilities. At the same time bankers initiated the foundation of the Dutch Bankers' Association (NBV) in 1948. The organization was built as an exclusive employer's organization, existing beside the Hoofdgroep Banken.

In 1952, the Hoofdgroep Banken was abolished. Its tasks were given to the NBV just at the start of the first discussions about a new act for the supervision credit system. Over time, the NBV became a vehicle for bankers' efforts to (re)gain their autonomy from state supervision and industrial concertation, to the extent that this was at all possible in the Dutch political climate.

The Policy Framework

The institutional backbone of banking supervision in the Netherlands has been provided by two laws: the Banking Act and the Act on the Supervision of the Credit System. This legislation encompasses three logics of supervision. First of all, there is supervision of financial institutions based on monetary considerations. Secondly, there is supervision from a prudential point of view. Thirdly, regulation and supervision have to serve structure policy, and predominantly the relations between banks and non-banks (Coljé, 1988). Having such an explicitly formulated structure policy makes the Netherlands a very unusual case in banking regulation.

This structure policy, dealing with the cooperative relations between banks and insurance companies, was explicitly formulated in 1981. In this year the first memorandum about policies to be implemented was sent to the representative organizations of the banking and insurance industries. As a juridical basis for this, the successive memoranda suited the WtK 1952 and 1956 Acts on the supervision of the credit system.

As in most industrial countries, the Dutch experienced a rapid economic expansion in the 1960s. The strong economic growth of the era created a disproportional demand for loanable funds. As a result, banks were confronted with different competitive challenges. First of all, they had to cope with the credit restriction policies of DNB and the government that were based on monetary considerations. Further, in order to satisfy the credit demand of business, banks had to attract more saving deposits than ever before. As a consequence, the general banks were facing fierce competition from insurance companies and so-called 'near' banks.

At this time the first postwar wave of mergers and acquisitions in banking occurred. During this period the tough struggle over attracting savings accounts between banks and insurance companies led to pressure on the government to relax the tax advantages on particular insurance products to customers of insurance companies. The dispute prompted a government memo entitled 'Broad Reorientation' (*Brede Herwaardering*), which entailed a reformulation of the different tax regimes for banking and insurance products. A last aspect of growing competition can be seen in the development of retail banking and the associated industry blurring (*branchevervaging*). These competitive pressures triggered further regulatory initiatives and legislation in the 1970s (WtK 1978).

Before the 1980s the main focus of structure policies was on the relations between banks and the issue of monopoly power. With deregulation and liberalization, this focus changed more and more to cross-industry relations between banks and insurance companies.

Changing Patterns in Bank Competition

The Dutch economy faced rapid economic growth in the 1960s. The existing high liquidity levels in the economy facilitated credit business with the private sector (Vlak, 1984). However, the continuous expansion of non-financial business led to increasing demands for funds in financial markets (Batenburg, 1984). One way to deal with these growing business opportunities was to expand by means of mergers and acquisitions. In 1964, the Nederlandsche Handel-Maatschappij and the Twentsche Bank formed the Algemene Bank Nederland (ABN). In the same year the Amsterdamsche Bank and Rotterdamsche Bank merged to form the AMRO Bank (AMRO). During the mid-1970s ABN incorporated Bank Mees & Hope and the AMRO took over Pierson, Heldring & Pierson.

In the 1960s, there was also a concentration in the category of savings banks. From 1960 to 1970, there was a reduction in institutions from 266 banks to 181 (Vlak, 1984). Beside mergers between general banks and mergers in the category of saving banks, there was also a trend towards closer cooperation in cooperative banking. In 1972, there was a merger of the Cooperatieve Centrale Raiffeisenbanken and the Cooperatieve Centrale Boerenleenbanken to form the RABO Bank. The concentration in the industry was not restricted to only the bigger institutions. In fact, the number of general banks was reduced from 117 in 1960 to 72 by the end of the 1970s.

The 1960s did not bring only concentration but also growing competition to financial institutions in the Netherlands. Retail banking gained importance for bank funding. It also reflected the spread of industry-wide competition on the different segmented markets and growing rivalry between specialized institutions and general banks. Liquidity reductions produced a competitive struggle for savings deposits. At the same time banks tried to extend their scope of business with the sale of insurance products.

After the first postwar wave of mergers and acquisitions in the 1960s, the liberalization of structure policy in 1990 caused a real merger mania. During the early 1990s different conglomerates were born in a second wave of postwar concentration of financial institutions. Basically, three types of conglomerates with different business foci emerged.

The first was a bank with a small insurance subsidiary: the ABN-AMRO Bank. In 1990, two major banks, the ABN and AMRO, merged to become ABN-AMRO Bank, a bank with the largest balance sheet total in the Netherlands (DFL550 billion) and 60 000 employees. The group has a strong national base, yet maintains a clear explicit international focus. ABN-AMRO is offering a broad range of financial products and has a broad client base. Before the mergers both banks were active in the insurance markets but only as intermediaries. In 1990, a new property insurance company was founded under the ABN/AMRO flag. Similarly, in 1993, a life insurance company was formed. Notwithstanding the growing insurance activities of the group, these activities remain modest compared to its banking business. The bank's strategy is strongly international, with a major position in the United States and a search going on for a new European home market.

The second conglomerate was a major bank with a large insurance subsidiary: RABO Bank Group. The RABO Bank was a cooperative bank which merged in mid-1990 with the insurance group Interpolis. With a balance sheet total of almost DFL300 billion and 37 500 employees, the RABO Bank intends to be a full service financial institution. In 1991, the RABO Bank created a strategic alliance with Europe's biggest investment fund manager, Robeco. Mid-1990s this alliance developed into a more integrated form of cooperation. The majority of the new body's activities are in the banking area. The main arguments for this merger have been derived from considerations of international competitiveness. Especially important here are the changes in the European financial service landscape. In the corporate philosophy of the RABO Bank Group, the increasing competition internationally can only be challenged from a strong national business base.

Finally, there is a holding with roughly comparable bank and insurance subsidiaries: ING Group and Fortis. The ING Group was founded in March 1991, with a balance sheet total of almost DFL400 billion and more than 50 000 employees. It was the result of a merger between the NMB-Postbank group and the insurance company Nationale Nederlanden. This merger was a classical example of the all-finance concept (Canals, 1997), since the supply of integrated financial services with a high cross-selling potential forms the backbone of its strategy. Although it is difficult to compare the absolute figures, the ING Group is just behind ABN-AMRO. With its all-finance approach, the group engages in highly integrated financial service provision. On 1 January 1990 the insurance company AMEV merged with the small VSB bank. At the end of the year this group merged with the Belgian AG Group and formed the Fortis Group. The emphasis in this group is predominantly on insurance activities. The group has a balance sheet total of almost DFL260 billion and more than 30 000 employees. The group does not have one particular home market. It has a strong position in the Netherlands and Belgium, and is an example of a 'successful' international merger. The group is less integrated than the ING Group.

3   THE RISE AND FALL OF FINANCIAL STRUCTURE POLICIES

Changing State–Sector Relationships

Financial regulation takes shape in interaction between regulators and financial actors. Historically, the state superimposed regulation on the sector, driven by its own political–economic needs and philosophies. However, there has always been a struggle over the power to issue money and allocate credit among state institutions and between state institutions and the banking community. The expansion of the exchange economy eventually forced the state to regulate money from a public interest point of view, since stable monetary and financial relations are a precondition for sustainable economic growth. Hence a balanced interplay between financial regulators and the sector is essential to achieve the fundamental regulatory policy goal of avoiding disruptive disturbances in the financial system. In the Netherlands, the main actors in this field are the ministry of finance, DNB, banking industry organizations and the financial institutions themselves.

The formation of financial conglomerates is a relatively recent phenomenon in the Dutch financial services industry that has an impact upon these regulatory interactions. Roughly speaking, there have been two main phases in Dutch structural policy since World War II. From 1945 until the end of the 1970s, there was a phase of 'strong' structural regulation. This phase broadly covers the periods of economic reconstruction (1945–50), the 'Golden days of Capitalism' (Boyer, 1999) in the 1960s, and the economic depression in the 1970s. It is characterized by a strong presence, if not an outright dominance, of the regulatory agencies in the policy process. This was followed by a phase of 'weak' structural regulation from 1980 to 1995. This phase comprises a period of manifest deregulation from 1980 to 1992, followed by a search for new tripartite relations under the now commonly accepted dominance of the financial institutions in the regulatory process.

From Central Bank Dominance to Liberalization, 1945–80

As we have seen, the Banking Act of 1948 brought an end to a debate about the postwar banking order.[7] The Act provided the juridical basis for the development of bank supervision through the implementation of the related Act on the Supervision of the Credit System (*Wet Toezicht Kredietwezen*, hereafter WtK). By this Act, DNB was empowered to supervise credit institutions in close connection with the representative organizations of the industry.

With the initial WtK of 1952, all financial institutions had to be sorted in a register of credit institutions. The main categories in this register were commercial banks and central credit institutions, agricultural credit institutions, general savings banks and brokers. This made it possible to differentiate the supervision regime for specific types of institutions. Following revisions of the WtK in 1956 and 1978, the components of the register changed in accordance with the envolving character of financial institutions.[8]

WtK 1952 prohibited credit institutions participating continuously in other registered and non-registered credit institutions without explicit DNB approval. Mergers with other companies or financial institutions were also restricted. DNB could refuse approval of mergers and acquisitions if it felt they constituted 'undesirable' developments in credit business or if they were judged to be in conflict with a 'healthy' banking policy. Also there was a strict regime which required all mutual participation in credit institutions to have a declaration of non-objection from the central bank. For participation in non-credit institutions, there was a somewhat lighter regime.[9] The WtK revision of 1956 was almost a complete copy of the 1952 Act except for one important innovation in its Article 13: a prohibition on takeovers of credit institutions.

At the time, the focus of structure policy was mainly on the banking industry. WtK's Article 13 comprised the legal formulation of the political wish to prevent an undesirable concentration of power in a few financial institutions. It was also intended to safeguard the high degree of transparency in ownership relations that was deemed necessary to maintain effective central bank control. However, there was never a clear formulation about what could be considered 'proper' and 'acceptable' levels of concentration.

In 1970, a new draft of the WtK was presented to the Lower House of Parliament. It proposed an extended and intensified form of structure policy.[10] The draft did not become law until 1978. It contained two important changes. First of all, there was an extension of structure policy to all banking businesses. The main reason for this extension was the wish to prevent a development of Dutch banking in the direction of '*banques d'affaires*'. A second change concerned the structure of decision making on declarations of non-objection. Until 1978, responsibility for this declaration lay with DNB. With the new Act this shifted to the minister of finance. More generally, WtK 1978 shifted authority and power in structure policy to the minister of finance. DNB's role was reduced to primarily executive tasks. Structure policy was brought back into the realm of political choice, that is, testing participations in view of the broader public interest instead of merely monetary policy considerations.

From Deregulation to New Tripartite Relations, 1980–95

It took from 1978 until mid-1979 before a government memorandum could be published with a concrete interpretation of the structure policy towards banks and insurance companies for the 1981–3 period. According to De Leeuw (1996) the regulatory agencies could not be blamed for this delay. The problem was more the rejection of the new regime by the banking industry organizations. Their main argument was that key elements of the proposed structure policy were too liberal. The intermediate organizations advocated a generic division between the banking and insurance industries in order to prevent an aggravation of their mutual competition.

In political terms, the banking industry simply wanted to preserve its position, and not only in respect to insurance companies. Fearing the continuing development towards fuzzier boundaries between different types of financial institutions, the banking industry wanted to 'freeze' the institutional status quo. Two critical issues in this debate concerned the issuing of mortgage bonds and the investment volume of insurance companies in banking institutions.

The 1981 memorandum maintained the generic separation between banks and insurance companies.[11] This separation did not forbid the two types of institutions acting as intermediaries for each other's products. Moreover, shortly after the publication of the memorandum, external developments forced a break in the prevailing structure policy. The memorandum had underlined the separate position of mortgage banks in issuing bonds. However, a crisis in mortgages financing occurred, triggered by an explosion of interest rates and a subsequent overheating and collapse of the housing market. This crisis forced the termination (in 1982) of all efforts to regulate the structure of mortgage banks (see De Leeuw, 1996).

In short, as an emergency measure DNB announced it would no longer compel banks and insurance companies that wanted to participate in mortgage banks to have a DNB declaration of non-objection (DNB, 1982). This ad hoc move had significant consequences: by 1986, all but one independent mortgage bank had been taken over by general banks and insurance companies.

Although these emergency actions boiled down to a softening of the strict structure policy regime, DNB and the ministry of finance confirmed in a press announcement their unchanged commitment to a policy of separating the banking and insurance business. At the end of 1983, it was decided to keep structure policy unchanged for the 1984–6 period. However, the supervisory authorities explicitly formulated the possibility of changing this policy if the circumstances so required. There was a second addition to the authorities' statement in terms of highlighting the requirements in the field of insurance intermediation by banks. The DNB wanted to prevent more insurance intermediation by banks for their 'own account'.[12] Important for the emerging discussion about deregulation was the requirement that DNB check all cooperation between banks and insurance companies for products with maturity of more than 12 years. This 12 year maturity limit was fiscally important and did lead to an uneven treatment of bank savings and tax-deductible premium payments for life insurance (De Leeuw, 1996).

This tax issue has been of great importance in the political debate about a new structure policy memorandum for the years after 1987. Just as in the early 1980s the ministry of finance advocated a gradual liberalization of the financial service industry. In an address to the Lower House of Parliament the minister said the government intended to abolish the generic separation between credit institutions and insurance companies. In order to do so, consultations were envisaged between the ministry of finance, DNB, the *Verzekeringskamer* (the supervisory body for the insurance industry, hereafter VK) and the supervised financial institutions (Tweede Kamer, 1986). During these negotiations, banks and insurance companies postured as advocates of further liberalization. They opposed the step-by-step approach proposed by the ministry of finance. If liberalization was unavoidable, they wanted a period of preparation followed by a quick and complete liberalization.

In Parliament there was strong opposition to liberalization from the three biggest political parties: PvdA, VVD and CDA.[13] As a result the minister of finance had to withdraw his proposals. The different parties agreed to depoliticize the separation issue by announcing that in the follow-up to the discussions 'the expected future developments in financial markets had to be taken into account' (DNB, 1987).

Eventually, the political momentum regained its pace. Since 1990, structure policy has swung definitively towards liberalization. All institutional barriers between banks and insurance companies have been removed. Important triggers for this liberalization have been developments at the European level: the EU Second Banking Directive, the Life Insurance Directive and the internal market for the financial service industry in 1993. In short, the challenge of the internal market has motivated the minister of finance to change structure policy, and has helped to convince the political parties that this was the road to take (De Leeuw, 1996, p. 67).

Liberalization did not imply a complete abandonment of structural policy, however. In cases of new participations, banks and insurance companies still need a declaration of non-objection from both DNB and VK. In order to link the policies of these two supervisory bodies the minister of finance drafted a protocol (agreed in October 1990) on supervision of financial conglomerates.[14] Basically, the supervisory powers regarding banks remained at DNB while for the insurance companies these powers rested at VK. Cooperative arrangements between DNB and VK were stipulated regarding supervision and reporting of conglomerates. Holdings as such are not subject to supervision (Coopers and Lybrand, 1997). The general requirements to holding companies are limited and explicitly formulated in Article 25 (2). These requirements can address the following (De Leeuw, 1996, p. 69):

- the amount of own capital of the financial holding in relation to the financial risks of the holding and the consolidated base of the group headed by the holding;
- the amount of mentioned financial risk;
- the spread of consolidation; and
- the information to be delivered by the holding.

The new Article 24 in WtK 1992 formalizes the supervision of bank–insurance conglomerates. It remains forbidden to perform banking and insurance business in one corporate body, or holding company. By means of this article DNB retains the right to impose requirements on non-bank participation in credit institutions. Through supervision of consolidated accounts it is possible to put requirements to the holding company of a bank–insurance conglomerate. A second important element of WtK 1992 is the easing of the rule for *banque d'affaires* activities. It is now accepted that the participation level of 5 per cent in the capital of a non-financial company can be raised to 10 per cent. Beyond this level a declaration of non-objection is necessary.

The Role of Bank Industry Organizations

The Dutch Bankers' Association (NBV) started in 1948 as the banking industry representative of the Dutch banking sector. The association was the discussion partner for DNB and minister of finance. For its participants the start of the association was not very easy. According to former minister of economic affairs Van den Brink (1948–52) who is also a former board member of AMRO bank, there were some frictions between DNB and NBV. He stated that, over time, different DNB presidents have changed the 'gentlemen's agreement culture' of the immediate postwar years. The bankers complained about DNB's policy to discourage the NBV from preparing papers for meetings of the two organizations. It would not be until the DNB presidency of Zijlstra (1967) that these papers were again exchanged in advance. Under this presidency, relations between NBV and DNB improved.

The former NBV and ABN chairman Batenburg has argued that there has always been a will to come to an agreement on monetary policy with DNB, because NBV wanted to avoid doing business with 'The Hague', the political actors in government and Parliament. However, there was one exception to this position: structure policy. In this field NBV tried actively to maintain bilateral discussions with the minister of finance and circumvent DNB, most likely because of its opposition to liberalization.

From 1948 until the early 1960s NBV was a closed organization, with strong personal relationships between its members. This cohesiveness came under pressure following the merger of the Nederlandsche Handel-Maatschappij and Twentsche Bank to ABN and the merger of the Amsterdamsche Bank and Rotterdamsche Bank to AMRO in 1964. Within the organization the differences between the giants ABN and AMRO and the smaller banks became more visible, also because the biggest bank in the association was to provide the chairman and vice-chairman. Although every board member of NBV has one vote, it became much more difficult for the smaller banks to oppose ABN and AMRO (Schipper and Wijnvliet, 1989, p. 111).

NBV was a bankers' association without representatives of cooperative banking and the state-owned *Postcheque en Girodienst*. For inter-bank consultations, NBV joined a discussion forum called the *College van Overleg* (Consultatory Council) with the cooperative RABO bank and the Dutch Savings Bank Association. The only meeting point with the *Postcheque en Girodienst* was through the *Raad voor het Betalingsverkeer* (Council for Payments). In Dutch bankers' representation, there has always been a world of cultural difference between NBV, the cooperative bankers and the representatives of the *Postcheque en Girodienst*. For almost eight years the merger of the public services of the *Postcheque en Girodienst* and the *Rijkspostspaarbank* (the public savings institution) into the Postbank was subject to intense discussion and massive obstruction by NBV members. Fearing intensified competition, NBV lobbied against the granting of full banking status to the Postbank (Cf. Schotsman, 1990).

At the end of the decade and in the wake of the liberalization of structure policies, the NBV became inactive. In 1989, the joint informal *College van Overleg* was reshaped into the Netherlands Bankers' Association (NVB), designed to coordinate various consultation activities within the banking industry.

4   CASE ASSESSMENT

The first 10 postwar years were crucial for the reinstitutionalization of public regulatory agencies. In the immediate postwar period, Dutch structural policy was to bring on a renewal of the national regulatory framework and financial institutions. In these years the main focus of the different government coalitions was on the reliance on social–economic planning instruments. There was a great emphasis on the management of credit flows from a macroeconomic perspective. During the early 1950s it became clear that the backbone of the associated reforms, the public-statutory industrial organization, had failed. Opposition from the banking industry reduced the industrialists' support for the government plans. The attempt to curb the banks in the *Hoofdgroep Banken* backfired and the banking industry gained recognition of the Dutch Bankers' Association (NBV) as the principal representative of the sector. NBV's position as the representative organization of the sector meant also a much reduced influence for cooperative bankers and representatives of the state-owned *Postcheque en Girodienst*. In the Dutch banking landscape this exclusion has exerted an enduring influence on competitive relations, in that market segmentation and product pricing have largely been in favour of the dominant banks.

The failure of the structure policies of the direct postwar governments to achieve an industry reconfiguration showed the limits of a *dirigiste* policy style. As a consequence, real supervisory structure policy powers were transferred to DNB. These powers, formally grounded in the different WtK legislations, created a special relationship between DNB and the banking industry. On monetary supervisory issues, such as the restrictive policies on credit creation, banks preferred to deal with the central bank and so avoided negotiating with political actors and bodies.

The main objectives of the Dutch structure policy have been the safeguarding of a healthy banking system and the avoidance of an undesirable concentration of power in the banking industry. In this respect, DNB supervision has played a pivotal role and has been successful. In the period reviewed, only two banks really collapsed. In 1981, a foreign bank, Amsterdam-American Bank, with a balance sheet total of DFL29 million ($15million) broke down. In 1983, the Tilburgse Hypotheekbank, with a balance sheet total of DFL700 million ($300million) defaulted. In this latter case, DNB's role as oversight body was strongly criticized (Rijnvos, 1987).[15] All further problems with mortgage banks in the 1980s were solved by takeovers by general banks and insurance companies.

In general, bank defaults or usage of guarantee provisions in the postwar period have been of minor significance in financial, macroeconomic and political terms. In terms of the evaluation criteria used in this research project (see Busch, Chapter 17 this volume), public policy to maintain the integrity of the Dutch financial system has been a success, although this was probably due more to the quality of prudential supervision than to structure policy.

When we come to controlling the concentration of power in the banking industry, two major transformations took place: the bank–bank merger in 1964 between ABN and AMRO, and the formation of the three major bank–insurance conglomerates during the early 1990s. In both instances the supervisory agencies were reacting to 'market developments' rather than shaping them. They could not withstand the pressure in the industry for mergers. In the restricted policy space of 1964, DNB agreed with the merger of ABN and AMRO with a special declaration of non-objection. This special declaration was quickly extended when other merger candidates applied.

The erosion of institutional segmentation in Dutch financial product markets and the expansion of retail banking networks fuelled a growing interest of banks in non-bank institutions. For DNB this became the point at which to start paying greater attention to structure policy regarding banks and insurance companies. In a letter to NBV, DNB presented its interpretation of WtK 1956. As we have seen, participation of banks in insurance companies with more than 5 per cent had been forbidden. A declaration of non-objection was necessary for every large participation. With this declaration DNB also claimed the prerogative to formulate special conditions to this type of participation. This amounted to a strengthening of structure policy and it reflected DNB's rejection of close bank–insurance combinations.

The first sign of a relaxation of structural policy came with WtK 1978. A doubling of the participation in insurance companies was permitted. Changes in the framework of international bank competition were expected from the implementation of European banking directives and internal market legislation. These indications of an impending liberalization prompted a strategic reorientation among banks and insurance companies. Before merging with AMRO Bank, ABN had negotiated with the insurance company Nationale Nederlanden (NN) about close cooperation. At the time, this 'rapprochement' did not succeed because of the mutual interests of both institutions in the United States (De Vries *et al.*, 1999). ABN Bank and NN feared a refusal from the American supervisory authorities. This is an interesting point because the combination of ABN-NN would have been totally different from the combination ABN-AMRO that emerged later. After this aborted marriage NN was behind the creation of the ING Group, one of ABN-AMRO's main competitors.

Nevertheless, the second wave of concentrations in the 1990s profoundly changed the financial relations between financial institutions, and between them and other key players in the national economy. In no time, the Dutch banking industry has become one of the most concentrated in the world. The conglomerates, ABN-AMRO, ING-Group and RABO Group dominate nearly all Dutch financial market segments, with market volumes of more than 80 per cent in the banking market (see Table 20.1).

Although the concentration ratio appears to be very high there are differences between the individual banking groups in market segments. ABN-AMRO occupied more than half the market for corporate credits. The top player in the market for consumer credits is RABO Bank which also maintains a strong position in payment services. The ING Bank was the leading bank in payment services with 40 per cent of the market (see Table 20.1). These figures are illustrative of the high level of concentration of the banking business in the Netherlands. Moreover, for almost 75 per cent of non-financial companies, this wave of concentration in banking was reason to reconsider their choice of their main banker (Schaper and Van der Zee, 1992).

Table 20.1   Market share of Dutch banks, 1991 (% of total)

	ABN-AMRO	ING Bank	RABO Bank	Total
Corporate credits	55	20	15	90
Consumer credits	17	23	40	80
Mortgages	16	22	30	68
Payment services	20	40	35	95

Source: LvE, *Financieel Economisch Magazine*, 27 June 1992.

Given these market shares it is difficult to claim that government and DNB structure policies with respect to the concentration of financial power have been successful.[16] However, one should assess the success of structure policies in the context of the growing international competition. In the years before 1990 the major Dutch banks were undervalued in stock market terms, and so they were relatively easy takeover candidates for foreign banks. So part of the banks' desire to pursue national mergers and acquisitions, and part of the regulatory authorities' willingness to acquiesce, was based on defensive considerations. However, at the same time a strong national base was also seen as a prerequisite for international expansion.[17]

DNB took a reactive stance in the two major postwar concentration waves. The bank–bank merger to respectively ABN and AMRO in 1964 changed the banking power configuration of the Netherlands. DNB accepted the merger as an exceptional case and thus paved the way for the next mega merger (to the RABO Bank). At the end of the 1980s, several financial institutions in banking and insurance were looking for closer cooperation. On the strength of arguments of international competitiveness, structure policy was liberalized. This led to the formation of three major financial conglomerates, ABN-AMRO, ING Group and RABO Group. Throughout this process DNB reacted to pressure from the banking community. In terms of the international competitiveness of Dutch financial institutions, state and central bank policy to lift the restrictions on bank–insurance combinations was successful. The national consolidation of Dutch banks provided the new conglomerates with a sound base for international expansion.

In the 1980–95 period the policy style of government shifted from a quasi-directive to a more policy-making one. Since the mid-1980s it has advocated cross-sector cooperation between banks and insurance companies. At the end of the 1980s this policy line was backed by DNB and opened the way for new and liberal structure legislation, de facto ending the era of public structure policies in the Netherlands.

As we have seen, structure policy is one of the three pillars of bank supervision and regulation in the Netherlands. The liberalization of this policy raises questions about its effects on the development of the national financial system. Structure politics is about the soundness of financial systems, but in a way also about the competition between financial institutions. The anticipation of international competitive pressures has been the major reason for this liberalization. Given the relatively small home market, this policy appears reasonable. However, it has also caused tensions in the triadic relations between state, central banks and banks. The governance structures of the first postwar decades have eroded, and nothing solid seems to have come in their place. When we accept the stable governance structures as a necessary precondition for sustainable economic growth, national public agencies have in other words acquiesced in the reduction of the sector's governability. One might question whether such national triadic relationships can at all be extended to the international institutional forms of banking of the current era. A way to cope with this problem can be found in the creation and deepening of international policy communities (Story and Walter, 1997).

5   CONCLUSIONS

In the period reviewed supervisory policies in the Netherlands have succeeded. Owing to the almost completely independent position of DNB there were no fixed and unmovable relations between the central bank, interest groups and the government. Since the early 1980s, liberal structure policies have paved the way for policy changes at the central bank and in the bankers' association. Internationalization of the financial services industry in general and the prospect of further financial integration in the European Community have been the main arguments for the shift from a directive to a liberal policy regime.

Overall, the prevention of high levels of concentration among banking institutions was subordinated to a policy of strengthening the international competitive power of Dutch financial institutions. Without any doubt this policy has been advantageous for these institutions. Their position on the home market has been safeguarded and they have been able to create new, North Atlantic home markets. It has also created a basis for the active and successful international acquisition strategy pursued by the Dutch conglomerates during the 1990s.

The degree of politicization of the sector has remained low throughout, paving the way for a shift to a predominantly consensual style. In the Netherlands, financial regulation politics has been shaped in the nexus between state agencies and financial institutions. To a lesser extent it has been the result of the role of party politics. With the exception of the immediate postwar years, the more adversarial style of left-wing politics has had little influence on the creation and working of banking structure policy.

Until the transformation of the Dutch Bankers Association (NBV) into the Dutch Association of Bankers (NVB) at the end of the 1980s, the representation of industry interests had been dominated by the general banks. Since liberalization, however, there has been a significantly greater influence of insurance companies and institutional investors on the sector's policies.

One should at all times remain aware of the thin line between the success and failure of banking structure policies. In the Dutch case, the implementation of the change to a more liberal and market-oriented financial system was a success, yet a serious international systemic crisis could quickly change this positive picture and turn it, retrospectively, into a failure.

NOTES

1. I would like to thank Andreas Busch and Paul 't Hart for comments and input on this chapter.
2. The remaining 20 per cent is due to the Special Financial Institutions. These institutions are channelling money from non-residents to non-residents. For the overwhelming part the transactions are payments of subsidiaries of foreign companies.
3. The Parliament of the Netherlands consists of an Upper and a Lower House (Staten-Generaal) and was introduced in 1815. From 1588 to 1795, the assembly of representatives was embedded in the (con)federal Republic of the United Provinces.
4. Emperor Napoleon regarded the Banque de France as '*ma banque*'. For William I, King of the Netherlands, the Netherlands Banks was his 'oldest daughter'.
5. One result was the creation of the Central Planning Office as an advisory council for government. Its first director was the economic planning specialist and Nobel Prize Laureate Professor J. Tinbergen.
6. Without any doubt the consensus-biased focus and the rejecting of the classical strike weapon are responsible for the 'friendly' labour relations and a low level of strike incidents. In the period 1960–95, the Netherlands lost, as a result of strikes and lockouts, per thousand workers in employment only 20 working days – quite modest compared to France, with 104 days, the United Kingdom, with 268 days, the United States, with 196 days and (West) Germany with 28 (Visser and Hemerijck, 1998, p. 95).
7. For the information about the development of legislation we have used the highly informative work of De Leeuw (1996).
8. In WtK 1978 the register comprised general banks, cooperative banks, security-credit institutions, saving banks, central credit institutions and capital market institutions.

9. Article 13, section 1(b).
10. Article 13 was replaced by an extended formulation of structure policy in Article 25.
11. By maintaining the so-called 'grandfather clause' for existing participations, the first memorandum (14 May 1981) upheld the generic separation between banks and insurance companies. Bank participation in insurance companies remained limited to the 5 per cent level. Under protest of the banking industry, insurance companies could participate in banks to a limit of 15 per cent of capital. This was only possible in the case of investment and excluded ownership governance.
12. In a letter (20 December 1983) to the representative organizations, DNB formulated three conditions: (1) from product specification it must be clear that the bank has only an intermediary role, (2) the bank cannot be the sole distributor of the product, (3) the premium invested by the insurance company in a bank can only be a fraction of the total bank balance sheet.
13. The CDA (*Christen Democratisch Appel*) is a merger of the Christian political parties: KVP, ARP and CHU.
14. A conglomerate consists of at least one credit institution or insurance company with a seat in the Netherlands, whose activities are, in the opinion of DNB or VK, in banking or insurance.
15. DNB was also criticized for being too lax in supervision in the case of the near-default of the Slavenburgs Bank in 1982. This unconventional bank, also active in black money transactions and suspect dealing, caused the greatest bank investigation in the Netherlands. As an emergency act, stimulated by the Netherlands Bank, the bank was sold to the French bank, Crédit Lyonnais.
16. This high level of concentration can restrict competition but financial innovation has reshaped all financial markets and reduced negative effects on competition (van Eerden and Graafsma, 1998).
17. In the international comparison of assets, ABN-AMRO is ranked 11th, RABO Bank Nederland 40th, and the ING Group 47th (*The Banker*, July 1998).

21. The liberalization of finance in Spain: from interventionism to the market

Sofía A. Pérez

1 INTRODUCTION

The principal event marking the Spanish financial sector over the last two decades has been the imposition of a programme of financial liberalization on a system that was based on the protection of a private banking cartel and a *dirigiste* model of state-directed credit allocation. This regulatory shift to the market was implemented in a highly protracted manner, extending from the beginnings of the transition to democracy in the late 1970s to the early 1990s. It was pushed forward by a network of reformers within the state elite (and, more specifically, the Bank of Spain) who gained control of public policy during the political regime transition and who were primarily interested in altering the institutional bases of macroeconomic policy making in Spain. Much of the character of the reform process can be understood in terms of the dual challenge faced by these reformers: that of pre-empting political opposition to their neoliberally oriented reform agenda while, at the same time, ensuring the financial system's soundness in the course of a lengthy macroeconomic stabilization process.

The process of financial liberalization in Spain was accompanied by two major episodes of banking crisis. The first, spanning the period from 1978 to 1985, involved a large number of smaller, industrial banks which, as a group, nonetheless accounted for a significant proportion of deposits. The second involved the failure of one of Spain's largest commercial banks (the Banco Español de Crédito, or BANESTO) in late 1993. These banking crises were quite costly in absolute terms. However, both episodes were also contained in nature and the stability of the financial sector as a whole never appeared to be threatened. Given the degree to which competition in the Spanish financial sector had been suppressed in the past (as reflected in very high cost and profit margins of Spanish banks during the 1970s and 1980s), the overall dimensions of the two banking crisis episodes seem relatively benign. From this particular perspective, the incremental and drawn-out approach adopted by Spanish authorities in their drive to liberalize the financial system may thus be deemed to have been a relative success.

However, as the following analysis will make clear, the banking crisis episodes do not represent the only important social costs incurred in the Spanish financial reform process. Indeed, the remarkably strong profit performance of the Spanish banking sector throughout the period may be largely attributed to a liberalization strategy that shifted a great deal of the burden of economic adjustment in the financial sector to other sectors of the economy by carefully limiting the pace at which disintermediation took place and the structure of the financial market was altered. Any assessment of financial liberalization in Spain must thus consider the impact of the reform process beyond the confines of the financial sector itself.

2   THE MAIN ACTORS IN THE SPANISH FINANCIAL SYSTEM

The principal actors in Spain's contemporary financial system during the period under review (1977 to 1994) were a small group of large commercial banks which came to dominate the Spanish financial system during the first quarter of the century. The Big Seven, as they were referred to at the beginning of the period (BANESTO, Banco Central, Hispano-Americano, Banco de Bilbao, de Vizcaya, Santander and Popular) operated as a cohesive cartel from the 1920s through the Franco regime, and for almost a decade after the regime transition. In the late 1980s, however, they entered a period of intense reorganization through a series of (mostly friendly) mergers, which by early 1999 had led to a new group of Big Four banks. These comprised the Banco Santander Central Hispano (BSCH), formed through a merger in early 1999 between the Banco Santander (which purchased BANESTO in 1994) and the Central Hispano (itself the result of a merger in 1991), the Banco Bilbao Vizcaya (BBV), formed through a merger of two banks (the Bilbao and the Vizcaya) in 1989, Banco Popular (the only one of the original Big Seven not to opt for, or fall prey to, a merger strategy) and Argentaria (a commercial bank formed by the state in 1991 by bringing together a series of public credit institutions and the postal savings bank, and subsequently privatized). As a group, these banks controlled more than 70 per cent of the commercial banking sector's deposits throughout the period. Constituted as universal banks, they also held significant equity stakes in Spanish industry, from which they retreated and to which they returned in a procyclical fashion over the last decades. The large commercial banks also have been historically the largest issuers of equity on the Spanish stock market, and they have come to hold a dominant position in other financial markets, including the insurance sector, pension products and mutual funds (see *European Banker*, August 1999).

While the large commercial banks have been the principal protagonists of the Spanish financial market, they are not the only financial institutions of significance in Spain. A second sector of importance is the savings banks, which are non-profit institutions controlled by regional authorities, and which, since the 1960s, have controlled about half of the market for total retail deposits. Several factors limited the political role of these institutions in the past. First, contrary to the high degree of concentration characterizing the commercial banking sector, the savings bank sector was historically highly fragmented (there are still 51 such institutions today). Secondly, given their subordination to political authority, these banks traditionally played a very passive role in the provision of finance, channelling the bulk of their deposits through the large commercial banks. And this subordinate role was reinforced by a highly discriminatory regulatory regime for these banks, which forced them to allocate a much larger part of their resources to state-directed aims (approximately 80 per cent of their deposits as opposed to 10 per cent for the banking sector) and kept them from expanding beyond their province of origin. Following the abolition of this discriminatory regulatory regime in the 1980s, two savings banks (La Caixa of Catalonia and Caja Madrid) pursued an aggressive expansion strategy that allowed them to rival some of the large commercial banks in terms of deposits and assets by the early 1990s.

The remainder of the deposit and credit market in Spain is accounted for by cooperative banks (which hold a very marginal share) and foreign banks, which were allowed to enter the Spanish market in the late 1970s, albeit under very restrictive conditions. One of the striking characteristics of the evolution of the Spanish financial market over the last decade is the limited success that foreign institutions have had in gaining market share even as these restrictive conditions have been lifted in compliance with European legislation. Indeed, in spite of substantial efforts to establish retail banking networks in Spain during the 1980s, several American banks (including Chase and Chemical) ended up withdrawing from the market by the end of the decade. Some European banks (in particular Barclays and Deutsche Bank) proved to have greater staying power. Nonetheless, the share of the Spanish retail banking market accounted for by foreign banks had fallen back to less than 5 per cent by the end of the 1990s, after reaching their peak at about 14 per cent in the mid-1980s.

The preponderant weight of the large private domestic commercial banks in Spain has also been reflected in the limited role that equity markets have played in Spanish corporate finance. Until the end of the 1980s, the Spanish stock market was subject to the monopoly of state-licensed agents who charged fixed commission on trades, and whose principal clients were in fact the private domestic banks (which also constituted the principal institutional investors in Spain). The overall level of stock market capitalization was low by international standards, and heavily dominated by banking and utility stocks. The stock market experienced a substantial modernization with the introduction of an electronic trading system and the abolishment of the monopoly of the state-licensed agentes in favour of brokerage firms in 1989. Nonetheless, total capitalization remained limited as a percentage of GDP until the second half of the 1990s, when the rise of domestic mutual funds spearheaded by the commercial banks and the massive entry of foreign institutional investors led capitalization to rise above 60 per cent of GDP. Even then, however, the composition of the Spanish equity market remained highly skewed in favour of banking sector stocks (which continued to account for 33 per cent of total capitalization in 1998), utilities (23 per cent) and telecommunications (15 per cent). Manufacturing firms continued to account for barely 10 per cent of total stock market capitalization in 1998 (Bolsa de Madrid, 1998).

3   THE POLITICAL AND INSTITUTIONAL CONTEXT OF THE REFORM

The Ancien Régime

The institutional context in which the present-day Spanish financial system had its origins (and which served as the starting point for the reform process) was one of state-sanctioned oligopoly combined, since the early 1960s, with heavy state intervention in the allocation of private bank credit. The first of these elements dated back to the Banking Law of 1921, which established a status quo in the banking sector by closing entry to the profession of banker and granting regulatory powers to a National Banking Council (CSB) controlled by the largest commercial banks. This status quo legislation was maintained through the years of the Second Spanish Republic (1931–9) and was reinstituted by the Franco regime at the end of the Civil War.

The introduction of this oligopolistic regulatory framework for the banking sector at the beginning of the century was linked to another aspect of Spanish financial regulation, namely the active involvement of private banking institutions in the inflationary financing of the Spanish Treasury. The grant of a monopoly of issue to the Bank of Spain in 1874, for instance, was tied to its commitment to finance all of the Treasury's demands. The establishment of the banking status quo and the self-regulatory powers granted to the CSB in 1921, similarly, came on the heals of the introduction of a new monetary mechanism, the so-called *pignoración automática* (or automatic collateral lending), whereby the private banks could monetize up to 80 per cent of the value of public debt that they subscribed. The *pignoración*, adopted in 1917 and reinstituted by the Franco regime at the end of the Civil War, also led the banks to become actively involved in the promotion and acquisition of new industries, as it allowed them to 'increase their ratio of productive to liquid assets ... at a negligible additional risk and cost' (Tortella and Palafox 1984, p. 88).

The second aspect of the institutional context that the reform process of the 1970s and 1980s sought to alter (state-directed credit allocation) had its origins in another Banking Law passed in 1962. That law, which followed the abolition of the *pignoración automática* and the imposition of an IMF-backed stabiliz-ation plan in 1959, nationalized the Bank of Spain along with a series of parapublic credit institutions and defined the banking system as an instrument of indicative planning. It set the stage for a new monetary policy framework that centred upon the rediscounting of private bank credit, and that was gradually expanded through the introduction of special rediscount lines for credits extended by banks to users earmarked by the planning authorities. The new law also led to a vast expansion of credit extended by the now public, or official, credit institutions, financed through the imposition of compulsory coefficients that forced private banks and regional savings banks (though overwhelmingly the latter) to channel a portion of their deposits to these institutions. These two mechanisms (the special rediscount lines and the expansion of credit channelled through the official credit institutions) allowed state officials to direct a very significant portion of the private banking sector's resources to specific users and activities in the Spanish economy from 1962 on.

The Banking Law of 1962 also purported to end the status quo in the banking sector by imposing a regime of banking specialization (separation of commercial and industrial banking) and opening the door to the creation of new industrial banks. Yet the implementation of the law was so calibrated as to severely limit any real challenges to the existing commercial banking cartel. The newly chartered industrial banks were prevented from actively competing with the large commercial banks through restrictions on branching and exceedingly high capital adequacy standards. Thus most of the industrial banks created between 1962 and 1972 were chartered by the large commercial banks, and independent industrial banks never attained the weight to offer any noticeable competition to the large mixed banks (Torrero, 1976, p. 863). The large commercial banks, moreover, were able to keep virtually all of their industrial holdings by simply issuing new stocks, because the only limit imposed on them was that their industrial holdings could not exceed the sum of their capital and reserves. Meanwhile, a 1962 decree authorizing the entry of foreign banks failed to be implemented. Thus state interventionism was made palatable to the banking cartel by the continuation of an extremely high level of protection from any real competition in the domestic market

Early Attempts at Change

This regulatory regime combining state interventionism in credit allocation
with a highly oligopolistic framework of banking regulation and a still rather
lax monetary policy framework began to undergo some changes at the end of
the 1960s. In 1969, reform-minded economists within the central bank managed
to push through a major change in the way in which interest rates were regulated,
so that all bank rates (previously set by the ministry of finance) were now linked
to the central bank's rediscount rate. Two years later, the same reformers were
able to get the government to abolish the special rediscount lines, replacing
these with a new coefficient on private bank credit that simply forced banks to
allocate specific portions of their lending to specific users. However, in their
two major objectives, that of creating a domestic money market in which the
central bank could exercise day-to-day control over liquidity, and that of
abolishing the ability of other state actors to interfere with a market-based
system of credit allocation, the reformers were blocked during the final years
of the Franco regime by the banking cartels' strong opposition to any major
regulatory overhaul.

A fledgling programme of financial liberalization hence produced little more
than a series of haphazard measures, including the liberalization of commissions
on bank lending in 1972 and that of bank branches in 1974. In the context of
an unaltered pricing cartel, these measures led the banks to vastly expand their
branch networks and raise their operating costs precisely at a time when the
Spanish economy was hit by the world recession. It was this context of a highly
cost-inefficient and protected financial system undergoing a massive expansion
in the midst of a mounting recession and a collapsing authoritarian political
regime that set the stage for financial sector reform.

4   FINANCIAL LIBERALIZATION:[1] THE REFORM PROCESS

Financial Reform and the Political Regime Transition

The agenda of institutional reform drafted in the Research Service of the Bank
of Spain during the late 1960s and early 1970s was powerfully bolstered by the
political regime transition that took place on the death of General Franco in
1975. The transition presented the reformers with a major opportunity, as it
propelled several of their key members into leading policy-making positions.
Key among these was the appointment of Enrique Fuentes Quintana, an
academic who had served as the principal mentor of most of the reformers on

the staff of Bank of Spain Research Service, as deputy prime minister and economics minister in the first government of Adolfo Suárez (1976–7). Fuentes initiated intense contacts with the heads of the Big Seven in the months leading up to the first democratic elections of June 1977 to discuss the reform of the financial sector, and he led the newly elected government of July 1977 to pass a major package of deregulatory measures just days after it took office.

The two principal objectives of the 1977 reform package were that of dismantling the system of state-directed credit allocation introduced with the Banking Law of 1962 and that of setting the bases for the creation of a money market. These objectives were critical to the central bank's agenda of transforming the institutional bases of macroeconomic policy and creating the tools whereby the central bank could control liquidity in a routine manner. The principal measures included in the 1977 package clearly reflected this concern: (1) the establishment of an auction system to allocate short-term bonds and credits to the banking sector through which the central bank was seeking to gain control of liquidity in the financial system, (2) the deregulation of interest rates on bank activities, and (3) two measures to eliminate the institutional bases of selective credit regulation (the abolition of the ministry of finance committee that had decided which sectors and activities were eligible for privileged financing, and the implementation of a schedule to dismantle the compulsory investment ratio on private bank lending).

The package of 1977 thus dealt a definitive blow to the system of state-directed credit allocation introduced by indicative planners in the 1960s. By contrast, it was remarkably devoid of measures that might have altered the highly oligopolistic nature of the market to which credit allocation was being devolved either by increasing competition in the credit market or by creating alternative sources of financing for companies. This failure to reform the structure of the domestic financial market was evident in several aspects of the reform process. The first of these was the treatment of foreign banks. The implementation of the 1962 decree opening the Spanish financial market to foreign banks was first postponed in 1977, and later implemented in such a fashion as to severely circumscribe the ability of foreign banks to exert any downward pressure on domestic credit rates. Those foreign banks approved for entry by the Spanish monetary authority were prevented from competing with domestic banks for deposits by being limited to just three branch offices, and made dependent on the inter-bank credit market controlled by the Big Seven for their resources. The avoidance of measures that might have increased competition in the credit market was also apparent in the reform of the official credit institutions that followed the 1977 package. A plan to merge these institutions into a single entity along with the postal savings bank (which would have given them a deposit base) might have allowed the government to end the collusive behaviour of the Big Seven in the credit market, yet it was rejected in favour of a far more limited reform that forced these institutions to raise their resources in the market while retaining their basic character as mere administrative bodies that were not equipped to compete with the banks in the capture of deposits. Thirdly, the failure to address the structural features of the Spanish financial market in the transition period was also evident in the government's indefinite postponement of capital market reform (see Pérez 1997, pp. 126–33 for more detail).

The 1977 package thus constituted an instance of credit deregulation (that is, market-oriented reform) in the absence of any accompanying effort to reform the underlying structure of the market (or what we might call market reform). The upshot in the 1977–8 period, during which the authorities implemented a monetary stabilization programme, was a particularly sharp rise in credit rates and a dramatic decline in the overall availability of medium- to long-term credit. This credit squeeze, the consequence of monetary rigour in a highly oligopolistic credit market, forced a record number of firms into failure, contributing directly to the sharp rise in unemployment that Spain was to experience during this period. Eventually, this crisis in the real sector would come to threaten the reformers' own agenda. As the ruling centrist coalition (UCD) entered a period of steady electoral decline, the government was forced to freeze the schedule to dismantle the compulsory investment ratio on bank credit in 1979. It was also forced to expand the amount of credit extended through the official credit institutions over the period 1980–81, and to monetize this expansion in a manner that seemed to run directly counter to the reformers' prime objectives.

The Reform Process following the Socialist Victory of 1982

At the end of the 1970s, the reformers' agenda thus appeared threatened by the centrist government's precarious hold on office and by the depth of the business crisis that the first phase of the liberalization programme had produced. The overriding electoral victory of the Spanish Socialist Party (PSOE) in 1982, however, was to put that agenda squarely back on track. Contrary to the expectation that the new government might pursue a less orthodox policy course, the new prime minister, Felipe González, appointed an economic team led by a prominent central bank-trained economist, Miguel Boyer, one of whose prime objectives was to fulfil the central bank's agenda for institutional reform. This choice by the PSOE leadership in favour of a neoliberal reform agenda was encouraged by the conspicuous failure of redistributive Keynesianism experienced in the early 1980s by the socialist government of France. It was also facilitated by the historical association between state interventionism and political authoritarianism in Spain, and by the heavy concentration of economic expertise in the Bank of Spain.

The reformers' strong position on the new government's economic team meant that an alternative programme of financial reform outlined in the party's electoral programme (calling for the use of the public credit institutions to break oligopolistic bank behaviour in the credit market) was abandoned outright. Instead, the process of financial reform pursued by the new government strictly adhered to the central bank's policy agenda. Having managed to limit the influence of other state actors over the financial system in the 1970s, this agenda now centred on finding a way to finance a growing budget deficit without compromising the central bank's ability to set monetary policy.

The problem that Spanish policy makers faced in financing the deficit derived from the continued absence of a market in short-term government debt (something the banks, who did not want government competition in the capture of short-term funds, had successfully resisted up to this point). This meant that the central bank was forced to monetize the Treasury's shortfalls and then to neutralize this monetization by issuing its own certificates of monetary regulation. From 1977 until 1982, more than 94 per cent of the deficit was first monetized, then neutralized in this way. But as the deficit grew, the central bank's ability to offset this monetization process was challenged, because the banks, who continued to hold an oligopsony (or position as a buying cartel) in the public debt market, were able to demand exceedingly high returns on the central bank's certificates.

The new government's approach to this impasse was obliquely enshrined in the creation of a new coefficient in 1983, which obliged the banks to invest up to 12 per cent of their deposits in government debt instruments. At first sight, this appeared to represent a blatant return to interventionism. In fact, however, it constituted a carefully negotiated solution to the deficit-financing problem that reconciled the central bank's objectives with the interests of the private banks. The new coefficient constituted an alternative to a more aggressive government effort to expand the public debt market and to open this market up to other institutions and individuals. Such a course of action would have led the government to compete directly with the banks in the capture of deposits. Moreover, in spite of its compulsory nature, the new coefficient did not constitute a binding constraint for the banks. Indeed, the latter had been increasing their public debt holdings independently, given the extremely depressed demand for credit from non-financial firms in the early and mid-1980s. An examination of the banks' balance sheets over the period 1984–6 reveals that the banks held far more public debt than the new coefficient required them to hold over this period (Pérez, 1997, p. 144). Thus, in fact, the solution to the deficit-financing problem enshrined in the new coefficient gave official sanction to a situation in which the banks were able to maintain their oligopolistic credit rates by shifting a large part of their resources into public debt at a point in the economic cycle when the fall in demand for credit by firms would otherwise have forced them to reduce their margins. At the same time, it allowed the reformers within the government to end the central bank's obligation to finance the Treasury's shortfalls.

The PSOE's first term in office was also marked by the intensification of a continuing crisis among many of the smaller industrial banks that had been created following the 1962 legislation. This banking crisis episode eventually affected 51 of the 102 banks existing in 1977 and accounting for 20 per cent of total bank deposits. However, it remained circumscribed to (mostly independent) industrial banks, forcing only one of the large commercial banks (the Hispano-Americano) to suspend its annual dividend payment in 1984. The persistence of net earning margins in the Spanish banking sector well above the OECD average through these years illustrates this rather limited nature of the crisis (which, in any case, was solved through a socialization of losses in the Deposit Guarantee Fund, created in 1978 and financed up to 50 per cent by the Bank of Spain). The ultimate upshot of the crisis was a new wave of concentration of the banking sector, as the large commercial banks eventually took over most of the relatively profitable banks rescued by the Fund.

EC Membership and Shifting Priorities in the Late 1980s

From the beginnings of the political regime transition through the socialist first term, the primary objective guiding the reform process had been that of altering the institutional bases of macroeconomic policy so as to make possible a stronger role for the central bank. By contrast, little emphasis had been placed on reforming the structure of the financial system itself. The accession of Spain to the EC in 1986 was to alter this ordering of goals in two important ways. It forced the authorities to pursue a modernization of the capital market, an objective long discussed yet equally long avoided. And it led the central bank to become involved in an attempt to restructure the banking sector so as to prepare that sector for the onset of a single European market in financial services after 1992.

In 1988, a decade after a government-charged commission had first delivered a report outlining the need for capital market reform, the government passed a major reform bill which, along with important technical changes (such as the introduction of an electronic continuous trading system), ended the privileges of state-licensed stock market agents in favour of brokerage firms. This belated reform bill (which also outlawed insider trading) achieved a categorical transformation of the Spanish stock market once it came into effect in 1989. Yet it also entailed limitations. Discriminatory tax treatment of mutual funds, for instance, kept new capital from flowing into the market during the first two years. And other regulatory provisions made it possible for the big commercial banks to corner the brokerage firm market (see Pérez, 1997, pp. 152–6). Given the banks' ambivalence in bringing new firms to the market (since they lost credit customers in doing this), these provisions may account for the fact that, despite two periods of economic boom, few firms outside the banking, utility and telecommunications sectors opted to seek capital market financing as an alternative to bank credit.

The second major effect of EC accession on the financial reform process was that it led the central bank to become actively involved in promoting a series of mergers among the large Spanish commercial banks. This process began with a hostile takeover bid (the first ever) by Banco de Bilbao for BANESTO in late 1987, backed (and it is widely believed, instigated) by the Bank of Spain. The bid was thwarted by a ruling of the Madrid stock exchange that required the Bilbao's shareholders to approve the share issue that the bank was offering to BANESTO stockholders (see Pérez, 1997, pp. 160–61 for more detail). Nevertheless, by raising the spectre of a breakdown in the cartel's cohesiveness, the attempt did set off a series of mergers that eventually led the Big Seven to be transformed into two much larger commercial banks (as outlined above) and one smaller bank (the Popular). Part of this process was the government's decision in 1991 to finally consolidate the public banking institutions into a commercial bank with a strong market presence (Argentaria), a move that was intended to instigate further mergers among the other commercial banks (as, indeed, it did).

While the government and the central bank thus began to promote a reorganization of the banking sector and a modernization of the Spanish stock market, this did not translate into a more generalized effort to break the still oligopolistic nature of the Spanish market for corporate finance. In allowing the banks to gain a clear position of dominance in the newly refurbished stock market, for instance, the government also allowed them to control the pace at which disintermediation would take place. Similarly, until the 1990s, the government eschewed a more aggressive effort to develop the public debt market such as might have helped to reduce the cost of the public debt, and thereby interest rates throughout the economy. It also maintained its restrictions on the operation of foreign banks for as long as EC legislation allowed it to do so. Rather than allowing competition to intensify rapidly, the strategy adopted by Spanish authorities on the eve of 1992 was thus one of allowing the banks to exploit their existing degree of oligopoly in the credit market for as long as possible, so that they could enter the Single European Market in financial services with the highest possible degree of capitalization. This, the authorities hoped, would help avoid a foreign takeover of the sector.

1992 and Beyond

By the end of 1992, the agenda of institutional reform set out by the Bank of Spain in the 1970s had been largely accomplished. The allocation of credit by private institutions had been deregulated and the public credit institutions had been transformed into a banking institution that was set to be privatized (as it would be over the course of 1993–8). The dismantling of external capital controls was about to be finalized and a money market had been created allowing the central bank to exercise operational control over domestic liquidity (to the extent that this was possible in a world of increased cross-border flows and exchange rate commitments). Indeed, the central bank's drive to establish the institutional bases for an orthodox monetary policy regime had been taken farther than the reformers' original agenda had stipulated with the peseta's entry into the European Exchange Rate Mechanism in 1989, and (eventually) Spain's acceptance into the club of countries that were to participate in the first wave of European monetary union (EMU) in 1999. The latter led the government to grant full statutory independence to the Bank of Spain in 1994 and to prohibit explicitly its financing the Treasury, thus taking the drive to establish the institutional basis for macroeconomic orthodoxy one step beyond the central bank's original blueprint

While the original agenda that had inspired financial sector reform had thus been put to rest, the second-order objective of preparing the sector for the onset of the Single European Market in financial services also seemed on track. Not only had the banking sector undergone a significant consolidation with the mergers leading to the BBV in 1989 and BCH in 1991, it also performed remarkably well over the course of the 1990s. This is particularly striking given the depth of the recession that the Spanish economy underwent following the ERM crisis of 1992–3 (a recession that led the unemployment rate to rise to a high of 24 per cent in 1994). Although profit margins declined gradually in the post-1992 period, they remained well above those of other European banks until the end of the decade. The large private banks also retained high capitalization levels, allowing them to engage in an aggressive campaign of acquisitions in Latin America. There they were able to continue to exploit much higher profit margins as these margins were gradually brought closer to European levels in the Spanish market. By 1997, Spanish banks (led by Santander and BBV) had thus gained control of more than 20 per cent of the banking market in countries such as Chile, Peru, Colombia, Venezuela and Puerto Rico, as well as very substantial shares in Brazil and Argentina (see Standard and Poor's *Credit Week*, 28 June 1997).

The major exception to this general rule was the fate of one of Spain's traditional banking giants, BANESTO, which became the subject of a Bank of Spain intervention and had to be rescued by the Deposit Guarantee Fund in early 1994. The failure of BANESTO, which suffered a shortfall of more than 600 billion pesetas (approximately 4.7 billion dollars) as a result of a surge in bad loans and a particularly vulnerable position in its equity holdings, was by far the most important banking failure since the initiation of the liberalization process (see *Financial Times*, 30 December, 1993; 11 May, 1994). Yet it, too, ultimately appeared to contribute to the process of consolidation in the domestic banking sector described above. BANESTO was purchased by Banco Santander, which thus established itself as one of two Spanish mega-banks (alongside BBV) and which eventually would take a clear lead in the Spanish banking scene by merging with the third-largest bank, BCH, in early 1999. By the late 1990s, the Spanish banking sector, one of the most protected and inefficient in Europe at the beginning of the period, thus appeared to have withstood the test of European integration and protected its position in the Spanish financial market at the same time as it had managed to acquire a veritable new economic empire in Spain's former colonies.

5 FINANCIAL LIBERALIZATION IN SPAIN: SUCCESS OR FAILURE?

The success of the programme of financial sector reform initiated in Spain in the 1970s may be assessed from one of several perspectives. The first is in terms of the key objectives of the central bank reformers who had designed and largely directed the process of institutional reform. As already noted, these objectives had most of all to do with altering the institutional bases of macro-economic policy. More specifically, the main aim of the reformers was to place the central bank in control of monetary policy and, to this end, eliminate those aspects of the regulatory framework that had allowed other state actors to exercise an influence over the credit market. From this first perspective, the reform process can be said to have been a clear success. The critical steps in establishing the regulatory authority of the central bank were taken with the reform package of 1977. Although the authorities had greater trouble with the creation of an efficient money market through which the central bank would be able to exercise day-to-day control over the level of domestic liquidity, this goal was also achieved by the end of the 1980s. Meanwhile, a series of negotiated solutions to the deficit-financing problem (most notably the public debt coefficient introduced in 1983) allowed the government to end the central bank's obligation to finance the Treasury's shortfalls. Well before the process of EMU led the Spanish government to grant full statutory independence to the central bank, the latter had thus gained de facto control of monetary policy. Indeed, it was able to exercise a great deal of influence over the course of economic policy and reforms more generally. As one of the original architects of the financial reform process (Enrique Fuentes Quintana) writes, after the the 1977 package of financial sector reform measures had been passed, no one, absolutely no one, was able to articulate a valid alternative to the reform criteria that the Bank of Spain had developed and begun to apply to the country's economic policy (Fuentes, 1991, pp. lx–lxii).

A second way in which the success of the Spanish liberalization drive may be assessed is in terms of the cost of failures within the financial sector that accompanied it. In terms of absolute figures, this cost was quite high. The total losses incurred by failing banking institutions amounted to 16.8 per cent of GDP for the 51 small industrial banks that went into crisis over the period 1978–83, and an additional 1.1 per cent for BANESTO in 1993, for a total of approximately 18 per cent of GDP. The resolution cost of these crises (that is, the cost to the Deposit Guarantee Fund) amounted to 5.6 per cent of 1985 GDP for the first wave of crisis, plus an additional 0.4 per cent of 1993 GDP in the case of BANESTO (Caprio and Klingebiel, 1996; *El Pais*, 10 January 1998), for a total of 6 per cent. These figures are moderate to high compared to the cost of the banking crisis in other European countries over the period (see Caprio and Klingebiel, 1996), yet they must be considered in the light of the extremely uncompetitive nature of the Spanish financial sector at the beginning of the period. If we consider this starting point, along with the fact that both crisis episodes remained contained in nature, the figures suggest that Spanish authorities were relatively successful in bringing about the transformation of the system from one controlled by a state-sanctioned cartel to one operating within the rules of the single European financial market.

If both the programmatic and the banking crisis-cost perspectives thus lead to a relatively benign assessment of the Spanish reform process, that process also entailed other costs not captured in either of these approaches. These are the costs that the Spanish reform process entailed for other sectors of the economy. As noted, much of the early phase of financial liberalization in Spain consisted of a process of deregulation without any accompanying reform of market structures. This biased course was maintained from the mid-1970s until the end of the 1980s, when capital market reform was initiated and foreign institutions were allowed to exert some downward pressure on credit rates. The choice of limiting the pace at which the banks would lose the benefit of a highly oligopolistic domestic market structure, and at which disintermediation (the shift of financial activity from financial intermediaries to capital markets) could occur, helps explain why neither of the two banking crises ever extended to the financial system as a whole. But it also placed an extremely heavy burden in the form of very high financial costs on other segments of the Spanish economy. The significance of this collateral cost to the Spanish economy is difficult to quantify, yet it is captured by the fact that Spanish industry had to face a negative leverage effect (a negative difference between the average cost of external financing and the average return on investment) of much greater proportion (and for a much longer time) than other countries undergoing an analogous deregulation process (for instance, France) (see Cuervo, 1980; Maroto, 1990;

Rivera *et al.*, 1993). Even in the absence of a specific quantifiable measure of the consequences of this negative leverage effect, this observation leads us to conclude that the success of the Spanish reform process was highly relative to the particular objectives that the reformers had set for themselves (those of establishing the bases for a more orthodox macroeconomic policy and of protecting the national character of the domestic financial sector).

Lastly, there is the issue of how successful the reform process was from a political perspective. The high absolute cost of the banking crisis, and the collateral cost to the Spanish economy of the incremental approach adopted by Spanish authorities, might lead us to expect a heavy political cost for the governments overseeing the process. The electoral collapse of the UCD may in fact have been affected by the impact of high interest rates on the economy. However, the greater part of the cost of the banking crisis and the cost to the economy in terms of high unemployment were incurred under the tenure of the socialist government. Yet the latter was able to weather both economic phenomena with remarkable ease until its eventual electoral defeat in 1996. This lack of political repercussions thus leads us to deem the reform process in Spain a remarkable political success. The cost to the economy of the incremental and drawn-out approach to financial reform adopted by the authorities had remarkably few political repercussions.

6 EXPLAINING THE COURSE OF FINANCIAL REFORM IN SPAIN

What explains the rather skewed ordering of priorities that guided the Spanish financial reform effort over the last two decades? As we have seen, this ordering secured certain important objectives, such as an early and rapid move to macro-economic orthodoxy in Spain. It also ensured the survival of the national financial sector in the face of European integration and a sharp rise in cross-border capital flows. However, the postponement for more than a decade of reforms that would have imbued the Spanish financial market with greater competition and forced domestic institutions to become more cost-efficient seems to conflict with the widespread notion that financial liberalization in formerly interventionist states is fundamentally driven by economic and political pressures to create more efficient capital markets (see, for instance, Frieden and Rogowski, 1996).

Part of the explanation for the peculiar course of reform pursued in Spain has already been advanced. The reform process, designed in the research service of the Bank of Spain, responded to an agenda that was primarily concerned with altering the institutional bases of macroeconomic policy, rather than with the adequacy of financial markets in providing financing in cost-efficient terms. The origins of this agenda are to be found in the way in which the identities and objectives of groups within the Spanish policy-making bureaucracy were shaped by the experience of the Franco regime, which combined authoritarianism with a high degree of paternalism in economic policy and the use of expansionary credit policies to diffuse social conflict. Yet why was such an agenda espoused by politicians such as Adolfo Suárez or Felipe González, whose own agendas had relatively little to do with these internecine battles within the bureaucratic elite?

The answer, as argued elsewhere (Pérez, 1998), has much to do with an asymmetry in the incentives that politicians in countries with formerly interventionist financial systems face in endorsing the agenda of neoliberal (or market-oriented) reform. Interventionist frameworks of financial regulation such as the one introduced in Spain in 1962 responded largely to the need to rationalize expansionary postwar credit policies whose ultimate objective in many cases was that of defusing the social conflicts inherent in rapid modernization. As postwar growth strategies premised on such credit expansion gradually exhausted themselves, the macroeconomic component of these strategies became far less sustainable. The interventionist frameworks created to support monetary expansion in the postwar period augmented the political costs of macroeconomic stabilization in the 1970s and 1980s by forcing state officials to allocate the cost of monetary rigour to specific users (those not tagged as recipients of privileged credit schemes). This created a strong incentive for politicians to opt in favour of market-oriented reform as a way to depoliticize the task of macroeconomic stabilization. However, the incentive to extricate state authority from the task of allocating the costs of monetary rigour to particular groups is essentially negative in nature (that is, it ends at the point at which credit is no longer subject to selective regulation). Other aspects of financial liberalization, such as the creation of efficient market structures, require an independent political will that is not necessarily forthcoming from politicians themselves. Much therefore depends on the nature of the broader policy-making community that charts the course of financial reform.

Where, as in Spain, this policy community is dominated by central bankers to the exclusion of other groups, financial reform is likely to become the subject of a search for accommodation between central bankers and their natural constituency, the domestic financial sector (Woolley, 1985, p. 338). Indeed, the search for such an accommodation is likely to be intensified by a fundamental tension between the two institutional imperatives of central banks: maintaining price stability and ensuring the stability of the domestic financial sector. The monetary restraint that market-oriented regulatory reform is intended to facilitate places direct pressure on the profitability of banks and brings to the fore potential conflicts of interest between the financial sector and firms in other sectors of the economy (in particular, firms in competitive sectors which cannot pass on costs). If banks are to remain profitable, they either have to become more cost-efficient or be allowed to exploit oligopolistic market conditions that allow them to pass on the higher cost of rediscounting without reducing their margins. Given that increased competition can threaten a shake-out in the financial sector (in particular, where banks have become accustomed to operating under limited competition and guaranteed liquidity), there is likely to be considerable pressure for central bankers to opt for the second solution: continued protection.

The particular course of financial reform in Spain is thus best understood as a consequence of the extent to which that process was dominated by the agenda of the central bank and not counterbalanced by other groups within the state or the broader policy community. The effort to establish their neoliberal reform agenda in the political transition period first led the central bank reformers to seek a powerful working alliance with the private banks, so as to bolster their political position within the state. This meant that the market-oriented reform process was strongly constrained by the effort to reconcile the agenda of institutional reform sought by the central bank with the interests of the private banks (as reflected most clearly in the 1977 reform package). The upshot was credit deregulation in the absence of market reform. Later, as the prospect of increased competition through the breakdown of cross-border barriers to financial activities in the EU became unavoidable, the concern of the authorities shifted to that of ensuring the survival of the national banking sector in the face of increased market integration. However, this did not mean a shift to a strategy that would have forced the banks to lower their margins and become more cost-efficient prior to 1992. Instead, the authorities chose to allow the banks to exploit the advantages of a still rather oligopolistic market in order to raise their capitalization levels, while also encouraging an intense process of consolidation in the sector. This strategy worked, in the sense that it discouraged foreign takeover attempts and allowed the banking sector to remain in national hands. Its flip-side, however, is a continued legacy of underdeveloped markets for corporate finance in Spain.

Lastly, it may be asked why, given the considerable costs imposed on other groups in the Spanish economy by the process of financial reform, there were no serious political repercussions for the socialist government overseeing most of the process. The principal answer to this paradox lies in the oblique manner in which these costs were passed on. The seemingly technical nature of much of financial regulation discouraged public debate on the subject in the 1980s. The matter was therefore left largely to central bank officials whose expertise was hardly ever challenged by the broader academic community. The contribution of an oligopolistic credit market to the high cost of financing for firms also was obfuscated by the simultaneous imposition of monetary rigour, a necessary evil to which the high cost of credit was attributed. The cost of the banking crises, on the other hand, was adroitly diffused through the combination of national deposit insurance and a pattern of insider rescues by the banking sector itself.

NOTE

1. This section is based broadly on chapters 5 and 6 of Pérez (1997).

22. The Swedish financial sector, 1985–92: policy-assisted boom, bust and rescue

Bent Sofus Tranøy[1]

1 INTRODUCTION

From the mid-1980s to the early 1990s, Swedish policy makers confronted a great challenge in formulating appropriate policies towards a financial market undergoing rapid change. Even though it was understood in more incremental and less dramatic terms at the time, in hindsight the task can be described as trying to manage and facilitate a smooth transition from one type of market order and governance regime to another: that is, from a severely regulated and largely insulated credit-based financial system to a liberal, competitive and internationalised financial system where capital markets played a greater role.

Today we can see that Swedish authorities, like many others in the 1980s and early 1990s, by and large failed in their policies towards the financial sector during transition. Policy contributed to asset price inflation, leading to a speculative bubble forming in the markets for real estate and shares. When the bubble burst and these markets crashed, they took most big banks and other financial institutions with them into a banking crisis of proportions only comparable to the great crisis of the 1920s. Although some banks fared better than others, it was a crisis for the Swedish financial system as such, partly caused by policy. That is why this chapter concentrates on policies with systemic ramifications, rather than on policies towards any individual institutions.

The failure could be described as macro destabilization combined with structural maladjustment – on the part of both the authorities and even more so the market actors themselves. Policies that affected financial market developments included fiscal and tax policy, interest and credit controls, and exchange rate and capital control policy. In sum these policies made for a violently procyclical stance which intensified both the boom and the bust phases. At the micro level, policy also failed. The state proved unable to formulate appropriate precautionary policy. Having thus labelled policy a failure because it helped cause the banking crisis, it should be added that the rescue operation which followed was a success. It was costly, but the financial system was soon back on its feet.

Most of this chapter is dedicated to a narrative on how policy affected the economy in a negative way. The underlying causal argument about why policy came to play this role is an institutionalist one. The point pursued is that the shift from one type of (stable) market order and governance regime to another brought with it severe problems of transition. This was so because coordinating policy across issue areas becomes much more difficult in a period where all crucial variables are 'in play'. Section 2 introduces the main institutional actors that participated in the policy making of the boom and bust episode, while Section 3 describes Swedish monetary policy and credit market regulation in its broader political context before the transformation of the second half of the 1980s. Section 4 tells the story of how policies stimulated the boom and bust sequence by being damagingly procyclical, with Section 5 evaluating and finding that this episode qualifies as a system-wide programmatic policy failure. Section 6 addresses the causes of this failure by highlighting its institutional origins, and the chapter closes with some concluding observations.

2   ACTORS, INTERESTS AND POLICY COORDINATION IN THE SWEDISH BANKING SECTOR

Policy contributed to the Swedish banking crisis because the Swedish polity – viewed as a decision-making entity – was unable to coordinate functionally interdependent policies. Thus it is crucial to appreciate that different institutional actors (and the interests and world-views they represent) play different roles in relation to different types of policy. Which actors dominate an issue area is of importance as regards how easy or difficult it is to adjust this policy to changes in other policies and the wider environment.

Theory could lead us to expect that technocrats will dominate the politics of credit controls because it is a technically difficult issue area. The opposite would be the case with interest rate deductions and tax levels. These issues engage the electorate directly and all the major parties have great stakes in them (Tranøy, 2000). To put it crudely, we can imagine a continuum between these two extremes, where all the other issue areas have their place. Fiscal policy in general would be close to the 'democratic politics' end of the spectrum; supervisory policy would be close to the other end, while exchange rate and incomes policy with its technical–corporative nature, fits in somewhere closer to the middle.

In the early 1980s, two main types of actors, commercial banks and savings and loans, dominated Swedish banking. The commercial banks were joint stock companies and their distinguishing feature was their relationship with the corporate sector. The legal form of savings and loans resembled that of foundations (Forssell and Jansson, 1996, p. 101). The commercial banks had almost 70 per cent of the banking market, while the savings and loans had slightly less than 30 per cent. *Föreningsbankar*, that is cooperative mortage banks for the rural sector, had a minor market share.[2]

The banking market amounted to slightly more than 40 per cent of all institutional lending or what we might call the credit market. Other institutional lenders were insurance companies, finance companies, pension funds or mortgage institutes. The commercial banks dominated the credit market also, because they fully owned most mortgage institutes, and these were, in turn, responsible for another 40 per cent of all lending in the Swedish credit market. The main actor representing (commercial) banking interests was the Swedish Bankers Association. According to central bank sources, this organization was more concerned with the day-to-day inconviences of a highly regulated regime, and had little to offer in terms of the overall policy discourse (Svensson, 1996, pp. 62–4).

3 THE POLITICAL AND INSTITUTIONAL CONTEXT OF SWEDISH BANKING: THE OLD REGIME

Before we turn to the dramatic events of the 1980s and the early 1990s, it is useful to try and understand the credit management regime Sweden left when her financial markets were liberalized and internationalized. To better appreciate this regime and why it was abandoned, it is also necessary to view it as a part of a broader macroeconomic regime and the troubles this regime ran into in the 1970s. Until the early 1970s, Swedish fiscal policy was fairly moderate, aiming at balanced budgets or small deficits. Wage settlements secured a relatively compressed wage structure, but more important was the goal of keeping real wage increases within the limits set by the productivity growth of the export sector.

The role of credit policy in the Swedish economic strategy of the first postwar decades was at least fourfold. It supplied a countercyclical element that fiscal and incomes policy lacked, it sought to provide fairly low interest rates and it sought to privilege housing construction and public borrowing. In order to achieve this, the maximum rates charged by banks were defined by the authorities, and the volume of credit was governed through credit controls. The state also regulated the supply of, and demand for, bonds. Further, extensive capital controls were employed to shield the credit market, and to hamper speculation against the currency.

The central bank had two main types of credit controls. Cash and liquidity requirements forced the banks to hold a discretely defined fraction of their balances in cash and other liquid forms. These requirements were used to constrain growth indirectly. For periods of very strong credit demand, the *Riksbank* had a more direct type of regulation, a 'ceiling' on all lending other than for the construction of homes. From the mid-1950s onwards, Swedish tax revenues began to increase faster than the OECD average (Steinmo, 1993, p. 132). This was reflected in high and increasing marginal rates. The system also allowed deducting interest payment from income tax. This brought real post-tax rates downwards and it reduced the real progressiveness of the tax system.

In the 1970s, Sweden went from moderate to unsustainable fiscal policies. The background to this was the twin external shocks of the breakdown of the Bretton Woods currency regime and 'OPEC 1' in 1973. The elections of that year also saw the infamous 'hung' Parliament of 175 seats on each side of the bourgeois–socialist divide, which did not facilitate economic governance. The ensuing international recession was met with expansionary monetary and fiscal policies. Defensive spending was continued and the budget deficit increased when a non-socialist coalition government took over after the 1976 elections.

The Swedish state also developed an incomes policy, that is, it engaged itself more directly in wage settlements. The government contributed to wage settlements with tax relief and increased transfers, thus further weakening its fiscal position. This was supposedly done in exchange for union moderation, yet it resulted in unprecedented growth of real wages (Mjøset, 1987, p. 423).

The deficits and the inflation of the mid-1970s were detrimental to the credit market regime that came to be abolished about 10 years later. Firstly, persistent deficits injected more liquidity into the system that could fuel 'grey markets', that is, transactions where the financial institutions try to hide their participation in order to avoid regulation. Secondly, inflation dragged real post-tax rates down, both as a direct effect and indirectly by bringing more people into higher income brackets ('bracket creep'). Higher income brackets meant higher marginal tax rates, increasing the share of interest rate costs paid for by the state. Thirdly, when seeking holders of its increasing debt burden, the government used market price to court households and non-financial firms. It could still, however, use regulatory instruments to make sure that financial institutions lent them money below market rates (Jonung, 1993, p. 332). The two-price system prompted opposition and evasive actions from the financial institutions.

In sum, Sweden entered the 1980s with a macroeconomic and credit policy regime under increasing pressure to change. The course chosen was one of liberalization. The results of this policy, as it interacted with other policies and changes in the market, will be revealed in the next section.

4 REFORMS AND THEIR CONSEQUENCES: BOOM, BUST AND RESCUE

The Boom Phase

After the elections of 1982 the Social Democrats returned to power under Olof Palme. Unemployment and inflation had both increased under non-socialist rule. Substantial fiscal and balance of payment deficits were also part of the inheritance. The government decided to make an offensive devaluation. This 'big bang' (16 per cent, coming on the heels of a 10 per cent devaluation the year before) was the centrepiece of a new strategy. The hope was to kick-start the economy through a profit-driven boom in the export sector. This was to be followed up by a commitment to a fixed exchange rate, more energetic incomes policies and fiscal moderation, all with the overriding goal of containing inflation. The strategy was dubbed the 'third road'.

It should be noted, however, that credit policy (understood as credit and interest rate controls) played no real part in the third road strategy. Erik Åsbrink, at the time under-secretary at the ministry of finance, was quite blunt: 'This [credit policy] was not a major issue for the incoming government' (quoted in Svensson, 1996, pp. 35–6). The post-devaluation economic policy discourse of social democracy was centred on the exchange rate commitment, the problem of persistent budget deficits and incomes policy (Wihlborg, 1993, p. 237). This relative political neglect of credit policy left the field open to central bank influence and Svensson's detailed historical investigation shows that its technocrats indeed made all the crucial liberalization initiatives that were to follow.

The growth of grey markets and the inflationary pressures this yielded were a key factor in convincing the *Riksbank* that credit controls could not work effectively. The fact that increasing efforts at regulation were continually circumvented constituted a learning process for central bankers. Reasoning within a neoliberal framework, they concluded that grey markets needed to be wiped out in order to control inflation. To dispense with the grey markets, central banks needed to be able to utilize the price mechanism in a uniform manner across different segments of the market.

First, liquidity quotas were repealed upon initiative from the *Riksbank* in September 1983. The core of the model, interest rate controls and the 'ceiling' on lending, however, survived another two years. During this time the staff at the *Riksbank* continued to work for the abolishment of this core as well, being able to refer to the arguments presented in a 1982 government report (Svensson, 1996, pp. 78–9; Wohlin, 1998, p. 24).

In May 1985, interest rate controls were finally scrapped. At the same time the credit ceiling was lowered (that is, banks were given less room for expansion). On 21 November, the *Riksbank* board decided to scrap the ceiling on new lending. The main argument was that the old regulatory devices were inefficient. It follows logically that, if the old regulatory tools were inefficient, their scrapping would not be of great consequence. As we shall see below, later developments proved this understanding to be faulty. The events of autumn 1985 have even been called the 'November revolution', but at the time liberalization was sold as a technical adjustment, not a dramatic political decision.

One individual who did not subscribe to this view was Lars Wohlin, a former central bank governor and in 1985 CEO at Sweden's largest mortgage company, *Stadshypotek*. When informed of the *Riksbank's* decision, he immediately ordered his organization to offer as many new bonds in the market as possible to be able to meet the increased demand for credit that he foresaw. In December, the monthly growth rate for credits from *Stadshypotek* quadrupled (Wohlin, 1998, p. 21). Assuming that property prices would rise faster, Wohlin also ordered that his institution move its upper limit from 75 per cent to 85 per cent of any mortgage object's value. Other institutions sooner or later did more or less the same. The aggregated result was a phenomenal growth period that may well be classified as a credit explosion. If we look at lending to households and businesses together, the average rate of increase (in nominal terms) was SEK 62 billion for the 1980–85 period. The average for the next five years was SEK 207 billion.[3] This corresponded to a doubling of the stock of loans (Lybeck, 1992, p. 64).

Asset price inflation
There are many reasons why credit growth of the size Sweden experienced in the latter half of the 1980s created problems from an economic management perspective. It was inflationary through stimulating demand. It put pressure on the administrative capacity of banks to handle risk at both the level of the individual credit and at the portfolio level. And it seriously destabilized the real economy through interaction with assets markets in driving asset price inflation into a speculative bubble.

The dynamic behind asset price inflation and bubble formation is simple: When the assets most commonly used as collateral for bank loans – shares and real estate – go through rapid price increases this can set off a spiral. Rising prices of collateral provide a rationale for extending credits, which in turn fuels inflation in these markets, and so on and so forth. Rising prices also have a wealth effect. This creates optimism that feeds on itself. The problem is that asset price inflation brings about a situation that is vulnerable to turns in market sentiment. Indeed, the stock of loans tracked Swedish asset prices all through the period of hyper growth in the mid-to-late 1980s and down again in the early 1990s (Bäckström, 1998, p. 11).

The most important market for this analysis is real estate because around 50 per cent of the subsequent losses experienced by banks was related to this market (Berglöf and Sjögren, 1995, p. 33). On the whole it is correct to say that real estate took off in the aftermath of the 1985 decision to scrap the credit ceiling. Commercial property, however, entered the 1985–9 period at high speed, riding on a corporate profits boom created by the 1982 devaluation. From 1982 to 1985, prices for commercial real estate grew by a factor of three. From 1985 to 1989, this market picked up even more pace, as these years saw a further quintupling of prices. Prices for residential property grew fast as well, but not that fast, with most of the increase coming after 1985 (Lybeck, 1992, pp. 63–4).

We saw above that Wohlin correctly predicted a phenomenal increase in the demand for credit from the real estate sector. His argument was that several decades of regulation had opened up a gap between the potential collateral value of Swedish real estate and the actual degree to which it was mortgaged. This is because in a market regulated like the Swedish the degree of mortgaging reflects historical building costs. Historical building costs will over time fall as a fraction of resale value even in a market with moderately rising prices. In 1985, the total stock of real estate in Sweden tied up around 40 per cent of the total stock of loans in the economy. In the UK market, which had been liberalized earlier, the corresponding figure was around 70 per cent (Wohlin, 1998, p. 25). After liberalization, this gap between the degree of mortgaging and potential mortgaging could be translated into business opportunities for house owners and their bankers, thus kick-starting the process of asset price inflation. The rapidly increasing prices, together with tax incentives and subsidies (see below) also produced a boom in the construction of new buildings. Fast growth also helped drive up costs in the sector, not the least labour costs (Petterson, 1993, p. 28).

Unlike the property market, the stock market was not the source of large losses when prices fell in 1989/90. Still, the indirect effect is not unimportant: a stock market undergoing hyper growth added fuel to the fire that overheated the Swedish economy in the last half of the 1980s. The primary effect the incoming Palme government hoped to achieve through its massive devaluation in 1982 was a profit-led boom in the export sector. The devaluation came just before an international upturn, and profits did indeed boom. This was reflected in stock prices. In real terms the market grew at a rate of 24 per cent per year during the 1980s, which made it one of the fastest growing markets in the industrialized world during that decade (Lybeck, 1992, p. 64).

Asset price inflation thrives on optimism. Another optimism-inducing factor was net pay increases. These were particularly high in the 1984–7 period (Agell and Berg, 1996, p. 580). A good indicator of the euphoric state of the Swedish economy in this period is the savings rate. This had been stable at around 4 per cent for much of the postwar period. During the early 1980s it was reduced and after deregulation the 'worst' years were 1987–9, when it averaged minus 4.3 per cent. The accumulated effect was impressive. In five years of boom, private sector debt shot up from 100 per cent to 150 per cent of GDP (Bäckström, 1998, p. 11).

The economy overheats and no-one tries to cool it

After 1985, the international upturn continued, but now domestic demand took over as the prime engine of growth, gradually leading to an overheating of the economy. One important question that arises then, is, what was done to cool off the economy? The short answer is not very much. The general picture is that other policies that are functionally interdependent with credit policies were maladjusted to the credit-led boom. And when policies finally were changed, it was a case of too much, too late (see below).

The first policy issue we should consider here is the right to deduct interest payments from taxable income. In a country with high marginal taxes this could translate into a substantial gap between post- and pre-tax real interest rates. The tax system also contained several other provisions that opened up plenty of room for arbitrage and tax-motivated investment choices. This held for both households and companies. These provisions constituted a structural bias in the Swedish economy: they heavily rewarded loan-financed investments compared to using savings and retained profits.[4] With the benefit of hindsight it thus seems obvious that repealing quantitative restrictions on the volume of credit without substantially reforming the tax system could release a powerful demand for credit.

In the late 1970s, after inflation and bracket creep had taken effect over a period of time, a realization did in fact take hold among the policy elites that the tax system needed reform (Steinmo, 1993, p. 182). The non-socialist coalition government(s) that ruled from 1976 to 1982, however, found it very difficult to move from a common understanding that something should be done to actually doing anything. In Steinmo's (ibid., p. 183) phrase: 'To oversimplify a bit: the Center party…wanted consumption taxes cut. The Liberal party wanted middle-class and salaried employees' taxes cut. The Moderate party wanted to cut taxes paid by high income earners.' According to Steinmo, the Social Democrats used this split among the governing parties to drive a wedge between them. They offered a compromise that entailed reducing marginal rates in exchange for putting a moderate cap on interest rate deductibility. The conservatives (the Moderate party) who opposed any such cap eventually left the government in protest, and thus the scene was set for the Social Democrats' victory at the 1982 election.

The night of the tax compromise was latter dubbed *underbara natten* (the wonderful night) but in reality the compromise was more of a paint job than a substantial reconstruction. Societal interests and coalition bargaining blocked the path for those politicians that wanted a substantive reform. Most of the incentives inviting loan-financed portfolio investments were kept, and although the cap on deductions was gradually raised so that in 1985 a household could deduct a maximum 50 per cent of its interest rate payments, the system still encouraged (over) investment in real estate. During the latter part of the 1980s, a substantial group qualified for the 50 per cent provision, which in reality made a nominal interest rate of, for instance, 10 per cent bite as if it had been 5 per cent.

On top of this came inflation. During the 1970s, Sweden built up a reputation as an inflationary economy and the country lived up to this in the 1980s too. Entering the decade at a level around 14 per cent, inflation fell in the middle of the decade before picking up again.[5] In 1990, Sweden once more saw double digits. In interplay with the tax system this had a severe impact on the real post-tax rates faced by normal income households, the perverse logic being that the more the economy boomed, the more inflation rose and the less it cost to borrow money. For mortgage loans for middle-income families the real post-tax rate went below zero in 1987, to around minus 2 per cent in 1990.[6]

Management through the nominal rate of interest also proved to be a problem. In a globalizing financial market, with a high degree of capital mobility, monetary policy choice is often couched in terms of domestic (countercyclical) management of the business cycle versus exchange rate objectives. If a country, like Sweden, tries to combine a previously established fixed exchange rate target with a liberalized credit market, it can only expect that exchange rate imperatives and considerations for the domestic business cycle will match each other sporadically. In the aftermath of liberalization, Sweden repeatedly encountered problems of this nature. Exchange rate considerations dictated that interest rates would be either too low or too high to constitute a sensible countercyclical use of monetary policy. In the first years after liberalization, downward pressure on interest rates was a recurring problem because of capital inflows. For example, in the winter of 1985–6, global interest rates fell and Swedish rates followed them downwards to the tune of four percentage points just as credit demand started to boom (Jonung, 1993, p. 313). Still this was not enough to stop Swedish banks from borrowing more and more abroad, a policy that added currency risk to the problem of credit risk.

Precautionary policies in an expansionist environment

The main contribution of policy to the banking crisis was the failure of macroeconomic management and regulation reviewed above. Still, practices and developments at the level of precautionary policies did not help things either. At this level the most significant problem was the awareness that a liberalized, fast-growing credit market demands more stringent measures to counteract increased risk taking. Two aspects of precautionary policy will be briefly addressed: capital adequacy requirements and the resources allocated to supervision of the credit market.

When it came to capital adequacy, the old Swedish regime was lax on at least two key points. The first point concerned the weighting of loans to homes. Under the old regime such loans were most often placed within a category that carried a capital requirement of 1 per cent. The corresponding figure in the new international standards, adopted by Sweden in 1983, is 4 per cent (Lybeck, 1992, p. 227; Wallander, 1994, p. 129).

The second point at which the old standards were more lax than the new ones was in regard to subordinated loan capital. This is an instrument that enjoys a legal status between equity (share capital and retained profits) and ordinary loan capital. In case the bank should fail it is subordinate to ordinary loans, but it is privileged compared to share capital. Also it cannot be written off against losses while the bank remains in operation. All this makes subordinate loan capital clearly inferior to 'real equity' as a buffer against losses. For this reason the new international standards only allow up to 50 per cent of a bank's own funds to be covered by this type of capital. This rule is meant to be absolute. In the old days, however, the practice had been to make the system more lax every time the situation demanded it. As Wallander (1994, p. 136) puts it: 'A bank's ability to expand was not regulated by its ability to accumulate or raise [own] funds. Rather, the need to expand governed the definition of adequate capital.' These weaknesses in the capital adequacy regime meant that directly and indirectly Swedish banks could expand in the market for home financing with less concern for their capital base than they would have been able to had standards been changed before rather than after the market was liberalized. Capital adequacy policy represented a missed opportunity because so many of the eventual losses were related to the property sector and because stricter standards would have made it impossible for the market to grow so fast in the first place.

Any major banking crisis will invariably lead to some critical attention being given to the action (and non-action) of the supervisory authority. It seems unreasonable to assume that it is within the powers of supervisory authority to prevent a banking crisis from happening, but some preventive effect can be hoped for through discovering problems early and generally seeing to it that proper craftsmanship is being exercised. The resources allocated to supervisory activities can also serve as an indicator of how seriously the degree of change undergone by the financial sector is taken.

Sjöberg (1994, pp. 181–213) has analysed the resource situation of *Bankinspektionen*. A key point is that, while the tasks of the institution grew in volume and complexity, new resources were hard to come by. In their budget for

1986–7, the supervisory body calculated that, with the same staff resources as in 1970, its workload was doubled. These sorts of constraints obviously forced its leadership to make some tough choices, and it is Sjöberg's conclusion that these choices were not always wise. On-the-spot inspections, for instance, were reduced just as the banks started on their accelerated growth path. Instead, work related to new instruments (derivatives for example) and 'new issues' (consumer protection and insider trading) was prioritized.[7] One could say that the supervisory authority followed 'newness' and innovation at the cost of not paying enough attention to the danger of the classic syndrome of hubris and poor credit judgment playing itself out.

Too Much Too Late: Bust, Crash and Rescue

This subsection tells the story of how Swedish policy makers finally managed to apply brakes to the economy, just as it was slowing down by itself anyway. After nine good years, the international business cycle fell away in 1989 and turned into a recession in 1990. This happened in a situation where Sweden's competitive position had been deteriorating fast, particularly since the period of overheating began in earnest in 1987. The current account showed sizeable red figures by 1988, and in 1990 Sweden's competitive position was between 10 and 15 per cent worse than before the great devaluation of 1982 (Wihlborg, 1993, p. 240). In May 1990, Sweden declared a unilateral link to the Ecu. This meant throwing the US dollar out of the basket, and as the dollar in this period swung wildly against the D-Mark, this made the Ecu basket less balanced than the old trade-weighted one. It also meant that Sweden to a larger degree 'imported' (rising) German interest rates while it loosened its ties to US interest rates, which were falling since the US economy was moving into a recession at this time.

That German interest rates were going up was due to a large extent to the struggle between the Bundesbank and the Kohl administration over the financing of reunification. Rising rates suited the other ERM countries poorly. This, plus the uncertainty over the Treaty of Maastricht caused by Danish and French popular reaction, and a falling dollar in the summer of 1992, put increasing pressure on the ERM. The troubles spilled over to Sweden. In addition, confidence in the SEK was particularly vulnerable to Finnish currency weakness since the two countries compete in price-sensitive export industries. Finland devalued against the Ecu in November 1991, while it gave up its linkage altogether in September the following year. All this contributed to a prolonged period of high nominal rates at a time when the economy and, in particular, the financial market were in free fall and clearly in need of lower rates.

Exchange rate troubles were also compounded by the fact that Sweden had scrapped its capital controls. This process had begun after internal deregulation was finalized in 1985. It was completed in line with the requirements of the single market for capital one year ahead of the EC's deadline in July 1990. Because of the need to finance budget deficits, Sweden had practised a fairly liberal policy on capital imports for a while. With the new round of liberalisation it became legal for virtually anyone to speculate against their own currency, for instance by borrowing at home and then taking this abroad to buy a more trusted currency. This sort of speculation is sensitive to extreme interest rate differentials. The *Riksbank,* with the full backing of its government, decided to defend the currency at literally any cost, which contributed to persistent high money market and rates to consumers. The peak was reached in September 1992. For a short time the *Riksbank's* overnight rates reached the absurd level of 500 per cent.

Also tax reform was finally achieved in 1991. This reduced marginal rates to 30 per cent, even for high-income earners (Steinmo, 1993, p. 189). The effect of this, falling inflation levels and an increasingly more desperate interest rate policy driven by exchange rate imperatives, was that the real post-tax interest rate rose steeply. Roughly speaking, it went from being marginally negative in the peak years up to as much as the 10 per cent mark for floating rate mortgages when the economy was in deep crisis in 1992. The accumulated fall in GDP from the middle of 1991 to the middle of 1993 was 6 per cent (Bäckström, 1998, p. 11). Manufacturing output declined dramatically, while total employment fell by about 11 per cent from 1990 to 1993 (Lindbeck, 1997, p. 1304).

Crisis signs in the financial sector had begun to show up as early as 1990. That autumn, several finance companies encountered severe liquidity problems. These institutions had specialized in transforming short-term borrowing into long-term lending to the real estate sector, and when assets prices started to fall and the cost of short-term finance went up, the squeeze was on. By 1991, these kinds of problems had spilled over to the banks. The logic of asset price deflation was now playing itself out. Credit supply was negative. Financial saving shot up from close to two-digit negative numbers to just above plus 10 per cent in only three years, and real estate prices plummeted. There was a wave of bankruptcies. The banks were caught directly through loans going bad at a time when the value of their collateral fell short because of the fall in assets prices, and indirectly because several banks had given credit to the finance companies that were now in deep trouble.

Although losses (as a percentage of total stock of loans) varied greatly (between 9.5 and 37.3 per cent), all of Sweden's seven biggest banks did experience severe losses in the 1990–3 period (Wallander, 1994, p. 80). The stock of bad loans (loans that gave no or close to no income) outweighed the capital base of the Swedish banking system. Six of the seven banks needed injections of fresh capital, either from the state or from their owners (Bäckström, 1998, p. 12). By the autumn of 1992, it was clear that the crisis had gained system-wide proportions, the measures taken against it reflecting this. These measures can be summarized in four points.[8]

1. A general state guarantee issued in the autumn of 1992. This said that the state would ultimately make sure that all liabilities (except shareholder capital) on Swedish banks (and certain other credit market institutions) would be honoured on time. The state actually issued guarantees and interest-free loans for two banks, *Första Sparbanken* and *Sparbanken Sverige* (later, *Första* was subsumed by *Sparbanken*). It also provided a guarantee for *Föreningsbanken*, which was vital in securing new private capital.
2. The establishment in 1993 of a special body, *Bankstödsnämden*, which had the task of securing the stability of the financial system through processing and handling any requests for state help to be able to meet capital adequacy requirements, and making sure that this help was given on equal terms.
3. The willingness to buy out private shareholders in banks that could not secure enough private capital to survive. In one case the shares that were taken over were considered worthless (*Gota Bank*) while, in another case, where private investors had been invited in by the state at a late date, these were compensated (*Nordbanken*).
4. The use of a 'bad bank' model. In the two cases listed under (3) above, this model was used to enable the 'mother bank' to continue day-to-day operations, while specialized organizations were established to concentrate on retrieving as much as possible from the bad loan portfolios.

5   ASSESSMENT: WHAT KIND OF POLICY FAILURE?

The Swedish banking crisis was not a policy failure in the sense that policy was unquestionably the prime cause of events. The actions of banks and other economic agents were arguably as, if not more, important determinants of the eventual outcome. The format of this contribution does not, however, allow me to pursue the problem of gauging the relative importance of different causal forces located at different levels of analysis. Such an exercise is not, however, necessary in order to classify this case as a policy failure,[9] because it is beyond reasonable doubt that policy made an important *contribution* to a multi-level process that resulted in the crisis. Policy issues such as the timing of the tax reform, the uncompromising hard currency stand and weak precautionary policy, amongst others, helped bring about the crisis. Furthermore, in hindsight, these actions and non-actions stand out as *foreseeable, avoidable* and *blameworthy*; thus the key criteria in Bovens and 't Hart's (1996, p. 15) definition of a policy failure are met.

What kind of policy failure was the Swedish banking crisis? Employing the typology presented in the introduction to this volume, the case presented here can be subsumed under the category of programmatic/system-wide failures. This assessment will be made in three short steps. First, however, key indicators will be presented that express the scale of the banking crisis in purely economic terms.

Losses on bad loans totalled SEK 175 billion for the four years from 1990 to 1993. This corresponded to about 12 per cent of GDP in one year. In the two worst years, 1992 and 1993, losses corresponded to 7 per cent of the total stock of loans (Wallander, 1994, p. 73). As we have seen, no banks were allowed to close down, but the three biggest losers (in absolute and relative terms) were no longer independent, becoming parts of bigger conglomerates as a direct result of the crisis. The rescue operation had a gross value of SEK 68 billion (Lindgren, 1994, p. 27). This corresponded to about 12 per cent of the state's budget for the fiscal year 1992–3, or about 5 per cent of GDP. The net cost to the taxpayer (after the state had been able to sell off most of the assets it acquired through its rescue operation) has been calculated at SEK 35 billion (Jennergren and Näslund, 1998).[10]

This outcome can be compared to the explicit and implicit goals of the liberalization policy. When advocating reform, the *Riksbank* explicitly argued that a more market-oriented regulatory model for the credit market should yield two primary benefits, a more efficient monetary policy in terms of stabilizing the economy and better resource allocation. The boom–bust sequence that followed makes it clear that the first goal was not met; likewise, the heavy over-investment of the boom period indicates that resource allocation did not improve over the 1985–92 period. What in hindsight must be considered the most important precondition of the liberalization policy, however, was so obvious that it remained implicit, namely that liberalization should not threaten the viability of the Swedish banking system. Thus none of the primary goals or preconditions of the liberalization policy were met, and therefore the case qualifies as a programme failure.

The Swedish banking crisis was to a much lesser degree a political failure, in the sense that it was not highly politicized. A large public investigation was undertaken in order to understand and draw lessons from the crisis, but none of the contributions focus strongly on the role of political decisions (Bankkriskommittén, 1994, 1995). To the degree that the role of policy is addressed in these reports (and in other books and articles on the crisis which are drawn upon in this chapter), this tends to be integrated into a description of broader economic trends. To my knowledge, no individual politician or bureaucrat (or groups of such) have been singled out for particular blame. In contrast to the débâcle over the ECU crisis in 1992 (Stern and Sundelius, 1998) and debates over the merits of Swedish economic performance in general,

Swedish politicians have been relatively modest in blaming each other for the banking crisis as such. Perhaps this has to do with it being easier to see a direct connection between the actions of bank managers and owners and the bad results, and that this group consequently has had to take more of the heat. A further factor that may have limited the politicization of the crisis is that it has been understood as a system-wide crisis. In this sense it involved all major players and parties. This also makes it easier to see why political blame could be diffused.

6   ANALYSIS: EXPLAINING FAILURE

Drawing on broader schools of thought in political science, Bovens and 't Hart (1996) distinguish between four analytical foci when explaining policy failures. These perspectives single out the management of problem solving, competing values, institutional interaction and structural constraints as the key challenges that have been (unsuccessfully) met, when explaining policy failures. The present case can best be explained by drawing on all four of these perspectives.

On the most general level, the case of the Swedish banking crisis as a policy failure has to be seen within an institutional perspective. The key point is that rapid and substantial change in some of the routinized policies that make up a policy regime can put insuperable pressure on the coordination capacity of the polity as a decision-making system. This can in turn lead to a situation where policies are allowed to undermine each other. This happens because policies that are tightly coupled in functional terms are only loosely coupled in the decision-making process. On this level this is an institutionalist story because it is about fragmentation, local (and therefore plural) rationalities and the unintended (and undesirable) consequences this brings about.

That functionally interdependent policies are formulated in relative isolation from each other is an everyday fact of political life in advanced welfare states. Time and attention are scarce resources, and together with specialization this induces sequential and sectorized treatment of issues. Thus in an institutionalist perspective loose coupling of functionally interdependent policies cannot in itself explain a policy failure. The link between loose coupling and failure lies with the fact that loose coupling continues to be the norm even in periods where the core policies change. In order to develop this argument we must engage another central tenet of institutionalist thought, namely the notion that institutional orders can be seen as alternating between periods of relative stability and periods with a high density of change, the so-called 'punctuated equilibrium metaphor' (Krasner, 1984).

This position implicitly assumes that any institutional order rests on a bed of functional compatibility between its constituent policy routines. This follows because, if policies invariably have impacts outside their primary domain, a minimum level of accommodation between policies must be built into the routines of the institutional orders. If not, such regimes would not be able to endure over time, and a certain endurance is a quality institutional orders have by definition. This implies that a change in core policies may create a functional need for mutual adjustments between the policies that together make up a regime. This is clearly brought out by the case at hand. A more liberal governance regime in the credit market created a functional need for coordinated adjustments of policies such as the tax system, interest rate policy, exchange rate policy and precautionary policies. The question then becomes what forces can drive wedges between these policies and the policies of credit market regulation? In order to understand this we can identify three mechanisms that draw on the other three perspectives identified by Bovens and 't Hart. Let us consider, briefly, what kind of mechanisms are involved.

According to Bovens and 't Hart, the *problem-solving perspective* tends to focus on information problems and cognitive incompetence when explaining policy failure. Translated to the case at hand, this perspective draws attention to a systematic ignorance by policy elites of the behavioural change that credit market liberalization produced and the underestimation of risk that this ignorance resulted in. The dynamics of asset price inflation and the willingness to assume risk on the part of market actors that this implied were not on the agenda of Swedish policy makers and planners before liberalization. Consequently, potential warning signals such as a dramatic rise in property prices and the dramatic fall in the savings rate were not heeded and precautionary policy did not come onto the agenda until it was too late.

The *competing values perspective* directs our attention to imbalanced conflict resolution. In the case of Swedish tax reform, we can speak of insufficient conflict resolution producing a long-standing deadlock. Meanwhile, credit market developments were allowed to be driven forward by the perverse incentives generated by a tax system developed in a different, more tightly regulated, credit economy.

Finally, a *structural constraints perspective* focuses on the contradictions and risks of failure inherent in complex systems. The modern, transnationalized economy can be seen as such as system, within which the Swedish economy makes up a subsystem. This type of perspective is one way of conceptualizing the dilemmas produced for Swedish policy makers at the intersection of exchange rate and credit policy. As we have seen, the commitment to a fixed exchanged rate (which in itself was entirely defensible) produced a procyclical interest rate policy which compounded the problems of domestic economic management in both the boom and the bust phases.

7   CONCLUDING REMARKS

This story of the Swedish banking crisis is not so much about the management of innovation as it is about the management of recurrence of old spectres. New instruments may have been crucial for convincing central bankers that credit controls were obsolete, but this freed the banks to assume what we might term old-fashioned risk. Aggressive lending and risk taking leading to bubbles forming in the markets for assets were at the heart of the problem, and these practices were not new: they were well known from the inter-war period and long before that. A preoccupation with new and more 'sexy' problems set against a background of more than 40 years of financial stability facilitated the unlearning of the lessons of the inter-war period.

The boom and bust sequence left Sweden's financial system badly hurt. From 1990 to 1993, Swedish banks accumulated losses corresponding to 16.8 per cent of total lending in 1990. Losses varied, of course, but even the two relative success stories among the five biggest banks (SE-Banken and Handelsbanken) suffered losses of just above and just below 10 per cent, respectively. The pervasive nature of the problems makes it more natural to see the Swedish case as one of system-wide failure rather than as a mere crisis of one or several banks.

Another distinguishing feature of this story is that, even though the Swedish polity failed to the degree that it helped bring the crisis about, it also displayed great strength through its ability to produce a consensual, yet decisive and effective, rescue operation. This is indicative of a more general phenomenon; that a great transformation may be difficult to spot while one is in the middle of it. Hence decisions were made in an incremental, often reactive and loosely coupled, manner until the crisis was manifest. At that point, however, key actors took a step back and managed to cooperate on a coherent response strategy.

At the beginning of the new century the economic policy regime seems to be gelling so that it is now entering another stable period. The responsibility for bank supervision was transferred from *Bankinspektionen* to *Finansinspektionen* (FI) when the former was merged with two other regulatory bodies to form the latter in July 1991. Tax reform is in place, public deficits have been greatly reduced and, since 1993, Sweden has pursued a flexible exchange rate policy which has put an end to the problem of procyclical monetary policy. One great unresolved issue, however, is that of Swedish participation in the EMU.

On the other hand, the financial market is developing along lines that are familiar to most advanced industrial nations. The trend is towards ever bigger units as there are mergers within and across previously separate sectors and countries. To an increasing degree, major corporate actors are seeing the Nordic financial markets as one, and whether or not Sweden (and Denmark) decides to join the EMU, the market actors are likely to continue to move towards a deeply integrated European financial market. This raises the possibility that the next banking crisis cannot primarily be analysed in terms of domestic policy choices and market developments.

NOTES

1. I would like to thank Andreas Busch, Adam Tickell, Sofia Perez, Paul 't Hart, Jon Pierre and other members of the project for comments on an earlier draft of this chapter. Outside the project, Mats Larsson and Torsten Svensson have also been very generous with help and comments.
2. Market share statistics are taken from Larsson and Sjögren (1995, p. 25).
3. Source: Petterson (1993, p. 36) Figures 2.5 and 2.6.
4. An eight-country OECD study from 1987 concluded that, in terms of its corporate tax system, Sweden had the greatest tax wedges of all the cases compared. (Quoted in Petterson, 1993, p. 56.)
5. Swedish inflation figures are depicted in SOU, 1996, p. 205, Figure 8.2.
6. Petterson (1993, p. 50, Figure 3.1).
7. See also Engwall (1997, p. 181).
8. This summary is based upon Söderström (1998, p. 647) and Dokument 17 (1997–8, pp. 257–61).
9. I have, however, addressed this problem more thoroughly in my study of the Norwegian banking crisis (Tranøy, 2000).
10. This estimate is modest. Jennergren and Näslund (1998, pp. 75–6) stress two cost components they were unable to include in their calculations. One is that the banks in general raised their net interest margins in the crisis years (from a previous average of around 5 per cent to more than 6 per cent). The other is the transfer of wealth from the public at large to shareholders of the banks that were able to survive because of the general guarantee issued by the authorities in 1992 (see Section 4 above).

23. The transformation of financial regulation in the United Kingdom: the Barings case

Adam Tickell[1]

1   INTRODUCTION

The City of London has been at the heart of global finance for two centuries. Although initially a product of British economic and geopolitical power, as Britain experienced relative economic decline during the twentieth century the City maintained its position. This resulted from a variety of factors, including the role of English as the dominant language of business, the City's geographic position in Europe between New York and Tokyo, the very size and liquidity of the financial markets themselves and the development of embedded financial knowledges within London. Critical too, however, were conscious policy choices by successive British governments and the Bank of England which aimed to maintain the City's pre-eminence with a liberal and welcoming regulatory environment. From the mid-1950s in particular, the Bank of England used mild regulation of international finance to vigorously promote the City as a site for banking. During the 1960s, for example, the development of the burgeoning Eurodollar markets was encouraged by a lax regulatory environment, while more recently it actively supported the development of the derivatives exchange at The London International Financial Futures Exchange (Kynaston, 1997). For the majority of the twentieth century, domestic institutions were supervised informally by the Bank of England while the industry was allowed considerable self-regulation (Moran, 1991; Hancher and Moran, 1989; Michie, 1992). While the Bank's governor had considerable power to influence decision making – a power underwritten by shared social backgrounds and economic power – the Bank itself was no less influenced by the City interests and consequently acted as the City's Praetorian Guard, maintained restrictive practices and supported exchange rate policies disadvantageous to British industry (Longstreth, 1979; Hutton, 1995). Entrance to the City's large, liquid and lucrative markets was often more dependent upon an 'establishment power' maintained by social networks and commonly understood discourses than upon financial power, a facet further strengthened by the geographical proximity of financial institutions (Amin and Thrift, 1992; Pryke, 1991).

The transformation of both the international financial system and the City in the period since the 1960s, however, brought pressures for regulatory change. Internationally, the financial system became progressively integrated, more coherent and characterized by rapid product innovation. The traditional business of banking, 'intermediation' between borrowers and savers, progressively gave way to a raft of complex new products which aimed to provide liquidity and to circumvent regulation: between 1972 and 1992, 31 major new financial products were created (Leyshon, 1992; Leyshon and Thrift, 1997; Lee and Schmidt-Marwede, 1993; Tickell, 1999). As London became home to more foreign financial institutions than any other city and as financial markets became increasingly competitive, the regulatory structure was formalized and codified in successive legislative moves (Moran, 1991; Amin and Thrift, 1992).[2] By the mid-1990s, then, the UK's financial system was more outward-looking and supervision was both liberal and codified. However, the transformations within the financial markets were more fundamental than policy makers had allowed for. The challenge for the regulatory authorities was simultaneously to protect the integrity of the financial markets and to supervise globalizing financial institutions in an era of increasing liquidity, taking due account of the effects of new financial products. Perhaps the sternest challenge to the British regulatory approach erupted in 1995 when, as a result of derivatives trading in Singapore, Barings Bank collapsed.

2   KEY ACTORS: BARINGS BANK AND THE BANK OF ENGLAND

The 'Old City'

Historically, the British financial system has been strongly bifurcated. While domestic financial markets were strongly segmented and enjoyed oligopolistic market conditions, wholesale financial markets were competitive and liquid. There are two main institutional actors in the Barings débâcle: Barings Bank itself and the Bank of England.

When, on 26 February 1995, the Bank of England put Barings Bank into administration, a bank which had epitomized British conservatism ended its independent existence. Barings was one of the few financial institutions which had matched the longevity of the City itself. It was founded in 1762 as a commodities trading house and rapidly became one of the most powerful institutions in Europe, during a period when London was at the hub of the international financial system (Michie, 1992; Kynaston, 1994). The City was not only the place where the vast majority of foreign currency, international loans and bullion trading was transacted, it was also the place where the 'rules' of the system were set and policed. The City was sustained by an unrivalled knowledge structure (Thrift, 1994) and a close-knit financial community, usually drawn from a narrow, upper-class, social stratum, which both 'strove towards endless expansion … so as to gain competitive advantage over rivals, and …tried to enlist non-economic power to regulate the system and to give monopolistic advantages to members' (Amin and Thrift, 1992, p. 581).

However, in 1890, Barings nearly collapsed as a result of an exposure of three times the bank's capital in Argentina, following a combination of bad luck and bad management. Emulating an operation the previous year by the Bank of France, the governor of the Bank of England agreed to subscribe £3 250 000 into a collective guarantee fund and successfully encouraged City merchant banks to contribute up to £500 000 each (Pressnell, 1968). From this point until the 1980s, Barings remained a conservative force in British finance, preferring not to join in the speculative frenzy that sent merchant banks out in expensive pursuit of stockbroking firms in the run-up to the 'Big Bang' and had a stated policy of conservative investment management. Although much of Barings' recent success had come in the so-called 'emerging markets' of the Third World, they developed a reputation for operational probity and had a stated policy of not trading on their own account.

The Bank of England was founded in 1694 and for the majority of its life it remained both a privately owned commercial institution and banker to the state, only slowly and fitfully taking on the usual characteristics of a central bank, such as lender of last resort and financial regulator. It was not until the election of the majority Labour government that in 1946 it became a full state-owned central bank, even then retaining its essential operational autonomy: governors could not be dismissed by the government, while the Bank retained the power to regulate commercial banks. Accordingly, the regulation of the British banking and financial systems has been described as 'meso-corporatist', as financial interest groups fused together the 'processes of interest representation, decision-making and policy implementation' (Cawson, 1985; see also Grant and Sargent, 1987; Moran, 1991). In finance, this was characterized by a mixture of informal regulation by the Bank of England and self-regulation on the part of the industry, and 'many of the important regulatory arrangements … in the financial community … were evolved in a political culture marked by a deferential attitude on the part of mass publics towards authority and a preference for informal and private regulation on the part of interest groups. These factors ensured that regulation was shielded from the attitude of democratic politics. This is what the characteristic British preference for "self-regulation" amounted to' (Hancher and Moran, 1989, p. 283; compare Wilson, 1984, pp. 224–5; Strange, 1986, pp. 129–31).

The reinsertion of the City of London into the international financial system as a key locus of activity from the late 1950s developed, in large part, as a consequence of this meso-corporatist regulation of finance. The growth of the Eurodollar market in London occurred as American banks sought to avoid stringent controls at home and because there was little formal regulation on overseas banks. Since 1951, when Harold Wilson made the British financial markets more open to overseas banks than in any other country in the world, Britain has always adopted a liberal approach to overseas banks (Coakley and Harris, 1983; Strange, 1986).

The informal regulation of banking began to come under pressure during the 1960s. The Bank of England was being slowly transformed from the City's representative in the state to the state's representative in the City, while the internationalization of finance after the collapse of the Bretton Woods system upon which London relied further undermined informal supervision, in five ways (Eichengreen, 1996). First, the inefficiency of British banks was exposed in the markets where they were competing with foreign banks (Gowland, 1990). Second, overseas bankers felt excluded from, and disadvantaged by, the regulatory decision-making process. Third, the development of new financial instruments and rapid technological development enabled banks to circumvent even the limited regulations that existed. Fourth, the sectional interests of some of the component parts of the financial sector were increasingly seen as undermining the wider interests of financial capital. Fifth, changes in the regulation of American securities markets and capital markets during the 1970s and 1980s put pressure on Britain to respond in order to retain London's relative position.

Accordingly, legislative change from the end of the 1970s began to codify supervision. The 1979 Banking Act aimed to prevent a recurrence of the conditions which led to the Secondary Banking Crisis of the mid-1970s by formalizing extant understandings on minimum capital, directors and depositor protection. Although these measures considerably tightened up regulation, breaches of the legislation by the Johnson Matthey Bank were not detected by the Bank of England and the 1987 Banking Act placed further formal powers at the disposal of the regulator (Norton, 1991). At the same time, regulatory change elsewhere in the financial sector stimulated intensified competition by opening markets to building societies, life insurance companies and foreign banks. Most important, however, was the abolition of restrictions on involvement in securities markets in the 'Big Bang' of 1986. The unifying theme, of regulatory codification, was bitterly resented by some of the older members of the financial community. For example, Lord Seebohm, a director of Barclays Bank, complained in 1987 that, 'If we go on chipping away at the flexibility and the old customs of the City, we shall sooner or later find that the City loses its prominent position as the financial centre of the world' (quoted in Roberts, 1995, p. 181).

The 'New City'

The City of London is, then, a very different environment from its nineteenth-century predecessor, yet it remains as one of the world's three most important financial centres because, as Amin and Thrift (1992) and Thrift (1994) point out, it has become one of the chief points for the scripting of the global financial services filière, it is a centre of the global corporate networks in the industry, and it is a proving ground for product innovation. In this new environment, long-established City institutions have seen their roles change. The Bank of England remains powerful, but the fear of incurring the displeasure of the governor is no longer sufficient to ensure responsible, prudent behaviour and the merchant banks which epitomized power in the City have seen their influence wane. While the 'Old City' valued stability, the 'New City' is more concerned with market efficiency (Leyshon and Tickell, 1994).

At the same time, securitization, disintermediation and the emergence of bancassurance undermined the clear divisions between banking and other elements of the financial sector. Yet, in keeping with the ideological predilections of the Conservative government, a plethora of organizations were created which had regulatory responsibility for different elements of the financial system. As Table 23.1 shows, while the Bank of England retained responsibility for the prudential supervision of banking, securities regulation 'belonged' to the Securities and Investment Board, derivatives regulation was within the remit of the Securities and Futures Authority, and the provision of investment advice to individuals was variously overseen by the Investment Management Regulatory Organisation and the Personal Investment Authority. Although this organizational structure meant that regulation was functionally oriented, as most financial institutions were involved in a range of different activities they had many different regulatory masters. Furthermore, while the Bank of England was a formal state body, many of the others were private self-regulating organizations (the, so-called SROs) which enjoyed delegated power from the state. Nevertheless, although no statutory powers existed, a principle that a lead regulator was responsible for the overall financial soundness of an institution had emerged. Such regulatory complexity was compounded by the fact that financial institutions operate across borders and, although international agreements ensured that there was a lead regulator based in the home country of an institution, host country regulators retained responsibility for activities in their territories. These responsibilities were both complementary and overlapping.

Table 23.1 The fragmented regulation of the British financial sector during the Barings crisis

Institution	Function	Status
Bank of England Supervision and Surveillance Division	Banking supervision (including wholesale money market regimes)	State body
Securities and Futures Authority	Securities and derivatives regulation	SRO
Securities and Investment Board	Investment business (including oversight responsibility for supervision of exchanges and clearing houses)	Statutory regulator
Investment Management Regulatory Organisation	Investment management regulator	SRO
Personal Investment Authority	Supervision of retail investment business	SRO
Insurance Directorate of the Department of Trade and Industry	Insurance regulation	Government department
Building Societies Commission	Supervision of building societies	Statutory regulator
Friendly Societies Commission	Supervision of friendly societies	Statutory regulator
Registry of Friendly Societies	Supervision of credit unions; registration and public records of building societies, friendly societies, industrial and provident societies, and other mutual societies	Statutory regulator
Society of Lloyd's; recognized investment exchanges and clearing houses; professional bodies	Self-regulation of relevant activities *but subject to regulatory oversight by a statutory regulator*	Various forms

3 THE FALL OF THE HOUSE OF BARINGS

In this changing landscape, Barings began to respond to the growing inter-nationalization of finance. In 1984, the group incorporated Barings Securities Ltd in the Cayman Islands which, in turn, operated a large number of subsidiaries, including Baring Futures Singapore (BFS). BFS was principally a derivatives trading house and operated both for clients and for the bank itself. Barings maintained a relatively conservative approach to dealing in derivative securities and relied upon strengths in corporate advisory work. Although the bank did use derivatives, the chair explained in 1993, they 'need to be well controlled and understood, but we believe that we do that here' (*The Economist*, 4 March 1995, p. 19). Indicative of such conservatism was the resignation of the architect of the BFS strategy in protest at the decision of the bank not to allow further capital exposures after losing £20 million on falling share prices in Tokyo.

Shortly after this resignation, Nicholas Leeson was appointed to head BFS. Leeson aimed to exploit the small margin between prices on the Tokyo and Singapore exchanges by selling options on the Nikkei index. These specialist options – known as straddles – gave purchasers the right either to buy stock from, or sell stock to, Barings if the Nikkei index moved outside a given range and effectively meant that Barings believed that the Tokyo market would remain stable. Leeson reported staggering success rates. In the year to September 1992, BFS made S$2.72m. By the end of 1993, Leeson's first year, the company's reported profits had risen to S$20.3m and contributed over a quarter of the Group's trading profits in the second half of 1994. However, even at this date, Leeson was circumventing the bank's audit procedures: the premium on the options went into an unauthorized and unmonitored account (Error Account 88888).

On 17 January 1995, the Japanese town of Kobe was hit by a massive earthquake. Within a month the Nikkei index fell from over 19 200 to under 17 500. Faced with escalating losses on his deals, Leeson began to execute increasingly large trades and fraudulently misrepresented his own trading as being on behalf of a client (BBS, 1995; Gapper and Denton, 1996). By 23 February, the Barings group treasurer realized that the bank's exposure was potentially unmanageable and called a board meeting to consider the problem. The board contacted the Bank of England and on 26 February Barings was put into administration. One week later, the Dutch allfinanz group ING bought the bank for one pound sterling and a commitment to meet all of its liabilities.

The bank initially responded to the crisis by portraying responsibility as belonging to Leeson alone. Barings was, it maintained, an innocent victim of a possibly fraudulent rogue trader: 'It's a cliché in our industry to say that we are all vulnerable to fraud … Let us suppose that the putative associate approached our trader and said: "you should build up a long position at Barings so great that when Barings discover it they cannot possibly sustain it and remain solvent. I, meanwhile, will build up a short position, and when Barings duly fails I will have a wonderful opportunity to cover my short at a profit.'"[3]

Although Barings' claims of criminal fraud proved unfounded, the bank was successful in presenting a picture of a cunning deceit which prevented managers from knowing what Leeson was doing. For example, a Barings official maintained that the company could have known that there was a problem only by looking at the paperwork for all contracts in the Singapore markets.[4] Yet this, too, turned out to be exaggerated, as there had been some internal criticisms of the arrangements around Leeson's unit. Shortly after Leeson was appointed as general manager of BFS, James Bax, the head of Baring Securities in the city had sent a letter to the bank's headquarters which expressed his 'concern ... that once again we are in danger of setting up a structure which will subsequently prove disastrous and with which we will succeed in losing a lot of money or client goodwill and probably both ... In my view it is critical we should keep clear reporting lines and if this office is involved in Simex [the Singapore Monetary Exchange] at all, Nick [Leeson] should report to Simon [Jones, a Barings director] and then be ultimately responsible for the operations side.'[5]

Despite this, there were no limits on the total number of contracts held for own-account trading for BFS until after summer 1994 and no action had followed an internal audit in August of that year which had concluded that Leeson had 'an excessive concentration of powers'.[6] While Leeson was undoubtedly deceptive, as he admitted in his own account of the affair (Leeson, 1996), he was poorly supervised and there was even some confusion as to who his line manager was. Moreover, BFS did not have a clear separation between dealing and settling, which meant that Error Account 88888 could operate undetected; warning signals were ignored; there was no risk management function at BFS; and the management of Barings Bank did not understand the culture of BFS (BBS, 1995, ch. 7). Furthermore, the Securities and Futures Authority, the SRO which regulated derivatives in Britain, had informed Barings that Leeson would not be able to trade in the City because he had not disclosed that he had a county court judgment against him. In moving Leeson to Singapore, the bank had effectively evaded the SFA's jurisdiction.

4   THE BANK OF ENGLAND: CRISIS MANAGEMENT?

The Bank of England first learnt about the scale of the problems facing Barings at a short meeting between Peter Baring and the Deputy Governor at noon on 25 February. Once alert to the possibility that Barings' capital base could be wiped out, the Bank moved rapidly. Eddie George, the governor, returned from holiday in Switzerland and summoned senior members of the financial community to his office. Over the weekend, they mounted a frenetic attempt to launch a 'lifeboat' for the bank. Although the problems facing Barings were substantial, it appeared as if the Bank of England would succeed, just as it had succeeded in persuading the banks to rescue Johnson Matthey Bank in 1986 (Clark, 1986).[7] The 'old rules' of the City, when it operated as a 'club' whose members would rally round in support of a colleague in trouble, were still expected to work, just as they had done in 1890.

At a meeting at the Bank of England on 27 February, the governor explained to assembled bankers that this was such a time. Although the meeting managed to raise pledges totalling £600 million, the open-ended nature of the derivatives contracts meant this was insufficient and that the governor was forced to admit defeat. From this moment, it was clear that the rules in the City of London had fundamentally changed. The gentlemen's club had failed to pull off a rescue and the Bank of England was unprepared to underwrite it. The ties that bound the City so closely together in the past had been unravelled by changes in the Bank of England, by the internationalization of the City and by the complexity and riskiness of new financial instruments. Global financial markets had undermined the City's regulatory space, highlighting the limits of 'gentlemanly regulation' and, in a very profound sense, the collapse of Barings symbolized the changes in the *modus operandi* of the City under way since the late 1960s (see Gowland, 1990; Cerny, 1991; Amin and Thrift, 1992; Hutton, 1995). The symbolism of 1995 was particularly acute in the light of the events of 1890: crises at Barings frame the period of effective Bank of England-led club regulation in the City.

On the day following the decision to put Barings into administration, the British regulatory authorities moved quickly to preserve the stability of financial markets and the reputation of the British regulatory authorities. These areas were defended by representing the Barings collapse as having no systemic implications for the effectiveness of a liberal regulatory approach. In the House of Commons, the Chancellor of the Exchequer claimed that 'there may be some falsification of the relevant records within the subsidiaries concerned. It will therefore take some time to unearth the full and detailed catalogue of events and methods employed to evade all the required management and regulatory controls. ... *it appears to be a specific incident unique to Barings centred on one rogue trader in Singapore.*'[8] The governor of the Bank of England was more explicit in a series of television and radio interviews throughout the day: 'It was simply a question of a dealer transacting outside of authority and being able to conceal that from his bank and from all his regulators for a period of three or four weeks ... in the best regulated market in the world you can have a rotten apple who will take on large positions outside his authority and can avoid detection for a little while and that's what's happened in this case.'[9] Such pronouncements attempted to foreclose any discussion which maintained that there were problems of supervision (or, indeed, of the financial sector in general) and, in so doing, were highly successful in calming the markets.

5   POLICY CONTEXT: THE SUPERVISION OF INTERNATIONAL FIRMS

Yet the City does not still operate under rules drafted in a very different era. Not only has the City been transformed socially, it has also simultaneously been at the transmitting – and receiving – ends of a transformation of the *geographical* rules. As financial markets have become increasingly globally integrated, national regulatory structures have had to change, further undermining their integrity. While, for example, the Bank of England had primary responsibility for supervising Barings, because Leeson was trading in Japanese stock futures in Singapore, regulatory responsibility was shared with authorities in both those countries. This is not, however, to argue that we should in some way 'naturalize' the international financial system (for example, Wriston, 1988) or to agree with those commentators who have argued that the global financial system is in an 'end of geography' state (O'Brien, 1992; on which see Martin, 1994; Clark and O'Connor, 1997). As Helleiner (1996) has stressed, nation-states have played a crucial part in the globalization of financial markets by liberalizing the constraints on private capital and by containing international crises. As such, national governments have contributed to those very developments which have undermined their ability to control events (Peck and Tickell, 1994; Tickell and Peck, 1995). Furthermore, even in the context of a globalized financial system, place remains important. The regulatory authorities in London had to respond to a crisis which emerged in Singapore as a result of offshore trading on Japanese markets. In this sense, the crisis at Barings was more than a local crisis in Singapore and London: it had ramifications about the very nature of financial regulation in an internationalizing financial system.

Far from being the result of the activities of a rogue trader or of simple control failures in one bank, the collapse of Barings exposed very real flaws in the Bank of England's approach to supervision. As consolidated regulator for Barings, the Bank of England was responsible for assessing the risks from all activities in all companies in the group. Consolidated supervision is enshrined in British banking law and international agreements under the auspices of the 1993 Basle Concordat, which aims to foster common standards and cooperation among national regulators. The Basle Concordat is legally binding on member states of the G10 industrial nations and was subsequently extended via a binding Document of Understanding with the 'Offshore Group of Banking Supervisors', which includes Singapore. Under these arrangements, the supervision of BFS was the responsibility both of Singapore and of London: 'Host authorities are responsible for foreign establishments operating in their territories, while parent authorities are responsible for them as part of larger banking groups. Such responsibilities are both complementary and overlapping' (quoted in BBS,

1995, p. 195). Nevertheless, as consolidated regulator, the Bank of England had a particular responsibility to ensure that Barings' subsidiaries were not endangering the group in any way.

In the Barings case, the Bank of England inadequately discharged its supervisory responsibility. While the 1980s and 1990s saw the erosion of informal regulation, it is clear that vestigial remains existed for the Bank of England's favoured institutions. With Barings, the Bank continued to trust verbal assurances from senior managers at the bank (ibid., p. 197) and catastrophically allowed Barings to exceed more than the normal limit of 25 per cent of its capital to particular overseas exchanges (ibid., pp. 244–5). These informal arrangements allowed Leeson to build up losses in Singapore without alarm bells ringing.

Nevertheless, it is important to emphasize that Barings collapsed as a result of losses on *derivatives* trading. Derivatives vary in complexity from simple futures and options to products which are based on complicated combinations of interest rates, currency movements and stock prices (Swyngedouw, 1996; Parsons, 1988; Tickell, 1999). Derivatives developed and are used widely as a risk management technique and by 1998 the notional outstanding principal of derivatives was estimated by the Bank for International Settlements as $86 382 *billion* (BIS, 1999, Tables 19–21).[10] The Bank of England has for a long time had a relaxed attitude towards the derivatives industry (much of which is based on the London money markets) and concurs with the views of Paul Volker, a former chair of the Federal Reserve Bank, who argued in 1994 that 'derivatives by their nature do not introduce risks of a fundamentally different kind or of a greater scale than those already present in the financial markets'.[11] Underlying such statements is the ideologically inscribed belief that financial markets are efficient and rational and that their further development demands a simple solution – more market information for participants – rather than a complex set of regulatory restrictions and interventions by central bankers across the world.

6 FAILURE AND SUCCESS: THE POLITICS OF BLAMING AND EXONERATION

Investigations and Political Judgments

While in public regulators were prone to play down the impact of the Barings crisis on their approach, behind the scenes it played a central part in recasting the British regulatory system.[12] Within the UK, two major inquiries were carried out into the affair: one was conducted under the aegis of the Board of Banking Supervision, the other by the House of Commons Treasury Select Committee.

The board was set up by the 1987 Banking Act as a response to perceived failures of supervision during the Johnson Matthey Bank affair in order to advise the Bank of England on how effectively it is exercising its supervisory powers. Members of the board included the governor and deputy governor of the Bank of England, the Bank's executive director in charge of supervision and six 'independent' members drawn from the world of finance themselves. As such, the membership of the Board of Banking Supervision illustrates the regulatory continuity with the older regime, as a Conservative MP, Anthony Nelson, pointed out in Parliament in 1986: 'I question whether we are involved in the cosmetic exercise of setting up a supervisory board to persuade people that something is happening but, in the end, it will be business as usual ... One needs experts. However, one needs a lay element, a common-sense element, to provide some input. ... [I would like to be assured that the board will be] not a cosy luncheon club but an effective watchdog body.'[13]

Nevertheless, the board conducted an exhaustive inquiry which looked into all of the roots of the affair, concluding that, while Leeson persistently acted beyond his authority and wilfully concealed evidence, his managers and supervisors within Barings 'must bear much of the blame' (BBS, 1995, p. 233). Not only did the managers permit a structure where one person had responsibility for both trading and settlement which allowed Leeson to conceal his losses, but they also placed few controls on the trader and set in place a line management structure which was at best, opaque. Furthermore, the Barings management was castigated for failing to respond to rumours in the market place and for inaccurate reporting of financial data to the British regulators.

Yet the Board of Banking Supervision report largely exonerated the Bank of England. For example, it pointed out that the Bank was not responsible for the overall supervision of the Barings: 'The supervision of other Barings entities (including their capital adequacy and the effectiveness of their systems and controls) remained the primary responsibility of the relevant regulator in the country or business sector in which the Group company operated ... The Bank is under no duty, indeed has no statutory power, to supervise other companies in a group to which a bank belongs' (ibid., p. 193).

The board did identify an 'error of judgement' (ibid., p. 245) in the Bank's decision to allow Barings to exceed exposure limits required under domestic and European agreements, yet concluded that the Bank needed only to tighten existing procedures. Therefore, it argued, 'the events leading up to the collapse of Barings do not ... of themselves point to the need for any fundamental change to the framework of regulation in the UK' (ibid., p. 251). As the finance minister relied upon this report to highlight any particular changes, it seemed as if the affair would lead to no fundamental change in the supervisory structure within the UK. In the short term, the board's conclusions and also those of the inquiry for Singapore's authorities (BBS, 1995; [Singapore] Ministry of Finance, 1995) stimulated the Bank of England to commission an audit into their internal supervisory culture. The 'Andersen review' highlighted a level of staff turnover within the Bank's supervisory team that was double the rate at comparable regulators, and the fact that the average age of British supervisors was 30, a full 10 years younger than the case in the USA and mainland Europe. It also recommended a series of changes which would ensure that there was a more systematic approach to supervision and strengthened the analytical basis on which judgments were founded, Andersen stressed the need for a cultural shift in the status of supervision (Arthur Andersen, 1996; Bank of England, 1996, 1997a, 1997b).

If the board had believed that the Bank had made minor errors, in the political arena the assessment was less sanguine. The Treasury select committee of the House of Commons carried out its own inquiry into the affair. British Parliamentary select committees are creatures of the legislature rather than the executive and only have the power to make recommendations. Nevertheless, their principal role is to hold the executive to account and they have developed an independence which, at its best, operates in a bipartisan manner. Thus, although the Treasury select committee was dominated by Conservative MPs, its report was agreed by all its members. The committee largely concurred with the Board of Banking Supervision that the immediate causes of the collapse were the fraudulent activities of Leeson and the failure of the Barings management structure to detect his losses. However, the Committee believed that the Bank of England had failed to keep pace with the emerging complexity of financial markets both within the nation-state and internationally. Furthermore, they argued that the degree of discretion the Bank allowed its supervisors failed to pay sufficient attention to behaviour in the financial markets. Underlying these specific criticisms was, however, a wider critique:

> We are concerned that, as a former bank itself and as a cheerleader for the City, the Bank may be in a position of 'regulatory capture'. Although the Governor saw no contradiction in the various roles of the Bank, we feel that the proximity of the Bank to the banking sector can act as a double-edged sword. While it is useful to the bank to have intimate knowledge of the banking sector (although not intimate enough to have picked up on the rumours circulating before the collapse of Barings) there is a risk that the bank could avoid introducing useful supervisory measures which would displease the banks or might be perceived to have competitiveness implications. It is not apparent that the banking sector has earned the soft touch provided by the Bank. The chairman of the SIB was clear that there should be a *quid pro quo* for such treatment and although the Bank has also referred to such an approach we remain concerned that the legacy of the 'old culture' will remain. (Treasury Committee, 1996a, p. xxxv)[14]

While the Committee applauded attempts to change the culture of the Bank, they were sceptical about the likelihood of such a cultural change emerging, pointing to similar assurances in the past. Therefore, the Committee argued,

> The Bank needs to demonstrate that it is able to separate its supervisory activities from its other functions and avoid any possible weakening of is regulatory effectiveness due to its proximity to the day to day banking markets. Otherwise it may be that in order to bring about the necessary cultural change banking supervision will have to be taken away from the Bank of England. (Treasury Committee, 1996a, p. xxxvi)

The election of a Labour government in 1997 set the conditions for this in place. On 20 May 1997, the new finance minister, Gordon Brown, announced a major set of changes:

> In today's world of integrated global financial markets, the financial services industry transcends geographical and political boundaries and the regulatory response must meet this challenge. The United Kingdom financial services industry needs a regulator which can deliver the most effective supervision in the world...
>
> At the same time, it is clear that the distinctions between different types of financial institution – banks, securities firms and insurance companies – are becoming increasingly blurred. Many of today's financial institutions are regulated by a plethora of different supervisors. This increases the cost and reduces the effectiveness of the supervision.
>
> There is therefore a strong case in principle for bringing the regulation of banking, securities and insurance together under one roof. Firms now organise and manage their businesses on a group-wide basis. Regulators need to look at them in a consistent way. That would bring the regulatory structure closer into line with today's increasingly integrated financial markets. It would deliver more effective and efficient supervision, giving both firms and customers better value for money, and would improve the competitiveness of the sector and create a regulatory regime to genuinely meet the challenges of the 21st century. Responsibility for banking supervision will be transferred, as soon as possible ... from the Bank of England to a new and strengthened Securities and Investments Board, which will also, as a result of forthcoming legislation, take direct responsibility for the regulatory regime covered by the Financial Services Act. (*Hansard*, 20 May 1997, col. 510)

In October 1997, the Securities and Investments Board was renamed the Financial Services Authority (FSA) which, in June 1998, assumed the supervisory responsibilities of the Bank of England. By the time the various legislative arrangements are in place, the FSA will be the sole supervisory authority for all financial services in the UK and will ensure that regulatory inconsistencies can be removed. Although many of the personnel implementing the new regime also worked at the Bank of England, the Financial Services Authority represents a sharp break with the past. Until 1997, the orthodoxy in the UK was that the central bank was the only appropriate regulator of banks, as the governor of the Bank of England had argued in 1994:

> Monetary and financial stability are inter-related. It is inconceivable that the monetary authorities could quietly pursue their stability-oriented monetary policy objectives if the financial system through which policy is to be carried on – and which provides a link with the real economy – were collapsing around their ears. The liabilities of banks in particular are money, and you cannot be concerned with the value of money without being concerned also with preserving public confidence in money in this broader sense. Equally though, the financial system is much less likely to be collapsing around the ears of the monetary authorities in an environment of macroeconomic stability than in one of exaggerated boom and bust and volatile asset values. This inter-relationship means that, whatever the precise institutional arrangements for financial regulation and supervision, central banks necessarily have a vital interest in the soundness of the financial system. (George, 1994)

Furthermore, the chair and board of the FSA can be removed by the British finance minister, unlike the governor of the Bank who is appointed for a fixed term; the clubbish regulation that persisted until the collapse of Barings is being superseded by a much tighter rules-based framework; trust structures are being replaced by enforceable norms; and fragmented regulatory oversight is being replaced by a mechanism which, in theory at least, ensures a holistic, coordinated response to the transformation of the financial markets.

The Ambiguity of Assessment

In narrow terms, the handling of the crisis at Barings was a programmatic success. Despite a considerable shock, the financial system remained largely unperturbed: none of Barings' counterparties encountered significant problems and derivatives trading reached new records in terms both of the number of contracts traded and of the value of those contracts by the end of 1995. Furthermore, that the bank was allowed to fail can also be considered a policy success. Although banks occupy a particular place in capitalism which oils the credit creation process, when governments conclude that banks are too important to fail, 'moral hazard' arises. Moral hazard refers to a state where excessive risks are taken because the risk takers are comforted by the thought that any resulting failures will not penalize them. The collapse of Barings gave a very clear signal that inadequate managerial control structures would not be sufficient cause for the Bank of England to step in to rescue a bank, however noble its pedigree or blue-blooded its clients. In a sense, it signalled that the Bank of England was willing to use its lender of last resort powers very carefully.

Furthermore, the collapse of Barings was a political success for a British government which remained largely insulated from any fall-out. There are a number of explanations for this. In the popular imagination the cause of the collapse was simple: in the mass circulation tabloid newspapers the collapse of Barings was presented as somehow being due to the failings of one individual rather than as being the result of systemic problems, while even more substantial treatments also tended to emphasize the failings of Leeson as an individual, probably in order to maintain the narrative account (Rawnsley, 1995; Fay, 1996; although see Leeson, 1996). More profoundly, although financial markets are intensely political, there is a bipartisan and depoliticized approach to the City in British politics. Financial capital occupies a privileged position in Britain and even before Tony Blair transformed it into 'New Labour', the Labour Party never seriously attempted to grapple with its power.

However, if our understanding of the policy framework is widened to that of a neoliberal approach to financial supervision, the collapse of Barings highlighted considerable problems in the regulatory approach. In contrast to classical economic theory, which underpins the liberal view, the collapse of Barings demonstrates that financial markets are *not* always efficient allocators of resources, but are vulnerable to a herd mentality and volatility (Thaler, 1993; Summers, 1986). In privileging non-state authority, the policy community has internalized an (accurate) assessment of the difficulties of reining in the markets and their belief in the desirability and rationality of efficient markets, and concluded that strong regulation is impossible. This was, in the terminology of Barry Turner, very much a 'man-made disaster' (Turner and Pidgeon, 1997). Yet the collapse of Barings and, more recently, the Asian financial crisis have truly shaken the mantra of liberal economists and it may be that the liberalization trends under way since the 1970s will turn out to be a historical curiosity (see Tickell, 1999).

7   ANALYTICAL QUESTIONS AND CONCLUSIONS

The collapse of Barings Bank was a seminal moment in the history of the British financial sector. Symbolically, it signalled that hitherto protected and privileged institutions are no longer able to operate as if the Bank of England will always be there to rescue them, while in more concrete terms it highlighted the ineffectiveness of a regulatory approach where the Bank of England's assessment of the integrity of a bank still relied heavily – if implicitly – upon outmoded notions of respectability forged during a different era. More fundamentally, the Barings crisis exposed the flaws in a regulatory system which treated the different elements of the financial system as discrete and essentially unconnected. Barings was a merchant bank, supervised by the Bank of England. Its nemesis arose in its trading of securities (which were regulated by a different authority) in Singapore, which was, of course, a separate regulatory jurisdiction. Although the Bank of England had primary regulatory responsibility in both the UK and, as the home country authority, globally, the complexity of the arrangements contributed to shortcomings arising from the informal regulation adopted by the Bank of England and enshrined in the regulatory structure set up by the Conservatives.

Furthermore, the collapse highlighted the fact that the established order is giving way to a new one in which financial rather than establishment power is the bottom line. In the months following the collapse of the bank, corporate customers began to move their assets away from British merchant banks to the clearing banks or to merchant banks which are part of larger groups. In concord with consolidation in the financial sector more generally, the collapse of Barings precipitated the decline of British financial institutions, even as central players in the City. Barings was just the first of four established British financial institutions to be taken over in 1995 by richer overseas companies.

Furthermore, as the international financial system has become more fully integrated, geography has assumed a different role. Financial institutions operate globally; product innovations in one place are soon copied elsewhere; and perturbations are rapidly transmitted throughout the system. Regulators are struggling, and in some respects unmotivated, to catch up. In the absence of an effective international regulatory authority, the Bank of England may appear powerless to control the activities of British banks, yet it is not the simple victim of a global financial system which has appeared from nowhere. Not only have the British authorities been among the most ardent advocates of untrammelled financial globalization, they also retain significant formal and informal sanctions.

In many respects the collapse of Barings was a 'non-event'. Although the bank was brought down by trading complex financial instruments, it was rescued a week later by one of Europe's largest financial institutions, the markets remained calm and there was no financial meltdown. Perhaps, as the governor of the Bank of England claimed at the time, the collapse of Barings really *was* unique to Barings. In this chapter it has been argued that this is not the case. The events that led to the collapse were specific, but by no means unique. The bank's profits relied upon trading in risky derivative instruments which have the capacity to become rapidly devalued. Furthermore, the attitude of the British regulatory authorities and, on the evidence that emerged after the collapse of Barings, bank managements towards derivatives instruments has been complacent.

Yet the Barings crisis also played a role in stimulating a fundamental rethinking of these regulatory approaches. Within the UK, the emergent regulatory system will incrementally but absolutely shift the balance between the City and the national state and the evisceration of the Bank of England undercuts the power of the City's representative in the state. However, this shift should not be overstated: the City of London remains above and beyond politics.

As one of the most dynamic elements of the British economy, it is highly unlikely that any government will consciously attempt to wrest real power from the financial sector. Nor should the differences in international approaches to derivative regulation be overplayed. As long as regulators insist on information and disclosure as being the building blocks of a new financial architecture, as they are, they remain bound by a market logic which cannot iron out the vicissitudes of market fluctuations. Yet perhaps we ask too much of our regulators, as the governor of the Bank of England argued before losing responsibility for supervision: 'I cannot sensibly give you an assurance that we will always pick up everything and I do not think it is realistic to expect that any system, rules-based or judgemental-based, will ever put you in that situation' (cited in Treasury Committee, 1996b, p. 156).

NOTES

1. I would like to thank Andreas Busch, Bent Tranøy, Hans Schenk and Paul 't Hart for comments on an earlier draft of this chapter and to acknowledge the support of ESRC for the Research Fellowship, 'Regulating finance: the political geography of financial services'. Any errors and omissions remain, of course, my own.
2. These include the 1979 and 1987 Bank Acts and the 1986 Financial Services Act.
3. Peter Baring, in L. Yoke Har, 'Chief talks of "major fraud"', *The Guardian*, 27 February 1995, p. 10; R. Lambert and J. Gapper, 'A low-risk business until "the fraud" says Barings chair', *Financial Times*, 28 February 1995, p. 2.
4. S. Vines, 'Leeson created bogus clients to hoodwink bank', *The Independent*, 1 March 1995, p. 2.
5. Cited in N. Tait, 'Failure is blamed on management in London', *Financial Times*, 6 March 1995, p. 2; P. Springett, 'Leeson warning "issued three years ago"', *The Guardian*, 6 March 1995, p. 12.
6. Quoted in N. Denton, 'The dangers were seen, but little was done', *Financial Times*, 3 March 1995, p. 2.
7. On that occasion, the Bank of England and City financial institutions bought Johnson Matthey Bank and met its debts. After the rescue, it emerged that fraud may have been involved in Johnson Matthey Bank's problems and that the 'lifeboating' institutions paid more money than the Bank of England but retained little control. The Johnson Matthey Bank affair led to fundamental questions about the role of the Bank of England and led to the creation of the Board of Banking Supervision.
8. Hansard, 1995, *Parliamentary debates*, 255, 60, c693–4; emphasis added.
9. Channel 4 News, 27 February 1995.
10. Although these data are very high, once counter-trades are netted off against each other the risk represented can probably be reduced to approximately 2 per cent of the total.
11. In J. Plender, 'The box that can never shut', *Financial Times*, 28 February 1995, p. 19.
12. The Barings collapse also had wide-reaching ramifications for international regulatory cooperation (Tickell, 1999).
13. Quoted in P. Martin, 'Labour keeps up attack on role of board', *Financial Times*, 7 March 1995, p. 22.
14. Such scepticism arose from the failures of the Bank of England to transform itself after the BCCI fraud case (on which see Kochan and Whittington, 1991).

Bibliography to part IV

Aggell, Jonas and Lermart Berg (1996), 'Does Financial Deregulation Cause a Consumption Boom?', *Scandinavian Journal of Economics*, 98 (4), 579–601.

Alsheimer, Constantin (1997), 'Die Entwicklung des Kreditwesengesetzes', *Die Bank*, 1, 27–31.

Amin, A. and N.J. Thrift (1992), 'Neo-marshallian nodes in global networks', *International Journal of Urban and Regional Research*, 16, 571–87.

Arthur Andersen (1996), *Supervision and Surveillance*, Report to the Bank of England.

Andrew, Jack (1998), 'Rescue plan for Lyonnais', *The Banker*, 148, 25–6.

Andvig, Jens. C. (1991), *Kredittkassen og Knut Wicksell*, Unpublished manuscript, Oslo: Norwegian Institute of Foreign Affairs.

Anonymous (1996), 'Taxpayers may foot $19bn Crédit Lyonnais', *The Banker*, 146. p. 848.

Anonymous (1997), 'The lesson of Crédit Lyonnais', *Economist* 344, 5 July, pp. 69–71.

Bäckström, Urban (1998), 'Finansiella kriser: Svenska erfarenheter', *Ekonomisk Debatt*, 26 (1), 5–19.

Bank of England (1996), 'The Barings collapse and its consequences', *Banking Act Report 1995/6*, 6–13.

Bank of England (1997a), Banks' Internal Control and the Section 39 Process, Bank of England, Consultative Paper, February.

Bank of England (1997b), 'The Bank's review of supervision', *Banking Act Report 1996/7*, 6–13.

Bankkriskommittén (1994), *Bankkrisen*, Stockholm: Fritzes.

Bankkriskommittén (1995), *Bankerna under Krisen: Fyra Rapporter till Bankkriskommittén*, Stockholm: Fritzes.

Barth, James R., Daniel E. Nolle and Tara N. Rice (1997), *Commercial Banking Structure, Regulation and Performance: An International Comparison*, Economics Working Papers, vol. 97–6, Washington DC: Office of the Comptroller of the Currency.

Batenburg, A. (1984), 'Bankieren op de golven van de conjunctuur', in J.H. Koning, G.P.L van Roij and J.J. Sijben (eds), *Zicht op Bancaire en Monetaire Wereld*, Leiden: Stenfert Kroese, pp. 27–45.

BBS (Board of Banking Supervision) (1995), *Report of the Board of Banking Supervision Inquiry into the Circumstances of the Collapse of Barings*, London: HMSO.

Becker, Jürgen (1998), 'Banking Supervision: Who is Doing What?', in Stephen F. Frowen and Robert Pringle (eds), *Inside the Bundesbank*, London, UK: Macmillan, pp. 56–67.

Berglöf, Erik and Hans Sjögren (1995),'Husbankrelationen i onivandling – forbindelsema mellan affärsbanker och storföretag i svenskt näringsliv 1985–1993', in *Bankerna under Krisen: Fyra Rapporter till Bankkriskommittén*, Stockholm: Fritzes.

Bergström, Hans (1991), 'Devalveringens politiska tillkomst', in L. Jonung (ed.), *Devalveringen 1982: Rivstart eller Snedtänding?*, Stockholm: SNS Förlag.

BIS (Bank for International Settlements) (1999), *International Banking and Financial Market Developments: March 1999*, Basle: Bank for International Settlements.

Bolsa de Madrid (1998), *Informe del Mercado 1998*, Madrid: Bolsa de Madrid.

Bovens, Mark and Paul 't Hart (1996), *Understanding Policy Fiascoes*, New Brunswick: Transaction Publishers.

Bovens, Mark, Paul 't Hart, and B. Guy Peters (1998), 'Explaining policy disasters in Europe: comparisons and reflections', in Pat Gray and Paul 't Hart (eds), *Public Policy Disasters in Western Europe*, New York: Routledge, pp. 195–213.

Boyd, John H., Chun Chang and Bruce D. Smith (1998), 'Moral hazard under commercial and universal banking', *Journal of Money, Credit and Banking*, 30(3), 426–68.

Boyer, R. (1999), 'Le politique à l'ère de la mondialisation et de la finance: Le point sur quelques recherches régulationnistes', in *L'Année de la Régulation*, Volume 3, Paris: La Découverte, pp. 13–77.

Brankin, Grainne (1995), 'Statement on Crédit Lyonnais', *Financial Regulation Report*, October, 24–5.

Brink, J.R.M van den (1989), 'De NBV en de organisatie van het economische leven: Terugblik', in J.J.M. Schipper, R.J. Schotsman and C.A.M. Wijnvliet (eds), *Veertig Jaar Nederlandse Bankiersvereniging 1949–1989*, Amsterdam: NIBE, pp. 30–35.

Canals, Jordi (1997), *Universal Banking: International Comparisons and Theoretical Perspectives*, Oxford: Clarendon.

Caprio, Jr., Gerard and Daniela Klingebiel (1996), *Bank Insolvencies: Cross-Country Experience*, vol. 1620 of Policy Research Working Papers, Washington, DC: World Bank.

Cawson, A. (1985), 'Varieties of corporatism: the importance of the meso-level of interest intermediation', *Organised Interests and the State: Studies in Meso-Corporatism*, London: Sage, pp. 1–21.

Cecco, M. de (ed.) (1987), *Changing Money: Financial Innovation in Developed Countries*, Oxford: Basil Blackwell.

Cerny, P.G. (1991), 'The limits of deregulation: Transnational interpenetration and policy change', *European Journal of Political Research*, 19, 173–96.

Clark, G.L. and J. O'Connor (1997), 'The informational content of financial products and the spatial structure of the global finance industry', in K. Cox (ed.), *Spaces of Globalisation*, New York: Guilford.

Clark, M. (1986), *Regulating the City: Competition, Scandal and Reform*, Milton Keynes: Open University Press.

Coakley, J. and L. Harris (1983), *The City of Capital: London's Role as a Financial Centre*, Oxford: Blackwell.

Coleman, William D. (1993), 'Reforming Corporatism: The French Banking Policy Community, 1941–1990', *West European Politics* 16, 122–43.

Coleman, William D. (1996), *Financial Services: Globalization and Domestic Policy Change: A Comparison of North America and the European Union*, Basingstoke: Macmillan.

Coleman, William D. and Geoffrey Underhill (1998), 'Globalization, Regionalism and the regulation of securities markets', in W.D. Coleman and G. Underhill (eds), *Regionalism and Global Economic Integration: Europe, Asia and the Americas*, London: Routledge, pp. 223–48.

Coljé, H. (1988), *Het Toezicht op de Banken in Nederland*, Amsterdam: NIBE.

Coopers & Lybrand (1997), *The strategic impact of the Euro – a survey of European retail banks*, Amsterdam.

Cox, Andrew (1986), 'The state, finance and industry relationship in comparative perspective', in Andrew Cox (ed.), *State, Finance and Industry: A Comparative Analysis of Post-War Trends in Six Advanced Industrial Economies*, Brighton: Wheatsheaf Harvester, pp. 1–59.

Cuervo, Alvaro (1980), 'Análisis económico-financiero de la empresa española', *Papeles de Economiá Española*, 3 pp. 150–61.

Dale, Richard (1992), 'Regulation of International Banking', in Peter Newman, Murray Milgate and John Eatwell, (eds), *The New Palgrave Dictionary of Money & Finance*, London, UK: Macmillan, pp. 320–23.

De Nederlandsche Bank, *Annual Report* 1982, Amsterdam.

De Nederlandsche Bank, *Quarterly 1982*, Amsterdam.

De Nederlandsche Bank, *Annual Report 1987*, Amsterdam.

De Quillac, Leslie (1995), 'A family affair', *The Banker*, 145, 22–3.

Dernirgüç-Kunt, Asli and Enrica Detragiache (1998), 'The determinants of banking crises in developing and developed countries', *IMF Staff Papers*, 45(1), 81–109.

Dennis, Bengt (1998), *500%*, Stockholm: Bokförlaget DN.

Deutsche Bundesbank (1976), 'Die Sofortnovelle zum Kreditwesengesetz', *Monatsberichte der Deutschen Bundesbank*, 28 (7), 18–23.

Deutsche Bundesbank (1985), 'Die Novellierung des Kreditwesengesetzes', *Monatsberichte der Deutschen Bundesbank*, 37 (3), 37–43.

Deutsche Bundesbank (ed.) (1988), *40 Jahre Deutsche Mark: Monetäre Statistiken 1948–1987*, Frankfurt am Main: Fritz Knapp.

Deutsche Bundesbank (1992), 'Die Einlagensicherung in der Bundesrepublik Deutschland', *Monatsberichte der Deutschen Bundesbank*, 44 (7), 30–38.

Deutsche Bundesbank (1999), *Bankenstatistik: Statistisches Beiheft zum Monatsbericht 1*, Frankfurt am Main: Deutsche Bundesbank.

Dokument no. 17. (1997–8), *Rapport til Stortinget fra Kommisjonen som ble Nedsatt av Stortinget for å Gjennomgå ulike Årsaksforhold Knyttet til Bankkrisen*, Oslo: Stortinget.

Dziobek, Claudia and Ceyla Pazarbaşioğlu (1998), 'Lessons from Systemic Bank Restructuring', in *Economic Issues*, vol. 14, Washington, DC: International Monetary Fund.

Eckstein, Wolfgang (1980), 'The Role of the Banks in Corporate Concentration in West Germany', *Zeitschrift für die gesamte Staatswissenschaft*, 136 (3), 465–82.

Edey, Malcom and Hviding, Ketil (1995), *An Assessment of Financial Reform in OECD Countries*, vol. 154 of OECD Economics Department Working Papers, Paris: OECD.

Eerden, L. van and C. Graafsma (1998), 'Een zoektocht naar nieuwe financiële verhoudingen', in B. van Riel, L. van Eerden, S. Stoop and C. van Diek (eds.), *Het Kapitalisme Sinds de Jaren '70*, Tilburg: Tilburg University Press, pp. 157–79.

Eichengreen, B. (1996), *Globalizing Capital: A History of the International Monetary System*, Princeton: Princeton University Press.

Eika, Kari H. and Ragnar Nymoen (1992), 'Finansiell konsolidering som en konjunkturfaktor', *Penger og kreditt*, 20 (1), 29–38.

Engwall, Lars (1997), 'The Swedish Bank Crisis: The Invisible Hand Shaking the Visible Hand', in G. Morgan and D. Knights (eds), *Regulation and Deregulation in European Financial Services*, London: Macmillan.

Ewijk, C. van and L.J.R. Scholtens (1999), *Geld, Financiële Markten en Financiële Instellingen*, Groningen: Wolters-Noordhoff.

Fay, S. (1996), *The Collapse of Barings*, London: Richard Cohen Books.

Federal Deposit Insurance Corporation (1997), *History of the Eighties: Lessons for the Future*, 2 vols, Washington, DC: Federal Deposit Insurance Corporation.

Fischer, Reinfrid (1997a), 'Das Recht der Bankenaufsicht', in Herbert Schimansky, Hermann-Josef Bunte and Hans-Jürgen Lwowski (eds), *Bankrechts-Handbuch*, München: Beck, pp. 3715–24.

Fischer, Reinfrid (1997b), 'Die Aufsichtsbehörden und ihre Instrumente', in Herbert Schimansky, Hermann-Josef Bunte and Hans-JürgeLwowski (eds), *Bankrechts-Handbuch*, München: Beck, pp. 3725—32.

Fitchett, Joseph (1996), 'The Crédit Lyonnais Debacle', *International Herald Tribune*, 13 October, p. 13.

Forssell, Anders and David Jansson (1996), 'The Logic of Organizational Transformation: On the Conversion of Non-Business Organizations', in Barbara Czarniawska and Guje Sevón (eds), *Translating Organizational Change*, New York: Walter de Gruyter.

Franke, Günter (1998), 'Notenbank und Finanzmärkte', in Deutsche Bundesbank (ed.), *Fünfzig Jahre Deutsche Mark: Notenbank und Währung in Deutschlandseit seit 1948*, Munich: Beck, pp. 257–306.

Freitag, Markus (1999), 'Globalisierung und Währung: Politisch-institutionelle Grundlagen unterschiedlicher Wechselkursentwicklungen in integrierten Finanzmärkten', in Andreas Busch and Thomas Plümper (eds), *Nationaler Staat und Internationale Wirtschaft: Anmerkungen zum Thema Globalisierung*, Baden-Baden: Nomos, pp. 143–66.

Frieden, Jeffry A. and Ronald Rogowski (1996), 'The impact of the international economy on national policies: An analytic overview', in Robert O. Keohane and Helen Milner (eds), *Internationalization and Domestic Politics*, New York: Cambridge University Press, pp. 25–47.

Fuentes Quintana, Enrique (1991), 'Prólogo', in Rafael Termes (ed.), *Desde la Banca v.1*, Madrid: Rialp, pp. ii–xcvii.

Gapper, J. and N. Denton (1996), *All that Glitters: The Fall of Barings*, London: Hamish Hamilton.

Gardener, E.P.M. (1992), 'Banking supervision', in Peter Newman, Murray Milgate and John Eatwell (eds), *The New Palgrave Dictionary of Money & Finance*, London: Macmillan, pp. 156–8.

General Accounting Office (1994), *Bank Regulatory Structure: The Federal Republic of Germany*, Washington D.C.: U.S. General Accounting Office. [GAO/GGD-94–134BR].

George, E. (1994), 'The Bank of England – objectives and activities', speech presented to Capital Markets Research Institute, Frankfurt University, 5 December.

Goodhart, Charles, Philipp Hartmann, David Llewellyn, Liliana Rojas-Suárez and Steven Weisbrod (1998), *Financial Regulation. Why, How and Where Now?*, London/New York: Routledge.

Gowland, D. (1990), *The Regulation of Financial Markets in the 1990s*, Aldershot, UK and Brookfield, US: Edward Elgar.

Grant, W. and J. Sargent (1987), *Business and politics in Britain*, Basingstoke: Macmillan.

Haas, Peter M. (1992), 'Introduction: epistemic communities and international policy coordination', *International Organization*, 46(1), 1–35.

Hall, M. (1987), 'UK banking supervision and the Johnson Mathey affair', in Charles Goodhart, David Currie and David T. Llewellyn (eds), *The Operation and Regulation of Financial Markets*, Basingstoke: Macmillan.

Hamilton, A. (1986), *The Financial Revolution*, Harmondsworth: Penguin.

Hancher, L. and M. Moran (1989), 'Organizing regulatory space', in L. Hancher and M. Moran (eds), *Capitalism, Culture and Economic Regulation*, Oxford: Clarendon, pp. 271–99.

Helleiner, Eric (1994), *States and the Reemergence of Global Finance: From Bretton Woods to the 1990s*, Ithaca, NY: Cornell University Press.

Helleiner, E. (1996), 'Post-globalisation: is the financial liberalisation trend likely to be reversed?', in R. Boyer and D. Drache (eds), *States Against Markets*, London: Routledge, pp. 193–210.

Herring, Richard J. and Robert E. Litan (1995), *Financial Regulation in the Global Economy*, Washington, DC: The Brookings Institution.

Hutton, W. (1995), *The State We're In*, London: Jonathan Cape.

Jennergren, Peter and Bertil Näslund (1998), 'Efter bankkrisen: Vad blev notan för skattebetalarna?', *Ekonomisk Debatt*, 26 (1), 69–76.

Jessop, B. (1990), *State Theory: Putting Capitalist States in their Place*, Cambridge: Polity Press.

Jonung, Lars (1993), 'Riksbankens politik 1945–1990', in L. Werin (ed.) *Från Räntereglering til Inflationsnorm*, Stockholm: SNS.

Josselin, Dapline (1997), *Money Politics in the New Europe: Britain, France and the Single Financial Market*, Basingstoke: Macmillan.

Kapstein, Ethan B. (1994), *Governing the Global Economy: International Finance and the State*, Cambridge MA, London: Harvard University Press.

Kareken, John H. (1992), 'Regulation of commercial banking in the United States', in Peter Newman, Murray Milgate and John Eatwell (eds), *The New Palgrave Dictionary of Money & Finance*, London, pp. 315–20.

Keman, H., J. Woldendorp and D. Braun (1985), *Het Neo-Korporatisme als Nieuwe Politieke Strategie: Krisisbeheersing met Beleid en (door) Overleg?*, Amsterdam: CT Press.

Klein, Dietmar K.R. (1991), *Die Bankensysteme der EG-Länder*, vol. 99 of Taschenbücher für Geld Bank, Börse, Frankfurt am Main: Knapp.

Knapp, Joachim (1976), 'Die Novelle zum Kreditwesengesetz', *Neue Juristische Wochenschrift*, 29 (20), 873–7.

Knoester, A. (1989), *Economische Politiek in Nederland*, Leiden: Stenfert Kroese.

Kochan, N. and B. Whittington (1991), *Bankrupt: The BCCI Fraud*, London: Gollancz.

Krasner, Stephen, D. (1984), 'Approaches to the State: Alternative Conceptions and Historical Dynamics', *Comparative Politics*, 16 (2), 223–46.

Kynaston, D. (1994), *The City of London: A World of its Own*, London: Pimlico.

Kynaston, D. (1995), *The Bank and the Government*, in R. Roberts and D. Kynaston (eds), *The Bank of England: Money, Power and Influence*, Oxford: Oxford University Press, pp. 19–55.

Kynaston, D. (1997), *Liffe: A Market and its Makers*, London: Granta Books.

Landesbank Rheinland-Pfalz (ed.) (1983), *Banken: Erfahrungen und Lehren aus einem Vierteljahrhundert 1958–1983*, Frankfurt am Main: Knapp.

Larsson, Mats and Hans Sjögren (1995), V*ägen til och från Bankkrisen*, Stockhom: Carlssons.

Lee, R. and U. Schmidt-Marwede (1993), 'Interurban competition? Financial centres and the geography of financial production', *International Journal of Urban and Regional Research*, 17, 492–515.

Leeson, N. (1996), *Rogue trader*, London: Little, Brown.

Leeuw, J. de (1996), *Financiële Conglomeraten in Nederland*, Amsterdam: NIBE.

Lehner, Franz, Klaus Schubert and Brigitte Geile (1983), 'Die strukturelle Rationalität regulativer Wirtschaftspolitik: Theoretische Überlegungen am Beispiel der Bankenpolitik in Kanada, der Bundesrepublik Deutschland, der Schweiz und den Vereinigten Staaten von Amerika'. *Politische Vierteljahresschrift*, 24 (4), 361–84.

Leyshon, A. (1992), 'The transformation of regulatory order: regulating the global economy and environment', *Geoforum*, 23, 249–67.

Leyshon, A. and N.J. Thrift (1997), *Money, Space*, Oxford: Blackwell.

Leyshon, A. and A. Tickell (1994), 'Money order? The discursive constitution of Bretton Woods and the making and breaking of regulatory space', *Environment and Planning A*, 26, 1861–90.

Lindbeck, Assar (1997), 'The Swedish Experiment', *Journal of Economic Literature*, 35, 1273–1319.

Lindgren, Carl-Johan, Gillian Garcia, and Matthew I. Saal (1996), *Bank Soundness and Macroeconomic Policy*, Washington D.C.: International Monetary Fund.

Lindgren, Håkan (1994), 'At lära av historien. Några erfarenheter av finanskrisen', in Bankkriskommittén, *Bankkrisen*, Stockholm: Fritzes.

Llewellyn, D.T., C. Goodhart and D. Currie (eds) (1987) *The Operation and Regulation of Financial Markets*, Basingstoke: Macmillan.

Llewellyn, D.T. (1992), 'Competition, diversification and structural change in the British financial system', in George G. Kaufman (ed.), *Banking Structures in Major Countries*, Dordrecht: Kluwer Academic Publishers, pp. 429–68.

Longstreth, F. (1979), 'The City, industry and the state', in E.C. Crouch (ed.), *State and Economy in Contemporary Capitalism*, London: Croom Helm, pp. 157–90.

Loriaux, Michael (1991), *France After Hegemony: International Change and Financial Reform*, Ithaca, NY: Cornell University Press.

Lütz, Susanne (1999), 'Globalisierung und der regulative Umbau des "Modell Deutschland" das Beispiel der Bankenregulierung', in Hans-Georg Brose and Helmut Voelzkow (eds), *Institutionelles Kontext wirtschaftlichen Handelns und Globalisierung*, Marburg: Metropolis.

Lybeck, Johan A. (1992), *Finasiella Kriser förr och nu*, Stockholm: SNS Förlag.

McClintick, David (1996), 'The Predator', *Fortune*, 135, 8 July, pp. 129–37, 165–77.

McClintick, David (1997), 'The Bank Scandal that Keeps Growing', *Fortune*, 136, 7 July, pp. 36–8.

Maroto, Juan Antonio (1990), 'La situación empresarial en España (1982–1989)', *Cuadernos de Información (FIES)*, 44/45, 1–17.

Martin, R. (1994), 'Stateless monies, global financial integration and national economic autonomy: the end of geography?', in S. Corbridge, N.J. Thrift and R. Martin, *Money, Power and Space*, Oxford: Blackwell, pp. 253–78.

Michie, R.C. (1992), *The City of London: Continuity and Change 1850–1990*, Basingstoke: Macmillan.

Ministry of Finance (1995), *Baring Futures (Singapore) Pte Ltd: The Report of the Inspectors Appointed by the Minister of Finance*, Singapore: Ministry of Finance.

Mjøset, Lars (1987), 'Nordic economic policies in the 1970s and 1980s', *International Organization*, 41 (3), pp. 403–56.

Moran, Michael (1986), *The Politics of Banking*, 2nd edn, London: Macmillan.

Moran, M. (1991), *The Politics of the Financial Services Revolution*, Basingstoke: Macmillan.

Newman, Peter, Murray Milgate,and John Eatwell, (eds) (1992), *The New Palgrave Dictionary of Money & Finance*, London, UK: Macmillan.

Niethammer, Thomas (1990), *Die Ziele der Bankenaufsicht in der Bundesrepublik Deutschland: Das Verhältnis zwischen 'Gläubigerschutz' und 'Sicherung der Funktionsfähigkeit des Kreditwesens'*, Berlin: Duncker & Humblot.

Norton, J. (1991), 'The EC banking directives and international banking regulation', in R. Cranston (ed.), *The Single Market and the Law of Banking*, London: Lloyds of London Press, pp. 151–72.

O'Brien, R. (1992), *Global Financial Integration: the End of Geography*, London: Pinter.

OECD (1992), *Banks Under Stress*, Paris: Organization for Economic Cooperation and Development.

Olsen, Johan P. (1992), *Analyzing Institutional Dynamics*, Norwegian Research Centre in Organization and Management, Bergen, working paper 92/14.

Parsons, J.E. (1988), 'Bubble, bubble, how much trouble? Financial markets, capitalist development and capitalist crises', *Science and Society*, 52, 260–89.

Pecchioli, Rinaldo M. (1989), *Bankenaufsicht in den OECD-Ländern: Entwicklungen und Probleme*, Baden-Baden: Nomos.

Peck, J.A. and A. Tickell (1994), 'Jungle law breaks out: Neoliberalism and global–local disorder', *Area*, 26 (4), 317–26.

Pérez, Sofía A. (1997), *Banking on Privilege: The Politics of Spanish Financial Reform*, Ithaca, NY: Cornell University Press.

Pérez, Sofía A. (1998), 'Systemic Explanations, Divergent Outcomes: The Politics of Financial Reform in France and Spain', *International Studies Quarterly*, 42 (4), 755–84

Petterson, Karl-Henrik (1993), *Bankkrisen Inifrån*, Stockholm: SNS Förlag.

Pozdena, Randall Johnston und Alexander, Volbert (1992), 'Bank Structure in West Germany' in George G. Kaufman (ed.), *Banking Structures in Major Countries*, Dordrecht: Kluwer Academic Publishers, pp. 555–90.

Pressnell, L.S. (1968), 'Gold reserves, banking reserves and the Barings crisis of 1890', in C.R. Whittlesey and J.S.G. Wilson (eds), *Essays in Money and Banking: In Honour of R.S. Sayers*, Oxford: Clarendon, pp. 167–228.

Pryke, M. (1991), 'An international City going global', *Environment and Planning D: Society and Space*, 95, 197–222.

Quinn, Dennis (1997), The correlates of change in international financial regulation', *American Political Science Review*, 91(3), 531–51.

Rawnsley, J. (1995), *Going for Broke: Nick Leeson and the Collapse of Barings Bank*, London: Harper Collins.

Reinicke, Wolfgang (1998), *Global Public Policy: Governing Without Government?*, Washington, DC: The Brookings Institution.

Richardson, Jeremy (ed.) (1982), *Policy Styles in Western Europe*, Boston: Allen and Unwin.

Rijnvos, J. (1987), 'Het structuurbeleid met betrekking tot de verhouding van bank- en verzekeringswezen in Nederland', in H.W.J. Bosman and J.C. Brezet (eds), *Sparen en Investeren: Geld en Banken*, Leiden: Stenfert Kroese, pp. 64–83.

Rivera, Olga, Francisco José Olarte and Mikel Navarro (1993), 'La situación económica-financiera de la empresa española frente a la comunitaria: Un análisis comparado a partir del proyecto BACH', *Economía Industrial*, 293, 59–77.

Roberts, R. (1995), 'The Bank of England and the City', in R. Roberts and D. Kynaston (eds), *The Bank of England: Money, Power and Influence*, Oxford: Oxford University Press, pp. 152–84.

Ronge, Volker (1979), *Bankpolitik im Spätkapitalismus: Politische Selbstverwaltung des Kapitals?*, Frankfurt/Main: Suhrkamp.

Rouban, Luc (1990), 'La modernisation de l'État et la fin de la spécificité française', *Revue Française de Science Politique*, 40 (4), 521–45.

Sauvé, Annie and Manfred Scheuer (eds) (1999), *Corporate Finance in Germany and France*. A Joint Research Project of the Deutsche Bundesbank and the Banque de France, Deutsche Bundesbank.

Schaper, H.N. and H. van der Zee (1992), *Bankrelaties Opnieuw Bezien: Gevolgen van Bakenfusies voor Nederlandse Bedrijven*, Amsterdam: Coopers and Lybrand.

Schimansky, Herbert, Hermann-Josef Bunte and Hans-Jürgen Lwowski (eds), (1997), *Bankrechts-Handbuch*, München: Beck.

Schippper, J.J.M. and C.A.M. Wijnvliet (1989), 'Nakaarten met dr. A. Batenburg, dr. J.R.M van den Brink, J.C. van Lanschot en mr. O.Vogelenzang', in J.J.M. Schipper, R.J. Schotsman and C.A.M. Wijnvliet (eds), *Veertig Jaar Nederlandse Bankiersvereniging 1949–1989*, Amsterdam: NIBE, pp. 106–15.

Schön, Donald A. and Martin Rein (1994), *Frame Reflection: Resolving Intractable Policy Disputes*, New York: Basic Books.

Schotsman, C.J. (1990), *De Postbank: Ontstaan en Ontplooiing*, Den Haag: SDU.

Simmons, Beth (1999), 'The internationalization of capital', in Herbert Kitschelt, Peter Lange, Gary Marks and John D. Stephens (eds), *Continuity and Change in Contemporary Capitalism*, Cambridge: Cambridge University Press, pp. 36–69.

Sjöberg, Gustaf (1994), 'Bank- och Finansinspektionens verksamhet 1980–1993' in Bankkriskommittén, *Bankkrisen*, Stockholm: Fritzes.

Söderström, Hans T. (1998), 'Bo Lundgren: När bubblan brast', *Ekonomisk Debatt*, 26 (8), 644–50.

Sozialdemokratische Partei Deutschlands (1976), *Framework of Economic and Political Orientation of the Social Democratic Party of Germany for the years 1975–1985*, Bonn-Bad Godesberg: Research Institute of the Friedrich-Ebert-Foundation, Translation by Diet Simon.

Statens Offentliga Utredningar (SOU) (1982), 52, *En Effektivare Kreditpolitikk*.

Statens Offentliga Utredningar (SOU) (1996), 158, *Sverige och EMU*.

Steinmo, Svein (1993), *Taxation and Democracy, Swedish, British and American Approaches to Financing the Modern State*, New Haven: Yale University Press.

Stern, Eric and Bengt Sundelius (1998), 'In Defence of the Swedish Crown: From Triumph to Tragedy and Back?', in P.D. Gray and P. 't Hart (eds), *Public Policy Disasters in Europe*, London: Routledge, pp. 135–51.

Story, Jonathan and Ingo Walter (1997), *Political Economy of Financial Integration in Europe: The Battle of the Systems*, Manchester: Manchester University Press.

Strange, S. (1986), *Casino Capitalism*, Oxford: Blackwell (reprinted 1999, Manchester University Press).

Studienkommission Grundsatzfragen der Kreditwirtschaft (1979) 'Bericht der Studienkommission 'Grundsatzfragen der Kreditwirtschaft'', *Schriftenreihe des Bundesministeriums der Finanzen*, in vol. 28, Bonn: Bundesministerium der Finanzen.

Suleiman, Ezra (1978), *Elites in French Society: The Politics of Survival*, Princeton: Princeton University Press.

Summers, L.H. (1986), 'Does the stock market rationally reflect fundamental values?', *The Journal of Finance*, 41 (4), 591–601.

Svensson, Torsten (1996), *Novemberrevolutionen: Om Rationalitet och Makt i Beslutet att Avreglera Kreditmarknaden i 1985*, Stockholm: Finansde-partementet.

Swyngedouw, E.A. (1996), 'Producing futures: international finance as a geographical project', in P. Daniels and B. Lever (eds), *The Global Economy in Transition*, Harlow: Longman, pp. 135–63.

Thaler, R.H. (1993), *Advances in Behavioral Finance*, New York: Russell Sage Foundation.

Thrift, N.J., S. Corbridge, R. Martin and N.J. Thrift (eds) (1994), 'On the social and cultural determinants of international financial centres: the case of the City of London', in *Money, Power and Space*, Oxford: Blackwell, pp. 327–55.

Tickell, A. (1999), 'Unstable futures: controlling and creating risks in international money', in L. Panitch and C. Leys (eds), *Global Capitalism Versus Democracy: Socialist Register 1999*, Rendleshem: The Merlin Press, pp. 248–77.

Tickell, A. and J.A. Peck (1995), 'Social regulation *after* Fordism: regulation theory, neo-liberalism and the global–local nexus', *Economy and Society*, 24 (3), 357–86.

Torrero, Antonio (1976), 'La evolución del sistema financiero', *Boletín de Estudios Económicos*, 30 (96), 855–87.

Tortella, Gabriel and Jordi Palafox (1984), 'Banking and Industry in Spain, 1918–1936', *Journal of European Economic History*, 13 (2), special issue, 81–111.

Touw, A.L. (1997), 'Ontwikkelingen in het bedrijfseconomisch toezicht op banken', in: *MAB*, 71 (12), pp. 624–34.

Tranøy, Bent Sofus (2000), *'Losing Credit': The Politics of Liberalisation and Macro-Economic Regime Change in Norway 1980–92*, PhD dissertation, University of Oslo.

Treasury Committee (1996a), *Barings Bank and International Regulation*, *minutes of evidence and appendices*, London: HMSO, HC65–1.

Treasury Committee (1996b), *Barings Bank and International Regulation: minutes of evidence and appendices*, London: HMSO, HC65–11.

Turner, B. and N.F. Pidgeon (1997), *Man-made Disasters*, 2nd edn, London: Butterworth Heinemann.

Tweede Kamer (1986),1985–1986, 19 200, IX B, no. 43.

Valdez, Stephen (1993), *An Introduction to Western Financial Markets*, Houndsmills Basingstoke: Macmillan.

Verkhovskoy, Pierre (1995), 'Controversy over rescue of Crédit Lyonnais', *Financial Regulation Report*, April, 10–12.

Visser, J. and A. Hemerijck (1998), *A Dutch Miracle*, Amsterdam: Amsterdam University Press.

Vlak, G.J.M. (1984), 'Structuurveranderingen in het Nederlandse bankwezen sinds 1960', in J.H. Koning, G.P.L van Roij and J.J. Sijben (eds.), *Zicht op Bancaire en Monetaire Wereld*, Leiden: Stenfert Kroese, pp. 97–117.

Vogel, Steven K. (1996), *Freer Markets, More Rules. Regulatory Reform in Advanced Industrial Countries*, Ithaca, NY: Cornell University Press.

Vries, J. de, W. Vroom and T. de Graaf (eds) (1999), *Wereldwijd Bankieren: ABN-AMRO 1824–1999*, Amsterdam: ABN-AMRO.

Wagner, Kurt (1976), *Stationen deutscher Bankgeschichte: 75 Jahre Banken-verband*, Köln: Bank-Verlag.

Wallander, Jan (1994), 'Bankkrisen: Ornfattning, Orsaker, Lärdomar', in Bankkriskommittén, *Bankkrisen*, Stockholm: Fritzes.

Warde, Ibrahim (1994), 'Financiers flamboyants, contribuables brûleś', *Le Monde Diplomatique*, juillet, 18–19.

Werin, Lars (1993), 'Instrumenten og marknadarna' in L. Werin (ed.), *Från Räntereglering til Inflationsnorm*, Stockholm: SNS.

Wihlborg, Clas (1993),'Valutapolitiken', in L. Werin (ed.), *Från Räntereglering til Inflationsnorm*, Stockholm: SNS.

Wijk, H.H. van (1988), *De Nederlandsche Bank: Functie en Werkterrein*, Amsterdam: NIBE.

Wijnvliet, C.A.M. (1989), 'De voorlopers, 1903–1949', in J.J.M. Schipper, R.J. Schotsman and C.A.M. Wijnvliet (eds), *Veertig Jaar Nederlandse Bankiers-vereniging 1949–1989*, Amsterdam: NIBE, pp. 15–30.

Wilson, G.K. (1984), 'Social regulation and explanations of regulatory failure', *Political Studies*, 32, 203–25.

Wohlin, Lars (1998), 'Bankkrisens upprinnelse', *Ekonomisk Debatt*, 26 (1), 21–31.

Woolley, John T. (1985), 'Central Banks and Inflation', in Leon N. Lindberg and Charles S. Maier (eds), *The Politics of Inflation and Economic*

Stagnation: Theoretical Approaches and International Case Studies, Washington, DC: The Brookings Institution, pp. 318–48.

Wriston, W. (1988), 'Technology and sovereignty', *Foreign Affairs*, 67 (1), pp. 63–75.

Zysman, John (1983), *Governments, Markets and Growth: Financial Systems and the Politics of Industrial Change*, Ithaca, NY: Comell University Press.

PART V

Managing crisis: HIV and the blood supply

24. Managing crisis: HIV and the blood supply

Erik Albæk

1 INTRODUCTION

When AIDS emerged in the early 1980s, it was a mystery.[1] In 1981, it was described as a syndrome, that is, a group of symptoms that together indicate a disease, but the precise character and causes were unknown. The first group to be affected was, oddly, hitherto healthy, young homosexual males, and the symptoms were equally odd: *Kaposi's sarcoma*, a rare skin cancer ordinarily only affecting elderly people or persons who had suffered long-term exposure to tropical sun, and *Pneumocystis carinii*, a pneumonia almost exclusively occurring in persons with severely suppressed or defective immune systems. The syndrome became no less mysterious when the group of symptoms as well as the group of patients expanded to include haemophiliacs, transfusion recipients, IV drug users, Haitians and Africans. Among the symptoms were swollen lymph glands, yeast infection and enormous weight loss, but the medical community and health authorities were unable to pinpoint a common denominator for patients and symptoms. At the same time, the explosive growth of new cases made it obvious that governments throughout the world faced a potential catastrophe of immense proportions, a major health crisis.

This section studies the public authorities' attempts to prevent HIV infection through the blood supply under the heading *crisis management*. When they realized that the entry of HIV into the blood supply constituted a potential health crisis, policy makers could not rely on known routines and standard operating procedures in their attempts to prevent further dissemination. Instead, the situation called for prompt action, fast adaptation and quick learning. At the same time, there was great uncertainty and minimal, confused or contradictory information. In other words, the health authorities faced the prototypical health crisis. Managing the threat of AIDS to the blood supply, however, did not present itself to policy makers in a self-evident manner. For instance, it took some time for relevant decision makers to realize that they were indeed facing a crisis. Until they did, their decisions were informed by well-established paradigms of blood safety, especially the one developed in response to hepatitis B (Marmor *et al.*, 1999; Shield, 1999). Even when the crisis was acknowledged, decision makers were confronted with ambiguous and inconclusive evidence and potential costs of both action and inaction. Furthermore, the entry of HIV into the blood supply was only a part – and, it seemed at the time, maybe only a very small part – of a much larger crisis: however catastrophic HIV in the blood supply might be, the major concern of the health authorities was the risk of AIDS spreading through sexual transmission in the heterosexual population.

Modern democratic governments increasingly find themselves in situations which call for crisis management. This is not necessarily because we live in more crises-prone times, but rather because more and more events today are construed and perceived as 'crises'. There are two reasons for this. First, with technological development and increased control over the environment, modern man has become still less fatalistic. Events, including sudden events, are no longer seen as the result of chance, fate or the will of gods. Instead, they are construed as problems which can be attacked and solved, especially by governments. Although people may not expect policy makers to solve all problems or prevent all crises 100 per cent effectively, today the burden of the argument seems to have shifted to policy makers: they must establish beyond doubt that they could not have solved a given problem or prevented a particular crisis, or they will be held responsible ('t Hart and Boin, 2001). Consequently, modern governance focuses increasingly on problems that may develop into crises – or rather, that can be construed as crises. No wonder a parallel increase can be observed in academic and professional literature prescribing crisis management.

Second, crises do not exist in any objective sense, only in the eyes of the beholder. With reduced fatalism it has increasingly become strategically advantageous for policy stakeholders – policy makers, political parties, bureaucratic agencies, scientists, interest groups – to present certain social conditions or clusters of events as 'crises', that is, as something in need of prompt public action. The very naming and framing of something as a crisis may generate an all-important political momentum for a specific issue definition or policy proposal. However, a cluster of events may also be constructed in retrospect as a crisis that was not discovered in time, not prevented to the extent possible or mismanaged. The greater the crisis mismanagement, in particular if mismanagement can be construed as a 'scandal', the greater the chances of delegitimizing and destabilizing the policy status quo. Thus the notion of crisis opens up windows of opportunity for policy reforms and political and institutional change. Such crisis management evaluations have become increasingly common in politics and therefore make crisis management an obvious object of analysis in the study of success and failure in modern governance (ibid.).

Transmission of HIV through blood and blood products was prevented very fast. Only three years passed from June 1981, when AIDS was first reported as an official clinical syndrome, before effective measures to prevent blood-borne transmission of this hitherto unknown disease were developed. One year later, most advanced industrial nations had implemented the two decisive preventive measures, testing of donor blood and heat treatment of blood-clotting products. It is difficult to think of another case where a mode of transmission of an infectious disease was stopped so effectively, so fast.

Even so, the fight against a disease has seldom aroused so much political controversy as did AIDS. In a number of industrialized democracies, the public authorities' preventive actions against AIDS turned into regular political scandals (Feldman and Bayer, 1999). In France, the blood scandal not only resulted in the first impeachment of ministers ever, including a former prime minister, but also in a change of the constitution. In Japan, the director of a pharmaceutical company was forced to go down on his knees and bow his head to the ground, one of the most humiliating gestures of apology in Japanese culture. In Denmark, the blood scandal had the most extensive and protracted judicial sequel in the country's political–administrative history. Similar scandals with parliamentary or judicial inquiries, litigations and total restructurings of the blood supply were observed elsewhere, while in other countries the political controversies were minor or non-existent.

How did an apparent medical success turn into such a phenomenal political failure? Could preventive measures have been introduced even earlier, had not political, bureaucratic, organizational or other illegitimate obstacles impeded the process? Or was the political evaluation of the way the HIV and blood crisis was handled by the health authorities guided by a separate logic unrelated to what in fact could have been known and done at relevant points in time? And why did the HIV and blood crisis become a failure only in some and not in other countries? These questions will be studied in this section.

The concept of programmatic success and failure in governance is used to study the capacities of the health authorities of the six governments to manage, with limited and highly uncertain information, the entry of a new, infectious and deadly disease into the blood supply. The concept of political success and failure is used to analyse the political evaluation of the authorities' programmatic crisis management. The object of this introduction to the crisis management part of this volume is threefold. The first is to describe the case, HIV and the blood supply. Knowledge of haemophilia and haemophilia therapy, transfusion medicine and HIV is essential to understanding the options that were available to the health authorities. Second, a number of indicators of programmatic, respectively political success and failure in managing the HIV and blood crisis are listed. Finally, possible explanations for variations across the six countries in their programmatic and political success and failure are presented.

2   HAEMOPHILIA AND HAEMOPHILIA THERAPY

Haemophilia is a hereditary bleeding disorder linked to the X-chromosome recessively. It is therefore transmitted from healthy mothers primarily to their sons, but a few women also have symptoms of haemophilia (known as von Willebrand disease). Haemophilia manifests itself in an extended coagulation period and abnormal bleeding tendency. There are two types of haemophilia caused by a deficiency of two separate blood-clotting proteins, called factors. Haemophilia A, which affects 85 per cent of haemophiliacs, is caused by a deficiency of factor VIII, and haemophilia B by a deficiency of factor IX. However, the symptoms of the two bleeding disorders are identical. Only a tiny fraction of the population suffers from haemophilia, around one per 15 000, and therefore very few families are affected by the disorder. On the other hand, many members of the same family may be affected simultaneously: brothers, uncles, cousins.

Haemophilia is divided into three categories according to severity. Patients with severe haemophilia (35 per cent of haemophiliacs) have less than 1 per cent of the clotting factor normally found in blood, patients with moderate haemophilia (15 per cent) between 1 and 4 per cent, and patients with mild haemophilia between 5 and 40 per cent.[2] Before the 1960s, when the first effective haemophilia therapy interventions became available, even negligible bruises might produce massive skin and muscular bleeding in patients with severe haemophilia. A tiny cut might lead to severe and unstoppable blood loss which sometimes went on for weeks, but often bleeding had no demonstrable external cause. The most typical symptom of haemophilia is joint bleeding which may initiate destruction of the joints and also considerable muscular atrophy if left untreated. Earlier, haemophilia patients frequently became disabled as a result of joint bleeding and had to use wheelchairs and crutches. Many died young. Patients with mild haemophilia usually do not suffer from severe spontaneous bleeding or from joint bleeding. They suffer blood loss primarily as a result of injuries or surgery. In the 1950s, the median life expectancy for haemophiliacs with severe haemophilia was estimated at 11–15 years. In 1980, it was close to the normal life expectancy in countries offering factor treatment.

Before the 1960s, one of the most effective therapies consisted in literally putting bleeding haemophiliacs on ice. The normal therapy for internal bleeding was immobility and encasing the limb in a plaster cast. Substitution therapy, that is supplying a haemophiliac with the deficient clotting factor, only existed in a very rudimentary form as whole blood transfusion, that is transfusion of blood as it exists in one person's body into another person's. However, the concentration of clotting factor in the blood of a single donor is not sufficient to make good a haemophiliacs' deficiency. Only when, in the 1960, it became possible to fractionate blood into its individual components and concentrate clotting factor from several donors did effective therapy become available. In the beginning, an unpleasant-looking yellow substance known as cryoprecipitate was to be administered intravenously, often over several days, and therapy required hospitalization. It was an ordeal, and many patients were small boys who had to be strapped to their hospital beds during therapy. Still, despite the burdensome process, the new therapy was a quantum leap into a bright new future for haemophiliacs.

In the 1970s, the manufacturing process allowed increasingly effective cleansing of factor products of other blood components, except clotting proteins. Around 1980, factor preparations were contained in small bottles to be kept in ordinary refrigerators and administered intravenously by haemophiliacs themselves whenever needed, or by parents of haemophiliacs under 10 to 12 years of age. Administration no longer required hospitalization and clotting factor concentrate could be brought along wherever haemophiliacs went, including skiing holidays. In a 10-year period, haemophiliacs had gone from no therapy, disablement and early death to effective self-administration of clotting factor and almost normal lives. They had reached what they felt was heaven on earth in no time.

3   TRANSFUSION MEDICINE AND BLOOD PRODUCTS

Although the first recorded attempt to transfuse blood was made as early as 1665, it was not until the identification in 1901 of the first blood group, the ABO group, that modern transfusion medicine began. This discovery solved the mystery why some, but not all, patients died from transfusion therapy: only if the patient received blood from a donor of the same blood group was a safe transfusion possible without the occurrence of clumping. Later, other blood groups were discovered, most notably the Rhesus system in the 1930s.

Transfusion techniques improved fast. By the 1960s, it had become possible to fractionate blood into its individual components. In traditional blood therapy, patients received whole blood with all its components even if they only needed one. In component therapy, blood drawings are fractionated into their individual components, and patients receive only the components they need. The remaining components are given to other patients. The blood components for which there is a special need in blood therapy are shown in Table 24.1.

Fractionation, in combination with a shift to plastic containers, also improved storage dramatically, in that the individual blood components tolerate varying storage techniques and periods. One storage technique was deep freezing of plasma. In 1964, it was discovered that slow thawing of plasma formed precipitate with increased clotting factor activity. By pooling plasma from several drawings, enough precipitate was produced to offer haemophiliacs the first effective substitution therapy. The product was named cryoprecipitate, in everyday parlance 'cryo', from the Greek word for freezing cold. From 1968, this method was used for commercial manufacture of clotting factor. Gradually, haemophilia therapy was improved by increasing the products' concentration of factor and by cleansing them of other blood components except factor. In the end, factor products were contained in a small bottle only a couple of centimetres tall. To produce a single batch of factor concentrate it was necessary to pool plasma from up to 20 000 units of blood. Thus patients with severe haemophilia would sometimes in one year be exposed to blood drawn from 100 000 different individuals. Needless to say, the costs of collecting, processing, testing and transporting blood and blood products were enormous. In the 1980s, experiments were made to produce genetically engineered recombinant clotting factor which are not based on human blood. In some countries, up to 98 per cent of the factor used in haemophilia therapy today is recombinant.

Table 24.1   Blood components: their bodily functions and medical uses

Component	Functions	Medical uses
Red blood cells	carry oxygen	to treat amnesia and replace blood loss during surgery
White blood cells	protect the body against infection	to fight bacteria and provide stem cells for transplantation
Blood platelets	help blood clot	to control bleeding caused by platelet deficiency
Plasma (the fluid portion of blood); contains the following components, among others:	carries proteins, salt and nutrients	
(a) albumin		(a) to neutralize shock
(b) immunoglobulin		(b) to fight infection
(c) antithrombin		(c) to neutralize thrombosis
(d) factor		(d) to help blood clot

Adequacy and safety of the blood supply have been major concerns throughout the history of modern transfusion medicine. Already during World War I, high standards of hygiene were recommended in transfusion practice to prevent the transmission of infection, and donor screening became the primary means to reduce the risk of blood-borne infections such as syphilis, malaria and hepatitis. Without techniques to test for the presence in blood of the causative organisms of these infections, efforts were made instead, to the extent possible, to select only healthy donors. The effectiveness of the screening procedures depended in large part on the honesty and truthfulness of the donor in reporting his health condition. Voluntary donation became the key to a safe blood supply: voluntary, non-remunerated donors who gave blood for altruistic reasons were regarded as more reliable than paid donors who had an economic incentive not to reveal their true health condition. As pointed out by Richard Titmuss in his famous study *The Gift Relationship* (1970), volunteer donation also carries fundamental meaning about social life and connectedness and allows donors to express social or national solidarity. Donor selection, however, could not secure a 100 per cent safe blood supply. Owing to long latency, for instance, donors may not be aware of their infection. Haemophiliacs were particularly exposed to transfusion-transmitted infection. They were treated with blood products derived from thousands of units of blood, and just one contaminated unit constituted a risk. In the end, almost all patients with severe haemophilia treated with factor contracted hepatitis. Although this may develop into a chronic condition, even haemophiliacs regarded it as an 'acceptable' and manageable risk in the early 1980s, compared to the alternative of limited mobility, crippling pain and early death.

Adequacy and safety concerns about the blood supply may clash if the demand for blood or blood products increase as it did in the 1970s. While transfusion services in developed countries were almost exclusively run on a non-profit basis, using voluntary, non-paid donors, manufacture of blood products was to a large extent run commercially and depended on paid donors. In the 1970s, the manufacture of blood products increased the need for plasma so dramatically that most countries that treated haemophilia patients with clotting factor were unable to generate enough plasma with existing transfusion technology. Therefore several private pharmaceutical companies established large-scale programmes for commercially based blood collection in developing countries which, among other things, meant an increased risk of infection. The World Health Organization, the European Council and International Red Cross therefore all recommended that national blood transfusion services not be run commercially, that voluntary, unpaid donors be used, and that countries strive for national self-sufficiency in blood and plasma. There were three reasons for the recommendations: (1) foreign-based commercial programmes for blood collection might jeopardize the establishment of effective and safe domestic blood collection systems in the developing countries, (2) sold blood was considered less safe than voluntary donations, and (3) infections might be exported across national borders.

Although efforts were made to increase plasma collection, many countries were not self-sufficient in blood products by the end of the 1970s. To meet domestic demand, they depended on imports, in particular from the United

States, the country with the largest production of factor preparations. Tragically, this was also the country in which a new, deadly disease first entered the blood supply. AIDS became a venomous serpent in haemophiliacs' newly found paradise.

4 AIDS AND HIV

The symptoms observed in 1981 in the first AIDS patients led medical experts to believe that the new disease was caused by a deficiency of the immune system exposing the patients to serious infections. They also believed that the deficiency was not inherited, but acquired. Hence the name of the disease: Acquired Immune Deficiency Syndrome. However, the causative agent was not known. It was presupposed that an explanation was to be found in the lifestyle of the first group affected: gay men. Only one year later, this turned out not to be the case: in 1982, the first American case of AIDS in a haemophiliac was reported and, in 1983, the first case of AIDS in a transfusion recipient. This was soon followed by reports on AIDS in IV drug users, Haitians and persons having stayed in Africa. These cases were first reported in the USA, but when reports on AIDS in the same groups soon after appeared in Western Europe, it was obvious that the world faced a major international health crisis.

At the time, there were many unknowns in connection with AIDS: causative agent, mode of transmission, contagiousness, latency period and life expectancy of persons with AIDS (which appeared to be very short). At this stage, the discovery of the causative agent and a test to identify its presence seemed very far away.

In 1983 in France, and in 1984 in the USA, a virus was isolated which was soon identified as the likely cause of AIDS. The French virus was termed the 'lymphadenopathy associated virus' (LAV), the American virus the 'human T-cell lymphotropic virus type III' (HTLV III). Later the two viruses were proved to be identical. A dispute between the French and the US research teams over ownership led to an international agreement on the name of the virus, 'human immunodeficiency virus' (HIV). The discovery of the virus enabled a firmer determination of its modes of transmission, namely 'bodily fluids', as they were called in an attempt to avoid offensive language and stigmatization: in other words, sexual contacts with the exchange of sperm and blood, blood transfusions and blood products, needle sharing and mother to foetus.

As early as 1984, a test to identify the presence of the virus was developed. In March 1985, the first test kit was marketed in the USA, allowing routine screening for HIV antibodies in donated blood. With the discovery of the virus and the development of tests to identify its presence, health authorities stood on somewhat firmer ground when deciding what actions to take.

5 METHODS TO REDUCE THE RISK OF HIV TRANSMISSION THROUGH BLOOD AND BLOOD PRODUCTS

Although knowledge on AIDS was scarce, highly ambiguous and inconclusive in the early 1980s, the international medical community successively considered and agreed on a number of measures to reduce the risk of HIV transmission through blood and blood products.

1. *Donor selection.* In the absence of tests to identify the presence of AIDS in blood, selection of donors became the first risk reduction initiative. Medical examination to detect donors with AIDS symptoms was not sufficient. As it was believed that AIDS had an unknown latency period, blood banks asked groups with a high prevalence of AIDS to exclude themselves from the donor pool. Even after the introduction of routine screening of donor blood, persons with high-risk behaviour are still asked to refrain from donating blood: antibodies to the virus can be detected at the earliest three months after infection and in some cases it takes several months for antibodies to develop.

2. *Surrogate screening.* Since gay men and IV drug users had a high prevalence of hepatitis B, which is also blood-borne, screening of donor blood for hepatitis B as a surrogate test for HIV was suggested. However, surrogate tests were generally rejected. The test would not at all be specific, and it was also very expensive at $5 per unit of blood (Shield, 1999, p. 334).

3. *Elimination of virus from blood products.* Since the late 1970s, attempts had been made to eliminate hepatitis from blood products, in particular by heat treatment. Initially, the loss of potency or yield (that is, factor protein) of the heat-treated factor VIII was enormous (between 50 and 90 per cent) and made the cost approximately 10 times that of non-heat-treated concentrate (Leveton *et al.*, 1995, p. 87). Consequently, heat-treated clotting factor was not generally used in haemophilia therapy. As soon as the causative agent of AIDS was known to be a virus, it was believed, but in no way certain, that the methods developed to eliminate hepatitis from blood products might also eliminate HIV. There were different methods to eliminate virus from blood products: heat treatment, chemical inactivation and elimination through adsorption, settling or filtering. Heat treatment may be wet, dry or steam, at varying temperatures and for varying periods of time. And finally, the two coagulation proteins, factors VIII and IX, might need different elimination methods. In the early 1980s, there was great uncertainty as to which methods were most effective. The US health authorities facing the world's highest prevalence of HIV among haemophil-

iacs were the first to react. By February 1984, all US fractionators had applied for and received licences for heat-treated clotting factor from the Food and Drug Administration. In October 1984, the US Center for Disease Control announced heat treatment effective in countering the AIDS virus and recommended that the use of non-heat treated clotting factor be limited.

4. *Screening of blood donations.* The methods to eliminate vira from plasma products are unsuitable for transfusion blood as red blood cells do not tolerate heat treatment. Instead, blood donations must be tested for antibodies to vira. Soon after the HIV virus was identified in 1984, the first experimental detection methods became available. In March 1985, the first commercial tests became available for blood banks and made possible, first, a screening of blood donors and, soon thereafter, when enough test material was available, a screening of all blood donations. Although it did not – and still does not – eliminate the risk of HIV transmission 100 per cent owing to the delayed production of antibodies to the virus, routine screening of blood donations in blood banks became the decisive method to protect transfusion recipients from HIV infection. Mandatory screening, however, also added to the safety of blood products which would eventually be derived from screened blood and, in addition, be heat treated.

A number of measures were not considered in general or at all in the international medical community, although in retrospect it would have been sensible to do so. Two types of measure in particular could potentially have reduced the number of persons infected through blood-borne HIV transmission. First, limiting the number of donors to whose blood a haemophilia patient or transfusion recipient was exposed would have reduced the risk of infection. In some countries, the transfusion paradigm of the early 1980s prescribed the use of more rather than less blood, and consequently the volume of blood transfused during surgery often exceeded the amount needed. As far as haemophilia therapy is concerned, one option would have been a switch to the burdensome and less effective, but much safer cryoprecipitate therapy; another to reduce the volume of clotting factor prescribed for the individual haemophilia patient, especially the use of factor for prophylactic purposes. For instance, haemophilia therapy in Finland had always relied on domestic products, and the health authorities decided early on to stick to haemophilia therapy based on cryoprecipitate produced solely from domestic donor blood. As a result, no Finnish haemophiliacs were infected with HIV. Second, putting a stop to the importing of clotting factor from countries with a high prevalence of AIDS cases also would have been a sensible preventive measure. However, had countries which relied on imported products opted for such policies in late 1982 or early 1983, we still do not know how many haemophiliacs might have avoided HIV infection. Many, and maybe most, were infected already at this time.

In the early 1980s, AIDS in general and HIV and blood in particular were extremely ill-structured policy problems haunted by lack of knowledge and high uncertainty. Writing with hindsight, after AIDS has become a well-structured problem in industrialized democracies, it is easy to see what could and should have been done. What today seems obvious, however, was not self-evident at the time. The response to the crisis was determined by a number of concerns which all claimed legitimacy at a time when there was no consensus on how to conceive the problem. Thus haemophiliacs and haemophilia therapists had difficulties accepting that a serpent had entered their newly found paradise. There was a great deal of denial which became all the more easy when the risk of dying from less effective or no haemophilia therapy compared to the risk of contracting and dying from AIDS was not known. The same was true of transfusion therapy. The health authorities decided to tone down the AIDS risk, not only out of concern for haemophiliacs and potential transfusion recipients, but also for adequacy reasons: many donors falsely believed they could contract AIDS by donating blood. Likewise, in certain parts of the USA, homosexual males accounted for a crucial part of the donor pool, and, if they did not donate, the result might be a blood shortage. Blood banks as well a haemophiliacs and haemophilia therapists requested that homosexuals refrain from donating blood, a request homosexuals saw as discriminatory: homosexuality as such was not a health risk, whereas a specific sexual behaviour might be. In France, prison management was reluctant to deprive inmates, many of whom were IV drug users, of a symbolically important rehabilitation tool: to express their willingness, through blood donation, to contribute altruistically and patrioti-cally to the well-being of the country. The combination of moral superiority (altruism) and economy in the dominant voluntary donor system biased decisions against heat-treated (foreign) commercial products. High numbers of false positive tests in early screening methods constituted an ethical dilemma: were gains in safety sufficient to justify the psychological strain on donors who would – wrongly – be informed that they were HIV positive?

6   MEASURING POLICY SUCCESS OR FAILURE

HIV in the blood supply was an ill-structured policy problem when, in 1982, AIDS was first known to spread via blood and blood products. A host of conflicting concerns had to be considered, each of which had a certain claim to legitimacy. At the time, no one knew the outcome. When the human immuno-deficiency virus was isolated in 1984, and methods to eliminate HIV from plasma products and to test for its presence in blood donations were developed over the next year, blood-borne AIDS turned into a relatively well-structured policy problem. With the exception of Spain, the countries included in the present study had implemented effective, preventive policy measures against HIV in the blood supply in the last part of 1985, although stocks of non-screened or non-tested blood products were still used beyond that point.

At the *programmatic* level, were the policies to prevent AIDS transmission through the blood supply a success or a failure? This question can only be answered on a comparative, not an absolute scale. One possibility is to compare the attempts to prevent blood-borne HIV transmission with policies to combat similar infectious diseases. Without doubt, the preventive measures taken by the health authorities to combat blood-borne HIV transmission will, in a historical perspective, come out as one of the most successful attempts ever to solve programmatically a major health crisis in the form of a rapidly spreading infectious disease. In few other cases, if any, has an infectious disease been stopped so effectively and so fast in one of its modes of transmission. However, a historical comparison would not say much about whether, in the early 1980s, effective policy actions could in fact have been taken earlier, neither would it reveal variations among countries in their capacities to deal with health crises of this type.

Alternatively, preventive policies across countries may be compared. Ideally, the effects of various policy actions should be compared: how successful were each of the six countries in their efforts to stop blood-borne HIV infection? However, valid indicators of policy effects do not exist and probably never can be generated as far as blood-borne transmission of HIV is concerned. Although one may compare the incidence of HIV infection among haemophiliacs and transfusion recipients in our six countries, the numbers say little about the effects of policy actions. In the vast majority of cases, haemophiliacs and transfusion recipients were infected before the mid-1980s when the first effective methods to prevent blood-borne HIV were developed. Therefore the proportion of, for instance, infected haemophiliacs in the total population of haemophiliacs in one country compared to another cannot be taken as an indication of the success of government action, only as an indication of differences in the epidemiology of AIDS in the six countries prior to the presence of effective preventive policies.

Rather than outcome indicators, process indicators will be used to compare the success of the programmatic HIV crisis management in the six countries. As indicators we will use the policy measures that the international medical community successively agreed were the most effective means to reduce the risk of HIV transmission through blood and blood products. We have also included the stop of imports of plasma products as an indicator, although this measure was not generally considered by health authorities across countries. The indicators of programmatic success are listed in Table 24.2, along with the date on which each indicator was recommended or introduced in the USA, the advanced democracy first hit by AIDS in general as well as by the tragedy of blood-borne HIV transmission specifically.

Table 24.2   Indicators of programmatic success

Measure	Date of US introduction
Donor selection	March 1983: Public Health Service recommendation
Screening of blood donations	January 1985: Public Health Service 'provisional' recommendations; April 1985: beginning of blood bank testing
Import stop of foreign plasma products	Not relevant
Heat-treatment plasma products	October 1984: Center for Disease Control recommendation that the use of non-heat-treated factor be limited
Recall of non-heat-treated blood products	1989: Food and Drug Administration mandate

At the *political* level, we search for indicators of whether the health authorities' efforts to manage the HIV and blood health crisis were considered legitimate. The indicators are as follows:

- media coverage,
- parliamentary, administrative or judicial investigations,
- parliamentary debates, questions to the minister,
- litigation,
- compensation schemes,
- political casualties,
- public opinion.

7   ASSESSMENT

The indicators just listed will be used to assess how successfully the blood-borne HIV crisis was managed. At the *programmatic* level, the introduction in the individual country case of preventive measures against blood-borne HIV transmission will be compared to corresponding introductions elsewhere. In general, the earlier a country introduced preventive measures, the more successful its crisis management. The assessment must, however, reflect

whether the individual country had good reasons at the time to postpone introduction of a particular measure. For instance, some countries decided to
postpone the introduction of heat treatment of plasma products. If the prevalence
of HIV in the country's donor pool was believed to be low or non-existent, a
postponement might, owing to the loss of clotting factor during heat treatment,
have been a very reasonable decision at a time when the effectiveness of heat
treatment was still doubted. A reduction in nationally produced plasma products
had to be replaced by heat-treated products manufactured from blood material
that was known to be infected.

Programmatic success or failure is one thing, the *political* legitimacy of programmatic decisions quite another. The programmatic and political levels need
not correlate. Policy and politics in this respect resemble the private firm in
which the logic guiding the production division is quite different from the logic
of the sales division (Simon, 1945; March and Simon, 1958). Thus successful
indicators at the programmatic level may easily be followed by indicators
proving high controversy, even 'scandals', and obvious political failure. Or
vice versa: something which is definitely a programmatic failure may never
attract the attention of the media, the population or important political actors.

The assessment cannot result in clear-cut yes or no answers, either at the
programmatic or at the political level. First, different indicators will point in
different directions. Second, neither in academic language nor in everyday
parlance do we find clear definitions of success and failure. Does the very lack
of failure – for instance if standard operating procedures work even in a crisis
– constitute successful crisis management? Similarly, inactivity in a crisis can
easily be construed as illegitimate and even scandalous, whereas overzealous-
ness – and waste of public funds – typically is not judged as harshly. But can
a wasteful response constitute a success?

The authors will overcome such problems to the extent possible by giving a
general, argued and balanced assessment of the crisis management in the
individual country cases. However, no common standard has been imposed on
the overall assessment of the success of crisis management in the six countries.
The individual authors are free to argue whether they find the management of
the blood-borne HIV crisis in their individual cases successful or not. Consequently, the comparison of crisis management success and failure presented in
the conclusion of this book may not fully agree with the assessments made by
the individual authors.

8   EXPLANATIONS

Each author was asked to look for explanations of success and failure in crisis
management in their individual country cases. Explanations may vary at the

programmatic and the political levels and across countries. Some explanations will be institutional. For instance, the organization of health care services and regulation will have important repercussions for health officials' capacity and autonomy to act in a crisis. Other explanations will be political. The conflicts of interests among actors in the blood supply can have an important impact both on programmatic solutions and for subsequent political evaluations. Policy style may be an important explanation both at the programmatic and the political level. A final example of the types of explanations presented in the analyses are historical and cultural explanations. For instance, the symbolic meaning historically given to blood in a country may have a decisive impact on who is included and who can and who cannot be excluded from the donor pool.

9   GLOSSARY

AIDS
Acquired immune deficiency syndrome. First observed in young homosexual males in 1981, AIDS was originally a group of symptoms believed to be caused by an acquired, as opposed to an inherited, deficiency of the immune system exposing the patients to serious infections. In 1982, AIDS was found in a haemophilia patient, in 1983 in a transfusion recipient. The causative agent of AIDS was later identified to be a virus, HIV. After the identification of HIV, AIDS characterizes the final stage of disease and is the definition of the syndrome caused by HIV. Four clinical symptoms must be identified in a patient to classify the infection as AIDS. The definition is used today essentially for epidemiological statistics.

Blood
The fluid that circulates in the principal vascular system, consisting of plasma in which cells and platelets are suspended. Originally, transfusion therapy transferred whole blood, that is, blood as it exists in a donor, into the body of the patient. Since fractionation of blood into its individual components became possible, whole blood is not used in transfusion therapy to the same extent as earlier. Often only the blood components therapeutically needed are transfused, for instance red blood cells in connection with surgery.

Blood products
Blood components or plasma products, that is, industrially purified proteins obtained from plasma, for instance clotting factors. Pharmaceutical products prepared from blood components are not classified as blood products: for example, alfa-interferon from leucocytes.

Cryoprecipitate ('cryo')
Factor concentrate derived from precipitate that remains when frozen plasma is thawed or by cooling plasma to very low temperatures. The discovery of cryoprecipitate made effective haemophilia therapy possible for the first time.

Factors I–XIII
A classification of blood clotting proteins. A deficiency of factor VIII and IX causes haemophilia A and B, respectively. By pooling blood drawn from large numbers of donors, factor can be concentrated into blood products used in effective haemophilia therapy.

Haemophilia
A hereditary bleeding disorder caused by a deficiency of two separate blood-clotting proteins, called factor: Haemophilia A caused by a deficiency of factor VIII, and haemophilia B by a deficiency of factor IX. Haemophilia manifests itself in an extended coagulation period and abnormal bleeding tendency.

Heat treatment
Method to inactivate vira in plasma products.

Hepatitis
Inflammation of the liver caused by different hepatitis vira. Blood-borne transmission of hepatitis A is rare, and the disease is of mild to moderate severity and never chronic. Hepatitis B and C can be transmitted by blood transfusion or by contaminated blood-clotting factor concentrate. Infection with both vira can be severe, chronic and sometimes fatal. The identification of the vira responsible for the hepatitis syndromes permitted the development of tests to screen blood donations for infection. Heat treatment inactivates hepatitis B and C in plasma products, whereas hepatitis A is hard to inactivate even with heat treatment and is therefore occasionally still transmitted via plasma products.

HIV
Human immunodeficiency virus, the aetiological agent causing AIDS.

Plasma
The fluid portion of blood carrying salt, nutrients and proteins, among others blood-clotting proteins known as factors.

Recombinant factors
Genetically engineered clotting factors not based on human blood and therefore not transmitting blood-borne human diseases. In the 1990s, an increasing share of factor preparations used in haemophilia therapy was recombinant. In some countries, up to 98 per cent of the factor preparations used in haemophilia therapy today is recombinant.

Screening
Various methods used to eliminate tainted blood from the blood supply. Selection/screening of blood *donors*: persons carrying symptoms of AIDS (or hepatitis) or belonging to groups with high frequency of AIDS (or hepatitis) cases are asked not to donate blood. Testing/screening of blood *donations*:

testing for the presence of antibodies to HIV or the presence of the hepatitis virus antigen in donor blood. Varying across countries, donor blood is today also screened for other vira.

Transfusion

The direct transfer of blood or its components from one person into another, for instance in connection with surgery.

NOTES

1. The description of haemophilia, blood therapy and HIV/AIDS presented in this chapter is based on SoU (1963), Leveton *et al.* (1995), Roberts (1996), Berridge (1997) and Martlew (1997). Claus Bohn Christiansen, Statens Serum Institut, Copenhagen, has provided helpful comments on the manuscript.
2. The share of haemophiliacs in the different categories varies across countries and has changed over time. The exact number of haemophiliacs in the population is not known because the vast majority of persons with mild haemophilia have never been in contact with the health care system because of their bleeding disorder. With improved diagnostic and therapeutic technology, a number of patients with mild haemophilia have been registered late in life and have increased the absolute and relative number of patients in this category.

25. Crisis governance in France: the end of sectoral corporatism?

Monika Steffen

1 THE MOST IMPORTANT POLITICAL SCANDAL SINCE DREYFUS

The 'contaminated blood scandal' was probably the most important political earthquake in France since the Dreyfus affair at the end of the nineteenth century. For the first time in history, three former ministers, including the prime minister, had to stand trial in a penal court for their action in government (1999). Four top executives of the blood transfusion system had already been sentenced to prison (1992) and a further trial, of 30 doctors, scientific experts and government advisers, is still pending today (May 2001). Six years had elapsed after the risk of HIV was eliminated from the blood transfusion system, before the scandal broke out. The blood transfusion system lost its legendary aura. What was previously considered as the world's finest example of medical achievement and social solidarity turned suddenly into a most negative picture, with corrupt doctors, incompetent public services and careless government officials.

A radical change in public perception followed press revelations.[1] Media impact, however, seemed insufficient to explain why the waves of the blood crisis were deeper in France than anywhere else.[2] The scandal had far-reaching consequences. Risk perception changed and the related policies were modified. The blood transfusion sector was reformed, the public health administration reinforced and the legal regime of responsibilities strengthened, all measures aiming to prevent similar problems in the future. The French case was a long story combining a high-profile crisis with important institutional reforms.

The French case presented surprising particularities. National risk management had a twofold result. As in many other countries, half of the haemophilia patients were HIV-contaminated, but France alone accounted for 60 per cent of all the cases of contaminated *transfusion recipients* recorded in the European Union.[3] The initial penal procedure, however, focused on the haemophilia issue. The HIV/blood story also seemed in contradiction with the institutional characteristics of the French political system. The strong powers of the executive, the hierarchical structure of public administration and the fact that the transfusion system was public, endowed decision makers with a substantial capacity for intervention which, nevertheless, proved ineffective.

2   THE POLICY CONTEXT: RISK PERCEPTION, POLITICIZATION AND COST CONTAINMENT

The AIDS epidemic arose in an unprepared policy field. The French health policy system was and, although to some lesser extent today, still is highly fragmented. It was composed of many specialized networks linking professional groups with their counterparts in the public administration. It was dominated by the hospital and university-based medical elite. Reforms were difficult to conduct in this context because of strong veto points and a large social and political consensus in favour of the access-oriented medical care system (Jobert and Steffen, 1994). The institutional context did not cater for comprehensive public health interventions, which would link different administrative and professional areas as well as care and prevention. The public health administration was the runt of the health care system, an 'administrative dwarf' (Morelle, 1996), lacking data systems and expertise capacity. Public health experts had little influence over policy issues. Their position was too weak to legitimize new intervention strategies in sensitive areas like sexuality, drug abuse or blood collection, all easily subject to ideological confrontation and politicization.

The political context contributed to shaping AIDS policies and the HIV/blood story in at least three ways. First, the rise of the socialists in 1981 led to unusually frequent elections and to the political cohabitation between a socialist president and a right-wing Parliament, both in 1986–8 and again in 1993–5: an unprecedented experience under the Fifth Republic. In a context of permanent electoral competition, decision making on AIDS campaigns was frequently delayed, almost throughout the 1980s. The Communist Party lost its traditional influence and a new extreme right-wing party, the National Front, gained substantial numbers of votes. The National Front launched a campaign on 'national decline' in which immigration, delinquency, drug abuse and AIDS were presented as parts of the same problem and proposed *'sidatoriums'* (sanatoria specifically for AIDS patients) to protect the French from the evil. The response of all major political forces was to defend individual freedom and promote solidarity with the victims of the epidemic, which in those early days meant gay men. In this context, the AIDS problem was framed as a political risk of stigmatization and minimized as a public health issue. The term 'at-risk groups' was banned from public use and policies. AIDS concerned citizenship and political values over and above public health (Steffen, 1996).

Second, during their initial period of government (1981–3), the socialists and their communist allies tried to stimulate the economy, with public investment to develop national production and growing social expenditure to favour consumption. The biomedical industry featured amongst the priorities. The national production of clotting factor VIII was launched at that time. A radical policy shift followed in 1983, with cost containment becoming the absolute priority. The new economic orientation enhanced power changes inside the government and between the social ministries. The health ministry lost its autonomy and was subordinated to the ministry of social affairs for all financial decisions. As a consequence, collaboration between the advisers of the two ministers, the so called *cabinets ministériels*, became extremely difficult.[4]

Inside the health ministry, power shifted to the department of social security, which was in fact more closely linked to the finance ministry than to that of social affairs. When the communists left government in 1983, the head of the general department of health (GDH), a communist appointed in 1981, remained isolated without any support within the decision-making structures. This, already the weakest, department of the health ministry responsible for public health and the blood sector, was particularly marginalized when the AIDS issue arrived on the agenda. No permission was given to the GDH to create a specific budget line for AIDS in 1983. Its general budget for prevention was even reduced in 1984 and 1985. In the same way, the first financial demand from the Pasteur Institute, to set up a high-security laboratory with the aim of cultivating the virus for the industrial production of test kits, was refused in 1983 (Roux, 1995, pp. 192–201).

Third, political alternation favoured the extensive growth of one of the particular features of the French government system, the 'ministerial cabinets', which meant the staff of personal counsellors attached to each minister. The total number of counsellors soared from 225 in 1981 to 428 in 1992. These 'shadows of ministers' had considerable influence but no precise legal status or responsibility (*Pouvoir*, 1994). They filtered access to the ministers and information submitted to them, gave orders to top civil servants and negotiated with the advisory staff of other ministers. Decision-making competence shifted from high public servants to political staff, from the permanently appointed heads of departments to temporary executives personally attached to a minister. The evolution led to increased centralization in decision making in which the prerogatives of the central health administration diminished.

3   GOVERNANCE IN THE BLOOD SECTOR AND THE HAEMOPHILIA WORLD

Within a segmented health policy field, the blood sector occupied a separate position. The institutional structures and the underlying ethical principles were rooted in history, going back to the end of World War II. Injured partisans secretly received free blood donations and enthusiastic mass collections accompanied the liberation army. This 'route du sang'[5] left a twofold legacy: the decentralization of the blood centres, and the voluntary donor who entered history as a national hero. After the war, the political forces of the Resistance[6] strove to generalize the war-born innovation into a national public blood service. The latter was formalized by a 1952 law, which prohibited commercial profits on the manufacture and distribution of blood. Paid donation[7] disappeared as a new system developed, together with health insurance.

The blood donor organizations became and remained, until the blood scandal, an influential policy actor,[8] generously subsidized by the blood centres. Together they ensured that chemists were excluded from the distribution of blood products in 1958. Only medical doctors were entitled to hand out such medicines. Exclusive distribution was thus reserved for the blood centres and the hospitals. In 1976, the only private firm active in the sector (Mérieux) had its licence withdrawn. Blood products were considered as part of the human body, not to be commercialized and therefore institutionally separated from all other medicines. Authority for blood products remained within the GDH, whilst the general system of surveillance and market authorization was located in the pharmaceutical department of the ministry.[9]

France had 170 blood centres when the HIV/blood challenge arrived, half of them with a private non-profit-making status,[10] all functioning within the framework of blood transfusion as a public service. Of these, 163, that is at least one for each territorial Department, acted as so-called 'transfusion centres' responsible for collecting blood and plasma and preparing labile products. They supplied the hospitals and the seven plasma fractionating centres which prepared the stable products and resold them to the hospitals and the transfusion centres which, in turn, supplied the patients. Prices were set by the GDH and were identical for all the centres. Possible differences in product quality, management or productivity made no difference to the administrative procedure. The 30 so-called 'regional centres' were attached to the university hospitals. Their directors acted as 'regional transfusion counsellors', whose responsibilities were not defined. All centres were legally and financially independent with no hierarchical links between them, because they were headed by a medical doctor entitled to professional independence.

The sector provided 11 000 protected jobs with public service status. Donation and the use of blood were extremely high, above European averages by up to 40 per cent (van Aken, 1993; Hagen, 1993). Transfusion medicine was not part of the syllabus in medical studies. It constituted a minor part of haemopathology (Ruffié, 1993), while the transfusion sector provided training for its own professionals. Transfusions in hospitals were mainly carried out with full blood, a practice favoured by the lack of specialized knowledge and the absence of regulating mechanisms (Setbon, 1993, p. 93). Blood was to be available without limitation.[11] Post-transfusion infections went largely unnoticed, since no organized feedback existed between the hospital services, the general practitioners and the transfusion centres (IGASS/IGSJ, 1992, p. 90). Poor communication with the other parts of the medical care system was described as the 'intellectual isolation' of the blood professionals (Sénat, 1992, p. 133).

The *Centre National de Transfusion Sanguine* (CNTS) was entrusted with tasks of national interest, such as keeping the list of donors with rare blood groups and importing specific items not produced in the country. Factor VIII concentrates were imported in small quantities for observation only. In 1982, funds were granted to the CNTS to set up a production unit for concentrates. Large-scale production was achieved in mid-1983 and increased by 60 per cent in 1984.[12] Simultaneously, six other centres were engaged in producing factor VIII concentrates. None had a virus inactivation process. During the rapid development, plasma provision became the main problem. The donor associations opposed plasmapheresis, which they viewed as a threat to the symbolic value of blood and to the institution of voluntary donation.[13] To meet needs, blood collection was intensified, including collection in risky places like 'red light' urban areas and prisons. Blood provision strategies also led to competition between the blood centres and to unofficial practices of overbidding and dumping with the fractionating centres (Hermitte, 1996, pp. 141–8). It proved difficult to conceive a coherent policy of industrial development in a context of independent agents, administratively fixed prices and a non-profit-making ideology.

The health administration had official authority over the sector but acted as a 'captured agency' (Bernstein, 1955). The CNTS occupied the central position, together with two institutions that emanated from it, the Transfusion Institute and the Transfusion Foundation. This set-up accumulated all strategic tasks: the leadership in plasma fractionating and the importation monopoly within the CNTS; fundamental research and scientific training within the Institute; professional training, coordination of regional policies, international relations and advice to the Health Ministry within the Foundation. By contrast, in the GDH, responsible for licensing the blood centres, controlling their activities and setting prices, only a single non-medical official was in charge of a task limited to administrative routine. Its official advisory body was the Consultative Committee on Transfusion, composed of the executives of the CNTS and the directors of the biggest blood centres. In the National Health Laboratory, which took charge of supervising technical procedures including quality control for blood-derived products and the approval of biological tests, only two officials were attributed to the work.

The French Haemophilia Association (FHA) was founded in 1955 by Professor Soulier, then the director of the CNTS, together with one of his haemophilic patients. Local groups were initiated by the regional blood centres.

The associations were accommodated and funded by the blood centres. The goal was to structure the sector and pressurize public authorities for free access to treatment, which was achieved in 1971. The majority of severe haemophiliacs were treated in the specialized services attached to the blood centres, often from their childhood. Home treatment with concentrates was publicized by the president of the FHA, who had learned about it in international meetings. At first doctors opposed the idea, arguing that intravenous injection was a serious medical act, but then supported it actively when it became known as prophylactic treatment. In the early 1970s, foreign firms tried to promote new treatments in France and trained French haemophiliacs during organized weekends and even holidays abroad, which were especially attractive to young patients seduced by sport (Carricaburu, 1999, p. 88). By the end of the 1970s, tension arose between the FHA and the CNTS over general access to the prophylactic treatment. The former, backed by the doctors from the blood centres, promoted a philosophy of 'normal life',[14] whilst the latter argued that the demand was excessive, financially and politically, and could not be satisfied by the voluntary donations. The CNTS was caught in the dilemma of either importing or producing concentrates on a large scale. The risk of transmittable disease played no part in this controversy. Hepatitis was widespead during the 1970s and was accepted, by doctors and patients alike, as the 'price to pay' for normal life (Carricaburu, 1999).

The institutional set-up was predisposed to governance problems for two reasons. First, the blood sector was not governed by a coherent set of institutions and the control agencies were captive bodies. Second, because of the ethical principles, an industrial empire was built into a traditional transfusion system. The two components of the sector had antagonistic interests, united only by the common goal of self-sufficiency. The case illustrated how ethics can contribute to policy failures.

4   GOVERNING THE FIRST CRISIS: RISK MANAGEMENT AT THE MARGINS[15]

At the beginning of 1983, only 60 haemophiliacs were undergoing prophylactic treatment. Professor Soulier answered the association's demand for increased importation with an 'open letter to haemophiliacs' in February 1983, warning them of the 'premature reliance on the new concentrates' and proposed a 'moratorium of two years'. He added that mysterious viral diseases could possibly be transmitted by 'commercial' plasma products. In May, the general assembly of the FHA, chaired by a most eminent medical professor, came to the conclusion that 'the potential risk due to AIDS objectively evaluated was not likely to modify current prophylactic treatment', that importation had to continue and that national production should be fully developed. At this crucial stage, hepatitis B served as a conceptual model, together with 'commercial' plasma, as a source of risk. This unrealistic vision was supported by at least three facts: the first identified case of AIDS in a haemophiliac in France happened to be a Haitian;[16] little information was given on the six cases of AIDS symptoms found in haemophiliacs of whom three had received exclusively French products; and the new topic of cost control in the health expenditure was perceived as an imminent threat by haemophiliacs.[17] The latter and their doctors were caught in the dilemma of 'cognitive dissonance' (Festinger, 1957).

Donor Selection

On 20 June 1983, the GDH issued an official order to the blood centres to screen donors. A month earlier, the CNTS and its providing blood centres had already introduced the measure, but the initiative was not publicized in the sectoral information channels. The GDH order included guidelines on the questions to be asked about sexual behaviour and the identification of clinical symptoms indicating possible AIDS infection. In February 1984, an inquiry showed that the official order had not been implemented. The professionals in the blood centres considered their donors as safe and the GDH's initiative as an unnecessary interference with their work. The donor association rejected it as an insult to their image. All opponents argued that it would lead to shortage of blood. The gay association and the journals close to the socialist left[18] criticized the 'anti-gay racism' and the 'indiscreet incursion into private life'. It was only in January 1985 that the GDH issued a reminder and recalled the legal responsibility of the blood centres.

The original version of the order, issued by Professor Roux, the head of the GDH, had been censured by the health minister's personal advisers. The two paragraphs referring to 'risky places' where collections had to stop were taken out. Blood collection in prisons had grown rapidly since 1982, reaching peak levels in 1984. In the administration of justice, blood donation was considered as an element of the social integration of inmates. Administrative authority over the subject was attached to the corresponding department in the ministry. It was only after a study by a prison doctor showed that nearly 60 per cent of the inmate donors belonged to high risk groups, mainly injecting drug users, that negotiation started between the ministries of health and justice. The recommendation to stop collections was made by telephone to the prison directors and blood centres in the summer of 1985. In order to 'avoid stigmatization', no written order was issued (IGASS/IGSJ, 1992, p. 176). As a result, several blood centres continued the risky collections, the last instance being recorded in 1991. Official estimates established that 0.4 per cent of the donations caused 30 per cent of the contamination (ibid., p. 105).[19]

Screening Blood

Mandatory screening became an urgent demand by the transfusion leaders and the Consultative Committee as the availability of test kits approached, in early 1985. In mid-February, the US firm Abbott had already filed an application for marketing authorization at the French National Institute of Health, prior to the submission of the French firm Pasteur-Diagnostics. The first pre-industrial test kits were used in the specialized haemophilia care centres in Paris, in 1984. Out of 400 patients tested, 45 per cent were HIV-positive. The results were published in international scientific literature, but not communicated to the haemophiliacs. In February 1985, a first survey of Parisian blood donors showed an HIV prevalence rate of six per thousand. On 12 March 1985, Dr Brunet, an epidemiologist in the GDH, issued a memorandum, which was immediately presented to the Consultative Committee and communicated to the minister's personal advisers. It stated: 'probably *all* the products prepared from pools of Parisian donors are currently contaminated'.

Screening out the HIV risk, however, represented a multifold policy issue. The major dilemma was the protection of the French market from US competition. Possibilities were explored either to delay market authorization, to allow the French producer to catch up with production capacity and competitiveness, or to arrange a centralized system of supply for all blood centres via the CNTS. Furthermore, supplementary budgets had to be found for the blood centres, which implied negotiations with the ministries of social affairs and of finance. Agreement had to be reached on the controversial question of whether and how to inform the donors found to be HIV-positive. Disagreement existed also, even within the small group of AIDS experts, over the opportunity to introduce blood screening before other free test facilities were provided outside the blood centres.[20]

On 9 May 1985, the prime minister's chief adviser organized an interministerial meeting to discuss the issues. The health ministry was represented by the minister's personal advisers; the GDH was not invited. The decision was taken to postpone the approval of the Abbott test. A different outcome would have been surprising. The prime minister's scientific adviser in charge of the file was a former research director from the Pasteur Institute and the lobbying director of Diagnostics-Pasteur a former head of the pharmaceutical control board of the health ministry. When informed of the meeting's outcome, the prime minister in person imposed a time limit for screening, 1 August (Morelle, 1996, pp. 80–81). He also arbitrated in favour of full information for positive donors. The press reflected the complex issue by running contradictory and alarming headlines.[21] Once the political decision was taken, everything went quickly. The prime minister himself announced screening in Parliament on 19 June; the National Institute of Health delivered marketing authorization to Pasteur on 21 June and to Abbott on 25 June; and on 1 August, all blood was systematically screened, throughout the country and the overseas territories.

Heat Treatment

The apparently confused story, which subsequently occupied legal investigation for many years, in fact comes down to two main questions: why did it take so long to introduce heat treatment, given that the public system was led by a national fractionating centre, and why were inactivated products, known to be largely contaminated, distributed during an 'intermediate period' of three months, from the end of June to 1 October 1985?

In early 1983, the CNTS received proposals from foreign companies to negotiate the massive importation of heat-treated concentrates, which was not considered. Instead, negotiations to produce under licence started with the Immuno company in October, but the contract was only signed in February 1985. Meanwhile, in 1984, the old director of the CNTS, Professor Soulier, retired and was replaced in the position by Dr. Garretta, his assistant manager who had had business training in the USA. The latter set up two new committees: the expert group of clinicians and biologists to monitor clinical trials on the effects of inactivated concentrates; and the National Haemophilia Committee, which included all parties – the clinical experts, the CNTS, the GDH, the FHA and the donor associations – with a mission to advise the Consultative Committee on AIDS-related questions. He tried to negotiate a licence which would cover all seven fractionating units, without success because the centres were independent. Many different inactivated products were imported, in small quantities, for clinical trials only. The latter continued after the end of 1984, although the efficiency of heat treatment was then proven according to the conclusions of the later court trials. The reasons for the time-absorbing studies were exposed by Professor Soulier in his hearing with the investigating judge. In fact, the CNTS was not looking for a good drug to import, or a simple transfer of technology, but for 'the best inactivation technique which would also eliminate the risk of hepatitis C'. The problem was not one of supply, he explained, but of a 'long-term industrial objective'. The most probable perspective for this was the approaching open European market.

Pressure on the CNTS grew, but then seriously increased, between March and June 1985, as information on the lethal HIV risk and the heat treatment spread among haemophiliacs, as Dr Brunet's memorandum circulated in the sectoral institutions and as domestic competition grew. The fractionating centre at Lille, whose executives only learned about the heat technique at a congress in Germany in the autumn of 1984, developed their own technique in collaboration with the French discoverer of HIV from the Pasteur Institute. Production tests were run in April 1985 and normal supply started in June. The Strasbourg centre also supplied heated products in July, produced under licence from Travenol, whilst the CNTS encountered technical problems. Supply was planned for June, but the Immuno technology proved incompatible with the fabrication techniques of the CNTS. Three months were needed to solve this unexpected practical problem.

Withdrawal of Non-heated Products

Dr Garretta turned to the classical strategies of invoking commissions and blame avoidance.[22] In early May, he met the FHA, informing them of delays due to technical adaptation. The haemophiliacs insisted on an ultimatum for 1 October. On 14 May, the expert group met to adopt a report prepared by Dr Habibi, responsible for distribution at the CNTS. The document concluded that the 'highly risky' products had to be withdrawn. Only imported inactivated or French products from exclusively negative donors should be distributed. At the session of the Haemophilia Committee, on 19 May, the FHA again insisted on the time limit of 1 October and agreed that until then unheated concentrates would still be distributed. According to the minutes of the meeting, no information was given to say that nearly *all* batches were at risk. The following day, the Consultative Committee met, without the haemophiliacs. It noted the agreement on 'the intermediate period' and took note of Dr Garretta's information that 'the probability of non-contaminated batches was small'. It was decided that inactivated products had to be reserved for HIV-negative patients and children under the age of four. On 26 May, an internal CNTS memo from Dr Garretta confirmed that 'unheated concentrates remained the standard procedure, as long as they were in stock'. The confidential minutes of an internal CNTS meeting held three days later stated that 'for highly contaminated products, the choice is between doing nothing or recalling them; it is the Health Authority's responsibility to decide and assume the consequences, financial losses for the CNTS and the departure from self-sufficiency'. The same text was added to the Habibi report, which was then immediately transmitted to the ministry (29 May) and later, much later, the Consultative Committee (26 June). On 3 July, a memo signed by Dr Habibi went out to the hospitals and haemophilia centres, publishing the rules for use of heated and unheated products, for HIV-negative and positive patients respectively. On the 23 July, the GDH issued an order for the exclusive use of heated products after 1 October. From mid-September, the CNTS provided heated products. The HIV/blood story should have stopped here.

5   GOVERNING THE SECOND CRISIS: MOBILIZATION, EVALUATION AND NEW RULES

Why did the scandal break out despite Dr Garretta's preventive blame avoidance strategy, and why did it involve the entire legal system which up to then had been absent from health issues? The second crisis arose from unexpected consequences of the ill-fated emergency solution adopted at the final stage of risk management: the standard distribution of contaminated concentrates during the 'intermediate period'. The structure of the second crisis appears similar to the first, in the sense that the risk was ignored and that the strategies to contain it failed, with the difference that the risk was now of a political nature. Four major elements explain the course of events: protest arose from individuals outside the established policy networks; the existing policy repertories offered no satisfactory answer to the grievances; an insufficient number of indictments existed to secure the legal action; resolving the crisis demanded major revisions in consumer protection. In fact, the HIV/blood issue arrived as an 'ill-structured problem' (Simon, 1973) not only for the sectoral decision makers, but also for those in charge of the political handling of the consequences.

A minor incident illustrated how little attention was given to the rights of patients. They were directly confronted by the donors, even in the local networks. When haemophiliacs expressed doubts about the French products in a television interview in 1986, the president of the Blood Donor Association immediately wrote to the president of the FHA to protest against these 'unwarranted attacks'. 'Haemophiliacs' total dependence on the donors' voluntary, free gesture,' he wrote, 'make their attitudes unjust and almost odious' (Casteret, 1992, p. 196). Also, the 1952 law obliged the blood centres to take out insurance only for the donors. This obligation was finally extended to recipients, in 1980, but the low coverage proved meaningless in the AIDS case. Furthermore, the majority of the French insurance companies were state-owned, until their privatization in 1993, either totally or for the majority of their shares. Still in 1986, the FHA approached the health minister, then from the right-wing RPR party, for financial support. She referred the demands to the law courts and commissioned a report, which led, two years later, to the part-time appointment of one social worker to assist families in need. Legal procedures were of little help. Apart from the heavy burden of accurate proof concerning the precise date of contamination, the product and its origin, the blood centres fell under different legal regimes, administrative courts for the public centres and private tort law for the private centres, with unequal conditions for the plaintiffs. It was also uncertain whether blood products fell under the responsibility of the public service, which was focused on provision and access, or under product liability, centred on the quality of the goods

(Hermitte, 1996, p. 275). The FHA also rejected the possibility of public disclosure.

Compensation became a tricky legal and political problem. In 1987, Jean Garvanoff, a haemophiliac with few links to the community structures, filed the first complaint, which was dismissed by the examining judge. The following year, together with other dissidents and a lawyer interested in the case, he filed a penal complaint against the CNTS, the Health Laboratory, the national advisory body for ethics and the FHA. In 1989, he founded a concurrent association to promote an activist policy style. Faced with internal tensions and threat of division, the FHA then sent an ultimatum to the health minister, in March 1989, after the socialists had returned to power. In July, a compensation scheme was published, with common funding from the state and the insurance companies. It was presented as an act of solidarity, not as compensation for damage, and was restricted to haemophiliacs. Allocations were limited to a maximum of FF 620 000 (94 600 Euros) for full AIDS, according to age and family responsibilities, and beneficiaries had to renounce further legal procedures. A government choice taken without consultation, in a field where no previous model existed which could foster consensus, was naturally exposed to criticism. Although the majority of haemophiliacs adhered to the scheme, it was criticized from all sides for reasons of principle: it would pervert the professional responsibility of doctors, open the door to new welfare allowances, be unjust for the victims of other medical accidents, make private insurance holders pay for the mistakes of the public service and even stigmatize other people with AIDS. Practical criticism focused on the exclusion of transfusion recipients. In 1990, a senator mobilized political support for a law providing full public compensation to all HIV/blood victims, according to the example set by the law for victims of terrorism adopted the same year. He personally helped to create the Association of Transfusion Recipients. The FHA then joined the stream of events and engaged in a campaign of political lobbying, with petitions and letters to all deputies and local politicians.

Political pressure rose to its maximum during 1991, a pre-electoral period. It was initiated by investigative journalism, a branch opened by the militant work of A.M. Casteret on the HIV/blood case. Competition between journals and journalists favoured high coverage (Champagne, 1994). The media drew a picture of corruption, accused Dr Garretta personally and criticized the alliance of interest between the state and the doctors. Dr Garretta resigned from his position in June, in protest. The publication of potentially compromising facts and documents led the government to demand reports, from the health as well as the financial inspectorates and a police investigation, whilst the parliamentary assemblies initiated their own inquiries. All aspects of the blood sector and its management were examined. The official reports fulfilled a twofold function. They prepared the basis for legal accusations and paved the way to reform. In

October 1991, four sectoral executives were charged in court: Dr Garretta and the scientific director of the CNTS (Dr Allain) for fraud, Professor Roux and the director of the Health Laboratory for non-assistance. After a trial in the summer of 1992, they were sentenced to four years' imprisonment, except the last, who was released.[23] In November 1991, President Mitterrand himself, who had requested the national decoration of merit, '*Ordre National de Mérite*', for Dr Garretta the year before, despite the reservations of his health minister, announced on television that every victim was entitled to full compensation and to public recognition, which could only be brought about by a law to signify the engagement of the entire nation. A law was adopted by vote in the national assembly on 31 December 1991.

The case still continued, on two fronts. Dr Allain appealed. The Appeal Court confirmed the sentences in 1993, with minor revisions only, but stated that the case contained elements of 'poisoning' which justified new procedures. The continuing controversy among legal specialists over the precise content of the different counts of indictment was thus legitimized. The final outcome was a new inquiry, covering this time the whole issue, including the collection methods, the information and negotiation strategies as well as decision making at all levels. It led to the recent charges against 30 people, all specialists from the blood sector and advisers of the ministers. In this forthcoming trial Dr Garretta and Dr Allain will be tried a second time, an unprecedented event in the history of modern law, with much heavier criminal charges: poisoning and involuntary violence. As for the former ministers themselves, they were finally tried in 1999, for involuntary manslaughter. The prime minister and the minister for social affairs were found not guilty, whilst the health minister was found guilty but not sent to prison.[24] The procedure started in 1991, initiated by the opposition during the political storm. However, judging members of government for their action in office demanded a joint vote of the two parliamentary assemblies, a special law court to be set up with deputies as judges. The practical attempt revealed a long series of incompatibilities concerning the procedures, the prescription periods and the indictments which changed several times. Most importantly, the unfruitful endeavours revealed the incapacity of the special court to adapt to modern society. As a final outcome, the special court was reformed, after necessary changes to the Constitution were introduced. The special court is now under the authority of professional judges and open to complaint from all citizens.

The *Conseil d'État*, the country's highest legal institution, played the major role in framing the legal problems and solutions. It suggested centralizing the nearly 2000 penal and administrative complaints to be dealt with by a single court for each legal track: one court for the administrative trials, one for the penal. It established product liability for blood products, confirmed the state's responsibility for patients in public medical services and introduced the obligation to act in the case of *potential*, not only confirmed, risks. The mobilization of the entire legal system contributed to designing the sectoral reforms, starting in 1993 with the complete reorganization of the institutional set-up of the blood sector. The main focus was on the creation of independent agencies and expert commissions and on effective surveillance and follow-up procedures. As a consequence, the hospitals were forced to find and check all transfusion recipients since 1980. Similar reforms reshaped the entire control systems of medicines and medical products. The new rules have since been extended to the food sector and related industrial procedures.

6 ASSESSMENT OF SUCCESS AND FAILURE

The French HIV/blood case illustrates a combination of *different degrees* of failure and success, on the programmatic as well as on the political level. It suggests no single criterion which would allow a conclusion on a clearly designed policy success or failure. It provides a complex puzzle with various elements of both.

Technical risk management was a *global failure*, although this was not noticed in the early stages and did not give rise to complaint at the time. It constituted a failure because HIV continued to enter the transfusion chain despite alarms being sounded about the risk. Adequate measures to limit the risk of transmission were not taken with the required urgency. The global failure was conditioned by the structure of the system, which was rooted in unquestioned intellectual paradigms, rhetoric accepting tranfusional risks, professional practices and also in part the financing procedures. The alarm was not understood in its full significance, which should be considered as a programmatic failure. Three elements of failure were common to the entire transfusion system and concerned haemophiliacs as well as transfusion recipients: the unsafe methods of blood collection, the late and incomplete application of the official orders for donor selection and the late provision of HIV test facilities outside the blood centres. The deficient risk evaluation was aggravated within the hospital services by the over-use of transfusions and the absence of systematic tracing back and warning systems.

In the specific field of clotting factors, risk management on the programmatic level was a *relative success*, despite many errors. The contamination rate of French haemophiliacs remained within the average range of most developed countries. The risk was under control within the normal time frame, as compared to international standards. The legal obligation to screen all blood units was even introduced earlier than elsewhere. In the specific French context, this nevertheless represented *a failure* because the scientific advance in HIV research and the public service structure of the entire blood sector should have enabled

France to do better. Existing opportunities were not fully used. Specific examples of this were the delayed support of the Pasteur Institute and, later on, the lack of support for the Lille fractionating unit. Further examples were the ambiguous messages given to haemophiliacs by their personal doctors and the CNTS, instead of adequate information delivered from the health authorities; failure to inform contaminated patients about the risk of transmission to their partners and new-born infants; and hesitation in importing purified products and/or returning to traditional treatments for an 'intermediate period'. The failure to officially recall the stocks of inactivated clotting concentrates and home-stored provisions also constituted a main element of the subsequent crisis and the penal blame shifting. However, since no case of haemophiliac con-tamination was attributed to inactivated medicines used after the official delay of 1 October 1985, this should not be viewed as a programmatic mistake, but rather as part of the political failure.

Assessment on the political level is also twofold. The outrageous scandal constituted without any doubt a *policy failure*, whilst the sustainable learning process resulting from it indicated a long-term *policy success*. The political failure was illustrated by a resignation and the penal trials of the four top executives as well as by public opinion polls, the dramatic press coverage, the official inquiries and, finally, by the public compensation scheme. The first penal trial coincided with the preparation of the reforms, as if the passage from the negative to the positive phases of the policy process, that is, from minimizing and denying the problem to acknowledging it and treating it institutionally, needed to be clearly highlighted through the legal judgement.

The political failure and crisis resulted from an interplay of institutional and sociological phenomena. The normal institutional functioning of the blood sector was not adapted to respond efficiently to the new risk. Decisions were therefore needed to introduce problem-oriented changes, but the centres of responsibility were not clearly identified or, in the case of the GDH, were too weak to impose their legitimacy. The ministers' trial in 1999 was entirely devoted to this question of the respective responsibilities of the medical, admin-istrative and political actors. Decision competence was in fact in the hands of the transfusion leaders, who tried to keep up previous policy goals. Incentives for problem-oriented change were non-existent. Case management was to remain marginal to preserve the global philosophy of the famous French model of blood transfusion. Therefore compulsory screening of blood samples seemed preferable to donor selection. This disturbed the internal functioning of the blood centres and the donor associations. In the same way, the first compen-sation scheme, proposing only a restrictive solidarity allocation reserved to haemophiliacs, remained in line with the traditional legal perceptions and did not provide any precedent for the costly compensation for other medical risks.[25]

The restrictive case management, however, did not work in *the long term*. New actors imposed new views: dissenting haemophiliacs, journalists and law professionals whose endeavours were favoured by the moving political context. Refusal to recognize contaminated patients as 'victims' and the secrecy surrounding decision making enhanced a deep sense of betrayal, widely shared by public opinion. The discovery that the unquestioned trust in medicine, the political elite and the public service was unrealistic had a heavy impact in the French context, because it called into question fundamental elements of national self-perception and the political culture.

Policy responses to risk and crisis stretched out over more than 15 years and still continue. The first phase of technical diagnosis and intervention extended from 1983 to 1985, cumulating in an acute crisis during May and June 1985. HIV was contained but it had not been prevented, which appeared unacceptable later on, when people actually died. The risk was accepted in the rhetoric of potential transfusion risks, not in reality. The second phase extended from 1989 to 1993, with an acute political crisis during one year, in 1991–2 up to the first penal trial. The aim in the first stage was to stop the fatal virus spreading in the blood supply. In the second stage, the goal was to examine the responsibilities for what went wrong and subsequently conceive a new framework for sustainable public health policies. The political management was *a story in two parts*.

In practical terms, the two periods were linked by mobilization and legal litigation. There was no 'crisis' when the risk occurred in the early 1980s, despite the uncertain nature of the problem and the sense of urgency among specialists. The absence of crisis can be explained by the fact that the dominant demands were rapidly satisfied: access to the new prophylaxis, the achievement of national self-sufficiency and, for risk containment, the introduction of compulsory blood screening and virus inactivation techniques. The victims were not yet visible in public terms and compensation was not yet formulated as a clear demand. From 1989 onwards, the context changed rapidly. The demand for compensation from the Haemophilia Association was barely satisfied and adopted without consultation. Journalists revealed confidential documents and proposed a new reading of the events. Last but not least, the socialists, who had been in charge of the initial risk management, were back in power and constituted an ideal target for political blame and contest.

In theoretical terms, the two parts of the story were linked by the difficult emergence of a different set of policy references.[26] The focus moved from a war-born philosophy of public service and a political perception of the AIDS risk towards a public health perspective and consumer protection. The change was made official by jurisdiction confirming the public responsibility for blood safety and, subsequently, risk prevention in general. The new 'principle of precaution' provided the legal support and an obligation henceforth imposed on all public authorities and decision makers, in any sector of activity that might affect human health.[27] The complete change of policy references, institutional actors and modes of regulation, together with new goals assigned to the blood sector, formed a new public policy, inaugurated by a prolific production of information widely diffused through public reports, judicial inquiries and the press. The quantity and quality of information as well as its controversial content contrasted with the previous situation where secrecy, confidentiality and homogeneous opinion prevailed. The case illustrated the crucial role of information and public communication in the success of reform policies (Schmidt, 2000a, 2000b).

7   CONCLUSION: WHAT MATTERED MOST?

From a comparative point of view, the most distinctive feature of the French HIV/blood case was the *crisis policy style*. To what extent can this be explained by case characteristics, sectoral specificities or the national context?

Blood is a vital fluid, heavily charged with symbolic values and ambivalent meanings. There is good and bad blood (Nelkin, 1999). Any risk concerning blood is likely to activate the register of 'bad' meanings and thus provoke passionate social responses. In France, the general sociological phenomena were aggravated by the historical commitment to a national philosophy of blood donation. It was precisely because the tragedy of blood in France was home-grown and could not be traced back to international business that the scandal had such exceptional dimensions.

On the institutional level, two elements in the organization of the French blood sector added to the specific challenge. The active presence in the policy sector of conservative blood donor associations discouraged the expression of criticism and worked against adaptation and marginal changes, especially as far as blood collection policies were concerned. The technological evolution introduced by the clotting concentrates had not been accompanied by adequate reforms of the supervising, control and decision-making systems. All this entailed uncertainty about who was responsible for what when the HIV crisis suddenly occurred. These governance problems were to a large extent connected with institutional outdating and updating (Steffen, 1999).

Everywhere, haemophilic patients were dependent on the medical establishment and were thus not easily inclined to disclose their problems in public. Professional paradigms still enjoy an important influence over health policies in most developed welfare states. International comparison, however, highlights the particular weakness of the French health system in controlling the doctors.[28] Until the early 1990s, both the blood and the health sectors offered an almost perfect example of sectoral corporatism, with little space left for policy alternatives or beneficiary participation. In the blood case, mobilization and criticism as well as problem framing and resolving were encouraged from outside the sector. The legal professions and the opportunities offered by the political context played a dynamic part in the crisis.

The French HIV/blood crisis was much more than a fatal virus in the blood transfusion system. It was the turning point in the policies and modes of governance of an extremely highly institutionalized and conservative sector. As subsequent developments suggest, it also became a starting point for accountability demanded from public authorities and politicians.

NOTES

1. 'The articles published in *L'Événement du Jeudi* were needed to highlight the cynicism, the lies, the mistakes (…). Pretentious French blood transfusion wanted to enlighten the world with its ethics like the statue of Liberty, but its flame hid problems' (haemophiliac interview, quoted by Bastin *et al.*, 1993, p. 155; translated by Steffen).
2. Japan was the only other case showing a wide-ranging public scandal. For an international comparison of eight developed countries, cf. Feldman and Bayer (1999).
3. In March 1995, 2664 cases of transfusion-related AIDS were declared in the EU, of which 1498 were from France. The number of transfusion-related cases per hundred thousand inhabitants: European average 0.81, France 2.64 (compared to UK 0.16, Netherlands 0.24, Germany 0.34, Spain 0.65). For declared AIDS cases in haemophiliacs per 100 000 inhabitants, France (7.76) remains close to the European average (7.2). (*Quarterly Report* of the WHO–European Union AIDS Centre, Paris, no. 45, 1995.)
4. This precise problem constituted an important point in the debates during the penal trial of the ministers, in February 1999.
5. Hermitte (1996, p. 91). For details on the history and the legal dimensions, see the excellent study of Hermitte (1996), from which the information used here is drawn.
6. Communists and militant Catholics formed the majority.
7. It was only in the 1993 reform that paid donation was formally prohibited.
8. 'When the Blood Donors' Associations sneeze, Parliament catches a cold' (interview, Setbon, 1993, p. 80).
9. The crucial problem of the integration of blood and derived products into the category of 'medicines and medical products' divided European policy makers for several years, from 1988 to 1995. The controversy directly concerned French policies, but cannot be treated within the scope of this chapter.
10. The description here refers to the situation up to the 1993 reform. Details given here are drawn from the official reports and the legal inquiries.
11. So-called 'comfort' or 'safety' transfusions were common practice in hospitals, to prevent post-operative shock (Soulier, 1992, p. 107). After the press campaign on the 'tainted blood', comfort transfusion declined by 50 per cent (ibid., p. 146). On national average, the quantity of labile units used dropped by nearly 20 per cent between 1986 and 1991 (Morelle, 1996, pp. 110–11).
12. Complete self-sufficiency was obtained in 1987 (Soulier, p. 90).
13. In 1984, plasmapheresis represented only 4.3 per cent of the donations, 10 times less than in neighbouring Belgium (Bastin *et al.*, 1993, p. 71).
14. 'Normal life' was the key reference also in social policies, for the elderly and handicapped.
15. The information used here is drawn from official reports, mainly Lucas, IGASS/IGSJ, from hearings during the legal procedure (Greilsamer), the press reports (mainly *Le Monde*) and the books written by the actors (Casteret, Roux, Soulier).
16. The case, published in *Le Monde*, 31 July 1983, was confirmed by the health authorities.
17. 'We did not believe it, we were afraid that health costs were being cut at our expense, because haemophilia is so expensive' (interview, FHA, 1993).

18. *Libération* and *Le Matin*.
19. The IGASS/IGSJ states 40 per cent, which includes a mistake; the agreed figure is 30 per cent.
20. HIV tests prescribed by doctors were covered by the health insurance in February 1986 only and centres for anonymous free testing were set up during 1987.
21. The heavyweight newspaper *Le Monde* printed a headline, '50 persons a week received HIV-positive blood in the Parisian area' (13 June 1985), expressed alarm at the 'persistent intolerance towards homosexuals' (20 June 1985) and presented blood screening as 'a very unusual ethical issue' (23–4 June 1985).
22. The following information originates from the Lucas report (1991) which provides a detailed documented chronology of the events. The quotations indicate passages from the minutes of the various meetings and documents.
23. In fact he was also sentenced by the Appeal Court a year later.
24. The health minister received an official reprimand as a punishment.
25. The issue is at present under discussion again, on the basis of a joint official report from the IGASS and the IGSJ (the General Inspection Boards of, respectively, the Administration of Social and Public Health Affairs and the Justice Administration), transmitted to Parliament in February 2000 (*Le Monde*, 17 February 2000).
26. The term corresponds to a change of the '*référentiel*' according to the perspective of French public policy specialists (Muller, 1998). For an international comparative perspective, see Boin and 't Hart (2000).
27. The diplomatic struggle within the European Union, opposing France and Britain over the embargo on beef importation, illustrates the far-reaching implications of the new 'principle of precaution'. It constitutes the official ground for the French government's refusal to raise the embargo.
28. Cf. David Wilsford's contribution to this book (Chapter 11). Also Jobert and Steffen (1994), Immergut (1992) and Steffen (2000).

26. The case of HIV and blood supply in Germany: programmatic failures and political successes

Patrick Kenis[1]

1 THE GERMAN CHALLENGE TO HIV AND BLOOD SUPPLY CONTAMINATION

The history of the HIV infection of haemophiliacs in Germany is a West German story. In contrast to West Germany, East Germany (the former German Democratic Republic, GDR) aimed at national self-sufficiency in blood and blood products. As result of this policy, only five HIV infections were detected among the estimated 1300 East German haemophiliacs (in 1986 and 1987). These infections were caused by imported, HIV-contaminated blood (Kiehl and Altmann, 1991).

In Germany, a total of about 550 haemophilia-associated and about 280 transfusion-associated AIDS cases have been reported as of 31 December 1999. A total of about 2000 HIV infections among haemophiliacs and about 600 transfusion-associated HIV infections are estimated to exist (Robert-Koch Institut).[2] This means that 50 per cent to 75 per cent of haemophiliacs who receive treatment with coagulation factors have been infected with HIV. The first AIDS case in a transfusion recipient was diagnosed in 1983. Also in 1983, in October, the first haemophiliac with AIDS was diagnosed. In 1984, seven haemophiliacs were diagnosed with AIDS. The majority of transfusion-associated infections and infections among haemophiliacs occurred before October 1985, and before mandatory HIV antibody testing for blood and blood products was introduced. There are data that suggest that the majority of infections among the haemophilic population occurred in 1984 (Erfle *et al.*, 1985).

At that time it was the responsibility of the former *Bundesgesundheitsamt* (Federal Health Office) to identify health risks for the general population (including risks from drugs, medical products and blood products) and to take adequate measures for preventing such risks. Formally and technically speaking, the Federal Health Office could have halted the distribution of possibly HIV-contaminated blood and blood products from 1984 onwards. As will be described later in this chapter, the Federal Health Office failed to take such measures. What turned out to be a major health related crisis (the contamination of many thousands of persons and the related severe illnesses and deaths) was not responded to by adequate crisis management. Later in this chapter, evidence will be presented demonstrating the programmatic failure in responding to the risk of the transmission of HIV via contaminated blood in Germany. As far as the political response is concerned, the picture looks quite different in Germany. As will be illustrated, the problem did not appear on any political agenda for some time but once there it was dealt with rather successfully. After providing an assessment of the programmatic and political response an attempt will be made to explain why the Federal Health Office did not take adequate measures for preventing the risk of HIV contamination through blood and blood products and why the political system was rather successful in gaining control over the issue.

2 THE INSTITUTIONAL CONTEXT OF THE BLOOD SUPPLY IN GERMANY

The actors involved in blood supply in Germany can be grouped as users, producers, administrators and therapists, and policy makers and controllers of blood and blood products in Germany. The following is a short overview of these actors.

Users

The users of blood and blood products are transfusion patients on the one hand and haemophiliacs on the other. Whereas the first group is not a clearly identifiable group since transfusion is generally related to certain incidents (such as operations or first aid in case of accidents), the second group is most clearly related to patients with haemophilia. Of these patients – an estimated 3500 to 6000 patients in Germany (Schramm and Schulte-Hillen, 1994) – between 2500 and 3500 require substitution therapy with coagulation factors. Anticoagulant treatment which uses concentrates of human coagulation factors, enriched for factor VIII, was widely available in Germany in the early 1970s. Since the product is approved for marketing, German health insurance covers the cost of treatment with this product since no equivalent product is available at a cheaper price.

The *Deutsche Hämophiliegesellschaft* (German Haemophilia Society) is an organization for people with bleeding disorder and for their relatives. Although the organization is generally described as a 'self-help organization' it is noticeable that physicians from haemophilia centres are members of the board of the organization. Another organization which could have represented the users of blood and blood products, the *Deutsche AIDS Hilfe*, did not play a major role in this context. As in many other European countries, the non-profit organizations which developed in the early phase of the AIDS epidemic concentrated mainly on homosexual persons and, later on, drug users (Kenis and Marin, 1997). It was generally felt that the problems of haemophiliacs are not understood by *AIDS-Hilfe* organisations (*Der Spiegel*, 1992, no. 24).[3]

Producers

The blood sector in Germany is a highly complex market, with an international component. The turnover is estimated at DM 500 million to 1 billion (*Der Spiegel*, 1993, no. 41). In 1992, blood products were imported from 28 countries with a value of about DM 220 million and exported to 80 countries with a value of about DM 300 million (*Die Zeit*, 1993, no. 47). Products include whole blood, blood components such as erythrocyte or platelet concentrates, and plasma-derived products such as fresh frozen plasma and clotting factor concentrates.

A highly differentiated set of organizations and producers are involved in blood provision and the production of blood products. As well as local public institutions (that is, hospitals and *kommunale Blutspendendienste* [local blood banks]) and the German Red Cross, private firms also are involved. The most important private firms are the Behringwerke-AG, the Immuno GmbH and the Troponwerke (of which Bayer is the parent company). The pharmaceutical industry is mainly active in plasma-derived products, such as clotting factor concentrates, anticoagulants and haemostatics. All these firms are at the same time internationally integrated.

Erythrocytes, thrombocytes and other blood products used for transfusion were mostly supplied through national resources, mainly by governmental institutions (such as local blood banks) and non-profit organizations. In the 1970s and 1980s, the majority of blood products such as coagulation factor preparations were imported to West Germany.

Since 1952, the Red Cross has operated blood banks (*Blutspendedienste des Deutschen Roten Kreuzes*). The Red Cross processed blood from more than 3.8 million donations in 1999 (www.drk.de/blutspendedienst). The blood banks are operated as non-profit organizations and blood donors do not receive financial compensation, while the blood products are sold on a full cost-recovery basis.

According to results from a survey on blood donors in Germany, they cannot be considered a homogeneous group. Whether commercial companies rely on a particular group of individuals who serve as plasma donors and whether this group is biased because certain persons (homeless persons or drug users) are attracted as donors even by the small amount of money paid for compensation is unknown (Dressler, 1999).

Also hospitals, university hospitals and specialized clinics often have their own blood banks. The products produced in these settings depend largely on local needs.

Administrators and Therapists

Blood and blood products are provided through the medical system. Blood is generally transfused in hospitals in the event of medical necessity. Anticoagulant treatment is administered through specialized haemophilia treatment centres, hospitals, ambulances or physicians in private practice. About 75 per cent of haemophiliacs who need treatment receive home care treatment (Dressler, 1999): a form of treatment where the patient receives a sufficient amount of clotting factors for self-administration. The clotting factor is stored in a refrigerator at home, and the patient keeps a supply that will last for a long period of time (approximately six months). The self-administration is performed according to a prescription by a physician, or according to the needs of the patient.

The therapeutic freedom of physicians in Germany allowed the use of high doses of coagulation factors, and physicians as well as patient felt that high-dose treatment should be administered in order to enable haemophiliac patients to lead a normal life. The same practice was followed by the majority of haemophilia centres and specialized physicians. In Germany, an average of 4 to 4.5 international units of factor VIII per capita of the general population per year is prescribed. This massive amount exceeds by far the doses of factor VIII that are being used in other European countries or in the United States (ibid.).

Policy Makers and Controllers

Under Germany's federal constitution (the *Grundgesetz*), health and health-related issues lie within the authority of the *Länder* (the states). The regulatory power of federal authorities is limited to certain issues delegated by the *Länder*. The federal ministry of health (*Bundesministerium für Gesundheit*) controls various federal institutes[4] and is the supervisory authority for federal health offices. Whenever a health-related decision is required at the federal level and when the federal ministry of health is involved, the federal agencies advise the ministry and prepare the scientific background for the political decisions. For example, federal agencies such as the Paul-Ehrlich-Institut (PEI) or the Institute for Pharmaceutical and Medical Products (BfArM) may license blood products or new drugs for marketing, but the direct control of production facilities is under the authority of the state where the producer is based.

Before responsibilities for blood and blood products were clearly regulated as a consequence of the HIV/AIDS scandal in 1994,[5] it was the responsibility and task of the former *Gesundheitsamt* (Federal Health Office) to identify health risks for the general population (including risks from drugs, medical products and blood products) and to take adequate measures for preventing such risks.

The history of the federal health office goes back to the *Kaiserliche Gesundheitsamt* (KGA), founded in 1876.[6] In the Weimar Republic it was renamed *Reichsgesundheitsamt* and in 1952 it was established as the federal health office and was put under the supervision of the home office. It was established as an independent federal administration, which is responsible for the entire state territory. It is different from a ministry because it is not directly involved in policy making but rather has implementation functions. In 1963, the supervision of the federal health office was transferred to the *Bundesministerium für Gesundheitswesen* (ministry of health). Before it was closed down in 1994, the federal health office incorporated six institutes[7] as well as the *AIDS-Zentrum* and a central department. Each of the institutes had its own goals and functions and was divided into a number of departments. The organizations had a staff of 3000, of whom 700 were scientists.

The federal health office was the federal agency which controlled not only approval of new drugs but also post-marketing control of approved pharmaceutical substances and drugs. The major purpose of post-marketing control is to ensure a positive risk–benefit ratio for new drugs. The procedure of post-marketing control involves not only federal agencies, but also state health offices and agencies as well as physicians who are obliged to report possible adverse effects of drugs and pharmaceutical products to the commission on pharmaceutical substances (*Arzneimittelkommission*) of the federal medical council (*Bundesärztekammer*).

The most important legal instrument for post-marketing control is the so-called *Stufenplanverfahren* (graduated plan procedure), introduced on 1 October 1980.[8] The first step of the *Stufenplanverfahren*, that is *Gefahrenstufe I* (risk level I) occurs when the federal health office (or today the *Bundesinstitut für Arzneimittel und Medizinprodukte*) receives initial reports on possible adverse effects or new risks of pharmaceutical substances. Consequently, the federal health office has to share this information with the producer of the substance and with the health offices of the *Länder*. In this way the information about the incidence of the adverse effects, its possible causes and the degree of risk can be collected. *Gefahrenstufe II* is activated when there are indications that the pharmaceutical substance is a health risk. Consequently, an expert commission (including representatives from federal health offices, the *Länder*, the pharmaceutical industry, health care professionals and external experts) will meet and discuss further actions.

The question of liability for blood-related injury or blood-related illnesses is regulated through the *Arzneimittelgesetz* (Medical Preparations Law) and through the *Bürgerliches Gesetzbuch* (German Civil Code). These laws require evidence of causation between a product and its use or administration on the one hand, and a possible injury or illness on the other. The burden of proof is with the person harmed.

3 DESCRIPTION OF THE EVENTS REGARDING HIV AND BLOOD IN GERMANY

This section provides a description of the way in which the problem of HIV in blood and blood products was perceived and reacted to in Germany from 1982 onwards.[9] In December 1982 an article published in the *Morbidity and Mortality Weekly Report* (MMWR, 1982) discussed for the first time the possibility of transmission of AIDS through blood. In the same month the federal health office reacted to this article. The working group on AIDS (composed of virologist and specialists on internal medicine and infectious diseases) of the federal health office published a *Schnellinformation* (rapid note) on AIDS (Weise and L'age-Stehr, 1982) which also explicitly mentioned the possibility of transmission through blood and blood products. It was published in the *Bundesgesundheitsblatt*, which meant that it was in the first place read by administers and therapists (that is, physicians).

As early as January 1983, the German Red Cross (being the most important supplier of blood) introduced measures to exclude donors at risk of AIDS (that is, people with weight loss, lymph node swellings and other clinical signs) from donating blood. The effectiveness of these measures is doubtful, but it indicates that the Red Cross considered the transmission of AIDS via blood to be a possible risk. From June 1983 onwards most Red Cross leagues and most other blood banks and transfusion centres started to exclude so-called 'risk groups' (intravenous drug users and homosexual men) from blood donation.

Also in June 1983, a decline of T (thymus) helper cells in German haemophiliacs was described for the first time (Marcus, 1993). In August 1983, the federal health office released an AIDS summary for physicians which pointed out the risk for recipients of coagulation factors and other blood products. At about the same time (the beginning of September 1983) a press release was distributed. At this time the federal health office started to take actions other than merely distributing information against HIV transmission via blood and blood products.

In November 1983, the federal health office introduced a *Stufenplanverfahren* (graduated-phase procedure) for the reduction of risks associated with coagulation factors. The *Stufenplanverfahren* was started for factors VIII. As usual the procedure started with a *Sachanhörung* (hearing) on 14 November. Representatives from pharmaceutical companies,[10] representatives of the *Bundesverband der Pharmazeutischen Industrie* (Federal Association of the Pharmaceutical Industry), representatives of several Red Cross leagues as well as representatives from different hospitals participated in this meeting, where representatives from the pharmaceutical industry emphasized that no proven AIDS case among haemophiliacs in Germany had been described and denied a causal link between factor VIII concentrates and AIDS, and the fact that AIDS is caused by an infectious agent. Several aspects, including donor selection in the USA and in Germany, documentation of products and an anti-hepatitis core test for potential donors, were discussed.

In June 1984, the federal health office announced that a hepatitis B core antibody test as a surrogate marker should become mandatory on 1 January 1985. The idea for the test was grounded on the belief that it could be a good marker for the risk of infections from sexually transmitted diseases. This test was not introduced because of objections from the blood industry. It was argued that these surrogate marker tests have only a limited validity, but also the expenses involved in the laboratory procedure played an important role.

On 8 June 1984 the federal health office issued a *Bescheid* (administrative decision) based on the November meeting. The *Bescheid* demanded a declaration of the country of origin of products, a declaration of the donor pool size, limited indication for use and warning with regard to a possible transmission of AIDS as well as a definition of criteria for donor selection and additional laboratory test (such as hepatitis B core antibody testing). The plan was to introduce these measures by 1 September 1984 but almost all regional Red Cross blood banks and many producers of blood products objected to these measures.[11] Because of these *Widersprüche* (objections) only some of the measures were implemented and then after a larger time delay. One major objection was that a limitation of the indication for factor VIII concentrates in treating severe haemophilia would interfere with therapeutical freedom of the physician. Other objections were that evidence about the country of origin, number of donors and pool size would not contribute to blood product safety. Moreover, a warning against AIDS was objected to because producers of blood products still believed, in the second half of 1984, that there was no evidence that AIDS could be transmitted through factor VIII concentrates.

On 12 December 1984 the federal health office issued a *Widerspruchsbescheid* (an administrative decision on the objectives) whereby the original *Bescheid* was changed in numerous ways: the use of factor VIII should not be limited to severe forms of haemophilia; evidence on the country of origin and of the factor concentrate was no longer required. Also products consisting of pooled plasma would be admitted, and only pools with material from more than 20 single donations had to be tested for quality and safety. From 1 March 1985 onwards producers of coagulation factors had to declare whether the product had undergone an inactivation procedure and, if so, which method was used.

Since February 1985 only factor VIII products which were heat-inactivated for hepatitis B virus have been used. In April 1985, the HIV antibody test was licensed for marketing and was immediately used by most transfusion service centres, although the test became mandatory only on 1 October 1985. At the same time some transfusion centres introduced a confidential donor self-exclusion form, asking donors to fill out a questionnaire and to declare that they did not belong to a 'risk group'. In the meantime blood 'on the shelf' was not rejected, but used for transfusion. On 1 October 1985, the HIV antibody test became mandatory. The introduction of HIV antibody testing was probably the most effective measure in preventing HIV infections via blood transfusions and in securing safety of coagulation factors.

In 1985–6 claims started to be made by persons previously infected. Most of these claims resulted in agreements with the insurers of the pharmaceutical companies. It was agreed that they would receive an average compensation of DM 70 000 (30 000 for medical costs, 30 000 compensating for lost incomes and 10 000 for the funeral costs), thereby excluding all acknowledgement of legal obligations for payment by pharmaceutical companies. Also, in 1986, Professor Egli and Dr Brackmann from the haemophilia treatment centre at Bonn University were sued by a patient. In this and similar cases it was almost impossible to find a physician for an expert opinion in court and no physician has been sentenced in the context of blood products and HIV infections.

Only in July 1987 was a confidential self-exclusion form as a mandatory procedure introduced for transfusion service centres. Blood donors filled out a questionnaire, received a leaflet about the possibility that HIV/AIDS could be transmitted through blood and blood products, and donors were asked to abstain from donation if they considered themselves to be at risk of an HIV infection. This procedure was recommended in 1987 but only became mandatory from the 1 April 1988.

On 1 June 1989, the second-generation HIV-1/HIV-2 antibody tests were introduced; and on 1 June 1990 the test for anti-hepatitis C virus antibodies was introduced, but not becoming mandatory until 25 April 1992. Only in 1993 did civil litigation against employees and civil servants from health authorities begin. However, it was not possible to prove that they had reacted insufficiently to the risk of HIV infection through blood products.

In October 1993, the case of the company UB Plasma shocked the German public. Even in the 1990s this company had used blood and blood plasma which were not tested for HIV antibodies. In order to save costs, UB Plasma sold blood products which were not tested or were inadequately tested for HIV. Costs were saved by using blood from countries such as Romania and by pouring together different blood donations before testing. This time problems were also identified by a virologist of the federal health office, who already in May had identified problems with the products of UB Plasma, but failed to inform the relevant institutions about his finding at that time. Soon after, products of UB Plasma were confiscated in 50 German hospitals and UB Plasma was closed down. On 29 October 1993, an investigation commission (*Unter-suchungsausschuß*) on HIV/AIDS and blood and blood products was established by the German Parliament (*Bundestag*) mainly as a result of the UB Plasma scandal.

In 1994, the federal health office was dissolved and from July 1994 onwards the Paul-Ehrlich-Institute became the central federal institution responsible for blood and blood products.

4 ASSESSMENT OF THE PROGRAMMATIC RESPONSE

The parliamentary investigation commission concluded that what had happened was a scandal and that pharmaceutical companies, physicians, blood banks and hospitals and the federal health office shared responsibility for the HIV infection of many PPSB (prothrombin) recipients, haemophiliacs and recipients of other blood and plasma products. Rather than asking how the responsibility for the scandal should be divided among these actors the main question was whether the *Bundesgesundeitsamt* as the major public institution formally responsible for avoiding health risks in Germany, as well as its controlling institution, the federal ministry of health, had failed in their functions. In a later section, when trying to explain the failure of the *Bundesgesundheitsamt*, the role other actors played will be brought in.

The Federal Health Office failed programmatically because it was incapable of implementing the necessary measures or because it has implemented them too late. The federal health office was very prompt in recognizing and informing physicians about the possibility of transmission of AIDS through blood and blood products (in 1982) but rather reluctant in formulating strategies and especially implementing strategies to prevent transfusion through blood and blood products.

The *Stufenplanverfahren* (graduated plan procedure) described above was never introduced with respect to whole blood and blood products or the transfusion of cellular components. There has only been a *Stufenplanverfahren* for factor VIII and not for factor IX concentrates or other plasma-derived products such as PPSB, despite the fact that a possible risk of transmission of viral diseases through these products had been reported. Moreover, in the case where a *Stufenplanverfahren* (for factor VIII in November 1983) was initiated, only some of the measures, which were according to international standards considered effective, were implemented and then even with a larger time delay.

It is also noticeable that it took the federal health office almost seven months to produce a *Bescheid* (administrative decision) on the basis of the *Sachanhörung* (hearing) in the *Stufenplanverfahren* for factor VIII.

In 1981, heat inactivated factor VIII (which was at that time known to lead to an inactivation of the hepatitis B virus and which also, as was learned in 1985, inactivates HIV) was licensed in Germany. The majority of HIV infections might possibly have been prevented if heat-inactivated factor VIII concentrate for treatment of all haemophiliacs had been mandatory since 1981 instead of a situation being tolerated where only haemophiliacs who tested negative for hepatitis B could receive reimbursement for heat-inactivated coagulation factors through their health insurance. The reasons why heat-inactivated factor VIII concentrate was not used for all patients were that in 1981 its price was twice as high as the price for regular coagulation factors and that producers argued that not enough heat-inactivated factor VIII concentrate would have been available (heat inactivation means a 40 per cent loss of the product). According to a parliamentary investigation commission, both arguments were invalid. It is stated that the extra cost would not have been an extreme burden to the health insurance and that, through reducing the high doses, which are common in Germany, enough coagulation factors would have been available. On the other hand, in 1981 nobody knew whether heat-inactivated factor VIII concentrate prevented AIDS. This relationship was, however, clearly seen and documented by many international and German experts from 1983 onwards. The federal health office also failed in taking measures to decrease the doses of units. Physicians argued that only this treatment would enable haemophiliacs to live a normal life, and denied that it increased the risk of HIV transmission. This issue remains controversial, even after the parliamentary debate (Eibl, 1995).

In April 1985, the HIV antibody test was licensed for marketing but became only mandatory half a year later, on 1 October 1985.[12] The producers claimed that there were not enough test kits available at that point, although it is difficult to know if this is true. By and large this again seems, however, a case where the federal health office delayed action instead of acting as the institution responsible for minimizing health risks for the German people. To many transfusion service centres this seemed to be totally unacceptable and irresponsible policy and they immediately started to use the test. On 1 October 1985, when the HIV antibody test became mandatory, the federal health office did not recall untested blood or coagulation factors since they seemed to be ignorant of the fact that many haemophiliacs who participated in homecare had stored large quantities of coagulation factors in their private refrigerators – supplies that would often last for another six months.

In summary, we find here that public administration seemed to have a lot of expertise on the problem of AIDS and the ways of transmission but often acted very slowly and passively and was ineffective in implementing decisions or policies. Consequently, the prevention of the transmission of HIV through blood and blood products should be considered a programmatic failure in the case of Germany.

5 ASSESSMENT OF THE POLITICAL RESPONSE

The assessment of the political response to the risk of HIV infection through blood and blood products should be divided into two periods. In the first decade of the crisis (1983–93) there was, generally speaking, a complete absence of any political response to the problem. From 1993 onwards, the situation changed radically, in that a rather elaborate political response developed.

In the period 1983–93, there was almost no public or political debate on the problem. Haemophiliacs or transfusion recipients did not play a major role in the public debate on AIDS in Germany, which otherwise reached its peak in 1987. Apart from some critical press articles and the first legal claims by persons infected (starting in 1985–6) there was no notable political response. In a detailed history written by two investigative journalists on the transmission of HIV through blood and blood products, the federal ministry of health (which was politically responsible, in contrast to the federal office, which was pro-grammatically responsible) is mentioned only twice. It is also indicative that, in the second edition of the book, which was published in 1993, Horst Seehofer, then minister of health, wrote a foreword (Koch and Meichsner, 1993).

It is difficult to assess this first period in terms of political failure or success. Can it be considered a 'success' that the political system survived the contamination and death of many persons? Moreover, success and failure can probably only be properly used as categories in those cases where the political system was actively involved in the policy. Characteristic of this first period, however, was the inactivity of the political system regarding the problem of HIV transmission through blood and blood products.

This situation changed dramatically in late 1993, when the press made it known that the company UB Plasma had used blood and blood plasma which was not tested for HIV antibodies as late as the 1990s. Not only the general public but also the minister of health, Horst Seehofer, learned these facts by reading the magazine *Der Spiegel* (6 September 1993). This fact, as well as the fact that it soon became known that the federal health office knew about this in May 1993, had major consequences. The scandal gained wide media attention and shocked the general public. An *Untersuchungsausschuß* (a parliamentary investigation commission on blood, blood products and HIV/AIDS) was set up, the federal health office was closed down (a unique event in German political history) and a foundation was established for patients who suffered from possible drug-related injuries or illnesses and for whom a proximate connection between the causes and consequences could be established.

The almost 700 pages of the final report of the *Untersuchungsausschuß* (which was made public in November 1994) provide a history of the HIV/AIDS-related events as well as a discussion of possible legal consequences. The report also contains recommendations about the safety of pharmaceutical substances and medical products in general as well as on compensation of recipients of these products. Many of the recommendations are generally considered ineffective and seen as resulting from the composition of the committee which reflected the different political parties in Parliament (Dressler, 1999).

A number of institutional changes followed the parliamentary investigation commission. In July 1994, the Paul-Ehrlich-Institute became the central federal institution responsible for blood and blood products. Moreover, a working group on blood and blood products was established at the Robert Koch-Institute in 1993. The purpose of the group is to support the work of the federal and state government and other health offices with expert advice.[13] Also the necessity of national self-supply of blood and blood products has been stressed repeatedly as a result of the HIV/AIDS crisis. Moreover, today, all plasma-derived products must be stored for a quarantine period of six months. The donor has to undergo a second HIV antibody test three months after donation, otherwise the blood product may not be used and will be rejected. Alternatively, virus inactivated plasma from one single donor may be used. Until this measure was introduced as a recommendation from September 1994 and became mandatory on 1 July 1995, blood and blood products were subject to the same laws and legal measures.

Generally speaking, the political response in this second period can be considered a success. Initiatives such as the parliamentary investigation commission and closing the federal health office were generally perceived as positive by the press, the general public and the politicians. Some results of the parliamentary investigation commission have been criticized as not going far enough and not contributing to structural change in such a way that a similar catastrophe could be prevented in the future (see Dressler, 1999). However, the drastic actions taken as well as the 'pacification' strategy which was the declared aim of the ministry of health and which generally fits the German political culture led to a perception that the crisis was dealt with in an adequate way.

6   EXPLAINING THE PROGRAMMATIC FAILURE AND THE POLITICAL SUCCESS

Why did the response to the risk of HIV infection in blood and blood products in Germany turn out to be a programmatic failure and a political success? This section will mainly introduce factors explaining programmatic failure. Explaining political success can only be done in a very rudimentary way because of the lack of data.

Two main arguments can be advanced to explain why the federal health office did not respond in an adequate manner to the challenge of HIV in blood and blood products. The first argument relates to the type of problem the federal health office had to deal with. It will be argued that the AIDS problem was an ill-structured problem and would have required a different response than routine problems. This situation was not adequately recognized by the *Bundesgesund-heitsamt*. The second argument relates to the type and structure of the external relationships of the *Bundesgesundheitsamt*. It will be argued that, in the first place, the type of relationship this organization had with other organizations can explain the response it developed to HIV and blood.

The problem of AIDS in the early 1980s can be characterized as an ill-structured problem. An ill-structured problem is, according to Simon (1973): (1) new, without familiar clues, (2) complex, with many clues to be taken into account, or (3) contradictory, with different elements suggesting different inter-pretations. The epidemiological pattern of what is known today as HIV infection was largely unknown in the early years of the epidemic, and the size of the epidemic was either over- or underestimated. At this time, it was uncertain how risky blood and blood products were. The main challenge in dealing with ill-structured problems is that imposing familiar structures upon them not only fails to solve these problems but often even exacerbates them. 'Business as usual' can thus be very harmful when confronting ill-structured problems. Ill-structured problems are best dealt with when common routines for problem solving are abandoned and integrative ways of problem solving are sought. Given the 'empty world hypothesis' of Simon (1969), where the structure of the problem is not known, the most effective solution is to use no more coordinat-ing apparatus than is absolutely necessary to bring about a satisfactory level of coordination; that is, favour lower levels of interdependence rather than higher, in order to minimize cognitive complexity. It is not clear whether the federal health office was incapable of judging the situation and problem adequately as an ill-structured problem or not. What they certainly did not do, however, was react to the problem in a way which would have been adequate. The situation at hand would have asked for facilitating decision-making structures, based on a problem orientation rather than on the common and classical bargaining structures between different stakeholders.[14] The fact that the federal health office could not create such a context for problem solving has in turn a lot to do with its position in the network of relationships of the different actors in the area of blood and blood products, as we will see below.

What Figure 26.1 illustrates is that the federal health office was, on the one hand, only controlled to a very limited extent by those one would have expected to control it; that is, its clients and its controlling institution, the federal ministry of health. On the other hand, the office itself had only very limited control over those it was supposed to control: the blood banks, the pharmaceutical industry and the administrators and therapists. Rather, the blood banks and the pharmaceutical industry seemed to have more control over the federal health office than vice versa. It thus becomes clear that the federal health office had far from a central position in this network and that the most significant influence in this network was the pharmaceutical industry and blood banks, which exerted substantial control not only over the federal health office but also over the administrators of blood products and indirectly over the receivers of blood products and the German Haemophilia Society. The control of administrators of blood products over patients is illustrated not only by the fact that on the board of the Haemophiliac Society (a so-called 'self-help group') a number of physicians had a seat but also by the fact that most physicians and haemophilia specialists did not inform their patients about the possible risk of AIDS. Some of them continued this (lack of) information policy as long as possible, declaring that AIDS was an insignificant risk for haemophiliacs. Cases have been reported where patients were told by their physicians as late as 1985 that AIDS was only a minor risk (Dressler, 1999).

Such an actor constellation seems to explain the following reactions. When using the national blood supply for production of coagulation factor concentrates

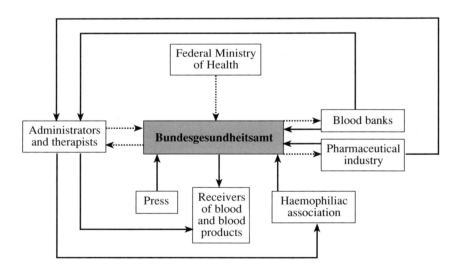

Figure 26.1   Direction and intensity of control relationships among the actors involved in HIV and blood in Germany between 1982 and 1986

was first discussed in the context of HIV/AIDS in the 1980s, representatives from the pharmaceutical industry as well as from self-help organizations for haemophiliacs argued that national resources would not be sufficient to meet the demand for coagulation factors. Thus a situation was created in which an adequate supply of coagulation factors seemed to be of greater importance than the safety of products. Physicians and their patients feared that a legal restriction on the use of imported clotting factors would lead to a shortage in supply. The federal health office seemed not to have the potential to contribute anything constructive to these discussions.

The importance of the pharmaceutical industry in this network is also illustrated by the fact that the perspectives of this industry are clearly represented in the final report of the investigation commission. It is consistent with the statement of Vogel, the executive director of the federal association of Germany's pharmaceutical industry, who stated in May 1987 that the HIV/AIDS scandal should be regulated in a way acceptable to the pharmaceutical industry (Koch and Meichsner, 1993, p. 140). The investigation commission had generally voted for changes, which could simplify the process of establishing proof of evidence, but detailed recommendations which would have had a major impact on the pharmaceutical companies were missing. The recommendations related in the first place to compensations and not so much to structural changes which could avoid similar problems the next time.

The reason why the pharmaceutical industry seems to have a stronger position towards the federal health office than vice versa seems to have something to do with the fact that a considerable information asymmetry existed between the pharmaceutical companies and the *Bundesgesundheitsamt*. Although the federal health office had a monopoly on the authorization of new drugs, the pharmaceutical companies themselves had (and still have) an important role in the definition of the authorization criteria, the implementation of the authorization process and controlling the incidence of adverse effects. It is clear that within such a system the federal health office becomes heavily dependent on the information provided by the pharmaceutical industry. In such a situation a climate develops where informal communication and a preference for solutions through bargaining becomes predominant. The reluctance to implement security measures, as described above, can be better understood in this context. In order not to harm its peculiar relationship with the pharmaceutical industry, the federal health office could have been reluctant to propose too radical and, especially, too costly measures.

Also the federal health office was only weakly controlled by the federal ministry of health. This control, for which Manfreid Steinbach was responsible, was extremely underdeveloped. According to an article in *Der Spiegel*, 'the easy-going way in which the former professional sportsman handled the security problems led, even among the pharmaceutic companies, to many raised eyebrows' *(Der Spiegel,* 1993, no. 41).[15] Also the different ministers of the federal ministry of health (Heiner Geißler, Rita Süsmuth and Gerda Hasselfeldt) did not consider the AIDS problem to be a very important one and therefore did not pay particular attention to what was occurring. It was only when the highly ambitious Horst Seehofer became minister that the relationship between the ministry and the federal health office became very different.

Also in the case of the relationship between the public and the press and the federal health office, a clear information asymmetry did exist. In this case it was to the advantage of the federal health office, which could provide information in a selective way. Consequently, only limited control by the public and the press became possible. As a consequence, the federal health office could be expected to take the pressure from the public and the press not too seriously.

Dismantling the federal health office in the end can be explained by Figure 26.1. The problematic compulsive marriage of the federal health office with the pharmaceutical industry led not only to specific resource dependencies but also to a certain blindness towards other relevant environmental aspects: the obvious and energetic action orientation of the new health minister was not considered significant, the significance of the product controlled, that is blood and its potential relationship to a health risk like AIDS, was underestimated, and the sensitivity to the AIDS issue among the public was not anticipated. Moreover, the potential influence of the media on such a 'thematic' issue was not properly recognized. This is a case where the behaviour of the organization and the issues at play in the environment drifted significantly apart.

As described above, the political response which developed from 1993 onwards can be generally seen as a success. One principal reason is probably that the minister in charge, Horst Seehofer, reacted quite differently from the way the federal health office reacted. Although he became increasingly sensitive to the critical information published in the press, he nevertheless still backed his administration on 23 September in the German Parliament: 'Anyone who claims that serious omissions have occurred and things have been concealed, should give concrete evidence. So far, that has not been done. Except for exaggerated claims, only hot air' (Koch and Meichsner, 1993, p. 319).[16] His position changed dramatically, however, on 5 October 1993, during a meeting with staff from the federal health office and the ministry in which the scale of the programmatic failures became clear. Seehofer was generally seen as a young and ambitious minister. This clear case of failure of the German health system was probably used by Seehofer to become involved in a system which was, generally speaking, rather inaccessible. Through this case he built up an active and dynamic profile which was rather uncommon for previous ministers of health in Germany.

It is interesting, however, that although Seehofer reacted in a rather drastic way (dismantling the federal health office and setting up a parliamentary commission) not much changed structurally in the system which produced the programmatic failures in the first place. Although the federal health office was replaced by another organization, there are no clear indications that the structure of the network described above changed substantially. This, and the general pacification strategy followed by Seehofer in the relationship with the other partners in the network, can probably also be considered as reasons why the 'political' response to the problem was a success.

7 CONCLUSIONS

It is difficult to make a definite statement about how many infections with coagulation factors and how many infections through blood transfusion could have been avoided if the German authorities had acted in a more positive way. It is clear that, even if all possible measures had been implemented at the time when there was at least some evidence about their effectiveness, the risk of infections could not be eliminated completely. On the other hand, it became clear that a substantial number of infections could have been avoided if a number of measures (such as excluding some donors from the donation of blood, the hepatitis B core antibody test, the uge of heat-inactivated factor VIII products and recalling and rejecting blood and blood products 'on the shelf') had been implemented more promptly and more effectively. It has been demonstrated that this failure has to do with the sluggishness with which programmatic responses have been developed.

Rather than concluding that this was the result of a 'cartel' of different institutions (such as pharmaceutical companies, health insurance, the Red Cross, the medical profession and state agencies), as has been argued by some (see, for example, Koch and Meichsner, 1993), it has been shown that it resulted from a lame duck policy. This lame duck policy resulted mainly from the network of relations in which the duck (the *Bundesgesundheitsamt*) was embedded. It received pressure neither from above (the federal ministry of health) nor from below (the patients, the haemophiliac society or the press). It was rather committed to assuring its relationships with the pharmaceutical industry and the administrators of blood products, relationships which were and still are characterized by resource dependency (in particular, information asymmetry). Instead of identifying health risks for the general population and taking adequate measures for preventing such risks, the federal health office was busier with securing its position within the network. This could be seen as a classical case of goal displacement leading to considerable programmatic failure.

The closed nature of this system went so far that even the minister of health (the supervisory authority) had to learn through the media about the programmatic failures within that system. Once the situation was clear to the minister, he took the necessary steps to deal openly and drastically with some of the consequences of the programmatic failures. This can be generally considered a political success, but whether he has dealt appropriately with the causes of the programmatic failures may be doubted and will, as sad as it is, become clear only after the next 'scandal'.

NOTES

1. I would like to thank Leo Huberts for his valuable comments.
2. As of 31 December 1999, a total of 18 524 AIDS cases have been reported in Germany. 11 959 cases have been reported among homosexual and/or bisexual men, 2768 cases among injecting drug users. The heterosexual transmission route accounts for 1127 cases. Annually, about 900 new AIDS cases and about 2000–2500 HIV infections are expected in Germany (Robert-Koch-Institut).
3. It should be mentioned, however, that the *Deutsche AIDS Hilfe* is a very decentralized organization and that local *AIDS-Hilfe* organizations may vary considerably.
4. The Bundesinstitut für Arzneimittel und Medizinprodukte in Berlin (BfArM), the Robert Koch-Institut in Berlin (RKI), the Bundesinstitut für gesundheitlichen Verbraucherschutz und Veterinärmedizin in Berlin (BgVV), the Paul-Ehrlich-Institut, Bundesamt für Sera und Impfstoffe in Langen (PEI), the Deutsche Institut für medizinische Dokumentation und Information in Cologne (DIMDI) and the Bundeszentrale für gesundheitliche Aufklärung in Cologne (BZgA). The three first institutes, the BfArM, the RKI and the BgVV, are the successors of the Federal Health Office which was, as a consequence of the HIV and blood scandal, closed down in 1994.
5. *Gesetz zur Neuordnung zentraler Einrichtungen des Gesundheitswesens* (GNG).
6. 'Seine Aufgabe wird es sein, das Reichskanzleramt sowohl in der Ausführung der in den Kreis der Medicinal- und Veterinärpolizei fallenden Maßregeln, als auch in der Vorbereitung der weiter auf diesem Gebiete in Aussicht zu nehmeneden Gesetzgebung zu unterstützen' (Von Stein, 1962, p. 442).
7. Robert-Koch-Institut, Institut für Arzneimittel, Institut für Wasser- Boden- und Lufthygiene, Max von Pettenkoffer-Institut, Institut für Sozialmedizin und Epidemiologie and Institut für Veterinärmedizin.
8. See the *Arzneimittelgesetz* (Medical Preparations Law) which regulates the production and distribution of medicines. Section 63 of the *Arzneimittelgesetz* prescribes an evaluation of possible risks and adverse effects of new pharmaceutical drugs after approval of these substances.
9. The information given here is mainly based on four sources: the 700-page final report of the investigation committee of the German Parliament which was published in 1994 (*HIV-Infektionen durch Blut und Blutprodukte. Schlußbericht des 3. Untersuchungsausschusses. Deutscher Bundestag*); press articles mainly from *Der Spiegel, Die Zeit* and *Focus*; and a book by the investigative journalists Koch and Meichsner, written in 1990. The second edition of the book which was published in 1993 includes a forward by the then Minister of Health, Horst Seehofer, and the case of the Koblenz-based company UB Plasma which, even in the 1990s, had used blood and plasma which was not appropriately tested for HIV antibodies (Koch and Meichsner, 1993); another source used is an article by Stephan Dressler (Dressler, 1999).
10. Alpha, Armour, Beecham, Behringwerke, Eurim, Hoechst, Hormonchemie, Intersero, Immuno, Medac, Mérieux, Nordisk, Rhône-Poulenc, Schering, Schwab, Serlac and Travenol/Cutter.

11. Two Red Cross leagues even filed a disciplinary complaint against the president of the federal health office. A disciplinary complaint is an appeal to the superior authority (in this case the federal ministry of health) and a legal control within Germany's administrative system. Professor Karl Überla was alleged of misconduct in his position and to be dangerous to the general public (Koch and Meichsner, 1993, p. 85). The complaint was rejected by the ministry on the grounds that the president's conduct was in accordance with existing laws and legal duties of the *Bundesgesundheitsamt*.

12. A similar delay between the availability of a test and its mandatory usage occurred with regard to the hepatitis C antibody test which became available in 1990 but did not become mandatory until 25 April 1992.

13. Members of the group are federal and state experts, representatives from the pharmaceutical industry and blood banks, as well as external experts.

14. For example, it is indicative for this situation that the alterations in the *Widerspruchsbescheid* were accepted with some feeling of relief, not only on the part of the pharmaceutical companies, but also by haemophiliacs and their physicians: treatment could continue as usual.

15. 'löste der frühere Leistungssportler durch seinen lässigen Umgang mit den Sicherheitsproblemen sogar in Kreisen der Pharmahersteller ungläubiges Kopfschütteln aus.'

16. 'Wer behauptet, es habe Versäumnisse gegeben, es seien Dinge verschwiegen worden, der soll die konkret belegen. Bis heute ist dies nicht geschehen. Außer pauschalen Behauptungen nur heiße Luft.'

27. The Dutch reaction to contaminated blood: an example of cooperative governance

Bert de Vroom[1]

1   THE HIV EPIDEMIC IN THE NETHERLANDS

The origin of the HIV epidemic in the Netherlands can be traced back to 1979, among men with homosexual contacts (STG, 1992, p. 59). The first AIDS case was diagnosed at the end of 1981.[2] Since then the cumulative number of AIDS cases increased to almost 5000 in 1999. Almost 75 per cent of this group have died. Since there is no notification and registration system for HIV infections, it is barely possible to reconstruct the size and development of the HIV epidemic in the same way as the AIDS epidemic. HIV infections in the Netherlands are estimated on the basis of the reported AIDS cases. These estimates have changed dramatically in recent years as a result of changing methods and assumptions. In early 1987, the number of HIV-infected people was estimated at 10 000–20 000. In early 1990, the number of HIV infections for 1989 was estimated at between 10 000 and 12 000. In 1995, the number of HIV infections was estimated at 8000 (Aids Fonds, 1996).

Haemophiliacs are the group at highest risk of HIV infections contracted through blood and blood products. Approximately 170 of the 1300 haemophiliacs in the Netherlands were contaminated with the virus from 1979 to 1985; that is, about 13 per cent of the total group. Out of the 170 contaminated haemophiliacs, 55 had actually developed AIDS by the end of 1994 (Nationale Ombudsman, 1995, p. 25). Scientific research among 328 haemophiliacs at the end of 1985 showed that 53 individuals were infected through blood products, most during the years 1982, 1983 and 1984 (respectively 12, 20, 12). The source of infection was both national and imported blood products (50 per cent each).[3]

In the period 1979–85, in addition to haemophiliacs, another 150 individuals approximately were contaminated with the AIDS virus via blood transfusion, of whom it is known that 47 had developed AIDS by 1 January 1996 (Aids Fonds, 1996). Thus the total estimated number of people contaminated via blood transfusion or via the blood products in the Netherlands in the mid-1990s is approximately 320, of which at least 102 people had already developed AIDS. In general, it is assumed that there were no more cases of contamination (of haemophiliacs) via blood products or blood transfusion after 1985. The percentage of reported AIDS diagnoses among haemophiliacs and individuals who have received blood transfusions is relatively low compared to the total number of AIDS diagnoses in the Netherlands (about 3 per cent of all cumulative AIDS cases). It has generally been assumed that the epidemic in this group has reached its limit.

When we compare the number of AIDS cases among groups at risk, men with homosexual contacts are by far the group most at risk, with 70 per cent of the cumulative AIDS cases. However, when the number of determined cases of AIDS is calculated on a per capita basis, then it is haemophiliacs, followed directly by the IV drug users, who suffer most from the AIDS epidemic (Kester *et al.*, 1997). We have yet another picture when we apply a country comparison perspective. From that perspective the rate of contamination among haemophiliacs in the Netherlands (13 per cent) compares favourably with the European average of about 35 per cent. The number of haemophiliacs in Europe as a whole is estimated at approximately 28 000, of which an estimated 10 000 have become HIV-contaminated. The differences between the European countries were large (in 1986) between the extremes of Poland, with 1.5 per cent, and France, with 81 per cent.[4] In the United States, the percentage of infected haemophiliacs is estimated at 70 per cent.

2   THE REGULATION OF THE BLOOD SUPPLY

The model of Red Cross blood banks controlling blood supply has existed in the Netherlands for a long period of time. The Dutch government had delegated its responsibility in this field to this private not-for-profit organization. The most important characteristic of the Dutch blood supply is the principle of voluntary and unpaid donors. The principle of voluntary, unpaid blood donation is highly valued because this system is believed to reduce the risk of the presence of pathogens. This principle has existed since the 1940s and was re-established in 1988 (during the first decade of the epidemic) in the new Blood Transfusion Act,[5] which mentions that the donor should only receive compensation for his or her real expenses. Furthermore, the Blood Transfusion Act contains a non-commercial principle, meaning that no profit should be made on blood products; they have to be supplied at cost price. In this way it prevents potential donors objecting to giving 'free of charge' something that is sold later.

The Dutch authorities have delegated donor recruitment and promotion of voluntary blood donation to the Red Cross. This non-profit organization has built a network of regional blood banks. In the second half of the 1990s there were 22 such blood banks throughout the country, collecting approximately 700 000 donations per year. In addition to the blood banks the Dutch Red Cross organizes about 400 blood circuit-collection events a year in places without blood banks, resulting in a further 100 000 donations. Finally, the Military Blood Transfusion Service delivers yearly an additional 15 000 blood donations. In total, more than 800 000 voluntary blood donations are collected in the Netherlands through these three channels, coming from more than 500 000 volunteers.

According to several publications by the blood banks the 'willingness of the Dutch population to donate blood is relatively large in comparison with the surrounding countries' (Baayen, 1997, p. 45). The quantity is almost sufficient to cover fully the raw material need and keeps imports of blood products to a minimum. That does not mean that there have been no imported blood products at all. Since the late 1970s, some new blood products have been imported, in particular from the USA. Most of those products were new types of medical treatment for haemophiliacs. The next section will describe how haemophiliacs' need for new products became a dilemma and (potential) conflict when the HIV epidemic started.

The fear that occasionally is expressed, that a non-commercial organization would not be able to respond adequately to an ever-growing demand for plasma products, seems unjustified for the time being, at least for the Netherlands. This seems to confirm a statement by Hagen that it is easier 'to organise an efficient blood transfusion organisation in countries with small or medium-sized populations than in countries with large populations' (Hagen, 1982, p. 83). In addition, he refers to sociological variables like social cohesion and centralization that seem more important than just the size of the population.

The production, distribution and delivery of blood and blood products in the Netherlands is not a 'free market and merchandise' but is restricted to a number of classified not-for-profit institutions (the Red Cross, for example), regulated by the Blood Transfusion Act and the Blood Products Regulation. These principles of the Dutch blood collection system were not abandoned because of the AIDS epidemic, but, on the contrary, have been strengthened. In the late 1970s and early 1980s, changing the voluntary unpaid system of blood collection into a paid and commercial model was considered, but in light of the AIDS epidemic and the expected threat to particular 'risk groups' this change appeared highly undesirable.

3   THE 1980s: THE 'PROGRAMMATIC' RESPONSE

The Actor Constellation

The actual HIV–blood policy in the 1980s was not an issue of strong central state involvement. The minister and state secretary of public health, normally the key responsible actors in matters of public health policy making, were not the key actors when it came to the interrelated issue of HIV and blood in the 1980s. Organizations in the 'state-periphery', 'quasi-state' organizations, various 'experts', 'organized groups at risk' and 'private firms' were all part of a 'cooperative' actor constellation around this policy issue. The particular 'policy choice' of a cooperative network of public and private organizations not only reflects the general style of Dutch policy making, with a strong emphasis on the role of intermediary, non-state organizations, it also reflects the particular context of the HIV/AIDS problem in the very first phase of the epidemic.

In this early phase of the epidemic, Dutch AIDS policy got its historical insignia.[6] In this period the most important choices as regards policy were made about the AIDS policy, and these have formed the foundation for the policy until the present. Attention was focused on two principles. On the one hand a compelling top-down imposed regulation and intervention style, in which the problem would be confronted through regulations and sanctions, was abandoned. Thus – unlike common practice in many other countries – the Dutch policy response was not based on forced exclusion or isolation, or on compulsory tests and compulsory registration of cases of HIV contamination. One clear example of this approach was the decision at that time not to bring AIDS under the operation of the Act on the control of infectious diseases and the tracing of causes of diseases (*Wet bestrijding infectieziekten en opsporing ziekte oorzaken*). This Act provides public health authorities with a legal basis to reduce risk of an epidemic by means of compulsory isolation or exclusion of (possible) infected people. In addition to arguments based on the right to private life and the prohibition of discrimination, this policy response was defended with the argument that there was no efficacious treatment for AIDS. The responsible minister of public health at that time, Elco Brinkman, formulated it as follows: 'by bringing AIDS under the operation of this act, the government deliberately participates in maintaining the illusion that this disease can be controlled by such measures'.

On the other hand, and as a more or less logical result of eschewing a hierarchical or coercive approach, a variety of public and private organizations were given an important role in trying to find a way to approach the AIDS epidemic. This particular actor constellation is summarized in Table 27.1, while Table 27.2 illustrates the way these different organizations were involved in their different policy networks.

As illustrated in Table 27.2 all the relevant actors (and their activities) were coordinated in an ever-growing and more integrated policy network. It started with some separate informal networks, but these were eventually integrated into one national coordination platform (NCAB). In addition to this national coordination structure for coping with the HIV–blood problem, a much broader

Table 27.1   HIV–blood actor constellations, Netherlands, 1982–6

Category	Actor
State policy makers	• Minister of public health • State secretary of public health
State bureaucracy	• Commission ex art. 1 • Inspection public health
State organizations (national)	• RIV(M) (not a 'policy organization' but an 'expert' organization: research)
State organizations (local)	• GGD (municipal health control authorities) • GVO (health information and education, Amsterdam)
State periphery[a]	• *Gezondheidsraad* (public health council)
Quasi-state organizations[b]	• Regional blood banks • CMBC (central medical committee for blood transfusion) • NRK (Dutch Red Cross)
Experts	• Different individuals • Organization of haemophilia practitioners (NVHB)
Groups at highest risk	• Homosexuals (COC) • Haemophiliacs (NVHP)
Producers of blood product, NL	• CLB (quasi-state)
Importers of blood products, NL	• Travenol • Tramedico

Notes:
[a]   autonomous organizations recognized (or established) by the state to advise state policy makers.
[b]   private non-profit organizations that fulfil a delegated state task/monopoly.

coordination network was developed in the second half of the 1980s, dealing with all kinds of HIV and AIDS-related issues and solutions. In that period the organizational network of 'AIDS organizations' was greatly expanded to more than 700 organizations (De Vroom, 1993; Kester *et al.*, 1997). Among these organizations are more than 40 regional AIDS platforms in which all kinds of organizations, including blood banks, exchange knowledge and experience and develop policies at a regional level. In addition to these AIDS platforms, AIDS and drugs platforms were established from the beginning of the 1990s, with a similar function. The national umbrella organization of the AIDS platforms is the NCAB, in which again all relevant interest groups, organized groups at risk, professional organizations and policy makers are represented.

Table 27.2   Policy networks in Dutch HIV/AIDS policy, 1982–6

Policy network	Involved actors (1982–6)

1983 (Jan.–Nov.)
Informal consultation network
    (formalized in
    November 1983 in LACT)
	• CLB
	• Regional blood banks
	• CMBC
	• COC (homosexuals)
	• GGD (some)
	• State public health inspectorate

1983–7
LACT (National AIDS
    Coordination Team),
    merged in NCAB, 1987
	• State public health inspectorate
	• GGD Amsterdam
	• GVO Amsterdam
	• SOA-*Stichting* (Foundation for Sexual
	• Transmittable Diseases Control)
	• *Schorerstichting* (The Schorer Foundation)
	• SAD (Foundation for Complementary
	    Services)

1983–7
Breed Beraad Aids ('Broad
    AIDS consultation'),
    merged in NCAB, 1987
	• Haemophiliacs (since April 1984)
	• Regional blood banks
	• Homosexuals
	• GVO
	• GGD
	• Drugs service organizations and other
	    'civil society organizations'

1984 (April)–1989 (Feb.) IAB (Intra department AIDS consultation)	• State public health inspectorate • Different departments • RIV(M)

1987 (Sep.)–mid-1995
NCAB (National Committee
    Combating AIDS)
Mid-1985–Mid-1995
Regional AIDS platforms (40)
	• See previous names (organizations were
	    represented by individuals who formally
	    had an autonomous status)
	• A variety of different private and public
	    actors (see De Vroom, 1993)

Source: Project, Managing Aids in the Netherlands; Geert Tillemans (1988); Nationale Ombudsman (1995).

The Definition of Problems

What were the main problems in the early phase of the epidemic? Who was involved in the problem definition and solution? And what was the dominant mode of interaction? Looking backwards it is relatively simple to indicate the dominant policy problem when it comes to HIV and blood in the early phase. In the end it comes down to the question of how to get a sufficient level of blood and blood products to fulfil the needs of Dutch society, without running the risk of transferring the HIV virus.

As in other countries the very first step in the problem definition was the general recognition and acceptance of a relationship between blood and HIV contamination. In the report of the Nationale Ombudsman (1995),[7] we find a fascinating account of the opinions of the various parties concerned about the question at what point the responsible actors could have known with certainty that AIDS was transmittable via blood. Was it as early as the middle of 1982? Or not until the middle of 1983, late 1983 or early 1984 (Nationale Ombudsman, 1995, pp. 42–9)? The answer was constructed afterwards as a consensus within the relevant scientific community. From that approach it was concluded that the end of 1983 or the beginning of 1984 should be seen as the historical point at which it became scientifically acceptable to expect (at least an epidemio-logical) relationship between blood and HIV contamination. The investigation of the ombudsman indicates that at that point all involved actors in the Dutch HIV–blood policy network were convinced of this relationship. But before that historical point many actors had already reacted with various precautions, as will be described below.

Six Solutions

The following sections illustrate how the different public and private actors have been involved in moving from problem definition to problem solution. Table 27.3 summarizes six relevant responses of the Dutch actor constellation to the problem of HIV-contaminated blood and blood products: (1) excluding 'high risk' donors; (2) terminating production of concentrated (not heated) blood products; (3) terminating import of foreign (not heated) blood products; (4) screening blood; (5) import of heated blood products; and (6) heat treatment of 'home-made' blood products.

These six responses can be clustered in two different groups, which also coincide more or less with the timing of their introduction. The first group represents so-called 'negative' interventions. These interventions restricted or dismantled existing practices and programmes. From that perspective the first issue debated was the exclusion of high-risk donors, in particular homosexuals. Almost at the same time the debate started on limiting the production of blood products from large samples (concentrated products) and stopping the import of concentrated products (from the USA).

The second group represents 'positive' interventions: new methods and policies to improve control and delivery of blood products. There were basically three responses. First was the introduction of blood screening, to test all blood donations for HIV contamination. The second measure was licensing of imported heated blood products. Almost parallel to this response the heating of 'home-made' blood products was another approach to resolving the problem.

Solution 1: excluding donors

Considering the risk of contaminated blood, the Netherlands decided in 1983 'as one of the first countries in Europe' (Olthuis and Stienstra, 1992) to exclude donors from the so-called 'groups at risk'. This concerned mostly men with homosexual contacts. Establishing this exclusion is a clear example of the consensus line of thought among the various groups involved at the beginning of the epidemic. Van Wijngaarden (1992) described this as follows:

> representatives of gay organizations, public health authorities, the blood banks, and the Dutch Haemophilia Association met for a period of three months. In April 1983, a compromise was reached. An information campaign would be organized to persuade gay men to refrain voluntarily from donating blood. To those who had participated in the successful process of resolving the controversy over the blood supply, this was to serve as a model for the future, one based on the avoidance of confrontation, one that would stress inclusion and negotiation. A committee of three gay men organized the campaign (....). Before donating blood, every blood donor received a leaflet that included information about AIDS and urged those who belonged to a group at risk to 'seriously consider refraining from donating blood' (...). Because the gay community had been involved in this process from the start, there was little opposition from those who might otherwise have interpreted the plea for withdrawal from the donor pool as an act of unacceptable discrimination.

However, it is not so evident in this quotation from Van Wijngaarden that it involved a compromise between the gay movement and other parties concerned (Nationale Ombudsman, 1995, pp. 59–60). The compromise reached in April 1983 started with a heated debate on Sunday, 30 January 1983 between representatives from the blood bank organizations, the gay movement, the haemophiliacs' organization, the public health inspectorate, the area health authority of Amsterdam and the local public health authority of Rotterdam. Later on, this day was referred to as 'the blood debate' or 'bloody Sunday'. At stake was the position taken by the blood banks that homosexual men should be excluded as blood donors. Under pressure from the gay movement, the compromise described by Van Wijngaarden was finally reached, after a few intervening steps. Although it was not a formal ban, this compelling recommendation clearly had an excluding effect (which was the intention).

Solution 2: termination of 'home-made' concentrated products

The 'consumption' of blood products in the Netherlands in the early 1980s was about 35.5 million units. The majority of these products (28 million units) were 'home-made' and only 7.5 million units were imported. The Dutch regional

Table 27.3   The Dutch response, by date and type of solution, 1981–6

	Response 1: restriction of existing practice			Response 2: 'innovations' to improve control and delivery		
	Excluding high-risk donors	Stop production of concentrated blood products	Stop import of blood products	Test (for screening blood)	Import of heated blood products	Heating of 'home-made' blood products
Jan 1983	Blood banks want exclusion of homosexuals as blood donors; organized homosexuals are against	NVHB advises medical professionals to reduce the use of concentrated products RIV advises reducing the use of concentrated products (31 Jan.)	NVHB advises halting imports of concentrated products			
Feb. 1983		RIV advises minister to halt use of concentrated products (14 Feb.)	Government considers stopping imports; haemophiliacs are against			
March 1983		Expert advises relying completely on 'cryo-precipitate' (small pool blood plasma)			In USA production of heated products has started (becoming available on Dutch market)	
April 1983	Compromise between blood banks, homosexuals, haemophiliacs: voluntary withdrawal of homosexuals CMBC guideline for blood banks: donors from high-risk groups should withdraw voluntarily		RIV advises not using factor VIII products from USA (because 'coming from paid donors')			

Date		
May 1983	Recommendation of public health inspector to stop imports of factor VIII and IX; possible withdrawal of import licensee (9 May)	Recommendation of public health inspector to take measures (9 May)
June 1983	First information leaflet of organized network: on HIV/AIDS and risks of particular donors (early June)	*Recommendation of Council of Europe: withdrawal of blood donors from high-risk groups (23 June)*
Aug. 1983		Travenol gets licence to import heat-treated Hemofil-1 (12 Aug.)
Sept. 1984	The Medical Chief Inspector of Public Health recommends not using foreign factor VIII	
Dec. 1984		NVHP asks for heat treatment of NL blood products (in USA and in NL) (10 Dec.) CMBC: heat treatment Seems effective (21 Dec.)

Table 27.3 (continued)

	Response 1: restriction of existing practice			Response 2: 'innovations' to improve control and delivery		
	Excluding high-risk donors	Stop production of concentrated blood products	Stop import of blood products	Test (for screening blood)	Import of heated blood products	Heating of 'home-made' blood products
Jan. 1985				Minister of public health requests blood banks to investigate possibilities of blood test	*International proof of effectiveness*	CLB gets licence to use heat treatment (8 Jan.)
April 1985				CLB: all donations will be tested for HIV (1 April)		
June 1985				All blood banks start HIV screening		CLB starts delivery of heat-treated factor VIII (3 June)
July 1985						CLB starts delivery of heat-treated protrombine complex (22 July) *HIV-tested not-heated cryoprecipitate from CLB and regional blood banks remain available* (22 July)
Dec. 1985						CLB starts delivery of heat-treated cryoprecipitate (2 Dec.)
April 1986					Hoechst and Bayer get licence to import	

Date			
June 1986	heat-treated products (8 April)		State Control Laboratory, CLB, blood banks and producers develop a 'norm registration document (NRD)' to regulate heat treatment of factor VIII products
July 1986		Travenol gets licence to import heat-treated factor VIII; withdrawal of licence to import not-heat-treated products (8 July)	
April 1987			Commission ex. art.1 advises state secretary to legally implement the NRD by the end of 1987
July 1987			State secretary advises blood banks to effectuate the NRD by 1 Jan. 1988
Dec. 1987			RIV(M) strongly advises the state secretary to implement the NRD
Jan. 1988			NRD comes officially into effect. *A number of regional blood banks continue the old practice*

Note: Some relevant international developments are indicated in italics.

519

blood banks and the Dutch central laboratory of blood banks (CLB) are the (non-commercial) producers of the Dutch blood products. Almost 75 per cent of the national production (19 million units) contain so-called 'small pool' products (cryoprecipitate). The remaining 25 per cent (9 million units) are 'large pool' products (factor VIII). These factor VIII products are only produced by the CLB, whereas the regional blood banks only produce 'small pool' products. Along with the 'home-made' factor VIII products another 7.5 million units of factor VIII products are imported from the USA (see below).

As soon as the possible relationship between AIDS and blood became obvious, the key actors in the Dutch actor constellation debated the use of non-concentrated (small pool) blood products. The central gatekeepers were haemophilia practitioners. These medical doctors advised and decided what products should be used for treating haemophiliacs. The organization of this group of professionals (NVHB) advised the professional group as early as January 1983 to reduce the use of concentrated products. At the same time the research organization for public health issues (RIV), and part of the ministry of public health, advised the minister of public health on two occasions against the use of concentrated products. Also the key scientific experts within the blood policy domain advised in March 1983 relying completely on 'small pool' blood products.

So far it is not clear to what level the use of 'home-made' concentrated products actually was reduced in the early 1980s, but, from the discussions at that time, as well as from the criticism in the 1990s (see section 4), the conclusion can be drawn that all actors within this blood policy domain had the idea that the use of concentrated products has been reduced to the minimum. As will be explained in the next section, the main concerns were the 'foreign' (imported) concentrated blood products from the USA, not the 'home-made' concentrated products. On the one hand, the actors had a high level of trust in the expertise of the medical profession to make the right decision about particular blood products. On the other hand, all actors were convinced that the voluntary and non-commercial blood system in the Netherlands, in combination with voluntary withdrawal of homosexual blood donors, substantially reduced the risk of HIV-contaminated blood.

Solution 3: stay on imports

Before scientific proof of a relation between HIV and blood became generally accepted, some actors within the relevant Dutch policy domain were already convinced about the threat of contaminated imports, and thought a stay on imports of particular blood products could possibly be part of the solution. In this case the initiative did not come from the state but from the professional 'field' (professional intermediary organizations). This 'field' 'took its responsibility at that time: practitioners and patients were advised from different sides [non-governmental parties, BdV] to change to products produced in the Netherlands' (Nationale Ombudsman, 1995, p. 171). One of the actors was the Organization of Haemophilia Practitioners (NVHB). This organization informed the relevant health practitioners in January 1983 not to use imported concentrated blood products; a similar reaction came in April 1983 from the state-owned research institute, RIV. This organization also advised against using 'factor VIII products from the USA' (Nationale Ombudsman, 1995).

There were basically two (interrelated) arguments to plead for such a halting of imports. One argument was that paid blood donation (which was used in the USA) would increase the risk of unsafe blood. Basically, the argument was that financial incentives attract particular risk groups (with low income and an unhealthy lifestyle). The other argument had to do with the characteristics of the new factor VIII products as developed in the USA. Since those products were produced out of a 'large pool' of blood plasma, and given the first argument of the paid blood donor system, the risk of contaminated blood products seemed statistically higher than in the case of the traditional small pool products. This argument was explicitly used in the above-mentioned RIV message.

In other words, already in early 1983 a policy in practice was developed to stop the import of certain blood products from the USA. The interesting point here is the absence of state regulation: no formal stay on imports of American products.[8] The question is, why not? Two explanations can be drawn from the investigation report of the Nationale Ombudsman. First, just because the relevant actors from the intermediary level and from the state periphery – as described – took their own responsibility, state intervention could be seen as something not necessary. And this was explicitly the argument of the ombudsman in concluding that the state at this point cannot be condemned for negligence (see next section) (Nationale Ombudsman, 1995, p. 171). Such an argument can of course only be defended within a society in which an intermediary 'actor constellation' has become institutionalized as an alternative 'mode of governance' (next to state intervention).

The second explanation has to do with one of the important 'problem owners' in the HIV–blood problems: the haemophiliacs. This group – at least their interest organization, NVHP – was against a formal stay on imports through state regulation. After the media reported that the state secretary of public health was considering a legal prohibition on the import of foreign blood products, the NVHP sent a telex to the state secretary asking him to delay his decision pending consultation. The NVHP had two arguments for opposing such a ban on foreign products. The first was the result of a debate from an earlier period about imports of commercial blood products.

The request of the haemophiliacs that commercial blood products be imported was not the result of a lack of blood products as such. The Dutch system at that time was able to produce the necessary quantities of blood and blood products (based on the voluntary, non-commercial principle). However, the commercial system in the United States did produce a number of innovations (such as the concentrated factor VIII products). These products were seen by haemophiliacs as real improvements. But, given the capacity of the Dutch blood system and the basic principles of the Dutch blood system (voluntary and non-commercial), importation was prevented for some time. Only after a legal procedure against the state was the importing of commercial factor VIII products allowed (Nationale Ombudsman, 1995, p. 73). In other words, the interest organization of haemophiliacs was afraid that 'the Aids-problem [was] used as a tool to settle a principle discussion'.[9] The second argument of the NVHP in opposing the ban was the trust they had in the 'self-regulation of haemophiliac practitioners and patients' in using those imported products.[10] In other words, (even) in the eyes of the problem owners, state regulation was not needed to solve this problem.

Solution 4: screening blood

All actors were convinced at an early stage that the introduction of an HIV test on donated blood would reduce the risk of contamination. When, in early 1985, the Abbott company got a licence from the US Food and Drug Administration to put the HIV test on the market, the introduction of that test in the Netherlands followed within a few months. After investigation of the effectiveness of this test, the CLB began testing in April 1985. All other blood banks introduced the test in June of that year.

Solution 5: import of heated products

The discussion about the principal question whether or not to import commercial blood products took another direction at the time that scientific research proved that heating the blood products could destroy the HIV virus in the product. In the first half of 1983, some commercial firms in the USA started to produce heated blood products. From then on the discussion was whether those products should be imported (instead of the non-heated products). Obviously, this issue did not result in a long-standing conflict. When different actors (NVHP, RIV and importers) asked for such an import, the Dutch government soon (from August 1983 on) approved the import of (different commercial) heat-treated blood products from the USA.

Solution 6: heating of 'home-made' blood products

Already in early 1985 some participants in the Dutch actor constellation were convinced of the effectiveness of heat treatment. At that time the national blood bank CLB received a licence to use heat treatment, and from mid-1985 the CLB actually started to deliver heat-treated blood products. However, the introduction of heat treatment did not mean that the availability of non-heated blood products was terminated at the same time. Those products (still HIV-tested) from both the CLB and regional blood banks were kept available. There was obviously no consensus at that point in time. So far, three arguments might explain why non-heated products were still available: first, the assumption that the voluntarily accepted withdrawal of homosexual donors was effective; second, the assumption that, as a result of the principle of voluntary and unpaid donors, other risk groups would be excluded; third, the assumption that the introduction of the HIV test was an extra safeguard.

But the debate continued among the actors involved. One year later, in June 1986, all involved actors (RCL, CLB, regional blood banks, and so on) agreed upon the so-called 'norm registration document' that clearly indicated heat treatment as the norm. But at the same time they agreed upon a 'period of habituation' of one year, indicating at least some lack of compliance capability, or probably even a lack of compliance readiness. However, one year later the 'norm' was still not implemented by all blood banks. In 1987, the Dutch government (the state secretary of public health) several times was strongly advised by a number of actors (see Table 27.3) to implement legally the norm registration document. The document did not come officially into force until 1 January 1988, almost a year and a half after the collective agreement, but even then some regional blood banks continued with their old practice, without any sanction.

Although after 1985 no new HIV contamination cases among haemophiliacs were observed, the relevant question is how to assess the failure of self-regulation in policy terms. Should the state have intervened more strongly and at an earlier point in time? According to the ombudsman, the state could be accused of negligence. From the perspective of the political and legal responsibility this judgment is logical. Another question is whether this judgment can still be defended if we consider the overall 'mode of governance' that has been developed in this policy domain. In the last section we will return to this sociological question.

4   THE 1990s: THE 'POLITICAL' RESPONSE

The End of Consensus

Looking back, the period of the 1980s can be characterized as the programmatic response to the problem of HIV and blood. During this period the different solutions to cope with this problem were developed and implemented. One decade later, in the 1990s, the programmatic response of the 1980s became the subject of a political debate and controversy.

Two main subjects were drawing public attention in the 1990s. First was the complaint by the Netherlands Society of Haemophiliacs (NVHP) that 'due to the negligence of the government policy during the first part of the eighties a number of haemophiliacs became infected with the Aids virus'. The second was a public debate about the 'solution' described in the previous section, that men with homosexual contacts should withdraw voluntarily from blood donations. The criticism is that in practice this policy solution led to a formal exclusion of this group as blood donors. This exclusion was brought up for discussion as a case of improper discrimination from the perspective of the excluded group. At the same time 'receivers of blood', represented by the interest organization of haemophiliacs, defended this exclusion as a necessary step to protect receivers of blood from the risk of HIV. In other words, looking back at these criticisms to the response of the 1980s, this response could be classified as a problem of both effectiveness and legitimacy. At the same time, it also seems to reflect the 'end of consensus' in this policy domain. In that sense those criticisms could be interpreted as indicating failing policy intervention during the 1980s.

Criticism 1: The Negligent Government

On 1 December 1992 the Netherlands Society of Haemophiliacs (NVHP) requested that the authorities begin an independent investigation into the origin of HIV contamination cases involving haemophiliacs during the period 1982–6. At a later stage a formal complaint against the Dutch authorities was filed in addition to the required investigation. The complaint read that, in the middle of 1982, after the announcement of the discovery of the AIDS virus, and after signals from experts in the field about haemophiliacs' risks of contamination by the AIDS virus, the reaction from Dutch authorities was inadequate. There are five points on which the Dutch authorities were accused of negligence:

1. The government should have gathered information about possible contamination, so that an adequate policy could have been developed in a timely fashion.
2. The government should have proclaimed import limits by the end of 1981/beginning of 1982 on American (non heat-treated) blood products because it could be assumed by then that these products most probably were contaminated with the AIDS virus.
3. The government should have given (timely) imperative directives to Dutch producers of blood products (the blood banks) to switch to heat-treated coagulation products.
4. The government should have decided long before 1988 to take heat-treated factor VIII blood products of the American company Armour off the market,

because an academic hospital in the Netherlands at the beginning of 1986 had already published evidence that these had led to contamination by the AIDS virus.

5. The government was blamed for not giving adequate information to doctors, haemophiliacs and donors in time.

In this case the organization of haemophiliacs did not opt for a formal legal procedure, but called in the national ombudsman. He made a thorough investigation of all aspects and developments relevant in connection with the complaint about contaminated blood that had occurred since the beginning of the AIDS epidemic in the Netherlands. The bulky report which resulted from this investigation assesses the responsibility of the authorities with regard to contamination in a detailed manner. Although the NVHP is not considered correct at all points, on some points the ombudsman accuses the authorities of negligence. The authorities are mainly reproached for having acted too slowly in two instances. The first instance was at the beginning of 1983, when it should have been known that blood products used in the Netherlands were not safe. The government should have banned all imports of these products. The second instance was at the end of 1984/beginning of 1985. By then it had become common knowledge that heat treatment of blood products was usually an effective method of destroying any HIV virus present.

The ombudsman emphasized that the first responsibility rested with the complete 'network' of producers, importers, the Central Laboratory for Blood Transfusion, the blood banks and those who treated the patients. However, they had made little use of their knowledge. Therefore the government – having final responsibility for the blood supply – should have intervened, according to the ombudsman. This difference between 'network' responsibility and governmental responsibility, as put forward by the ombudsman, is an interesting point, to which we will return at the end of this contribution. The minister of public health, Els Borst, who was in power at the time this report was published, has also officially recognized the liability of the government, and without reservations. Because of this, the report recommended raising the compensation for haemophiliacs to a significantly higher level than awarded until then.

At that time the compensation rate was DFL25 000. Along with Hungary (DFL15 000) the Netherlands belonged to the most 'niggardly' countries. In most countries amounts often exceeded DFL100 000, from DFL200 000 in Germany to more than DFL600 000 in France. After the recommendations from the ombudsman, a tug-of-war arose over determining the new level of compensation, but finally, in accordance with good Dutch 'trade practice', an average of the various amounts awarded in other countries was fixed; that is, an amount varying between DFL100 000 and DFL200 000.

The question of when and whether the minister and state secretary might have known that blood products might be contaminated by the AIDS virus was crucial to the ombudsman's burden of proof. This is an interesting and highly relevant question concerning liability. At which moment and based on which statements and by whom may we assume that the politically responsible officials might have known that there were unacceptable risks at stake? As illustrated in the previous sections, the ultimately crucial date was constructed as the end of 1983/beginning of 1984. The politically interesting question is whether and to what extent the situation in the Netherlands is different from the situation during the French blood scandal. It is well known that in France criminal proceedings were instituted against the politically responsible officials, and some were even sentenced to imprisonment. Why has this not happened in the Netherlands?

It is safe to say that the French blood scandal is different from the Dutch in terms of the number of casualties. This number was much higher in France. The difference, however, lies mainly in the way that the responsible officials in both countries reacted to the knowledge with regard to the contamination. In the Netherlands the decision was taken to intervene, albeit too slowly (in the eyes of the ombudsman). In France the responsible medical authorities allowed blood to be administered, although they were fully aware of the fact that it was contaminated. This can be regarded as a penal offence, which is something different from negligence.

Criticism 2: The Excluded Group

In the previous section the consensus between the relevant actors to 'exclude' 'risk donors' from giving blood has been described. More than 10 years later this exclusion became subject to public discussion. At the beginning of 1994, the manager of the Central Laboratory for Blood Transfusion Services (CLB) expressed the view in a television programme that it might be wise to change the rule that excludes men who have had sexual contacts with other men as blood donors.

In his opinion it would be advisable for blood banks no longer to exclude homosexuals as a group, but instead to take sexual behaviour as a basic principle. A few months later a charge from a donor against the Utrecht blood bank concerning discrimination was dismissed by the public prosecutor. Two years later this discrimination perspective was aired again in a national newspaper in a reader's letter. The argument highlighted a demonstration in Jerusalem at the beginning of 1996 of more than 10 000 Ethiopian Jews against the policy of the Israeli blood bank, which does accept them as donors, but destroys their blood automatically. According to the author of the letter:

Exclusion based on the sole fact that a man is having gay sex is not right. By changing the risk factor 'homosexual contacts' to 'unsafe sexual contacts' blood banks could kill two birds with one stone. Not only will this be an actual contribution to pursuing optimal safety, but in addition one is no longer guilty of suggesting that the risk of HIV infection lies in gay sex (Van Zuijlen, 1996).

This article was promptly followed by a reaction from the Dutch Society of Haemophiliacs (NVHP) (Hulst and Smit, 1996).[11] The statement of the Society is that the interests of (potential) blood and blood products recipients should outweigh those of the potential donors of blood. The discrimination argument was used erroneously, according to NVHP. They refer to a verdict of the *Bundesgerichtshof* in Hamburg of 30 April 1991, in which the interests of the receivers preponderate over the interests of the donors. A further reference is made to the above-mentioned dismissal of a Dutch claim. All this leads to the conclusion that there is no support for a possible reproach with regard to discrimination to be found in the international human rights treaties. In addition, there are still major risks involved and it is 'advisable that the Dutch blood banks maintain their present strict pre-selection for blood donors'.

This example illustrates a number of things. First, there is a precarious balance between 'effectiveness' and 'legitimacy' in these kinds of policy solutions. Secondly, it is not only the old debate for and against exclusion of donors, as debated during the 1980s: In the meantime a number of technological developments (blood testing, heating and so on) have changed the situation. Third, this conflict also illustrates how social construction of problem definitions and solutions is a continuing process.

5   ASSESSMENT AND CONCLUSION

To assess the policy response to the problem of HIV and blood in the Netherlands we should first of all make a distinction between the early phase (1982–6) and the reactions and interpretations of the 1990s. These two periods have been labelled here as respectively the 'programmatic' and the 'political' response. This distinction of two 'historical phases' is deduced from the idea that a particular policy response should be analysed as part of a social construction within the boundaries of a given institutional (cultural and historical) context.

At this point the question of success or failure becomes interesting. What would be the basis for judging policy decisions in terms of success and failure? On what basis should we decide what issues should be characterized as the 'real problems' and what solutions should be characterized as 'good solutions'? There are two interrelated ways to escape this normative dilemma. First, the process from problem definition to problem solution and judgments about effectiveness of chosen solutions can be analysed as social constructions in a given institutional and cultural (historical) context. From such a perspective, policy effectiveness can be defined as the extent to which feasible solutions for observed social or policy problems have been or can be realized (Hoekema *et al.*, 1998, p. 74). Such a definition refers both to the particular institutional setting and to the process of social construction. Feasibility refers to the classical distinction of Zald (1978) between compliance readiness and compliance capability. In other words, policy solutions are based on both the available technical possibilities and social acceptance. And it will be clear that those conditions might be different and can change over time and between different social systems. The term 'observation' refers explicitly to the actual social context in which relevant actors should at least recognize a particular phenomenon as a problem.

Social constructivism does not mean that we could not say anything from an 'outsider's' point of view. In this respect the approach of Fritz Scharpf is a helpful one. He stresses the importance (for political sociology) of analysing the general capacity of specific policy-making institutions to produce policy choices that come close to the 'common good' (Scharpf, 1997, p. 15). This capacity varies, according to Scharpf, with respect to the type of problem that should be solved, the actor constellation involved in the problem-solving activities and the institutionalized mode of interaction.

Looking back, and applying the definition of policy effectiveness and the concept of capacity, how should the programmatic response of the early phase be assessed? The central question, from the perspective of effectiveness, is, did the 'policy system' produce 'feasible solutions' for 'observed problems', and in time? As illustrated, the involved actor constellation did define both the key problems and a number of relevant and feasible solutions (see Table 27.3). Compared with international developments and reactions at that time, one might conclude from that perspective that the relevant problems were recognized and the relevant solutions were applied.

The fact that the policy system produced policy choices that came close to the 'common good' (at that time) can be explained by the 'capacity' of the system. In the Dutch case this capacity was based on a particular organizational model of high horizontal differentiation and integration of the actor constellation at the same time. A variety of public and private organizations became involved in the process from problem definition to problem solution. At the same time all those actors were coordinated within a particular organizational structure of horizontal 'platforms'. These 'platforms' were not just spontaneous networks but were at the same time recognized, facilitated and otherwise supported by the state. As such these networks were part of the 'governance model' to cope with this problem. However, the important characteristic was that the state did not play a hierarchical role, in the sense of hierarchical or coercive 'steering'. Further, in the 1990s this lack of state control became one argument used in the political response to 'explain' the 'failures' of the early phase and to accuse the state of negligence (see section 4).

How can the lack of coercive state control in this policy domain be explained? In my opinion there are two interrelated sociological arguments to explain, and even justify, the lack of coercive state control: the nature of the problem and the particular mode of governance developed to cope with the problem. Let us start with the first point.

The HIV/AIDS epidemic started as an issue of high uncertainty, which from a sociological perspective is different from a risk. What we label as 'risk' is already the result of a complex institutional process in which particular (selected) dangers and uncertainties have become classified, limited and defined. At this point dangers can be 'calculated', and it is then that we can classify them as a risk (see Douglas and Wildavsky, 1982; Evers and Nowotny, 1987). Thus, in the early phase, the HIV/AIDS epidemic could not be classified as having a defined risk and a corresponding solution or approach. On the contrary, the epidemic was characterized by an extreme level of uncertainty. There was uncertainty about the source, uncertainty about the use of existing problem-solving 'tools' and 'mechanisms', and uncertainty about the development of feasible, acceptable and legitimate new solutions. We have argued elsewhere, that, in this early phase of the epidemic, 'traditional' institutional approaches did not work, and for this reason the 'organizational approach' (the establishment and involvement of a variety of so-called 'AIDS service organizations') became almost a necessary and logical one (Kenis and De Vroom, 1996).

In other words the nature of this particular problem (the high level of uncertainty) mobilized a particular institutional (organizational) process in which the state was not the dominant or authoritative actor. This empirical fact seems to coincide with a trend discussed in the debate on modern types of governance, such as cooperative or interactive governance (by, among others, Mayntz and Benz). One of the arguments in this debate is that, in a situation where, on the one hand, the societal need for an effective solution is high, but on the other hand 'the state' is not able to solve the problem, 'the state becomes dependent on social co-operation' (Grimm, 1986, p. 104).

This brings us to the second point, the 'mode of governance' developed in the Dutch case. This particular mode, as described in the earlier sections, can be characterized as an example of cooperative governance. This is a type of governance where 'state and non-state actors participate and co-operate in a more or less durable mixed public/private network in which the definition, formulation and implementation of a public policy have been made dependent upon the outcome of a process of consultation, negotiation, exchange and communication' (Hoekema *et al.*, 1998). In such a constellation and given the 'logic' of this form of governance, a dominant and authoritative role of the state is hardly possible and might be counterproductive. This seems the case particularly in situations of complex problems with a high level of uncertainty. The interesting point, when we analyse the judgment of the ombudsman, is that precisely the existence of this particular mode of governance in the 'AIDS–blood policy domain' in the Netherlands, becomes an argument for the ombudsman to use to defend the lack of state intervention in certain instances.

This observation on governance still leaves us with the problem that in some instances the state was blamed for negligence. In those cases the argument of the ombudsman was that the state should and could have acted in a more authoritative way. Is he right from the theoretical perspective chosen here to analyse the effectiveness of the policy response? To answer this question we need to distinguish different phases in the policy process. There is the phase of the selection and definition of particular problems and the formulation of particular solutions (programmes) and there is the phase of implementation. Following the arguments in the theoretical debate and the results of empirical research, one might conclude that the horizontal mode of interaction is a necessary one in the first phase of finding a problem-solving strategy in situations of complex issues with a high level of uncertainty. However, when it comes to implementation of collectively agreed-upon solutions, a vertical (hierarchical or authoritative) mode of coordination might be a functional or even a necessary complementary mechanism.[12]

When we analyse the Dutch response in the early 1980s we might conclude that the horizontal mode of governance developed at that time was quite effective in developing relevant programmes to cope with the problem of HIV-infected blood and blood products. As debated in the previous sections, and illustrated in Table 27.3, the Dutch response was in line with the international developments and reacted relatively fast through a number of interventions. It has also become clear that the development of these solutions was not primarily a state activity. From that description of the actor constellation in the 1980s, and also from the critics in the 1990s, the conclusion can be drawn that the state did not play an important role in the sense of either policy initiatives, strict state regulation or coercive interventions. The most important initiatives were developed by intermediary organizations; the input of the state was basically delegation and facilitation. Because this 'intermediary network' did function quickly and effectively, the state itself thought that intervention was not needed.

However, when it comes to the implementation stage of the solutions, more authoritative state intervention might have been necessary and possible. This was particularly the case with the implementation of the sixth solution discussed: the heating of 'home-made' blood products (see section 3). At this point we touch upon a relevant and interesting problem in the theoretical debate about the distinction between 'network responsibility' and 'governmental responsibility', or, to put it in other words, how can horizontal and vertical modes of interaction be combined in such a way that the advantages of both mechanisms become complementary instead of excluding each other? It is a precarious balance, since hierarchical intervention should not be used in the phase of problem definition and the development of relevant programmes that comprise both compliance readiness and compliance possibilities. Because both the state and the other, non-state, actors in the HIV–blood policy domain in the Netherlands did not clearly distinguish these two phases of the policy process, the possibility and necessity of an authoritative intervention in the second phase was not realized.

Can we blame the state and other actors for this? From a legal (and formal) point of view one could blame the lack of state intervention at that time. This was the line of reasoning of the ombudsman. However, from a sociological point of view, this conclusion is less obvious. As stated, the 'lack' of state inter-vention was not the result of 'negligence' but the result of the relative high effectiveness of the actor constellation at that time. As we also realize that scientific knowledge at that time about these complex modes of governance – and in particular the knowledge of how to combine horizontal and vertical modes of interactions – was still not very well developed, we can follow the same line of reasoning as the ombudsman did when it came to the scientific insight about the relationship between blood and HIV.

NOTES

1. I am in particular grateful to Marjo Baayen and Eva Schulte for their contribution of relevant empirical evidence.
2. *Nota inzake het Aidsbeleid* (TK, 1986-1987, 19218, no. 2:3). In other sources early 1982 is mentioned as the year of the first registered AIDS case (WHO, *Aids surveillance in Europe*).
3. Research by E.P. Mauser-Bunschoten, cited in Nationale Ombudsman (1995, p. 127).
4. The report from the Nationale Ombudsman (ibid., p. 29) refers in this connection to the 17th International Congress of the World Federation of Haemophilia, in June 1986 in Milan, where the percentages mentioned were published.
5. This law came into force in phases starting on 23 February 1989. This law replaces the Human Blood Act of 1961.
6. The term 'historical insignia' is borrowed from Stinchcombe, who developed this term in order to indicate that organizations often bear the stamps of the time they were founded (Stinchcombe, 1965).
7. The report of the ombudsman (1995) was the result of an investigation that year, requested by the organization of haemophiliacs. This organization accused the government of negligence in the early phase of the epidemic (see section 4 for more details).
8. At that time, heated factor VIII products were not yet available.
9. Letter to the CMBC, 4 March 1983 (cited in Nationale Ombudsman, 1995, p. 78).
10. Ibid.
11. The authors are respectively chairman and coordinator of the NVHP.
12. This argument is brought forward in the 'older' neocorporatist debate (see the work of Schmitter and Streeck), as well as in the modern governance debate (see the work of Scharpf and Mayntz).

28. Coping with HIV transmission in Spain: the case of blood control failure

Jacint Jordana[1]

1 THE CONFIGURATION OF THE BLOOD PROBLEM IN SPAIN

The political decisions regarding AIDS between 1983 and 1987 in Spain were very reactive, and were largely the product of media exposure of problems in this policy sector. Two of the clearest examples of the scarce capacity of the Spanish public health system to react were the delay in the obligatory control of HIV in products, and later the even longer delay in controlling HIV in all the blood transfusions and transplants. This chapter will analyse these two cases. The impact of the crisis was limited primarily to the medical professionals and patients linked with haemophilia and blood banks, because politicians and the public did not focus their attention intensively on these problems. Also after 1987, when this issue became more widely known, its impact was only partial because other AIDS-related problems dominated the Spanish agenda from the late 1980s.

It is necessary to keep in mind that these two cases were not the only examples of late reaction or simply incapacity in the Spanish health system during the initial years of the epidemic. The absence of information campaigns, the lack of assistance to organizations serving members of risk groups or the absence of innovative approaches towards initial attitudes of discrimination also facilitated the intense expansion of the epidemic in Spain during those years. The Spanish rate of AIDS increased very quickly in the 1980s. Then, beginning in the next decade, a growing sense of a major crisis emerged, and a broad political and moral debate appeared, in which the question of blood banks and the haemophiliacs remained only as a small part of the tragedy.[2] Nevertheless, new preventive effective measures needed time to be implemented, and Spain had the highest rate of AIDS cases per capita in Europe during most of the 1990s.

2 THE SPANISH POLITICAL AND INSTITUTIONAL CONTEXT

In the 1980s, political responsibility for the Spanish health care system moved from the Francoist highly centralized health care administration to a complex distribution of responsibilities among different levels of government. Starting from the transition to democracy and the promulgation of the new constitution in Spain, an important process of decentralization began, based on the development of new political and administrative regional bodies. The nationalist demands of some areas, such as the Basque Country or Catalonia, accelerated this process. The PSOE, the Socialist Party in government during the 1980s, introduced a broad health care reform that changed the corporatist Francoist system to a model of universal health care coverage financed mostly through general taxation.

Thus health care decentralization in Spain during the 1980s was a result of two separate developments: public health care reform and the territorial decentralization of the state. The former implied an important institutional shift from the limited coverage model to a National Health Service. The latter was a consequence of the emergence of the new democratic regime during the 1970s and the appearance of some nationalist movements, and involved adoption of some features of a federal model, with a special asymmetrical character, in the new constitution (1978). The constitutional differences in the distribution of powers among special and standard regions were especially significant. Initially, during the early 1980s, there were four special regions (Andalusia, the Basque Country, Catalonia and Galicia) with constitutional powers in some public policy fields. Somewhat later three other regions obtained similar status, while the health policies of the remaining 10 standard regions were mostly controlled by a central state agency. As a result, in the late 1980s, about 60 per cent of the Spanish population was governed by special autonomous communities that enjoyed a high degree of political control over some public policies, such as health care and education.[3]

In the case of health, the main difference was that the special regions have almost full legislative power for public health – only limited by the basic legislation from the central state – and manage directly the public health care services, including public hospitals. In the standard regions, public health was regulated by the central state legislation, and health care services were managed by a common agency (INSALUD) directly from central government, with a common organizational structure.[4] However, some few responsibilities in public health were devolved to all regions by the constitution of 1978. Among them were prevention policies (health education, disease surveillance, environmental health and so on), while the central administration only maintained some basic regulatory powers on these issues, including the coordination tasks and information procedures. As a consequence of these transformations, many new public health organizations emerged in Spain during those years at the regional level, with different sizes and functions, developing new procedures and models of intervention. At the same time, the health ministry in central government modified its role and reformulated its activities.[5]

Confronted by a complex topic such as AIDS policy, these processes of institution building hindered reaction by public authorities to the epidemic. Formally, both the central government and the special regions could legislate about blood banks, transfusions or haemophilia therapy: if the regulation had the character of basic law, the central government could legislate; in other cases special regions could exercise their own regulative responsibilities. Only for surveillance of infectious diseases did the central government not have any regulative capability, apart from maintaining some type of coordination among the regions. Facing AIDS-related problems, these very new and complex institutional settings – which were not fully completed until the end of the 1980s – neglected continuous coordination needs, and internal differences about risk perception appeared, especially over responsibility for financing the new programmes. Also the new public health regional administrations were mostly inexperienced, given that under Francoism there had been no central prevention administration with strong capabilities that could serve as a model for the formation of new regional administrations.

Although political parties during the 1980s attempted to maintain a low profile in all aspects of AIDS policy, significant differences among them emerged, mostly in their reactions when they were in charge of a regional government, with different perceptions of the problem producing significantly different priorities. Besides public actors, active organizations in this emerging field were professional associations of doctors and health specialists (fundamentally epidemiologists and public health practitioners, but also virologists, for example) and the associations of the people affected. Among the latter group the most significant was the association of haemophiliacs: the *Asociación Española de Hemofilia* (hereafter AEH).[6] The press was also very important in diffusing information about the problems related to AIDS prevention policies in Spain, using its capacity to provoke political scandals. Media behaviour was to some extent quite sensationalist during certain periods, while remaining quite uninterested in the problem most of the time. Also the associations of donors were not active and there were no associations of people affected by blood transfusions, or of drug users.[7]

3   BLOOD SUPPLY POLICIES PRIOR TO THE AIDS CRISIS

During the Franco period, the first steps in constructing a rudimentary blood transfusion service were taken during the 1940s, with the creation of the *Instituto*

Nacional de Hematologia y Hemoterapia in 1942 (as a research and advisory body) and the establishment of several territorial services. These services, however, covered only part of Spain, and had to be financed outside the state budget by local governments. During the 1950s and 1960s, most blood donors in Spain were paid, and only a few associations at the local level existed, in order to promote altruistic blood donation (frequently, these initiatives were prompted by physicians belonging to blood transfusion services in hospitals). In 1967, these local initiatives were able to establish some national coordination, creating the *Federación de Asociaciones Españolas de Donantes Altruistas de Sangre* (FAEDAS). As an administrative reaction to improve the situation, in 1970 the health ministry created a commission focused on increasing the number of voluntary donors (in that year, only 23 per cent of the blood was collected on a voluntary basis).[8] One central initiative of this commission was to expand local associations of blood donors across the whole Spanish territory. The aim was to stimulate the multiplication and consolidation of more local groups of frequent voluntary donors, based on the example of the already existing voluntary blood donors associations. So, in 1975, there were established the *Hermandades de Donantes de Sangre de la Seguridad Social*, which augmented the number of blood donors associations existing across the Spanish territory or reinforced previously existing ones. These efforts during the 1970s helped to increase the number of donations, and resulted in a reduction of paid donations during the late 1970s and early 1980s.[9] At the beginning of the 1980s no blood transfusion service or coordination body existed at either the regional or national level. In some cases the new regional administrations began to regulate and coordinate to some extent blood donation and blood supplies during those years. In particular, the special regions tried to encourage altruistic donations, with the aim of eradicating paid donations. However, the central government had retained the capacity to establish the basic regulation on blood transfusion and blood donation.

Since the mid-1980s, the Spanish policy had accepted voluntary donation as the only way to obtain blood, and the new legislation on blood banks enacted in 1985 only accepted limited paid donations. In fact, the legislation itself was an early reaction to the AIDS crisis. Most blood banks were established inside the hospitals – especially the large ones, both public and private – to provide their internal needs. Also the Red Cross organization was very active in collecting blood and creating new blood banks. In spite of this, self-sufficiency for blood transfusions was not always achieved, and some commercial blood banks remained, with paid donors, to solve supply problems in small hospitals, and especially to supply the needs of several small Spanish plasma manufacturers. Nevertheless, the manufacture of blood products in Spain remained only as a small part of total blood products consumption in the country throughout the decade. Because of these problems, during the 1980s it was necessary to import most of the blood products used; more than 80 per cent of blood products used had to be imported from abroad, usually from the United States. Few private firms made blood products in Spain, and there were no public manufacturers, although many projects were launched at that time. These manufacturers received unused blood from hospitals, paying the cost of extraction and conservation, and also had their own blood collection facilities (on the basis of paid donors).

There were roughly 2500 Spanish haemophiliacs at the beginning of the 1980s. Since 1976, their blood products requirements had been completely covered by the public health care services and, in fact, almost all hemophiliacs were treated at public hospitals, especially at the bigger ones, in which there existed specific haemophiliac reference centres (about 32). In 1982, the health ministry also agreed to pay for the self-administered daily treatment of haemophiliacs. Both measures improved the quality of life of haemophiliacs in Spain. However, it is interesting to note that, when AIDS appeared, the haemophiliac community in Spain had only very recently become fully dependent on public health institutions and resources.

4   THE POLICY CHRONICLE: HIV AND BLOOD SUPPLY IN SPAIN

The Beginning, 1983–5: Establishing Controls on Plasma

The first information about the risks of transfusions and plasma infected by HIV appeared in the Spanish press in May 1983.[10] The recommendations of experts were quite clear: it was desirable to refuse blood donations from people belonging to high-risk groups, and to avoid imported plasma, especially from the USA, where more cases of AIDS had already appeared. Immediately, the AEH took advantage of the information to make public its concern on the topic, and asked for more attention to be given to the problem by the public authorities. The AEH had already approached the Spanish health care authorities, at the beginning of 1983, expressing its concern about the possibility of using infected blood products – especially factor VIII – coming from the USA, since most Spanish consumption was imported from there. The World Federation of Haemophilia had also alerted the AEH to this possibility. However, the AEH had not obtained any response from the ministry, an indication of the great ignorance about the illness that then existed. At that time, the intention of the AEH was not to mobilize their nearly 2500 members, and especially not to create an alarmist situation among them.

The publication of this information in the influential newspaper *El País* produced an immediate reaction from the health ministry, and its general director of health planning quickly summoned E. Galinsoga, the general secretary of the AEH, to a meeting. The interview did not produce the results desired by the haemophiliacs, since a few days later, with media interest in this new illness and its relationship to haemophilia still lively, the AEH summoned a press conference in which it introduced a more dramatic tone to the situation that was taking place. The AEH pointed out to journalists that the health administration had hidden the problem of the infections until then. The proposal for preventive action launched by the association was based on quickly creating Spanish self-sufficiency in blood-related products, with the objective of avoiding imports. In short, the AEH sought to establish a large number of paid blood banks in Spain, and to manufacture all blood products directly in Spain, in the briefest possible time. The health ministry was completely against accepting the formula of general payment for blood, at the time when paid blood donation was diminishing in Spain. The ministry agreed to stimulate self-sufficiency, but by improving the organization and the promotion of voluntary blood donation.

The reaction of the health ministry to the news of AIDS was to constitute a commission of experts to attack the new illness, and to study how to reach self-sufficiency in blood products. The general director of health planning promised an operative plan before the end of 1983, centred on promoting voluntary blood donation.[11] However, the AEH insisted openly on the need to encourage the establishing of a paid system, to reach self-sufficiency more quickly. The AEH assumed that the risk of HIV infection would be eliminated or greatly reduced, given the belief that almost no AIDS existed in Spain at that time. In June 1983, the first research on voluntary blood donation in Spain, carried out by the health ministry, revealed the existence of confused management of blood by some hospitals. Especially puzzling was the sale of unused blood from hospitals to industrial manufacturing, for its conversion into blood products. The ministry recognized that the legal regulation of blood donation was faulty, but rejected facilitating paid donation of blood, and insisted on the plan to encourage altruistic, unpaid blood donation.[12]

This first episode involving AIDS and haemophilia in Spain, occurring at a relatively early date in the international expansion of the epidemic, was an important alarm call for the health ministry, and generated a state of high anxiety and uncertainty among Spanish haemophiliacs, who were already quite aware that they were being infected on a massive scale by transfusions of blood products. Therefore a possible preventive measure to reduce the probability of receiving infected blood products was to avoid importing blood products from countries with a known high number of AIDS cases. Another measure was to avoid blood donations from special groups of the population, such as homosexuals, who were identified as a high-risk group at that time. However, no formal decision on preventive measures was taken by the health ministry during 1983 and 1984, either as a recommendation to the hospitals, or in the form of additional resources in order to increase voluntary blood donations. Only one year after the first media report of a relationship between AIDS and blood, on March 1984, a periodic publication of the health ministry treated the topic, and some means of prevention were suggested. It proposed to control blood donors from risk groups, to inform individuals belonging to those groups and to decrease the dependence on factor VIII and other blood products from abroad.[13] Nevertheless, during those years the health minister, helped by the AIDS commission, only monitored the epidemic of new cases.[14] The topic almost disappeared from the media and only some very timely declarations of political authorities and medical experts hinted at the importance of the new illness, highlighting the small number of cases already detected in Spain, and its links with some special risk groups.

We should point out that, since October 1983, some Spanish blood banks, especially those in the larger hospitals with larger haemophiliac units, alarmed by the medical information already available, began to introduce some preventive measures. This occurred spontaneously, using a bottom-up logic derived from a mixture of medical responsibility, local haemophiliac pressure and the resources available to each hospital; it expanded after it was discovered that HIV caused AIDS. However, it is very difficult to measure exactly how many blood banks and haemophiliac units introduced concrete measures, and exactly when, during the period from October 1983 to October 1985 (when finally the health ministry made some preventive measures mandatory). In some cases, the hospitals opted for administering exclusively heat-treated factor VIII.[15] However, in many cases, nothing was done.

The promises of those responsible for the Spanish health policy, in May 1983, to prepare a plan to reduce dependence on imported blood products, and to create new public blood laboratories, were not met. In general, the topic of AIDS did not cause too much interest in Spanish society in 1984. After the first media reports in May 1983, Spanish public opinion had been convinced by politicians and experts that it was a very minor illness, with risks concentrated in certain groups of individuals and, therefore, of little interest to the population in general. The information on the spread of the disease abroad, in spite of appearing in the press, did not seem to cause much concern among the public. Thus, during all of 1984, the only activity by the health ministry regarding this topic was to maintain the AIDS commission.

The discovery of HIV opened the possibility of identifying infected patients through tests for the detection of HIV antibodies. Once proven effective in 1985, the detection tests opened up a quite different horizon regarding the application of preventive measures, and especially regarding the possible HIV infections from blood transfusions, organ transplants or administration of blood products. However, the development and commercialization of the test to detect HIV antibodies in March 1985 did not produce a reaction in Spain. During the first half of 1985 the slight interest on the topic remained as it had throughout 1984. Most public health authorities were very optimistic; diverse declarations in the newspapers highlighted the possibility of finding a vaccine quickly, starting from the identification in the laboratory of the HIV virus.[16] Nevertheless, given the appearance of new cases, arguments emerged about the necessity of introducing serious preventive measures. The first pronouncement of this sort was made by the health minister of the Basque government, J. Azúa, in April 1985. He noted the appearance of the first case of AIDS in the region, and said that 'although we could have doubts about whether all the preventive measures are necessary in view of the scarce incidence of AIDS in the Basque Country (...) we should carry out the maximum effort, especially in its prevention'.[17] Starting in April–May 1985, some hospitals introduced the HIV antibody test, although they did not obtain funds from the health ministry or regional health authorities. The test was applied in some blood banks as an experiment, to discover exactly the HIV prevalence among the paid and unpaid donors.[18] Because of its low cost and expected utility, many blood banks had tested blood in order to select blood donors during the months before (especially those located at the hospitals and on the basis of altruistic donors). In July 1985, the health ministry made it known that it was preparing to require preventive measures for all the blood banks, as well as requesting from all blood producers and importers a control certification guaranteeing the absence of the HIV virus in its products.[19]

In August 1985, a new media storm broke in Spain over the epidemic. A study carried out in the USA, analysing more than a million samples of blood, allowed researchers to have quite exact data about the infection probabilities through blood, as well as the proportion of infected haemophiliacs.[20] Although in the USA the situation was quite different, many people began to perceive that Europe would reach the North American levels within two or three years, since the infection pattern could not differ a lot. Therefore, during that summer, numerous European countries implemented new norms to control blood products better. At the same time, the media reported the concern of Spanish health authorities about the existence of HIV-infected stocks of blood products that could be marketed (the decision to purchase blood products with heat treatment or without it was made separately at each hospital). Then several new regional health authorities reacted very quickly. The Madrid region established a commission to plan preventive measures, Catalonia announced measures to control blood products – recommending the heat treatment – and to discriminate among prospective blood donors. Also the Basque Country was the first region to regulate legally some aspects of AIDS prevention.[21]

With this new information and the reactions of some regional health authorities, the health ministry responded in an unusually urgent manner in mid-August. The minister, E. Lluch, announced rigorous norms over transfusions of blood, and the *Subsecretario* (actually the vice-minister) announced that a law had already been prepared for approval in September by the council of ministers. The law required HIV testing of all blood products consumed in Spain.[22] Regarding control of blood donors, the health ministry preferred implementing selective controls, as well as the exclusion of donors that were from risk groups. Presumably for economic reasons, the application of the HIV test to all blood donors was rejected. The *Subsecretario* openly defended these measures with the following statement: 'In the blood banks, in those in which we detect a high index of positive results of AIDS, the tests will be obligatory, and they won't be carried out in those where the incidence is minimal.'[23] While waiting for approval of the law, the health ministry transmitted a note to the regional health authorities which advanced its proposal to prohibit by law paid donations of blood and announced the establishment of a system for selection of blood donors.[24]

Following declarations made by the political authorities, in September 1985, the administrative machinery began to turn. The health ministry mandated from 1 October HIV tests for all blood products (the whole samples of individual donors), imported as well as those produced by local manufacturers, and also made compulsory the analysis of all stocks of blood products, looking for HIV.[25] Only blood intended for plasma production was to be screened with the HIV test, by the manufacturers, whether it came from blood banks or from the manufacturers' own blood collection facilities. On 9 October, an ordinance (*Real Decreto*) was promulgated regulating blood donation and the management of the blood banks, making mandatory discrimination among blood donors (excluding those belonging to risk groups), but not blood screening with the HIV test. A National Commission of Haemotherapy was also set up as an advisory organ, with the participation of haemophiliac associations and representatives of the health ministry and the regional health administrations. Finally, and contrary to previous declarations, the law permitted paid donations in some blood banks.[26] With these measures, a certain satisfaction was given to the haemophiliacs, who, after many years of insistence, finally obtained dependable mechanisms of control for blood products in order to avoid HIV infection.

Second Phase, 1986–7: Control of the Blood Banks

After the promulgation of the ordinance, the problem of infection among haemophiliacs diminished as a resut of control over blood products that the manufacturers exercised. However, this was not true of blood transfusions. The health ministry opted for low-cost mechanisms of identifying blood donors, excluding those belonging to high-risk groups, but discarded the more expensive measure of a systematic HIV testing of all blood donors. The ordinance did not make checking for the HIV virus obligatory in all blood banks. However, at the same time, the more expensive measure was imposed in many European countries. In addition, two months more were required before the appearance of concrete instructions from the health ministry, developing the ordinance, that specified numerous technical aspects of managing blood banks.[27] Also it was required that blood banks should not accept 'any candidate belonging to population groups with a risk of transmission of AIDS' and each donor was to be asked about symptoms and signs of AIDS. It is clear that, for blood donations, this new regulation left some areas exposed.

This regulation was effective from February 1987, and led to an important scandal about transfusions of blood contaminated with HIV in Spain. However, owing to other factors that we will analyse later, the scandal was confined to the practices of the blood bank at a single hospital, in Bellvitge (Barcelona). Yet similar situations could surely have occurred in many other blood banks across the country; also, as we have explained, the decision on low-cost preventive measures of the health ministry in October 1985 was very controversial. After the ordinance of October 1985, there were no policy changes in the health ministry for more than a year. The opinion of the health authorities was that this topic was already under control, and that new efforts should be focused on the development of other preventive measures.[28] Nevertheless, it was leaked to the press that the AIDS commission had already called numerous times on the health ministry to impose compulsory HIV antibodies tests.[29] Hence, during the autumn of 1986, the health ministry announced that it had included in the 1987 national budget the money to impose a mandatory HIV test for all blood donations in Spain.

Given the system of political and administrative decentralization already mentioned, some regions introduced regulations that modified those of the health ministry (in a formal sense, these regional regulations complemented the basic central government laws). In the case of the Basque Country, Navarra and Catalonia, their respective health authorities established norms making HIV tests compulsory for all blood donors before the health ministry did the same in February 1987 (October 1985: Basque Country, Navarra; October 1986: Catalonia). Therefore, over a relatively extended period, different approaches existed in Spain, according to region. In February 1987, a concerned editorial of *El País* characterized this situation as bizarre, highlighting the scarce political interest on the topic in Spain. Finally, a few days later, a ministerial order established the obligatory HIV tests for all blood donations in Spain. This was promulgated on 18 February 1987 by the health ministry.

The preparation of this preventive measure was carried out in coordination with the regional health authorities, and it was even approved previously in a special meeting with the politicians in charge from all the regions (since in many cases they had to implement the measure). At that time, the extent of HIV positives in blood donations in Spain since 1985 was already known with accuracy. The laboratories that produce blood products in Spain were forced – from October 1985 – to test all the batches of blood that they received from the hospitals, and then passed on the results to regional health authorities and to the health ministry. In fact, this information was the very direct cause of the reactions of some regions in imposing a compulsory HIV test before the health ministry did. Surprisingly, the media did not discuss this unusual situation. However, the question was clear. Almost a year later, the president of the Catalan Association of Haemophiliacs outlined the problem very acutely: 'I don't understand why, if in 1985 the HIV test was ordered to check plasma, it took almost two more years to do the same thing for donations made in the Spanish blood banks.'[30]

5   THE POST-CRISIS: CLARIFICATION OF RESPONSIBILITY AND COMPENSATION

As mentioned above, the first blood scandal occurred in February 1987 in Catalonia, and was the only one with a significant impact on public opinion. A big public hospital, near Barcelona (Princeps d'Espanya Hospital), managed by the Catalan public health administration, acknowledged that its blood bank did not use the HIV test after it had been declared mandatory by the regional government in October 1986.[31] Here it is necessary to remember that the Spanish health ministry did not enforce the HIV test until February 1987. Citing financial problems, the director of the hospital had not authorized funds to buy the products necessary to run the test during those months. Also the Catalan health administration had not supervised the implementation of its own regulations on HIV tests sufficiently in this case.

The scandal was immediate. The national press, especially the newspaper that discovered the failure, *El País*, ran extensive coverage of all the aspects, and the editorial of the newspaper called for a serious investigation and demanded clarification of responsibility for the case. In response to the media demands, the Spanish justice ministry decided immediately to nominate a special public prosecutor to investigate the case. Two months later, the public prosecutor accused the management team of the hospital, and also physicians who ran the blood bank. During the next two years, every step of this judicial process was covered by the newspapers in full detail, until trial sessions were held at the Provincial District Court in Barcelona.[32]

Another, smaller scandal occurred at the beginning of 1988, when the office of the Provincial District Court in Barcelona heard the accusation of a person infected by HIV through a transfusion administered in May 1986 in a large Barcelona hospital (Vall de Hebrón Hospital). At that date, the HIV test was still not mandatory in Catalonia, nor in Spain as a whole. The accusation was based on the argument that, if the test existed, the hospital should have assumed responsibility to use the test, although it was not required legally. The accusation represented the first stage of a problem that began to take on bigger dimensions. At that time, in Catalonia alone, a minimum of 15 other people who had received HIV-contaminated blood by transfusion in the period from summer 1985 to October 1986 had been identified. However, the stigma of AIDS, at all levels of Spanish society – and especially at that time – surely reduced the appearance of similar judicial demands.[33]

At the end of 1991, there had been around 25 single claims presented by HIV-infected people who had had blood transfusions, some appearing to occur before the detection test was available, and others after this was available. A judgement of the Supreme Court recognized this year, for the first time, the right of an HIV-infected patient to claim compensation before the appearance of regulations making HIV tests compulsory, because this had already been known and broadly disclosed among the medical community since the summer of 1985. In the early 1990s, more decisions of Spanish tribunals on individual cases of transfusions with HIV-infected blood appeared, requiring the administration to reimburse the victims, but without condemning the individuals responsible. The doctrine of the Spanish Supreme Court was to consider HIV infections caused by a transfusion of blood before controls were declared mandatory as a fortuitous case, denying blame to politicians and public health officials. However, the Supreme Court decreed that the state had an objective responsibility regarding HIV infections, and therefore that harmed patients should be reimbursed by the health administration.[34]

During the second half of the 1980s, contacts between Spanish haemophiliacs and the health ministry had been quite discreet, although the number of haemophiliacs infected with HIV was very high. The rare mention in the media of haemophiliacs, in spite of their being well organized, was put into relief by a representative of the association: 'for a long time we have remained silent because to have AIDS or the suspicion of being able to be infected created for us a much bigger social problem'.[35] However, in April 1987, the AEH announced that it would take out legal proceedings against the health ministry and eight pharmaceutical manufacturers for their responsibility in the massive contamination. They argued that the Ministry and the laboratories knew that HIV-infected factor VIII had its origin in blood donors belonging to high risk groups. In the end, however, they did not sue.

On 28 June 1989 the Social Policy Committee of the Spanish Congress of Deputies debated a proposal on the possibility of paying compensation for haemophiliac deaths caused by AIDS. All groups voted in favour, except the socialist group, which had absolute majority, and the proposition was rejected. The argument of the socialists was that 'the anguish, the physical and psychical sufferings cannot be interpreted differently depending on the means of infection (...) it could represent an attack against justice'.[36] In spite of this, during all this time, silent negotiations between the AEH and the health ministry were undertaken, focusing on the possibility of establishing some type of collective compensation for haemophiliacs. The proposal to create a foundation seemed to be acceptable to both sides; however, strong discrepancies appeared over the amount that should be donated by the public sector. A short time later, the AEH again threatened to sue the health ministry, for 9500 million pesetas, as compensation for all the infections that occurred before 1985. Also the AEH leaked to the press a report of the health ministry, in which it recognized that 1509 Spaniards had been infected by blood products or transfusions from 1981. Separate negotiations also took place between haemophiliacs' regional branches and regional health administrations. In Catalonia, the Catalan health administration offered 50 millions pesetas, while the Catalan haemophiliacs expected 1000 million pesetas. Because of these discrepancies, in May 1991 a collective action on the part of haemophiliacs was brought against the Catalan government and several laboratories. The lawsuit argued that methods of eliminating the HIV contamination in blood products existed from 1983 (by means of heating) but that until October 1985 the administration did not take the measures that it was necessary to impose in an effective way to safeguard factor VIII.

At this time the argument of the health ministry was that the Spanish health administration was not responsible for the infection, because it was not responsible for the import centres and the private manufacture of blood products. In this way, it could oppose the possibility of individual law suits. However, the AEH pressed its petition in a determined fashion. The negotiations continued for two years more and finally, in Spring 1993, after some months of final disputes over the total amount of compensation, the ministry and the haemophiliacs reached an agreement. The agreement was confirmed in an ordinance establishing governmental aid for a total of 1056 infected haemophiliacs, or their relatives if they had already died.[37] Government aid consisted of a fixed amount for each victim or relatives (around 60 000 Euros) and also monthly pensions for the people infected and their sons until the age of 24. It is important to note that, at the same time, the ordinance extended governmental aid and benefits to people infected as a consequence of blood transfusion or transplant, although their actions against the government were always individual, and only a few dozen presented their demands in court. However, the favourable decision of the Supreme Court in 1991 opened the door to more demands, and probably the government also considered this possibility when extending public benefits. In sum, leaving aside pension funds, the total amount of the compensation awarded by the Spanish government to the HIV victims or relatives reached 43 million Euros during 1993 and 1994.[38] However, neither before nor after this compensation agreement did any politician, government agency or public servant assume openly the responsibility (nor was any convicted of negligence by the courts or parliamentary investigations) for not introducing mandatory screening of transfusion blood much later than other Western countries.

6 ANALYSIS OF THE CASE: WHY DID PREVENTION FAIL?

The available data at present on the number of people that developed AIDS in Spain show that those infected by blood products or transfusions constituted a small part of the total number of cases (1.4 per cent and 0.6 per cent respectively). These percentages are similar to the European average in the case of the infections for blood products and much smaller for transfusions (1.6 per cent and 1.7 per cent respectively). However, these data hide the magnitude of the failure of the preventive policies on the infection of blood in Spain between 1983 and 1987. The difference is partly due to Spain having the highest per capita incidence of AIDS in Europe, partly due to its great volume of cases among injectable drugs users (40.4 per cent of all the declared European cases) that decreases the relative incidence of other risk groups. Nevertheless, if we analyse the absolute number of people infected by blood products in Spain, we find that this is the highest in Europe, and greater by 20 per cent than the number of cases present in other countries with larger populations: France, Italy or Great Britain. With respect to blood transfusions, the number of cases declared in Spain was only lower – in terms of per capita infections – than France and Romania (countries where there were enormous scandals as a consequence). The data of the rest of European countries – separating Italy, Portugal and Belgium, with very similar figures to Spain – show much lower figures.[39]

HIV infection among haemophiliacs was higher because of the lack of self-sufficiency in blood products in Spain. As most blood products were imported during the early 1980s, the possibility of infection was much greater in comparison to other European countries. From late 1983, in some cases, Spanish haemophiliacs benefited from heat treatment, but it depended on the purchasing policy of each individual hospital. Only from October 1985 were controls fully mandatory, and based on HIV test screening for all blood products. For the small proportion of blood products made in Spain, in most cases the local manufacturers did not introduce voluntary HIV controls before October 1985, although some did some months before, in April.

As we illustrated, HIV infections from blood transfusion or transplants were also high in comparison to other European figures. Although a completely effective control (using HIV tests for all donations) was introduced extremely late in most parts of the country, probably donor selection was partially effective. Also the number of people living with HIV in Spain during the early 1980s was quite low among the population in general (but present to a certain extent). Thus the number of infected blood donors was not extremely high. The delay in the introduction of the HIV test for all donors could help explain the high Spanish figures in this case. Throughout 1986, the topic of imposing mandatory HIV tests for blood donations in Spain was becoming a question of economic costs for decision makers. Between summer 1985 and autumn 1986, most European countries had already imposed compulsory tests for donors, but the Spanish government had not yet taken any formal decision, and the previous system continued in force, based on discrimination by risk groups.

It seems clear that Spanish indicators permit us to make the assessment that blood management in face of the AIDS threat could be understood as a major programmatic failure. The delays experienced in implementing effective controls on blood banks and blood products between 1983 and 1987 were substantial, and political attitudes were highly reactive. There was some public attention to this problem, but it did not produce a great scandal in Spain, as it had in other places, although similar reasons existed. However, the level of public uproar remained very low during the period and political reactions were very few. Finally, after many years of quiet bargaining, in 1993 the government succeeded in striking a peaceful deal with haemophiliacs, without assuming any political responsibility.

We can try to explain why all this happened, as we do in the next section, but the reason for long delays in introducing mandatory controls is something that escapes our analysis. Many factors – institutions, culture or lack of accountability, among others – combined to produce the unsuccessful reactions of those politically responsible for the prevention of the epidemic. Thus we focus our analysis only on some aspects that could help explain why politicians were so limited in their ability to solve AIDS-related problems during the first years of the epidemic.

7   LOOKING FOR EXPLANATORY ELEMENTS: POLITICAL DECENTRALIZATION AND REACTIVE HEALTH POLICY

For the Spanish public health administration, the very moment that AIDS was appearing coincided with the most intense period of constructing a decentralized public health system. This was clearly an important obstacle to a rapid reaction to the AIDS epidemic. Instead of creating a strong, centralized taskforce to cope with all aspects of AIDS prevention, problems like defining central and regional responsibilities, lack of coordination, political struggles and so on often paralysed any initiative to establish better preventive policies. Politicians' main attention was focused on building the newly decentralized public health system, and they often interpreted concrete action on AIDS prevention as a way to gain more institutional power, either for centre or periphery. If we add to this problem the Francoist legacy of weak public health preventive policies and institutions (low blood self-sufficiency, few regulations and so on) it is easier to understand the central role of the media as an agenda setter and the predominance of reactive health policies during those years.[40]

It is necessary to remember also that an important information problem exists when analysing the course of the epidemic of declared cases of AIDS, since they represent infections that happened about five years earlier. Especially for a reactive policy style, this problem complicated decisions on AIDS prevention, since perceptions of risk became very diffuse. This perception hindered decision makers in favour of active prevention measures (using economic and political costs) since the benefits in terms of fewer infections were only seen in the long term (with the reduction of the number of future cases). However, from a situation where the probabilities of infection were based only on identification of the donors belonging to the groups at risk, in 1985 the situation changed to a new one with the existence of the HIV test. Then infection probabilities could be calculated better, and the donors and recipients could be clearly identified. This modified the policy context: from a perception of quite diffuse risks, difficult to separate from subjective distortions, it moved to a perception of the risks that could be quite exact. In this new situation, the cost–benefit calculus – although in an intuitive form – could be made quite clearly by public decision makers. The costs of using the test, in a widespread way, for all blood donors and all blood products, could be balanced against the human lives that would be saved. On this last point, there was still a margin of uncertainty; at that time it was not known exactly what percentage of those infected would develop AIDS, and how many of these would die before effective treatments could be developed.

Reactive policies are usually guided more by external pressures than are anticipatory ones, because they have more difficulties in processing information internally and in making new decisions. This is clear for the two cases examined, where the role of the processes of collective action in the results obtained by two groups was very important. While haemophiliacs finally obtained compensation as a result of their collective action, they also more quickly had the mechanisms of control over HIV imposed (but not so quickly when compared with other European countries). In contrast, it took a long time to eliminate completely the possibility that patients might be infected by transfusions. Also compensation that the HIV-infected patients from blood transfusion got was basically an indirect effect of the haemophiliac pressure on the health ministry.

The differences among well organized groups and collectives without any organization appear to be very significant, especially if one keeps in mind the role of their lobbying activities and political pressure on the Spanish political and administrative system. Given the nature of their health problem and their dependence on public resources, all Spanish haemophiliacs were already members of the AEH before the AIDS problem appeared and that allowed them to negotiate this problem in a continuous way throughout the period. On the other hand, recipients of infected transfusions did not have any basis of organization; nor did they have a way of being identified to each other (also keeping in mind the social rejection of AIDS). The possibilities that collective action would emerge were much reduced in this case, and the dependence on public initiative was much stronger than for the haemophiliacs who could gain their objectives by means of pressure and insistence against a reactive state.

NOTES

1. I am very grateful to Elvira Mendez and Andreu Segura for their helpful comments on earlier versions of this chapter. I would also like to thank Alberto Valdivia for research assistance.
2. For an overview of the history of AIDS prevention problems in Spain until the early 1990s, see Álvarez and Hernandez (1994); Zunzunegui (1994).
3. Since the transition to democracy Spain has had three territorial levels of government: local, regional (the autonomous communities) and central (the state).
4. On the Spanish health care system, see the chapter 'Por un consenso en la Sanidad', in CECS (1997). For the specific aspects of health decentralization policies, see Rico (1997).
5. Since 1987, an intergovernmental political body (*Consejo Interterritorial*) has been established to coordinate health policies among the central and regional levels of governments. One of the most important fields of activity of this body was precisely to set up agreements in order to coordinate public health prevention policies.
6. The AEH was created in 1971; in 1989 it became the *Federacion Espanola de Hemofilia* (FEH). This change involved an organizational transformation adapting the association to the new decentralized political framework in Spain. However, some regional associations did not join the Federation – as in the case of the Catalan organization.
7. For a broader analysis of AIDS preventive policies in Spain, see Jordana and Méndez (1996).
8. Martin Villar (1980).
9. Camara Mendizabal (1980). From 1970 to 1997, blood donation in Spain rose from seven donations yearly for every thousand habitants in 1970, to 14.3 in 1980, 27.6 in 1990 and 36 in 1997 (see http://www.msc.es/salud/epidemiologia/ hemoterapia.htm).
10. The correspondent of *El País* in London published an article based on information that had appeared in *The Lancet* that a Spanish haemophiliac had died of AIDS in a Seville hospital. The correspondent used this news to introduce the opinion of the British specialized press on the topic (*El País*, May 1985, p. 29).
11. *El País*, 13 May 1983, p. 32. The creation of commissions for the monitoring of the epidemic was also impelled in some regions. For example, the autonomous government of Catalonia created a commission in September 1983, in which all hospitals were represented.
12. *El País*, 16 June 1983, p. 29.

13. Ministerio de Sanidad (1984).
14. When AIDS was more clearly understood, the epidemiological and surveillance authorities continued the commision's practice. The AEH's opinion of the commission was very negative. A. Gomés, its president in 1985, declared: 'The commission meets little and without effectiveness, because they don't study the cases conscientiously.' He argued that, from 1983 onwards, the AEH had insisted that better plasma controls be implemented. In those years, a deep conflict existed between the AIDS commission and the AEH. The AEH wanted to join the commission but was constantly being denied membership. The conflict came close to a rupture in the relationship between the AEH and the health ministry (*El País*, 7 September 1985, p. 20).
15. For example, at La Paz, a large hospital in Madrid with the biggest haemophiliac unit in Spain, treating around 12 per cent of all Spanish haemophiliacs, heat treatment was introduced in October 1983 and was used exclusively thereafter (Magallon *et al.*, 1987).
16. See, for example, the comments of the official responsible for the coordination of AIDS medical research in Spain, R. Nájera, who stated that it would take only two years to develop a treatment against AIDS (*El País*, 6 January 1985, p. 36).
17. *El País*, 20 April 1985. p. 36.
18. In September 1985, in a meeting of the Spanish Hematological Society, medical researchers presented data that HIV was present among both paid and unpaid blood donors. However, the differences were great. While only 0.2 per cent of unpaid donors were HIV positive, a total of 3.3 per cent of paid donors, recruited by the Spanish plasma laboratories, were HIV-positive (see Hernandez *et al.*, 1986; Gutierrez *et al.*, 1986).
19. *El País*, 14 July 1985, p. 36.
20. *El País*, 4 August 1985, p. 26.
21. *El País*, 11 August 1985, p. 21; and 14 August 1985, p. 18. In the Basque Country, the regional government made it illegal for homosexuals and other risk groups to donate blood (*La Vanguardia*, 7 August 1985, p. 3).
22. *La Vanguardia*, 12 August 1985, p. 3.
23. *El País*, 14 August 1985, p. 18. The elaboration of this norm was long underway. Sources at the Ministry have revealed that it took more than two months of preparation, including several meetings to coordinate the measures with the regional governments.
24. Ibid., p. 16.
25. RCL 1985/2205, *Resolución de la Subsecretaria*, Ministerio de Sanidad y Consumo, 6 September 1985.
26. RCL 1985/2549, *Real Decreto*, 9 October 1985.
27. RCL 1985/1959, *Orden*, 4 December 1985.
28. In particular, to cope with the rapid spread of HIV in the jails. The news got to the press and generated enormous attention, since it contradicted the official discourse of scarce presence of HIV in Spain. (*El País*, 13 April 1986, pp. 16–17; 30 June 1986, p. 6.)
29. *El País*, 10 February 1987, p. 18.
30. *La Vanguardia*, 15 January 1988.
31. In fact, this information got to the press as a result of internal disputes among the hospital managers.
32. Punishments were mild. Two years after, in an appeal to the Supreme Court, the sentences were reduced even further. However, in all the cases the government was held responsible for the damage inflicted upon the HIV-infected persons.
33. *La Vanguardia*, 14 January 1988; *El País*, 14 January 1988, p. 23. The woman was infected in May 1986, but she was not able to obtain information on her infection until late 1987 because she had not received any test results from the hospital for a long time.
34. Sentence of the Supreme Court (RJ 1991/5131).
35. *La Vanguardia*, 11 January 1991.
36. *El País*, 14 September 1989, p. 34.
37. *El País*, 10 March 1993, p. 22; 22 April 1993, p. 34; 19 January 1994, p. 23. (See *Real Decreto Ley* 9/93, 28 May 1993.)
38. The government established several conditions for receiving compensation: (a) that the infection occurred as a consequence of a treatment provided by a public health care agency,

(b) that the infection occurred before the HIV test was declared mandatory, and (c) that compensated persons renounced their right to sue public health agencies or their employees. (See *Real Decreto Ley* 9/93, 28 May 1993.)

39. See CESES (1998).

40. However, it could be said that the complex problem that AIDS prevention represented for the Spanish public health agencies was also a challenge that had a positive side. The difficulties associated with the problem made clear a need for more coordination between the central state and the regions – politically and technically. As a case of policy learning, it seems clear that this aim has progressively been reached from 1987 onwards. Also it is interesting to observe that learning how to coordinate these policies was applied not only to AIDS-related problems, but also to many other public health issues. On the key role of coordination in AIDS public policy, see Anand (1997).

29. Protecting the Swedish blood supply against HIV: crisis management without scandal

Erik Albæk

1 INTRODUCTION

The most conspicuous aspect of HIV in the Swedish blood supply is its inconspicuousness on the public and media agendas.[1] If Mr and Mrs Swensson had any knowledge of policies to secure the blood supply, they would have it from news reports on 'blood scandals' abroad, in particular neighbouring Denmark (Albæk, 1999). In Sweden, HIV in the blood supply became the forgotten aspect of the public record of the AIDS tragedy, not even mentioned in analyses of Swedish AIDS policies (Henriksson, 1988; Fox *et al.*, 1989; Henriksson and Ytterberg, 1992). What instead made Swedish AIDS policies famous not only at home but around the world were Sweden's policy measures to prevent HIV transmission through sexual activity and sharing of needles, some of which were the most restrictive measures implemented in the Western world. They squarely contradicted the European Council's recommendation on AIDS policies, and Sweden refrained in 1989, the only member country to do so, from signing and supporting the Council's recommendations (Henriksson and Ytterberg, 1992, p. 328).

AIDS became known in Sweden soon after it was first reported in the United States as an official, clinical syndrome. Although Sweden's first case of AIDS was diagnosed as early as 1982, only medical professionals and social groups perceived to be at risk, in the first instance gay men and later haemophiliacs, knew of AIDS in the early 1980s. But even amongst medical professionals and at-risk groups, only a limited number of people had intimate knowledge of the disease. Not until the mid-1980s did AIDS attract the attention of the media and thereby the public at large, and, by then, technicomedical solutions to prevent blood-borne HIV transmission had already been found and implemented. Because blood-borne HIV had already found its programmatic solution before AIDS reached the agendas of the media and the public, it never became more than a marginal health problem in the public arena. With only one exception, the programmatic solutions to prevent HIV transmission through the blood supply were never questioned politically in Sweden.

2   THE POLICY CONTEXT

Health care in Sweden is divided among the central and local levels of government. At the central level of government, the Ministry of Health and Welfare (*Socialdepartementet*) is charged with overall health planning and policy formulation, whereas regulation and control is the responsibility of the relatively independent National Board of Health and Welfare (*Socialstyrelsen*). Until 1990, when it was established as an independent agency (*Läkemedelsverket*), the board's Department of Drugs (*Socialstyrelsens läkemedelsafdelning*) was charged with regulation, control and inspection of pharmaceutical products and their manufacture, whereas the board's Department of Health and Hospitals (*Socialstyrelsens hälso- och sjukvårdsafdelning*) was responsible for the corresponding functions with respect to medical therapy. However, all legislative matters, orders and general recommendations were decided by the board's central management.[2] As far as the blood supply was concerned, all administrative decisions on the quality and safety of blood products were taken by the Department of Drugs, whereas blood donation and blood transfusion were the responsibility of the Department of Health and Hospitals. Although they were both units within the same agency, the two departments worked relatively independently of one another, but did cooperate on an ad hoc basis on matters of common interest. With regard to HIV, a special taskforce was set up which met on a weekly basis.[3] In Sweden, health service delivery is the responsibility of the local levels of government, first and foremost the regional county authorities. Throughout the history of HIV in Sweden, the county hospitals have been charged with transfusion services and haemophilia treatment as well as running the blood banks. The blood banks have also delivered plasma to Kabi, the only Swedish pharmaceutical manufacturer of clotting factor concentrate.

Until the mid-1980s, virtually all AIDS policy initiatives, including initiatives on blood, were taken within the medical policy subsystem. In 1985, the Swedish government, in effect the Prime Minister and the Minister of Health and Welfare, did take the initiative to formulate a comprehensive AIDS policy with the creation of the National Committee on AIDS (*AIDS-Delegationen*) intended to advise the government on policy. Not only was this initiative taken at a comparatively very early stage, it also had a remarkably high political profile. The committee chairman was none other than the Minister of Health and Welfare, and committee members included Social Democratic and opposition leaders, medical experts, civil servants and interest group leaders, including the Swedish Association of Local Authorities and the Federation of County Councils. This high-profile policy body dealt with practically all aspect of AIDS, except blood. At the time the committee was created, the crisis of HIV in the blood supply had been technically overcome with the implementation of donor blood screening and heat treatment of blood products.

3 PROTECTING THE SWEDISH BLOOD SUPPLY AGAINST HIV

Prophylactic factor VIII treatment was introduced in Sweden as early as 1958 (SoU, 1993, p. 16). Prior to the epoch-making American discovery of cryoprecipitate in the mid-1960s, Swedish researchers had produced a factor VIII concentrate in cooperation with the pharmaceutical company Kabi. Since then Kabi, which holds a dominant position in Swedish blood products manufacture, is the only Swedish pharmaceutical manufacturer to uphold production of clotting factor concentrate. Kabi's production method required thousands of litres of plasma in a pool, whereas the production of cryoprecipitates only required small pools of plasma derived from few donors. Prior knowledge of Kabi's product biased haemophilia therapists and haemophiliacs against cryoprecipitate therapy. So did the health care funding system: industrially manufactured pharmaceutical products were paid for by the central government, whereas blood components, the technical category to which cryoprecipitates produced in blood banks belonged, were paid for by the county council via blood bank budgets. Although several blood banks wanted to produce cryoprecipitates in the 1970s and 1980s, the county authorities had no incentive to support such production.[4]

As raw material, Kabi used plasma collected in Sweden and abroad. Until the 1980s, the supply of Swedish plasma was limited, and Swedish blood products manufacturers depended on the import of plasma from abroad, in particular from neighbouring Finland. The share of Swedish raw material increased at the beginning of the 1980s and made up 85 per cent of the plasma used by Kabi in its 1984 production. At the time, Kabi satisfied 50–60 per cent of the Swedish demand for factor VIII. The remaining demand was satisfied by imported preparations, in particular from the United States. As far as factor IX concentrate is concerned, Kabi's production was, on the whole, sufficient to satisfy the domestic demand (SoU, 1993, pp. 25–6).

The first case of AIDS in Sweden was diagnosed in September 1982. Information that AIDS was not only a sexually transmitted but also a bloodborne disease quickly reached Swedish transfusion specialists and haemophilia therapists. At first there was great confusion about how to handle this previously unknown, infectious and deadly disease. Only in 1983 was a new retrovirus,

HIV, discovered in the USA and France, and during the spring of 1984 it became possible to isolate the virus from AIDS patients. The idea that this new virus was the cause of AIDS gained support and was presented as a plausible theory in articles in June and September 1984 in *Svensk Läkertidning,* the journal of the Swedish medical association (Biberfeld and Biberfeld, 1984; Biberfeld *et al.*, 1984). At the same time, epidemiological data from the USA indicated that AIDS infection could be transmitted through blood even from persons with no or only vague symptoms of AIDS. Soon after, the aetiology of AIDS seemed clear: the disease was caused by HIV.

Before the aetiology of AIDS was fully known and, accordingly, before there were technicomedical measures to prevent blood-borne HIV transmission, there was great uncertainty among the health authorities as to what possible preventive steps to take. Interestingly, as early as January 1983, two months before the US centers for disease control delivered a similar recommendation, the Swedish Federation of Gay and Lesbian Rights, together with a few physicians, recommended that gay men refrain from donating blood. The federation's recommendation provoked the National Board of Health and Welfare to accuse the federation of creating hysteria. The suggestion that AIDS might be transmitted though blood could, according to the board, deter people from donating blood and frighten those who needed blood transfusions (Henriksson and Ytterberg, 1992, pp. 321–2).

Only on 12 July 1984 did the board issue an order that certain at-risk groups be excluded from the donor pool, but even then AIDS was only mentioned briefly and the order to specifically exclude heterosexuals or homosexuals with many sexual partners and IV drug users was based allegedly on high incidences of hepatitis (and syphilis), not AIDS, among these at-risk groups. The recommendation was sent from the printer on 21 September and came into effect on 1 October 1984 (SOSFS, 1984). Not until 19 March 1985 did the board issue an order with general recommendations on AIDS, including an addendum to the board's order on blood donation, blood transfusion and so on of 12 July 1984 clearly specifying exclusion of at-risk groups from the donor pool (SOSFS, 1985).

In September 1984, Kabi initiated heat treatment experiments of its factor VIII concentrate, Octonativ. As a result of international information, the company changed its heat treatment method in November and expected to initiate a clinical study in March 1985. However, in February 1985, Kabi was notified by a blood bank that a donor whose blood had been used in the production of Octonativ had later tested positive for HIV antibodies. In a letter of 20 February, Kabi passed this information on to the National Board of Health and Welfare. In a letter of Friday 22 February, the company notified the board that it had decided to withdraw all Octonativ from the shelves. The very same day, the board decided that all factor VIII sold in Sweden must be heat treated before use. After 25 February, Kabi only delivered factor VIII concentrate that had been heat treated, in accordance with the board's regulations, at 68°C for 24 hours (SoU, 1993, p. 30). Thus, over one weekend, the company managed to introduce heat treatment as a standard procedure in its production and, over the same weekend, to supply enough virus-inactivated clotting factor concentrate to cover the demand.

At that time, the question of screening donor blood also emerged. In letters of 5 March and 2 April 1985 to the National Board of Health and Welfare, the Swedish Haemophilia Society requested that all donor blood be screened for HIV antibodies. In its 19 March 1985 order with general recommendations on AIDS, the board announced that steps had already been taken to find out how testing for the presence of HIV antibodies in blood and blood products might be introduced in Sweden (SOSFS, 1985, p. 2). In March, methods to test blood for HIV antibodies became available in Sweden. The methods immediately attracted the attention of the blood banks, and in mid-May a number of blood banks started to test their donors. In a letter of 3 May to all county health and hospitals committees, the board recommended that screening for HIV antibodies be implemented as soon as possible. In similar situations, the board would normally issue an order. In this case, the board decided to issue a recommendation because an order required a number of technical tests of HIV screening techniques before final approval, a procedure that might prolong the introduction of HIV screening for several months. The committee advising the board on HIV screening was divided into one group which found screening methods too unreliable and untested for the board to recommend general implementation, and another group, the majority, which shared these concerns, but found that the media and political attention to AIDS called for extraordinary steps by the board. By issuing its recommendation, the board speeded up the introduction of screening in Sweden considerably.[5] On 12 June, the first county council decided to introduce testing of all donors. Other county authorities followed suit, and at the end of September all blood donations in Sweden were tested (SoU, 1993, p. 34). After the de facto implementation of donor blood testing by 1 October, the National Board of Health and Welfare found no reason to issue a formal mandatory order until 19 December 1989 (SOSFS, 1989).

In addition to the blood banks' screening, Kabi initiated screening of blood donations in order to improve the safety of its blood products. In a letter of 4 June to the Swedish blood banks, Kabi announced that it planned to test donations that had not been screened by the banks. The company expected to start its screening procedures by 1 July. By 1 August, all new plasma used in Kabi's clotting factor would be tested either by the blood banks or by the company itself. The date was later postponed to 15 August, which was also the date from which imported products were to be based on screened plasma only.[6]

However, Kabi had stocks of unscreened plasma and, in order to keep up with demand, the company decided to use both screened and unscreened plasma in its production of blood products during a transition period of a couple of months. This decision was not communicated to the National Board of Health and Welfare. Kabi appears to have used unscreened plasma in its production until 15 November 1985, and factor VIII concentrate based on unscreened plasma produced by Kabi was on the market until mid-April 1986, factor IX concentrate until 14 March 1986 (SoU, 1993, pp. 36–7).

On 14 March 1986 – a year after the national board of health and welfare had mandated heat treatment of factor VIII concentrate – it was reported that a 17-year-old haemophilia B patient had tested HIV-positive during a routine check.[7] The young man had been treated with Kabi's factor IX product, Preconativ, and other patients treated with Preconativ were immediately checked. Four patients tested HIV-positive. It quickly became apparent that a deficient virus elimination method used by Kabi in its factor IX production was the cause of the four patients' HIV infection.

On 25 May 1973, Kabi had had a factor IX product registered at the National Board of Health and Welfare's Department of Drugs under the name of Preconativ. At the same time, the company had started the development of a special virus separation technique intended to minimize the risk of hepatitis transmission through Preconativ. In July 1975 and again in March and May 1976, Kabi applied for a patent on its technique. On 24 July 1983, the company applied to the National Board of Health and Welfare's Department of Drugs to introduce the virus separation method into the manufacture of Preconativ. Permission was granted on 28 April 1983.

When subjected to the heat treatment methods used for virus inactivation in factor VIII in the 1970s, factor IX concentrate had tended to increase the risk of thrombosis in patients undergoing therapy. Heat treatment experiments for factor IX concentrate were therefore not initiated until much later, and instead Kabi used another elimination method, gel adsorption. The original intention was to eliminate hepatitis virus from factor IX concentrate, as stated by Kabi in its 1983 application to the board to introduce the gel adsorption method into its production of Preconativ. It was soon discovered that the method also eliminated HIV from factor IX concentrate. This method proved less suitable for eliminating the virus from Kabi's factor VIII product, Octonativ, because factor VIII components were adsorbed to the gel as well, thereby reducing production output. When, on 20 February 1985, a Swedish blood donor was reported HIV-positive and Kabi decided to introduce heat treatment for Octonativ, the company at the same time judged that the gel adsorption method was sufficiently effective to eliminate HIV from Preconativ and therefore continued using this technique in its production of factor IX concentrate.

The 14 March 1986 disclosure that a haemophiliac had tested HIV-positive after Preconativ therapy caused hectic activity at Kabi. That very Friday night the company started a chain of telephone calls to pharmacies throughout Sweden which was to be continued the following morning to pharmacies that were open on Saturdays. The chain was re-established on Monday morning. As early as Saturday 15 March, Kabi had sent a letter to all Swedish pharmacies informing them that the sale of Preconativ had come to a halt, pending an investigation. On Monday 17 March, Kabi sent a letter to, among others, its own warehouses, wholesalers and pharmacies informing them of the decision to withdraw Preconativ from the market and requested a complete stock count. As its reason for withdrawing the product, Kabi said that the preparation was to be heat treated.

The National Board of Health and Welfare also acted fast and immediately allowed a still to be registered, heat-treated Austrian factor IX product onto the Swedish market. On 22 December 1986, Kabi was permitted to remarket heat-treated Preconativ. The board also immediately initiated a number of activities to investigate what had gone wrong at Kabi. These investigations disclosed irregularities in the procedures at Kabi and in the communication between the company and the board. For instance, it was not until 27 March 1986 that the board's Department of Drugs found out that there were still products on the Swedish market based on non-HIV-tested raw material. The board had interpreted Kabi's decision to test, at the latest from 15 August 1985, all plasma used in its clotting factor production to mean that, after that date, only HIV-tested coagulation products would be on the Swedish market. Kabi's decision to use its stocks of unscreened plasma during a transition period had not been communicated to the board. On 27 March, the board immediately mandated that only tested products were to be sold by Kabi. Also the board discovered that earlier, in August 1985, a test programme initiated by Kabi had indicated that the company's gel adsorption method was not 100 per cent effective. This information was never communicated to the board either. However, Kabi avoided both sanctions and official reprimands, and the irregularities disclosed by the board's investigative activities were not communicated to the media or the public until years later.

The four patients were the last haemophiliacs and the only haemophilia B patients to become infected during therapy in Sweden. In all, 94 haemophilia A patients were infected during therapy in Sweden, primarily owing to infection in imported products, and the vast majority were infected between 1979 and 1983 (Svensk Förening för Transfusionsmedicin, 1988, p. 7). After the implementation of heat treatment and donor blood screening, no haemophilia A patients were HIV-infected during therapy in Sweden. A total of 80 transfusion recipients are positively known to have become infected during therapy in

Sweden, primarily from 1982 to 1985 (ibid.) and none after the implementation of blood donation screening.

4   THE AFTERMATH

Compensation

The universalist Swedish welfare state has always provided generous benefits to persons who cannot support themselves, for instance the sick or disabled. On top of this, various compensation schemes were available to persons who became HIV-infected through blood. On 1 January 1975, Sweden introduced, as the first West European country, a patient injury insurance scheme run and financed by a consortium of the central government, the county authorities and the district authorities. On 1 July 1978, a corresponding medicines injury insurance scheme was set up by a consortium consisting of all pharmaceutical companies on the Swedish market, domestic manufacturers as well as importers. The idea behind the schemes was to make possible compensation for injuries caused by treatments and medicines even if the very restrictive common compensation rules did not apply.

When the two compensation schemes, the medicines injury scheme in 1986 and the patient injury scheme in 1988, decided that HIV infection in itself warranted compensation, infected Swedish haemophilia patients and transfusion recipients were some of the first HIV victims in the world to obtain compensation. Out of the 104 persons in Sweden who had become HIV-infected due to haemophilia treatment, six were positively infected abroad and were not compensated by the Swedish medicines injury compensation scheme. Of the remaining 98 infected haemophiliacs, 94 were compensated. Of the 86 infected transfusion recipients in Sweden, two were positively known to have become infected during transfusion therapy abroad, while in four cases the source of infection is not known. The remaining 80 transfusion recipients were all compensated by the patient injury insurance scheme. Furthermore, six persons infected through sexual contact with HIV-infected haemophiliacs or transfusion recipients were not formally entitled to compensation, but were nevertheless compensated by the two compensation schemes (SoU, 1991, 34).

The decisions by the two schemes to compensate were fairly automatic. HIV infection was compared to other medical injuries which were eligible for compensation, and the medical condition was judged to be such that it warranted compensation. Medicines and patient injury compensations in Sweden are calculated on the basis of very detailed tables according to seriousness and age. However, the calculations for HIV were complicated because of the very special nature of the infection and the associated diseases, that is the diseases making up the AIDS syndrome. In 1986, representatives from the Swedish Haemophilia Society and haemophilia therapists agreed with the medicines injury insurance scheme on a lump sum compensation for infected haemophiliacs. However, this compensation was increased in 1988 and in 1991, partly because a number of non-economic injuries were now included in the compensation calculations, for instance fear and social isolation inflicted upon infected haemophiliac patients. Similar increases were seen in the compensation paid to infected transfusion recipients. In 1988, the government had established a royal commission to investigate non-economic injuries in general. In 1991, the commission issued a special report on non-economic injury compensation to HIV-infected persons (SoU, 1991). The report concluded that HIV was a very special disease that made comparisons to other medical injuries difficult and recommended an increase in compensations paid to HIV-infected haemophilia patients and transfusion recipients. This recommendation was adopted in 1991 by the two insurance schemes and the government, both parties paying an additional ex gratia compensation of SEK 100 000 to infected haemophilia patients and transfusion recipients on top of the compensations paid by the two insurance schemes in accordance with normal calculation procedures (*Svar på interpellationerna*, 1992/93: 92 och 97). In 1995, Swedish haemophiliacs had been compensated with a minimum of SEK 487 750 and a maximum of SEK 603 250. As of 1 January 1995, the highest compensation given for a pharmaceutical or patient injury in Sweden was SEK 650 000 (FIBS, 1990; 1995). Compensation, including ex gratia compensation, to infected Swedish haemophilia patients and transfusion recipients was given without political controversy and without much public attention. The same is true of the government's decision to subsidize programmes run by the Swedish Haemophilia Society to support HIV-infected haemophilia patients and their families.

Factor IX 'Scandal'

On 12 February 1993, the local newspaper *Upsala Nya Tidning* published a number of articles with interviews with the four haemophiliac patients who had been infected in the autumn of 1985 during treatment with Kabi's factor IX product, Preconativ. From 22 to 27 February, the national tabloid *Aftonbladet* ran a series of highly critical articles accusing Kabi of negligence and unethical conduct and blaming the company for the four haemophiliacs' HIV infection. Among other things, the articles revealed that Kabi had already been notified by the researchers conducting the company's test programme in August 1985 that its gel adsorption method to eliminate HIV virus from Preconativ was deficient. *Aftonbladet*'s articles attracted enormous public attention. As early as 1 March, the Minister of Health and Welfare was questioned in Parliament about the action he planned to take to prevent similar incidences in the future (Interpellation, 1992/93:92). On 9 March, the government was asked in Parliament whether it intended to investigate the National Board of Health and Welfare's handling of the Kabi affair (Interpellation, 1992/93:97). The minister responsible responded on 19 April that the government had authorized him to initiate an inquiry already on 4 March, and he had appointed the chairman and members of the inquiry team on 18 March (*Svar på interpellationerna*, 1992/93: 92 och 97).

The inquiry commission was given less than three months to complete its investigation (Dir. 1993) and issued its report on 31 May 1993 (SoU, 1993). The commission concluded that the contaminated Preconativ products used to treat the four haemophiliacs were known to have been manufactured by Kabi in April 1985 and that the tainted blood donation was known to have been drawn at a hospital in June 1984. The commission was asked to evaluate specifically whether HIV infection of the four haemophiliacs could have been avoided, had the National Board of Health and Welfare and Kabi taken different actions. The commission noted (a) that this question can be answered only hypothetically and (b) that no clear 'yes or no' answer can be given. The commission considered HIV testing of blood plasma, measures to reduce the volume of HIV in blood plasma, substitution preparations and product information, and concluded that, had measures been introduced which in retrospect seem sensible, the four haemophiliacs could likely have avoided HIV infection. However, given the information available to the actors at the time of decision, it was highly unlikely that infection could have been avoided.

At the same time, the commission found reason to criticize a number of practices and procedures both at Kabi and at the National Board of Health and Welfare. Kabi was criticized for not passing on to the board a preliminary report from the company's test programme indicating that the gel adsorption method was deficient. According to the report, this inaction clearly violated Swedish regulations on pharmaceutical manufacture and prevented the board from assessing whether Preconativ could remain on the market if virus elimination was done only by the gel method. The report found no reason to criticize Kabi's practice of mixing screened and non-screened plasma, although it did find the practice inexpedient.

However, the report attracted little public attention when it was published, it stirred no political controversies and no sanctions were imposed on the company or the board. The four infected haemophilia B patients sued Kabi, but the case was settled out of court with little public attention.

5   ASSESSMENT

In the early 1980s, the Swedish health system was well connected to the international blood therapy community. Shortly after the first reports from the USA that AIDS is transmittable through blood, this information was available to Swedish health care professionals. However, Swedish physicians and health officials were as confused as their international colleagues about the way to interpret this information. On the one hand, they faced a potential health crisis of immense proportions if the blood supply became infected with AIDS in an uncontrollable manner. On the other hand, the risk of blood-borne transmission was highly uncertain. It was equally uncertain what could sensibly be done to prevent blood-borne AIDS transmission.

The Swedish health authorities never favoured policy options that could have reduced the number of blood donations to which the individual transfusion patient and, in particular, the individual haemophilia patient were exposed. One option would have been a switch to the considerably less plasma-demanding, however therapeutically much less effective and much more inconvenient, cryoprecipitate therapy; another option was to reduce Sweden's comparatively extensive use of clotting factor in prophylactic treatment. Both options would also have drastically reduced the need to import plasma products from the USA. It is uncertain how many Swedish haemophiliacs could have avoided HIV infection had Sweden quickly opted for such policy solutions. A number of Swedish haemophiliacs are known to have become HIV-infected as early as 1979 and 1980 (Svensk Förening för Transfusionsmedicin, 1988, p. 7). The remaining factor VIII-treated haemophiliacs who became infected up to and including 1984 were primarily treated with imported clotting factor preparations. Thus it is likely that a fast switch to cryoprecipitate manufactured from Swedish plasma might have reduced the number of HIV-infected Swedish haemophilia patients. In the early 1980s, however, when the risk of contracting and dying from AIDS was not known and therefore could not be compared to the risk of death or invalidation from less effective or no haemophilia therapy, a switch to cryoprecipitate therapy did not present itself as an option to Swedish health officials, haemophilia therapists or haemophiliacs. The Swedish decision to stick to (imported) clotting factor concentrate was the rule among countries offering factor therapy to haemophiliac patients in the early 1980s.

In the absence of tests to detect AIDS in blood, selection of donors became a risk-reduction initiative that quickly resonated in the international blood therapy community, although it also met with opposition, in particular from at-risk groups, who found the policy initiative discriminatory, and from health officials who feared that the population at large might start to doubt the safety of the blood supply. As early as January 1983, the Swedish Federation of Gay and Lesbian Rights surprisingly recommended that gay men refrain from donating blood. The policy recommendation was rejected by the national board of health and welfare, and not until the autumn of 1984, much later than most comparable health authorities, did the board officially request that at-risk groups withdraw from the donor pool, and even then the recommendation was not straightforward.

As soon as the causative agent of AIDS was known to be a virus, the only domestic blood products manufacturer, Kabi, as well as the health authorities, reacted comparatively fast whenever they had information on which they could act. At an early stage, Kabi started to develop methods to eliminate HIV from its clotting factor products. When the first case of HIV in a Swedish donor became known, Kabi withdrew all its factor VIII concentrate from the market. The company not only changed its production over one weekend, it was also capable of fully supplying the market with heat-treated factor VIII instantly. Likewise, the health authorities responded by immediately mandating that only heat-treated clotting factor concentrate be used in haemophilia therapy in Sweden, thereby making Sweden one of the first countries in the world to introduce mandatory heat treatment. However, the method used to eliminate HIV from Kabi's factor IX product, Preconativ, later turned out to be deficient. Irregular and suboptimal operating procedures at Kabi and the regulatory National Board of Health and Welfare allowed the non-effective gel adsorption method to be used beyond reasonable limits before it was withdrawn from the market. However, as soon as it discovered the ineffectiveness of its gel adsorption method, Kabi withdrew Preconativ from the market, and the National Board of Health and Welfare instantly allowed an unregistered, heat-treated Austrian product onto the Swedish market.

Screening of donor blood was introduced early in Sweden. At the end of September 1985, all donor blood was screened. This made Sweden one of the first countries to fully secure transfusion blood. By 15 August 1985, before all donor blood was screened in the Swedish blood banks, Kabi had secured its blood products by screening all plasma that had not been screened by the blood banks. However, during a transition period of a few months, Kabi mixed screened and non-screened plasma in its clotting factor manufacture. Even so, from 15 November 1985, Kabi used only screened raw material. This made Sweden one of the first countries to produce only heat-treated *and* screened blood products. However, there were still heat-treated products based on non-screened material on the Swedish market until the National Board of Health and Welfare found out by chance and immediately mandated that only tested products be sold.

Although there were occasions, in particular in the very first years of the AIDS epidemic, when the Swedish health authorities could have taken actions which in retrospect turned out to be wiser, the general conclusion on the Swedish efforts to manage programmatically the HIV and blood crisis is that Sweden, on a comparative scale, fared well, especially with respect to the introduction of the two decisive measures to secure blood and blood products: heat treatment of factor concentrate and screening of donor blood.

At the time of decision, the programmatic policy actions just mentioned were primarily known to professionals within the blood supply policy subsystem – not to the media, the general public or other policy subsystems. Thus the most important steps to secure the blood supply in Sweden were taken just before AIDS became a major issue in the media and some time before AIDS reached Sweden's political agenda.

The absence of public awareness in Sweden of the health authorities' policies to manage programmatically the HIV and blood crisis in the early and mid-1980s did not differ from the situation in most advanced industrial democracies, but the absence of a retrospective politicization of these policies in the late 1980s and early 1990s makes Sweden unique. First, in contrast to what happened in a number of countries, including the other five case countries of this book, the actions taken by the Swedish health authorities to prevent blood-borne HIV infection were never questioned by the media, by politicians, by the courts or by the Swedish Haemophilia Society. Only Kabi's failure to eliminate HIV from its factor IX preparations effectively reached the media and then only briefly. When the ineffectiveness of the heat treatment method was disclosed to the public – years after the company had introduced a new, effective heat treatment method – the government acted swiftly and closed the case politically by appointing an inquiry commission. In its report, the commission did criticize procedures at Kabi and the controlling health authorities, but its criticism was not fatal to public officials or to employees at Kabi. No sanctions were imposed, nor were there any official reprimands.

Second, also in contrast to the situation in a number of countries, compensation for HIV-infected haemophiliacs and transfusion recipients never became a political or judicial issue in Sweden. As patient and medicines injury insurance schemes were already introduced, Sweden in 1986 became the first country to compensate infected haemophiliacs and, in 1988, transfusion recipients. Although HIV infection among haemophiliacs and transfusion recipients remained a non-issue in the media and in Parliament, the level of compensation was increased on a couple of occasions. The fast inclusion of HIV-infected haemophiliacs and transfusion recipients in the medical injury compensation schemes also meant that only the four infected haemophilia B patients sued a blood products manufacturer for compensation.

In the late 1980s, AIDS became a high-profile policy issue in Sweden, but even then HIV and blood attracted marginal attention from the public, the media and policy makers, as the blood supply basically had been secured at the point in time when AIDS reached the political agenda. In a sense, HIV and blood became the forgotten part of the larger AIDS story told in Sweden. This makes it difficult to characterize the Swedish management of the HIV and blood health crisis as a political success, because terminologically a success normally requires some form of active action. It would be more correct to conclude that the Swedish policies to manage the crisis programmatically never turned into a political failure.

6   ANALYSIS

In general, policy implementation in Sweden is the responsibility of agencies entrusted with a high degree of political autonomy. Swedish health policy is no exception; in fact, the autonomy of the national board of health and welfare is probably even greater than that of other agencies. An important explanation for the comparatively successful programmatic management of the HIV and blood crisis in Sweden was the existence of an internationally well-connected professional blood policy community which, in combination with the political autonomy of the blood policy subsystem, allowed actors in the national board of health and welfare, the blood banks, the haemophilia therapy centres and the blood products manufacturer Kabi to react swiftly and effectively to international information on HIV infection in the blood supply as it changed almost from month to month. Kabi launched heat treatment experiments at an early stage for professional reasons, but also because the company knew that the regulatory national board of health and welfare would mandate heat treatment in the not too distant future. As early as February 1985, the company managed, over a single weekend, to submit its entire production of clotting factor concentrate to heat treatment when evidence emerged that Swedish blood had become infected by HIV. Likewise, the board had the capacity to act promptly and mandate heat treatment immediately. It also had the freedom to speed up the introduction of screening in Swedish blood banks when it decided to circumvent its normal procedures by issuing a recommendation rather than an order. In mid-1985, various actors in the Swedish blood supply system had the capacity to follow the board's recommendation to introduce screening of donor blood at different stages, with the result that screening had been effectively introduced throughout the entire system by 1 October 1985.

However, there are also indications that the Swedish medical community reacted counterproductively in their attempts to respond to the entry of HIV into the blood supply, precisely because they were internationally well-connected, highly professional and autonomous. Thus, in the early 1980s, Sweden was one of the international front-runners in haemophilia therapy, for instance with respect to prophylactic use of factor concentrate in haemophilia therapy. Having just experienced the tremendous advances of modern haemophilia therapy, Swedish medical professionals engaged in haemophilia therapy were prevented from seeking policy options outside the most recent therapy paradigm. They did not, for instance, consider a switch to cryoprecipitate therapy, even though their colleagues in neighbouring Finland opted for this policy, nor did they consider a temporary halt to prophylactic factor treatment. Also the government commission's inquiry into the Preconativ 'scandal' revealed how health regulators in the national board of health and welfare presumed that their fellow professional colleagues in the pharmaceutical industry automatically followed the best manufacturing practice for pharmaceutical products, and how they were therefore too lax in their control of Kabi's factor production.

Swift action and comparatively successful programmatic policies may partially explain the almost total lack of political controversies in Sweden over the nature of the preventive policy measures and the timing of their implementation. However, it can only be part of the explanation. As is evident from the history of blood-borne HIV in other countries, programmatic success does not automatically generate political success. To explain why Sweden so conspicuously avoided a failure in the political evaluation of the government's policies to prevent blood-borne HIV, two types of explanations present themselves.

The first is policy style. Sweden's national committee on AIDS only marginally dealt with HIV in the blood supply, but by establishing this committee at a comparatively early stage and with an unusually high political profile, the government sent the signal that it took AIDS as a policy problem very seriously. Furthermore, in accordance with the Swedish tradition of corporatist consensus politics, all relevant interested parties, including the parliamentary parties, were represented on the committee. Although some of Sweden's extremely restrictive AIDS policies did stir opposition, in particular from the Swedish Federation of Gay and Lesbian Rights, the committee forged a strong policy consensus among all relevant interested parties in Swedish politics. Nobody with any political clout in Swedish society could offer opposing views. A situation in which the government clearly indicated that it took AIDS seriously, and in which a strong policy consensus prevailed throughout the political landscape, meant that there was little room for haemophiliacs to attach themselves to broader conflicts over AIDS, had they wanted to.

Second, policy history seems to be an important explanation. The fact that Sweden had already introduced patient and medicines injury insurance schemes in the 1970s and immediately applied them to infected transfusion recipients and haemophilia patients meant that Sweden avoided all the controversies over compensation that raged in other countries. Also the tradition of government support for the activities run by all sorts of idealistic or interest organizations was quickly applied to the Swedish Haemophilia Society, whose efforts to help, advise and support its infected members and their families are almost exclusively funded by the Swedish government.

NOTES

1. The Swedish Haemophilia Society and the Swedish Federation of Gay and Lesbian Rights gave me access to their archives. Ingvar Sjöholm, professor and director of the Department of Drugs, National Board of Health and Welfare from 1982 to 1996, and Claes F. Högman, professor and former director of Uppsala University Hospital's blood bank and scientific adviser on transfusion medicine to the National Board of Health and Welfare, both provided information on HIV and the Swedish blood supply and commented on the manuscript. Lars van Dassen, Uppsala University, and Jakob Jensen, University of Aarhus, assisted in gathering information. I am grateful to all of them.
2. In the following, the National Board of Health and Welfare will often be referred to as the board, and only occasionally will the two departments be referred to as independent units.
3. Information on the division of labour within the National Board of Health and Welfare was provided by Professor Ingvar Sjöholm in personal correspondence of 16 April and 27 May 2000.
4. Personal correspondence of 13 May 2000 with Professor Claes F. Högman.
5. Personal correspondence of 14 April 2000 with Professor Claes F. Högman. Professor Högman was a member of the committee advising the National Board of Health and Social Affairs on HIV screening.
6. In personal correspondence of 16 April 2000, Professor Ingvar Sjöholm pointed out that standards applying to Swedish pharmaceutical products would automatically also apply to imported products.
7. The following description of Kabi's production of factor IX concentrate is based on the SoU (1993) report.

30. HIV and the blood supply in the United Kingdom: professionalization and pragmatism

Richard Freeman

1 INTRODUCTION

There is a narrative of crisis in writing about British AIDS politics, but the securing of the blood supply against HIV figures in it only marginally. HIV infection by means of contaminated blood is only one of several themes in a complex and continuing story, and it is rarely, if ever, the dominant one. The technical and administrative issues raised by the risk to the blood supply were resolved before what is acknowledged to be the crisis period of AIDS policy making in Britain in the mid-1980s, and played relatively little part in that generalized sense of crisis; they belonged to a 'pre-political' period lasting from 1983 to 1985. Ministers were troubled less by blood than by sex or drugs; in context, the contamination of the blood supply represented at most a relative problem. By the time the issue of compensation for those infected with HIV in the course of medical treatment began to be raised after 1987, AIDS policy making was in the process of 'normalization'. It remained a political issue, certainly, but not a critical one. Nevertheless, for all the subsequent ramifications of AIDS politics, it was through blood and related issues that AIDS first came to constitute a public policy problem (Small, 1988; Berridge, 1997).[1]

2 THE POLICY CONTEXT: ACTORS AND INSTITUTIONS

In the 1980s, and perhaps even now, health and health care in the UK were governed by what was in comparative terms a highly centralized and integrated set of institutions. These were replicated and expressed in arrangements for the supply of blood and related products and for the treatment and care of those who needed them. The presence of HIV in the blood supply constituted an acute and specific problem in a context in which the quality, viability, organization and funding of public sector health services was being called into question, not

567

least by the government responsible for it. The period 1979–97 was one of sustained single-party Conservative government; in the 1980s, that government was effectively unchallenged at the polls and at its strongest and most confident after 1983, coincident with the high politics of AIDS.

Governing Health and Health Care

Reform of the National Health Service (NHS) in 1974 (the first major reform since its foundation in 1948) was an act of bureaucratic rationalization. In England and Wales, a hierarchical structure of regional, area and district health authorities was introduced,[2] responsible for hospital services, some community and public health functions, and health planning; general practitioner (GP) services were administered at local level by separate bodies. In 1979, a Conservative government was elected, espousing a set of radical neoliberal commitments meant to reverse Britain's widely acknowledged economic decline. This was attributed to the undermining of market relations by an overblown public sector and inefficient social investment. Key measures in respect of health care included the introduction of general management from 1984 and, at the end of the decade, systemic change introducing what was known as an internal market in the supply of health services.

Health reform illustrated some of the defining features of British government in this period. In a political system dominated by Parliament, Parliament itself was dominated by one party: government was insulated from some of the ordinary pressures of pluralist democracies, as posed for example by interest group activity and public opinion. In what were both a centralized political system and a centralized structure of health administration, government decision making was unusually autonomous. Major decisions could be made in an ad hoc way, with minimal consultation. The exercise and maintenance of ministerial authority, specifically prime ministerial authority, was paramount. Ideology was unusually important during the Thatcher administrations in particular, both in defining policy problems and in formulating solutions to them. Each of these elements was expressed in the nature and timing of policy responses to AIDS, and is discussed later in this chapter.

Governing Blood

The symbolic significance of blood is near-universal. In the UK – though this is not unique either – it carries a secondary level of particular institutional symbolism. It was through a comparative study of the UK and the United States that Titmuss's ideas about the value of what he described as the 'gift relationship' (Titmuss, 1970) were worked out.[3] The virtue of a system of voluntary, altruistic blood donation like Britain's was not only moral, but economic; it was not only right, but efficient and effective, too. More broadly, the gift relationship was the hallmark of the integrity of the NHS and the ideology on which it rested. At the end of the 1970s, however, institutional imagery did not correspond to practical reality. Though the UK was self-sufficient in whole blood, supplied by volunteer donation, the supply and distribution of blood products – which, with advances in medicine, were becoming increasingly widely used – was a commercial activity undertaken in international markets (Berridge, 1997).

The national blood transfusion service was established in 1946, born (like the NHS itself) of the emergency medical services arrangements made in wartime. Like health care, too, blood transfusion in England and Wales continued to be organized on a regional basis (ibid.). Until changes made in the 1990s, the service was organized and funded by regional health authorities (RHAs), which were essentially the middle tier of the administrative hierarchy connecting local districts to central government. Functional disparities between regions were an acknowledged problem, making for a differential pattern of scarcity and glut across the country (in Scotland, by contrast, the organization of health care in general and of the blood transfusion service in particular were always more centralized). Following a review of regional transfusion centres in England and Wales in 1987, which recommended some national coordination, a national director was appointed in 1988 with a brief to promote efficiency and cost-effectiveness in the service and a degree of coordination both among the different centres and between them and the recently regenerated blood products laboratory (Martlew, 1997). A new national blood authority assumed managerial responsibility for the regional centres from 1994, taking budgetary responsibility from the RHAs at the same time.

Factor VIII concentrate, the blood-clotting agent used in the treatment of haemophilia, was first licensed for use in the UK in 1973. Part of the NHS's requirement was produced by the blood products laboratory at Elstree, outside London, though the country remained a long way short of self-sufficiency: by the end of the decade over half of all concentrate used was imported (Berridge, 1997; Garfield, 1994). Not least because the commercial product was expensive, and because access to it was controlled by the local decisions of NHS providers, British use of Factor VIII remained comparatively very low (Berridge, 1997).

Criticism of the government for its slow progress in achieving self-sufficiency in blood products was strengthened by an outbreak of hepatitis at a special school in Hampshire in 1981, which was linked to the use of commercial supplies. At the same time, government itself put pressure on the Elstree laboratory to move away from its habitual service orientation, fixed on the needs of the NHS, to a new entrepreneurial approach to the potential market for its products (ibid.). New investment was announced in November 1981, as well as the creation of a central blood laboratories authority. The Bio Products

Laboratory, a new facility with the capacity for national self-sufficiency, opened at Elstree in 1986 (Martlew, 1997).

Haemophilia treatment in the UK is provided by 110 regional centres; specialist support for these is provided by 10 haemophilia reference centres. Service guidelines taking account of the impact of AIDS on the use of blood products and on patient counselling began to be drawn up from 1982–3 (Bennett and Ferlie, 1994).

A disease-specific patient organization, the Haemophilia Society, was formed in 1950 (Berridge, 1997). The national body is organized into local branches (Bennett and Ferlie, 1994); it has had a paid secretary since the 1970s, as well as established parliamentary connections; it has also received some financial support from the pharmaceutical industry. For a time, the society struggled with the idea of being linked with AIDS: its honourable, deserving voluntarism – reinforced by something of a 'family' identity derived from the genetic transmission of haemophilia – was at odds with the community activism and inherently sexualized identity of the gay organizations with which it came into contact. Where much of the society's work was concerned with the denial or overcoming of an unwanted identity, that of many gay activists focused on the construction and protection of it.[4]

3   HIV AND THE BLOOD SUPPLY IN THE UK: A POLICY NARRATIVE

The story of the securing of the UK blood supply against HIV infection can be told in two parts. The first (1983–5) was a technocratic process culminating in the heat treatment of all imported factor VIII from January 1985, and the screening of all donated blood from October. This crisis, if it was such, was a programmatic or technical one, and it was resolved before the more general issues of HIV and AIDS prevention became intensely politicized during 1986–7. The second part of the story (1987–92) concerns compensation for haemophiliacs who had received contaminated factor VIII before 1985. Claims for compensation were first rejected by government, then met by a £10 million ex gratia payment in November 1987. Continued lobbying of MPs, paralleled by litigation proceedings, brought a further payment of £19 million in November 1989. A final out-of court settlement was accepted in April 1991, and compensation for non-haemophiliac recipients of infected blood agreed in February 1992.[5]

Control, 1983–5

The first diagnosis of AIDS in the UK was made in 1981, and the first reported death occurred in 1982 (Berridge and Strong, 1992). In the United States, the first case reports of AIDS among haemophiliacs were made in July 1982, and the first documented link with blood transfusion in December of that year (Small, 1993). The possible transmission of AIDS through infected blood was reported in the UK medical press early in 1983; in October, details were published of the first known haemophiliac case of AIDS in the UK (Berridge, 1997; Bennett and Ferlie, 1994). As a public health issue, AIDS presented first as a local problem of infection control, especially in hospital settings (Bennett and Ferlie, 1994). It then became a question of preventing infection through contaminated blood;[6] only later were transmission through sexual and drug-taking behaviour to become problematized as public issues.

There were two ways of controlling blood-borne HIV infection: by screening the blood supply and by heat treating blood products. The blood supply, in turn, could be protected by asking individuals thought to be at risk of AIDS not to donate blood and then, later, when a viral cause was identified and a test available, by blood testing. The DHSS leaflet, *AIDS and How it Concerns Blood Donors*, was produced in September 1983,[7] reflecting a decision made by the regional directors of blood transfusion services earlier in the year. These guidelines were revised and made more explicit in December and again in January 1985, when practising homosexual and bisexual men were asked not to give blood. A subsequent revision in September, reflecting the availability and introduction of the HIV test, asked donors' consent for blood to be tested for HIV. The risk of HIV infection was detailed more explicitly again the following year, in September 1986.

The viral cause of AIDS was identified by a team led by Luc Montagnier at the Pasteur Institute in Paris in 1983 and in 1984 by Robert Gallo and a team from the National Institutes for Health in Bethesda. Prototype versions of tests were developed in mid-to-late 1984; the first to become widely available anywhere in the world was marketed in the USA by Abbott Diagnostics and approved by the Food and Drug Administration there in March 1985 (Bennett and Ferlie, 1994; Berridge, 1997). After trials, two tests were licensed for use in the UK, one manufactured in the UK (by Wellcome) and one in the Netherlands, by Organon. All blood donated in the UK was screened for HIV from October 1985.[8]

Evidence of the role of contaminated blood products in AIDS transmission in the UK began to emerge in a disconnected way in 1983 and 1984. In May 1983, a tabloid Sunday newspaper ran a story about two men, in hospital in London and Cardiff with suspected AIDS following routine treatment for haemophilia (Berridge, 1997). The paper drew a link with the use of commercially produced, imported factor VIII. The Medical Research Council's working party on AIDS met for the first time in October 1983: its discussion acknowledged the use of factor VIII and blood transfusion as risk factors for AIDS infection. The first parliamentary question on AIDS, in July, had asked about self-sufficiency in blood and related products; in November, health minister Kenneth Clarke argued that there was no conclusive evidence of AIDS infection through contaminated blood products. In the autumn of the following year, 1984, HIV antibodies were found in sera taken from haemophilia patients in various parts of the country who had been using factor VIII.

Heat treated Factor VIII first became available from a US commercial source at about the same time. At the beginning of January 1985, the Department of Health and Social Security (DHSS) recommended that only heat-treated factor VIII be used in the treatment of haemophilia. Owing to a delay in mass production, heat-treated NHS products only became widely available in the summer, though it had first been produced by the blood products laboratory at the end of the year before (Berridge and Strong 1992). In September, the *British Medical Journal* reported a study of HIV seropositivity among haemophiliacs which showed a high rate of infection among haemophilia A patients, who had received commercially produced factor VIII concentrate, and none among haemophilia B patients, who had received NHS-produced factor IX. A commercial batch of factor VIII produced in the USA was withdrawn early in 1986, after two UK haemophiliacs who had used it seroconverted. These and similar measures notwithstanding, the *BMJ* reported in July 1986 that NHS-produced blood products could not be guaranteed to be free from contamination.

Meanwhile, at the end of 1985, the government had begun to provide a certain amount of infrastructural investment and support for AIDS-related services. Plans to dismantle the Public Health Laboratory Service (PHLS) were reversed in September, soon after being revealed by some of the experts the government had asked for advice. New funding was made available for counselling at haemophilia reference centres as well as for the Haemophilia Society in October, and for the PHLS, for some of the RHAs in and around London which were providing most AIDS-related treatment and care and for the principal haemophilia reference centres in December.

Crisis, 1986–7

Blood and related issues contributed to the construction of a generalized health political crisis which took place in Britain in 1986–7, though they did not then constitute much of its substance or political processing. This happened in a number of ways. First, instances of infection among the partners of seropositive haemophiliacs made it clear that HIV could be transmitted heterosexually. Second, and unlike the concentration of HIV among gay men in London and other large cities, cases of haemophilia – and so of HIV infection among haemophiliacs – are much more evenly distributed geographically (Garfield, 1994). Third, the link with haemophilia changed the age profile of HIV infection, making it clear that children were also affected.[9] In September 1985, there was much public anxiety about a child with haemophilia who was also HTLV-III positive attending a local school in Hampshire (ibid.). Underlying these shifts of perception lay a normative understanding that there might be 'innocent' as well as 'guilty' victims of AIDS. In February 1985, for example, the general media took up medical press reports of a nurse who had become HIV-infected as a result of a needle-stick injury. In technical, programmatic terms, nevertheless, matters concerning the blood supply had been more or less dealt with by the end of that year.

The crisis period of AIDS politics in the United Kingdom[10] – which for present purposes represents something of a critical interlude – was marked by the establishment of a Department of Health AIDS unit (formed to deal with the volume of calls the department was getting) at the end of 1985; the formation of AIDS action groups at local level in late spring 1986, and of a cabinet committee on AIDS in October; the first formal parliamentary debate on AIDS took place in the House of Commons in November, and was followed by the allocation of £20 million to a public education campaign. The National AIDS Helpline was set up in December; an information leaflet titled *Don't Die of Ignorance* was delivered to all households in January 1987 and a coordinated broadcast media campaign marked 'AIDS week' in February. The Commons' Select Committee on the Social Services published its review of *Problems Associated with AIDS* in May, and the AIDS Control Act was passed at the same time, obliging health authorities to provide reports of AIDS case numbers and accounts of local prevention schemes and facilities for HIV testing and AIDS counselling, treatment and care.

What was at issue in 1986–7 was the extent of the epidemic, which meant its prevalence in the heterosexual population. Debates about prevention centred on the relative merit and efficacy of health education as opposed to (or sometimes complemented by) various forms of compulsion directed at 'risk groups'; in turn, this entailed defining the various responsibilities of government, individuals, the media, voluntary sector and community organizations, health services, schools and employers. Debates about treatment, counselling and care as much as education centred on the resources required to provide them.[11] Debates about the blood supply went little further than the technical requirements of infection control. Although, at the end of 1986, two-fifths of reported HIV infections in the UK were attributable to blood transfusion and/or the use of blood products, 'it looked as though haemophilia was all over as a political issue. The blood supply had been made secure, almost all haemophiliacs had been tested and the view from Westminster was clear: terrible tragedy, great sympathy, but these things happen' (Garfield, 1994, p. 207).

Compensation, 1987–91

The Haemophilia Society's campaign for compensation for those of its members who had become infected with HIV in the course of their treatment began in earnest in the spring of 1987 (Garfield, 1994). At local level, letters were written to MPs and threats were made to sue health authorities. The society's initial focus rested on a claim for a non-means-tested allowance for haemophiliacs with HIV. In November, some of its representatives met John Moore, secretary of state for social services, who simply referred them to existing entitlements. Without accepting liability for HIV infection in the course of NHS teatment, but under pressure from its own backbenchers, the government made a £10 million ex gratia payment to a fund administered by the society's Macfarlane Trust.

Over the following two years, a number of legal aid applications were granted to haemophiliacs seeking to press their claim for compensation in court; preliminary hearings took place in mid-1989. In November, a group of senior backbench Conservative MPs met the prime minister to press the haemophiliac case, and an additional £19 million for the Macfarlane Trust was announced the following day.

Almost a year later, in September 1990, the judge in charge of proceedings in the High Court wrote both to those bringing the action and to the government urging an out-of-court settlement. In November, pressure was brought to bear on the new health secretary, William Waldegrave, by an all-party group of MPs. In the end, money seemed more important than the clarification of liability: as the leader of this group declared, 'We are not asking the government to admit legal liability – in this case we want to quantify its moral responsibility' (ibid., p. 213). It was the new prime minister, John Major, who approved an out-of-court settlement in December, providing £42 million early in 1991.

Over the next 12 months, a campaign took place on the part of the estimated 170 non-haemophiliac NHS patients who had become infected with HIV by blood transfusion between 1981 and 1986. The Whole Blood Transfusion/AIDS Campaign was set up in Edinburgh. It used the media in a much more direct way than the Haemophilia Society, which had a much better developed infrastructure and established political connections. In April–May 1991, the *Observer* ran stories of individuals infected with HIV through blood transfusion. As with haemophiliac infection, compensation was first ruled out by the government early in 1992, but a settlement was awarded a month later, in February, on a basis similar to that for haemophiliacs (Small, 1993; Garfield, 1994).

This meant that, but for one or two footnotes, the policy issues to do with HIV and the blood supply were effectively resolved. In the spring of 1992, the tabloid press made much of accusations that a Birmingham man, a haemophiliac who, having used factor VIII concentrate had tested positive for HIV in 1985, had deliberately infected four women through sexual contact (Garfield, 1994). The issues raised now were about the effectiveness of health education and the possible criminalization of HIV transmission; they had little, if anything, to do with the blood supply. In 1994, a new strain of the immuno-deficiency virus, O HIV, was identified (*Guardian*, 4 April). The risk it represented was played down by medical commentators: cases were extremely rare and standard tests would be modified. In 1990, similarly, new tests had been introduced after a British blood donor was found to be infected with HIV-2.

4 ASSESSMENT

Programmatic

It is difficult to write about AIDS policy and politics anywhere as a story of success. In comparative terms, nevertheless, the British case may be read as one of relatively limited failure.

Given how much is now known about AIDS and the virus which causes it, it is important to remember that any assessment of the programmatic success of AIDS policy making must be marked by uncertainty. Even now, the extent of the epidemic can only be estimated, not measured. But when health care professionals and their haemophiliac patients began to be confronted by HIV and AIDS in the period 1983–5, they as much as public policy decision makers had other, now sometimes forgotten, but then much more salient and specific, uncertainties (Berridge, 1997; Garfield, 1994). To begin, professionals and patients alike were reluctant to acknowledge that the use of factor VIII concentrate – which had been the source of real gains in health and quality of life for many haemophiliacs – might be a problem (Berridge, 1997).[12] These afforded strong reasons to continue factor VIII treatment until the point at which negative indications became incontrovertible. Furthermore, it was known that the heat treatment of a blood product – a technique used in the late 1970s to inactivate non-A non-B hepatitis – reduced its clotting factor. This required a much larger supply of blood in order to produce the equivalent volume of product, which in turn made it much more expensive. Once the first heat-treated factor VIII was produced commercially in the USA, and until the NHS product became available in mid-1985, the choice for clinicians lay between using heat-treated product from what was taken to be an unsafe pool (the USA) or an untreated product from one which was thought to be relatively safe (the UK). Even when tests began to be developed in 1984–5, there was continuing uncertainty about their accuracy, as well as about the clinical significance of testing positive: was a positive result an indication of infection or of resistance and immunity to it? In any case, by March 1985, only three of 5000 haemophiliacs in the UK had been diagnosed with AIDS (Garfield, 1994; Department of Health/Welsh Office, 1988, table A2.3).[13]

For their part, health service officials were as concerned to protect the much-prized system of volunteer blood donation as to address the specific needs of haemophiliac and other users of blood and related products (Berridge, 1997). This amounted to balancing the competing needs of the supply and demand sides of the blood transfusion service. On the supply side, even before a viral cause was known, the problem was to explain to donors that certain behaviours should be understood as risk factors for AIDS and that some people should not give blood. Initially cautious information for donors, given in a pamphlet which was revised and rewritten several times between 1983 and 1986, needed to be widely intelligible without being confusing, specific without being stigmatizing. When, early in 1985, it became clear that donors were beginning to stay away from transfusion centres, the government invested money in a campaign to encourage blood donation (ibid.). On the demand side, that of haemophiliac users and their specialist physicians, the issue was much clearer: it was for access to blood and products derived from it which were demonstrably safe.

Political

Abbott Diagnostics' HIV test first became available in the USA in March 1985, though it was not licensed for use in the UK; it was not until the beginning of October that all blood donated in the UK was screened as a matter of course. Commentators acknowledge that 'questions were raised' about this six-month discrepancy (Street, 1988; Berridge, 1997), though they produced little political effect. The delayed introduction of testing in the UK was justified by officials on grounds of reliability, in that the Abbott test was known to give high numbers of false positive results, and trials were conducted on alternatives (Berridge, 1997; Garfield, 1994). Interviews with officials have brought a rejection of the claim made by some that the evaluation of different testing kits was instrumental, allowing a domestic company (Wellcome) to enter a valuable market; this denial appears to have been generally accepted. Later, it was argued that haemophiliacs with HIV and AIDS would have become infected before March 1985 rather than between March and October (Berridge, 1997).[14]

In other respects, the safety or otherwise of the blood supply generated nothing like a political – as distinct from programmatic – crisis. The blood transfusion service in England and Wales was known to be disorganized but, though it was reviewed and reformed in 1987–8 and again in 1993–4, no effective blame for avoidable HIV infection seems to have been laid at its door. The programmatic failure of which the government, then as now, has been most often accused – that of not providing health education specifically for gay men – has been of virtually no political consequence. AIDS brought no ministerial casualty, but instead some credit to the key actors of the early-to-mid-1980s, notably chief medical officer Donald Acheson and to some extent secretary of state for health Norman Fowler. In the later period, especially that of the quest for compensation for those infected with HIV by contaminated blood, there is an enduring impression of the government moving more or less in its own way, more or less in its own time.

5   ANALYSIS

'AIDS' is no single thing. Even in clinical terms, it is a syndrome not a specific pathology, though it appears to have a single viral cause. In any event, the structure of natural scientific explanation cannot be expected to map easily onto the policy world. Sociologically speaking, AIDS is not a single phenomenon but a nexus of issues, questions, tensions, stories and meanings; it can only be accounted for, if at all, by a complex set of models, metaphors and interpretations. Even when, as here, the crisis is defined in a limited way – as a problem of the control of the blood supply – there are different ways of understanding different parts of that story. In respect of the UK, the institutional framework of health politics and the patterns and habits of government mattered at different times in different ways. Each, in turn, may be understood as a different way of dealing with uncertainty.

Institutional Framework

The NHS functions as a mechanism of both centralization and decentralization, which are in turn closely connected to processes of politicization and depoliticization. HIV and AIDS first emerged in the UK (as in other countries) as local, even individual, problems; first responses to them were necessarily made at local level, often by those directly affected or by others with immediate reponsibilities for medical care and infection control. As in other countries, too, what 'crisis' meant, in practice, was the generalization or universalization of a problem which in turn seemed to require central government action. Elsewhere, that process took some time. In Britain, the hierarchical governing structure of the NHS, separate from local government and subordinate to the centre, ordinarily means that central government tends to be held responsible for what might otherwise remain local issues – hospital closure, for example. Government responsibilities for health and health care can be identified more quickly than elsewhere and, if somewhat less quickly, taken up. Unsurprisingly, what holds for health politics in general held also for AIDS politics in particular.

AIDS was governed in a centralized and exclusive way, led by an identifiable policy elite (Street and Weale, 1992). The department of health's expert advisory group on AIDS met for the first time at the end of January 1985 (and one of its first tasks was to manage the introduction of the screening of donated blood: Garfield, 1994). It had 22 members, mostly doctors (clinicians, scientists, epidemiologists) who had worked on AIDS since it had first appeared, and department of health officials. The group's function was to advise the chief medical officer; he, in turn, produced a confidential paper on AIDS for secretary of state Norman Fowler in June (ibid.). Later, government decision making was removed to a cabinet committee, which was first convened in October 1986 under Lord Whitelaw and included representatives of the department of health and social security, the department of the environment, the ministry of defence, the foreign office, the home office and the Scottish, Welsh and Northern Ireland offices.

Furthermore, in the course of dealing with AIDS, centralized institutional responsibilities were extended, rather than avoided or dismantled. There is evidence of this in the reform of the blood transfusion service, as of the health education council; in the reform of the public health service (following a review led by Acheson) which clearly located managerial responsibility for it in the NHS rather than in local government; in the administrative separation of health from social security which created a single-purpose, ministerial level department of health for the first time; in the more general and more or less autocratic reform process of 1988/9 to 1990/91.

In the last instance, the introduction of market elements into the organization of health care, it is arguable that central responsibilities were assumed in order to be dispersed. In respect of AIDS, the pre-existing order in the NHS served also as an institutional tool of depoliticization, as it does for broader and more persistent distributional issues. Almost paradoxically, public health care is a way of turning over to the private government of medical professional decision making and regional and district resource allocation the intractable problems of who gets what, when and how. This matters most when what is at stake is expensive treatment, but it holds just as well for operational measures such as infection control. The resource allocations and administrative circulars which began in 1985 were a way of flushing responsibilities back down the managerial hierarchy of the NHS.

Policy Style

For present purposes, it is helpful to disaggregate the concept of 'policy style' into the practical interactions of political interests, on one hand, and the ideology by which the political process and its outcomes are legitimated, on the other.

By 1990, the government came to see a High Court tussle with HIV-infected haemophiliacs as potentially damaging in political terms. In the event, the settlement followed fairly quickly on the replacement of prime minister

Margaret Thatcher by John Major. The issue offered a ready opportunity for the new leadership to be seen to be doing 'the right thing' (Street, 1993; Garfield, 1994). To this extent, party and electoral considerations belong more clearly to the later period of the politics of the blood supply described in this chapter, but their introduction now is not at odds with the reading of the effects of the institutional framework outlined above. For interests operate in and through institutions. The institutional framework of British politics, both in respect of health care and more generally, served to identify not only government responsibilities but also government interests. Almost inevitably, government responsibilities were disbursed in ways which maximized government interests. In general terms, and again in comparison and contrast with other countries, British AIDS policy has been described as 'political', meaning that decisions taken were expedient, 'politically feasible or desirable' (Moerkerk and Aggleton, 1990).

At the same time, the government response to claims for compensation on the part of haemophiliacs was shaped in part by the conservative moral framing of the issue. Backbench support was predicated on the perceived legitimacy of the haemophiliac case, on the 'innocence' of their infection in contrast to others; similiar lobbying on behalf of gay men or drug users was (and remains) almost unthinkable. Significant, too, is that the resolution of the compensation isues was a pragmatic rather than a principled one. Getting money out of the government – even though it was less than what was asked for – was more immediately useful than an acknowledgment of its legal and/or moral liability. AIDS policy and politics in the UK has been described as pragmatic and ad hoc, influentially so by the social services committee's report of 1987,[15] as well as 'groping, incremental' (Day and Klein, 1989, p. 351). In this, very specific sense, it may be described as in large part non-ideological.[16]

At least until 1986–7, and as soon as possible again thereafter, government AIDS policy tended to be presented as a professional, technical matter, engaging different parts of what was a standard repertoire of tools of medical science and public health; in this it was only typical of much of UK health policy making as a whole (Street, 1988; Fox *et al.*, 1989; Day and Klein, 1989). And for the most part, professionalization meant depoliticization. Importantly, too, this complex process was supported and protected by cross-party consensus. In Britain, the uncertainties surrounding AIDS, both technical and political, made for collaboration and consensus between parties, rather than polarization and conflict. Parliament as such was more or less indifferent to the topic, its debates on AIDS poorly attended. Much more significant was the formation of an all-party parliamentary group (APPGA) following the social services committee's report of May 1987 (Street, 1993).

6   CONCLUSION

In programmatic terms, HIV infection in the UK attributable to contaminated blood and related products was contained, but not prevented. In political terms, damage both to the government and to the National Health Service was kept to a minimum. Both outcomes are explained by a set of complementary factors. Throughout the period reviewed here, government and health service responses to HIV infection in the blood supply were marked by uncertainty and pragmatism. These were suffused with certain preconceived ideas of morality and legitimacy, which applied as much to the established system of blood donation as to blood-related HIV infection. Accounting more specifically for the first phase of the story focuses on the centralized, authoritative institutions of health administration in the UK, replicated in responding to AIDS. The second phase reflects a more pluralist politics, centred on Parliament, which is characteristic of other areas of public policy making in Britain: at each stage, decisions about compensation were expedient ones, often shaped by governmental and party political (electoral) interests. Its subdued aspect reflects at least in part the way in which claims for compensation were pressed by backbench lobbying rather than by inter-party and other conflict in the public domain.

NOTES

1. For introductory accounts of AIDS policy and politics in the UK, see Small (1988), Street (1988, 1993), Day and Klein (1989), Strong and Berridge (1990), Berridge and Strong (1992), Street and Weale (1992). Berridge (1996) is an authoritative full-length study. Revealingly, issues to do with the blood supply barely figure in Street's specific review of the period 1986–1990 (Street, 1993).
2. Area health authorities were abolished in 1982.
3. Two of the principal sources for this chapter (Berridge, 1997; Martlew, 1997) are published in a new edition of *The Gift Relationship* (Titmuss, 1997). For a treatment of the impact of HIV and AIDS on understandings of blood donation as gift giving, see Murray (1990).
4. Garfield (1994) draws a distinction between the Haemophilia Society and many of its members, according to which, over time, the society forged and maintained close links with other AIDS organizations but made little of them to its members.
5. The narrative account presented here is distilled from secondary sources. The chapter owes particular debts to Berridge (1997) in respect of the earlier period, 1983–5, and to Garfield (1994, pp. 60–73, 207–14) for the later period, 1987–91.
6. There have been six cases of HIV infection in the UK in tissue recipients; these are included in PHLS figures for infection attributable to the contamination of the blood supply and are treated as part of the more general narrative presented here.
7. Bennett and Ferlie (1994), Street (1988) and Berridge and Strong (1992) give August.
8. Berridge (1997) gives 1 October; Martlew (1997) and Street (1988) give 14 October.
9. The 1050 HIV infections reported in England and Wales up to mid-1988, and which were attributable to haemophilia treatment and other uses of blood and blood products, included 157 children aged 14 or under (Department of Health/Welsh Office, 1988, table A2.6).
10. For specific accounts, see Street (1988), Day and Klein (1989) and Schramm-Evans (1990).

11. 'The substance of AIDS policy is largely money – money for research, treatment, education' (Street, 1988, p. 491).
12. Berridge draws a parallel here with the difficulty faced by gay men, given recent advances in sexual liberation, in accepting the reality of a sexually transmitted and fatal infection.
13. At the same time, there had been 69 HIV infections attributed to the use of contaminated blood and related products by haemophiliacs and others, from a total of 225 infections (Department of Health/Welsh Office, 1988, table A2.6).
14. There is an argument that institutional integration makes for some functional efficiency, though its political significance is probably just as great (see 'Analysis', below). Routine HIV testing of donated blood, for example, 'was introduced into the United Kingdom on 14 October 1985; all transfusion centres started on the same day with a common procedure' (Martlew, 1997, p. 46). This may have pre-empted claims against the government which might have arisen in the event of disparities among users of different services in different parts of the country. What is fascinating, too, is the celebratory, quasi-religious tone in which the claim is made; there are echoes of the 'appointed day' on which the NHS was instituted in July 1948. The quotation is taken from a paper written by a consultant haemotologist and former director of a regional transfusion service.
15. Cited by Street (1993, p. 227).
16. Of course, the denial of ideology itself might be better described as a very British ideology. Berridge (1996, p. 236) describes the resolution of the compensation issue as a 'classic liberal compromise'.

Bibliography to part V

Aids Fonds (1996), *Aids-Bestrijding*, March.

Aken, W.G. van (1993), *The Collection and Use of Human Blood and Plasma in Europe*, report for the Council of Europe and the Commission of European Communities, Strasbourg: Council of Europe Press.

Albæk, E. (1999). 'The Never-Ending Story? The Political and Legal Controversies over HIV and the Blood Supply in Denmark,' in E.A. Feldman and R. Bayer (eds), *Blood Feuds: AIDS, Blood and the Politics of Medical Disaster*, New York and Oxford: Oxford University Press, pp. 161–89.

Alvarez, C. and 1. Hernandez (1994), 'AIDS in Spain: lessons learned from a public health disaster', *Journal of Epidemiological Community Heath*, 48 (4), 331–2.

Anand, P. (1997), 'A note on co-ordinating the AIDS crisis: issues for policy management and research', *International Journal of Health Planning and Management*, 12, 149–57.

Baayen, M. (1997), *Bloed in Beeld: Een onderzoek naar de vraag of altruïsme een garantie is voor een voldoende en veilige bloedinzameling in Nederland*, (afstudeerscriptie), Enschede: Universiteit Twente.

Bastin, Nicole, Geneviève Cresson and Jean Tyberghein (1993), *Approche Sociologique de la Demande en Réparation du Préjudice Thérapeutique: Le Cas du Sida*, Research report, CLERSE, IFRESI, Universities of Lille.

Bennett, C. and E. Ferlie (1994), *Managing Crisis and Change in Health Care: The Organizational Response to HIV/AIDS*, Buckingham: Open University Press.

Benz, Arthur (1994), *Kooperative Verwaltung: Funktionen, Voraussetzungen und Folgen*, Baden-Baden: Nomos.

Bernstein, M. (1955), *Regulating Business by Independent Commissions*, Princeton: Princeton University Press.

Berridge, V. (1996), *AIDS in the UK: The Making of Policy, 1981–1994*, Oxford: Oxford University Press.

Berridge, V. (1997), 'AIDS and the gift relationship in the UK', in R.M. Titmuss, *The Gift Relationship. From Human Blood to Social Policy*, original edition with new chapters, edited by A. Oakley and J. Ashton, London: LSE Books.

Berridge, V. and P. Strong (1992), 'AIDS policies in the United Kingdom: a preliminary analysis', in E. Fee and D. Fox, (eds) *AIDS: the Making of a Chronic Disease*, Berkeley: University of California Press.

Biberfeld, Gunnel and Peter Biberfeld (1984), 'Aktuellt om AIDS – virologi, immunologi, epidemiologi,' *Läkertidningen*, 81, (26–27), pp. 2595–8.

Biberfeld, Gunnel, Ulla Bredberg-Rådén, Blenda Böttiger, Peter Biberfeld, Linda Morfeldt-Månsson, Jukka Suni, Antti Vaheri, Carl Saxinger and Robert Gallo (1984), 'En enkel metod för bestämning af antikroppar mot AIDS-associerat virus (HTLV-III),' *Läkartidningen*, 81, (39), pp. 3482–3.

Boin, Arjen and Paul 't Hart (2000), 'Institutional crisis and reforms in policy sectors', in H. Wagenaar (ed.), *Government Institutions: Effects, Changes and Normative Foundations*, Dordrecht/Boston: Kluwer Academic Publishers, pp. 9–32.

Camara Mendizabal, G. de la (1980), 'Presente y futuro de la hemoterapia en España', *Sangre*, 25 (5C), 925–9.

Carricaburu, Danièle, (1999), 'Innovation thérapeutique et acceptabilité du risque iatrogène: l'introduction des produits antihémophiliques concentrés dans les années soixante-dix', *Sciences Sociales et Santé*, 17(4), 75–97.

Casteret, Anne-Marie (1992), *L'Affaire du Sang*, Paris: La Découverte.

CECS (1997), *Informe España 1997*, Madrid: Fundación Encuentro.

CESES (1998), *HIV/AIDS Surveillance in Europe*, 58, June.

Champagne, Patric and Dominique Marchetti (1994), 'L'information médicale sous contrainte à propos du "scandale du sang contaminé"', *Actes de la Recherche en Sciences Sociales*, 101–2, March, 40–62.

Day, P. and R. Klein (1989), 'Interpreting the unexpected: the case of AIDS policy making in Britain', *Journal of Public Policy*, 9 (3), 337–53.

Department of Health/Welsh Office (1988) *Short-term Prediction of HIV Infection and AIDS in England and Wales. Report of a Working Group*, London: HMSO.

Dir. (1993), *Utredning Angående Överföring av HIV-smitta Genom Läkemedlet Preconativ*, Beslut vid regeringssammanträde, 1993–03–04. Dir. 1993:29.

Douglas, Mary and Aaron Wildavsky (1982), *Risk and Culture: An Essay on the Selection of Technical and Environmental Dangers*, Berkeley: University of California Press.

Dressler, S. (1999), 'Blood "Scandal" and AIDS in Germany', in E.A. Feldman and R. Bayer (eds) *Blood Feuds: AIDS, Blood, and the Politics of Medical Disaster*, Oxford: Oxford University Press, pp. 192–212.

Eibl, J. (1995), 'Bonner Konstruktionen (Interview)', *Edition Zeitthema-Dossier*, July, 13–17.

Erfle, V., R. Hehimann, W. Mellert, G. Kruger, E. Seifried, H. Heimpel, H. Rasokat, E. Lechler, E. Holzer and P. Hellstern (1985), 'Prevelance of antibodies to HTLV111 in AIDS risk groups in West Germany', *Cancer Research*, 45, 4627–9.

Evers, A. and H. Nowotny (1987), *Über den Umgang mit Unsicherheit: Die Entdeckung der Gestaltbarkeit von Geselischaft*, Frankfurt am Main: Suhrkamp.

Feldman, Eric and Ronald Bayer (eds) (1999), *Blood Feuds: Aids, Blood and the Politics of Medical Disaster*, Oxford: Oxford University Press.

Festinger, L. (1957), *The Theory of Cognitive Dissonance*, New York: Harper & Row.

FIBS (1990), *Ersättning till de Blödarsjuka HIV-bärarna*, Mimeo: Förbundet Blödarsjuka i Sverige.

FIBS (1995), *Ersättning till de HIV-positiva Blödarsjuka*, Mimeo: Förbundet Blödarsjuka i Sverige.

Fox, D.M., P. Day and R. Klein (1989), 'The power of professionalism: AIDS in Britain, Sweden and the United States', *Daedalus*, 118 (1) 93–112.

Garfield, S. (1994) *The End of Innocence. Britain in the Time of AIDS*, London: Faber & Faber

Greilsamer, Laurent (1992), *Le Procès du Sang Contaminé*, Paris: Edition Le Monde-Documents.

Grimm, Dieter (1986), 'The Modern State: Continental Traditions', in Franz-Xavier Kaufmann, Giandomenico Majone and Vincent Ostrom (eds), *Guidance, Control and Evaluation in the Public Sector*, New York: De Gruyter, pp. 89–111.

Guitierrez, M., M.S. Romero, L. Larrad, L. Callén, P. LaSierra, H. Soler and F. Gomez (1986), 'Prevalencia de anticuerpos anti HTLV-111 en donantes de sangre y poblaciones de riesgo en Zaragoza', *Sangre*, 31 (2), 261.

Hagen, P.J. (1982), *Blood: Gift or Merchandise: Towards an International Blood Policy*, New York: Alan R. Liss.

Hagen, P.J. (1993), *Transfusion Sanguine en Europe: un Livre Blanc*, Strasbourg: Editions of the European Council.

't Hart, P. and R.A. Boin (2001), *From Crisis to Normalcy: The Long Shadow of Post-crisis Politics,* in U. Rosenthal, A. Boin and L.K. Comfort (eds) *Managing Crises: Threats, Dilemmas and Opportunities*, Springfield: Charles Thomas (forthcoming).

Henriksson, B. (1988), *Social Democracy and Societal Control: A Critical Analysis of Swedish AIDS Policy,* Stockholm: Glacio Bokförlag.

Henriksson, B. and H. Ytterberg (1992), 'Sweden: The Power of the Moral(istic) Left,' in D.L. Kirp and R. Bayer (eds), *AIDS in the Industrialized Democracies: Passions, Politics and Policies*, New Brunswick: Rutgers University Press, pp. 317–38.

Hermitte, Marie-Angbèle (1996), *Le Sang et le Droit. Essai sur la Transfusion Sanguine*, Paris: Seuil.

Hernandez, J.M., J. Piqueras, C. Martín Vega, E. Argelagues, M. Ribas Mundo, M. Canivell and M.T. Lopez (1986), 'Anti- LAV/HTLV-1 11 en donantes voluntarios de sangre y donantes retribuidos de plasma de Barcelona', *Sangre*, 31 (2), 260.

'HIV-Infektionen durch Blut und Blutprodukte' (1994), Schlußbericht des 3. Untersuchungsausschusses, *Deutscher Bundestag*, Drucksache 12/8691, Bonn, November.

Hoekema, A.J., N.F. van Manen, G.M.A. van der Heijden, I.C. van der Vlies and B. de Vroom (1998), *Integraal Bestuur: De Behoorlijkheid, Effectiviteit en Legitimiteit van Onderhandelend Bestuur*, Amsterdam: Amsterdam University Press.

Hulst, Jos and Cees Smit (1996), 'Belang patiënt gaat voor dat van bloeddonor' (Patient's interest outweighs blood donor's), *de Volkskrant*, 22 February.

IGASS/IGSJ, (1992), *Rapport d'enquête sur les collectes de sang en milieu pénitentiaire*, (Joint report of the Inspection Générale des Affaires Sociales and the Inspection Générale des Services Judiciaires), IGASS: SA 07 92 119; IGSJ RMT 13 92, Paris.

Immergut, Ellen M. (1992), *Health Politics: Interests and Institutions in Western Europe*, Cambridge: Cambridge University Press.

Interpellation 1992/93:92 av Birgit Henriksson (m) till socialministern om hiv/aidssmitta, fremställts den 1. marts.

Interpellation 1992/93: 97 av Berith Eriksson (v) till statsrådet Bo Könberg om KABI och blodprodukten Preconativ, fremställts den 9. marts.

Jobert, Bruno and Monika Steffen (1994), *Les Politiques de Santé en France et en Allemagne* (Espace Social Européen, 4), Paris: Observatoire Européen de la Protection Sociale.

Jordana, J. and E. Méndez (1996), 'Les politiques de prevenció de la sida a Espanya: el seu desenvolupament institucional', *Revista Catalana de Sociologia*, 2 (1), pp. 27–49.

Kenis, Patrick and Bert de Vroom (1996), 'HIV/Aids – Defizite und neue Formen der Wohlfahrstätigkeit', in Adalbert Evers and Thomas Olk (eds), *Wohlfahrtspluralismus*, Opladen: Westdeutscher Verlag, pp. 323–47.

Kenis, Patrick and Bernd Marin (eds) (1997), *Managing AIDS –Organizational Responses in Six European Countries*, Aldershot: Ashgate.

Kester, Ineke, Bert de Vroom and Armand van Wolferen (1997), 'The Netherlands: The Strong Civil Society Response', in Patrick Kenis and Bernd Marin (eds), *Managing Aids: Organizational Responses in Six European Countries*, Aldershot: Ashgate, pp. 65–115.

Kiehl, W. and D. Altmann (1991), 'AIDS- und HIV-Infecktionen im Gebiet der ehemaligen DDR', in H. Jäger (ed.), *AIDS und HIV-Infektionen*, Landsberg: Ecomed, pp. 1–18.

Klein, R. (1989), *The Politics of the National Health Service*, 2nd edn, Harlow: Longman.

Koch, E.R. and I. Meichsner (1993), *Böses Blut – Die Geschichte eines Medizim-Skandals*, Hamburg: Hoffmann und Campe.

Leveton, Lauren B., Harold C. Sox, Jr., and Michael A. Stoto (eds) (1995), *HIV and the Blood Supply: An Analysis of Crisis Decisionmaking*, Washington, D.C.: National Academy Press.

Magallon, M., F. Ortega and J. Martin Villar (1987), 'Status VIH hernofílicos: Experiencia de tres años con preparados tratados por calor', *Sangre*, 32 (3), 394–5.

March, J.G. and H.A. Simon (1958), *Organizations*, New York: Wiley.

Marcus, U. (1993), 'Die HIV-Epidemie bei deutschen Blutern: eine Chronologie', *AIDS Nachrichten aus Forschung und Wissenschaft*, 4, 1–10.

Marmor, T.R., P.A. Dillon and S. Scher (1999), 'The Comparative Politics of Contaminated Blood: From Hesitancy to Scandal,' in E.A. Feldman and R. Bayer (eds), *Blood Feuds: AIDS, Blood and the Politics of Medical Disaster*, Oxford: Oxford University Press, pp. 349—65.

Martín Villar, J. (1980), 'Esfuerzos realizados en el pasado', *Sangre*, 25 (5C), 930–46.

Martlew, V (1997) 'Transfusion medicine towards the millennium', in R.M. Titmuss, *The Gift Relationship. From Human Blood to Social Policy*, original edition with new chapters, edited by A. Oakley and J. Ashton, London: LSE Books.

Mauser-Bunschoten, E.P. (1995), *Complications of Hemophilia Care*, Houten: Ibero.

Mayntz, R. (1997), *Soziale Dynamik und politische Steuerung*, Frankfurt am Main: Campus Verlag.

Ministerio de Sanidad (1984), *Boletín de Indicadores Sanitarios*, Madrid, March.

Moerkerk, H. and P. Aggleton (1990), 'AIDS prevention strategies in Europe: a comparison and critical analysis', in P. Aggleton, P. Davies and G. Hart (eds) *AIDS: Individual, Cultural and Policy Dimensions*, London: Falmer

Morelle, Aquilino (1996), *La Défaite de la Santé Publique*, Paris: Flammarion.

Muller, Pierre (1999), *Les Politiques Publiques*, 3rd edn, Paris: Presses Universitaires de France.

Murray, T.H. (1990), 'The poisoned gift: AIDS and blood', *Milbank Quarterly*, 68, suppl. 2, 205–25.

Nationale Ombudsman (1995), *Openbaar Rapport 95/271*, The Hague: De Nationale Ombudsman.

Nelkin, Dorothy (1999), 'Cultural Perspectives on Blood', in E. Feldman and R. Bayer (eds), *Blood Feuds: Aids, Blood and the Politics of Medical Disaster*, Oxford: Oxford University Press, pp. 273–92.

Nota inzake het Aidsbeleid, Kammerstukken TK, 1986–1987, 19218, no. 2.

Olthuis, Henk and Stef Stienstra (1992), 'Er komt geen Nederlands "bloed-schandaal"' (There won't be a Dutch 'blood scandal'), *Intermediair*, 20 November, p. 27.

Pouvoir (1994), 'La mise en examen des cabinet ministériels', 68, Paris: Seuil.

Rico, Ana (1997), 'Regional decentralization and health care reform in Spain (1976–1996)', *South European Society and Politics*, 1 (3), 115–34.

Robert Koch-Institut, Fachgruppe Infektionsepidemiologie/AIDS-Zentrum (ed.) (1998), *AIDS/HIV Quartalsberichte*, Berlin: Robert-Koch-Institut (Eigenverlag).

Roberts, S.S. (1996), 'Blood Safety in the Age of AIDS,' *The FASEB Journal*, 10 (4), pp. 391–402.

Roux, Jacques (1995), *Sang Contaminé. Priorités de l'État et Décisions Politiques*, Montpellier: Cditions Espace.

Ruffié, Jacques (1993), *Rapport sur l'Enseignement, la Formation et le Recrutement en Transfusion Sanguine*, Report to the Ministers of Health and of Education, Ministère de la Education Nationale et de la Culture, and Ministère de la Santé et de l'Action Humanitaire, Paris.

Scharpf, F. (1997), *Games Real Actors Play: Actor-Centered Institutionalism in Policy Research*, Boulder, CO: Westview Press.

Schmidt, Vivien A. (2000a), 'Democracy and Discourse in an Integrating Europe and a Globalizing World', *European Law Journal*, 5 (2).

Schmidt, Vivien A. (2000b), 'The Role of Values and Discourse in Welfare State Reform: The Politics of Successful Adjustment', in F.W. Scharpf and V.A. Schmidt, *Welfare and Work in the Open Economy, Vol. 1 From Vulnerability to Competitiveness*, Oxford: Oxford University Press.

Schramm, W. and J. Schulte-Hillen (1994), 'Todesursachen und AIDS-Erkrankungen Hämophiler in der Bundesrepublik Deutschland', in I. Scharrer and W. Schramm (eds), *25. Hämophilie-Symposium Hamburg*, Berlin/Heidelberg/New York: Springer, pp. 7–17.

Schramm-Evans, Z. (1990), 'Responses to AIDS: 1986–1987, in P. Aggleton, P. Davies and G. Hart (eds), *AIDS: Individual, Cultural and Policy Dimensions*, London: Falmer Press.

Sénat (1992), *Rapport de la Commission d'Enquête sur le Système Transfusionnel Français en vue de son Éventuelle Réforme*, C. Huriet and J. Sourdille (19 December 1991), Document no. 406, Paris.

Setbon, Michel (1993), *Pouvoirs contre Sida. De la Transfusion Sanguine au Dépistage: Décisions et Pratiques en France, Grande-Bretagne et Suède*, Paris: Seuil.

Shield, Sherry (1999), 'The Circulation of the Blood: AIDS, Blood, and the Economics of Information,' in E.A. Feldman and R. Bayer, eds, *Blood Feuds:*

AIDS, Blood and the Politics of Medical Disaster, New York and Oxford: Oxford University Press, pp. 323–47

Simon, Herbert A. (1945), *Administrative Behavior*, New York: Free Press.

Simon, H.A. (1969), *The Sciences of the Artificial*, Cambridge, MA.: MIT Press.

Simon, H.A. (1973), 'The Structure of Ill-Structured Problems', *Artificial Intelligence*, 4, 181–201.

Small, N. (1988) 'Aids and social policy', *Critical Social Policy*, 21 (1), 9–29.

Small, N. (1993), *AIDS: The Challenge*, Aldershot: Avebury.

Soulier, Jean-Pierre (1992), *Transfusion Sanguine et Sida. Le Droit à la Vérité*, Paris: Frison-Roche.

SOSFS (1984), 'Socialstyrelsens föreskrifter om blodgivning, blodtransfusion m.m.' *Socialstyrelsens Författningssamling*, 1984, nr. 27. SOSFS 1984:27.

SOSF (1985), 'Socialstyrelsens föreskrifter och almänna råd angående AIDS.' *Socialstyrelsens Författningssamling*, 1985, nr. 4. SOSF 1985:4.

SOSFS (1989), 'Socialstyrelsens föreskrifter om blodgivning, blodtransfusion m.m.' *Socialstyrelsens Författningssamling*, 1989, nr. 38. SOSFS 1989:38.

SoU (1991), Statens offentliga utredninger. *HIV-smittade – Ersättning för Ideell Skada*. Delbetänkande av kommitté om ideell skade. Stockholm: Justitiedepartementet. SOU 1991:34.

SoU (1993), Statens offentliga utredninger. *Överföring av HIV-smitta Genom Lekemedlet Preconativ*. Stockholm: Socialdepartementet. SoU 1993:61.

Steffen, Monika (1996), *The Fight against AIDS. An international public policy comparison between four European countries (France. Great Britain. Germany. Italy)*, Grenoble: Presses Universitaires de Grenoble.

Steffen, Monika (1999), 'The Nation's Blood. Medicine, Justice and the State in France', in E. Feldman R. and Bayer, (eds), *Blood Feuds. Aids. Blood and the Politics of Medical Disaster*, New York: Oxford University Press, pp. 95–126.

Steffen, Monika (2000), 'Les modèles nationaux d'adaptation aux défis d'une épidémie. France, Grande-Bretagne, Allemagne, Italie', *Revue Française de Sociologie*, 1, 5–36.

STG (1992), *AIDS in Nederland tot 2000, Epidemiologische. sociaalculturele en economische scenario-analyse*, Houten/Zaventem: Bohn Stafleu Van Loghum.

Stinchcombe, A.L. (1965), 'Social Structure and organizations', in J.G. March (ed.), *Handbook of organizations*, Chigaco: Rand McNally.

Street, J. (1988) 'British government policy on AIDS: learning not to die of ignorance', *Parliamentary Affairs*, 41 (4), 490–507.

Street, J. (1993) 'A fall in interest? British AIDS policy, 1986–1990', in V. Berridge and P. Strong (eds), *AIDS and Contemporary History*, Cambridge: Cambridge University Press.

Street, J. and A. Weale (1992), 'Britain: policy-making in a hermetically sealed system', in D. Kirp and R. Bayer (eds), *AIDS in the Industrialized Democracies: Passions, Politics and Policies*, New Brunswick: Rutgers University Press, pp. 185–220.

Strong, P. and V. Berridge (1990) 'No one knew anything: some issues in British AIDS policy', in P. Aggleton, P. Davies and G. Hart (eds), *AIDS: Individual, Cultural and Policy Dimensions*, London: Falmer.

Svar på interpellattionerna 1992/93: 92 och 97 om Kabi och blodprodukten Preconativ av statsrådet Bo Könberg (fp), 19 April.

Svensk Förening för Transfusionsmedicin (1988), *Kartlägning av Sveriges Blodförsörjning*, Sammenställd av Blodcentralen, Regionssjukhuset i Örebro.

Tillemans, Geert (1998) *AIDS, beleid en organisaties*, PhD thesis, Katholieke Universiteit Nijmegen.

Titmuss, R.M. (1970) *The Gift Relationship. From Human Blood to Social Policy*, London: George Allen & Unwin.

Von Stein, L. (1962, first edition 1882), *Die Verwaltungslehre: Teil 3*, Stuttgart.

Vroom, Bert de (1993), 'Aids: nationale patronen van organisationele respons' (Aids: national patterns in organizational response), in Jacques van Doom, Pauline Meurs and Ton Mijs (eds), *Het Organisatorisch Labyrint*, Utrecht: Aula, pp. 183–214.

Weise, H.J. and J. L 'Age-Stehr (1982), 'Schnellinformation: Unbekannte Krankheitserreger als Ursache von tödlich verlaufended erworbenen Immundefekten', *Bundesgesundheitsblatt*, 25, 408.

Wijngaarden, Jan K. van (1992), 'The Netherlands: A Consensual Society', in David L. Kirp and Ronald Bayer (eds), *Aids in the Industrialized Democracies: Passions, Politics and Policies*, New Brunswick: Rutgers University Press, pp. 252–77.

Zald, Mayer N. (1978), 'On the social control of industries', *Social Forces*, 79–102.

Zuijlen, Bo van (1996), 'Bloed homo's is niet per se onveilig' (Blood of gays is not necessarily unsafe), *de Volkskrant*, 20 February.

Zunzunegui, M.V.(1994), 'Sida y salud pública en España', *Gaceta Sanitaria*, 8 (40), 1–2.

PART VI

Comparisons, conclusions, reflections

31. Patterns of governance: sectoral and national comparisons

Mark Bovens, Paul 't Hart,
B. Guy Peters, Erik Albæk,
Andreas Busch, Geoffrey Dudley,
Michael Moran and Jeremy Richardson

1 TOWARDS COMPARISON

In these two concluding chapters we attempt to pull the results of the individual chapters and sections together. The comparative issues we address are those originally outlined in Chapter 2. The first main task we have set ourselves is to *evaluate* how well six European states managed to handle a number of key governance challenges that states and other public institutions regularly face: managing decline, reform, innovation and crisis in sectors of society for which the state has taken at least part of the responsibility. In order to do so, we shall examine the results of the 24 empirical studies of state performance across four different policy sectors. Each policy sector was selected to represent a particular governance task, yet at the same time the sectors also constitute different institutional configurations of state, private and international actors, rules and practices as well as environmental contingencies that are likely to influence their 'governability' by national policy makers. Thus we are always comparing countries and policy areas at the same time, although at any one time the emphasis may be on one or the other.

In making this overall assessment of governance successes and failures, we shall differentiate between the programmatic and the political dimensions of state performance. For each sector, we have specified in Chapter 2 the evaluation criteria used, taking into account the intricate nature of each governance challenge. In this chapter we shall systematically check to what extent programmatic and political judgments about performance coincide or diverge. Cases where discrepancies arise between programmatic and political performance are particularly intriguing. As we shall see, this happens more in some sectors than in others, raising questions about the nature of sectoral governance, or perhaps the nature of the particular governance task they represent. We therefore also address the issue of policy style along the two axes presented in Chapter 2.

Our second objective in these final chapters is to *explain* the patterns of governance success and failure that emerge from the comparative assessment exercise. More specifically, we look at two questions that represent potentially competing hypotheses (Freeman, 1985). The first is: to what extent can idiosyncratic national policy styles be identified consistently across the sectoral cases studied, suggesting that certain states conduct policy in certain typical ways, irrespective of the governance task and sectoral context they face? The second is: to what extent do the four policy sectors studied here bear cross-national institutional resemblances that can account for the success–failure patterns we have found, suggesting that there are certain ways to govern certain sectors irrespective of the country in which the governing takes place? The reality is, as always, more diffuse than these two ideal–typical explanations suggest. In the final chapter we shall try to see just how clear the overall picture is as it emerges from these studies.

In this chapter we summarize the results of each of the sectors separately, both in terms of programmatic and political performance and of policy style. In the next chapter we integrate the sectoral findings into a comparative assessment of governance performance across sectors and nations. There we also reflect upon the yield of this research project in view of the original questions we asked at its outset.

2   MANAGING DECLINE: FROM RESCUING TO RESTRUCTURING NATIONAL STEEL INDUSTRIES

Beyond Decline Management

We have chosen the steel sector as our example of the typical challenges that governments face when a major industry or sector of society experiences decline: a steady and thus relatively foreseeable but robust and therefore perhaps less controllable downturn. This downturn has different dimensions: at the *industrial* level, there is decreasing competitiveness resulting in diminishing profits or even losses, which trigger 'downsizing' and raise the prospect of major firm collapses; at the *societal* level, the economic problems of major industries or strategic firms may generate considerable collective stress in the communities that depend on their survival – industrial workers as a social group, but often also entire towns and regions where these industries are sometimes concentrated; at the *political* level, these circumstances bring about potentially debilitating tensions as the dominant issues in the policy arena switch from distributive to redistributive, putting pressure on the triangle of government, industry and labour that constitutes the heart of the political arena in traditional sectors such as steel. In our comparative study design, we were interested in how the various national governments coped with decline management. We wanted to study how particular national and sectoral institutional configurations and governance styles affected the nature and the programmatic and political effectiveness of government policies vis-à-vis the steel policy community in this context of decline.

The case studies demonstrated the limitations of this design, in various ways. First, the economic and sociopolitical developments in steel were not monotonously set in the key of decline. The general trend towards increasing competition, declining profitability and major cyclical demand fluctuations was at times punctuated by more manifest symptoms of crisis. These pertained to, among others, insolvencies or other symptoms of imminent collapse of major firms, the publication of corporate plans for rationalization and 'downsizing', or government plans for mergers or the withdrawal of state support. In these cases, the ongoing policy process was put under pressure by shortened time horizons, public protests, industrial action, increased media attention and political controversy. So in practice the management of industrial decline was sometimes intertwined with the management of industrial crisis, with all its paraphernalia of last-minute rescue plans, street disturbances, marathon negotiation sessions and political blame games. On the other hand, and ultimately more important, the management of decline was in most countries eventually redefined as the governance of restructuring and innovation. From trying to salvage endangered plants and established firms, public policy makers in most countries found themselves drawn into collaborating with industry to 'reinvent' steel production and steel governance. This involved schemes to adopt new production methods, penetrate new markets, seek out international alliances and attract investors – worlds apart from the messy politics of 'downsizing'. Thirdly, the original study design put the emphasis squarely on national governments. As Dudley and Richardson point out in the introduction to the steel section, it is impossible to understand steel policy making without taking into account the prominent role of transnational considerations and governance mechanisms, which shaped and constrained national policy options. Steel policy lies at the roots of the institutional history of the EU, and national policy makers in the steel sector had been practising the art of multi-level governance long before political scientists discovered it. In the case studies, the shadow of European governance, and the mixed motives for national policy makers that it entailed, come out clearly, particularly in the British and Spanish cases. Hence the governance challenge in restructuring steel was to create policies that were viable in the domestic politicoeconomic context and at the same time were in tune with, or at least sustainable in, the European steel policy arena.

Although the nature of the governance task in steel policy proved to be more complex, and perhaps less distinctive, than originally envisaged, the case studies bear out one other crucial design assumption, namely that governance does indeed matter for outcomes in the public sector. The various national steel industries and the policy communities associated with them experienced rather different fates, both in programmatic and political terms, and there are sufficient reasons to presume that this had to do with the ways in which they were being governed. As we have noted already, the challenges facing these six countries in this policy area were quite similar, but the outcomes were rather different.

Assessment: Differential Performance

Before we return to this conclusion, let us first document the policy outcomes for the six countries (see Table 31.1). The results suggest that, on the programmatic level, three modalities can be found: countries where restructuring went ahead relatively soon, swift and successful and with minimal political contestation (Sweden, Netherlands, Germany); countries where economic restructuring proceeded effectively but harboured some political costs (Britain, France); and countries where economic restructuring was slower and less comprehensive, and took place against a backdrop of political game playing (Spain). Overall, only one country (Spain) scored negatively on the programmatic indicators. This may be an astounding result, given the size of workforce reductions that took place in the 1970s and 1980s and the devastating effects these have had on the economic and social fabric of the regions involved. It may be more accurate to label steel restructuring as a matter of non-failure than to speak of straightforward success. Especially in truly big steel-producing countries such as France and England, and to some extent Germany, restructuring did involve massive employment losses and major public investments and subsidies. Since even the most successful countries experienced significant reductions in the workforce, this fact alone – however painful and politically volatile it was at the time – cannot be a sufficient reason for a more negative programmatic assessment. The industry experienced technological innovations and international competition that made it essential to achieve major productivity gains. Faced with the choice between long-term survival and short-term maintenance of pre-decline employment levels, policy makers sooner or later preferred the former, even if political and institutional constraints in some countries may have prevented them from saying so timely and publicly.

On the political side, it is perhaps most remarkable that, given the aforementioned workforce reductions and the often very marked regional concentration of the burdens of redundancies, there has not really been a major, debilitating political crisis on the steel issue in any of the countries. Things were tense on the shop floor and in the affected regions and communities in France and Britain at times, particularly during the early 1980s, but government policies never suffered from enduring national public or parliamentary legitimacy shortfalls. In Germany and Sweden, broad government–industry concertation combined with proactive social and re-employment initiatives effectively mitigated politicization. In the Netherlands, the structural simplicity of the steel sector (one firm only) facilitated pragmatic deal making, in contrast to France, where internecine warfare between the two main steel conglomerates produced an adversarial climate, and relations between communist and socialist partners in Mitterrand's early government were tense. In Spain, the politics of steel were most complex and sensitive: steel restructuring took place in 'nested games' (Tsebelis, 1990) of tripartite (government–industry–unions), intergovernmental (central versus regional governments) and transnational (the 'shadow of the future' of imminent EU accession) bargaining. This was an institutional environment rich in potential 'decision traps' (Scharpf, 1988, 1997), yet policy makers eventually succeeded in overcoming political sensitivities and rent-seeking behaviour, and gradually set the industry on the wider European path of increased productivity and international competitiveness, albeit much later and less vigorously than in other countries.

In the case of steel governance, reaching overall assessments is less straightforward than Table 31.1 might suggest. On the programmatic side, there is the question of how to combine microeconomic rationality (which dictates that policy is successful when the industry is either made viable again or terminated swiftly when this is clearly impossible) with broader social considerations (which workforce reductions are really 'needed' to revitalize an industry). There is also the matter of calculating and valuing the amount of money involved in direct or indirect state support. Figures on this issue are almost by definition controversial, since they are used strategically by steel policy actors at the transnational level when defending or attacking past and planned policy initiatives by national governments. On the political side there is a classic value trade-off problem: do we consider steel policy to be politically successful if major 'downsizing' has taken place without the government getting into trouble for letting that happen (as in Britain)? Or should we rather emphasize the social dimension of restructuring and tie political success to the capacity of governments to mitigate effectively the 'pain' of restructuring, for example by insisting on a slow pace and attendant social programmes (as in the early stages of the Spanish case) or by proactive re-employment and 'reskilling' strategies (as in Sweden and Germany)? We have tried to steer a middle course here and include both logics of evaluation side by side without prioritizing one over the other.

With this caveat in mind, we can now compare the political and programmatic outcomes for each country, and identify any asymmetries. This is done in

Table 31.1 *Managing decline and restructuring in the steel industry: outcome assessment*

	France	Germany	Netherlands	Spain	Sweden	UK
Programmatic dimension	+/–	+	+	–	+	+
Public money spent on restructuring and flanking measures	Major state investments and subsidies	Major subsidization between 1975 and 1985, thereafter sharp decline	Relatively moderate subsidization; more substantial state ownership	Major state subsidies and expensive 'crisis packages' over >20-year period	Major state spending on restructuring plans	Significant state support initially, but relatively quick move to self-sufficiency
Viability of the industry after restructuring	Slow but steady efficiency gains and reduction of indebtedness	Successful diversification strategies and stable profitability	Successful internationalization and diversification	Slow and low efficiency gains; loss of domestic market share to foreigners	Successful restoration of competitive industry	BS (now merged with Dutch Hoogovens) as strong corporation
Employment losses	High workforce reductions during crisis periods (>50%)	Significant workforce reductions in 1970s, later stabilization and successful reskilling	Comparatively low workforce reductions during crisis periods (<25%)	Eventually high workforce reductions	Successful proactive re-employment strategies	Major workforce reductions in 1960s–80s but not since privatization in 1988

Political dimension	+/−	+	+	+/−	+	+/−
Absence of political crisis	Major tensions and policization during crises	Consensualist corporatism	Public–private partnership; union cooperation	High politics (inter-governmental and EU context)	No partisan politics re state role in decline management	Consensual policy making; later state–BS rift
Fair distribution of 'pain'	Strong regional variations	Regional variations in re-employment strategies	Unilocation; aborted regionalized production	Affected regions hard hit; decreasing social policies	Initially very, later less active state safety net	Affected regions hard hit
Current political status of steel industry	Steel remains 'national champion'	Steel no longer a national but a regional political issue	Depoliticized: steel as ordinary economic sector	Politics of attrition: steel community split open	Steel no longer a 'strategic industry'	Steel no longer a 'strategic industry'

Comparisons, conclusions, reflections

Figure 31.1, which shows Spain to be the single most problematic overall case, and Sweden, Germany and the Netherlands to have been relatively successful in meeting the combined challenges of decline and restructuring in the steel industry. A clear asymmetry between programmatic and political performance can be seen in Spain. Programmatic failure manifested itself in a tardy and incomplete restructuring of what has long been an inefficient and uncompetitive steel industry, yet it did not produce political fatalities. This was probably due to the gradualist, and initially consensual, approach to restructuring. Painful decisions were not so much made as they were forced upon policy makers during crisis episodes. Moreover, throughout the entire process delicate inter-governmental bargaining took place between Madrid and the state capitals of the country's steel regions, mitigating the inflammatory potential of this issue in the Spanish federalist system. In Britain, too, there is some degree of discrepancy between the programmatic and the political outcomes, but of an opposite nature. There was programmatic success in reviving and privatizing British Steel, yet this success was marred by the subsequent souring of the political atmosphere in the once so consensual steel policy community. This discrepancy is explained by Dudley and Richardson as the gradual growing

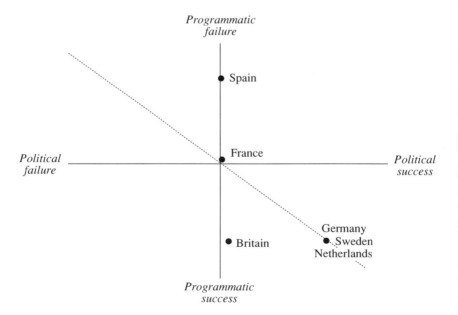

Figure 31.1   Managing decline and restructuring in the steel sector: an integrated assessment

apart of the state and BS management in terms of the policy frames they used in looking at steel policy issues: BS managers adopted a squarely market-oriented, maximum competition framework, whereas the government could not and would not completely ignore the broader industrial and trade policy context in which steel issues were being negotiated at the EU level, and sometimes took positions that were anathema to BS interests and desires. These tensions amounted eventually to what Dudley and Richardson describe as a 'breakdown' in governance, that is the political failure in the wake of privatization to adapt the institutional structure of steel politics to the changed ownership and market conditions.

Policy Learning and Evolving Policy Styles

Of all the four sectors studied in this volume, steel policy is the one that evolved most gradually, over two decades or more. On the other end of the continuum sits HIV/AIDS policy, where the key governance challenge was clearly concentrated in time and space, and quick responses were essential, even if this became clear in part only in retrospect (see further). The management of innovation in the banking sector in most countries was speeded up by technological developments, the rapid emergence of new financial services, a global trend towards deregulation, and finally the occurrence of 'accidents' (that is, individual banks threatening to go under) that required immediate responses (see below). The management of reform in health care is, like steel policy, a continuing affair, but in this study we have chosen to focus on individual reform attempts regarding the position of medical professionals, which tended to be processed in less than a decade.

   The drawn-out nature of decline management and restructuring in steel policy has an important consequence for the analysis of policy styles: it allowed plenty of opportunity for learning from experience, and produced changes of style in one country over time (see Olsen and Peters, 1996; Rose, 1993; Hall, 1993; Sabatier and Jenkins-Smith, 1993). In three of the six cases, France, Spain and the UK, there is clear evidence of stylistic changes (see Figure 31.2). In France, the early problems of the steel industry were met by classic Keynesian forms of government intervention: major financial support, production-oriented reorganization plans and nationalizations. When industrial decline persisted, new plans and firm reconfigurations were experimented with, with varying degrees of success. Sometimes, new policy initiatives were launched more as a matter of political expedience (electoral cycles were important here) than as deliberate learning. Over time, the French state moved from a classic anticipatory and imposed style towards a more reactive and more consensual mode. In Spain, the policy paradigm of steel policy makers and some of the corporate managers slowly but surely moved from Keynesian interventionism to market liberalism,

but this frame change was neither universal nor uncontroversial in the classic
corporatist setting of the Spanish steel community, which is why the leading
advocates of more ambitious restructuring had to tread carefully and sometimes
had to wait for crises (cyclical downturns) and external forces (EU accession
negotiations) as windows of opportunity to gain support for politically painful
moves (Kingdon, 1984; Keeler, 1993; cf. Boin and 't Hart, 2000). In the UK,
BS management proved rapid learners and were among the first, along with
Hoogovens management in the Netherlands, to fully embrace neoliberal norms
of free trade, competition and, most importantly, a bias against government
subsidization and intervention in the industry. It is perhaps not exaggerated to
claim that, in the British case, the Conservative government was moved along
the path to privatization by the industry instead of vice versa. When privatization occurred, it posed unforeseen challenges to the prevailing modes of
governance, initiating a search for new institutions and interaction patterns that
has yet to end.

In contrast, in Germany, the Netherlands and Sweden, the policy style
remained relatively constant. In Sweden, both social–democratic and liberal
governments adopted a mix of proactive decline management combined with
an emphasis on creating the conditions for renewed international competitiveness of the industry as a whole. The eventual privatization of SSAB therefore

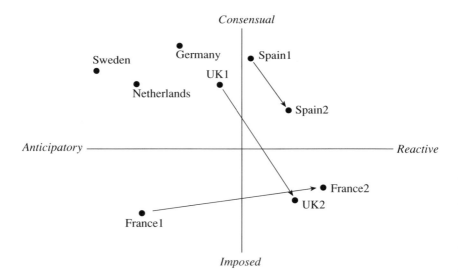

Figure 31.2   Managing decline and restructuring in the steel industry:
*   national policy styles*

constituted less of an institutional rupture than the privatisation of BS did in Britain. The Swedish state did evolve in its attitude towards the management of the social consequences of decline: whereas central government had in the early stages of the process projected itself as the first and last resort of communities distressed by plant closures, by the late 1980s it had extricated itself from that role, leaving subnational authorities and networks of local actors to fill the gap. In Holland and Germany, the modus operandi of government was most robust. In Germany, corporatist consultation has been and still is the predominant mechanism of managing the steel sector. The Dutch found their unique blend of 'laissez-faire interventionism', as Schenk calls it in his chapter, to be working well. This was made easy by the fact that 'the steel industry' consisted of one firm only, and a relatively well-run and forward-looking one. In other words, the Dutch government was never really faced with the kinds of political trade-offs and risks that French and Spanish policy makers had to struggle with, since Hoogovens withstood the crises of the 1970s and 1980s much better, and took successful initiatives to hedge its bets (aluminium production, strategic alliances), therefore reducing the burdens of 'downsizing'.

Explaining Success and Failure: From Governments to Governance

Taken together, the steel case studies provide few surprises for students of comparative public policy in western Europe. Most states' policy styles conformed, at least initially, to the general expectations formulated in Chapter 2. The most interesting analytical questions are:

(a) why were there policy style changes over time in some countries,
(b) why did some states perform better than others, and
(c) why were there discrepancies between programmatic and political performance, notably in Britain and Spain?

Explaining policy style changes
Why did three of the states studied here change their approach to governing the steel sector in the course of the last 30 years, and why did three others refrain from doing so? A straightforward explanation might be that the former showed the capability to learn from experience, and the others did not. The evidence suggests, however, that the reverse holds true: the three that did *not* change their governance style were also the most successful in meeting the combined challenges of managing decline and restructuring. Moreover, lack of style change did not necessarily mean an absence of learning. For example, Schenk shows that Dutch policy makers in the Ministry of Economic Affairs based their approach to steel governance in part on experiences gained with other forms of industrial policy, including conspicuous failures in trying to rescue other sunset

industries. Pierre does the same for Sweden: the recommendations of the royal commission that formed the core of the steel policy strategy were heavily influenced by the lessons from decline management in shipbuilding. Instrumental learning did take place in both these countries, but in France, Spain and the UK learning went further and affected the fundamentals of the prevailing steel policy paradigm, including the institutional logic of state–industry relationships in the sector. In our view it was not so much the better capability but rather the more strongly felt need to change approach that prompted these states to adapt their policy approaches more profoundly. Two types of stimuli may have triggered this. The first was situational pressures: the cyclical slumps in global demand and the increasing foreign competition revealed that the steel industries of France, Spain and the UK were simply in worse shape than some of their European counterparts. The second was trial-and-error dynamics: especially in France and Spain, the early policy responses to decline just did not do enough to put the sector back on its feet. In France, grand plans came to naught, and there were some costly and politically sensitive failures, whereas in Spain the actors in the steel arena slowly became aware of the costs of the policy immobility that resulted from rent-seeking corporatism and tenuous intergovernmental relations. In the UK, the situation was different: its brand of consensualism went a long way in managing the sharp decline of the industry in the 1970s and 1980s. As Dudley and Richardson argue, the need to rethink the governance approach arose, not because of failure, but because of governance success: in privatizing a now successful and strong British Steel, the British government unwittingly altered the structure of the policy community for good. It now found itself confronted by an assertive, even aggressive corporate player that had become progressively less dependent upon concertation with the government, and more upon keeping up with global market changes.

Explaining differential performance

Why did some states fare better than others in the transformation of their national steel industries? It would be far too simple to ascribe this simply to the superior capacity of the policy makers or the government agencies in question. As in the other sectors, policy successes and failures are made by a mixture of 'virtu' and 'fortuna', that is, prudent governance and external forces that elude the policy makers' grasp (Dror, 1986). More specifically, policy makers in steel as well as in the other sectors operate within more or less given institutional contexts with set rules, roles, policy frames and power relationships. These facilitate and constrain the policy choices they can feasibly make, as well as the likelihood that their policies are successfully implemented. Policy makers are, moreover, always confronted by things that happen in their political, economic and international environment which they cannot influence but which impinge upon their policy spaces. In that sense, successful governance is always a combined product of good sense and good luck.

Taking this into account, the case studies suggest four crucial factors that influenced the course and outcomes of steel governance in the six countries studied. As pointed out above, the structure of the industry varied greatly from country to country: the number of key firms, their location, their embeddedness in the regional or national industrial self-image and strategy. Doing business with one firm only or within a well-organized government–industry consultative framework is much more simple than dealing with various, unorganized and mutually competitive firms or conglomerates. Secondly, the political structure has an impact: in federal systems, the territorial politics of restructuring are potentially more complex and risky to national policy makers than in a unitary system. The difference between Spain and Germany is interesting with respect to both these factors: both countries had heavy concentrations of steel production in two regions and both are federal systems; yet the crucial difference between them was the presence of a well-functioning consultative, corporatist structure in Germany that served to counteract the dangers of policy paralysis, whereas in Spain the restructuring process was slowed down because it was lacking such an institutional framework at the sectoral level.

The prevailing policy ideas among government (both national and subnational), industry and unions are also quite important. The crucial question there is when and to what extent these players shifted from a conservationist desire to preserve firms and jobs by means of government subsidies and protectionism towards the neoliberal position that restoring competitiveness by productivity gains and product innovation was the key to the long-term survival of the industry, even if this came at the cost of plant closures, job losses and liquidation of non-performing firms. In Spain, some of the national policy makers converted to neoliberal thinking much earlier than most of their counterparts in the steel sector. In Britain, in contrast, BS seemed to be leading even the Conservative government in this respect. In Holland and Germany, the policy ideas of the key actors appear to have been more in tune throughout the process. In Sweden, there was broad consensus at the national level but, given the dispersed nature of the industry, central government found itself in delicate talks with regional and local authorities who were less prone to adopt the microeconomic point of view and simply feared the consequences of the impending closure of major local employers. In France, there were definite mismatches of policy ideas not only between the government and the industry, but within each of them.

Finally, the quality of corporate management is a factor that cannot be underestimated. Internationally oriented, forward-looking firm managers played a pivotal role in the British, Dutch and Swedish restructuring processes, whereas in France and Spain the steel bosses were more likely to be quasi-political figures. They seemed at times less interested in improving their firms' competitiveness than in maintaining the political networks necessary to sustain the inflow of government subsidies and to keep in place cushy but economically ultimately unviable protective belts. The steel case shows that, for better or for worse, what company managers think and do may have a crucial impact on the programmatic and indirectly also the political success of industrial policy. The same goes for the impact of supranational policy makers, notably the European Commission. Dudley and Richardson are therefore right to stress the importance of looking beyond 'government' and focusing squarely on 'governance' in analysing the evolution of the European steel industry and steel policy.

Explaining an assessment asymmetry
In Chapter 2 we have formulated five tentative hypotheses that help explain why programmatic successes may not always be political successes, and vice versa. These referred to the impact of political structure, political culture, policy frames, the type of governance task, and the symbolic potential of the issues in question. In the steel sector, unlike what we will see later on in the finance and HIV sectors, the asymmetric case that needs explanation is Spain. The political culture hypothesis appears to be most relevant here. The programmatic short-comings of steel policy never became a major political issue because of the consensual approach to 'downsizing' and restructuring that the government had opted for in the early 1980s. Since all of the key players were involved in the policy-making process, and were sometimes able to exercise de facto veto powers against proposals for change they did not like, they were not free to criticize the resulting policy stalemates and soft compromises that emerged. Moreover, the broader political context in which steel restructuring took place for a long time conduced to moderation in attacking the government: the continuing process of transition to democracy, the application for EC membership, and the strong political dominance of the social–democratic party, particularly during the first two Gonzales governments.

3 MANAGING REFORM: CONTROLLING THE MEDICAL PROFESSION

Controlling Institutional Gatekeepers

Health care is a key sector in the modern welfare state, in terms of budgetary importance, public interest and political focus. Within this vital sector, the medical profession has a pivotal role. In most of the countries studied, doctors traditionally have been well organized, they exercise large professional and political powers, and their professional interests are firmly established in the legal, political and financial systems. They are among the most important formal and informal gatekeepers of the medical system. Any attempt to reform the medical sector at large will have to reckon with their institutional dominance. In most countries, a reform of the health sector in practice is tantamount to a reform of the institutional powers of the medical profession. The studies presented in this sector therefore focused on a key episode in the reform of the medical profession in the last two decades of the twentieth century. Each study started with the same research question: what did the policy episode do to the power of these institutional gatekeepers?

Within this broad framework, however, the nature and the context of these reform attempts varied. By contrast with the HIV and blood supply crises, which struck the health sector at approximately the same time, the specific governance challenges for the national health authorities in these reform cases were not always similar.

In Germany, France, the Netherlands and the UK, the attempts to control the professional dominance of the medical profession were basically driven by a desire to contain the increasing costs of health care. Each of the reform attempts studied in these countries was only one of a series of more or less successful attempts at financial or professional reform. In Germany, France, the Netherlands and the UK, the policy goals and the policy history were quite comparable – even though the institutional structure and political context were quite different, as has been explained by Moran in his introduction to Part III.

The reform attempts in Spain and Sweden were driven by different motives. In these countries, the government tried to increase the accessibility and quality of primary health care. In Spain, the socialist government aimed at a structural and comprehensive reform of the inefficient and fragmented Francoist system of health care. Thus the issue was not cost control in a well-established sector of the welfare state, but the very establishment of a modern, efficient and equitable system of public health care in the first place. In that respect, the Spanish reforms were by far the most ambitious and far-reaching. In Sweden, the Liberal Party intended to extend and improve the system of public health care which had already been introduced in the late 1960s. In these countries the reform attempts therefore did not focus primarily on the financial structures, but on the institutional make-up of the sector at large.

However, what was crucial in each of these cases for the success of the reform attempts was the power of the medical profession to resist these institutional reforms and, likewise, the political capability of the state to prevail over these well-organized interests.

Assessment: Incremental Successes, Radical Failures

How did each country fare in controlling and reforming the medical profession? In Table 31.2 the programmatic dimension of success and failure is assessed on the basis of various indicators. First, we have looked at the duration of the reform attempt. This was based on the assumption that swiftness is an important element of reform capabilities. Moreover, it can be an indicator of the power of the medical profession to halt or hinder reform attempts. The longer it takes to get the reform proposal accepted, if at all, the smaller the power of the health authorities to manage the reform of the medical profession. It is not a very solid indicator because time is a relative notion in the context of reform. The demarcation of the reform period is particularly arbitrary, as was already mentioned in the introduction to Part III. In the cases of Germany, France, the Netherlands and the UK, we see a series of attempts to reform the medical sector, starting in the early 1980s. In each of these countries only one particular attempt was chosen for analysis. These reform proposals more or less built upon the earlier attempts at reform, both in substantive and political terms. Elements of earlier proposals were incorporated in these new reform attempts and political actors saw the new proposal as another episode in a continuing story of reform. In some of these countries the picture would have looked quite different if an entire series of attempts at reform, undertaken by successive governments, had been taken as the unit of analysis, as has more or less been done in the Spanish case.

We have also looked at the level of ambition that was achieved. Did the authorities manage to reach the goals they had set themselves in these reform proposals? And how ambitious were these goals? Did they aim at incremental adjustments or did they go for structural reforms? We have also distinguished between short-term and long-term successes to get a more subtle assessment of what happened. In the Spanish case, for example, the federal government met strong resistance when it initially launched its ambitious proposals. It subsequently changed its reform strategy and moderated its proposals, which in the long run led to a successful implementation of the proposals in most of the regions. On the other hand, Burau, in discussing the German case, and Trappenburg and De Groot in discussing the Dutch, express doubts whether the initially successful reforms of the national health ministers Seehofer and Borst prove to be sufficient in the long run. They managed to achieve the policy goals they had set themselves, but it remains to be seen whether this will lead to structural cost containment in the health sector. In most countries structural factors, such as ageing and technological change, are at work which will jeopardize incremental attempts to contain the cost of medical care. A long-term assessment of the reform attempts is difficult to make in these countries, as the stories are still unfolding. However, it may very well be that in the long run the Seehofer and Borst reforms indeed will turn out to be just a minor episode in a much longer story of cost containment.

The third programmatic indicator looks at the reduction of professional dominance. What did the episode do to the financial and clinical autonomy of

Table 31.2 Managing reform, controlling the medical profession: outcome assessment

	France[1]	Germany	Netherlands	Spain	Sweden	UK[2]
Programmatic dimension	–	++	+	+	– –	+
Length of reform attempt	Long (1970–99)	Short (1/1/1992–1/1/1993)	Medium (1994–8)	Long (1982–93)	Medium (1992–5)	Long (1989–97)
Achieved level of ambition:						
Short-term	+/–	++	+	+/–	–	+
Long-term	– – (policy paralysis)	+/–	+/–	++ (except two regions)	n.a.	n.a.
Reduction of professional dominance (financial, clinical political)	– – Traditional remuneration system and clinical autonomy intact; political stalemate	++ Limits to self-administration; reduction clinical autonomy; shift of power to state	+ Output pricing; employment relations; more guidelines	++ Shift from private practice to public health care centres	n.a. (Failed plan aimed to increase autonomy)	+ Professional autonomy challenged by managerial function; insider role of associations weakened
Political dimension	?	++	+	–/++	–	+/–
Political consequences	?	Increased legitimacy of state governance	Political credit to minister (short-term)	Short-term: fierce political battle; two ministers step down; electoral costs. Long-term: strong increase in public satisfaction; erosion of opposition	Strong opposition; electoral losses	No direct adverse consequences; some electoral damage in the long run

Notes:
1. The French study focused more on the entire series of health care reforms than on one particular attempt to control the medical profession. The assessment should be interpreted accordingly.
2. For the UK only the introduction of the purchaser/provider split is represented, because this was the single most important reform attempt in that case.

individual doctors in health institutions and to the political power of their professional associations? Did the health authorities indeed manage to get more control over these institutional gatekeepers? This is the most solid measure of the overall capability of government to reform the medical profession.

The overall picture of the cases studied here is positive. Except for Sweden and France, the attempts to reform the financial or institutional make-up of the medical sector were quite successful. In France, the state has failed in recent decades to reform the ambulatory care system in general and the institutional arrangements for the medical profession in particular. Despite some major attempts at reform, French medical professions have managed to defend the status quo with regard to its financial and clinical autonomy. In spite of its political powers, the French state is tied to path dependency and has not been able to achieve lasting institutional changes.

Given the power of the medical profession in Germany and the bleak history of health care reform, the *Gesundheitsstrukturgesetz* was an unqualified and impromptu success, at least in the short term. It contained many far-reaching reform measures, which minister Seehofer managed to get politically accepted in an unusually short time span. It was widely heralded as a successful and speedy reform both by political actors and by policy analysts. As yet, it is still less certain whether all of these structural reforms will be implemented and effective in the long run. Likewise, in the Netherlands, minister Borst was quite successful in her short-term attempts to control the medical specialists when compared with her, often far more ambitious, predecessors. With regard to the first two indicators, the assessment of the Spanish reform attempts produces diametrically opposite results. Initially, the socialist government was not very successful with its radical proposals for a comprehensive system of public health care. It subsequently modified its proposals and adjusted its political strategy. In the long run, Spanish policy makers achieved considerable successes and managed to establish an extensive system of public primary health care in most of the regions. In Sweden, the family doctor scheme, which aimed to attract more doctors to primary health care through the introduction of private practices and market elements, and thereby to enhance the access to family doctors in rural areas, was a downright failure. None of its ambitions were reached and most of the reforms were repealed as soon as their most ardent political sponsor, the Liberal Party, left the government. Finally, in the UK the introduction of the 'purchaser/provider split' in the 1990s was a successful attempt to improve the professional and financial accountability of general practitioners.

Strikingly, in most of the countries studied the professional dominance of doctors and their associations within the medical institutions was reduced to a greater or lesser extent. In most countries the financial and clinical autonomy of individual doctors has decreased through the introduction of fixed diagnosis-related and lump-sum payments, employment relations and fixed contracts instead of private practice, medical guidelines and clinical models. Increased managerial control of the working conditions of doctors also weighs in. In many countries the professional associations experienced a loss of institutional power. Insurance funds, GP fundholders, health authorities and general managers have seriously challenged their insider role in the governance of the sector. The only exceptions are Sweden, where most doctors are already publicly employed and where the Liberal Party actually intended to increase their economic freedom (albeit against their will), and France, where the medical associations seem to have managed, to some extent, to defend the institutional status quo.

What is even more important, given the governance challenge at stake here, is that in all of the countries – again with the exception of France – the collective power of doctors vis-à-vis the state seems to have been reduced. All authors report a diminishing political power of the professional medical associations. In most countries the influence of the medical associations on the policy process has weakened, often as a result of internal divisions within the medical profession itself. Even in Sweden, according to Garpenby, the collective voice

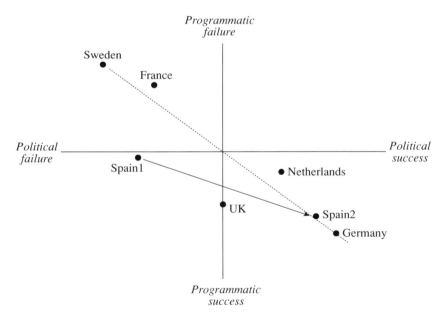

Note: The dotted line indicates full symmetry between programmatic and political outcomes.

Figure 31.3   Managing reform of the medical profession: an integrated assessment

of the profession is weaker at the end of the 1990s than it was at the beginning of the decade.

Table 31.2 also provides an assessment of the political success and failure of the reform attempts. The political outcomes are more or less symmetrical with the programmatic outcomes, as can be observed from Figure 31.3. This is not very surprising, given the inherently political nature of the governance challenge at stake here. The reform of an entrenched profession is not a technocratic but a political enterprise. Crucial for its success is not the technical quality of the policy proposal, but the amount of political support it receives, not only in the sector itself, but also in the political realm and with the public at large. Policy makers therefore have to invest in political alliances and to deploy strategies for depoliticization and political risk management. Political aptitude, therefore, is an important element of programmatic success and programmatic successes eventually can be transformed into political capital.

Overall, Figure 31.3 confirms the optimistic vision of governance, represented by Candide in the first chapter and by our null hypothesis in the second chapter. Policy makers who succeed in substantive programmatic reforms, such as Seehofer in Germany and the socialists in Spain, are rewarded by an increase in political legitimacy and public satisfaction, according to our authors.

Policy Style: From 'Blueprint' to 'Bright Idea'

On the issue of national policy styles, the picture is less clear. Figure 31.4 gives the policy style configuration for the cases of health reform. This configuration does not confirm the hypothesized national policy styles, with the exception of the Netherlands and the UK. However, it is questionable whether the cases studied here were representative for either the national or the sectoral policy style. Several authors note that the policy-making style in the specific case was at odds with the usual style.

We see a shift in policy style in a number of countries. In Germany, for example, the policy style at the federal political level was strongly consensual, as was to be expected. Minister Seehofer invested much energy in the creation of a cross-party political consensus. However, in stark contrast with the previous reform attempts and with the hypothesized corporatist policy style, the lobbyists for the medical professional organizations and for other interest groups were almost completely excluded from the policy-making arena. The consensual style only applied to political actors. In the Netherlands, Borst used a consensual and incremental approach which left ample room for self-regulation. This is in line with the hypothesized Dutch policy style. Again, this was in stark contrast with the approach of some of her predecessors who had confronted the health sector with detailed and far-reaching schemes for reform. A similar shift, from detailed proposals to a general set of ideas, is reported by Harrison for the UK. To complicate things further, in the specific policy episode studied in the UK this shift is accompanied by a shift along the other dimension of policy style: from a style which seeks consensus with interest groups to the imposition of policy. It is not yet clear whether this represents a structural shift in health policy making in the UK; it is certainly consistent with the more general alteration in policy style associated with the triumph of Thatcherism in British politics. In the Spanish case, too, we see a shift in policy style. The socialist government started with a confrontational style of policy making and tried to impose a detailed proposal for primary care upon the sector. When this grand scheme met with fierce opposition from the sector, policy makers gradually moderated their proposals and shifted to a pragmatic and moderate style of policy making. Eventually, they adopted a consensual policy style and managed to steer a middle course, avoiding open confrontations with the professional medical associations on the one hand and the unions on the other. In Sweden too, the Liberal Party's family doctor scheme broke very obviously with the sector-specific policy style that had hitherto been established in the health sector. The failure of this top-down reform attempt may therefore be interpreted as a confirmation of the hypothezised strongly consensual Swedish policy style.

The overall picture in these cases suggests a tendency to move away from imposed, grand designs to more experimental, adaptive styles of policy making. From blueprint to 'bright idea', as Harrison calls it.

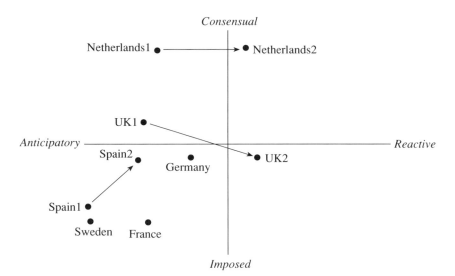

Figure 31.4 Managing reform of the medical profession: national policy styles

Explaining the Successful Reduction of Professional Dominance: United they Stand, Divided they Fail

In most of the episodes studied here, we see a reduction of the professional dominance of doctors, both individually within the medical institutions and collectively within the political system at large. The most important issue to be explained in these cases of managing reform is therefore the following: why were most governments, to a greater or lesser degree, successful in reducing the power of the medical profession?

The management of medical reform, as defined here, is more or less a zero-sum game with two major players, health policy makers on the one hand and the medical profession on the other. Their successes and failures are to a large extent complementary. The medical professions' failure to maintain the institutional status quo constitutes a policy success and vice versa. Therefore, what is to be explained here is both the failure of the medical profession to maintain or increase its professional dominance and the success of the health authorities in enhancing public control.

Explaining the loss of professional political power
The overall picture of the medical profession is one of increasing heterogeneity and a gradual loss of political power. The case authors offer several explanations for this.

- In the past decades the structure of the medical profession in a number of countries has changed, mostly owing to demographic factors. In the 1970s and 1980s, in the wake of the baby boom, sizeable new generations of doctors entered the profession. They held different views about the status and nature of medical work and were less focused on private practice and financial autonomy than the traditional middle-aged general practitioners and specialists who had dominated the professional organizations until that time. Although no systematic evidence is brought to bear in the case studies it is almost certainly the case that these national professions are seeing an increase in feminine participation that is both decreasing internal solidarity and, probably, is an indicator of declining collective occupational status. The increased heterogeneity within the profession weakened its institutional and political strength. The new generations created their own professional associations, which usually were more cooperative in the design and implementation of state plans for health reform. This was most conspicuous in Spain, where new generations of young, progressive doctors became the allies of state reformers and often participated in the design of the health care reform from below. Similarly, in the Netherlands and France, the medical specialists' association split up into more progressive, state-oriented and more conservative, private practice-oriented parts. Technological change, which encourages the development of new medical specialisms, also probably reduces the internal homogeneity of medical professions in the long run.

- The rising number of doctors and the cost containment measures have also generated an increase in distributional struggles within the profession itself. This is particularly true of those countries where one finds a coexistence of hierarchical and market systems of remuneration. In Germany, for example, there were deep divisions between the self-employed office-based doctors and the salaried hospital doctors, as well as between general practitioners and specialists. Similar divisions have risen in France, the Netherlands, Spain and the UK. The professional associations seem to have increasing difficulty uniting the various interest groups and adopting a uniform stance. This was even the case in Sweden where the leadership of the dominant Swedish Medical Association was strongly in favour of medical self-employment, but eventually had to retreat because it turned out that the majority of its members preferred to maintain their public employment security.

- Another reason for the diminishing political power of the professional medical associations may also be a decrease in public acceptance of their professional status. Harrison, in his analysis of the UK, points to a certain general antipathy to the medical profession, which may have weakened its position vis-à-vis the government.

Explaining the success of the reform attempts

In most countries the circumstances for institutional reform were favourable. However, this alone is not sufficient to bring about the more or less successful control of the medical profession. What were the main explanatory factors on the policy-making side?

- *Institutional factors*   In Germany, the Netherlands, the UK and, to a lesser extent, in Spain, we see a high degree of path dependency and continuity. At least part of the successes of both Seehofer and Borst can be explained, paradoxically, by the failures of their predecessors, as Burau points out in her analysis of the German case. In the first place, the earlier attempts facilitated policy learning, because they served as a sort of negative blueprint. Seehofer and Borst were able to learn from the political and programmatic mistakes made by their predecessors. Secondly, these earlier failures helped to create a sense of urgency, both in the political arena and in the medical sector. Thirdly, these earlier failures had gradually changed the institutional landscape and the balance of power. They more or less paved the way for the subsequent successful attempts, which were in fact quite consistent with the earlier proposals. As was already mentioned in the introduction to Part III, the institutional frameworks of the health sector vary in their capacity for reform. The institutional framework of the NHS in the UK was a key factor in facilitating the successful implementation of the purchaser/provider split, according to Harrison. The combination of its tax-financed, budget-capped, central government-control character and its dominant position as the provider of medical care gives policy makers levers that do not exist in more pluralist systems such as Germany or the Netherlands.

- *Policy style*   In their analysis of the reasons for success or failure of the reform attempts all authors mention elements of policy-making style as an important factor. In most of the cases, with the exception perhaps of Germany, policy making by detailed blueprint was no longer feasible, as it had been in the 1960s and 1970s. The failure of Borst's predecessors, the retreat of the Spanish socialists and the demise of the Swedish Liberal Party testify to this. Policy making by bright idea, by the swift promulgation of a core set of ideas combined with an invitation to relevant actors to participate in the implementation of these ideas through experiments, seems to be a much more promising road. Some of the key characteristics of this new process, which are described by Harrison, can be found in other cases too. First, the process of initial design of the reforms is short, largely conducted in secret, and shielded from lobbyists of the professional interest groups. This pattern can also be found in the German case and to a lesser extent in the Netherlands. The elaboration of these bright, but rather vague, ideas is left to the implementation phase in which there is ample room for experiments and voluntary participation. Harrison calls this 'manipulated emergence'. Elements of this strategy could also be found in the Netherlands. In both countries this turned out to be a highly successful strategy for the implementation of the reforms. The absence of an institutional blueprint blunts potential opposition to the reforms. Voluntary participation in experiments is far less threatening and it allows for psychological adaptation and unannounced policy adjustment. By orchestrating experiments, both the British and the Dutch policy makers also managed to bypass the official professional organizations and were able to do business directly with individual hospitals or practitioners who, at the local level, saw opportunities in the proposals. In this way the policy makers made optimal use of the increasing divisions within the medical profession and managed to create bandwagon effects.
- *Political tactics*   Since most authors focus on a particular reform episode instead of examining a long series of reforms, some of the explanations for the policy making successes are quite specific and deal with issues of personal leadership style and political tactics. In managing short-term

reform, individual political skills matter. This is most conspicuous in the German case, where the clever manoeuvring and determination of minister Seehofer tipped the scale. He managed to keep the political initiative and effectively set limits to the influence of the medical lobbyists. In the Netherlands the incumbent minister, Borst, had a substantial amount of credit with the sector because of her background as a medical doctor and former health official. Initially, she managed to enhance it by stating repeatedly that the Dutch health care system was doing a great job. In the UK, political tactics, notably the manufacture of a crisis, contributed to the successful introduction of the purchaser/provider split, according to Harrison. The Conservative government successfully exploited the public perception of an NHS funding crisis in 1987 to create a sense of urgency. In France, in contrast, according to Wilsford, neither Juppé nor Aubry managed to open a window of opportunity in health care reform.

In the political realm, as with the medical sector, the motto is: united they stand, divided they fail. Cross-party consensus is important to create a platform for reform. This was a major element in Seehofer's success and the failure to invest in it contributed greatly to the failure of the Swedish Liberal Party. In most of these cases of health reform we see few acute crises that spur a search for blame. Rather, we see long incremental struggles with an occasional window of opportunity. At these critical junctures individual political skills can help to speed up the policy-making process.

This leads to a somewhat paradoxical conclusion to our review of the health sector. This is one of the most institutionally densely populated policy sectors in modern states. There exist an abundance of policy networks and policy communities. It is a sector in many ways made for immobility, and one where we might expect human agency to be a slight influence on policy change. Yet this very weight of institutions and interests means that human agency – one important source of short-term variation in all this stability – can have an important influence. In these health sector policy histories people matter and, above all, people called politicians matter.

4   MANAGING INNOVATION: REGULATING FINANCE IN AN ERA OF GLOBALIZATION

A Shifting Governance Challenge

The world of finance has been in a state of flux for some time. As Busch has pointed out in his introductory chapter, the release of national controls on the mobility of capital during the 1980s and 1990s has profoundly changed the structure of the financial sector, as well as the role that national governments (can) play in managing it. Firstly, banks have lost their self-evidently central role in lending and investment. A host of new financial products have been developed and delivered by other entities, such as insurance firms and investment companies. Financial markets have diversified, and so have the regulatory structures put in place to supervise their operation. This means that, today, central banks are by no means the only institutional watchdogs in the financial sector. A host of other, partly self-governing oversight bodies have sprung up. Moreover, not only have financial markets diversified, they have also internationalized. Capital is now a completely decommodified, deterritorialized phenomenon, and the banks and other operators on the now global financial markets have been adjusting to this. They have gone offshore, they have made takeovers in other countries, they collaborate in multinational consortiums on specific projects, and so on. As a consequence, it has become much more difficult, if not impossible, for national policy makers to demarcate the boundaries of their financial systems, let alone regulate and control the behaviour of the financial players that operate in it or interact with it.

These developments have led to a profound change in the public governance of financial markets. National policies have traditionally been twofold: measures to prevent bank failures, motivated by the desire to secure the viability of the national banking system and protect the safety of deposits; and measures to ensure that their financial sectors operated in such a way as to promote economic growth and employment. In the newly emerging globalized financial system, this is no longer tenable. From the case studies reported here a clear picture emerges of the new governance challenges triggered by innovation in the financial sector. First of all, the *objective* of preventing bank failures has gradually given way to the need to safeguard the stability of the system as a whole, given that serious fluctuations and collapses by individual banks and other players are likely to happen from time to time. In Wildavsky's (1988) terms, the logic of policy making has shifted from anticipation to resilience: no longer can policy makers hope to prevent shocks from happening by fine-tuning their regulatory oversight or taking a direct hand in running the system; they have to accept that bigger, stronger forces are at play now that ensure that from time to time accidents will happen; all that public policy can do is to make sure that the damage done by these shocks is minimal, and that the right lessons are learned from these collapses. Secondly, the relevant *level of governance* at which these objectives are to be accomplished has been shifting away from national governments or central banks towards European and indeed global regulatory institutions. In an open, deregulated economy there is only so much that states can do to affect the operation of their financial sectors as well as to achieve their macroeconomic aims.

The case studies document this process of shifting governance challenges. One is set relatively early in the process (Germany, mid-1970s) and shows how an early crisis induced effective learning by both the state and the sector. In contrast, the UK case study takes us to the mid-1990s and shows what happens when 'old' governance bodies face challenges brought about by the 'new' conditions. Other case studies are more longitudinal. The Spanish and Dutch cases encompass the decades in which the critical changes to the global financial system took hold and show what it took to get Spanish and Dutch financial policies to adapt to these changing realities. Underlying all of the cases is the critical need for policy makers to balance microeconomic concerns of running a sound financial system with macroeconomic priorities of keeping the nation as a whole afloat, but nowhere does this come out more clearly than in the Swedish case study, where the limits of classical macroeconomic management in the volatile economy of the late 1980s and early 1990s are exposed and analysed in terms of their effects on the banking system.

Assessment: Policy Failures without Political Consequences

In keeping with the evolving nature of the critical governance task, the programmatic dimension of financial sector governance involves a mixture of anticipation (can states prevent serious bank collapses from happening?), resilience (can states effectively dampen the scope and systemic impact of the failures that do occur, and at what price?) and institutional re-engineering (besides dealing with its volatilities, have states been proactive and successful in adjusting their regulatory approach to the newly emerging financial order?). On the political side, we simply ask to what extent policy making for deposit protection – whether in its institutional engineering or incident management guise – has become the subject of political controversy and has resulted in political sanctions against crucial policy makers. In Table 31.3, we present the results of the national case studies.

Inevitably, a table collapses a complex reality into a simple set of boxes. In Table 31.3 a major simplification has occurred in the programmatic dimension of policy assessment. The overall judgment of programmatic performance is actually a composite evaluation of two very different policy strands: the institutional re-engineering of the banking system, in response to critical environmental changes affecting its operation, and the preventative and emergency measures taken with a view to specific (series of) bank failures. Although generally the same actors and institutions deal with both these issues, in some of the cases there are rather marked differences in how well they did in both spheres. This makes for the rather ambiguous +/– summary judgments at the top end of the table. In France, institutional redesign was proactive and generally effective, but policy makers were unwilling to accept its consequences

Table 31.3 Managing innovation in the financial sector: outcome assessment

Programmatic dimension	France (1980–98)	Germany (1974–84)	Netherlands (1980–95)	Spain (1977–95)	Sweden (1985–92)*	UK (1994–5)
	+/–	+	+	+/–	–	+/–
Prevention:						
• Number and relative size of bank failures	Failure of only one but a big (US$31 billion asset loss) bank	Failure of three relatively small banks Key case: DM 1.2 billion lost	Two minor bank collapses (plus one foreign-owned bank)	51 minor bank collapses and later collapse of one big bank; losses: 18% GDP	Macroeconomic mismanagement triggered bank failures	Failure of one moderately sized but symbolically crucial bank
Response:						
• Costs of bailout	Public money: US$20 billion	Public money: none	Public money: none	Public money: 6% GDP	Public money: ??	Failed bank taken over by Dutch bank
• Timing of state action	Slow and non-vigorous response	Effective, if restrained, state response	Ongoing process of legal reform	?	Relatively vigorous response	Bank of England took lead in crisis management
• Containment of systemic impact	No cascade effect	No cascade effect despite temporary crisis mood	Not applicable	No cascade effect	No bank failures	No cascade effect
Re-engiering:						
• Timing/duration of institutional change	OECD leader in market deregulation	Prompt, crisis-induced response by banking community	Incremental change process, partly driven by EU developments	Two-stage, protracted reform struggle to ensure liberalization and end oligopolies	??	Gradualist move from 'old' to 'new' City without adequate assessment of regulatory consequences

Political dimension	+/-	+	+	+	+	+
• Perceived adequacy of new regime	Market deregulation not matched by less incestuous governance structures	High: further crisis avoided	High: Dutch financial conglomerates very successful globally	Macroeconomic and Eurostrategic objectives achieved at considerable collateral costs		Bank of England's regulatory role diminished without clear institutional alternative
Judgment of official investigative bodies:	Common opinion that government mismanaged; criminal proceedings against bank officials	Commission report vindicates the basic structure of the banking and deposit insurance system	n.a.	n.a.	??	Bank board, Commons committee reports blame bank management v. Bank of England
Political consequences for policymakers:	Exploitation of scandal by opposition	No political damage to government	n.a.	No discernible electoral costs for successive socialist governments	??	No political damage to government

Note:

* The Swedish case study focuses more on macroeconomic management than on the management of the financial system; the assessment should be interpreted accordingly.

to the full: they held on to state influence in some of the biggest banks, and allowed mismanaged within one of them to go unchecked, with dire consequences for the taxpayers. In Spain, policy makers succeeded in unsettling a deeply entrenched statist–oligopolic system, but fared less well in mitigating the vulnerabilities that resulted from the incremental nature of the institutional overhaul. In the UK, institutional adaptation was hardly done by concerted policy action, yet when a crisis occurred the Bank of England and the key players in the City were effectively able to contain the damage. Still, despite these mixed results, the three countries just mentioned do contrast rather sharply with (particularly) Germany and also the Netherlands, which are clear-cut programmatic successes. The question is how these differences in programmatic performance can be explained.

The most remarkable finding, however, relates to the discrepancy between the sometimes huge financial (and macroeconomic) costs caused by the failure of banks and the almost complete absence of adverse political consequences for incumbent governments (see Figure 31.5). The Swedish and Spanish cases

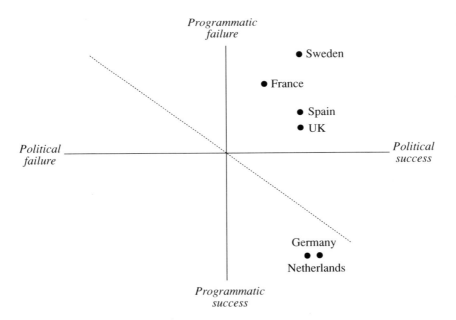

Note: The dotted line indicates full symmetry between programmatic and political outcomes.

Figure 31.5   Managing innovation in the financial sector: an integrated assessment

are most remarkable here: in Sweden, macroeconomic mismanagement caused microeconomic problems in the banking sector, in Spain the reverse was the case; yet in both countries hardly a ripple resulted in the political arena. In short, in the banking sector the programmatic and political dimensions of policy evaluation appear to be disconnected, where in other sectors, such as HIV and steel, a weak programmatic performance is more likely to spill over into political controversy.

Policy Style: The Limits of Imposition

Mapping the policy styles in the financial sector is also somewhat complicated by the fact that, as in the steel sector, 'policy' here has a dual meaning: institutional redesign and the management of bad banks. We have, nevertheless, placed the six countries in the policy style matrix since there did not seem to be major discrepancies between the way in which both tasks were handled in each of the countries (see Figure 31.6). The most remarkable finding here is that all of the countries are located in the upper, consensualist half of the table. For consensual democracies such as Germany, Holland and Sweden this was to be expected, but less so for the UK and particularly for Spain and France, who deviate significantly from their hypothesized generic national policy styles (see chapter 2, Figure 2.2). The conclusion has to be that, at least in the 1970s–1990s

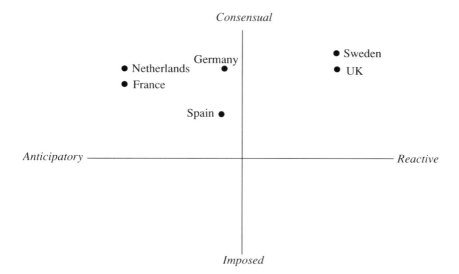

Figure 31.6   Managing innovation in the financial sector: national policy styles

period, the financial sector was hard to regulate and control 'from above' by the state. Below we shall examine why this was the case.

Explaining Success and Failure: Contextual Volatility and Sectoral Autonomy

In sum, the empirical findings from the financial sector present us with the following analytical puzzles:

1. Why do some countries do better than others in the management of innovation in the financial sector?
2. Why the discrepancy between the relatively significant incidence of programmatic weaknesses, if not outright failures, and the complete absence of political failures in any of the cases studied?
3. Why the marked absence of more top-down forms of state intervention in the sector, even in countries with a tradition of state imposition?

Explaining differential programmatic performance

The country chapters do not provide us with a basis for clear-cut generalizations. The reasons for programmatic failure, for instance, seem to be manifold and cover the full range of individual, organizational, regulatory, systemic and situational variables identified in the literature on policy fiascos and man-made catastrophes (cf. Anheier, 1999; Bovens and 't Hart, 1996; Gray, 1998; Reason, 1997; Turner and Pidgeon, 1997; Vaughan, 1996). In the British case, for example, there is some justification for arguing that 'human error' (that is, Leeson's solo flight into financial disaster) played a significant part in the collapse of Barings. Yet, at the same time, organizational failures were at work, since Leeson was allowed to go adrift by a negligent if not implicitly complicit management at the bank. Barings management, in turn, could be so lackadaisical because it did not feel sufficiently monitored by the regulatory bodies, thus exposing weaknesses in the institutional fabric of the 'new' City. Yet, at the same time, global events and unforeseen economic contingencies played a role: the Kobe earthquake, which in turn affected Asian markets, which triggered the collapse of Leeson's trading scheme. In France, too, human, organizational and systemic factors seem to have interacted: well-designed and promptly executed changes in regulatory structure interacted in unforeseen ways with an ambitious bank president encouraged by his political protectors to set his organization on an adventurist and ultimately fatal course of risky deals. In France and in Spain, part of the failure had to do with 'politics' interfering with 'sound finance': in France, geostrategic political considerations prompted policy makers to want to position Crédit Lyonnais as a counterweight to German dominance of the European financial scene; in Spain, unravelling the closed shop arrangements of the Franco era required a protracted struggle between neoliberal reformists and the guardians of the status quo within the financial establishment. The need to compromise was hard to ignore, but the half-baked nature of the early reforms strongly contributed to the bank collapses that followed later. Interestingly, as in the steel sector, the wider political context – the impending accession to 'Europe' – played an important part in bringing about institutional changes in Spain in the first place. The Swedish case perhaps best illustrates the multicausal nature of failure in this sector, Tranøy's key argument being that Sweden drifted into recession (and its banking system into crisis) as a result of several different, uncoordinated macroeconomic and fiscal policies. In this sense, the core of the problem was an error of omission: Swedish policy makers and financial institutions either failed to grasp or to act upon the inflationary spiral springing from the interaction effects between apparently loosely coupled economic developments and policies.

Likewise, the 'success' cases do not demonstrate clearly how prudent financial policy ought to be made. In the German case, 'luck' was combined with virtue. The financial system was lucky in that it received a serious warning about the vulnerability of existing deposit protection schemes fairly early on, that is well before the neoliberal watershed in the world of finance had taken place, which could have raised considerably the price of the Herstatt and the other two bank failures that took place in 1974. The system was virtuous in the sense that both the state and the key financial institutions proved willing and able to learn from the Herstatt fiasco, and put in place new institutional arrangements that have since proved their viability. In the Dutch case, the absence of crises affecting Dutch banks (there was one instance in which the French-owned Slavenburg's bank collapsed owing to bad management practices), the regulatory regime could be adjusted slowly but surely to the international and technological changes. Within the Dutch finance policy community there were at times some tensions (between the ministry of finance and the national bank, for example), but these were neither very intensive nor politically significant in pursuing the liberalization path.

Explaining the depoliticization of failure

As mentioned above, several hypotheses were formulated in Chapter 2 purporting to explain discrepancies between programmatic and political assessments. More specifically, the politicization and depoliticization of programme failures was held to be contingent upon a number of factors.

- *The political structure* Following Lijphart (1999) we can expect political actors in consensual systems to be more inclined to 'absorb' programme failures without major political controversy, and those in majoritarian systems to be more combative about them, increasing the likelihood of political failures. In the financial sector, this hypothesis is not supported: in all of the six countries (three majoritarian, three consensual) the degree of politicization of bank failures and the attendant economic adversity was low.

- *The political culture*   The more a country or sector is characterized by norms of pragmatism and consensus the lower the likelihood of political failure. This hypothesis appears to have some relevance. In most of the countries studied here, policy towards the financial sector seems to have been a rather low-key affair, with strongly corporatist traditions (Germany) or cosy informal networks between government officials and bankers (UK, France, Spain). The sector traditionally enjoyed either a high degree of autonomy (Germany, Netherlands, UK) or was tightly embedded in the intricate machinery of the state's macroeconomic policy (Spain, France, Sweden). Whichever way was followed, policy was made in 'iron triangle'-like cliques of Treasury bureaucrats, central bankers and banking representatives, where norms of professionalism prevailed (Heclo, 1977). This was a world far removed from the more complex and open networks to be found in, for example, health policy.

- *Policy frames*   In such a world there was a relatively high degree of consensus about how the system should be governed. Policy actors may have argued about the settings of certain policy instruments (such as interest rates or credit allowances) but not about the fundamental objectives of policy, let alone about the definition of the situation created by the changes in the international financial system (see Hall, 1993). The protracted struggle that took place in Spain to reform the system was only partly an exception to this rule: reform was initiated by a new generation of post-Francoist technocrats, and in a sense it was not so much a political struggle as a transition from one type of institutional consensus in the epistemic community of economic management to another (cf. Haas, 1990).

- *Governance task*   The original hypothesis is taken from Lowi's (1964) typology and suggests that the more redistributive the nature of the policy, the higher the likelihood of politicization of programme failures. In the bank collapses and financial turbulence that occurred in the cases studied here, a lot of money was lost, including a lot of taxpayer money. Directly or indirectly, the (opportunity) costs of the programme failures that helped produce them were, therefore, considerable. Significant (sometimes double-digit) percentages of GNP evaporated or had to be used for bailouts in Sweden, Spain and France. However, the fact that this de facto entailed serious redistributive consequences never made it into the public imagination. Probably this had to do with the fact that the pain was spread across all taxpayers rather than concentrated in certain communities, as in the steel cases. It seems we need not Lowi, but Wilson (1980) to explain this. He hypothesized that this dimension (diffused v. concentrated) pay-offs or costs was a crucial one in determining the political interaction with regard to an issue.

- *Symbolic potential*   The final hypothesis postulated that an emotive subject matter would be more conducive to politicization than a technical one. The case studies, especially when compared to the findings of the other three sectors, seem to bear out this expectation.

Explaining universal consensualism

In the financial sector, all of the national policy makers studied here proceeded more or less in concert with the private actors. Neither the country nor the political identity of the incumbent government turns out to be a good predictor of its macroeconomic and microeconomic policy style. Why? There are various reasons:

- A more directive approach simply did not work: this was clearly proved by the experience of the early Mitterrand government (1981), whose Keynesian interventionist policies failed markedly in the increasingly open and deregulated economic environment. The French government was forced to make a quick U-turn in economic policy. In turn, the failure of state imposition in France was a key factor in converting Felipe González's Spanish social democrats to neoliberalist restraint in dealing with the markets.

- A more directive approach was not programmed into the sector's insti-tutional hardware. As mentioned above, in most of the countries the banking industry had enjoyed considerable leeway in running its own affairs within the parameters set by macroeconomic policy. When these controls were gradually released and their freedom to operate on the global markets was increased dramatically, none of the states took com-pensatory measures in the sense of improved facilities for monitoring the banks' behaviour or more stringent oversight of their modus operandi. If anything, the trend was towards a further disentangling and depoliti-cization of financial governance, including efforts to increase the independence of central banks from the national government. In the German case, the state was moved by political pressures in the immediate wake of the Herstatt crisis to assume a more directive role. Yet the sector effectively forestalled such intervention by showing prudent self-government and ensuring that public policy objectives were met through cooperation between financial actors, in concert with, but at a 'safe' distance from, the state.

At least up to the mid-1990s, it appears that regulating finance was just not an issue for forceful state action. Since that time, critical incidents such as the Barings collapse, the Asian crisis and the Latin American economic collapses have made it clear that the matter has now transcended the scope of national institutions and governance mechanisms altogether. The money flows have simply become too vast, too rapid and too volatile. The latent instabilities introduced into the global financial system by the rapid innovations made possible by liberalization and advanced information technology will now have to be dealt with by regional (European, Asian) and/or global (IMF) financial institutions.

As an aside, it should be observed that the normative superiority ascribed to consensualism by Lijphart (1999), who demonstrated empirically that consensual democracies performed better in terms of effectiveness and legitimacy, is not replicated in the banking cases either. Consensualism in one way or another prevailed in all the national approaches to financial sector governance but, as we have seen, their effectiveness differed markedly. This finding shows that Lijphart's claim is probably too wide: when coming down from the Olympic heights of entire political systems and entering the murky realities of individual policy sectors within those systems, a much more differentiated picture is likely to emerge, both empirically (policy style) and normatively (government performance).

5   MANAGING CRISIS: HIV AND THE BLOOD SUPPLY

Governing an Ill-structured Problem and a Political Crisis

With hindsight, the rise of the HIV/AIDS epidemic in the early 1980s can be defined as an extremely ill-structured problem. All of the authors of the case studies point out that the health authorities were faced with a new disease about which they had hardly any familiar clues. The epidemiological pattern of the disease was largely unknown until the discovery of the HIV viruses. It was unclear how many people were infected with HIV and how many of those infected would actually develop AIDS.

Within this critical challenge, the particular issue of preventing HIV contamination through blood transfusions and blood products presented health authorities with its own complexities. Given the initial uncertainties about the cause and patterns of HIV infections, authorities were faced with tragic choices when dealing with haemophiliacs. Treating them with the factor VIII and factor IX blood products might result in HIV infection and, possibly, in a premature death from AIDS. Denying them these highly effective treatments would strongly affect the quality of their lives and would seriously increase the risks of disablement and early death because of unstoppable bleeding. In several countries haemophiliacs initially opposed a ban on the use or import of factor VIII blood products. Similar ethical dilemmas rose with regard to transfusion blood. Excluding homosexuals or prison inmates from donating blood would decrease the likelihood of HIV contamination, but it might also lead to serious damage to the legitimacy of the voluntary donor system and to a shortage of blood.

Initially, in the early 1980s, the case of HIV infection through blood and blood products was not an acute, but rather a creeping crisis. There was a high level of uncertainty, but not always a corresponding sense of urgency among the health authorities, haemophiliacs or the general public. In the first years of the epidemic, the risks of the transmission of HIV through blood and blood products were not immediately clear. From a European perspective, the epidemic might very well have been only a North American phenomenon. Reliable tests and treatments of blood and blood products became available only gradually. The incubation time for AIDS was long. As a result, it took years before the major health crisis among the haemophiliacs and transfusion recipients actually materialized.

Because of this latter aspect, health authorities in a number of countries were in fact faced with two different crises. The initial, rather creeping, programmatical crisis was more or less resolved by the mid-1980s. By then, the issue of preventing AIDS and HIV had become a well-structured problem, at least in the Western world. A few years later, in the early 1990s, a much more acute political crisis broke out, when it became clear that many people had become fatally ill because they had been treated with HIV-contaminated blood or blood products in the early 1980s. This was most conspicuous in France, and to a lesser extent in Germany, the Netherlands, the UK and Spain. The nature of this second, political, crisis was very different from the first. It was a manifest crisis of legitimacy, but not an ill-structured problem. In most countries, except France, this second crisis could be handled by using routine strategies for crisis containment, depoliticization and blame avoidance.

Assessment: Disjunctures between Programmatic Performance and Political Legitimacy

Programmatic assessment

The fascinating thing about these case studies is their high level of comparability. In all of the countries studied, health authorities were faced with a similar problem at more or less the same time. They all had to struggle with the medical uncertainties and moral intricacies surrounding AIDS and HIV. In order to assess the effectiveness of their response, we have to take into account these uncertainties and intricacies. Paraphrasing De Vroom in Chapter 27 (on the

Netherlands), the central question is: did the policy system produce feasible solutions for problems that were observable at that time?

What differed was the context. The nature of the blood supply systems varied among the countries in our sample and therewith the risks of HIV contamination. In the early 1980s, Spain did not have a well-established system of voluntary donations and had to rely on paid donors and imports of transfusion blood. Germany, too, relied to some extent on paid donors. This strongly increased the risks of HIV contamination. France relied on voluntary donations, but the quality of its transfusion blood was not as high as in other countries with a system of voluntary donations, because blood was also collected in prisons, where a great number of inmates turned out to be HIV-infected intravenous drug users. With regard to the factor concentrate blood products, few countries were self-sufficient. Most countries imported blood products from the United States, which in hindsight turned out to be a major source of contamination. The level of the imports varied, however. Germany imported a majority of its blood products and Spain imported more than 80 per cent. France was self-sufficient and so was Sweden with regard to factor IX concentrate, but Sweden depended on imports for 40–50 per cent of its factor VIII consumption. Britain imported about half of its stock of factor VIII concentrate, but its use of this product was fairly limited. For these reasons, as Albaek has already pointed out in the introduction to Part V, output indicators, such as the number of HIV-infected transfusion patients or haemophiliacs per capita in each country, are unreliable indicators for success and failure of the governance task of managing the HIV and blood crisis.

Instead, we have looked at the timing of a number of preventive measures that became feasible during the early 1980s. When did the health authorities effectively implement feasible measures to prevent the spread of HIV through blood or blood products? We have scored each country on five preventive measures, two with regard to blood donations and three with regard to blood products. These scores are presented in Table 31.4.

At the top of the table we have given each country an overall programmatic assessment, on the basis of these comparative indicators. France scores below average when compared to the other countries studied. However, on the programmatic side, France is certainly not a downright failure. Local health and prison authorities were very late in effectively implementing the order to screen blood donors, which greatly added to the relatively high level of contamination of blood and blood products. On the other hand, France was comparatively early in testing all its blood for HIV – which is a surprising conclusion given the fact that the postponement of the Abbott test was one of the major contributing factors to the political crisis in France. France was, in fact, among the first to authorize and apply the American Abbott test, notwithstanding the political lobby for the home based Pasteur Diagnostics test. The major failure

Table 31.4 *Managing crisis, HIV and the blood supply: programmatic assessment*

Programmatic dimension	France	Germany	Netherlands	Spain	Sweden	UK
	–	+/–	++	– –	+	+/–
Effective donor selection	Mandatory 20/6/1983; implemented 1985–91	Informal practice 1/6/1983; mandatory 1/4/1988	Self-regulation 1/4/1983	Mandatory 9/10/1985; implemented 4/12/1985	Mandatory 1/10/1984	Informal practice 1/9/1983; guidelines 1/1/1985
Testing of all blood	1/8/1985	1/10/1985	1/6/1985	18/2/1987	1/10/1985	1/10/1985
Import stay on untreated blood products	Not relevant	?	Early 1983 (informal agreement)	1/10/1985	25/2/1985 (non-heated) 15/8/1985 (non-tested)	1/1/1985
Heating blood products	1/10/1985	1/2/1985	3/6/1985	1/10/1985 (?)	25/2/1985	1/7/1985
Untreated products off market*	1/10/1985	Early 1990	1/6/85 (non-tested) 1/1/88 (non-heated)	1/10/1985	15/4/1986	1/1/1986

Note:
* By this is meant an end to the delivery or sale of untreated products by manufacturers. It did not always imply a total recall of all untreated products from hospitals and patients.

in France has been the postponement of the mandatory heat treatment of blood products from June until October 1985 and the subsequent failure to withdraw unheated products from the stocks. Germany scored more or less the average. Effective donor selection was informally realized at an early stage and Germany was among the first to introduce the heat treatment of factor products. It took a very long time, however, before all the untreated products were effectively withdrawn from the market. The Netherlands did comparatively well on all counts. At an early stage, health authorities effectively implemented tests and treatments. Donor selection and a stay on imports of untreated products could also be realized early through informal agreements between health authorities, blood banks and intermediary organizations. Spain's handling of the HIV and blood crisis was by most standards a clear failure. This is particularly so with regard to blood donations. The authorities were very late in taking measures to select donors and, on top of that, ordered the screening of blood almost two years after this became feasible. Also Spain was relatively late in implementing a stay on imports of untreated products. Sweden did relatively well, although factor IX products which were not fully virus-inactivated were still on the market at a late stage. Finally, the performance of the UK is more or less average on most indicators.

The overall programmatic assessment of the management of the HIV and blood crisis, the governance challenge studied here, should be positive. The prevention of HIV dissemination through blood and blood products happened very fast. Most European countries adopted most of the preventive measures not long after they were introduced in the USA. From June 1981, when AIDS was first reported as an official clinical syndrome, only three years passed before effective measures to prevent blood-borne spreading of this hitherto unknown disease were developed. One year later most countries offering effective factor therapy to haemophiliacs had implemented most of these preventive measures, with the exception of Spain. It is difficult to think of any other infectious disease for which one of its modes of infection has been stopped so effectively, so fast.

With hindsight one can argue whether there may have been other feasible solutions available at that time that could have reduced the amount of HIV infection through the blood supply even further. A number of measures were not considered in general or at all in the international medical community, although in retrospect it would have been sensible to do so. The enthusiasm for the 1970s' formidable technical advances in blood therapy was such that it hindered a consideration of the obvious alternative in preventive policy to adopt less blood-consuming – and thereby safer – transfusion and haemophilia therapies. For instance, a temporary switch to the less effective, but much safer, cryoprecipitate therapy would have seriously reduced the chance of HIV infections. Effective therapy was given priority over safe therapy. The medical paradigm that effective therapy necessarily involved higher consumption of blood later turned out not to be universally true. Internationally, only a few countries and none of the six countries in this study, in their choice of policies diverged from the dominant policy understanding of the international blood community.

Political assessment

The governance challenge in most of the countries studied in fact consisted in managing two different types of crisis. We have therefore also asked the authors to assess whether and why the issue of HIV and blood turned into a political crisis in the early 1990s. The results of this political assessment are presented in Table 31.5. Again, we have given an overall assessment of the political appreciation of the issue in each country. This is followed by a more detailed assessment on the basis of a number of parameters that indicate whether the way the issue was handled by the national health authorities has been considered legitimate in each particular country. In most countries the political outcomes do not parallel the programmatic outcomes. This is most conspicuous in the case of France and Spain. By all standards, the issue of HIV and blood has resulted in a major crisis of legitimacy in France, notwithstanding the fact that French health authorities only performed below average on some of the programmatic indicators. The opposite has happened in Spain. The Spanish authorities have a very bad track record, but nevertheless hardly suffered politically. The issue of HIV and blood only stirred a minor scandal in Barcelona and has never jeopardized the legitimacy of the Spanish political or health system at the national level, as it has in France. Similar asymmetries can be found in Germany and the UK, both average performers programmatically, where incumbent health officials, like minister Seehofer in Germany and chief medical officer Acheson in the UK, even managed to gain political credit by acting in an expedient way once they found out about the issue. In none of the cases studied could a full symmetry be found between programmatic performance and political legitimacy, as can be seen from Figure 31.7.

Policy Style

In most countries studied, both the programmatic and the political crises were handled in line with the hypothesized national policy styles. Not surprisingly, in the Netherlands and Sweden the AIDS epidemic and the issue of safe blood were handled in an inclusive, strongly consensual way (Figure 31.8). All relevant actors, public organizations, private companies and intermediary organizations of haemophiliacs and homosexuals, were involved in the policy process. The blood policy subsystem was given considerable leeway in handling the issue in a cooperative and expedient way. The same was true of the political

Table 31.5 *Managing crisis, HIV and the blood supply: political assessment*

	France	Germany	Netherlands	Spain	Sweden	UK
Political dimension	– –	+	+	+/–	++	++
Media coverage • Judgement • Intensity	Very negative High	Mild Medium	Mild Low	Negative Incidental	Neutral Very low	Mild Low
Judgment of official investigative bodies	Negative reports by health, financial and police authorities	Negative report by parliamentary commission	Ombudsman investigation; negative on some points	Penal inquiry into Catalan case; no general inquiries	Mild report on Preconativ by health ministry	No specific official inquiries
Litigation	Nearly 2000 complaints; 34 executives on trial; four convicted so far	Most claims were settled; civil litigation against some officials; no convictions	None	Some civil litigation; two light penal sanctions of hospital officials	None	Some civil litigation; settled out of court
Compensation paid	1992, high	1986, medium	Late 1980s, low; 1996 medium	1993, low	1986, medium; 1991, high	1987, low; 1991, medium
Political casualties	Three former ministers on trial; major crisis of legitimacy	Federal health office dissolved; health minister Seehofer gets credit	None; formal excuses by minister of health	None; no major scandal	None; no scandal	None; credit for some officials
Public opinion	Very negative	Mildly positive	Neutral	Neutral	Absent	Mildly positive

634

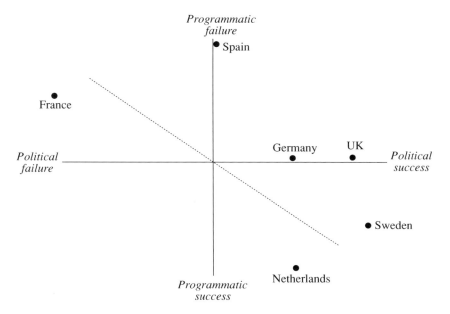

Note: The dotted line indicates full symmetry between programmatic and political outcomes.

Figure 31.7   Managing crisis in HIV and the blood supply: an integrated assessment

management of the crisis. The governments in both countries acted in a non-confrontational, consensual style, and therewith effectively managed to depoliticize the issue. To a lesser extent, this has been true of the UK and Germany. In both these countries a consensual style prevailed, although this was mixed with hierarchical elements in the UK or forced through by corporatist arrangements in Germany. The health authorities in Spain and France were far less responsive, and sometimes even hostile, towards the associations of haemophiliacs and other victims. A highly institutionalized and conservative blood sector dominated the health system and effectively locked out new actors or beneficiaries.

On the other axis we also see clear differences in the way policy makers responded to the crisis. The authorities in Sweden and the Netherlands were actively engaged at an early stage in discussing measures with the sectoral actors. We have labelled this as an anticipatory style, although we are aware that in a crisis like this anticipatory policy making is, almost by definition, not possible. Partly for the reasons just mentioned, the authorities in both Spain and, to a lesser extent, France acted in a reactive way. In Germany, too, regulatory capture contributed to a dominantly reactive style, with the exception of health minister Seehofer, who quickly responded when the issue hit the press.

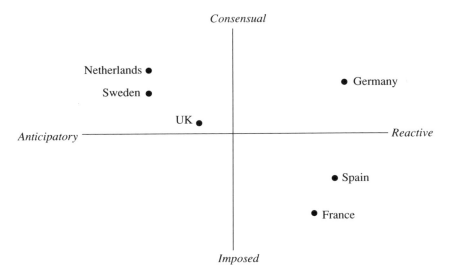

Figure 31.8   Managing crises in HIV and the blood supply: national policy styles

Explaining Patterns in Success and Failure

In sum, the assessment of the HIV and blood supply cases leaves us with two analytical questions: (a) why were the health authorities in some countries much swifter in solving the ill-structured problem of dealing with HIV in the blood supply, and (b) how can we explain the asymmetries in programmatic performance and political legitimacy?

Explaining the variations in programmatic performance
The health sector in general, and the blood subpolicy system in particular, is highly professionalized. This is the main reason why most countries succeeded in effectively preventing the dissemination of HIV through blood and blood products within a relatively short period. The existence of an international network of blood therapists allowed information on the contamination, and on tests and treatments, to travel at great speed and across national borders. Within most countries firmly institutionalized professional networks of researchers, therapists, manufacturers and regulators existed. These operated on the basis of

medical expertise and were given considerable autonomy in devising and implementing new technologies and therapies. At the same time, the very existence of a professional community of blood experts is, paradoxically, also one of the main causes of the perceived failures.

The clue to this paradox seems to lie in the relative institutional and intellectual openness of the professional policy community. The major explanation for the relatively swift response to the issue of HIV and blood in the Netherlands, according to de Vroom, lies in the specific mode of governance that was developed in the Dutch case. Public and private actors, vested professional institutions and intermediary organizations of haemophiliacs and homosexuals cooperated on an equal basis in the definition, formulation and implementation of preventive policies. The role of state actors was limited to a horizontal coordination of the discussions and negotiations. In the early phase of the crisis, when the policy problem was ill-structured and when uncertainty was rampant, this was the most effective way to develop feasible, acceptable and legitimate solutions (although de Vroom adds that a more hierarchical approach might have been more effective in the later, implementation stages of policy making). Similarly, in Sweden professional autonomy and cooperation between central and local actors as well as public and private actors is the major explanation for the swift and effective responses with regard to the developing crisis. But even in open professional communities such as the Dutch and the Swedish, professionalism may also have been an obstacle to effective problem solving. The professional agreement on the advantages of the dominant therapeutic paradigm in haemophilia treatment was so overwhelming that its wisdom in the face of the AIDS epidemic was never questioned. In Sweden, the discovery of the deficient method used to treat factor IX products demonstrated that medical regulators too uncritically presumed that professional responsibilities would automatically overrule commercial incentives in the pharmaceutical industry.

In contrast, in France, and to a somewhat lesser extent in Germany, the professional community was characterized by institutional closure and regulatory capture. Donor associations and pharmaceutical companies, who had a vested interest in maintaining the status quo, dominated the policy networks. Health authorities were dependent on these actors for expertise and information. Processes of cognitive dissonance and goal displacement could develop because dissident opinions or outsider perspectives were effectively blocked. Secrecy, confidentiality and intellectual homogeneity prevailed. The latter was also the case in Sweden, with regard to factor IX concentrate.

The bad performance of Spain can partly be explained along these lines too. The Francoist health system was particularly badly adapted to solve an ill-structured problem like the rise of HIV and AIDS. Institutional structures and practices for preventive health care were mostly lacking. When the AIDS epidemic struck, civil society in Spain was still very weak. Transfusion patients did not have any public voice whatsoever and the haemophiliacs, although better organized, remained very passive politically throughout the 1980s. To make things worse, the transition from a centralized to a decentralized system of health care badly interfered with the crisis as it blurred responsibilities and eroded the capacity of central authorities to implement and monitor effectively the preventive measures that were ordered. In the early 1980s, public health authorities' attention was focused on the construction of a new balance of power between the state and the regional institutions. This prevented the development of a more cooperative style of policy making, as most preventive measures were interpreted as moves in the struggle for institutional power.

Explaining asymmetric politicization

In Chapter 2, we formulated the Candide interpretation of governance as our null-hypothesis: if authorities do well programmatically, they will be rewarded politically, and if programmes fail to perform as expected, this will lead to commensurate negative political feedback. This hypothesis is not supported in any of the case studies. In none of the cases can a full symmetry in outcomes be found. Of the two rival hypotheses, the Cassandra hypothesis is not supported either. In most cases in which the political legitimacy remained high, this is not primarily caused by the deliberate deployment of manipulative strategies for blame avoidance by the authorities. More importantly, the asymmetries between programmatic performance and political perception go both ways, as could be seen in the case of France. Even health authorities that performed comparatively very well, for example in the Netherlands, were nevertheless confronted with some political headwinds.

How can we explain these discrepancies between programmatic performances and the level of politicization? In Chapter 2 we also formulated propositions with regard to a number of relevant factors.

- *The political structure*   The hypothesis that consensual democracies will show lower levels of politicization than majoritarian systems is partly supported in the HIV and blood crises. In the three countries with strong consensual and corporatist traditions, Germany, the Netherlands and Sweden, no major political crises occurred. In Sweden, for example, all relevant political actors were represented in a high-profile committee that was established to deal with the rise of AIDS at an early stage. This committee forged a strong consensus and forestalled the emergence of any serious opposition. In France, on the other hand, no cross-party cooperation and consensus occurred. On the contrary, the HIV and blood crisis was played up in the election campaign and used by the opposition to discredit the socialist government. The UK is the atypical case in this respect, a majoritarian political structure in which nevertheless a cross-party consensus emerged over AIDS and HIV, which resulted in low levels of politicization.

- *The political culture* Here the hypothesis was that a country or sector in which pragmatism, consensus and cooperation prevail would show lower levels of politicization. This hypothesis is basically confirmed in the cases of HIV and blood. In Sweden, the UK, Germany and the Netherlands, which all did well politically, the claims and complaints of the various affected groups were handled in a pragmatic, non-confrontational way. In Sweden, the Haemophilia Society was effectively coopted into the policy subsystem, and the government offered to fund all its programmes for the infected members. Also the Swedish government pragmatically applied existing medical insurance schemes to infected haemophiliacs and transfusion patients. In the UK, too, according to Freeman, pragmatism is the dominant policy style in much of health care policy making and this was particularly so in the case of AIDS and HIV. Most of the issues that arose were framed as non-ideological, professional matters and handled in an expedient way. In Germany, minister Seehofer effectively controlled the political damage by using a pacification strategy that befitted the German, consensual political culture. In the Netherlands, too, the policy subsystem was very open to the intermediary organizations of haemophiliacs and gays, and they were effectively coopted into the policy-making process. As in Sweden, they were in fact made partly responsible for the policies that were pursued. Moreover, the Dutch minister of health, Borst, acted in a non-confrontational fashion. She immediately acknowledged government liability, offered public apologies and was willing to offer more generous compensation. In France, however, the political crisis was handled in a rather different key. In France, secrecy, confidentiality and closure prevailed. Donor associations and the blood centres dominated the blood sector. According to Steffen, little attention was given to the rights of patients. They were not coopted but confronted by the donor associations and the health authorities. Public authorities were very late and reluctant in offering compensation or any other form of assistance to HIV victims or their associations. Thus the latter were more or less forced to turn to the courts. The result was a litigation explosion, extensive media attention and a high level of politicization. Spain is the odd case in this respect. Despite its relatively bad performance, public upheaval remained limited to two Catalan cases of negligence. The Spanish organizations of haemophiliacs, although well established, chose to negotiate discretely with the authorities and refrained from litigation, except for Catalonia. Blood transfusion patients were not organized collectively and were even more reluctant to come out in the open. Only a few dozen chose to litigate against the government. According to Jordana, this can be explained by the social stigma which was attached to AIDS at the time. In general, it is safe to say that, even until the early 1990s, Spanish civil society was relatively weak, and its political culture reactive or even passive, when compared to most of the other countries studied.

- *Policy frame*   Here the hypothesis was that an inverse relation would exist between the epistemic homogeneity within the policy sector and the level of politicization. This is hardly supported here. In all of the countries studied, the blood sector was originally characterized by professionalism and epistemic homogeneity. Nevertheless, the levels of politicization varied. In France, the country with by far the highest level of politicization, the blood sector was extremely institutionalized and offered an almost perfect example of sectoral corporatism with high levels of paradigmatic consensus.
- *Governance task*   In the aftermath of the HIV and blood crisis, redistributive issues became of great importance. Unlike what happened with the crisis in the financial sector, the costs of the failure of governance had to be borne by specific groups. HIV-infected haemophiliacs and transfusion patients were clearly identifiable (and 'innocent') victims, and the stories of their wretched lives and miserable deaths triggered media attention and the subsequent political crises. In line with the hypothesis, those governments (Sweden, UK, Germany) which quickly responded to the redistributive issues by offering compensation schemes had the lowest levels of politicization.
- *Symbolic potential*   Here the hypothesis was that the more emotive the subject matter is, the higher the likelihood of an intense politicization of the failure. This seems an important clue in both the French and the Spanish asymmetries. In France, the institutional structure and ethos of the blood provision system went back as far as World War II. Its self-sufficiency was a source of national pride and donating blood was seen as a matter of citizenship. Thus, in France, the contamination of this vital fluid with the deadly HIV viruses, which could not be attributed to foreign sources, shocked the national self-image. And worse still, a sector that hitherto had always been associated with altruism and citizenship turned out to be tainted with commercial interests. In Spain, the negative stigma that was attached to AIDS, which was perceived by the general public as a disease of sexual perverts and drugs addicts, kept many victims from going public with their cases. In that particular case the negative emotions effectively hindered politicization.

32. The state of governance in six European states

Mark Bovens, Paul 't Hart and B. Guy Peters

1 COMPARING PERFORMANCE ACROSS COUNTRIES AND ACROSS SECTORS

With the information we have amassed to this point we can begin to make some comparisons concerning the relative governance capacity within the four policy sectors we have been examining, as well as the apparent governance capacity of different political systems. These comparative points must be considered very tentative generalizations, given that they are based on a limited number of cases and a limited number of policy areas. Still, this is perhaps the most systematic comparison of these two dimensions of governance that is as yet available, given that for each policy area we have closely matched case studies in the six countries. Likewise, these four policy areas were not selected at random but were chosen to represent important dimensions of governance capacity and the six countries also were selected to represent variations in political structures and political styles.

2 NATIONAL STRENGTHS AND WEAKNESSES

If we begin with the conventional comparative question of which country performs best, the winner on the programmatic dimension appears to be the Netherlands, with the United Kingdom also scoring rather well. This is interesting given that these two countries have rather disparate approaches to governance. The Dutch style (see below) tends to be one of building consensus between state and society, and within the public sector itself. Consultation is central to this governance approach, and the case studies report on consultations in most of the policy areas. Consultation should be expected to be important for the political success of a policy, but also appears (again based on a limited 'sample' of cases) to be useful in producing programme success as well. As well as building consensus, the consultative style of governing appears to open up government to the full range of information available, and therefore improve the probability of finding a 'correct' policy choice. This impact of the quality of decisions was particularly evident in the HIV case in the Netherlands. Interestingly, however, Sweden tends to utilize much of the same consensual style of governing but this has enjoyed somewhat less success. In reading the cases, one sees that Sweden actually has blended its consultation with a strong portion of *étatisme*, a blend that does not appear to be particularly successful.

Politically, the overall results were not much different from the programmatic outcomes. France and Spain tended to be less successful in constructing their actions in ways that were acceptable to the public, or to other political actors. This was particularly evident in the case of France and HIV blood, but was found in several of the cases. Again, the tendency not to consult, and to proceed along paths determined largely by the interests of government organizations or politicians themselves, characterized policy making in these countries. While there were notable political failures in the other countries, the more open and consultative styles of all the other countries produces greater political responsiveness and apparently greater political success.

The differences (both positive and negative) are not so great that one can make definitive statements about the governance capacity of these governments, but the two southern European countries do appear to have been more likely to fail when faced with significant challenges to their governance capacities. This has been true both programmatically and politically. If the argument about the role of consultation in the more successful cases is correct then the centralized and *étatiste* character of these two countries might have been expected to be associated with less successful governance, and indeed it is. The political failures in particular appear to be a function of the tendency to use *raison d'État* to justify actions and thereby to ignore effectively public opinion and the role of pressure groups. The centralized, government-dominant system seems particularly ill-suited to novel and poorly defined issues, just the types of issues that are likely to become more common in present-day governing. It was perhaps particularly telling that these two governments were notably less successful than the others in coping with the HIV blood crisis. One might hypothesize that the more centralized and didactic regimes might be much better at dealing with crises than would other types of governments, but that does not appear to have been the case.

The Lijphart (1999) distinction between majoritarian and consensual *structures* appears less useful in this explanation than does the more cultural explanation. That is, the UK as the only real majoritarian case in this group of countries was rather successful both politically and programmatically, while several of the consensual countries were not so successful. Spain and, especially, France are less clearly majoritarian but do have some characteristics of that type of political system and have tended to be the least successful cases in this sample. On the other hand, the clearest consensual cases of the Netherlands and Sweden have been successful while the somewhat less clear example of consensual democracy in Germany was somewhat less successful. One preliminary conclusion that could be drawn from these findings is that either of the two forms of governing can be successful, but that mixtures of the two types may not be as viable.

When we turn to examine the outcomes of these cases across the policy sectors, the first thing that is apparent, and rather heartening for students of the public sectors, is that there are perhaps more successes than might have been expected, given the conventional wisdom about the prevalence of failures and fiascos in the public sector. There are some notable failures, but the large majority of the cases are considered by the authors to be programmatically successful. Somewhat fewer cases were deemed by the analysts to be political successes as well, but even in this category the public sector did not perform as badly as Cassandra might have expected. The Candide interpretation of (de)politicization, formulated in the second chapter, is, by and large, supported by our cases too. The number of symmetrical cases is much larger than the asymmetrical ones. In most cases there is a fair symmetry between the programmatic performance and the political credit of policy makers.

These findings are particularly interesting given that these policy areas were selected to represent serious challenges to the governance capacity of these systems. Governments have been capable of responding to a variety of challenges and to generate reforms that were both effective and politically palatable.

3   SECTORAL STRENGTHS AND WEAKNESSES

Moving from the generalities to look at the relative level of success in the four policy areas it seems that governments were most successful in managing decline in the *steel industry*. In some ways this is to be expected, given that these governments had been in the steel business for some time and therefore understood the issues involved in making steel and the labour-management issues, even if they did not fully comprehend the dynamics in the international political economy that were producing the decline in the industry. Further, the relatively gradual and, to some extent, foreseeable nature of this problem may have made it substantially easier for governments to manage. The decline in this industry occurred over a long period of time, but a good deal of the political decision making occurred during a period in which government intervention in the economy, especially to bail out 'sunset' industries, had become less politically acceptable.

Interestingly, the management of health cost containment and control of the *medical profession* was also relatively successful. Policy making in this field might have been expected to be less effective programmatically as well as politically, given that in each country the government was confronting extremely powerful professional interest groups with relatively few countervailing groups to support its attempts to control health costs. Policy makers effectively made use of the increasing heterogeneity within the medical sector. In this sector Sweden appears to have been perhaps the only significant failure, although it might be argued that the major successes for Sweden in this field had occurred some years earlier. Moreover, the particular case studied in Sweden was rather at odds with the prevalent policy style. Also the experience of France is certainly not a model of success in controlling the medical profession. In part the continuous and nagging nature of the problem appears to have enabled the government to wear down the resistance of these powerful groups and to mobilize public resources to confront the issue.

As noted, there are some disjunctures between programmatic and political assessment. It is easy to see why cases that are programmatic successes are also political successes, and why failure on one dimension is related to failure on the other. The more interesting cases are when the two dimensions diverge and the political reactions to government action are different from the actual performance of government. This divergence reflects the capacity of governments to depoliticize the problems they encounter in making and implementing policies, as well as the control that governments have been able to take over the sources of information about many policy areas, especially those about which there is less reliable information available within the private sector. The management of innovation in *financial regulation* represents the most interesting policy area demonstrating the disjuncture between programmatic and political criteria for evaluation. In this policy area all the countries could be counted as political successes even though four of the six were probably programmatic failures. In these latter cases governments had several positive aspects of the cases favouring their political success. First, compared to HIV blood or even control of the medical profession, this was not an emotive issue. Much of the high-level 'wheeling and dealing' in the financial sector is remote from the experience and understanding of the average citizen, so that he or she had difficulty becoming involved. In addition, governments could put much of the blame for programmatic failure on individual weaknesses rather than on the weaknesses of their governance apparatus. Thus governments could construct these failures, even those involving huge amounts of money, as simply the products of greed and incompetence among the private actors, rather than incompetence in the public sector. This means that the capacity to *de*politicize is perhaps even more crucial for the political success of a government than the capacity to construct political events as it would like (Edelman, 1971, 1988).

The other sector in which disjunctures between programmatic and political assessments were found was in the management of HIV in the *blood supply*.

Unlike financial regulation, this is a very emotive issue, especially in France, which had the greatest political fall-out over the issue. Further, this issue was one which many citizens appeared to understand, even if only at a visceral level. The depoliticization strategy was therefore less viable and governments had to think of ways to manage the issue politically in a more direct manner. The strategy (whether adopted wittingly or not) that appears to have been successful is to be non-confrontational and to accept responsibility even when the actual culpability of the public sector was less than complete. While some politicians 'stonewalled' and denied that they or the government had any responsibility for the negative outcomes, the more successful politicians avowed that the public sector was indeed culpable at least in part and attempted to respond positively to the human crisis involved. The odd case out was Spain, for which the Contingentia hypothesis, formulated in Chapter 2, seems to apply. In the late 1980s, federal health policy makers were just lucky that civil society was still reactive and that the negative stigma of HIV infection effectively hindered politicization.

We should also look at cases in which adequate performance by the public sector resulted in a less than favourable political rating. The problem is that there are really no clear cases of this type. The closest is the UK and management of the medical profession. Although this was far from a manifest political failure there were still some political repercussions. The fact that programmatic successes in most cases lead to an assessment of political success is to some extent a heartening finding for those who, like Key (1966), argue that 'the ordinary voter is no fool'. A less positive assessment of this finding would be that governments have developed a substantial capacity to control the presentation of their policies to the public and to manage the news. The Blair government in the UK may be the principal example of control and 'spin-doctoring', but all governments now are capable of ensuring that such good news as is available is in the hands of the public. As noted above, the Candide interpretation is not supported fully, but there is some hope for the capacity of governments that do perform well to be rewarded for their policy successes.

4   COMPARING POLICY STYLES

We have also discussed these cases in terms of the policy styles being used. We have already noted that the concept of policy style has been questioned by critics, and this research provides an opportunity to look more carefully at the utility of the concept. That utility can be twofold. First, the concept of style may be descriptively useful and may be employed to characterize the policy process in different political systems. Does the same style appear in the same country in the same way in all policy areas, or are the findings more varied than that? The concept may be predictively useful as well. Can we predict the success and failure of a policy (programmatic, political or both) based on the policy style adopted, or are the outcomes of these cases too disparate to support such theory building about public policy?

The empirical evidence here seems to allow us to argue that the policy styles of some countries are more stable and clearly defined than are those of others. In particular, the Netherlands and Sweden emerged as consensual in almost all the cases, as would be expected from the conventional discussions of politics in these two countries. Germany also emerges as relatively consensual, as does Spain. The latter case is the more interesting: given its political history and its majoritarian governments it might be expected to rely more on imposition. In general, the governing style of all these countries emerged as more consensual than might have been expected from the literature, reflecting perhaps continuing changes in the style of politics in all industrialized democracies.

If we examine the other dimension of policy style, reactive versus anticipatory, there was considerable variation among the policy areas in the way the actors involved attempted to deal with the future course of policies. For most of the policies the Netherlands, Spain and the UK tended to be relatively anticipatory, while the other states tended to be reactive. The findings for financial regulation were somewhat the reverse, with Spain and France being more anticipatory systems. If the concept of policy style is to be a robust description of the manner in which policy is made in the individual countries, there should not be the degree of variation across policy areas that was found. Further, in the cases of steel and health there was a good deal of movement of countries from one style to another – in some cases to diametrically opposed styles – in the course of the time period investigated. While this is indicative of a substantial learning capacity on the part of these governments, it does not lend much support to the policy styles argument.

There seems to be some covariance between policy area and policy style, just as there is for countries. In particular, the financial regulation example had a large majority of consensual policy styles adopted, even for countries for which this was not expected. Further, this was a policy area in which we might have expected rather strong interventions by government: regulation (as well as deregulation) tends to involve the use of the legal authority of the state to achieve its policy goals. On the contrary, the fundamental policy style in this area was building consensus among the actors involved. It may be that this policy area was sufficiently new and innovative for the interests involved to be insufficiently entrenched to require the imposition of government authority.

The use of policy styles as an explanation for performance receives somewhat more support in these data. The most important element in the discussion of the above findings is that consensual politics tends to be more successful than the politics of imposition in almost all our policy areas. This is true whether the consensual style is implemented by countries in which it should be expected (the Netherlands) or by countries in which it is not expected (Spain). Thus it appears that the nature of modern politics is that attempts to build consensus when making policy are more effective than attempts to impose authority. The reactive versus anticipatory dimension, on the other hand, does not appear to have much relationship to the success or failure of a programme, or of its politics. This may reflect the difficulties encountered by any government attempting to anticipate socioeconomic change and create responses prior to that problem actually manifesting itself.

The idea of policy style is intuitively appealing, and appears to capture a great deal of what we know about policy making in a range of political systems. Despite the face validity of the concept, it has not proved itself to be very robust or effective in this analysis. In particular, it is not effective in differentiating among countries. There is a range of available political systems in this selection of countries, but these do not emerge in the analysis. These countries do at times display some of the behaviour expected of them, but they are almost as likely to act in the opposite manner. These styles do have a somewhat better record in predicting the success of policies, and in explaining their political palatability. In many ways, however, policy style may be better conceived of as a dependent variable, the product of other political forces rather than a more free-standing explanatory concept.

5   EXPLANATORY FACTORS

Each of the discussions of policy sectors addresses the several hypotheses we developed earlier as possible comparative explanations for the findings concerning differences in the policy choices and the success of governments. There are five major explanations with which we have been working throughout the analysis of these 24 cases in public policy making (see Chapter 2, as well as the sector overviews in Chapter 31). From Chapter 31 it becomes clear that some of these clearly did not work well, particularly the governance task and symbolic potential hypotheses. The most crucial explanatory angles contained in the original five hypotheses appeared to be the following.

- *National political structure and culture*   As Arend Lijphart (1999) argues, the best explanation of differences in policy choices is the insti-tutional apparatus responsible for making the decisions; or, as Sven Steinmo (1993) put it, 'It *is* the institutions, stupid.' In the Lijphart version of the structural explanation, the institutions in question are conceptual-ized primarily in rather formalistic terms, and are defined primarily in terms of the nature of parliamentary majorities and the interactions of actors in legislative and political executive institutions.

- *Sectoral traditions and institutions* It may be that there are more differences across sectors than there are across countries. The constellation of interests, ideas and institutions that shape each policy area may have more influence than differences in political structures. To some extent the ideas governing these policy areas are the same across countries, as with the ideas of the medical profession, for example, but in others there may be national variations in those ideas. The same goes for the networks of actors associated with sectoral traditions and institutions, which surround all policy areas. All policy areas have networks of interest groups and other state actors surrounding them, and these can be seen as the repositories of some of the ideas and policy frames that influence policy, as theorized by Sabatier in his work on advocacy coalitions (Sabatier, 1998). The difficulty is that the network explanation itself is rather indeterminate (Dowding, 1995; Marsh and Smith, 2000), and simply saying that networks exist does very little to improve the strength of network explanations. For example, there were networks at work in all the HIV blood cases we have presented but the strength and content of those networks was sufficiently different to produce widely different outcomes.

From the discussion of Chapter 31, we can also infer several other possible explanations for the policy outcomes within and across various sectors and countries.

- *Situational contingencies and trends* An alternative explanation, in some ways almost the null hypothesis, is that the particular situations and confluence of events may have greater influence than any more systematic relationships. This 'explanation' is also very much like the garbage can model (Cohen *et al.*, 1972) in placing the explanatory burden on particular, almost random, combinations of opportunities and solutions.
- *Leadership and statecraft* Another possible explanation is that people matter at least as much as institutions, so that the best way to explain the different outcomes observed among these countries is that the men and women in power are crucial, be they the classic figure of the strong political leader or government minister, or the more contingent figure of the policy entrepreneur (Kingdon, 1984). This explanation should be extended to include the government capacity of the systems in question, meaning in particular the capabilities of the public bureaucracy and its ability to make and implement policy.

- *Transnational dependencies and governance mechanisms*   We have focused attention on national governments, and indeed do believe that this level remains significant in understanding public policy. That having been said, however, these countries are all members of the European Union and a host of other international regimes. In addition, the international market place has an increasingly important influence on a range of public policies, and countries also have the capacity to learn from one another how to improve their policies (Rose, 1993).

Let us briefly review what can be concluded about these various analytical angles. The general problem we face is part and parcel of the rather loosely structured comparative case method used in this project: each of these explanations is plausible and each of the factors probably has at least some influence over each case for which we have data. Therefore presuming to reject any of these hypotheses on the basis of the relatively small data set is at best risky, and at worst simply foolish. Still, these 24 cases do enable us to say which of the alternatives is the more likely to yield theoretical fruit in the future and which seems to merit somewhat less future attention.

We have already noted the extent to which institutional explanations, at least those based on the rather simple and formal differences among institutions, do not have much credibility based on these results. This is in part a problem with the notion of institutions used here. The consensual/majoritarian difference is probably too gross a conceptualization to use for explaining policy, even if it is useful for explaining political stability and resilience. The same sort of finding, that the ability to use the rather broad differences between presidential and parliamentary regimes or between different types of parliamentary regimes to explain policy is limited, has been demonstrated in other research projects (Weaver and Rockman, 1996).

On the other hand, however, we can recognize that the consensual style of policy making (taken perhaps more broadly than in the Lijphart characterization) is important for understanding success and failure in policy making. This broader conception of consensualism may be as much cultural as it is structural, and involves the way in which political systems, taken rather broadly, choose to involve civil society in policy. Political culture is as least as slippery a concept as the institutional variables we have been discussing (Wildavsky, 1987), so we should not immediately resort to the cultural level to find an explanation. Still the consensual element of the policy style explanation does appear to reveal a good deal about the way government is able to perform its tasks. This explanation may also be related to the positive utilization of networks to link state and society. Also networks should be seen as at least as useful in linking different parts of government as in linking that government to the society. Successful governments increasingly need to be able to link different policy areas and to coordinate a range of policy interventions. We see this somewhat less in these cases (with the exception of steel) than we might in many others, but as we think about explanations the need to manage across the public sector should not be forgotten.

Following from the above comment, we should also remember that institutions can be conceptualized as something more than just formal structures. March and Olsen (1989), for example, argue that institutions are defined more by their ideas – 'logic of appropriateness' – than they are either by 'logics of consequentiality' or by their formal structures. For the policy areas we have examined, each policy within each country has its own version of what actions are considered appropriate, closely related to the idea of sectoral traditions mentioned above. In this view, normative institutionalism and historical institutionalism (Steinmo *et al.*, 1992) are more closely related than is usually assumed (Peters, 1999). The historical institutionalists' assumption that initial policy choices made in a policy area tend to be largely determinative for future policy making may simply be a way of saying that a logic of appropriateness exists. Those logics of appropriateness are to some extent similar across countries, based on the existence of epistemic communities (Haas, 1990). Yet there are also national differences based on national variations in the interpretation of the knowledge base of the policy field, as well as political differences in the various countries.

The concept of the 'logic of appropriateness' within a policy area emphasizes the importance of ideas in explaining policy choices. That having been said, the mechanisms through which ideas come to influence policy are not always clear. In some cases there does appear to be a *Zeitgeist* that has a pervasive influence over policies. This may be seen, for example, in the financial regulation cases, given that there was a powerful and pervasive set of ideas in place about the primacy of markets and the need to rethink government involvement. Still those ideas must be converted from simply a set of ideas into operational concepts. This process of using ideas is still rather poorly understood in the policy sciences, especially when these issues are considered comparatively. Paul Sabatier (1998) has looked at the use of ideas within the context of learning theory, while Schon and Rein (1994) discuss the utilization of ideas more in terms of 'policy frames' that define the realm of possible, or at least conceivable, outcomes. Ideas do appear to be useful in explaining stable policy regimes in which the ideas have been institutionalized over a period of time, but they appear somewhat less useful in explaining policy change. That is, if governments must cope with a rapidly changing set of ideas (as in the case of HIV/AIDS) they may not be able to bring those ideas into the process readily.

To this point the argument has been that ideas and logics of appropriateness do have some impact on policy choices as well as on the success and failure of those policies, with the implicit assumption that the issues involved are rather clearly defined and the information available is unambiguous. We might argue, however, that one of the principal governance tasks facing any political system is shaping the issues and defining just what the nature of the issue is. Take, for example, the steel issue we have used here. We have initially dealt with this as an issue of managing decline. This seemed a reasonable and useful construction, but in doing the studies we discovered that in most countries a lot of the action evolved around efforts by some participants in the process to define the issue rather differently. Further, the definition of the policy issue can influence the range of actors who are involved and which actors they are. If it is a regional policy issue it will invoke a very different set of actors than it might if it were defined more as a labour issue or simply an industrial issue. This point leads to an analytic question for policy analysis: the need to think about policy issues not so much in terms of the functional titles such as steel or agriculture but more in terms of the dimensions of these issues.

If we can place less reliance for explanation on formal institutional structures than we might have thought when initiating this analysis, we also should be somewhat dubious about the globalization/Europeanization explanation. It is clear that in the steel cases, as well as in the financial regulation cases, the international market was crucial in creating the need for policy interventions. That finding is not, however, the same as providing explanations for differences among national interventions or differences in the success of those interventions. In the financial regulation cases in particular the international environment did create different opportunities for countries depending upon their access to that market and the general strength of their economies. Despite those external pressures for some convergence, several countries still responded in somewhat distinctive, national manners (see also Scharpf, 2000). If we had used different policy areas for our examples, say if the cases had been drawn from agriculture or competition policy, then 'Brussels' would have been a much more important influence on the policies selected by governments. However, even in the finance case here the European influence was not nearly as strong as might have been expected from all the popular and academic concern about internationalization.

As well as the policy styles that influence policy choices, there may also be administrative traditions that influence the ways in which governments implement policies, and which may also contribute significantly to the success or failure of the programme. Most of the literature on public policy focuses on formulation to explain the nature of policies and their success. There is, however, a significant independent impact of implementation and administration on programmes and their success. Among the countries we have in this sample there is a wide range of administrative styles, just as there is a range of policy styles. Further, just as policy styles are more or less inclusive and consensual, so too are administrative styles, so that bureaucracies more willing to negotiate and discuss their activities may be more successful than those that continue to govern through *fiat* and imposition. In particular, the French and Spanish administrations coming from the Napoleonic tradition have found it difficult to adjust to a more democratic style of management. Thus, if we want to use policy styles as an explanatory factor, it appears that we need to spread the net somewhat more broadly and create a broader conception of what 'style' means (see Peters *et al.*, 2000).

The case studies we have presented here focus more on structural and institutional explanations of policies and their successes, and tended to emphasize the role of individual decision makers somewhat less. This is true both for the programmatic successes and failures and for the political dimension. This focus on structures is in contrast to the usual journalistic and even historical literature that focuses on individuals and their impacts on policy choices. There were certainly some instances among these 24 cases in which individuals did become crucial, not only as agents of policy change, such as health minister Seehofer in Germany, but also as political scapegoats for failures, such as his colleague in France. We therefore need to think about the way in which to incorporate the individual element into the analysis in a systematic manner. Otherwise, like the culture explanation above, this could simply be a residual explanation that is used when others have failed. The contrary danger, however, is that this becomes simply a more systematic version of the 'great man [person]' theory of history.

Also, as intimated above, any explanation based on individual factors should also take into account the role of public administrators as well as political officials. This is often difficult to do, given the self-effacing nature of most public servants in these democratic systems and the tendency of politicians to be substantially less self-effacing. Still modern political systems – especially the complex systems discussed here – tend to be subject to major influence from their bureaucracies and individual public servants within them. Likewise, there may be a need in some instances also to include the role of individuals in the private sector who have a pervasive impact on policy. However, as we discussed with regard to the role of ideas and networks, we will need to specify the ways in which these individuals work their way through the policy-making system.

6   SOME QUALIFICATIONS

This chapter has demonstrated, if nothing else, that explanation in comparative public policy is an extremely difficult undertaking. The findings that we have would be, in the terms of statistical models, overdetermined, with at least as many explanations as observations, so that it is difficult to distinguish any clear causal patterns. Even in these carefully selected cases there is sufficient variance within to make generalizations suspect. Comparative analysis presents a number of particular problems for this study, given that we get the countries involved as huge 'packages' of potential independent variables, and have little opportunity to control for the range of factors influencing the outcomes. This problem arises in any attempt at comparative analysis, but is perhaps even more evident here, given the range of possible influences on public policies, especially policies such as HIV and blood that have such strong emotive and cultural elements bound up in them.

We have been placing much of the blame for failures in developing strong conclusions about comparative policy on the comparative politics dimension of the analysis, but we might also raise questions about the other dimension of analysis: policy sciences. One of the most important dimensions of policy analysis that has yet to be attacked systematically is the definition and analysis of policy problems (Dery, 1984; Rochefort and Cobb, 1993; Hisschemöller and Hoppe, 1995). We have constructed the discussed governance challenges here in particular ways, but these were by no means the only fashion in which they could have been analysed. Further, even with these constructions we may need to move the discussion in an even more analytic dimension to ask what are the underlying dimensions of problems. Are the goods involved divisible or more classic public goods? Are the issue areas captured by interest groups or are they more subject to control by government itself? This list could be extended, but the point would remain the same: both comparative politics and policy sciences are challenged by these findings.

All the above having been said, we have been able to tease out some preliminary conclusions and generalizations. Perhaps the clearest of these is the importance of building cooperative and collaborative structures within the public sector, and between the public and private sectors, if one wants to enhance one's probabilities of policy success. We might have expected more consensual systems to have been capable of averting political problems, but it appears that this pattern of governing is also crucial for achieving programmatic success in governing. It is perhaps particularly interesting that this style of governing appears successful even in political systems that are generally characterized as more centralizing and hierarchical.

Despite the somewhat indeterminate nature of these findings, we are not yet ready to say that this is a garbage can in which outcomes are purely situational and random. There are some regularities in these data, and some countries do tend to perform better than others, and some policy areas do appear more amenable to being managed than others.

7   ANOTHER CHANCE MEETING

After a gap of over three years Candide and Cassandra happened to meet again, this time in a coffee house in Leiden. After exchanging pleasantries and expressing their mutual surprise at again meeting by accident, they returned to the old subject of the governance capacity of the public sector in European countries. They had both heard that a major research project had been launched soon after their initial encounter, designed to investigate their concerns about the possible failures of public programmes, and each had been able to get his or her hands on copies of the papers in the project. Although they had looked at the same 24 academic papers, their judgments of what those papers demonstrated varied, and varied as one might have predicted from their previous conversation in Oxford.

Cassandra initiated the discussion with a casual comment about the glaring governance failures that this research had demonstrated. She had noted with particular glee severe failures such as HIV and blood in France and Spain, and the reform of the medical profession in Sweden. These demonstrated, at least to her, the basic incapacity of governments to cope effectively with major problems, especially problems that dealt with complex problems such as medicine. Further, she considered some of the judgments made about the cases as suspect. In a number of cases that, on balance, had received a positive evaluation she commented that a negative assessment could have been made just as easily. She recognized that the common finding in studies of the public sector had been to identify problems and failures, and accepted that some of this concentration on failure had biased the public understanding of government. Still she thought that the present studies perhaps had gone too far in the other direction.

While Candide accepted that there were some glaring failures in the 24 cases the researchers had examined, he did consider that the overall findings demonstrated the ability of governments to govern rather effectively in a variety of settings. Few of the examples had been perfect cases, as governments were often groping with poorly defined problems, with rapidly changing information, with scarce resources and with numerous and conflicting interests in the private sector. Still most governments in most cases had been able to navigate these minefields successfully and produce reasonable responses to those extremely difficult questions. Further, even if there were less than perfect scores on all the dimensions of success, the evidence was fairly weighed and the balance was in favour of success. Success and failure in public programmes is rarely so clearly defined as it might be in the private sector, with its clear measure of profit to determine whether there had been success, so governments (and analysts) have to understand and balance a range of criteria to say that an outcome is a success or failure.

Cassandra was not to be convinced so easily about the abilities of the public sector, and began to attack the very definition of success employed in the studies they had read. For example, for the steel cases she argued that the successful management of decline was a very minimalist standard of adequate performance by the public sector, given that at least some of the reasons for decline in that industry actually resided with public sector involvement in the industry in the first place. Therefore outcomes that were considered as successes were simply tidying up a mess that government had helped to create. A more adequate measure of successful governance would be the capacity to avert problems like the inefficiency of the steel industry, an excessively powerful medical profession, and even the HIV contamination of the blood supply. Likewise, the authors of the financial regulation cases appeared to be more sanguine about the significant financial losses incurred in the private sector than certainly the investors involved would have been.

Cassandra continued her attack on policy making in the public sector. She was concerned about the time dimension for declaring success or failure in public programmes, and thought that most of the studies she had read tended to take too much of a short-term perspective on the outcomes of those programmes. For example, the health cost and professional control cases did not assess the long-term effects of reducing the autonomy of the medical profession, even supposing that the control was implemented as well as the authors of these papers assume it has been. The problem may be that successful controls, given the criteria advanced in the case, may in the longer term make the practice of medicine less attractive to well-qualified people and therefore in the end reduce the quality of care available to citizens.

Candide found it difficult to accept the extremely high standards of success that Cassandra was now advancing, and accused her of moving the goalposts for the public sector. When the only cases of success and failure available – largely gross failures made known through sometimes sensational media coverage – tended to support their views, she was quite comfortable with more minimal standards. However, once more systematic evidence was available and it demonstrated that, on average, governments were not doing so poorly, she rather quickly made the standards for success more demanding. Indeed, if the same standards were applied to organizations in Cassandra's beloved private sector many, if not most, firms might be found wanting. Firms in the private sector have been, if anything, more guilty of taking short-term profits at the expense of longer-term growth and success. Quoting the eminent social philosopher Yogi Berra, Candide told Cassandra that the future hasn't happened yet, so that governments must govern in the here and now and to some extent discount future unknowns. Indeed, spending too much time considering the long-term consequences of each action could paralyse government and make its policy making both slower and less likely to address issues in an effective manner.

Candide also pointed out the difficulty and severity of the issues being assessed in these studies of policy success and failure. In the HIV/AIDS cases, for example, governments were forced to make policy in an area with rapidly changing and sometimes conflicting scientific information, strong vested interests with different types of information, and at least two different client groups. Further, in some of the countries, those in one of the client groups were considered pariahs and the valuable information and opinion that they had, and their possible role in solving the problem, were often discounted. The issue involved was one of life and death, and was also vested with symbolic as well as material importance. Attempting to govern effectively in a thicket such as this is a severe challenge for any organization, public or private, and on balance governments had done well, or so Candide thought.

Still not agreeing on the objective success and failure of the programmes being studied, Cassandra shifted attention to the political dimensions of evaluation. Cassandra thought that the measures being applied were perhaps too easy here as well. She wondered whether simply escaping blame was an adequate measure of success or if there needed to be a more positive conception of the political performance of a government. Few if any of the cases reported, she argued, demonstrated that governments were able to build positive support for their policies. Likewise, reelection was, she thought, a dubious measure of success for any one policy, given that elections tend to be fought over a range of issues, so that attributed success or failure to any one could be highly suspect. In her view governments needed to be held to higher standards of probity and efficiency if they were to pass political tests.

Even if avoiding blame for policy failures were a sufficient criterion for political success, Cassandra was surprised that governments were being given so much benefit of the doubt by the public in these studies. Therefore she shifted her attention to this second dimension of the political assessments. Although there was no firm pattern emerging from the studies, she found that citizens were letting governments off somewhat too easily when they considered programmatic performance in the public sector. She was personally appalled at the ease with which governments were able to convince their publics that these significant policy problems were being handled adequately, and by the capabilities of governments to convert negative outcomes (both objectively and in her view) into political successes. She found this disheartening finding (to her) especially apparent in the case of financial regulation. The political successes to her reflected the capacity of governments to manage the media and consistently to deceive the public and present a series of (at best) half-truths to citizens for their political purposes.

Not surprisingly, Candide thought that Cassandra was again being extremely unfair, both to the public sector and to the analyses that she had read. In the first place, while avoiding repercussions was certainly a major component of the political assessment criteria, other values also were considered in these evaluations. The major political dimension is indeed avoiding blame and severe electoral consequences, but that may simply be another ways of stating that these governments functioned in modern democracies. Policy questions are now so complex and the chances of error so strong, and the chances of errors being exposed also so high, that if a government can perform well enough to remain in office it has not governed badly. This is especially true when governments must deal with highly emotive issues such as HIV and blood, or must distribute losses rather than gains for citizens, as in the case of the national steel industries.

Also there were some cases in which governments were able to enhance their legitimacy through programmatic success, as with the German government exercising greater control over the medical profession. Likewise, the management of decline in steel in several countries demonstrated a capacity to build support around policies that were difficult and yet necessary. This finding might be considered good news for individuals concerned about the decline in public trust of government. It seems that even if citizens do say that they no longer trust their governments, when they are confronted with real cases they are more willing to provide governments with some latitude for action. Therefore, in practice, governments in this set of countries continue to have substantially more legitimacy than most public opinion studies indicate. Candide thought that governments deserved perhaps even more credit politically than they were being given by the public, rather than less, given the severity of the challenges that they had been able to overcome.

As they debated the issues raised by these 24 cases, the one thing that Candide and Cassandra could agree upon readily was that their opposing conclusions were at least in part a function of fundamental differences in what they considered to be 'good government' or 'good governance'. Cassandra had what might be called an 'assembly line' conception of good government. For her this term meant setting clear goals, fulfilling unambiguous measures of achieving those goals, strict evaluations of economy and efficiency, and the creation of popular legitimacy through programmatic success. The general style of governing she was advancing appeared hierarchical, with ministers in the centre of the system providing direction and taking responsibility for the outcomes. Government should, therefore, be considered as performing like a successful firm in a well-defined private market, with customer satisfaction and profits being the clearly understood goals for its actions.

Candide, on the other hand, had a more of an 'arts and crafts' conception of what constituted good government. He did not think that producing good government was possible in such an unambiguous and linear manner as did Cassandra. Rather, he conceptualized good government as being working one's way through a complex series of challenges in the most effective and politically sensitive manner possible. When doing so, people in governments would be working with incomplete information (both programmatic and political) and would be attempting to please a public with diverse and often conflicting values. These governments would also be faced with a number of internal governance problems, not the least of which is attempting to coordinate the activities of the numerous organizations working within the public sector. In this view governing was much less determinate than the idea of activities in the public sector that Cassandra advanced. Governance in this conception is the exercise of judgment and also the use of networks and other means of collecting information and creating consensus.

As they parted, they could also agree that the research that had been completed had revealed a good deal more about success and failure in governing than most of the research on the subject that they had read previously. These cases were not selected because it was already known (or assumed) that they had been a failure or, less likely, a success, but rather they were chosen to demonstrate a range of challenges faced by modern governments. With this range of issues there was a better opportunity to determine what government actually can do. Further, these cases were examined within a wide range of political systems with the possibility of better understanding what factors may influence success and failure. Finally, these cases have been more careful than most in differentiating the political and the programmatic dimensions of success and failure, developed a number of dimensions of each, and provided rather nuanced judgments about how well governments had performed on each dimension. Still, despite the contributions made here, they could both think of new questions, and different but equally interesting policy areas, to extend the research. They promised to meet again soon and continue their conversation.

References to part VI

Anheier, H.K. (ed.) (1999), *When Things Go Wrong: Organizational Failures and Breakdowns*, London: Sage.

Boin, A. and P. 't Hart (2000), 'Institutional Crises and Reforms in Policy Sectors', in H. Wagenaar (ed.), *Government Institutions: Effects, Changes and Normative Foundations*, Dordrecht: Kluwer Academic Publishers, pp. 9–32.

Bovens, M. and P. 't Hart (1996), *Understanding Policy Fiascoes*, New Brunswick: Transaction Publishers.

Cohen, M.D., J.G. March and J.P. Olsen (1972), 'A Garbage Can Model of Organizational Choice', *Administrative Science Quarterly*, 17 (1), 1–29.

Dery, D. (1984), *Problem Definition in Policy Analysis*, Lawrence: University of Kansas Press.

Dowding, K. (1995), 'Model or Metaphor? A Critical Review of the Policy Network Approach', *Political Studies*, 18, 136–58.

Dror, Y. (1986), *Policymaking Under Adversity*, New Brunswick: Transaction Publishers.

Edelman, M. (1971), *Politics as Symbolic Action: Mass Arousal and Quiescence*, Chicago: Markham.

Edelman, M. (1988), *Constructing the Political Spectacle*, Chicago: University of Chicago Press.

Freeman, G.P. (1985), 'National Styles and Policy Sectors: Explaining Structured Variation', *Journal of Public Policy*, 5 (4), 467–96.

Gray, P.D. (1998), 'Policy Disasters in Europe: An Introduction', in P.D. Gray and P. 't Hart (eds), *Public Policy Disasters in Europe*, London: Routledge, pp. 3–20.

Haas, E.B. (ed.) (1990), *When Knowledge is Power: Three Models of Changes in International Organizations*, Berkeley: University of California Press.

Hall, P.A. (1993), 'Policy Paradigms, Social Learning and the State: The Case of Economic Policymaking in Britain', *Comparative Politics*, 25 (3), 275–96.

Heclo, H. (1977), *A Government of Strangers: Executive Politics in Washington*, Washington, DC: The Brookings Institution.

Hisschemöller, M. and R. Hoppe (1995), 'Coping with Intractable Controversies', *Knowledge and Policy*, 8 (4), 40–60.

Keeler, J.T.S. (1993), 'Opening the Window for Reform: Mandates, Crises and Extraordinary Policy-Making', *Comparative Political Studies*, 25 (4), 433–86.

Key, V.O. (1966), *The Responsible Electorate: Rationality in Presidential Voting*, Cambridge, MA: Harvard University Press.

Kingdon, J.W. (1984), *Agendas, Alternatives and Public Policies*, Boston: Little, Brown.

Lijphart, A. (1999), *Patterns of Democracy: Government Forms and Performance in Thirty-Six Countries*, New Haven, CT: Yale University Press.

Lowi, T.J. (1964), 'American Business, Public Policy, Case Studies and Political Theory', *World Politics*, 16 (4), 676–715.

March, J.G. and J.P. Olsen (1989), *Rediscovering Institutions: The Organizational Basis of Politics*, New York: Free Press.

Marsh, D. and M. Smith (2000), 'Understanding policy networks: Towards a Dialectical Approach', *Political Studies*, 48 (1), 4–21.

Olsen, J.P. and B.G. Peters (eds) (1996), *Lessons from Experience: Experiential Learning in Administrative Reforms in eight Democracies*, Oslo: Scandinavian University Press.

Peters, B.G. (1999), *Institutional Theory in Political Science: The 'New Institutionalism'*, London: Pinter.

Peters, B.G., R.A.W. Rhodes and V. Wright (eds) (2000), *Administering the Summit: Administration of the Core Executive in Developed Countries*, Basingstoke: Macmillan.

Reason, J. (1997), *Managing the Risks of Organizational Accidents*, Aldershot: Ashgate.

Rochefort, D. and R. Cobb (eds) (1993), *The Politics of Problem Definition*, Lawrence: University of Kansas Press.

Rose, R. (1993), *Lesson-Drawing in Public Policy: A Guide to Learning Across Time and Space*, Chatham: Chatham House.

Sabatier, P. (1998),'The Advocacy Coalition Framework: Revisions and Relevance for Europe', *Journal of European Public Policy*, 5 (1), 98–130.

Sabatier, P.A. and H.C. Jenkins-Smith (1993), *Policy Change and Learning: An Advocacy Coalition Approach*, Boulder, CO: Westview Press.

Scharpf, F. (2000), 'The viability of Advanced Welfare States in the International Economy: Vulnerabilities and Options', *Journal of European Public Policy*, 7 (2), 190–228.

Scharpf, F.W. (1988), 'The Joint-Decision Trap: Lessons from German Federalism and European Integration', *Public Administration*, 66, 239–78.

Scharpf, F.W. (1997), *Games Real Actors Play: Actor-Centered Institutionalism in Policy Research*, Boulder, CO: Westview Press.

Schon, D.A. and M. Rein (1994), *Frame Reflection: Solving Intractable Policy Disputes*, New York: Basic Books.

Steinmo, S. (1993), *Taxation and Democracy: Swedish, British and American Approaches to Financing the Modern State*, New Haven, CT: Yale University Press.

Steinmo, S., K. Thelen and F. Longstreth (1992), *Structuring Politics: Historical Institutionalism in Comparative Analysis*, Cambridge: Cambridge University Press.

Tsebelis, G. (1990), *Nested Games: Rational Choice in Comparative Politics*, Berkeley: University of California Press.

Turner, B.A. and N.F. Pidgeon (1997), *Man-Made Disaster*, Boston: Butterworth-Heinemann.

Vaughan, D. (1996), *The Challenger Launch Decision: Risky Technology, Culture and Deviance at NASA*, Chicago: University of Chicago Press.

Weaver, R.K and B.A. Rockman (eds) (1996), *Do Institutions Matter? Government Capabilities in the United States and Abroad*, Washington, DC: The Brookings Institution.

Wildavsky, A. (1987), 'Choosing Preferences by Constructing Institutions: A Cultural Theory of Preference Formation', *American Political Science Review*, 81 (1), 3.

Wildavsky, A. (1988), *Searching for Safety*, New Brunswick: Transaction Publishers.

Wilson, J.Q. (ed.) (1980), *The Politics of Regulation*, New York: Basic Books.

020000 048572 020

Index

Index